TEMPEST

TEMPEST

THE ROYAL NAVY AND THE
AGE OF REVOLUTIONS

JAMES DAVEY

YALE UNIVERSITY PRESS
NEW HAVEN AND LONDON

Published with assistance from the Annie Burr Lewis Fund.

All reasonable efforts have been made to provide accurate sources for all images that appear in this book. Any discrepancies or omissions will be rectified in future editions.

For information about this and other Yale University Press publications, please contact:
U.S. Office: sales.press@yale.edu   yalebooks.com
Europe Office: sales@yaleup.co.uk   yalebooks.co.uk

Set in Garamond Premier Pro by IDSUK (DataConnection) Ltd
Printed in Great Britain by TJ Books, Padstow, Cornwall

Library of Congress Control Number: 2023931520

ISBN 978-0-300-23827-3

A catalogue record for this book is available from the British Library.

10 9 8 7 6 5 4 3 2 1

CONTENTS

CONTENTS

ILLUSTRATIONS AND MAPS

PLATES

1. Title page of *Rights of Man* by Thomas Paine, 1791. British Library.
2. Front page of London Corresponding Society handbill advertising a petition to the House of Commons for parliamentary reform, 1793. TS 24/3/34, The National Archives.
3. Portrait of John Nicol by William Home Lizars, 1822. © National Portrait Gallery, London.
4. Volunteer poster, *c.* 1797. © National Maritime Museum, Greenwich, London.
5. *Manning the Navy*, 1790. © National Maritime Museum, Greenwich, London.
6. Union Flag flown on the *Queen Charlotte* at the Battle of the Glorious First of June, *c.* 1794. © National Maritime Museum, Greenwich, London.
7. French Republic banner captured during the Battle of the Glorious First of June, *c.* 1794. © National Maritime Museum, Greenwich, London.
8. *Visit of George III to Admiral Lord Howe's Flagship the Queen Charlotte, Following the Battle of the 'Glorious First of June'*, 1828. © National Maritime Museum, Greenwich, London.
9. *The Point of Honour* by George Cruikshank, 1825. © National Maritime Museum, Greenwich, London.

33. Naval pillar, 1804. © National Maritime Museum, Greenwich, London.
34. *The Sailor's Orphans or Young Ladies' Subscription* by William Ward, 1800. Yale Center for British Art, Paul Mellon Collection.
35. *Sailors Conversation* by William Ward, 1802. Yale Center for British Art, Paul Mellon Collection.
36. Portraits of *Temeraire* mutineers from the pamphlet *Trial of the mutineers, late of His Majesty's Ship Temeraire*, 1802. British Library, London. © British Library Board. All Rights Reserved / Bridgeman Images.

MAPS

The following sources have proved helpful when researching the maps used in this book: Brian Lavery, *Nelson's Navy: The Ships, Men and Organisation, 1793–1815* (London: Conway Maritime Press, 1990); N.A.M. Rodger, *The Command of the Ocean: A Naval History of Britain, 1649–1815* (London: Allen Lane, 2004); Sam Willis, *In the Hour of Victory: The Royal Navy at War in the Age of Nelson* (London: Atlantic Books, 2013); Roger Knight, *The Pursuit of Victory: The Life and Achievement of Horatio Nelson* (London: Allen Lane, 2005).

ACKNOWLEDGEMENTS

This book has been written during 'interesting times'. In Britain, the last few years have seen near-constant political turmoil, a major global pandemic, the death of a long-serving monarch and now a cost-of-living crisis, and it would be strange indeed if these events had not affected the words that follow. Every book is influenced by the period and environment in which it was written and I have no doubt that these episodes have shaped the way I think about the equally tumultuous 1790s. I have done my best not to let contemporary issues affect my treatment of the historical evidence, and throughout I have questioned 'why' something happened, rather than whether it 'should' have happened. That said, this is a book with politics at its heart and, as I write, widespread industrial action is taking place across the country. These issues of pay and living standards are not so dissimilar to those that confronted eighteenth-century sailors, for all that the immediate contexts are very different. I am sure that in the pages that follow my sympathy for those attempting to improve their lot in life will be evident, something that I am happy to acknowledge.

Tempest is a product of its time, but it also owes its existence to the help and assistance of countless organisations and individuals. Support from the Huntington Library in Pasadena, California, was essential, encompassing a three-month Mayer Fellowship in the summer of 2019 and a one-year Kemble Fellowship in Maritime History in 2020–1. This last survived the pressures of the Covid-19 pandemic, and while my time in Pasadena was shorter than initially planned, it remained crucial for allowing me time to think, write and discuss my ideas. Special thanks must go to Steve Hindle for his generosity and unswerving support of my project. I am also grateful to Juan Gomez, Natalie Serrano and Catherine Wehrey-Miller for their expert assistance with administrative matters before, during and after my fellowships. Roy Ritchie and Vanessa Wilkie offered advice on the Library's collections that proved incredibly useful. I must also thank two different cohorts of Huntington scholars with whom I shared many lunches and walks, and in particular the group of hardy fellows in 2020–1 who read one of the chapters and helped my thinking on a number of points. To use Californian parlance – I appreciate you.

I was also fortunate to receive a short-term fellowship at the National Maritime Museum in Greenwich, which allowed me access to its material culture collections and its unrivalled archive of sailors' letters. I want to thank the Trustees and academic committee of Royal Museums Greenwich for the award of the fellowship, and in particular Stuart Bligh and Lizelle de Jager for their flexibility arranging access to the stores and archives amid the pandemic. Librarians and archivists at the Caird Library made strenuous efforts to allow me access to materials at a time when Britain was only just coming out of a lockdown, and special thanks must also go to Stawell Heard and Magdalena Schedl for their assistance. It was also great to see former colleagues: Sally Archer, Robert Blyth, Lucy Dale, Aaron Jaffer and Megan Barford offered good-humoured support.

I have benefited from the opportunity to consult a wide range of primary materials at a host of other record offices and archives. I want to thank the staff and volunteers of the British Library, Cambridge University Library, the Devon Heritage Centre, the Dorset History Centre, the Somerset Record Office, the Suffolk Record Office and the United States National Archives. Particular thanks must go to The National Archives (TNA) in London, a never-ending treasure trove for any historian who seeks to research the history of the Royal Navy. Countless days were spent researching this book at Kew, and I am indebted to the staff who produced records with speed and efficiency. This was particularly true during the pandemic, when TNA was one of the first repositories to reopen and allow grateful researchers to consult materials. This book would not have been feasible were it not for my visits in the autumn and winter of 2020, and my sincere thanks go to all the archivists and retrieval staff who made accessing documents possible.

At Exeter, I owe debts to many. Firstly, I want to thank my under-graduate and postgraduate students who have allowed me to wax lyrical about the Navy and the Age of Revolutions without complaint, espe-cially those who took my 'Britain and the Age of Revolution, 1775–1832' special subject, which has been a pleasure to teach. Discussion in seminars has helped clarify my thinking about numerous subjects, while students' work has challenged my ideas. The quality of work produced has often been exceptional, and eagle-eyed readers will note that some students' work is referenced in what follows. I also want to thank colleagues who have offered support – professional and emotional – since I joined the Department of History. I don't have space to mention all my workmates, but my thanks go to those who helped with the book, whether an idea, a debate or a well-timed trip to the pub: Jonathan Barry, Helen Berry, Helen Birkett, Emily Bridger, Gemma Clark, Gareth Curless, James Fisher, Henry French, Maria Fusaro, Freyja Cox Jensen, Jon Lawrence, Camille Mathieu, Marc Palen, Stuart Pracy, Laura Rowe, Laura Sangha, Gajendra Singh, Martin Thomas, Richard Toye, Richard Ward and Hannah Young. Ryan Hanley offered advice on a number of points and was kind enough to hand over source material from his own research that was highly relevant to this project. I also want to single out my colleague Elin Jones, with whom I help run the maritime history programme at Exeter, and whose research on eighteenth-century sailors aligns neatly with my own. Elin's advice and friendship have been a real solace as the book has taken shape, and her critical commentary on the book's structure, as well as specific chapters, has been invaluable.

I was fortunate to present different chapters of the book at a number of conferences and seminar series. My thanks go to the Centre for Early

Modern Studies at Exeter University, Peter Wilson's 'Mobilizing War' conference at Oxford, the History Department of the University of Portsmouth, the Consortium on the Revolutionary Era, the Devon History Society, the British Society for Eighteenth Century Studies, the McMullen Naval History Symposium at the US Naval Academy, the North American Conference on British Studies, the University of California Early Modern Studies Institute British History Seminar Series, and the Maritime Cultures and Environments Reading Group. In each case, I am grateful for the opportunities provided, and for the useful feedback and suggestions I received on different sections of the book.

Throughout the writing process I have also enjoyed correspondence, chats and (increasingly) Zoom calls with other historians whose work speaks to the subject of this book. I am grateful for written and virtual communications with Isaac Land, Niklas Frykman and Callum Easton, all of whom have offered advice over the past years. In places I take a contrasting line, or interpret the evidence slightly differently, but I'm grateful for the ideas and encouragement they have offered. Evan Wilson has proved an expert sounding board throughout, and I owe a debt of gratitude to him for his advice and cheering messages from across the Atlantic. Tawny Paul offered an introduction into forbidding economic history debates, and equally important guidance on the taco stands of Los Angeles. Joanne Begiato gave me a sneak preview of her chapter on Jack Crawford months ahead of its publication, and Lee-Jane Giles sent me her BA dissertation on the marine mutiny of 1797 – for both I am thankful. Nick Rogers generously sent me his lengthy list of impressment riots and affrays across the eighteenth century, and I am grateful to him for a number of other references, suggestions and chats as the book has taken shape. Elsewhere, a range of other scholars have offered advice and examples, and I also want to take this opportunity to thank Katy Barrett, Brad Beavan, Cat Beck, Richard Blakemore, Sara Caputo, Erica Charters, Quintin Colville, Stephen Conway, Joe Cozens, David Cressy, Marianne Czisnik, Jeremiah Dancy, David Davies, Kevin Dawson, Jonathan Fennel, Aaron Graham, Doug Hamilton, Mark

Hanna, Alan James, Kenneth Johnson, Kay Kearsey, Paul Kennedy, Jane Knight, Andrew Lambert, Brian Lavery, Margarette Lincoln, Carrie Long, John McAleer, Kevin McCranie, Anna McKay, Peter Mancall, Zoe Mercer-Golden, Ryan Mewett, Renaud Morieux, Steve Murdoch, Elaine Murphy, Lindsay O'Neill, Susannah Ottaway, Katie Parker, N.A.M. Rodger, Sujit Sivasundaram, Hannah Stockton, Sally Voelcker, Tim Voelcker and Peter Wilson.

At Yale I am indebted to Heather McCallum, who has proved a wonderful – and patient – editor as the pandemic created unexpected delays. Her team have provided excellent assistance throughout, starting with Rachael Lonsdale and Lucy Buchan who oversaw the production stage. Katie Urquhart lent her considerable expertise to help market the book, and it is largely through her efforts that the book is so lavishly complemented with colour images. I am grateful to Alice Greaves for her thorough job copy-editing the manuscript, to Martin Brown for designing the maps, and to Lucy Isenberg who proofread the final set texts.

Special thanks should go to those who read chapters and commented on the substance of what follows. The two anonymous peer reviewers devoted considerable time to commenting on the first draft of the manuscript, and their responses have made this an immeasurably better book. I've also been fortunate to share chapters with friends and academic colleagues. Callum Easton knows more about the 1797 mutinies than anyone, and I was delighted that he agreed to comment on the full manuscript as it neared completion and save me from a few embarrassing errors. Mike Duffy read a number of chapters, and his genial support and critical eye have improved the manuscript significantly. He also presented me with some initial archival research conducted by David Syrett, uncompleted due to his passing, to which I hope I have done justice. Lastly, Roger Knight has long been a tireless supporter of my work and kindly offered to read the manuscript as it neared its final submission; the book has benefited hugely from his wise and learned counsel. No doubt some errors remain, the responsibility for which is entirely mine.

ACKNOWLEDGEMENTS

On a more personal note, I want to thank my family and friends. My parents have long supported my love for history, though it remains a surprise to all of us that I am able to make a living from it. My sister, brother and friends outside academia have offered support in ways they probably do not understand, but for which I am eternally grateful. The last words, though, should go to my partner and my daughter, who arrived just as the book manuscript neared completion. My life is very different now to when I started this work, but it is all for the better because you are both in it. To Hannah and Anwen, with love – this book is dedicated to you.

NOTE ON CONVENTIONS

This book concerns Britain's experience of the 'Age of Revolutions'. It focuses squarely on the 1790s, a period in which the spread of revolutionary ideas shaped naval and national life in manifold ways. This is not to say that radical political opinions did not exist before or after this period, but in the pages that follow I suggest that it was in the decade after the French Revolution that Britain faced the genuine possibility of political and social disunion as a result of revolutionary ideology. Furthermore, throughout the book I also use the plural phrase 'Age of Revolutions' rather than the singular 'Age of Revolution'. This was the term predominantly used by contemporaries and it serves an important analytical function too. Protest and rebellion manifested themselves in distinctive and unique ways around the globe, and even within Britain, popular engagement with the revolutionary era was not monolithic and depended on nationality, class and geography. There were many different experiences of the Age of Revolutions, and so I use the plural throughout. Additionally, in this tumultuous era, many place names also changed, most notably the French colony of Saint-Domingue, which became the Republic of Haiti. For the purposes of this book, I use the most accurate chronological term, so 'Haiti' when discussing the nation that later emerged, but Saint-Domingue during the period of the 1790s.

A similar clarification is also necessary in regard to the military conflict that dominated this decade, the French Revolutionary Wars. This began in April 1792 when the French National Assembly declared war on Austria and Prussia, but it wasn't until February 1793 that

Britain entered the conflict. In the fighting that followed, Britain and France were constant antagonists until peace was signed in 1801. However, other nations entered and left the war – Spain, for instance, fought on both sides at different points – and there were at least two distinct coalitions of European powers fighting against French Revolutionary forces. Their experience of the war was a series of conflicts, rather than a continuous one. While most scholars would use the plural 'Wars' rather than 'War', this is a book primarily about Britain, and in the writing that follows I generally use the singular noun to refer to the specific clash between Britain and France fought between 1793 and 1801.

There are a number of other terms that warrant a little justification, not least the notion of 'Britain' itself. In 1793 Britain was a relatively new political entity, brought together following the Act of Union between England and Scotland in 1707. In 1801, a further Act of Union with Ireland, prompted primarily by the religious and political turmoil unleashed during the revolutionary era, saw this composite kingdom grow ever larger and become the United Kingdom of Great Britain and Ireland. The Royal Navy was a 'British' institution in almost every respect: it was funded by the British Parliament and primarily manned by men from across the British Isles in vessels that had little allegiance to localities, unlike the army where regiments drew specifically from individual counties. Nonetheless, the individuals who made up the Navy's crews did not always see their world through 'British' eyes: some came from abroad and, as we will see, Welsh, Scottish and Irish nationalism remained powerful forces throughout this period. Throughout the book I use 'Britain' to describe the political state and 'British' to describe its people, but I am conscious that many contemporaries would not have agreed with these descriptors.

As might be expected in a book about the Royal Navy, the pages that follow contain a number of maritime phrases, not all of which are common in twenty-first-century parlance. I have taken care to steer clear of complicated nautical terminology and offer brief explanations were necessary. I naturally refer to a large number of ships, which are italicised throughout. Elsewhere I have moved away from tradition and describe them as 'it' rather than 'she'. Naval vessels were and are inanimate objects, and it seems both antiquated and problematic to see them as feminine. I have also avoided using the prefix 'HMS' (His/Her Majesty's Ship), an abbreviation that was occasionally employed from the 1790s onwards but was not in common use until about 1820.

Lastly, and most pertinently to this book, it's worth saying a few words about vocabulary. This book deploys a wide variety of quotations, but eighteenth-century spelling was far from uniform and there is a natural tendency to want to modernise or standardise spelling. Throughout, however, I have presented the words of contemporaries without alteration, as they were written and recorded. Where meaning is unclear I have added a clarification in square brackets and in rare cases have used 'sic' to denote a spelling that might otherwise look like a mistake. One notable exception here is the word used to describe the men who worked in the lower deck of naval ships. They would have used 'seaman' to describe themselves, as opposed to the word 'sailor', which was in use but like 'mariner' generally denoted any individual who went to sea, including officers. For a modern-day audience, however, 'sailor' is the more familiar term for a member of a ship's company (and generally prompts fewer sniggers too). In this book I use the two interchangeably but for the most part deploy the more modern, latter version.

PROLOGUE

In June 1797, naval sailors stationed at the mouth of the Thames Estuary wrote an impassioned political declaration. In angry, heartfelt prose, they painted an appalling picture of life at sea amid a war that had already lasted four years, and which showed no sign of coming to a conclusion. Their efforts, they argued, could not be doubted. Since 1793 they had 'confounded' and 'terrified' Britain's enemies at sea, guarded the coasts from invasion, and protected the nation's children from 'Slaughter' and its lands from 'Pillage'. In return they had only received 'Acts of cruelty' and attempts to deprive them of their 'Common Rights'. They posed a simple question. 'Shall we . . . who have endured the Toils of a Long Disgraceful war', continue to 'Bear the Shackles of Tyranny and Oppression'? Their answer was bold:

No. The Age of Reason is at Length arrived. We had long been Endeavouring to find ourselves Men. We now find ourselves so. We will be Treated as such.

The declaration then concluded with a threat. The sailors demanded an increased salary alongside other grievances and made clear that they were prepared to take extreme measures to secure them. 'We will sell our Lives Dearly to Maintain what we have Demanded,' they declared, and they blocked the River Thames to all passing commerce. They then offered a further warning: 'A few Days will probably Lead us to something more.'[1]

Written at the climax of what came to be known as the Nore mutiny, the declaration offers a fascinating window into the varied – and often conflicting – political minds of eighteenth-century sailors. Their prose was layered with references to class and the inequities of society, with mentions of 'vile gilded pampered knaves' who were 'wallowing in the Laps of Luxury' and 'Tyrants who derive from us alone, their Honours, Titles and Fortunes'. It also demonstrated political astuteness, offering a form of conditional patriotism carefully designed to paint their demands as reasonable, and the stubborn stance of the government as deeply unfair. 'Have we not a Right to Complain?', they asked. The authors took pains to profess their 'highest opinion of our Beloved Sovereign' and stated that they had had no desire to 'subvert the Government of Our Beloved Country', making clear that once their demands were met they would return to their duty and 'enter with alacrity upon any employment for the safety of our Country'. Alongside this careful positioning, though, came damning criticism of the ministry of William Pitt, critiquing the honesty and decorum of those 'at the Helm of the State', and a further warning that they were alive to 'tricks of Government' and 'attempts to Deceive us'.[2]

Perhaps the most startling aspect of the sailors' prose was the use of overt political terminology. By referring to the 'Age of Reason', and more subtly in its allusions to 'Rights' and 'Tyranny', it explicitly referenced the radical ideas underpinning recent upheavals in America, France and Haiti that historians have come to refer to as the Age of Revolutions. This declaration was but one example of sailors' political activity in the 1790s, and across the decade, sailors read newspapers, sang political ballads and produced rousing documents that called for redress. In this, the sailors at the Nore were channelling the ideas of the age, characterised by a movement for constitutional reform and the remarkable growth of popular political engagement. Nor was this limited to words. On numerous occasions, ideas were transformed into action, as sailors wrote petitions, went on strike and fought back against the hated policy of impressment. With other avenues exhausted, they also raised the red flag of mutiny with greater frequency than ever before, not just at the Nore, but repeatedly across the decade. Mutiny was not a new phenomenon, to be sure, and sailors had their own traditions of workplace dispute, honed over centuries. However, the regularity of the rebellions of the 1790s, as well as their explicitly political nature, augured something quite different. They had become active participants in the Age of Revolutions, taking the ideas and mores of the era and applying them to their own situation.

Sailors' political activity, in turn, became a problem for the state. On 7 June 1797, a copy of the declaration arrived at the office of Evan Nepean, First Secretary to the Admiralty, where frantic work was being done to isolate the mutineers at the Nore and force them to return to their duty. Nepean understood only too well that this was a document made for public consumption and took steps to ensure it was not circulated any further. He was well aware that it had the potential to sway minds. Across the 1790s, the contested loyalty of sailors infiltrated – and at times came to dominate discussion within – the public sphere. Journalists, pamphleteers and songwriters followed events closely, and while the government's propaganda organs could be relied upon to present a sanitised version of events, naval crews continued to offer stark examples of political action. Sailors were only too aware of these debates and intervened to control their own image. As such, the declaration of June 1797 was an attempt not only to lay down their grievances, but also to correct a media narrative and state their case to the British public. 'The publick prints teem with falsehood and Misrepresentation' it noted, and it repeatedly called on the sailors' 'Countrymen' for their support.

These themes – the political activities of sailors, the response of the British state and the Navy's wider place in British popular culture – are the subject of this book. *Tempest* traces the relationship between the Navy and the wider Age of Revolutions, focusing particularly on the French Revolutionary War of 1793–1801, in which Britain faced a new and threatening enemy. The French Republic stood for liberty, equality and fraternity, while in comparison the British state came to represent more traditional notions of king, constitution and the protection of the status quo. In this war the Navy took centre stage, its role as the nation's defender placing it at the heart of British attempts to subdue Revolutionary France. However, deployed in an ideological war against revolutionary ideas, the appearance of dissent – and in 1797, widespread mutiny – in the Navy's ranks threatened the entire edifice of the war effort, and the British constitution itself. At a time when the loyalty of the population was monitored more closely than ever before, the activities of naval sailors were objects of both governmental and public concern. For many, the result was brutal punishment, and in extreme cases, execution at the yard-arm of their ships.

What follows is the story of a naval war, but also of the political maelstrom that consumed the British nation across the 1790s. At its heart are the sailors who navigated these extraordinary times and who found themselves, as the authors of the 1797 declaration put it, 'in the Midst of Tempest'.

INTRODUCTION

The 'Age of Revolutions' is a long-standing historical concept that defies easy categorisation. There is little scholarly consensus on when it began or ended, or on its causes or its legacies, and the phrase has become a malleable term deployed to signify a period of widespread global change in the decades either side of 1800.[1] Whatever its chronology, there is greater consensus about what this period represented. The Age of Revolutions saw politics, society and culture transformed, as growing political consciousness gave people new principles and frameworks with which to question the existing order and challenge authority.[2] Alongside this came a series of political upheavals that redefined the practice of politics. The revolutions in America (1775), France (1789) and Haiti (1791) are only the most famous examples, and increasingly scholars have moved away from Western-centric approaches to ones that consider global developments in this period, based around the concept of a 'World Crisis'. These include other momentous events such as Pugachev's Revolt in Russia, the White Lotus Rebellion in China, the Wahhabi Movement in Arabia, as well as anti-colonial protests in South Africa, the Dutch East Indies, India and South America, to name but a few.[3] Contemporaries were well aware that they were living through a period of remarkable change. 'This being the Age of Revolutions,' wrote the British *Morning Post* in 1795, 'changes must be expected in most parts of the world.'[4]

Britain, however, was one of the few nations not to experience a revolution. A number of scholars have suggested moments where

Britain came close to political upheaval, and indeed, the great social historian E.P. Thompson argued that the naval mutinies of 1797 offered 'the greatest revolutionary portents for England'.[5] Certainly there were Britons who hoped for a revolution of some description, and throughout this period, a series of British governments were paranoid that one was likely to break out. Alongside the 1797 mutinies were numerous other moments where a full-scale revolt seemed nigh: the Gordon Riots of 1780, the food riots in 1795, the Luddite Rebellions of 1811–12, the Peterloo Massacre of 1819, the Swing Riots of 1830 and the Reform Act Crisis of 1831–2. None escalated in the same way as events in Boston, Paris and Saint-Domingue, but Britain was still a major partici- pant in the Age of Revolutions. For a start, as the world's leading impe- rial power it was the defining force against which many rebellions were fought – in Britain's empire in North America, at the Cape of Good Hope, in Ireland as well as across a series of Caribbean islands. More than this, though, there is an emerging consensus that the Age of Revolutions impacted Britain in more subtle ways. While there was not a 'Bastille moment' that ushered in an overthrow of the status quo, the era was nonetheless defined by the circulation of new ideas, the intensi- fication of calls for reform and the growth of extra-parliamentary polit- ical activity.[6]

These developments did not come out of the blue, but built on long- standing political traditions. Radicals such as John Wilkes, unhappy with the electoral system created during the political settlement of 1688–9, called for reforms from the mid-eighteenth century onwards. This was a system defined by 'pocket' or 'rotten' boroughs, the most notorious of which was Old Sarum, where there were no voters other than those chosen by the landowner, Lord Camelford. Other electoral injustices were found across the country: large industrial cities such as Manchester had no representation, while Cornwall's twenty-one boroughs returned forty-two MPs, far in excess of the more populous Lancashire and Yorkshire. Altogether half of the 513 MPs in England and Wales were returned by a mere 11,000 electors.[7] Reforms of this system were frequently suggested, but it was difficult for this movement to gain traction against a resilient establishment, and the political structures of the 1780s were little changed from a half-century earlier. True, the American Revolution of 1775–83 created remarkable political partisanship as the middling and elite classes clashed over the cause of American independence, and in its aftermath, campaigns for the abolition of the slave trade and parliamentary reform briefly grew in strength.[8] Nonetheless, these failed to secure the necessary legislation and the status quo remained.

It was the French Revolution of 1789 that re-invigorated the pressure for reform in Britain. By the late 1780s France's finances were in a parlous state, a relic of a ruinously expensive intervention in the American War and a deeply inefficient and unfair tax system. Louis XVI's attempts to resurrect his financial position came to nought and in 1789 he called an Estates General in the hope of gaining support for much-needed reforms. He and his advisors quickly lost control of proceedings, first to an 'aristocratic' revolt, and then to the growing political authority of the 'Third Estate', who in June 1789 declared the creation of a National Assembly to represent the wider French people. They were supported by the actions of the Parisian 'Sans Culottes', the politically literate class of artisans who led the attacks on the Bastille prison in July and who marched on the Palace of Versailles in October to protest the price of bread. The revolution in Paris became ever more radical, and by 1792 a new democratic nation had been created. The monarchy was abolished, and the following year Louis XVI was executed. All remnants of feudalism were eliminated, and political power was centred in a new National Convention that saw delegates selected by near-universal male suffrage as the 'Jacobin' faction took control. In just three years, one of Europe's largest and longest-standing autocratic monarchies had been toppled, and the new French Republic became a beacon of modernity both in Europe and across the globe.[9]

The onset of the French Revolution was initially welcomed in Britain, with some observers happy to see the nascent French democracy aping

British parliamentary institutions, while others were content to spectate as Britain's great rival was consumed by civil strife. However, as events in Paris became ever more violent, culminating in the Reign of Terror in 1793–4, conservatives became increasingly concerned that unchecked popular radicalism might spread across the English Channel. Edmund Burke's *Reflections on the Revolution in France*, published in 1791, represented the Revolution as a menace to the political, social, religious and moral order of Europe, and a number of crusading pamphleteers and commentators sympathised with Burke's views. In response came a string of more progressive political tomes that painted a very different picture, such as Mary Wollstonecraft's *A Vindication of the Rights of Men*, which offered a strident defence of the French Revolution.[10] This 'revolution debate' was held primarily by the propertied elites, but there were signs that radical ideas were being disseminated among the plebeian classes too. The anniversary of the fall of the Bastille was celebrated in numerous towns and around Britain, and more radical ideas were starting to take root. At Leicester, for instance, handbills were found on churches and other public places with the words 'Revolution for ever', while in Sheffield treasonable inscriptions were written on walls. In the countryside too, dissent was becoming widespread: in Tattenhall, near Chester, a local cheesemonger declared his opposition to tithes in the hope that the clergy would be stripped of their privileges as they had been in France.[11]

Nothing signals the arrival of the Age of Revolutions in Britain better than Thomas Paine's *Rights of Man*. Published in two parts in 1791 and 1792, this extraordinary volume offered not just a refutation of Burke, but also a detailed programme for republican, fully democratic government. Paine had already played a vital role in the American Revolution, producing pamphlets such as *Common Sense* that had done so much to assert the colonists' cause, and his latest publication promised to usher in a similar transformation in Britain. It argued forcefully for the idea of popular sovereignty, universal suffrage and representative government based around an assertion of the equal 'rights of man' – a key contrast with Burke's philosophy, which refuted the existence of abstract rights. Paine's views grew more strident as he developed a sophisticated argument for citizenship and economic equality: the second part of *Rights of Man* advanced plans for redistributive taxation, while his *Letter Addressed to the Addressers* (1792) called for the formation of a British Convention to design a new constitution for Britain. Paine's works sold in unprecedented numbers – believed to be in excess of 100,000 copies in Britain – easily outselling Burke's book, and they offered a radically different progressive plan than the constitutionalist writings of earlier in the eighteenth century. Only a revolution could achieve the ends he sought, and by 1791, Paine thought Britain's time had come. 'It is an age of Revolutions,' he wrote, 'in which every thing may be looked for.'[12]

Not only did *Rights of Man* offer a radical departure from the moderate constitutional reformers of the mid-eighteenth century; it also presented, for the first time, a political vision that emboldened the artisanal and working classes across the country to engage with politics. Democratic organisations for political reform were created in over thirty towns across Britain, including Belfast, Dublin and Cork. In Norwich there were no fewer than forty-two clubs discussing Paine's ideas.[13] The most prominent national organisation was the London Corresponding Society (LCS), which assumed a leading role in the reform efforts of the 1790s. Its driving force was the radical Thomas Hardy, the eldest son of a merchant seaman who had worked as a shoemaker and bricklayer before moving to London and immersing himself in political education. From 1792, the LCS campaigned for parliamentary reform, comprising annual parliaments, universal manhood suffrage and uncorrupted elections, and it soon had a membership numbering in the tens of thousands. Membership of the LCS cost only a penny, and its public events attracted crowds of 2,000–3,000 at a time. It also played an important role in disseminating Paine's work, including abbreviated pamphlets that summarised his ideas concisely. What followed was a dramatic spread of Paineite radicalism, offering displays of radical solidarity, including the planting of 'liberty trees' and the organisation of marches, such as one in Sheffield that brought an estimated 5,000 people together to condemn Burke.[14] This represented the most significant popular political programme in Britain since the Levellers of the mid-seventeenth century.[15]

The reform movement, as it has become known, initially hoped to achieve its aims through petitions, a common political tactic by the late eighteenth century. By May 1793, thirty-six petitions had been sent to Westminster from London, Norwich, Sheffield, Nottingham and especially Scotland, displaying a broad pool of support for the cause of parliamentary reform. Their rejection by the House of Commons made clear the limitations of petitioning, and instead the LCS planned for a National Convention, advocated by Paine and Joseph Gerrald in a pamphlet called *A Convention the only Means of Saving us from Ruin* (1793).[16] This remained a fragmented movement, though. There was disagreement about whether such a convention was a means of bringing reformers together, or a genuine attempt to create a more democratic and representative rival to Parliament. Some British radicals continued to draw inspiration from the long-standing constitutional criticism of John Wilkes.[17] The publications and correspondence of the LCS were similarly disjointed, torn between a moderate reform of Parliament and more extreme republican policies. More violent plans were also concocted: in 1794 a plot to kill King George III was discovered, and while there was no connection to the LCS, it signified that there were those prepared to consider extreme means.[18] It followed that the LCS was only the most well-known – and among the better organised – reform groups, but it did not represent the entirety of radical thought.

In Parliament, efforts for reform prompted contrasting reactions. For the majority of the Tory faction who governed Britain throughout the 1790s, the swirling radical currents of the early 1790s were an alarming challenge to the status quo that directly threatened their wealth and power. Prime Minister William Pitt, who earlier in his career had himself dabbled with attempts to reform the voting system, was discomforted by the intensity of radical activity, not least when more moderate calls bore a striking resemblance to his own earlier plans. He privately admitted that Tom Paine was 'quite in the right' but feared that were he to encourage his ideas 'we should have a bloody revolution'.[19] The Opposition Whig faction was similarly unsettled by events in France. Its larger-than-life leaders Charles James Fox and Richard Brinsley Sheridan celebrated the early successes of French revolutionaries, but this left them vulnerable when the Revolution took a more violent turn from 1791 onwards. Dismissive caricatures of the 'Jacobin' Fox with blood on his hands, or wearing a revolutionary 'bonnet rouge', formed part of a media campaign designed to isolate and ridicule him, and by 1797 he had temporarily retired from mainstream politics. A handful of MPs such as Samuel Whitbread, elected to his seat in 1790, took up more radical positions, including proposals for a national education system and, in 1795, an attempt to introduce a minimum wage. For the most part, though, Parliament was dominated by MPs who favoured the protection of the existing status quo.

Conservatism was not limited to Tory grandees sitting in Parliament. Alongside LCS events came a wave of public gatherings that preached a very different politics, as reformers were met and countered by a loyalist movement that promoted king and constitution. In July 1791 there were riots in support of church and monarchy in Birmingham, which some newspapers presented as spontaneous and emotional outbreaks of popular fervour. *The Times*, for instance, reported the Birmingham riots as coming from 'the LOYALTY of the people and the utter abhorrence in which the principles of a REPUBLICAN SYSTEM OF GOVERNMENT are held by the people at large'.[20] Between November 1792 and March 1793 there was a series of public burnings of effigies of Tom Paine, with the *Leicester Chronicle* noting that this 'revealed the sincere loyalty of the populace at large'.[21] Historians caution us not to take these events at face value, and certainly they were not as organic as they were made out to be, but part of a wider programme instigated by the state and its allies.[22] Many were organised by the Association for Preserving Liberty and Property against Republicans and Levellers, also known as the Crown and Anchor Society, founded in late November 1792 by John Reeves. The organisation had close links to Pitt's ministry: it received government money, and the first advertisements (in the government-aligned *Sun* newspaper) were arranged by the undersecretary at the Home Office, Evan Nepean. As many as 2,000 loyalist associations were founded up and down the country in 1792 and 1793.[23] Alongside this came a tide of loyalist propaganda, through address, sermon, tract and festival, while publications such as Hannah More's *Village Politics* and later her *Cheap Repository Tracts* were written to directly combat radical literature in the new marketplace of ideas.[24]

The state's propaganda push was a reaction to very real concerns about the spread of radical and reforming ideas. William Windham, a moderate Whig MP, thought Britain had been infiltrated by French sympathisers: 'In every town, in every village, nay almost every house, these worthy gentlemen had their agents,' he later wrote.[25] In response, the government tightened its powers of surveillance. The British Secret Service, a small and peripheral organisation at the start of the 1790s, rapidly grew into the Alien Office, which monitored the entry of people into Britain. Government expenditure on intelligence increased sixfold across the 1790s: Nepean dispersed £50,571 on Home Office 'secret business' between June 1791 and March 1795, and Pitt later explained to the House of Commons that overall secret expenditure in 1795 totalled £150,000.[26] The Alien Office also took over control of domestic surveillance, and in particular the activities of the LCS, with none other than John Reeves at its head. His Crown and Anchor Society, ostensibly a conduit for loyalist thought, was also a policing operation designed for the surveillance and prosecution of Paineite radicalism. This involved mobilising local authorities and employers against radical sympathisers, observing taverns and alehouses, and organising extensive correspondence with Whitehall about individuals who merited closer inspection. In 1794, Reeves's close relation James Reeves was employed to spy on the LCS and was crucial in helping to bring to trial a number of its leading figures.[27]

The state also acted to close down radical literary space. Panicked by the content and success of the second part of *Rights of Man* – the Attorney General complained that it had been 'thrust into the hands of subjects of every description' – on 21 May 1792 the government issued a Royal Proclamation Against Seditious Writing. Paine was indicted for libel and sedition, though a delay in organising the trial allowed him to escape across the Channel where he was given honorary French citizenship and elected to the National Convention. The prosecution went ahead in his absence, and the jury found him guilty. Paine was not alone in feeling the wrath of the state, though. In the aftermath of the proclamation, bookshops, taverns and coffee houses were watched by informers and by men of property alarmed by the spread of popular radicalism. John Frost, a close friend of Paine, was overheard declaring his support for 'Equality, and no King' in a coffee shop and was convicted and sent to Newgate prison for six months. Publishers such as James Ridgeway and H.D. Symonds were sent to Newgate in 1793 for publishing Paine's work and Charles Pigott's satirical *The Jockey Club*, which mocked Britain's social elites. Earlier in the eighteenth century the Court of King's Bench had witnessed on average two prosecutions a year, but by the 1790s this had multiplied to over ten, with nineteen in 1792 alone. Through legislation, and with the support of loyalist observers, the state's ability to quarantine texts only grew.[28]

The government also targeted the meetings of the London Corresponding Society. The first general meeting of the LCS in October 1793 had to change its venue when the landlord was threatened with the loss of his licence. The second, held a month later in the open air at Spitalfields, was so heavily policed that the number of constables and magistrates almost equalled the number of LCS members present.[29] When it was clear this would not halt the movement, the government encouraged more legalistic tactics. In 1794, Scottish courts handed out draconian sentences against radical activists attending a British convention for reform in Edinburgh, and the LCS's plans to call a 'Convention' in England that same year gave the government a pretext to arrest its leaders. Thirty men, including the secretary of the LCS, Thomas Hardy, were taken into custody, and the government established two secret committees to examine the papers seized, on the basis of which they suspended habeas corpus. From this point, any Briton could be arrested by the state without the need to provide cause. A second report produced months later concluded that radical societies had been planning what amounted to high treason: at the very least attempting to achieve a reform of Parliament by overawing sovereign power, and at worst planning a full-scale revolution. Following a subsequent open-air meeting in Copenhagen Fields in October 1795, the government pushed through the Seditious Meeting Act and the Treasonable and Seditious Practices Act (collectively known as the 'Gagging Acts') that made it illegal to criticise the king and restricted the size of public meetings to fifty people.[30]

This era of state repression has been termed 'Pitt's Terror', a deliberate attempt to equate the actions of the British government with those brought in by the Jacobin committees in France. Certainly, being a radical in the 1790s meant constant fear of arrest, and draconian sentences were possible: William Skirving, Maurice Margarot and Joseph Gerrald were each given fourteen years' transportation for calling for the organisation of a British convention, sentences that shocked many impartial observers. However, the inconsistency of sentencing for sedition in the 1790s, and the regularity with which those accused were acquitted, are also marked.[31] In November 1793, Daniel Isaac Eaton was tried for publishing a speech by John Thelwall which referenced a tyrannical gamecock, 'King Chanticleer', beheaded for his despotic behaviour, but he was acquitted when his attorney pointed out that it was the Attorney General who had committed sedition by linking the publication to George III. Following the arrests of 1794, Thomas Hardy, John Horne Tooke and John Thelwall were all charged with high treason, but they were also acquitted when the prosecution failed to offer any evidence of armed insurrection or a conspiracy against the king. These 'Treason Trials' revealed the great risk the government took in trying radicals in such a public way, and the defendants made much of the fact that their plan for parliamentary reform was similar to one proposed by Pitt himself a decade earlier.[32] The acquittals were greeted with delight in radical and opposition circles and were deeply embarrassing for the government. If the sinewy arm of the state was flexing more than it had done previously, it could not always grip its target securely.

This heated political climate was stirred further by the coming of war with Revolutionary France. In February 1793, the French Republic's avowed motive of spreading revolutionary ideas across Europe led to a declaration of war on Britain. War with France was not a novel concept to eighteenth-century Britons; indeed, they only had to look back a decade for the last time the two nations had fought. It was clear to all onlookers, however, that this was not the traditional enemy of old, but a new and more threatening revolutionary adversary. Cuthbert Collingwood, a naval captain from the North East and an avowed conservative, understood its ideological nature only too well:

> This war is certainly unlike any former, both in its object and execution. The object is a great and serious one, to resist the machinations of a mad people who, under the mask of freedom, wou'd stamp their tyranny in every country in Europe, and support and defend the happiest constitution that ever wisdom formed for the preserving order in civil society.[33]

War against Revolutionary France helped justify some of the government's more repressive legislation, and the slow mobilisation of Britain's military machinery offered further propagandist potential. However, war also brought with it food shortages, increased taxation and invasive recruitment activities, and in the process it opened up new political fault lines. Opposition Whigs spoke out against the war, while radicals opposed it even more vigorously.[34] Throughout the conflict, which lasted until 1801, critiques of the British war effort became commonplace, and the war was by far the single most-discussed topic in political pamphlet literature.[35]

The 1790s, then, brought the Age of Revolutions to Britain, marked by radicalism, loyalism, state repression and, in 1793, war with an ideologically driven neighbour. While each had precedents, this was a fundamental step change from what had come before, with the French Revolution as its spark. Britons were confronted with the spectre of mass political activity, and the state was forced to acknowledge that it needed to attend to the opinions of a much wider portion of society than those who cast votes in elections.[36] Even the most repressive legislation prompted an engaged and critical response from the British public. Opposition to the Gagging Acts in Derby, Nottingham and Sheffield, as well as London, represented the last great constitutional protests of the eighteenth century, and petitions against the legislation drew four times as many signatures as did those in its favour.[37] Similarly, despite the attempt to limit speech, attacks on the government found other avenues, whether through anonymous handbills or other forms of media that proved hard to censor. It was in this context of war, political engagement and extra-parliamentary activity that the Navy took centre stage.

Within the vast historiography on the Age of Revolutions, the Royal Navy is frequently a supporting character, its relevance to wider scholarly debates confined to its role as a fighting force that propped up the British state. This book challenges this framework, bringing the social and political developments of the era into the maritime world. Amid the wide scholarship on the emergence of political radicalism and state repression outlined previously, the political sympathies of naval sailors, and the wider impact of these political developments on the Navy, have been overlooked. Here the Navy suffers in comparison with its shore-based equivalents. There have been countless studies that place the activities of the army, militia and volunteer forces in the political culture of the 1790s, land-based forces whose centrality to issues of domestic loyalism and subversion are obvious.[38] Naval fleets that for the most part served at one remove – and often at great distance – from most Britons have rarely been given the same attention. J.E. Cookson, whose *British Armed Nation* represents one of the finest examples of scholarship on the militarisation of British society in the 1790s, argued that 'the navy does not seem to have impinged on politics, government, and society to nearly the same extent as the land forces, perhaps mainly because of the physical remoteness of seamen in comparison with soldiers and auxiliaries'.[39] In recent years, this notion has come under attack by scholars such as Isaac Land and Nicholas Rogers, who have offered studies that position naval sailors more firmly within Britain's wider political culture.[40] However, it remains the case that historians of Britain's revolutionary era rarely think about the men who worked on the Navy's ships, and who came to affect British politics in numerous ways.

This is all the more surprising when one considers that the Navy was one of the largest communities of labour in the country, with almost 130,000 sailors serving in its ranks during wartime, alongside thousands of officers. What is more, these were mobile, cosmopolitan people. It was the sailors' lot to travel, to experience new places and sights beyond the comprehension of those Britons who remained at home. John Jupp marvelled in 1798 at the sight of the 'Burning Mountain' of Mount Vesuvius, and later 'Pompeys Pillar', a solid stone column measuring 114 feet in height that he declared 'one of the 7 Wonders of the World', as he sailed across the Mediterranean.[41] Ships were also spaces where men of different backgrounds, communities and even nations came together: naval crews were remarkably diverse, with a range of different nationalities present on board; only half identified as 'English'.[42] Added to this, a high proportion of sailors were also literate, with the most recent scholarship suggesting that 62 per cent of sailors in this period were able to write letters to loved ones; even those who could not were able to ask better-educated messmates to act as their scribes.[43] The acts of writing, reading, exchange and discussion were commonplace on a naval ship, and attempts to prevent sailors from engaging in these activities could have severe consequences. In July 1797, one of the complaints of the mutineers of the *Saturn* was that they had been cut off from shore and received 'no Newspapers'.[44] Throughout Britain's Age of Revolutions, the maintenance of lines of dialogue, communication and news was essential to any naval community, and naval sailors offer a fascinating case study into political engagement in the era.

Not only did the Navy represent a large and significant body of labour; it was also a social community that mirrored hierarchies on land. There is now a vast body of work that explores the social worlds of the Navy in the late eighteenth century and reveals a complex hierarchy of rank and status.[45] This was not one interchangeable mass of men, but a conglomerate of different levels of authority and expertise that did not always map directly onto the Navy's pecking order. There was a vast difference in status between a raw landsman new to the service and an able seaman who had years of experience under his belt. Alongside these men of the 'lower deck' came petty officers such as the coxswain, the master-at-arms and the quartermaster, as well as specialist positions such as the cook and schoolmaster. Further up the naval hierarchy came warrant officers, representatives of the burgeoning British mercantile middling classes: these included the ship's master, who navigated the ship, and the purser, who was responsible for the vessel's supplies, alongside the surgeon, gunner, carpenter and boatswain. Command of a vessel was entrusted to commissioned officers, lieutenants and a captain, who had been through an intense period of practical training and passed an examination in order to hold their position. While there were officers of blue blood, for the most part they were also drawn from the ambitious middling classes.[46] Taken together, this was a layered and complex social world, and a microcosm of wider British society.

With the outbreak of war in 1793, it was assumed that the Royal Navy would be a prominent counter-revolutionary force. National security rested upon its ships and fleets, defending against a French invasion of the country while also protecting British trade and extending the country's imperial position around the globe. As one pamphlet noted:

> Whosoever considers the position of England, and of its Colonies, will perceive that our very existence depends on this circumstance alone, viz. that we should be superior at sea; all our politics ought therefore to be directed to that object singly.[47]

In the aftermath of the disastrous American War, government and public alike were content to pay for fleets, funded by high levels of taxation that promised protection from external threats. William Pitt's government invested vast amounts of money in the infrastructure and fighting ships of the Royal Navy, allocating the astonishing sum of £39.96 million on naval expenditure between 1784 and 1792, allowing dockyard workers to be kept on, new docks to be built at Portsmouth and Plymouth, and the fleet to be rebuilt.[48] The Navy's strategic significance was matched by its cultural prominence. Across the eighteenth century, a series of 'Admiral heroes' had offered compelling symbols around which notions of Britishness coalesced, while its seamen – 'the bulwark of Great Britain' – were represented as brave, loyal and constant servants to the national interest in numerous forms of media.[49] A pamphlet from 1790 spoke for many when it stated that 'The Nation loves the Navy; it is a favoured Service'.[50]

It followed that when revolutionary activity seemed to appear in the service, it not only struck at the heart of the nation's security but also undermined its greatest patriotic symbol. For all these reasons, then, the Navy offers a fascinating window into thinking about wider developments in political engagement, state and society during the Age of Revolutions. However, just as historians of Britain have frequently ignored the Navy, scholars of the maritime world all too often have failed to think about the political contexts in which its sailors and officers operated. On the contrary, historians have been quick to dismiss sailors as political actors: Michael Lewis suggested that the 'real British Seaman was usually a simple soul, obstinately conservative, ill-educated', and more recently, Stephen Taylor's study suggested that the British sailor had little awareness or interest in 'political designs'.[51]

Certainly, sailors happily played up to their 'simpleton' stereotype when it suited them. In the aftermath of shipboard disorder, sailors claimed not to understand, or remember, what had happened in a deliberate attempt to avoid punishment.[52] However, scholars who have emphasised sailors' naïveté have usually followed the cultural trope, rather than the reality. More sophisticated analyses, such as N.A.M. Rodger's study of the mid-eighteenth-century Navy, stress the fundamental loyalty of sailors and depict the naval ship as a place of consensus.[53] However, the deluge of political activity that emerged after the declaration of war in 1793 denoted something very different. If the traditional eighteenth-century naval community was marked by mutual reliance between ranks, this was shattered by the revolutionary upheavals of the 1790s.

There is a competing body of scholarship based around the idea of a 'revolutionary Atlantic'. This stresses the transnational nature of sailors' activity, emphasising class struggle and the exploitation of labour by developing capitalist systems. For Marcus Rediker, the maritime proletariat that emerged in the eighteenth century was driven by a fundamental 'class confrontation' between common sailors and their officers over 'issues of power, authority, work and discipline'. Rediker, with Peter Linebaugh, has gone on to argue that the political culture of the maritime working classes represented a marginal, alternative order, or a 'hydrarchy', defined by its proletarian roots and opposition to the authority of the state.[54] More recently, Niklas Frykman's work on the

British, Dutch and French naval mutinies of the 1790s offers a transnational take on naval rebellion, exploring how naval rebellions across European nations overthrew the 'absolute rule' of naval officers.[55] This remains an important framework for understanding the nature of maritime labour and the variety of ways in which sailors could resist authority across the eighteenth century. However, not every sailor saw shipboard conflict in terms of class, and many chose not to rebel against their officers; for every potential revolutionary, there was also a loyalist who chose to protect the status quo. What is more, even those sailors who did take part in shipboard protest understood their 'rights' in a defiantly 'British' patriotic context.[56] Daniel Campbell, seaman of the *Tartar*, offers one telling example. In his complaints about his officers in 1797, he made it clear that this 'was not the way to use a British seaman', a stance that was replicated across the nation's fleets.[57]

One commonality of these works, whether stressing the fundamental loyalty of sailors or their links with Atlantic radicalism, is that sailors were unique. In Rediker's view, 'maritime radicalism' offered something fundamentally different from that of land-based society, while N.A.M. Rodger stresses the longer tradition of maritime protest, distinct from shore-based customs.[58] While these two schools of thought hold dimorphous views in almost every respect, here, at least, they agree: the sailor was a peculiar and different beast. In this, both owe something to the Foucauldian vision of the ship as a 'heterotopia', a 'floating piece of space . . . that exists by itself'.[59] And yet, while the working lives of sailors were distinctive in many respects, the distance between ship and shore was never as large as is often thought. Sailors remained firmly connected to communities on land; as we will see, the politics, social hierarchies and labour practices of the maritime world remained rooted in land-based cultures. Indeed, ideas moved the other way too. Just as naval personnel were shaped by societies ashore, so too were land-based practices influenced by sailors' activity. The English term 'strike' is itself inherently maritime in origin, the first instance recorded in 1768 when sailors referred to the act of striking (dismantling) the rigging to communicate their refusal to sail and protest their working conditions.[60] From the outset, then, this book argues that sailors' lives were distinct, but not separate.

Tempest attempts to bridge these competing bodies of scholarship and place the Navy at the forefront of Britain's Age of Revolutions. From the outset, the Navy was a vital actor in the war against Revolutionary France, and this book discusses its major contributions to the war effort. There is a vast scholarship on individual battles and personalities (predominantly officers) but there have been few attempts to think about the naval operations of the 1790s collectively.[61] Certainly, they are rarely viewed outside the triumphalist lens that so often dominates naval historical writing. At the same time, this is not a book about 'how the Navy won the war', not least because Britain ended up on the losing side. When peace preliminaries were signed in 1801, French continental successes far outstripped those achieved by the Navy at sea, and the Treaty of Amiens that brought the conflict to an end saw France granted exceedingly favourable terms in return for an end to the conflict; France was left not just intact but in a stronger position in Europe than it had been in 1793. Furthermore, while the Navy won a series of victories fervently celebrated by swathes of the British public, the conflict was also marked by calamitous imperial expeditions and a series of naval failures that prompted the very real fear of a French invasion of the British Isles. Added to this, the revolutionary age saw, for the first time, the prospect of a full-scale naval revolt, one that was threatened in the early years of the war and which finally came to pass in 1797. For the most part, this is a book about a Navy in crisis.

Tempest moves beyond operational considerations and also uses the Navy to explore wider processes of popular political engagement. It argues that naval sailors had a sophisticated understanding of contemporary politics and redeployed this in a maritime context. This was not a new phenomenon, for sailors had long framed their appeals in terms of 'usage' and 'liberties' that drew on an established tradition of British intellectual thought. However, this was turbo-charged in the intellectual and political watershed of the early 1790s. Sailors engaged with political theorists like Rousseau, Paine and Godwin, and they used the language of 'rights' and 'tyranny' to justify their actions. In 1795, the naval officer Philip Patton made a direct connection between political upheaval and naval rebellion, noting that France had presented itself 'under a new aspect to Seamen' as a 'Land of Liberty' and that it would 'affect the Maritime world in general'. He worried about the impact on the sailors: 'now the times are changed . . . the day seems not to be very distant . . . when a general disposition to Mutiny takes place'.[62] This prediction came to pass, and the 1790s was defined by sailors' increased engagement with politics, whether through swearing oaths, writing petitions and political declarations, or planning mutinies on a scale hitherto unseen. Naval sailors were but one community of labour, but together they offer an insight into the different ways Britons in this period participated in political culture.

It is important to stress here that this engagement took many forms, and that sailors did not act as one united group. On the contrary, there were deep divisions among the Navy's crews, divisions that can be mapped onto the wider currents of the era. Some sailors were undeniably radical, whether adopting new forms of protest or adapting long-standing traditions. Many sailors were aware of – and sometimes participated in – the literature and activities of societies like the LCS, or rebellious organisations such as the United Irishmen. Others were less explicit in their ideology but hoped for moderate reform of the naval world. Some identified more with the Whig political tradition, arguing against Pitt's repressive measures or the justness of the war. We should also note that many other sailors chose not to protest or rebel; indeed, it is possible to draw out a thick seam of loyalism in the ranks of naval crews. These were not unthinking, pliant men, but individuals who made a conscious choice to oppose mutiny or other attempts to undermine officers' authority on board a ship. In the most heated moments, sailors violently disagreed with each other about aims and means, and the consequences of rebellious activity also brought these divisions to the fore. Sailors testified against each other in court, often with horrendous consequences – a far cry from the solidarity on show elsewhere in the decade. Their views, therefore, were far from monolithic and instead represented a kaleidoscope of opinion that changed according to time and place. Whether radical, reformist, Whig or loyalist, they were fully participating in Britain's Age of Revolutions.

Tempest also considers how the naval arm of the state, primarily the Admiralty, responded to sailors' political engagement during the revolutionary age. There is a vast literature on the relationship between the Navy and the development of fiscal institutions, as well as research on the ways in which naval logistics contributed to the development of the British state, in terms of its size, its professionalism and its relationship with the private sector.[63] There is also a sizeable scholarship on how the state intervened in markets, in particular the food market.[64] Only recently, however, have historians begun to think about the ways in which the Admiralty attempted to control its sailors.[65] Confronted by the spectre of mass naval resistance and numerous naval failures, the Admiralty ushered in new legislation and practices, including more oppressive recruitment methods and mass executions of naval mutineers designed for the express purpose of deterring further rebellion. The government also organised naval propaganda designed to instil loyalism in the population. We have already seen how John Reeves's association acted as a hub of loyalist thought, but alongside this came an array of government sponsored or supported media. Newspapers aligned with – and sometimes owned by – politicians disseminated pro-governmental takes on recent events, while a tide of loyalist ballads, broadsides and tracts were distributed by local notables, many paid for with government subsidies.[66] Taken together, this represented a concerted attempt by the state to appropriate the Navy as a cultural tool.[67]

Lastly, the book shows that debates over the political activities of sailors, officers and the Navy alike infiltrated – and at times came to dominate discussion within – the public sphere. In recent years, scholarly attention has focused increasingly on the impact of warfare on British society, demonstrating that while Britain's many conflicts were for the most part fought away from British soil, they still left a considerable imprint on the British people.[68] At the same time, there is a burgeoning literature on the cultural contexts in which the Navy operated, and an increasing number of studies have explored the ways in which the Navy could be used in popular media.[69] *Tempest* seeks to build on this and to show how the revolutionary period eroded public faith in the Royal Navy. Here too there were continuities with the previous decades, for while the eighteenth century saw numerous celebrations for naval victories, the American War prompted critiques of the Navy's contributions to the war effort, and disputes among the officer corps. Throughout the 1790s, this became ever more widespread, and the Navy was mocked for its failure to protect national interests. There was also a more fundamental breakdown, however, as the public image of the sailor transformed from that of the loyal patriot to a more problematic image that emphasised his troubling political allegiances. While the idea of a strong, successful Navy manned by a loyal workforce remained resilient in the early years of the war, the public's relationship with the Navy was tested to its limits by the challenges of the revolutionary era.

Taken together, then, *Tempest* offers the first sustained, comprehensive treatment of the Navy that links it to the wider political contours of the revolutionary age. It is a study of battles, blockades and imperial warfare, but also of mutiny and resistance, of politics and propaganda, consistently bringing the analysis back to the wider social and cultural contexts in which the Navy acted. As such, it represents a 'new' naval history that uses this institution to explore a larger scholarly issue.[70] Studying the Navy of the 1790s offers a lens through which to view wider processes of political engagement, the growth of the state, and the fluctuations of public opinion. At the same time, this book argues that it is impossible to understand the Navy's history in the 1790s without also comprehending the wider revolutionary upheaval in which it operated. After all, every sailors' voyage started on land, and it is to these first steps that we now turn.

ONE

LAWLESS MOBS AND A GORE OF BLOOD
Naval Mobilisation and Impressment

The outbreak of war in February 1793 found John Nicol hiding from a press gang. He had just arrived in Gravesend after a long trading voyage and was determined to make his way to London, where he hoped to find work on an East India Company ship. As a sailor of long experience, Nicol was a prime target for the Royal Navy, and he was terrified at the prospect of being impressed. When a naval ship came alongside his vessel, Nicol took evasive action: he and another sailor stowed themselves so deeply among bags of cotton that they were 'almost smothered', and the two men escaped detection. Alarmed at this close call, Nicol decided to travel over land, this time using a disguise to evade the Navy. He changed into his shore-going clothes and complemented them with a powdered wig, cocked hat and cane purchased from a customs officer, with which he hoped to impersonate a clerk going about his daily business. 'I am confident my own father, had he been alive, could not have known me,' he recalled. His impersonation required no little initiative: at one point he called for a pen and ink when dining at an inn to throw a suspicious local off the scent, and under their watchful gaze he made himself busy 'writing any nonsense that came in my head'. Throughout his journey, the threat to Nicol's liberty was very real. 'Had [he] suspected me to be a sailor,' he later wrote, 'he would have informed the press gang in one minute. The waiters at the inn would have done the same.'[1]

Nicol's tactics of evasion were colourful, to be sure, but his narrative of fear, avoidance and popular surveillance was typical of countless sailors operating across the British Isles in the spring of 1793. In years of peace the Royal Navy could rely on a small, skeletal workforce of only a few thousand men, but the coming of war brought mass mobilisation and the need for tens, if not hundreds of thousands of sailors.[2] Most in demand were skilled sailors such as Nicol, identifiable by their muscular frame, tarry hands and distinctive gait fashioned by years spent on a rolling vessel, who could be integrated into the complex world of the naval ship with little difficulty. Such men were not easily produced, however, presenting the Admiralty with a problem its military counterpart did not have. Nicol himself noted that 'could the government make perfect seamen as easily as they could soldiers, there would be no such thing as the pressing of seamen'.[3] While the Admiralty hoped for volunteers, there were never enough to fill the Navy's ranks, and the British government instead resorted to impressment, a deeply controversial practice by which seamen were forced into the Navy against their will. This began a cat-and-mouse game, played out around the world, as press gangs searched for recruits, and sailors attempted to resist.[4] Impressment had long been a tried-and-tested means of securing maritime labour, but it became all the more intense in the heady political environment of the early 1790s, when it came to represent the worst excesses of a tyrannical and undemocratic government. In the minds of ruling elites, opposition to impressment aligned ominously with escalating levels of political protest, prompting an unprecedented response from the British state as the Navy used ever more intrusive and violent means to secure maritime labour.

Nicol himself soon discovered that the reach of the state was difficult to avoid. Having escaped the press gang's clutches in 1793, he arrived in London and found work on board a merchant ship, the *Nottingham*, bound for China. On its return to Britain the following year, he once again began to work on a disguise in the hope of avoiding naval service. Nicol allowed his beard to grow longer and he stopped washing, hoping to make himself as unappealing as possible to the naval crews that intercepted and searched mercantile vessels returning to Britain. Briefly, it seemed that fortune was on his side. The *Nottingham* was examined by a naval recruitment party in the English Channel but Nicol was down in the hold and avoided being selected. However, his luck soon ran out. One of the sailors who had been seized had an injured leg, and the naval officer returned to the vessel and took Nicol in his place. 'Thus were all my schemes blown into the air,' he wrote, and 'I found myself in a situation I could not leave, a bondage that had been imposed upon me against my will . . . Remonstrance and complaint were equally vain.'[5] Like many thousands of others, Nicol found himself coerced into the Navy, his liberty removed and his future prospects uncertain.

War brought an urgent need for maritime labour. In an ideal world, the Royal Navy would be manned solely by enthusiastic volunteers determined to serve their country, and judging by the propaganda of the time, there was every expectation that such men existed. Recruitment posters appealed to 'Royal Tars of Old England' and called on all those who 'love your country' to repair to their local recruiting officer.[6] Local rendezvous points, usually inns or taverns, acted as recruitment centres where dedicated Regulating Captains flew flags, dispensed alcohol and displayed literature that was designed to appeal to the patriotic and xenophobic instincts of potential volunteers. One such appeal called on 'Englishmen willing to defend their country' and created an alarmist picture of a French enemy who would imminently 'invade Old England' to make 'whores of our wives and daughters' and to 'rob us of our property'.[7] Britain was also awash with loyalist ballads, written and performed in the hope of encouraging further recruits. The song *The British Tars*, for instance, advocated that 'true hearts of oak' will 'put to sea again' and offered an example for all to follow:

When War at first assail'd us,
I quickly left my trade,
Our Country was in danger,
I flew to lend my aid . . .[8]

The balladeer Charles Dibdin was paid a pension by the British government to produce patriotic ballads that celebrated the simple loyalty and
manly courage of the British sailor, and he went on to produce over one
hundred such songs in the course of the French Wars.[9]

There is evidence that this propaganda – and culture more generally
– did inspire some hearts and minds. John Nicol had been encouraged to
go to sea in the first place having read *Robinson Crusoe* 'many times over',
though given the nature of Crusoe's trials there is some question about
whether he got beyond the first chapters.[10] Another sailor, John Gibbs,
was so determined to join the Navy that he lied on his recruitment form,
stating that he was 'entirely free from all Engagements' and that he
'voluntarily enlisted myself to serve His Majesty King George'.[11]
Enlistment activities went hand in hand with loyalist celebrations:
recruitment parties were prominent during an effigy-burning of Thomas
Paine in Plymouth in early December 1792 that was attended by thousands. Newspapers, particularly those of a pro-government bent,
published numerous stories that described volunteers marching happily
to recruiting stations with flags flying and drums beating.[12] In reality,
more pragmatic decision-making probably lay behind volunteering.
Most recruitment literature also advertised the pecuniary rewards available, and it seems likely that these were more important motivators.
Edward McGuire, for instance, came to England in the early 1790s as a
labourer, but finding 'the work being slack & times very dear', he volunteered for the Navy. Financial considerations also prompted the Jamaican
sailor Thomas Ottery to join, to help pay a debt of £40.[13] Sailors could
also expect to receive free medical care, and well-manned naval ships
were less arduous workplaces than their mercantile equivalents. In this
sense, the naval labour market was much like any other, with a complex
mix of social and pecuniary incentives offered in exchange for work.

The problem for the Navy was that patriotism and a steady wage
only went so far. An able seaman (someone with more than two years'
experience at sea) earned 24 shillings a month, while an ordinary seaman
(someone with more than one year's experience) earned 19 shillings. A

raw 'landsman' was paid a mere 18 shillings. These wages were not entirely representative, for naval sailors were given free food and shelter as part of their service, and prize money allowed fortunate sailors to supplement their wages.[14] Even taking this into account, however, their salaries placed them squarely among Britain's 'lower sorts', on a par with agricultural labourers, who in the early 1790s could expect to earn around 26 or 27 shillings per month, and below the estimated average male wage of between 39 and 45 shillings per month.[15] What is more, the Navy could not compete with rival professions, in particular commercial shipping, where skilled sailors could earn as much as 60–70 shillings per month.[16] Rather than increasing pay, the Navy's solution was to offer one-off enlistment bounties of £5, £2 10s, and £1 10s for able seamen, ordinary seamen and landsmen respectively. Only reluctantly did the government seek to intervene directly in the labour market for seamen, and not until March 1795 when manning concerns forced their hand. The 'Quota Acts' were intended as a limited form of conscription in which maritime counties were instructed to provide a set number of trained seamen. They too resorted to bounties to encourage men to come forward, and the best estimate is that around 31,000 seamen were recruited in this way.[17]

Further bounties were provided by local associations, keen to play their part in the war effort. This was a truly national endeavour, with successful subscriptions held at Carnarvon, Great Yarmouth, Ashburton, Wrexham and the Isle of Wight, to name but a few locations.[18] In each place, lists of subscribers were published in local newspapers, allowing the middling classes to demonstrate their patriotic zeal in the most public way possible. The *True Briton* made particular mention of Manchester, for while there was 'the greatest possibility of that Town being the first to suffer by a War', due to its reliance on foreign trade, 'such is the spirit of patriotism that pervades the Country . . . that a large sum was very soon subscribed there, for the purpose of raising men for His Majesty's Service'. Eleven 'gentlemen' subscribed 100 guineas each to raise a regiment of Royal Marines, and within the week 1,100 people had come forward to serve.[19] Later in the war – and somewhat less altruistically – naval recruitment also provided a means for local authorities to rid themselves of 'undesirable' people. A new statute introduced in 1795 allowed them to raise 'able bodied and idle persons as shall be found within the said counties to serve in His Majesty's Navy': in April 1795, thirty such people were presented to the Navy at Newgate, and a further forty-two at Dublin in November.[20] In Liverpool, the regulating officer Captain Worth admitted that one sailor, George Wood, had been forcibly entered into the Navy because he was a 'common disturber of the peace'.[21]

Who were the men who came forward for the Navy? A register of sailors recruited in the maritime county of Dorset offers a fascinating window into the backgrounds of the men who volunteered. It reveals that these were overwhelmingly young men between the ages of seventeen and twenty-two, with a few older hands in their late thirties and early forties; the median age of those coming forward from Bridport, for instance, was twenty-one. For the most part they were local men from Dorset or neighbouring Somerset and Wiltshire, their options limited by the economic dislocations of the era. Half of the men recruited in Sturminster and Sherbourne were labourers struggling to find work amid an agricultural depression. Recruits were not limited to the labouring classes, however, and among the other recruits we find skilled workers adrift amid a downturn: a mason, a sawyer, a weaver and a thatcher, alongside two cordwainers. In the small town of Wareham, five of the twelve men who came forward were stonemasons, suggesting a quite specific regional decline. Some volunteers had some experience of the maritime world and were able to leverage their skills for higher bounty payments. A few described themselves as 'mariners', such as Joseph Lucas, who received £9 9s, a vast sum. Labourers also declared that they had previously 'used the sea for some years' in order to command higher bounties.[22]

The enrolling officers scribbled details of each volunteer's distinguishing marks, revealing brief flashes of humanity. Some men had tattoos, such as Thomas Bates, who had depictions of Adam and Eve on his left arm. Joshua Cox had anchors engraved into his skin, while Hillery Viell had a crucifix, suggesting that he was Catholic. Both of these men also marked their bodies with the initials of loved ones: Cox had the letters 'J.C.' cut across his hand, while Viell marked his arm with the letters 'F.N.' and 'R.F.' Sailors' physical appearance was also noted, giving us glimpses of what these recruits looked like. The majority were described as being 'fair' or 'ruddy', but Adam Davey, William Mitford and Joseph Jones were described as having a 'Dark Complexion', and may therefore have been Black. These are fragmentary details, and we are left attempting to reconstruct lives based on very little. Take, for example, the thirty-six-year old James Burk, who is recorded as having lost the tips of two fingers on his left hand, and whose home parish was Cork in Ireland. We know nothing else about him, and quite why he found himself in Dorset in 1795 is a mystery. Still, there was something about the Navy – whether the lure of steady wages, a generous bounty (he received £5 12s) or other inducements – that encouraged him to come forward as a volunteer.[23]

The simple truth, however, was that the Navy could not rely on market forces to man its ships. As a result, from the outset of war, the Admiralty authorised widespread impressment in an urgent effort to find skilled labour. This was organised by the Impress Service, which by 1795 consisted of 32 Regulating Captains overseeing 85 press gangs and a total of 754 men, stationed across Britain and Ireland. Their instructions gave them incredible licence to find men wherever they could, with specific orders to procure volunteers and impress such 'Seafaring men ... as will not enter voluntarily'.[24] Impressment itself happened in two ways. Firstly, press gangs operated in maritime communities and seaports where they targeted mariners waiting for their next voyage. The second – and as the war went on the most common – means of impressment was to take sailors directly from merchant ships.[25] At the start of a given war an embargo was placed on trade which allowed the Navy to take sailors from mercantile vessels, while for the remainder of the conflict commercial ships were searched and sailors forcibly

N

Atlantic Ocean

North Sea

Glasgow Edinburgh

Londonderry

Newcastle South Shields
Sunderland
Belfast Whitby

Irish Sea Hull

Dublin Liverpool

Yarmouth

Waterford London

Cork Deal

Haverfordwest Gravesend
Swansea Portsmouth
Pembroke Bristol

Dorchester Folkestone
Bridport
Exeter
Plymouth Poole
Wareham

0 km 100
0 miles 100

English Channel

Map 1: Britain and the impress service, 1793–5.

removed. There was a balance to be struck here, and politicians tried to ensure that the mercantile trade on which Britain also relied was not decimated by shortages of labour.[26] Some officers took this consideration seriously: Admiral Richard Howe was desperate for trained seamen in the early months of the war, but he insisted on leaving at least forty sailors on returning Indiamen to ensure they got back to port safely.[27] However, there were others who cared little about the consequences of removing large numbers of men from trading vessels. The merchant master Samuel Kelly described a near-permanent conflict as naval officers attempted to take men from his ships. At one point his vessel avoided the port of Liverpool altogether when he had heard that extensive impressment operations were under way there.[28]

There were clear rules about who could be impressed. Only men aged between eighteen and fifty-five who 'used the sea' could be taken, though this was a subjective term at best. The Navy was also allowed to take those men who worked 'in vessels and Boats upon rivers', a capacious definition that included a range of occupations, not just deep-sea sailors. Numerous groups – including apprentices, masters and first mates of merchant ships, pilots, government officials, foreigners and those working in the Greenland fisheries and east coast coal trade – were given specific protections for fear of upsetting the rhythm of commerce crucial to the British economy. In each case, sailors were presented with a document that explicitly banned them from being impressed.[29] The administration of protections took up a lot of government time, and some regulating captains took the regulations seriously.[30] Jaheel Brenton complained in June 1794 that he had been forced to discharge many recruits as they were 'old & inferior' or 'young apprentices', while in Hampshire, William Yeo bewailed that fishermen were not liable to be taken.[31] The rules could be bent, however. At times of great labour shortage, the government could declare a 'hot press', which allowed regulating captains to waive certain restrictions. Furthermore, naval officers were given incredible licence to distrust protections and a number ignored them altogether.[32] Samuel Kelly remembered that two Swedish sailors signed to his ship were impressed, and that the regulating captain simply ignored his appeals. The American sailor Prince Edward testified during a court martial that he had shown his protection to the press gang officer, who 'tore it before my face' and subsequently impressed him.[33]

One of the most difficult tasks for the historian is to discover exactly how many of those recruited in this period were impressed, and attempts to construct a reliable figure are riven with methodological issues. A recent quantitative study of naval muster books across the 1793–1801 period concluded that only 16 per cent of sailors overall were impressed, and that the great majority of the remainder were volunteers.[34] However, there are numerous problems with this analysis, not least the definition of 'volunteer'. Even if a sailor was recorded as a volunteer, the reality was often somewhat different. When press gangs went aboard a merchant ship, they asked first for volunteers and offered a generous bounty to those who came forward. They also announced that if the sailors on board 'refuse to go voluntarily, they will be excluded from those advantages', and likely pressed anyway.[35] These demands were often backed up with the threat of violence. When Lieutenant Dillon went on board a merchant ship, he made sure his men's muskets were visible and ordered that the guns of his schooner be loaded and readied to fire. Only then would he demand that 'volunteers' came forward: 'I shall order my men in the schooner to fire into you', he would shout, 'here I am, and will not quit you until I have at least 10 or 12 seamen out of this vessel'.[36] With escape unlikely and recruitment near inevitable, many people took the money and were logged as volunteers, albeit in name only.

The government was well aware of the practice, and its moral ambiguity. In 1794 two apprentice master mariners, Thomas Allan and Alexander Fairweather, were impressed but, resigned to their fate, later 'volunteered' in order to receive the bounty. When they appealed for their release, the Admiralty solicitor was forced to admit that 'These Men are pressed' and that 'a Jury would never condone their continuing under such circumstances as a Voluntary Act'.[37] Nonetheless, the Admiralty encouraged a fluid understanding of what a 'volunteer' was, and it seems that officers acted accordingly. In September 1793, Captain William Carthew noted that he had received nineteen seamen who had come to him as pressed men but who were 'desirous of becoming Volunteers'. He thought they were 'worthy of such indulgence' and that they ought to get the bounty as well 'for the purpose of more effectually attatching [sic] them to the Service'.[38] One naval midshipman happily admitted to a court martial that he had allowed a sailor to take the bounty when it became clear to them that they were 'obliged to go'.[39] The smuggler John Rattenbury was caught by a press gang, and with escape impossible he volunteered, 'if that can be called a voluntary act, which is the effect of necessity, not of inclination'.[40] While muster books report any number of 'volunteers', this is a misleading description of their status.

We will therefore probably never know exactly how many people were pressed, but even the most conservative estimate suggests that tens of thousands of men were forced into the Navy against their will during the 1790s.[41] Moreover, the focus on calculating a specific number diverts our attention from the significant emotional trauma that impressment caused. Countless testimonies make clear that it was a brutal and damaging act. William Richardson recorded how 'Some of the poor fellows shed tears on being pressed after so long a voyage and so near home', while another later recalled his fellow sailors' 'pitiable plight' in the hours after being impressed.[42] The long-term psychological impact was no less severe. The naval physician Thomas Trotter observed coerced sailors succumbing to despondency and wrote extensively about how impressment created a 'mind diseased' with hatred. In his view, impressment was 'a most fatal and impolitic practice ... the cause of more destruction to the health and lives of our seamen, than all other causes put together'.[43] Even years after sailors had returned home, the traumatic impact of impressment remained. Following his discharge from the Navy at the end of the French Revolutionary War, John Nicol spent the early 1800s paranoid that the press gang would come for him again. 'I dared not to sleep in my own house, as I had more than one call from the gang', he later recalled. He had to give up his trade, uproot his life and retire to the countryside before he could shake the fear.[44]

For every man impressed, countless others were affected. Parents, partners and children often had no idea where their sons, husbands and fathers were stationed, or even if they were dead or alive.[45] With limited means of communication, the emotional stress for sailors and their loved ones could be devastating. In October 1793, Frederick Hoffman helped impress sailors returning from the West Indies and witnessed their turmoil first-hand:

> They had been absent nearly eighteen months from their wives and families, and were fondly looking forward to a meeting with those for whom they lived and toiled, but, alas! they were doomed to return to that foreign climate they had a few months before left, and from whence it was impossible to know when they would come back.[46]

John Marlow, a seaman of the *Bellerophon*, was 'pressed into the service', leaving his wife and small family 'without being able from Bounty or any thing else to give them the smallest assistance'.[47] Mary Quick's coach-maker husband Michael had never worked on water but was impressed in April 1791. She was left to fend for herself, pregnant and with two small children, with no paternal support or indeed any idea of when he would return: it would soon, she predicted, 'bring her and them to ruin'.[48] On a larger scale, these absences reshaped local economies and networks of philanthropy. Richardson returned to his native South Shields towards the end of the war and found it far from 'that merry place we had hitherto known ... every one looked gloomy and sad on account of nearly all the young men being pressed and taken away'.[49] On Tyneside, poor relief tripled in the early 1790s to accommodate the families of seamen taken up by the press.[50]

Even those who volunteered for the Navy quickly found themselves trapped. William Robinson recalled how his ideas about naval life did not survive long on the receiving ship:

... it was for the first time I began to repent of the rash step I had taken, but it was of no avail, submission to the events of fate was my only alternative, murmuring or remonstrating, I soon found, would be folly.[51]

Once on board, there was little prospect of leaving the service until the end of the war. There were brutal punishments designed to intimidate potential deserters – the standard penalty was a flogging – and repeat offenders could be punished even more severely. Such punishments meant that even a sailor who volunteered found he could not later change his mind, and the many sailors who did come forward of their own volition found it nearly impossible to leave the service until the Royal Navy allowed it. There were no maximum terms of service, and the Navy proved expert at holding onto men once it had them. Its policy of 'turning over' men allowed it to take sailors from a ship at the end of its voyage and discharge them into another naval vessel preparing to go to sea. Through such means, even enthusiastic recruits found themselves imprisoned in the Navy for the entirety of a conflict, and by the end of the 1790s, 'turned over' men represented the largest proportion of manpower onboard British warships. William Richardson was one such victim of the Navy's strong-arming, turned over into the *Prompte* after two years away at sea 'without a moment's liberty on shore', along with thirty-six others.[52] Even for volunteers, then, naval service could become a form of coerced labour, and impressment was often just the first in a long series of injustices that curtailed a sailor's agency and freedom.

Sailors were well aware that impressment was a fundamental violation of their liberty. Naval service removed any control over their immediate future and compelled them to earn lower wages while suffering long-term separation from family.[53] Some historians have attempted to offer a more consensual take on impressment, suggesting that sailors saw it as an incident of their profession, 'soon to be got over', or that they acclimatised to naval service after about a year.[54] Certainly, sailors could be pragmatic about their immediate prospects, and the threat of severe discipline no doubt concentrated many minds. For every reference to acquiescence, though, there are others that offer critique. William Richardson recalled that he had initially resigned himself stoically to his fate on being impressed: 'I was young', he said, and as he 'had the world before me', did not 'fret much'.[55] Elsewhere, though, we find him despondent at his 'hard fate' or even offering dissenting utterances: 'Here was encouragement for seamen to fight for their king and country!', he declared after he was turned over in 1794.[56] William Spavens voiced bitter realism, noting impressment was 'a hardship which nothing but absolute necessity can reconcile to our boasted freedom'.[57] As we saw earlier, John Nicol had no compunction in referring to his impressment as a form of bondage, a very deliberate reference to chattel slavery.[58]

Sailors understood the value of their work and how this fitted into wider patterns of forced labour in the Atlantic world. In the mid-1790s the Admiralty was bombarded with petitions from naval sailors appealing for higher pay and better conditions, in which they frequently compared their plight to that of enslaved Africans. Sailors on board the British frigate *Shannon* protested that their treatment was 'more than the Spirits and Harts of true English Man can Cleaverly [Cleverly] Bear for ... we Are Bound free men and we are Determined not to be Slaves'.[59] Another petition complained that the Admiralty had:

> ... the Smallest idea of the Slavery under which we have for many years Laboured ... [We] Labour under every Disagreement and affliction which African Slaves cannot endure ... Most of us in the Fleet, who have been Prisoners ever since the war Commenc'd ... Have we not a Right to Complain?[60]

The analogy to chattel slavery was contrived: sailors received wages, and they would likely be released from their 'bondage' at the end of the war. In this sense, the comparison was a rhetorical device, used by protesting workers across the Atlantic world to advertise poor working conditions and draw attention to their plight. However, these petitions reveal sailors' assertion of their 'freedom', a critique of their coercion and imprisonment, and speak to a growing acknowledgement of their rights.

These concerns were not limited to sailors, and across British culture impressment was a deeply controversial issue; indeed, until the late eighteenth century, it inspired more widespread opposition than slavery. Impressment violated the 39th chapter of the Magna Carta, which stated that 'No man shall be taken, imprisoned ... or in any way destroyed ... except by the lawful judgement of his peers and by the law of the land'. However, the constitutionality of impressment was never challenged, and even when individual cases came up in court, judges ruled that national necessity overrode any legal issues. Away from the courtroom, coerced naval labour sat uneasily in a nation that lauded itself for a love of liberty, and whose unofficial national anthem, 'Rule Britannia', declared proudly that 'Britons will never be slaves'.[61]

It followed that numerous publications repudiated impressment, most famously James Oglethorpe's *Sailors Advocate*, published repeatedly across the eighteenth century, which denounced it as a fundamental violation of English freedom.[62] Caricaturists such as James Gillray produced bitter swipes at the practice, while Samuel Collings's 1790 print *Manning the Navy* depicted a press gang armed to the teeth attacking a would-be sailor.[63] Ballads, particularly from the 1780s onwards, paid particular attention to impressment. 'The Press'd Sailor's Lamentation', for example, tells the tale of an Irish farmer hauled away by a press gang, while 'True Blue' attacked the incongruence of impressment in a country proclaiming to be a land of liberty. It argued that 'to be prest is not due to a Briton / Whose bosom sweet liberty warms'. Press gang songs were particularly prevalent in the North East, the most famous of which was 'Here's the Tender Coming', in which the sailor's duty to his family falls foul of a press gang.[64]

Despite this hostility to the practice, it is notable how infrequently impressment became a parliamentary issue. Opposition Whigs attempted to abolish the practice in 1787, with Richard Brinsley Sheridan introducing a bill to that effect, but it was defeated by the Tory majority. There were also numerous attempts to find new solutions to the problem of naval manning, but none was deemed practical without substantially raising naval wages or reordering the British economy, a step no government was willing to take.[65] Part of the explanation for this is that for every critical statement, there were others who saw impressment as a 'necessary evil', and even loyalist statements that defended or even sympathised with press gangs. The *Sun* newspaper noted approvingly in 1794 that a lieutenant at Harwich had 'secured many useful Seamen for the supply of His Majesty's Navy', while another reported the 'unlucky circumstance' of a midshipman belonging to the press gang in Bristol being wounded and hoped that 'the greatest possible care' would be taken to prevent other disturbances.[66] A number of patriotic plays offered supportive takes on the practice. *Love and Honour; or Britannia in Full Glory at Spithead*, performed to large audiences in Covent Garden in 1794, featured a press gang that behaved responsibly and even altruistically, sympathetic to the circumstances of the individuals it met, and selective in terms of the men it recruited. Similarly, Robert Benson's *Britain's Glory*, also performed that year, presented press gangs positively at a time when riots protesting military recruitment were alarming the capital.[67]

Indeed, the tumultuous political climate of the 1790s brought new meaning to critiques of impressment. Thomas Paine, a former sailor himself, made specific mention of impressment in the second part of his *Rights of Man*, when he hoped for a world in which the 'tortured sailor' would be 'no longer dragged along the streets like a felon' and allowed to 'pursue his mercantile voyage in safety'.[68] The London Corresponding Society saw impressment as an unnecessary consequence of an unjust war, noting that for 'fresh supplies of blood' the 'liberties of our country are invaded! the seaman is torn from his family!'[69] Charles Pigott's ribald *Political Dictionary*, published in 1795, characterised the Navy as a 'floating hell', manned by sailors who were 'torn by force from their wives and families'.[70] The publisher Edward Rushton, whose bookshop in Liverpool acted as a hub of intense networking for radical writers and intellectuals, was a relentless critic of impressment throughout the 1790s, culminating in his 1801 epic poem 'Will Clewline', subtitled 'Tale of the Press Gang', in which 'the poor enslaved tar / Is to combat for freedom and laws'. Its most memorable passage described a powerful scene of family life shattered by the actions of a press gang:

> They seize on their prey all relentless as fate,
> He struggles – is instantly bound,
> Wild scream the poor children, and lo! his loved Kate
> Sinks pale and convulsed to the ground.[71]

Another radical writer, Mary Wollstonecraft, saw impressment as a practice that impacted women most keenly and championed the cause of impressment widows. Her novel *Maria*, published posthumously in 1797, told the story of Peggy, who loses her husband Daniel to impressment. Following his death, Peggy is left alone and vulnerable, but 'Had Daniel not been pressed . . . all this could not have happened'.[72] Radical literature such as this reached a wide audience and raised public awareness of the brutality of impressment.[73]

Critics could do little to resolve the immediate issue of the severe labour shortage, however, or the government's policy of impressment. Sailors therefore faced a choice: to acquiesce, or to resist. Many chose the former option, intimidated by the threat of violence or making the best of a bad situation. However, countless others chose to defy the press gang. Here, sailors could also fall back on a number of proactive schemes, the most common of which were those employed by John Nicol: fleeing, hiding and disguise. Sailors paid close attention to newspapers, and reports of a declaration of war would prompt many to flee from maritime communities. In Jamaica in 1793, the news of war was 'discovered by the public papers' and a mass of sailors 'fled into the Country'.[74] Those who could not run attempted to fool or trick their would-be pursuers. Disability, mental illness, women's clothing, self-harm and even feigning death were used to avoid impressment. Sailors on merchantmen returning to Britain were frequently hidden in the dark recesses of ships, though the Navy gradually became wise to this trick. During one search William Dillon found a seaman concealed behind mahogany bulkheads in the master's cabin, and another three 'stout fellows' hiding elsewhere. The sailor Jacob Nagle recalled twenty-seven men being hidden 'among the cargo' of the ship to prevent them being pressed.[75]

Rather than relying on merchants or local authorities, sailors could use the law to avoid capture. One such tactic was the loophole of debt, and in particular a 1758 Act of Parliament that prevented sailors from being arrested for debts under £20 but allowed them to be held for sums over that amount. With war on the horizon, enterprising men quickly went on a spending spree and racked up bills of precisely £21, though not every sailor read the memo correctly: James Seaton was arrested for a debt of £19 and was subsequently released from prison and presented to the Navy.[76] Even those who gained a temporary reprieve soon found that the Admiralty was unwilling to give up potential recruits. Peter Kendle was imprisoned for a debt of £21, and while the authorities found 'there to be no Reason to believe there was any collusion in it', he was discovered to be a deserter from the Navy and so was handed over all the same.[77] John Stormy was no more fortunate. It was decided that there was 'no Room for doubt' that his actions were 'for the sole purpose of getting him out of the Service'. He was bailed, at considerable expense to the government, to make him liable once again for naval service. From the Admiralty's perspective it set an example for others considering a similar evasion: they hoped that a few such instances would 'tend very much to lessen the number of them'.[78]

A more secure means of evasion was to take advantage of statutory and customary legal loopholes. Quick-thinking seamen joined a protected trade or found proof of foreign nationality, and in 1796 the United States Congress passed legislation directing federal customs collectors to issue US citizenship certificates to American sailors. There was a thriving black market in false protections, with the US Minister to Britain, Rufus King, reporting on fees changing hands and acknowledging that 'some of those who have applied to me are not American Citizens'.[79] Similar business existed around the UK: in Sunderland, a fee of 8s 6d could solicit a forged document.[80] On rare occasions, cases of corruption came up before a court martial. In September 1793, Lieutenant Ralph Ridley was tried for receiving a bribe not to press a man; found guilty, it was deemed that he had 'behaved in a fraudulent and scandalous manner unbecoming the character of an officer' and was dismissed from the service.[81] Still, the Admiralty faced a dilemma when it came to punishing guilty men. In 1793 Henry J. Hardacre was discovered to have been selling fraudulent protections using forged signatures. Rather than trying Hardacre and setting an example for others, the Admiralty solicitor recommended dealing with the issue more quietly, noting 'the danger there may be in making publick, by means of such a trial, the easy manner in which such frauds may be practised'. Instead, it was suggested that they 'dispose of this offender on board one of the King's Ships that he might not soon be in a situation to practice similar frauds'.[82] We do not know what became of Hardacre, but there was nobody of that name tried for selling a forged certificate that year.

Sailors were on much stronger legal ground after impressment had occurred, when they could use writs of habeas corpus to protest an unlawful seizure. This long-standing device gained increased significance in the heated political climate of the 1790s, for even after the suspension of habeas corpus in 1794, cases that pre-dated the legislation continued to be heard. These appeals proved a continuous thorn in the side of the Admiralty, as attorneys clustered around naval ports to help seamen and their families apply for writs.[83] From January 1795 a steady stream of cases arrived with the Admiralty's solicitor James Dyson, which listed the manifold ways naval officers had impressed men illegally in the early years of the war. In almost every instance, the Navy was found to have wrongly impressed the individual in question: in a sample of cases from January to July 1795, only one individual was found to have been correctly detained, and Dyson's repeated recommendation was that the men should be released to avoid a damaging court case. Indeed, by March 1795 it is possible to detect a hint of irritation in his replies, not least in the case of James Smith, who was impressed despite being underage, an apprentice *and* a foreigner.[84] In some instances the threat of legal action could be very profitable. John Nicolson threatened to sue the Admiralty for the losses incurred by a year-long confinement, and Dyson recommended that the press gang officers offer a settlement out of court, for if it came to trial 'no Defence could be made for them in such actions'.[85]

Not every sailor had access to such legal means, however, and the majority relied on more basic forms of resistance. Some simply fought off their would-be imprisoners: Michael Thomas, a caulker who was impressed in Castle Street, Minorca, was dragged away, his clothes torn and watch broken, before he finally made his escape. Others were helped by loved ones. The partner of one sailor attacked a press gang with 'the assistance of some of her female friends', injuring one and allowing her lover to escape.[86] Attempts by a press gang to board an East India Company vessel lying at Gravesend were abandoned when sailors on board appeared with weapons in their hands, swearing they would injure anyone who came on board, after which the press gang rowed off to find easier prey.[87] It took time to move impressed men to waiting warships, and flight was a constant risk. The accounts of the local regulating officer at Greenock, near Glasgow, Jaheel Brenton, reveal almost constant desertion: in one week in late July 1793 he suffered the indignity of losing more men to desertion than he had secured.[88] Rescues were also attempted. In July 1793, one press gang was attacked by twenty seamen with blunderbusses, pistols and cutlasses, injuring two men of the press gang and forcing the release of two impressed men. The following year, a large body of shipwrights assembled and, using a spar as a battering ram, broke into the prison where a colleague was being kept, liberating all the men held within.[89]

In some instances, sailors were able to organise mutinies on board the tenders that transported them to waiting warships. They were particularly common in locations where anti-impressment fervour was high, and a few examples here will suffice. On 20 November 1793, thirty-two men escaped from the *Mary* tender in the harbour at South Shields, and in March 1794 impressed men took over the *Eleanor* tender while the crew were at dinner, though on this occasion the majority of the escapees were recaptured.[90] In Liverpool the following year, twenty-three men escaped from the *Ann* tender at 4 a.m., catching the sleeping guards unaware. In the subsequent court martial, the midshipman left in charge, Mr William Johns, acknowledged that this was not the first time the men had tried to run. In this last instance we also hear the political language of the era, for officers testified that the sailors shouted 'liberty or death' and that 'it was liberty they wanted' as they overtook the vessel. The combination of violence and radical language proved a terrifying prospect for the eight naval officers charged with trying the case. Two 'ringleaders' were subsequently court-martialled: they were acquitted of mutiny but found guilty of desertion and received a severe punishment of 300 lashes.[91]

As these examples suggest, sailors were prepared to fight fire with fire and respond to physical coercion with violence of their own, often acting collectively.[92] Throughout the 1790s, the volume and variety of anti-impressment riots and affrays were remarkable: there were at least 104 such incidents reported between March 1793 and April 1802, and the real number is likely to have been much higher, as not every incident was reported and gangs had a disincentive to report embarrassing failures or defeats.[93] Furthermore, the unrest of 1793–4 was different from anything that had come before. Whereas impressment protests had long operated in a reactive way to individual injustices, in the 1790s we see sailors organising proactively and in combination with local communities. For instance, at the very beginning of the recruitment effort in

Newcastle in 1793, the sailors 'bound themselves to each other to resist any attempt to suppress them at the hazard of their Lives'.[94] Moreover, their activity was concentrated in areas where political unrest was most apparent – for example in South Shields, Greenock and Liverpool – and harnessed the language of protest and radicalism.[95] As we will see, sailors showed no little political skill, developing petitions and appeals, collaborating with other communities of sailors, and using the local and national press to further their ends.

The earliest example of mass resistance came in Whitby in January 1793, when as many as 1,000 sailors assembled at the regulating captain's rendezvous spot and threatened to pull it down unless the press gangs were dismissed. The local regulating officer John Shortland Philip Stephens decided it was prudent to disperse the press gang 'until order has been re-established'.[96] Subsequent efforts to secure men in Whitby proved equally futile: two days later, John Oaks's gang was met by 'a great Body' of sailors who had assembled, 'signing papers and sticking them up signifying they would not be pressed'. Oaks wrote to the Admiralty in some distress: 'I was told by a party of seamen that stood in the street, that if I returned with them, I and they must not expect to live.' This protest lasted for three days, until the press gang was driven out of the town and the rendezvous destroyed.[97] The local magistrates offered little in the way of protection to naval officers and drew a direct line between these events and wider fears of political agitation: in a declaration aimed at calming tensions, they chastised the actions of the 'lawless mob' as 'Sedition & Insurrection' that served only to 'gratify the Enemies of this Country'. The local community paid little heed, however, and Whitby's opposition meant that it was virtually impossible for the Admiralty to recruit there.[98]

There were similar scenes 40 miles to the north, on the River Tyne, where uprisings broke out at Newcastle and South Shields. This had long been a site of political unrest, and sailors' capacity for collective action in the North East had been demonstrated the year before when seamen and keelmen organised strikes protesting their pay. The naval officer Cuthbert Collingwood, a Newcastle man himself, had earlier commented on the local sailors' eagerness to strike and their 'enthusiasm for liberty', while in 1792 a local correspondent had reported to the Home Office that a thousand 'six penny copies' of Thomas Paine's books had been sold by a local bookseller.[99] Sailors at that port produced a petition that not only signalled their desire for collective action but also showed how political language could be deployed against the policy of impressment:

> We the Seamen of Newcastle upon Tyne ... declare ... we are shock'd to observe, that ... we alone are deprived of the Rights of personal protection ... [and] ... it is our opinion that we are deprived of an equal Participation of those Rights by the cruel mode of manning the Royal Navy by Impress, a mode though countenanced by Precedents and supposed to have been a part of the common Law has never been sanctioned by the authority of Parliament; we think ourselves justified in endeavouring to resist this species of cruelty.

They resolved to communicate their resolutions to sailors in the 'Principal Ports of this Kingdom' and to print their declaration in newspapers. The editor of the *Newcastle Chronicle* duly obliged, an act condemned by local politicians increasingly concerned about the spread of potentially revolutionary ideas.[100] The situation grew steadily more tense – the local gang was told that if any of its members returned 'they should be torn Limb from Limb'.[101]

At the same time, links to radical politics in the North East became ever more apparent. During one press gang riot a liberty pole was erected in the marketplace and the local magistrate reported that hundreds of rioters had driven the press gang through the streets under a banner carrying the message 'Liberty For Ever'. Sailors seem to have consulted the local Magna Carta Club, one of several political societies in the town.[102] Local authorities became highly concerned: the Mayor of Newcastle appealed for a detachment of dragoons to be sent to their area, while local MPs appealed to Home Secretary Henry Dundas that 'no time should be lost in taking decided steps to quell the spirit of resistance which the sailors manifested'.[103] Just as alarming to the British government was the strong possibility that anti-impressment resistance was spreading. The rhetoric used by sailors suggested cohesion and solidarity, for while those operating on the Tyne spoke of themselves as 'the Seamen of Newcastle', increasingly sailors' declarations referred to one large community, united by common interests: one written in February 1793 began 'Friends and Fellow Seamen!'[104] Nervous correspondents noted the sailors' 'Firmness', while Dundas was informed that the unrest at South Shields had 'arisen from the Example set at Whitby', and that 'Two of the Ringleaders in that Tumult were seen at Shields a few days ago'.[105]

Little could be done to prevent news and information travelling, or to stop sailors acting in combination with local communities. A few days later, in the nearby town of Sunderland, the press gang was warned that they 'had better take care of themselves' for 'if they do not we will take care of them . . . We fully design that we will destroy them and very soon.'[106] In a printed declaration the sailors laid out their complaints in less foreboding language, framing their struggles within a broader discourse on patriotism and their fundamental rights as Britons:

> . . . We have always shown a Readiness to meet the Enemies of our Country, so that our present Objections do not proceed from Cowardice, but from the dreadful Miseries which we have known, seen, and felt . . . therefore we cannot conscientiously, either as Men, Britons, or Christians, any longer countenance by Compliance, such a shocking Abuse of Power. – Twenty-two Shillings a Month, Fellow Seamen, is Five Shillings a Week! . . . For these we are *torn* and *compelled* to accept this small sum, which is not Half what we receive in the Merchants' Service . . . But this is not the worst – our Children and Dependents are neglected: They are exposed to all the Miseries of Poverty, and are hindered in the Courts of Life by Want of Protection

and Education. These are great calamities ... we only seek the same Rights of Protection from seemingly abused Power, as the rest of our Fellow-citizens.[107]

Impressment attempts continued, however, and the local community followed through on their threat, attacking local troops brought in to keep the peace with 'Stones, Bricks, Tiles and everything that could be picked up'. On 18 April 1793, Lieutenant Boulton was besieged at his rendezvous by 'hundreds of Seamen, Soldiers and Women', until an army regiment was brought in to dispel the uprising.[108]

Resistance was not confined to the North East, and press gangs and their associates became targets across the country. In Greenock, a meeting of 'all the Carpenters, Beggars, Caulkers and Seamen of the Town' resolved to stand together and 'Support Each Other in case an Impress should take place', and they threatened the local magistrates that 'if they ... Countenance the Impress, they must abide by the Consequences'. By June, the matter had got entirely out of hand, with locals burning one of the boats belonging to the rendezvous in the town square.[109] Here, sailors also benefited from the protection of local and regional authorities, demonstrating the importance of negotiation between state and community for effective impressment efforts. The regulating officer Brenton was initially assured that he could rely on 'every assistance' of the magistrates of Greenock, but his arrival panicked a community dependent on maritime trade for its livelihood, and six months later he was complaining to the Admiralty that 'they give them no support when attacked by the Mob' and he was forced to suspend recruitment efforts.[110] The following month the magistrates were still refusing to back his press warrants: 'from what I learn', wrote Brenton, 'the Town in general are determined to oppose any Impress on Shore'.[111]

Elsewhere, local communities worked together to prevent specific individuals being impressed. In Swansea, a printer who had volunteered to be the 'master of ye Press Gang' was threatened by a local crowd who placed the struggle of impressment within its wider political context.

They promised that he would find his house 'pulled about your ears, by ye unanimous multitude' if he persisted in 'that diabolical act' on behalf of 'a war, which more than half ye nation think to be most unjust & unnecessary', carried on with no other real intention than to 'stop the progress of civil & religious liberty'.[112] In October 1793, as many as 500 seamen tore down the rendezvous at Strand Street in Liverpool in retaliation for the death of a merchant master who had resisted impressment: here, the mayor turned a blind eye to the disturbances and no ringleaders were prosecuted. In late 1793 a ropemaker working in Plymouth dockyard was illegally impressed, and after insulting the regulating captain he was dismissed from his job; 300 ropemakers went on strike in sympathy, and he was reinstated within three days.[113] Nor was this confined to Britain. In Newfoundland, a local crowd acted in a 'Riotous and tumultuous manner' to liberate two impressed sailors and beat a naval lieutenant, Richard Lawry, 'in so unmerciful a manner' that he was killed. The government's response was swift and strong: dozens of suspects were rounded up, and two men were tried and hanged.[114]

By August 1794, underhanded recruitment practices were generating protests in the nation's capital. Shortages of naval and military labour had led to a profusion of 'crimping houses', where vulnerable men were tricked into joining the Army or Navy. Often operating out of alehouses, 'crimps' plied potential recruits with alcohol and encouraged them to rack up large debts, which could only be paid off by enlisting and securing the bounty. When, on 15 August, a mentally ill man named George Howe jumped to his death from a second-floor window in Charing Cross while trying to escape impressment, it sparked riots across London, and three crimping houses were torn down on the night of 20–21 August. The links to radical politics were there for all to see. A handbill circulating during the riots lambasted the policy of impressment and questioned 'Is this the land so famed for liberty?', while one of the ringleaders of the riot, an unnamed Black man, was heard justifying his actions in the context of the revolution then in motion in Saint-Domingue. 'Now or never is the time to be free,' he shouted, 'the black men are already made free in the West Indies by their exertions, and why should white men continue slaves in their own country?' He was one of twenty-three arrested for their part in the disturbances, four of whom were later executed. The crimping riots were the most serious unrest the capital had seen since the Gordon Riots of 1780, and a reminder of the ongoing links between revolutionary politics and opposition to naval and military recruitment.[115]

The scale and nature of sailors' resistance, charged as it was by political radicalism and the wider threat of sedition and subversion, placed unique pressures on the British state. The threat was twofold. Firstly, sailors' defiant activities in the first years of the war defied its authority at a time of revolutionary upheaval, when concerns about the growth of radical politics were most pronounced. Secondly, resistance to impressment specifically challenged the state's ability to man its ships and defend the country from a potential invasion: the autumn of 1793 saw the first of many invasion scares in Britain as Revolutionary France expanded its military might. The British government's response was subtle and sinister. It utilised unprecedented state surveillance, collecting information about anti-impressment activities, as part of a wider campaign to observe the growth of a radical and increasingly subversive political culture.[116] The state went further, however, ramping up its impressment activities and excusing – and sometimes even protecting – those who committed violence in its name.

The British government watched anti-impressment activities closely. Letters from regulating captains arrived regularly at the Admiralty, while correspondence from local politicians about anti-impressment activity was sent directly to Dundas at the Home Office. This was but one part of wider surveillance activities taking place in the febrile climate of 1792–4. Regular reports of spies and informers flooded into the Home Office, reporting the formation of societies, meetings of potential revolutionaries, the publication and distribution of radical texts, and the movements of possible French agents.[117] It is not clear how far the government was able to keep track of all this information, or indeed how much of the information they received could be counted upon. Certainly, some of it was sensationalist, for example John Stockdale's report of twenty-five revolutionary Frenchmen 'sent over to the country armed with daggers for the purpose of assassinating and cutting off any obnoxious characters'.[118] We do know that this information was actively solicited: Dundas's secretary Evan Nepean wrote to one correspondent in 1792 thanking him 'for the information conveyed' and asked him to 'watch over the conduct of the disaffected people in your neighbourhood', as he could not at this moment 'render a more acceptable service, than by transmitting from time to time your observations on the conduct of people of that description'.[119]

The government took a special interest in radical activity in ports and maritime communities. In Liverpool it was noted that 'a society for Parliamentary Reform' had been formed, while in Newcastle it was reported that the city was 'ripe for revolt' and that the magistrates were afraid to act. In Glasgow, the government learned that 'Great numbers' had signed a reformist declaration for parliamentary reform, estimated at 50,000 people.[120] That these were all areas of intense anti-impressment activity was not lost on a government paranoid about the spread of radical ideas and fearful of the prospect of sedition and subversion. In 1793, Britain's military resources were spread across the country not only to defend against external threats, but also to monitor internal disturbances. They were concentrated particularly in port towns and in areas where there had been press gang disturbances.[121] By the summer of 1794, 'riots against the press gangs' remained one of the most concerning domestic threats discussed by Pitt's Cabinet, represented as being both menacing and politically motivated.[122] Just as correspondents informed the government, on a more local level distrustful citizens let local magistrates know about suspicious arrivals or shady behaviour, or informed on sailors to local regulating captains. It was this climate of suspicion that John Nicol observed as he took extraordinary steps to hide his identity from wary locals in 1793. Nor was he alone in these thoughts, and his recollections chime with a memorable passage in Jane Austen's *Northanger Abbey*, likely written in 1794–5, in which Henry Tilney describes a country 'where every man is surrounded by a neighbourhood of voluntary spies'.[123] This was intended to be comforting, but it was also an uneasy recognition of national anxiety and paranoia.

The state's role went beyond surveillance, and extended to protecting those who committed violence on its behalf. One example concerns a sailor named Richard Tuart, who in October 1793 was indicted for the murder of a Swedish man named Lars Holmstans. Tuart was a member of a press gang that had attempted to seize Holmstans and beat him with sticks when he resisted impressment. He suffered severe injuries and died one month later. At the subsequent trial, one witness testified that he had seen Richard Tuart assaulting Holmstans: 'I saw Mr Tuart beating the deceased . . . he was beating him with a stick in the street . . . In consequence of being beat he tumbled down, and then he came and crawled to the bar, and then he tumbled down again . . .' Another witness, a fellow Swedish sailor named Lawrence Leymon, stated that he too had been attacked:

> I was shoved out of doors . . . and three of them were jumping on my breast with their knees, and beating me over my head with sticks; I saw no more of the deceased, till I was brought into the house, when I saw a man laying over a chair, and all over a gore of blood.

Three more witnesses, Michael Hedges, Eleanor Newton and Sarah Clark, testified that they had seen a number of men attacking Holmstans, 'beating him over the head with sticks', but could not identify the specific individual responsible.[124]

The trial then took an unexpected turn. A surgeon and his assistant took the stand and suggested that the link between the assault and

Holmstans's death was not at all clear-cut. They noted that during examination Holmstans's lungs were found to be much diseased and that 'The immediate cause of his death was a bleeding of the lungs'. While admitting that 'An inflammation might be produced there in consequence of violence', the surgeon suggested that it could have come from 'many other occasions', and while it was likely that the assault had played a role, they could not say for sure that the disease and bleeding were the 'result of the blows'. This assertion transformed the prospects of the accused. The judge intervened and ruled that 'the indictment charged the prisoner with killing the deceased, by blows inflicted with a stick; now the evidence by no means proved that, and there was therefore an end to the indictment'.[125] The defendant, Richard Tuart, was found not guilty of murder; more surprisingly still, he was not charged with a lesser crime, such as manslaughter or even assault.

Had Richard Tuart's assault on Holmstans been an isolated event, it might be considered exceptional, but earlier that month Tuart had been in court for assaulting another Swedish sailor who had resisted impressment, Lars Nyman. Nyman accused Tuart of a 'violent Assault upon me', in a case that was heard in early October 1793. In this case too Richard Tuart escaped without punishment. The injured party, Nyman, was paid the sum of £30, and he therefore decided to drop the charges against Tuart. Quite who covered this fee is not clear: this was an extraordinary sum, and there is little chance an ordinary sailor would have access to this sort of money.[126] What is evident is that Tuart was acting under the auspices of the state and doing so with impunity. He was able to commit repeated assaults on sailors and avoided any punishment: acquitted and once again a free man, Tuart returned to his duties working on a press gang in the maritime boroughs of London. Even aside from the violence inflicted, the attempted impressment of Holmstans was illegal: as a Swedish national, he wasn't liable to be pressed, something that was also mentioned but was not followed up in the subsequent trial. It was heard that Leymon had protested that 'I am a protectioned man, I have got this protection', upon which the press gang hit him again and called him a 'Scotch buggar', while another swore that the press gang had cried 'Swedes, Swedes, come out!'[127]

We also see here the role of the establishment: two surgeons and a judge, figures of authority, had intervened to sway a trial. We know that judges could use cases to set examples, such as when a judge in Whitby sentenced one Hannah Hobson to death 'as an Example' for her part in an anti-impressment riot in Whitby in 1792. He considered Yorkshire to be 'prone to riots' and hoped (in vain, as it turned out) that Hobson's punishment would deter others from defying the state.[128] The judge in Tuart's case was well aware that it would be reported in the press, and knew that the ruling would embolden those who used violence as part of impressment activity, This is not to suggest that this incident was a state conspiracy, or that politicians, lawyers and surgeons were acting together to acquit the accused. Instead, we should think of it as an example of institutional protectiveness, in which men of the establishment could influence trial proceedings in a way that favoured the status quo and those in power. As we have seen, they were operating in a culture in which resistance to impressment was deeply threatening, and popular media frequently took the side of the state. Of the two newspapers that reported on the trial of Tuart, the *Sun* and the *World*, neither saw any reason to query the curious intervention of the judge; the *Sun*, a government-sponsored newspaper, did not see fit to mention his role at all.[129]

Although Tuart's assaults produced little public outcry, state protection also occurred in cases in which local opinion was inflamed. William Yeo was a regulating captain on the south coast, and like his fellow regulating officers in Liverpool and the North East, he came up against obstructive local magistrates. In January 1794 he accused them of 'throwing obstacles in the way of the Officers employ'd on the Impress Service', and by April he was still complaining that they were complicit in impressment evasion, refusing to back press warrants and declining to answer his increasingly irate letters of protest.[130] As a result, his officers began to take ever more drastic measures to locate trained seamen.

In November 1794, an impress tender attempted to search a merchant vessel named the *Maria*, anchored at Poole in Dorset. The crew of the *Maria* refused to let the press gang on board, arming themselves with handspikes to defend themselves and threatening the naval vessel with violence if they attempted it. A change of tide allowed the *Maria* to weigh anchor and try to escape the Navy, but at this point, seeing their prey about to get away, the naval tender began to fire on the merchant ship. The first shot caused considerable damage, and despite pleas from the *Maria* to stop the bombardment, the naval vessel continued to fire its guns: the next volley killed the pilot of the ship on the spot. The naval crew kept up the fire, and two more men were killed, and seven wounded, before it submitted.[131]

The action caused fury among the townspeople of Poole. The crew of the *Maria* had not used firearms, and the local community saw the naval response as illegal and hugely disproportionate. The *Courier* newspaper noted that the funeral of the pilot who was killed, Thomas Allen, was attended by thousands:

> an assemblage of persons, amounting to upwards of three thousand, with countenances full of fury and revenge, had surrounded the quay, and but for the timely and well-tempered interference of Mr Jeffrey the Magistrates, the lieutenants and their gangs would certainly have all been butchered in their own way.[132]

The coroner's inquest into the event declared the action 'wilful murder', and the three men in charge of the press gang, Lieutenants Arthur Glover and Nathaniel Philips and Midshipman John Oliver, were tried for murder. Once more, though, the apparatus of the state served to protect the perpetrators of violence; once again, there were no convictions. In February 1795, as the Dorchester Assizes began to arrange for the trial, the Admiralty solicitor James Dyson rushed there to deal with the 'late unfortunate Affair' at Poole, and successfully intervened to move the trial to London. Since the offence had taken place at sea, he suggested that the Admiralty had jurisdiction. He also made the point that the significant public outcry meant that 'the Prisoners are not likely to obtain a fair and impartial Trial there, by reason of the prejudices entertained against them by the Person who would compose the juries'.[133]

At the ensuing Admiralty court trial, the three men were acquitted of any wrongdoing: it was deemed that their press warrants were accurate, their attempt at entering the ship legal, and therefore that they were not at fault for the murders.[134] The people of Poole were furious, and bowing to public pressure, the Corporation of Poole offered fresh Bills of Indictment at the ensuing Dorchester Assizes against the offending officers 'for the several murders of Thomas Allen, Peter Rake and John Housley'.[135] Once again, though, the Admiralty's solicitor intervened, travelling to Dorchester to offer counsel to the accused and once again meeting Yeo, 'whose evidence may be wanted', at the King's Arms Inn at Dorchester, bringing with him press warrants issued to Lieutenants Philips and Glover, and His Majesty's Order in Council for impressing seamen. Dyson ensured that the defendants pleaded 'autrefois acquit'; namely, that they had already been tried. The twelve judges presiding over the case agreed, and the prisoners were once again set free.[136] The Navy took some steps to calm local tensions: the three accused officers were moved to different regions, and the regulating captain, William Yeo, was offered a position as regulating officer of Haslar Hospital; his position in Southampton had become untenable.[137] Other than that, though, there was no justice for the three victims of the attack.

Not every case saw courts take the side of the state, and we should recognise that local conditions and agendas played an important role. In Hull in February 1794, Mark Bolt was tried after resisting impressment, in which he shot and killed one of the sailors, Charles Darley. The coroner's jury recognised 'the principles of the Bill of Rights that every Englishman's house (or apartment) is his castle' and returned a verdict of homicide in self-defence.[138] But elsewhere, we see repeated examples of the practitioners of state violence being excused and protected. In 1794 a press gang from the frigate *Aurora* boarded the merchant ship *Sarah and Elizabeth* of Hull, killing a carpenter's mate, which the local coroner judged as murder. However, no punishment was rendered, although the captain was transferred to another ship and sent to the West Indies. In 1797, a pregnant woman was struck on the head by a naval lieutenant and so 'ill-treated' by his press gang that she died the following morning. Two of the gang were arrested, but there is no record of a trial for either.[139] Two years later, an Irishman named Joseph Leahey was stabbed to death in a struggle against a press gang, but the gang pleaded that they had feared for their lives and were found guilty only of manslaughter and fined a shilling each. The lenient sentence caused public uproar, not least because a contemporaneous trial saw another man, Charles Eyres, fined 40 shillings for merely 'stealing coal'. A crowd gathered and one rioter was killed before the Wapping and Union Volunteers mobilised to keep the peace.[140] As this suggests, the state's support – both tacit and direct – of cruel recruitment practices did little to calm social tensions.

Countless sailors operating in the 1790s were confronted with a political institution able and willing to use violent means to secure maritime labour. Furthermore, the actions of those employed on press gangs, and those of the British government, allow us to think again about the reach of the state in the 1790s. At a time when leading radicals such as Thomas Hardy, John Horne Tooke and John Thelwall were tried very publicly and acquitted of any wrongdoing, the examples laid out here suggest a far more powerful – and even insidious – state. We see press gangs acting with impunity, committing violence and avoiding punishment. In this sense, impressment was a form of state-sanctioned violence: officers were given exceptional means to seize men and combat opposition, while those who took part in press gangs and committed excessively violent acts were acquitted in courts of law. Scholars of state-sanctioned violence have noted that it need not take the form of an organised conspiracy. On the contrary, it can occur when an institution creates conditions in which individuals are able to act free of persecution from the letter of the law.[141] These examples suggest that we ought to think about the much murkier, 'soft' or hidden strength of the eighteenth-century British state.

The primary defence put forward by contemporaries was that impressment was necessary. By 1795, shortfalls in skilled sailors prompted Pitt to try increasingly controversial fixes, such as forcing shipowners to supply men to the Navy, but here too the response was hostile, and merchants at Whitehaven petitioned Parliament pointing out the disastrous consequences this would have for their trade. The following month they introduced the Quota Acts, in which the challenge of manning the Navy was offloaded onto counties. Although partly successful, this too was abandoned in 1797 when many counties chose to pay a hefty fine rather than disrupt the local labour markets. One solution to the problem that seems to have completely eluded Admiralty and government officials was raising the wages of naval seamen, which had not been increased since the seventeenth century. The government had clearly made a connection between financial incentive and national service and had been happy to throw money at the problem in the form of bounties, and it is peculiar that they didn't see this through to its logical conclusion. Nor was the government entirely ignorant of the needs of sailors: in 1795 the Seaman's Relief Bill was passed, allowing sailors to send a portion of their wages to their families on shore.[142] Nonetheless, there was no enhancement of the sailors' wage until 1797, when sailors took matters into their own hands.

Necessary or not, the government's approach to recruitment slowly bore fruit. The wave of community resistance that emerged in 1793–4 was unprecedented, and in some regions it severely hampered recruitment efforts, but the number of men serving in the Royal Navy steadily rose throughout the 1790s. A force that amounted to 14,303 seamen in

October 1792 reached 55,843 men in April 1793, 79,703 by October 1793 and 94,499 by October 1794. This still was not enough, however, and throughout the decade the Navy struggled to man its ships; it was not until the summer of 1799 that numbers reached a peak of 129,884 men.[143] Even allowing for the fact that a proportion of these men came forward of their own volition, we are left with the uncomfortable truth that tens of thousands of men serving in the Royal Navy during the Revolutionary Wars were there through coercion.

Sailors were not, however, pliant, unthinking cogs in a martial machine. While some resisted, others chose to adapt and survive: John Nicol later rationalised that 'he was as happy as a man in blasted prospects can be', and he fought with valour at the Battle of the Nile in 1798. Even sailors who conformed, though, remained critical of impressment, and Nicol explained his new-found dedication as offering the quickest route to winning the war and thus being allowed to return home.[144] As the next chapter will demonstrate, in the first years of the war, many sailors followed Nicol's lead and found ways to endure a conflict unparalleled in its scale and scope.

TWO

WAR OF PRINCIPLE
Naval Conflict in Europe, 1793–5

In many respects, the war that broke out in February 1793 bore a remarkable similarity to Britain's other conflicts of the eighteenth century. France had long been Britain's 'natural' enemy, and the two nations had locked horns on no fewer than five occasions since 1688. As before, British war aims remained inherently traditional, focusing on the maintenance of a balance of power in Europe (not least keeping hostile powers out of the Low Countries), the defence of the British Isles and the protection of its trade.[1] As in previous conflicts, British strategy centred heavily on its Navy. In the first year of the conflict there were uncertain efforts to influence the war on land, but none proved successful: attempts to support a royalist revolt in Brittany came to nought, while military expeditions to Dunkirk and Flanders in 1793 secured little.[2] For the most part, British strategy focused on the oceans, and all that remained was to decide where Britain's naval forces should be deployed. Here again the Admiralty followed an established pattern. Small fleets were stationed in the Caribbean, the East Indies and off Britain's Canadian possessions, where they maintained and expanded its commercial empire, a 'blue-water strategy' by which colonial acquisitions were acquired and exploited, ready to be traded at the end of the war.[3] With these secured, the bulk of British naval strength was concentrated in Europe, targeting the destruction of French naval power. By October 1793, four-fifths of its ships were concentrated in European waters.[4]

If war aims and strategy were similar, in other respects the war that broke out in 1793 was fundamentally different from anything that had come before. For the first time, Britain faced not an absolute monarch, but a newly forged republic with a revolutionary ethos, committed to exporting democratic values abroad. In the early years of the Revolution, William Pitt's government had attempted to adopt a policy of neutrality and avoided having an 'official' view about French politics. In February 1792, Pitt had declared, somewhat hopefully, that 'there never was a time in the history of this country, when . . . we might more reasonably expect fifteen years of peace than we may at the moment'.[5] When war arrived a year later, Britons were all too aware that they were entangled in a new type of conflict against a novel and threatening adversary. As one pamphleteer put it, Britain was facing 'an Enemy of a new kind . . . who fights not to subdue States, but to dissolve society – not to extend Empire, but to subvert Government – not to introduce a particular Religion, but to extirpate all Religion'.[6] Many of the Revolution's early defenders in Britain were forced to abandon their prior positions as alarming reports of political violence arrived in London. France's declaration of war came a week after the execution of King Louis XVI, while a few months later the French Convention declared that 'Terror' was the 'order of the day'.[7]

In the years that followed, revolutionary ideology and nationalism fundamentally altered the ends and means of warfare. More than ever before the full resources of society were mobilised, while the line between combatants and non-combatants became increasingly blurred (and at points was completely erased).[8] In 1793 the French Republic proclaimed every male citizen a soldier and created vast armies of conscripted soldiers. Rhetoric about a 'war to the death' intensified. The revolutionary Bertrand Barère declared in 1794 that the British were 'a people foreign to Europe, foreign to humanity. They must disappear', while orators throughout France called for the 'extermination' of their enemy across the English Channel. On 26 May 1794, the French National Convention issued a 'no quarter' decree, effectively declaring that all prisoners of war were to be executed.[9] Leading revolutionaries were clear about what this meant: Minister of War Lazare Carnot noted that 'War is a violent state of affairs' and that 'It must be waged to the utmost'. Maximilian Robespierre defended the 'no quarter' legislation on the basis that 'Those who make war on a people to halt the progress of liberty and destroy the rights of man must be attacked by all, not as ordinary enemies, but as assassins and rebel brigands'.[10] Nor was this escalation in the intensity of warfare limited to France, for Britain too planned extreme means to secure victory. In 1793 the British considered starving France by extending the category of 'contraband of war' to include foodstuffs, and in 1794 it attempted to do just that by intercepting its grain imports. This was economic warfare on a scale not seen before.[11]

A new vernacular was needed to explain this new form of fighting. As early as 1791, Edmund Burke had predicted that old modes of 'civilised war' were on the way out and looked forward apprehensively to 'the hell-hounds of war' being 'uncoupled and unmuzzled'. By 1793 he had come up with a term for this novel, ideologically charged conflict: 'Our War is not a War of Ambition', he wrote, but a 'War of Principle'.[12] The writer Robert Nares saw it in similar terms:

> Thus is the present War a new phenomenon, for, besides being a necessary War for self-defence, it is A WAR OF PRINCIPLE – a War in defence of all the Rights of Nations, against the Arbitrary Usurpations of a Gallic Mob.[13]

The nature and course of the French Revolution continued to shape the conflict, as increasingly large French armies clashed with the forces of European kings. It did not take long for revolutionary ideas on land to transfer to the oceans. One of the more perceptive naval officers, Cuthbert Collingwood, noted to his friend Horatio Nelson in late 1792 that 'The times are turbulent; and the enthusiasm for liberty is raging even to madness', and that 'The success of the French people in establishing their republic has set the same principle, which lurked in every state of Europe, afloat'.[14] From Britain's perspective, the war of principle conducted between 1793 and 1795 was fought overwhelmingly on the seas around Europe as its naval forces clashed with those of the French Republic.

For most of the 1790s, the Royal Navy faced a French opponent of near-equivalent size and strength.[15] During the 1780s France had brought a number of new ships into service, and by 1793 it had sixty-five battleships to call on; Britain's eighty-five battleships were stretched much further due to its global commitments, meaning near-parity in European waters. Beyond the arithmetic, however, the French Revolution had created a number of problems for its fleet. A service built on discipline and strict obedience to orders struggled to conform to a new political culture built on the idea of popular sovereignty, and for the first years of the Revolution it was beset by rebellions: mutinies were common, and to the admirals' fury, the National Assembly refused to condemn them. By 1793 this conflict between democratic and disciplinary values reached a breaking point, and there was another mutiny when the French fleet stationed at Brest was ordered to operate against royalist forces in the Vendée. Amid the upheaval, many experienced French officers left the service in protest, and by 1794 very few officers had experience in their post.[16]

The integration of democratic principles did lead to a far more meritocratic institution, as in the French army, allowing many talented men to reach a rank hitherto unattainable. However, anything that hinted at harbouring royalist ideals was thrown out with the bathwater: the elite corps of specialist gunners was perceived as an aristocratic threat and abolished. Moreover, the Revolution did little to assuage France's chronic shortage of trained maritime manpower. Recruitment continued to be imposed through a deeply unpopular system of 'classes' that required men from the coastal provinces of France to serve a term every three, four or five years, depending on the size of the province and the needs of the fleet, but even this could not furnish the men required.[17]

As we have seen, the shortage of trained maritime manpower was a common problem in Britain too. Despite ferocious impressment, the Royal Navy also remained undermanned, crippling its early mobilisation. The situation grew worse as additional ships were mobilised, and by 1794 nine of the ships in the Channel Fleet were missing at least one-sixth of their crew.[18] What is more, many of those encouraged or compelled into the Navy were raw recruits. A high proportion of merchant sailors who entered the service were new to naval warfare, while the many thousands of 'landsmen' who were recruited had never been to sea before. In the summer of 1793, Lieutenant Robert Mends of the *Colossus* complained that his men knew 'so little about a ship', while the Navy's desperation is also revealed by some of the men Howe recruited. Charles Underwood, John James and John Jones, all aged between sixteen and seventeen, were found to be too weak to hold a musket and were dismissed, being deemed not competent 'for maritime [sic] Service'. Nor were the officers themselves exempt from criticism. In one of many preventable accidents, in July 1793 the *Bellerophon* collided with the *Majestic*, and a set of 'Additional Instructions' had to be circulated to prevent future blunders.[19] The impact on the operational ability of the Navy's ships was considerable. Collingwood complained that 'we do not manage our ships with that alacrity and promptness that used to distinguish our Navy' and noted a 'tardiness ... and a sluggishness ... that is quite new'.[20]

Unlike France, Britain was able to find enough men to at least send fleets to sea in 1793, and of these forces without doubt the most important was the Channel Fleet. Its commander, Admiral Richard Howe, was a controversial choice. He had made many enemies during his service in the American War and his time as First Lord of the Admiralty (1783–8), and some officers refused to serve with him.[21] Nor was he a man in good health. Aged sixty-eight and suffering terribly from illness – his letters frequently referred to his 'gouty sensations' – he was only

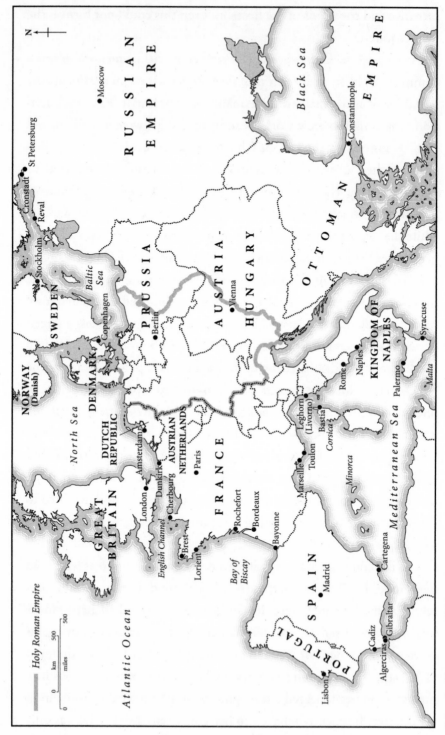

Map 2: Europe in 1793.

persuaded to take the command following a direct request from King George III.[22] Howe's chief task was to prevent the French Brest fleet from escaping, and his methods proved contentious. Howe favoured a policy of 'open blockade', by which only a few frigates would be left to watch the French fleet, while the main fleet withdrew to the safety of Torbay and Spithead, ready to move if needed. It left his forces vulnerable to French sorties, however, and also clashed with the expectations of the British press who were agitating for a naval victory. Howe's perceived lethargy saw him dubbed 'Lord Torbay', while more radical publications represented him as an aristocratic incompetent.[23] Some critics accused Howe of treason: James Gillray's print *A French Hail Storm* depicted Howe as a Neptune-like figure being bombarded with a hail of French gold, much of which fell into his coat pockets.[24]

The first shot of the naval war was fired on 13 March 1793, when the appropriately named French privateer *Sans Culotte* was captured by the brig *Scourge* after a three-hour fight. However, there was little other naval activity out of Brest, and the intelligence the British received suggested this state of affairs would continue. Howe noted that 'The accounts from the Continent received this last week promise little occasion for business in our Line' and doubted that the call for 'naval exertions' would be considerable.[25] For the most part the French ships that ventured out were small privateers, capable of predatory actions against smaller naval vessels and merchants. One of these was the *Cléopâtra*, which met Captain Edward Pellew in the frigate *Nymphe* on 18 June. This fight also offered signs of the revolutionary warfare to come: the French captain nailed a cap of liberty to the main truck of the French ship as it approached, and its crew shouted 'Vive la Republique' as the two vessels engaged. The *Cléopâtra* surrendered after a fifty-minute fight, but casualties were high and almost even: the British suffered fifty killed and wounded to the French sixty-three. In a similarly hard-fought action a few months later (24 October 1793), the British frigate *Thames* was beaten to a standstill by its French equivalent *Uranie*.[26] Otherwise, the operations of the Channel Fleet followed a well-worn pattern, with third rates and frigates keeping to the seas to watch for movement out of the French Atlantic ports of Brest and Rochefort, while the bigger ships of the line remained in port, especially during the winter.[27]

Further to the south, the Mediterranean Fleet was commanded by Vice Admiral Samuel Hood. A veteran of the Seven Years' War and American War, Hood had a reputation for drive and attention to detail, qualities essential in a command that stretched from Gibraltar in the west to the shores of the Ottoman Empire in the east. Britain's only naval station was at Gibraltar, from which it was expected to project power across the whole basin, requiring considerable diplomacy alongside expert fleet management. The kingdoms of Spain, Naples and Sardinia offered important military and naval support, while sizeable quantities of food and water came from North African states. In this vast sea, the threat of French privateers was pressing and, as in the north, French resolution and revolutionary spirit in battle were not in doubt. In late September 1793, Horatio Nelson watched a French frigate at the neutral port of Leghorn depose their captain and appoint new officers from the crew. 'What a state,' he wrote to his wife, 'they are mad enough for any undertaking ... I shall be surprised at nothing they may attempt.'[28] The following month Nelson was confronted with French fighting spirit first-hand when his 64-gun *Agamemnon* was fought off by the weaker 38-gun *La Melpomène*. Chastened, he privately thanked God for his survival. The Admiralty was embarrassed enough that his letter recounting the action was not printed in the *London Gazette*, as was the custom with successful actions.[29]

Hood's orders directed him to protect British trade in the Mediterranean but also allowed him to use his initiative if an occasion arose to offer 'some decisive Blow against the Naval Power of France'.[30] His force had scarcely arrived in the Mediterranean when just such an opportunity presented itself. In August 1793 he was approached by envoys from Marseille and Toulon who sought protection from Hood's fleet. In Paris the expulsion of the 'Girondins' faction on 31 May–2 June 1793 had prompted communities across France anxious about the

Revolution's violence and radical direction to overturn local Jacobin regimes.[31] The Committee of Public Safety's response was typically severe, sending armies south under General Carteaux to crush the cities in rebellion. Cut off from supplies from both land and sea, local representatives were caught between the British and the revolutionary armies, and on 23 August a delegation from Marseille approached Hood asking for a military alliance. The following day they were joined by commissioners from Toulon who offered up the harbour and surrounding forts to Hood. The British admiral, never short of confidence, decided not to look a gift horse in the mouth and agreed to offer assistance on the condition that the city declared its loyalty to the deposed Bourbon monarchy. Hood was too late to save Marseille, which fell to revolutionary forces on 25 August, but on 28 August British and Spanish ships began to occupy the harbour at Toulon. Many French sailors loyal to the Revolution were disgusted, drafting a petition in defiance and demonstrating with a placard declaring 'La Constitution ou la Mort!' There were mass desertions of republican sailors on the night of 27–28 August before the British and their Spanish allies took control of the town.[32]

France's second most important naval base had been secured without firing a shot. At a stroke, thirty-one ships of the line were captured, as well as several smaller vessels, and French naval power in the Mediterranean was paralysed. In Britain, newspapers trumpeted the success. 'The capture of Toulon is the most important event of this campaign,' wrote the *London Chronicle*, 'since it has cost not a drop of blood' and 'destroys all the naval force of the French in the Mediterranean'. The news was framed within the wider ideological battle, with the *St James's Chronicle* declaring it a victory that promised to 'shake off the Tyranny of a mad Democracy, and to restore that Monarchy which they had sworn to maintain'.[33] The *Sun* took the opportunity to rail against opposition Whigs – whom they termed 'English Jacobins' – who had suggested concentrating naval forces in the Caribbean. Indeed, conservative organs expected Toulon to be the first of many 'great Towns and

Provinces' to declare their independence from the Revolution and avow their detestation of the 'worst of Tyrants'. Also prominent was the idea that those who remained loyal to the Revolution could now with justification be starved into submission. The *London Chronicle* noted that the British capture of Toulon deprived Marseille and all Provence of crucial food supplies from the Levant and expected that 'This want of corn will be the most severely felt ...'.[34] In a war of principle, ever more extreme means were used to achieve victory, and economic warfare of this nature became part and parcel of naval efforts over the coming year.

The capture of Toulon was exactly the sort of opportunistic operation the Admiralty had hoped for in the Mediterranean.[35] However, it served as a useful reminder that the celebratory declarations of newspapers did not always tally with the views and ideas of the public. The bloodless surrender of French forces without a shot being fired failed to seize the imagination of many Britons: the *St James's Chronicle* that had earlier boasted about Toulon's seizure reported a few days later that 'The capture of this important Arsenal and fortress does not appear to have made all the impression upon the minds of the people of this country which might have been expected from an event by far the most fortunate of the campaign'.[36] In government too there were mixed reactions as the enormity of what Hood had agreed to were realised. In making a Bourbon restoration a condition of his assistance, now trumpeted by the press, Hood had committed the British government to clarifying its position on the post-war settlement, something it had been avoiding since the outbreak of war. Pitt and the Foreign Secretary, Lord Grenville, had been initially supportive of the French Revolution, and neither was keen to see the restoration of the *ancien régime*. For the first time in the conflict, they were forced to commit to clearly stated goals: by the end of December 1793, 'the destruction of the atrocious system now prevailing in France' had been added to the government's list of official war aims, and Pitt's ministry remained committed to a Bourbon restoration until late 1795.[37]

What is more, having seized Toulon, the prospect of holding onto the town in the face of the advancing revolutionary armies was challenging to say the least. Toulon was not designed to be defended from the land, surrounded as it was by several hills from which artillery could wreak havoc. Hood had only 1,200 troops with which to mount a defence of these heights, and he wrote to the Admiralty bluntly pointing out that he did not have the forces to defend the town. The response from London was muddled: the government planned to send 5,000 troops and at one point hoped to try and induce other French regions to hand themselves over to British protection. These reinforcements were delayed, however, and were too trifling a force to make a significant difference: Lieutenant General Charles O'Hara thought that 25,000 troops were needed for proper defence. The French siege began on 8 September and gradually encircled Toulon as the hopelessly outnumbered defenders were gradually forced from the heights around the town, and a young artillery officer named Napoleon Bonaparte organised devastating artillery barrages on the naval vessels at anchor. The British ships in the harbour could do little to respond, hampered by shallow water and unable to gain the necessary elevation for their guns. Naples and Sardinia sent troops, as did the naval base at Gibraltar, but the promised Austrian soldiers never materialised, and it was only on 9 December 1793 that reinforcements from Britain set sail.[38]

It was too little too late. British and Spanish commanders had already decided upon an evacuation, including 7,500 political refugees who faced the guillotine were they to be captured by the republican armies. There was also the question of what to do with the French ships seized when Toulon was first occupied. Hood lacked the manpower to crew these vessels and so ordered Captain Sidney Smith to organise their destruction. In total, eight ships of the line were burned, along with vast quantities of naval stores, a significant setback for the French navy. The blow might have been greater still, as amid the chaos fifteen other vessels escaped with varying degrees of damage.[39] Smith was later blamed for this missed opportunity to wipe out the French

Mediterranean fleet once and for all; just under five years later, eight of the thirteen ships that survived took part in Napoleon's expedition to Egypt and fought in the Battle of the Nile.[40] Furthermore, what had been destroyed could be rebuilt using the remaining naval stores. French shipbuilders quickly replaced the ships that had been lost, and Nelson later wrote in some wonder of how 'the French have put together a fleet at Toulon, which could hardly be credited'.[41] The capture of Toulon was therefore a blow from which the French soon recovered. More serious was the damage done to the French navy's reputation. News of the surrender of the Mediterranean fleet arrived alongside reports of the 1793 mutiny in Brest and confirmed for many in Paris that the navy remained a hotbed of royalism.[42]

In the aftermath of the Toulon evacuation, the winter of 1793–4 offered a momentary pause to both Britain and France. To the north, Howe's 'open blockade' saw the bulk of his fleet stationed in Torbay and Spithead. Frigates were sent 'from time to time' to Cherbourg, Guernsey and Brest to gain intelligence on the preparations of the French, with mixed results.[43] Captain Sir Andrew Douglas wrote that bad weather had prevented him from looking into Brest and he returned to Spithead having gained no information.[44] To the south, Hood's fleet returned to Gibraltar for repairs. His young nephew, also named Samuel Hood, did not get the memo, however, and arrived at Toulon in his vessel *Juno* under the impression that it was still in British hands. It was not until he had sailed into the harbour and saw sailors wearing revolutionary tricolour cockades that he realised something was wrong: 'It may be more easily conceived than any words can express what I felt at that Moment', he later wrote. A fortuitous change of the wind allowed his crew to quickly set sail and escape by moonlight before the bewildered Frenchmen knew what had happened. A canny operator, Hood sent a dashing account of the action to his uncle, and also to the Admiralty, safe in the knowledge that it would make its way into the national press. Unlike Nelson's unsuccessful action of 1793, it was published in the *London Gazette* the following month and served as a public relations model for other officers to follow.[45]

In the Channel, the French used the hiatus in naval action to good effect. Jeanbon Saint-André, a representative of the French Convention, was sent to Brest to restore order, and over the course of two 'missions' there between October 1793 and June 1794, he transformed the Brest fleet. Understanding that there needed to be reconciliation between ideas of popular sovereignty and military effectiveness, he developed a new penal code in which obedience to authority was repackaged as devotion to '*la patrie*'. Petitions to commanders were forbidden, and mutiny was to be punishable by death, performed in front of the whole fleet. 'It is just,' he wrote, 'but severe.' Those that erred or failed to show enough revolutionary enthusiasm would also suffer death, and seventy men – dockyard workers, sailors and administrators – perished in this way.[46] Uncompromising in the extreme, the impact was remarkable. French dockyards outfitted or repaired warships in record time, located stores with efficiency, and levied workers and sailors in ever greater numbers.[47] Government authority was restored, and for the first time since the start of the war, the French navy was ready to seriously challenge the British at sea. Four French vessels entered the Channel in April 1794 and were intercepted by a frigate squadron under John Borlase Warren; outnumbered, three French vessels were captured in the subsequent battle. This did not dissuade the French from further action. The commander of the Brest Fleet, Louis-Thomas Villaret de Joyeuse, a liberal nobleman who had survived the French Revolution, noted that things were 'starting to come together' and that they could now approach the British 'with some confidence'.[48]

Heartened by the reports from Brest, in early 1794 the Committee for Public Safety began to develop ambitious plans. At Cancale on the north coast of Brittany were assembled 20,000 men, 154 transports and 6 ships of the line intended to attack the Channel Islands, and for the first time in the war the prospect of revolutionary armies landing on British soil became a distinct possibility.[49] More pressing for France, though, was the protection of food convoys from across the Atlantic Ocean. The price of bread had been a crucial factor early in the

Revolution, and supplies had been further strained by the inflated demands for food from the vast armies operating on France's frontiers. The government introduced a legal maximum price for bread but understood that the best solution was to boost supply. A vast convoy of over 100 ships was arranged carrying 67,000 barrels of flour from the grain-rich United States, while Rear Admiral Vastabel was ordered to take his squadron and escort it across the Atlantic.[50] The French were aided by the fact that other powers, unhappy about the British claim to a right to search their vessels for French property and contraband, appeared to be moving towards a more hostile stance. Sweden and Denmark discussed an 'Armed Neutrality' in March 1794, and the United States House of Representatives placed a temporary embargo on trade with Britain (subsequently defeated in the Senate) and threatened to raise an army of 50,000 men.[51]

In this climate, the convoy of grain intended for France took on added significance. On 7 March 1794, the Admiralty ordered Howe and his fellow officers to detain shipments of corn and naval stores; this was economic warfare in all but name, targeting the population of its enemy. The Navy pursued this policy with enthusiasm: a few weeks later, Captain Sir Andrew Douglas captured a Danish brig, the *Venus*, laden with wheat from Wismar, with no evidence that it was actually sailing to France. 'I consider it to be of so much Importance to prevent Corn getting to France that I am enduced [sic] to take this step,' he wrote to Howe.[52] By early April, intelligence on the French convoy of American grain had also reached the Admiralty's ears. An American merchant captain in the pay of the British sent word, while Pitt's ministry also learned that France had deposited $1 million in the Bank of the US to buy flour and other provisions. The Admiralty directed Howe to put to sea immediately and intercept the 'very large and valuable fleet of merchant ships' that 'may be shortly expected from America under convoy of a French squadron'.[53] On 2 May he sailed from St Helens with thirty-four ships of the line, the largest fleet yet assembled by the British in the war. The plan was to cruise off Brest and keep a careful watch in case the French fleet came out to protect the inbound convoy. Rear Admiral Montagu was ordered to sail to the south of Brest with a squadron of six 74-gun ships and three frigates to locate the convoy and, if possible, capture or extinguish it.[54]

Thus began an operation to search and destroy. Howe arrived off Brest and checked that Villaret's main French fleet remained at anchor. Concerned that Montagu might be outnumbered and in danger, he abandoned his position off Brest and began to comb the Bay of Biscay. For two weeks both Howe and Montagu searched in vain for the convoy, bombarded the whole time with conflicting intelligence from the Admiralty and captured ships about its location.[55] They were searching a vast space without a firm idea of where the French convoy was aiming for: France's western coast was 400 miles long, and the convoy could have been heading to a number of places – Brest, Lorient, Rochefort, Aix Roads, Bordeaux or Bayonne. On 18 May, Howe returned to Brest having failed to intercept the French fleet, only to be forced off station three days later by prolonged westerly winds. He retreated to the safety of the open sea, allowing Villaret to escape from Brest, under direct orders from Robespierre to ensure the safety of the convoy. Howe raced back to Brest as soon as the weather improved, and found the harbour empty.[56] On board the British fleet, news that the French had escaped 'caused greatest excitement ... and nothing was heard but bringing the French to action'.[57] With little time and no crew to spare, Howe ordered all the enemy merchant ships recently captured to be burnt, another sign that Britain was fighting a new type of warfare.[58]

On 28 May, 400 miles west of Ushant, Howe's force of twenty-five ships of the line finally spotted Villaret's force of twenty-six vessels. After months of stasis the two largest fleets in Europe were at sea and willing to do battle. They were almost equal in size but in other respects were very different. The French had spent the majority of the previous year in port with little opportunity to drill, and their officers remained inexperienced. Only one of their commanding officers had ever seen action before, while the three flag officers had been lieutenants prior to the Revolution. By contrast, all of Howe's captains had seen fleet action, seventeen of them on two occasions. The British had had the opportunity to practise manoeuvres and gunnery, though it seems this was done in a very slipshod fashion: only six vessels had practised more than five times in the six weeks preceding, and nine of the fleet, around a third, recorded either one or no gunnery practice before meeting the French in battle.[59] Moreover, in other respects it was the British who were deficient. Howe's fleet remained seriously undermanned, reduced further by a sickness that ran through the fleet in March 1794 and which Howe described as a 'calamity'.[60] What the French lacked in experience they hoped to make up for in enthusiasm. Indeed, perhaps most surprising is that the French had been able to assemble a fleet at all. Collingwood was certainly astonished that despite ruined finances, limited stores and with almost all of Europe at war with them, the French had met them at sea with a fleet that he deemed superior.[61]

As the British force approached that of the French, each had different aims in mind. Villaret's overriding objective was to occupy Howe for as long as possible to allow the convoy to get through: as the Committee for Public Safety noted, 'it is not a naval victory we need at the moment, but our convoy'.[62] By contrast, Howe had to hope that the convoy would be captured by Montagu and instead aimed at delivering a telling blow against French naval power in northern Europe. A scholar of naval tactics, Howe had spent the preceding years planning for such an opportunity. He was very critical of 'The looseness of our present System of Tactics in the Navy, if any System may be properly said to exist' and worked closely with his naval friend and colleague Captain Roger Curtis to develop a new method of fighting. He was ahead of his time, fully expecting battles in 'a future War' to involve as many as sixty sail of the line, and despaired that there was no doctrine to guide how such a vast force should be trained and conducted in battle to act with 'uniformity & effect'.[63] In 1793 he had issued a fleet order that proposed an entirely new form of attack. Rather than fighting at distance in a gunnery duel, the fleet would attack from windward and at a chosen moment would turn together to cut through the enemy line at many different points, engaging the enemy from the leeward side and thus preventing their escape.[64] It was far from prescriptive, but it was a bold and aggressive plan, fully in keeping with the demands of total war.

With daring came risk. Howe's plan relied on pinpoint manoeuvring and communication, and as the two fleets neared on 28 May, the challenge of directing vast fleets in rough conditions quickly became evident. The French were disorganised – in Howe's words they were 'seemingly unapprized that they had the British fleet in view' – but it was some hours before the British could take advantage.[65] Howe made the signal to attack the enemy's rear, intending to bring about a general action, but it was not until 2.30 p.m. that the *Russell* opened fire on the French *Révolutionnaire*. For nearly four hours the *Révolutionnaire* fought alone against six British ships; the *Audacious* and the *Bellerophon* were so badly damaged they had to pull away and attend to repairs. The overwhelming numbers began to tell, however, and the French vessel was only saved by rising winds, roughening seas and the arrival of night, which allowed the *Révolutionnaire* to drift back to the French fleet.[66]

The following day, Howe's communications were again followed haphazardly. Those ships that did obey orders struggled to execute them: the *Queen*, for example, tried four times to cut through the line and failed on each occasion, while Howe's own attempt to lead by example also ended in failure, hampered by a heavy squall and falling mist. His vessels fell into disordered chaos during their approach. 'Scarcely any two ships were on the same tack,' remembered one midshipman, 'and many were near running on board each other ... Nothing but confusion was visible in our Fleet, whilst the enemy's line was in perfect order.'[67] By contrast, Villaret organised a successful manoeuvre when he sailed to the support of the *Tyrannicide* and the *Indomptable*, which had briefly been separated from the main fleet. The British ships were too disordered to intervene.[68]

A thick mist prevented further action over the next two days, and it was not until 1 June that the two fleets confronted each other once again. This time Howe's plan directed every ship to steer for its opposite number, and he reorganised his line of battle to ensure that his vessels would be matched against ships of similar firepower. As the British fleet approached, they were subjected to intense French gunnery, and officers, nervous about the loyalty of the men they commanded, patrolled the gun decks and attempted to reassure their crews. On the *Defence*, Captain Gambier 'spoke to all the men at their guns in terms of encouragement' and encouraged them to 'fight for their country', and he was gratified to see that a 'determination to conquer prevailed throughout the ship'.[69] Indeed, Gambier's ship was the first to meet the French line, followed soon after by Howe's flagship, the *Queen Charlotte*, which forced its way through a gap in the French line left by the *Jacobin*. Howe came up alongside Villaret's flagship, the massive 120-gun *Montagne*, and was quickly surrounded by three other French vessels, which allowed the *Montagne* to break away and create havoc elsewhere. Others were less successful at breaking the line: towards the centre, the *Brunswick* crashed directly into the *Vengeur du Peuple* and the two ships drifted off, locked together in combat.[70] The *Brunswick* suffered the worst casualties in the British fleet, with 40 dead and 113 wounded. Despite numerous attempts, the French line was broken only four times, and the battle fractured into individual actions between vessels.[71]

Along the line the fighting was intense, befitting a battle fought for principles and ideals. 'These Republica[n]s fought with a degree of perseverance and obstinacy bord[er]ing upon madness,' wrote one sailor, 'for when their masts were gone, they nailed their colours down to the stumps of the masts ... and even when lying a-wreck upon the wat[er].'[72] Collingwood recalled that the French fought with 'a savage ferocity' expected of a fleet instructed not to take prisoners, while William Parker observed a French officer striding upon the deck attacking sailors who flinched from the battle and claimed that he saw French ships signalling to 'give us no quarter'.[73] Some sailors saw the fight in almost apocalyptic terms. After the battle, Jonathan Wilkinson wrote that 'in the time of the action you would of thort [thought] the

Ellement ad [had] bene all on fire . . . it was all the same as a hale Storme a bought [about] the Ship'.[74] Officers on both sides were astonished at the resolution and endurance of their men. Thomas Mackenzie of the *Gibraltar* commended their performance 'which far surpass'd my most sanguine expectations as I may venture to say not above one in twenty ever saw a gun fired prior to the later periods'.[75] Exhausted sailors found new reserves of strength. Lieutenant Beecher on the *Defence* brandished his sword at sailors he believed to be shirking their duty. They explained that they had been fighting for two hours and were naturally fatigued; this pacified the lieutenant, and the men soon returned to their guns.[76]

Within an hour of combat beginning, smoke had engulfed the scene, obscuring the wider battle.[77] British gunnery began to gain the ascendency, able to fire more quickly and accurately as a result of more extensive practice and the lighter weight of British cannons, making them easier to reload.[78] Such ferocity was impossible to maintain for long: at midday exhaustion had set in across the fleet, and by 1.15 p.m. general firing had ceased. Many ships had been completely disabled: France had twelve dismasted vessels, and Britain eleven. Several ships had to be towed clear of the action by frigates to avoid them falling into French hands. A number of French vessels remained isolated from the remainder of the fleet, but still they refused to surrender, and it was only when Villaret manoeuvred eastwards and demonstrated that he would not come to their aid that they finally capitulated. In particularly poor condition was the *Vengeur*, which had been holed in numerous places and slowly sank; it took the efforts of the *Culloden* and the *Alfred* to come to the rescue of the drowning French sailors.[79] One anonymous sailor on board recalled the 'lementable [sic] sight to see and hear the cries of the poor wretches' and noted that 'humanity must shed a tear on behold in the terrible devastation of war'.[80] Here, at least, was a degree of humanity among the violence, as boats from the two ships saved the lives of around 500 French sailors. On other prizes the devastation was far more gruesome. The sailor John Morris went on board a captured French vessel and found its decks 'Coulard [Coloured] with blood and dead bodys and limps [lumps] of men' so much so that 'we Could not walk'.[81]

The surrender of the *Vengeur* was the final act in the battle, and by 6.15 p.m. the remainder of the French fleet was out of sight and heading back to France. Howe decided not to make any attempt to pursue the French for fear of leaving his damaged ships vulnerable to a French counter-attack, a decision that allowed Villaret to recover four of his stranded vessels before escaping. The casualties testified to the intensity of the battle: British losses of 290 killed and 858 wounded exceeded those of every other naval battle of the eighteenth century up to that point, while the French suffered an estimated 4,200 deaths, roughly 10 per cent of their available seamen.[82] For those that survived, the relief was palpable, though almost every sailor faced strenuous activity repairing devastated ships and recovering prizes. Many had gone days without warm food, catching only snatches of sleep on deck whenever they could. One seaman, John Davies, wrote to his parents that between the 29 May and 1 June 'we did not let our hammocks down, only lay any where upon deck, and we had not time to cook our meat'.[83] We also see the first glimmers of war weariness. The day after the battle Jonathan Wilkinson wrote that he had 'bene this three years at seea and as but ad my foot on shore 5 times' and hoped fervently that 'I hope this whar will not be long and then I meane to Cum down to See you plas God to Settel at home'.[84] A few months later, he deserted from the Navy.[85]

On the face of it, the action appears to be a singular British success. France had lost seven ships – the biggest loss to Britain at sea in a century – and its maritime manpower had been decimated. Britain had removed any threat of a French invasion – for the moment at least – and also brought to an end the Baltic 'Armed Neutrality'. The British envoy at Stockholm referred to the battle as a 'decisive stroke, the effects of which will be felt in every part of Europe'.[86] However, if the initial aims of the protagonists are considered, it was the French who were the real winners. Villaret had successfully drawn Howe's fleet away and allowed the grain convoy to get through: it arrived amid much celebration on 12 June, having lost just one vessel during its passage. Indeed, looking beyond the simple arithmetic of ships captured and lost, a significant proportion of Howe's fleet were forced into port for extensive repairs, rendering them temporarily useless.[87] What is more, rather than being checked or contained by the battle, the French continued to threaten at sea. While the Channel Fleet remained in port, devastated by a typhus outbreak – it was only at sea for one month between June and December 1794 – French frigate squadrons terrorised shipping off Ireland, while in November Admiral Nielly took a squadron into the Western Approaches and captured the British 74-gun *Alexandria*. On 31 December 1794, the Brest fleet left port for more than a month of cruising, during which it lost five ships but took more than a hundred British prizes and a ship of the line.[88]

In truth, neither claim to victory was secure, and the fighting of 28 May–1 June 1794 prompted much recrimination. In Villaret's fleet, two officers were accused of deserting the fleet; Captain Bombard of the *Montagnard* was acquitted, while Captain Gassin of the *Jacobin* was found 'guilty but excusable' and was fortunate that a change in the political situation in France meant he avoided a visit to the Revolutionary Tribunal in Paris. Similar accusations were levelled in the British fleet. Many British officers were unhappy that Howe and Curtis had refused to chase the retreating French fleet, and historians continue to debate what might have happened had he been more aggressive during the afternoon of 1 June. Nelson later referred dismissively to 'Lord Howe's Victory' – in other words, a missed opportunity.[89] Blame was also directed towards individual ships' captains. Several vessels had fired into each other during the fighting, and in total twelve British ships suffered from friendly fire. Few captains had actually executed Howe's orders to break through the line, and the admiral's attempts to usher in a new method of naval tactics had met with, at best, limited success.[90]

Some British officers' careers were terminated after the battle. A whispering campaign against the conduct of the *Caesar*'s captain, Anthony Molloy, prompted him to request a court martial to clear his name. In the subsequent trial, he offered a persuasive defence, claiming that his rudder had been too badly damaged to follow Howe's orders, and secured the support of many serving officers. However, although exonerated of cowardice, he was found guilty of failing to follow orders and dismissed from his ship. Howe, who had long disliked Molloy, worked hard behind the scenes to ensure the verdict. He wrote the lengthy opening statement at the trial, sent the prosecutor a list of witnesses he hoped would be called and correctly predicted how each juror would vote.[91] Nor was Molloy alone in feeling the wrath of an unimpressed Admiralty, as the Navy took the opportunity to quietly rid itself of others who had performed poorly. Montagu, who had searched in vain for the French convoy before returning to Spithead, was made a scapegoat for the Navy's failure to intercept this vital shipment, and was never given another sea-going command.[92]

Howe's dispatches also caused controversy. In his first letter to the Admiralty, written on 2 June, he had offered superlatives about the conduct of the fleet, praising the officers and ships' companies in broad terms for their bravery and 'spirited exertions'.[93] His subsequent letter named specific captains who had distinguished themselves but left out many others, which infuriated those not mentioned. Rear Admiral Caldwell left the service in protest the following year, while Collingwood, who had captained Rear Admiral Bowyer's flagship by himself when his superior was wounded and might have expected an honourable mention, was equally furious. Blaming Curtis for advising Howe poorly, he dismissed him as 'an artful, sneaking creature' and complained that 'while all England was rejoicing in a great victory, the hearts of those who won it were sinking with disappointment'.[94] A gold medal was issued by the Admiralty but was only presented to captains that Howe and Curtis had selected, and Collingwood refused all future awards until it was presented to him too; he eventually received one three years later, when his conduct at the Battle of Cape St Vincent forced the Admiralty to cave. Even Howe found a reason to feel slighted. He was initially promised the Order of the Garter by Pitt, but the vicissitudes of politics meant the prime minister was forced to give it instead to the Duke of Portland to secure his support in Parliament. A livid Howe turned down the marquisate he was subsequently offered.[95]

All these concerns were swept away, however, by the tide of celebration that followed the news of the battle arriving in Britain. The young politician George Canning was at the opera when the news arrived:

> We had not been there above half an hour when we perceived a degree of bustle and hurry in the lower boxes – presently the Opera stopped – people stood up, some knowing, but the greater part wondering for what reason . . . I never saw a finer or more affecting spectacle than the almost electric and universal sensation that seemed to pervade every part of the House – the transport and triumph which burst forth as soon as their astonishment subsided.[96]

The press delighted in celebrating Britain's first major victory in the war. What is more, it was a *naval* victory. The *St James's Chronicle* reminded its readers that 'our true security consists in the dominion of the sea' and stated that the outpouring of joy that followed the news of victory 'proves how much more Britons are delighted by success at sea than on land'. As it explained, 'The sea is our protecting element, and as long as *Britannia rules the waves* nothing can hurt us. A Victory at sea must ever give us more heart-felt pleasure than twenty victories on the continent.'[97] Lost in their bombast, most newspapers neglected to mention that the French convoy had got through, and that French naval power had at best been only temporarily checked. *The Times* reported a victory which, they predicted 'with confidence, has so crippled the navy of France, that it will be impossible for the French to send another grand fleet to sea, at least during the present campaign'.[98] The reality, as we have seen, was rather different.

For the moment, though, the British were happy to celebrate a largely meaningless victory. Across London, church bells pealed merrily amid the 'constant discharge of cannon', while theatre performances added the songs 'Rule Britannia' and 'Britons Strike Home' to performances. Three nights of patriotic celebrations followed in which loyalist mobs roamed the city, demanding that houses illuminate their windows in celebration and offering violence to those who refused. This 'plebeian wave' saw many broken windows, and the radical opponent of the war Thomas Hardy was viciously attacked; his wife, pregnant with their sixth child, only escaped with the help of neighbours.[99] Certain aspects of the battle were recounted with loyalist glee: observers noted the symbolism of the fact that the aristocratically named *Brunswick* had defeated and sunk the French ship *Jacobin*, either unaware of or ignoring the fact that this had not actually happened.[100] Whereas commentators had hitherto mocked Howe for his lethargy, now they celebrated him as a 'fighting admiral' who, in the words of the *Oracle*, had won such a victory that 'the NAVAL POWER of our ENEMY is most probably ANNIHILATED FOR EVER'.[101] Sketches of the battle were produced for the *Morning Herald* that outlined Howe's skilful manoeuvres on the day, while the thanks of the House of Commons, Lords, Guildhall and City of London were circulated widely. More traditional images of the triumph also proved popular, and the battle produced at least thirty-three identified prints, more than any prior action.[102] At Sadler's Wells, the artist Robert Andrews produced a 'Historical and Scenic Display' that placed Howe in a long line of successful naval admirals going back to the Spanish Armada.[103]

It was left to other, more subversive media to tell a more nuanced story. Caricatures, ever the most reliable window into popular mentalities, saw explanations of British success not with Howe, but in the actions of Britain's sailors. Isaac Cruikshank's print *Lord Howe they run* offered a simple image of British sailors beating their cockaded-French counterparts bloody, while Howe himself was visible by his absence.[104] Martin Saunders's play *The Crimps; Or, the Death of Poor Howe* told the story of a sailor who had fought at the battle on 1 June only to return to Britain and fall victim to a crimp house scheme; it was considered so seditious that it was censored by the government and never performed. The prominent Whig Richard Brinsley Sheridan produced a theatrical production which he titled *The Glorious First of June*, a term that came to define the fighting of 28 May–1 June. His point, though, was that the fight was anything but 'glorious', and instead he used the battle to reveal the distressing impact war had on families.[105] In the play sailors consider their mortality and the 'friends they ne'er may see again', while one female character pleads with her sailor husband not to go to war:

Thy country's cause and honour call,
Are words that but deceive the,
Though seest my tears, how fast they fall
Though must not, William leave me . . .[106]

The play was the first of its kind, intended specifically to raise funds for the relief of widows and orphans created by the battle. Not everyone approved of its content – the artist Joseph Farington complained that the play dwelt too much on the consequences of war – but the benefit night took £1,526 11s in funds, the largest sum gained by any single theatre performance at either Drury Lane or Covent Garden during the eighteenth century.[107]

This was a sign, at least, that the public were alive to the costs of the war, not just the 'glory'. Sheridan's play was but one part of a wider subscription effort intended to help the hundreds of injured sailors and their families. Schemes such as this had been in place since the start of the war, with a 'Society for the Relief of the Widows and Children of Seamen and Soldiers' set up on 19 February 1793, with the intention of offering monies 'beyond the provision made in certain cases by the State'. It proved popular: by January 1794 it had raised £19,197 and had expanded to provide clothing to seamen and funds to the Foundling Hospital to help them take in orphaned children of sailors.[108] The *Glorious First of June* sparked renewed interest, and a new committee dedicated to those who had lost loved ones between 28 May and 1 June was set up. Donations also came in from Lloyd's of London and Trinity House, while specific parishes – such as that at St Martin in the Fields – also sent over £600.[109] A 'Ladies Subscription' for the relief of seamen and soldiers was set up, with a lengthy list of subscribers printed in the press.[110] The battle also boosted schemes intended to raise bounties for volunteer seamen, which saw a range of contributions, large and small. The Earl of Sandford publicly committed £500 towards it, but there were also more 'ordinary' contributors, such as Mary Price, who gave £5 5s, and John Compton, who offered the relatively minor sum of £2 2s. Charitable contributions of this nature offered men and women the opportunity to amass social capital, among the middling classes at least. By September 1794, over £10,000 had been raised, while 343 men and 70 boys had been recruited.[111]

These efforts also offered succour to those who had been given little reason to think patriotically. Dillon saw this first-hand when he went to visit wounded sailors in hospital. One midshipman who had lost a leg told him bluntly: 'Never mind the honour and glory of the Country. Give me my leg back again.'[112] Statements such as this carried even more weight in a climate of political tension; as we saw in the previous chapter, in August 1794 London was rocked by 'crimping riots' protesting unfair recruitment practices in both the Navy and the Army. The recent battle offered the British government an opportunity to cast a different light on the war effort, and they lost no time in claiming that it had vindicated their policies. Parliamentary 'votes of thanks' were published in newspapers, a traditional response to a military victory, but one that was used increasingly during the 1790s: between 1714 and 1793, Parliament voted thanks on only fourteen occasions, but it did so forty times between 1793 and 1815.[113] Whig politicians also attempted to appropriate the battle for their own ends, suggesting that naval forces would be better employed in the Caribbean, and the opposition *Morning Chronicle* was one of a few organs to note that it was France that had actually attained its objectives by securing the safe passage of the convoy, raising doubts about the 'victory' that had been achieved.[114] Pitt's response was to create set-piece events that celebrated the Navy in the most public way possible. Pitt and Dundas arranged for George III to visit Howe's fleet in Portsmouth and adjourned Parliament to allow its members to attend in full view of thousands of spectators, a scene later captured by the artist Henry Perronet Briggs. This was followed by the triumphant launch of a new ship, the three-decker *Prince of Wales*, in an unsubtle attempt to boost loyalism.[115]

If the aftermath of the battle proved politically impactful in Britain, the same was also true in France, where the recent action was presented as a fantastic success for the Revolution. Jeanbon described the battle as 'glorieux' to the French Convention, and returning officers joined a celebratory parade that marched from Brest to Paris. Not only had the convoy got through, but the battle had provided a number of glorious moments for the people of France to fête, all the more important after the embarrassments at Toulon. Chief among these was the sinking of the *Vengeur* following its bitter fight against the *Brunswick*. Barère, who months earlier had used incendiary rhetoric to vilify the British, understood the need to raise the prestige of the Revolution and saw in the *Vengeur* an opportunity to create a narrative of fearless republican virtue and courage. As he said to the Convention:

> Imagine that ship, the *Vengeur*, riddled by cannon-balls and cracking at every seam, surrounded by the English tigers and leopards, a crew now composed of the dead and dying, struggling against waves and cannons both . . . on every side cries of *Vive la République! Vivent la liberté et la France!*[116]

Reports of its engagement were distributed through the Jacobin clubs of France and, as in Britain, a new three-decker ship was ordered. This was to be called the *Vengeur*, a symbolic nod to the vessel that had given the Revolution new meaning.

In the first two years of the French Revolutionary War, all sides adopted rhetoric that suggested a new era of fighting had dawned. In deeds too, both protagonists tested the boundaries of conflict further than ever before. The British adopted an unprecedented policy of economic warfare intended to starve the French into submission and were only unsuccessful because of the failure of Montagu's squadron to find the merchant ships, the skill of the French admiral Villaret and the bravery of his crews. For the most part, French forces largely ignored the 'no quarter' decree, but there were combatants that followed the Revolution's legislation more fervently. On 12 July 1794, a British merchantman was taken off Algiers and every member of the crew was executed according to the 'no quarter' rule.[117] It was not until the fall of the Jacobins and the creation in 1795 of a more moderate revolutionary government, the Directory, that the rules of war returned to the more traditional mores of the eighteenth century. This moderation also promised the possibility of conciliation between the two countries. In a speech in December that year Pitt suggested that 'such an order of things' had been established in France to allow for (ultimately unsuccessful) negotiations for peace.[118] Only then, though, was Britain's 'War of Principle' abandoned for something far more familiar, a competition fought for the balance of power in Europe and global colonial possessions, rather than a conflict of ideals.

Even as more moderate voices came to the fore, the political character of the conflict remained. In the summer of 1795 the Navy transported an army of French loyalists and émigrés in Quiberon Bay in the Vendée, an area of resistance to the Revolution where the British hoped to support and further encourage the royalist cause. After a successful landing, the attempted invasion ended in calamity following an assertive republican counter-attack, and it fell to naval vessels to evacuate the force. Around 2,400 troops were saved, but 6,332 émigrés were taken prisoner by the revolutionary armies, 750 of whom were executed by Revolutionary Tribunal.[119] The French navy resumed its threatening activity: during the operation, a fleet under Villaret went to sea again with fourteen ships of the line and eleven frigates, where he engaged with Vice Admiral Cornwallis's small squadron off the coast of Brittany. Lord

Bridport's much larger force quickly came to its rescue, and outnumbered, the Battle of Groix saw Villaret fight a determined retreat in which he lost three ships before finding safety in the harbour at Lorient. The action prompted a mix of disappointment at the lost opportunity and satisfaction that a disaster had been avoided. Lord Spencer, the First Lord of the Admiralty, referred to the 'anxiety which we all felt very naturally' on hearing of the French fleet, but also of the 'essential importance to the successful issue of the contest at this very critical moment'.[120]

Britain still faced a fight against a determined French revolutionary enemy. The Republic's ambitions grew as its military success confirmed its dominance of the European continent. By 1795 Austria and Prussia had been compelled to sign peace treaties, and Britain was fighting alone, bringing ever greater stresses on the state. The last months of 1794 and early months of 1795 saw serious unrest, with the wrath of the crowd directed at the high price of food, while impressment activities continued to spark social tension. In February 1795 there was a 'warm skirmish' between press gangs and would-be recruits in Deptford, and at Cambletown Lock local residents resisted the efforts of the local press gang. In March a deserter from the *Anson* was rescued from the press gang by a crowd, while in June shots were fired to prevent Lieutenant Miller impressing sailors.[121]

These protests came to a head on 13 July 1795, when an estimated 12,000 rioters marched down Whitehall and gathered outside 10 Downing Street, throwing stones through windows and attacking suspected recruiting houses, a reprise of the 'crimping riots' of the year before. The crowd was dispersed by the military and two protesters were killed; the remainder marched over Westminster Bridge to St George's Fields, to chants of 'Pitt's Head and a quartern Loaf for Sixpence'.[122] By the end of 1795 domestic matters were almost out of control, and the prospect of revolution in Britain reached fever point. The king's coach was jeered at and pelted with stones as it moved through London, and Pitt pushed through the repressive 'Gagging Acts' in an attempt to stem the tide of popular protest: the Treason Act expanded definitions of treason and the Seditious Meetings Act limited meetings to no more than fifty people.[123]

In the face of this turmoil, the Navy appeared as a rare, successful bulwark against the forces of revolution and radicalism. The Duke of Portland, now in government following his deal with Pitt, imagined it in almost mystical terms:

> It opens scenes to my mind, where I can contemplate with a sort of satisfaction which I think no other Event could have afforded me – I think I see an English fleet covering the coast of France and the white Plumes and Standards erected and advancing to restore Order Religion and law to that unhappy Country and tranquillity and security to the rest of the civilised world. Don't say that I dream and I shall indulge this vision with confidence and make every exertion in my power to realise it.[124]

That was about to change, though. Murmurings of discontent in the Navy had been heard throughout 1794, and in April the Admiralty received an unsigned petition from the ship's company of the *Theseus* complaining of 'very ill treatment' by the officers and asking for redress.[125] A brief investigation found no evidence of discontent, and the Admiralty was comforted further by the sailors' performance at the Glorious First of June.[126] Indeed, throughout the fighting of 1793 and 1794, naval sailors had fought bravely against the naval forces of Revolutionary France, and officers had been encouraged, and even surprised, at the loyalty they displayed.

In December 1794, however, a far more threatening letter was written. The sailors of the *Culloden* who had taken part in the Glorious First of June wrote a letter to their commanding Admiral complaining of their treatment and, more specifically, that their ship was not seaworthy. They demanded 'terms' and signed the letter not with a name, but with a far more threatening label: 'a Delegate'. This moniker had strong overtones of revolutionary committees and was the term used to describe the representatives sent by the London Corresponding Society and Society of Constitutional Information in their attempts to create a 'British Convention' in Edinburgh in 1793.[127] The naval establishment was horrified. 'I can hardly image [sic] consequences more necessary to be guarded against, than those not unlikely to be expected from the introduction of <u>Delegates</u> amongst us,' wrote Howe.[128] After two years of war spent fighting French revolutionary forces, it appeared as though a radical threat was also brewing in the Navy's own ships.

THREE

'WE THE SEAMEN'
Protest and Resistance at Sea

A naval ship was a weapon of war, but also a floating society. Hundreds of people from a range of different backgrounds were crammed into individual vessels, where they lived, worked and recreated alongside each other. It was, as sailor Samuel Leech put it, 'a little community of human beings, isolated, for the time being, from the rest of mankind'. On the ideal ship, Leech wrote, 'each task has its man, and each man his place', describing its crew as a set of human machinery that moved 'with wonderful regularity and precision to the will of its machinist – the all-powerful captain'.[1] These movements, however, rested upon a set of relationships that were anything but mechanical. Like any community, the social world of a naval ship was governed by informal and long-standing customs that shaped interactions up and down the naval chain of command. At its heart lay an unwritten contract, in which seamen and petty officers acquiesced in the hierarchical system of the Navy but in return had certain expectations of fair treatment or 'usage': quality food, even-handed discipline, regular pay and a seaworthy ship. When these expectations were not met, there were customary forms of protest and resistance that could be employed by sailors to negotiate better terms of service.

Sailors operating in the early years of the French Revolutionary War could draw on all these practices, honed over the previous century, to register their grievances. However, the 1790s ushered in new ways of thinking about and employing political power. Firstly, sailors increasingly framed their actions in language that focused on their rights and 'usage', and by the mid-1790s they were directly employing revolutionary terminology and deploying the language of Enlightenment philosophers and radical writers. Secondly, the nature of protest also changed. While in the early years of the war customary forms of dissent were used frequently, these were replaced by new methods more in keeping with the age: long-form political petitioning was employed across the fleet, while naval mutinies became far more regular, and far more extreme. We also see sailors learning to act collectively, communicating with other ships and across fleets, learning lessons and sharing common grievances. If in the early 1790s naval protest was confined to individual ships, by 1797 sailors of the Channel Fleet were composing a blunt petition to the Admiralty that channelled the Preamble to the United States Constitution and spoke for all sailors serving off the British Isles. 'We the seamen of His Majesty's Navy,' they declared, 'take this liberty of addressing your Lordships . . . shewing the many hardships and apprehensions we have laboured under for many years.'[2]

This chapter explains how sailors found new means, and growing confidence, to register grievance between 1793 and 1797. It offers a taxonomy of protest, outlining the different ways sailors could bring grievances to bear, beginning with a study of long-standing, customary forms of protest. These were the 'weapons of the weak', a form of 'everyday resistance' by which a subordinate group could negotiate the terms of their labour.[3] It then moves on to discuss how sailors adopted new means of protest, firstly through a form of petitioning that built on wider contemporary practices, and then arguing for a fundamental change in the way that mutiny was used by sailors. These activities brought them into conflict with the Navy's system of discipline, which again offered something distinct to those on land. As Leech explained, the social world of the Navy was 'governed by laws peculiar to itself', a reference to a set of regulations known as the Articles of War that laid out clear rules for all members of the crew to follow.[4] The crimes of disobedience, neglect of duty and most obviously mutiny were very specific to the naval world and the Articles represented a means of creating control and order on naval ships. As sailors' protest changed across the 1790s, so too did the interpretation and application of these rules. The Admiralty and its commissioned officers of the Navy responded with ever more violent tactics to subdue dissent, representing a heightening of tension and fundamental fracturing of shipboard consensus.

If the Navy was in many respects a contained social environment, these changes were still shaped by developments on land, and particularly by British political culture. As we will see, the social community of the naval ship was not nearly as isolated as Leech suggested: the vast majority of naval vessels, stationed as they were in home waters, were never more than a few days away from a friendly port, and sophisticated logistical chains meant that information in the form of orders, intelligence and newspapers regularly arrived on board a ship. All members of a crew had the opportunity to send and receive letters from friends and loved ones, assisted by the Navy's penny post system that allowed correspondence to travel great distances for only a small fee.[5] And indeed, when arriving at a port, friendly or otherwise, news would quickly spread through a ship via papers and word of mouth. Information was also passed between ships, allowing the latest political news and information from home to quickly spread through a ship's crew, and increasingly from ship to ship. It was by such means, for example, that sailors of the *Eurydice* learned in the summer of 1796 that other vessels' grievances had been met and used this information to argue for their own.[6] These bridges between ship and shore were easy to maintain, and hard to break; no ship was an island.

Throughout the eighteenth century, sailors had numerous legitimate means of registering complaint. The Articles of War directed the sailor to quietly address any complaints to 'his Superior or Captain or Commander in Chief', who would then be responsible for dealing with the issue.[7] Seamen serving in the early years of the Revolutionary War certainly took advantage of this. In 1793, William Abbot was cut in two places on his face when he was struck repeatedly by Lieutenant Horace Pine, and shortly thereafter he wrote his complaint.[8] Some well-meaning officers, such as Captain James Cranstoun, encouraged their men to come forward with any grievances so that they could be settled quickly and amicably. Not every officer was this supportive, however. In 1795, one sailor complained about the quality of the food and was threatened with a flogging and then beaten when he refused to eat. Additionally, addressing a complaint to a captain proved impossible when the officer was the object of the grievance: the men on board the *Windsor Castle* had to wait until they were in port before they could complain to a higher authority.[9] Either way, it was a risky decision for an individual seaman to come forward alone, and so often a group of sailors – or an entire crew – would come forward to make a complaint. In 1793, for instance, the crew of the *Illustrious* accused the surgeon's mate of beating a seaman, prompting his court martial.[10]

Any member of the crew could ask for legal redress through a court martial, seamen included. In March 1796 Thomas Brown was put in irons when he refused to go to bed when ordered, and, deeming this 'a real rascally officer trick', wrote to his captain 'for a Court Martial' and to 'try every B——r of a Lieut'.[11] John Cooper similarly requested a court martial when he was accused of desertion as it allowed him to bring witnesses to bear and, he hoped, improve his chances of acquittal. Sailors who requested a court martial ran the risk of more severe punishments. David Coleman said that 'he would rather be tried by a Court Martial than be flogged' when he was accused of using mutinous language, and following a trial he was sentenced to a much harsher flogging of 200 lashes.[12]

Seamen were most likely to call for a court martial in cases of excessive or repeated brutality and could be successful: Lieutenant Humphrey Faulkner of the sloop *Peterell* was dismissed from service in 1796 for 'cruelly inflicting punishment on two Boys'. That said, justice of this kind was rare. Not only did sailors face unsympathetic officers keen to defend their colleagues, they also confronted a disciplinary system in which a degree of violence was both expected and accepted. The practice of 'starting', whereby a sailor could be struck by an officer with a cane or piece of rope, was entirely within the rules. John Grant, a Master of Arms on board the *Janus*, argued successfully in 1796 that he had a right to strike any member of the ship's company whenever he pleased, while one naval captain did not consider striking a sailor with a stick to be unusual.[13] Many sailors acknowledged that a degree of discipline was necessary: William Richardson, for one, stated that seamen 'like to see subordination kept up, as they know the duty could not be carried on without it', but they also recognised 'good usage', as well as officers who overstepped the mark.[14]

However, there is evidence that naval punishments were growing more severe during the 1790s: rates of flogging increased threefold as increased dissent prompted a spike in levels of punishment.[15] Specific incidents reveal that officers were all too happy to use savage violence to maintain discipline. In 1794, for instance, the midshipman George Glanville investigated a gathering of men below deck and felt free to attack the nearest sailor, hitting him with a rope, without fear of punishment himself.[16] In this context, proving cruel treatment by an officer became ever more difficult. In 1795, numerous individuals testified that Captain Richard Bridges had 'beat his servant ... with his fist', and others saw him drive the man's head 'against the Door', but the charge was 'not proven'.[17] Two years earlier, in 1793, Jonathan Pascoe was beaten by the surgeon's mate William Batty so badly that he died, and a number of individuals testified that while they had seen him strike Pascoe, they could not say that Batty's blows caused his death. It was decided that the charge was 'totally void of foundation' and Batty was acquitted. James Allen, cook of the *Medusa*, beat his 'boy' so much that 'his Cloaths all over Blood & Bleeding at the mouth and nose', but he was only court-martialled when he subsequently insulted Second Lieutenant James Lloyd, who had queried his actions.[18]

Sailors also knew that if they failed to prove the charge, they themselves were then open to a charge of insolence or contempt. Thomas Brown, who wrote to his captain to demand a court martial, saw his accusations dismissed and was subsequently punished with fifty lashes.[19] Nonetheless, seamen were able to make the Articles of War, and courts martial, work in their favour. In 1794, Jeremiah Squirrel was accused of disobedience and insolent behaviour, but it became clear in the court martial that he had been repeatedly beaten by his boatswain. Squirrel brought forth a number of witnesses who testified to his oppression, and it was decided that the charge against Squirrel was 'not sufficiently proved'. Through such means, courts martial were a form of resistance, through which seamen could have their own voices heard and make their own arguments for what was deemed just and fair.[20] Those at the lower end of the ship's hierarchy could also work together, collectively, to show up more powerful accusers, especially those who abused their position. In 1793 the boatswain of the *Porcupine* accused the seaman Edward Patten of stabbing him, a serious charge that carried the death sentence. The boatswain could find few to corroborate his story, and other sailors testified that they had seen him beating Patten and had not even seen a knife. The boatswain could not show any evidence of a wound, and Patten was acquitted.[21]

Beyond the court martial, there were numerous other tactics seamen could employ to make their complaints heard. One technique was a form of hunger strike, whereby sailors would refuse to eat food they believed had gone off. On the *Terrible*, sailors' criticisms of the quality of bread were ignored, and so between 10 and 12 September 1795 they refused to eat any until their grievances had been heeded.[22] While the crew suffered from a lack of victuals, the longer-term impact was to render the ship inoperable. A similar approach was followed when sailors on board the *Sheerness* refused their grog rations. The ship's crew confronted the captain, William Hanwell, after hearing a rumour that the ship's supply of spirits would soon run out. Rather than eke it out with half or quarter rations, they insisted that they should have the full allowance of grog straight away, even if this meant it ran out sooner. The captain refused 'from the impropriety of the request', outraged that sailors had the temerity to ask for redress in a way that 'appeared to me to be a demand'. A group of sailors gathered on the quarterdeck to make their feelings known, shouting loudly that 'We will have All or None'. The following day the only people who came for their grog ration were quartermasters, boatswains and marines; the rest of the crew stayed below, making a very clear point to the captain.[23]

Sailors could also refuse to take part in traditional shipboard rituals. Dancing was a common recreational activity, encouraged by officers as a non-threatening form of exercise that could be conducted in plain sight; it followed that withdrawing from these rituals upset the normal social rhythms of a ship of war. On the *Minerva*, sections of the crew were outraged when newly pressed men were ordered by the young captain to tack the ship without speaking or making a noise, an almost impossible task for inexperienced recruits. Many failed at the attempt and were punished with six or seven lashes the next morning. This infuriated the crew: not only was it an affront to their sense of fair treatment, but it undermined the unwritten contract between seamen and officers. That evening, the men of the lower deck refused the captain's standing order to dance on the deck and remained below. This was a peaceful but pointed protest: gunner's wads flew about 'in all directions', lights were extinguished and a wad was rolled into the admiral's cabin. The admiral's steward was asked to investigate, and the sailors reported pointedly that 'there was too much dancing at the gangway in the morning to keep them dancing in the evening'. The chastened captain never employed such brutality again: in the subsequent voyage only one man was flogged, and that for striking an officer.[24]

There were numerous other forms of non-violent resistance that could be exercised. One such ploy was the use of sound to register complaint. Amid the cacophony of shipboard noise – the bells which called the men to watch, the bosun's whistle and the orders of officers, not to mention the never-ending creaking of a ship's timbers – there were opportunities for seamen to share and communicate grievance. In the first instance, seamen could whisper and mutter to each other, using the darker, quieter recesses of the lower deck to discuss their plight with fellow sailors. This remained risky, though, for even in the lower reaches of the ship sound could travel easily: as one sailor later noted, in a ship 'every thing can be heard'.[25] For this reason, furtive conversations also occurred up in the rigging, out of earshot of the main deck and commissioned officers. Thomas Lawrence and David James met high in the rigging to discuss their grievances and utter 'words of a seditious tendency', and used the same space as a safe haven to write a letter critiquing the ship's officers.[26] In this way, sailors exploited the murky depths and giddy heights of the ship for their own ends, transforming these peripheral areas of the ship into spaces in which dissent could be voiced. Even a keen-eared officer struggled to pick out voices, let alone identify a specific individual. On the *Winchelsea*, officers listening out for seditious statements were just able to make out accents and occasionally seditious words but found it impossible to identify individual voices well enough to tie them to mutinous statements.[27]

Sailors could also use sound in a collective manner, not least through 'murmuring', in which they uttered complaints in an almost wordless form. Unlike shouting or whispering, murmuring was a vocal but nonverbal noise, a collective rumbling of voices, that ensured no one individual could be blamed and punished. This was not new to the 1790s, and indeed the polyphony of sailors' voices and 'noyse' on ships had caused consternation for officers since the seventeenth century.[28] Murmuring therefore represented a long-standing and discomforting subversion of authority, and it was incumbent on officers to be able to understand and interpret sounds emanating from the ship's crew. The sound of murmuring was a sure-fire sign of dissatisfaction, and often a signal that further upheaval was afoot. In 1794, able seaman James Calaway was given twenty-four lashes for mutiny and contempt of his superior officers, an action that prompted 'murmerings among the people'. Shortly after, the crew of his ship, the *Culloden*, revolted against their officers and began a mutiny that lasted five days.[29] The connection between 'murmuring' and mutiny became so well established that by 1797 London newspapers were commenting on the connection between murmuring and shipboard protest – a sure sign that a rebellion was about to start.[30]

Cheering was another form of collective sonic protest that made a clear point while disguising the identity of the protesters. For much of the eighteenth century, cheering was associated with celebration, whether of a military victory or a ship's safe arrival after a long voyage. In the 1790s, however, it took on new meaning as a rallying cry for other sailors on board.[31] In 1793 around forty-four men of the *Winchelsea* cried 'three cheers' to alert the rest of the crew before barricading themselves below decks. Two years later, the crew of the *Terrible* and then the *Pompee* gave three cheers before attempting to take over their ships.[32] By 1797, the sound of sailors cheering had become a weapon of protest likely to terrify any officer who heard it. On the *Kingfisher*, the crew were assembled to watch the punishment of a man they believed to be innocent and offered a series of cheers to signal their disapproval. Thomas Carr, a seaman who had been present, testified that their aim was 'To give the Captain warning about flogging the people'.[33] Alongside the cheering, sailors also hissed at the captain, a form of dissent more usually associated with the London stage by which theatregoers could signal disagreement or disapproval of a performance.[34] Hissing and cheering were therefore highly performative forms of dissent, closely aligned with land-based customs but re-employed for use at sea.

Members of the crew could offer more direct oral protest by audibly – and sometimes openly – critiquing a ship's officers. These tended to be men of warrant rank who were likely to be better educated and had the benefit of seniority to protect them from the most brutal punishments. One such man was Richard Parke, the purser of the *Gibraltar*, who in 1796 stood on the quarterdeck and was publicly critical of the ship's commander. Told by a lieutenant that this 'was not a place to give his

Opinion', Parke disagreed, stating that 'he had a right to give his opinion when ever it was asked'. This appeal was powerful and demonstrated Parke's awareness of contemporary debates in Britain about the meaning of sedition; as we saw in the previous chapter, the Treasonable Practices Act and Seditious Meetings Act of 1795 severely restricted Britons' free speech. Parke's words were directly at odds with the Articles of War, however, and in his subsequent court martial for 'making use of seditious speeches' he framed his argument in the language of his individual rights. More concerningly, he spoke of liberal traditions in both Britain *and* France and referred to the whole proceeding as 'a perversion of the British Law & Justice, which as a British subject I have a right to expect'.[35] Nonetheless, the charges were proved 'in part' and he was severely reprimanded.

Naval personnel could go beyond seditious utterances and directly disobey an order. Those who did so also tended to be men of warrant or commissioned officer rank: of the twenty-four cases of disobedience that came up before a court martial during the 1790s, only four involved seamen, though it is likely that many instances of disobedience were dealt with without recourse to a trial.[36] Regardless of rank, this was an individual act of resistance against a superior officer. Naval personnel could also be accused of the more serious charge of contempt, and there was a clear distinction between the two: at one court martial in 1793, a midshipman testified carefully that the accused man had spoken 'in disobedience, but not contempt'.[37] Quite what constituted disobedience and contempt was at the discretion of the court martial, but small deviances could be harshly punished. In 1795, the boatswain Henry Jackson was dismissed and rendered incapable of holding any employment or office in the Navy for clenching his fist at Lieutenant Thomas Smithies and refusing to go on board ship. Indeed, careers could be ended by a few careless words. Michael Passmore, master of the *Daedalus*, told a lieutenant that he was rigging the ship wrongly – 'you are a Fool you know nothing about it' – for which he was reprimanded and dismissed from his position.[38]

Disobedience was often the result of a disconnect between social status and naval rank. Men were highly conscious of their position on board a ship, and anxious to defend it. Insubordination was clear in cases when a sailor challenged a superior officer, such as Edward Chambers's challenge to Robert Bloye, a master's mate. Bloye declared that he was 'in a higher station and therefore would not suffer such Language from him', and Chambers received fifty lashes for his indiscretion.[39] Elsewhere, class and status did not map easily onto the naval hierarchy, and countless clashes were caused by disagreements over who had authority. This was particularly true among warrant officers, who were men of considerable expertise and often had good reason to question their superiors. John Dick, the carpenter on *La Concorde*, told a lieutenant that it was 'not his business' to determine defects in the ship, and when threatened with reprisals he said the lieutenant 'might do his worst'. George Passmore, the master of the *Woolwich*, laughed at his captain's threat to court-martial him, telling him 'to do as [he] pleased' and that it was 'out of [his] power to hurt him'. These disagreements could also be couched in terms of individual rights. In 1794, a lieutenant told John Barry, sergeant of marines, to be quiet, and he responded that the officer had 'no rights' to give him orders, for that was his business.[40]

The Articles of War were therefore a form of control that extended to officers as much as sailors, especially in the early stages of a career. Commissioned officers had to serve six years as a midshipman or master's mate before they were allowed to take the lieutenant's exam; only if they passed were they granted access to the Navy's upper echelons. During this period they performed many of the lowly tasks on board, and they were often reliant on sailors and petty officers to learn their craft. In these difficult years, master's mates and midshipmen on course to become commissioned officers could find their status challenged, certainly if they lacked connections and the patronage of more senior officers. Young, well-connected midshipmen were treated very differently to those who had struggled up from the ranks, creating resentment and insecurity. One such individual was Richard Parker, the son of a baker who had spent the 1780s working on a series of naval vessels and who by 1793 had laboured hard to achieve the rank of master's mate. That year he refused an order to take his hammock up on deck, dismissing it as menial labour and unfitting work for 'an officer on board the ship'. He was reduced to the rank of a common seaman, though the court martial held out hope that 'future good conduct' would allow him to be reinstated.[41] The experience left a bitter taste, and four years later he became the face of a fleet mutiny that shook the Navy to its core.

Perhaps the most definitive form of individual resistance came through desertion, whereby a sailor would simply run away from his ship. While at sea this was all but impossible, but any vessel stationed in port ran the risk of losing men, and many officers took extreme steps to prevent sailors from running, whether through increased numbers of sentries or by handing out severe punishments. While the precise numbers are unclear, we know that desertion was rife. On the *Ceres*, a ship for which we do have data, as many as forty sailors ran from the vessel in the course of 1795.[42] By 1796 Rear Admiral William Parker was complaining of the 'frequent practice of desertion' and desperately encouraged his captains to 'keep up good order & discipline in the squadron'.[43] As escape became harder, sailors used a multiplying variety of tactics. Some took advantage of gullible officers, gaining permission to go onshore to pick up tools or supplies, or by faking illness or injury. James Coleman, for instance, declared to his ship's surgeon that a wagon had run over his knee many years previously and was sent ashore to sick quarters in Yarmouth, from where he absconded a few days later. William Saunders made himself sick by taking medicine so that he would be sent ashore to the naval hospital at Haslar, and there he escaped by climbing over the wall.[44] Sailors who could swim simply dived over the side; others took temporary command of the ship's jolly boat and rowed to shore.[45]

Sailors ran for a range of reasons. The pull of family was powerful, and many left when a more financially lucrative offer came along. Ships serving in the Caribbean and Mediterranean frequently lost men enticed by the lure of a merchant sailor's wage, while some sailors deserted only to re-enlist in the Navy and receive a second lucrative bounty. There were also political motivations. Some seamen, for instance, deserted in protest at having been impressed. William Taylor, formerly a carpenter, was impressed in 1796 and immediately sought a way out. He gained permission to pick up stores on shore only to disappear; when caught, he proclaimed that 'a Carpenter ought not to be impressed'.[46] Similarly, sailors deserted in protest at poor treatment. In the case of the *Ceres*, so many men ran from it 'merely and solely from the ill treatment & severity of Discipline', and by 1796, sailors caught running frequently mentioned poor treatment or 'usage' as part of their defence. John Skene justified his running as the natural reaction to an officer 'giving me such usage on Shore', while William Dixon stated that a number of men had deserted from the *Maidstone* 'on account of ill usage'.[47] Sailors made a clear connection between the conditions of their service and rates of desertion, with one noting that the 'barbarous' treatment they had received must be a 'singular disadvantage to the Service', discouraging as it did other sailors from coming forward. 'As soon as men can escape from such Barbarity,' he wrote, 'they will do it.'[48]

Those sailors that did escape from the Navy's clutches then came up against a further hurdle. Britain's increasingly militarised society was a hostile environment for deserting sailors, with militia and volunteers roaming the nation's towns and main roads. Such was the state's desire to control naval manpower that militias and army units were given sizeable sums for capturing deserting sailors, and others had their expenses covered. In 1794, Benjamin Johnstone of the Irish Regiment claimed a bounty to return a runaway and asked for £2 6s 6d for cart hire and accommodation to bring them back to port.[49] As we have seen, long-serving sailors were easy to spot, and military bounty-hunters were particularly active in seaports and maritime communities. The

Hampshire Militia was particularly active, securing sums as high as 20 shillings for each sailor returned to the Navy, while an Act of Parliament allowed local authorities to award as much as 40 shillings, more than a sailor's annual wage.[50] Sailors were also recaptured much further afield. David and William Read were located in Edinburgh, where they were found 'sitting in a house with some of their friends'.[51] In imperial regions, locals could be enlisted to help bring back runaway sailors. On San Domingo, escaping sailors were apprehended by Spanish locals, who brought them in as prisoners five hours after they deserted, and in Lisbon, John Hayes and John Matthews were arrested by the 'Police of Lisbon' as stragglers.[52] Even away from the naval ship, then, sailors found that they could not always escape the reach of the state.

So far we have considered the customary modes of resistance available to sailors that were built on a long tradition of maritime protest. In the 1790s we begin to see different forms of protest taking root, such as through the tactic of writing a petition. This was on the face of it a long-standing practice in which sailors would produce a written document that stated their complaints and called directly for redress, representing a deliberate escalation of a grievance to a higher authority.[53] In the first instance, a petition could be written to the fleet's commanding officer as a way of formally announcing discontent; this at least allowed the crew to imagine they were still following the 'proper channels' of legitimate protest, by addressing a superior officer and listing their problems. In reality, though, commanding officers found these letters easy to ignore. In early 1797 the crew of the *Syren* wrote a petition to the commander-in-chief at Portsmouth, Admiral Peter Parker, and received no reply. They followed it up with another petition sent directly to the Admiralty that pleaded their case, and only then was the Admiralty concerned enough to send a naval captain to investigate and take action.[54] Many subsequent petitioners cut out the middlemen and wrote directly to the

Admiralty. In this sense, petitions were articles that allowed negotiation, or bartering, between social groups, and on land there was a longstanding tradition of petitioning dating back to at least the seventeenth century by which people could appeal for restitution or charity. Paupers, for instance, had considerable power when claiming poor relief. Similarly, the wives and families of sailors who had been killed or injured could appeal to the government and local justices of the peace for financial restitution.[55]

The nature and extent of petitioning were transformed in the 1790s. Firstly, whereas before they had been rare and isolated events, written complaints were sent to the Admiralty with remarkable frequency, particularly as the war developed. Secondly, while petitioning had always been a highly political act, this was heightened in the latter decades of the eighteenth century. From the 1770s on, the petition was increasingly utilised not as a claim for assistance, but as a collective document that allowed political campaigns to communicate ideas and build pressure.[56] Between 1775 and 1778, some 60,000 people signed their names to petitions and addresses either opposing or supporting the government's use of force in America, and contemporary observers began to view petitions as valid indicators of informed public opinion.[57] Petitioning efforts were also central to the campaign for the abolition of the slave trade in the 1780s. In 1788 the Manchester Abolition Committee initiated a mass petition drive to put pressure on Parliament, and in the subsequent year between 60,000 and 100,000 signatures were collected, the largest petition drive Britain had seen.[58] By 1795, the *Critical Review* saw a direct connection between petitions and a wider desire for reform: 'When the table of the house of commons is covered with petitions from counties, cities and towns, we shall begin to think that the PEOPLE have expressed their will'.[59] Sailors' petitions therefore adopted the tactics – as well as the language – of the revolutionary age.

Petitions allowed sailors to present their concerns directly, and anonymously, to their officers. Writing a petition was a potentially mutinous act, and so the vast majority of petitions took care to ensure that no individual was named. Letters were therefore signed by ships' companies: 'The Whole ships Company belonging to his Majesty's Ship Nassau'; 'We the Company of HM Sloops Fly'; 'Yours, Ceres Frigate Ship's Company'; or more simply, 'We the Ships Co'.[60] This also gave collective weight to any address, giving the impression that the entirety of the crew was behind the petition, and some went out of their way to give this impression. A petition of the crew of the *Reunion* in 1796 was signed 'One & All', while the crew of the *Eurydice* stated explicitly that the letter was 'signed unanimously'.[61] It is not clear how representative these petitions actually were, and there is evidence that some sailors on board ship wanted nothing to do with petitioning attempts: Thomas Conway, for one, refused to contribute as he 'saw no bad usage' on board the vessel.[62] Certainly many officers understood that petitions might represent a minority opinion, such as George Home, who referred to a document 'purporting' to be from the ship's company.[63]

In some instances, a petition had more weight if sailors *did* sign with their real names. This demonstrated that their grievance really did represent the views of the entire ship's company, though care was taken to ensure no one individual could be deemed the 'ringleader'. One technique was to use a 'round robin' petition, whereby sailors added their names in a circle, making it impossible to determine the order in which it was signed. This was a long-standing tactic, first recorded in the Navy in 1731 but used by mercantile sailors as far back as the seventeenth century.[64] Ideally used on vessels with small crews, it proved difficult to arrange on larger ships where it was impossible to fit even a proportion of a crew's signatures onto one page. It remained very effective on smaller ships, however, allowing virtually the whole crew to sign their names. In 1794, thirty-one sailors of the armed sloop *Lady Taylor* wrote a petition complaining of the 'bad usage' they had received, while a round robin of around eighty sailors of the *Vestal* pleaded to be allowed to join their favoured officer, Captain McDougall, who had been transferred to a different ship, as they 'would be very Happy to Sail along with him'.[65]

Officers, for whom the jeopardy of signing a name was somewhat reduced, also used round robins. In 1795, officers about to be sent to the West Indies were furious about new regulations that forced them to seek military approval to discipline troops being transported on naval ships. Amid the furore, seven of eight admirals wrote a letter of protest, while all but one captain signed a round robin petition protesting. The new regulations were quietly shelved, and it is interesting to speculate how much of an example this set for other ranks.[66]

For the most part, though, writing a petition was a risky act. Naval officers kept a careful eye on literate seamen who wrote letters or helped crewmates craft correspondence. In early 1797 James McCoy was accused of writing a seditious document, and a key part of the evidence against him was that he had been seen composing a number of personal letters to his family. On a different ship, Bryan McDonnough had been spotted writing 'several Letters for different Men on board who could do so well write themselves'.[67] Given the possible punishment for writing a seditious letter, seamen went out of their way to avoid being linked to petitions, and it follows that we know relatively little about who crafted these documents. Certainly, a ship's company spent considerable time finding the right person to write a petition. On the *Caesar*, Thomas Ryan approached his crewmate John Conway to write a letter to the Admiralty as he had been told 'he knew not a fitter Person to do it' than he.[68] Continuities of tone and language within these sources suggest that some petitions were written by one individual, but sailors could also write specific sections of a document. In 1795, William Rogers admitted writing the 'middle bit' of one such letter but said he had no idea who wrote 'the beginning or end of it'.[69] This was another means of ensuring a degree of anonymity, by which sailors could deny writing more incendiary sections.

Petitions tended to focus on incidental rather than structural grievances. They rarely referred to overarching injustices, such as impressment, and they refrained from calling for reform of naval discipline or the Articles of War. On the contrary, one petition acknowledged that punishment in some cases was 'absolutely necessary, and that the service absolutely requires it'. Here again, seamen objected to moments when the social contract between sailor and officer was broken, for example where punishment was excessive or unfair. The same petition went on to complain that they were 'struck down like so many oxen' in a manner that was not 'right, reasonable or humane' and 'a disgrace to the name of Britons'.[70] Sailors wrote to the Admiralty in increasing numbers, framing this broken contract as 'bad usage'.[71] By 1795–6, complaints to the Admiralty were coming thick and fast, and each petition took care to list in graphic detail the sailors' treatment. The men of the *Nassau* wrote that the 'ill usage we have on board this Ship' was so bad that it was 'almost impossible for us to put it down in Paper as cruel as it realy in Fact is' before detailing 'flogging and abusing above humanity'. A petition from the sloop *Weasle* complained of the 'Bad usage' of one lieutenant who made them strip and repeatedly beat them with the end of a rope. Some went as far as to demand that specific officers be replaced.[72]

Frequently, the sailors' concern was less their treatment and more the affront to their honour and sense of fairness. On the *Atlas*, sailors complained that they had been blamed for an accident on board the ship that was the fault of Mr Woodford, the ship's master. Woodford had attempted to pass the blame on to the crew, citing their 'inattention to . . . duty', which outraged the sailors and prompted an irate letter in which they laid the blame squarely at his door, attacking his status as a gentlemen and demanding a master who 'knows his Duty' and who would acknowledge any mistake he made.[73] Similarly, sailors expected their ship to be safe and dependable, and the crews of the *Fly* and the *Syren* were happy to write to the Admiralty about those vessels they deemed deficient. They could also expect a certain quality of food: the sailors of the *Squirrel* complained about the poor quality and quantity of their victuals, noting that 'you are obliged to take what ever the purser serves out Good or Bad and Dare not say one word against it'.[74] Nor were all petitions focused on the needs and wants of sailors: some focused instead on other injustices. In May 1794 around thirty petty officers of the *Alfred* wrote a petition to the Admiralty in support of a popular master's mate who lacked the contacts to advance his career, expressing their hope that the Admiralty would intervene.[75]

As these examples demonstrate, there was a power imbalance at the heart of any petition. Seamen frequently offered a blunt acknowledgement of the disparity in social status and education between themselves and naval elites: the petition of the sloop *Fly* in January 1795, for example, apologised for troubling the Admiralty 'with these few unpolished lines'.[76] In this, sailors' petitions demonstrate some engagement with land-based petitioning cultures, following conventions laid down by etiquette and conduct books.[77] Beyond an acknowledgement of differences in wealth and status, some asked forgiveness for taking up the Admiralty's time: the sailors of the *Reunion* apologised for 'giving you the trouble we are now about to give you'.[78] Petitions also wished the receiver good health, often in fawning tones. The crew of the *Atlas* in 1797 referred to 'your Lordship's Goodness' when addressing the Admiralty, while another petition stated that the sailors were 'for ever bound in Duty to pray for your Lordships long life and eternal welfare'. In some instances, sailors referred to an almost paternal relationship between officer and crew. The ship's company of the *Nassau* stated that they wrote to the Admiralty 'the same as a child to its Father'.[79]

Sailors also used other tactics of late-eighteenth-century petitioning to make their appeals seem more reasonable. Firstly, they adopted the language of patriotism, portraying themselves as men who fervently wished to serve king and country. The sailors of the *Ceres* noted their 'utmost endeavour to stand in defence of our lives, for our King & Country's cause, as we have no intention to quit the service', while those of the *Winchelsea* noted that 'Nothing gives us more Pleasure To serve His Majesty king George the third'.[80] The author of the *Atlas* petition went out of his way to declare the sailors' patriotic zeal, referring to 'the name and character of free born British Subjects, and Seamen, men who are unanimously willingly to lose the last drop of their blood in defence of their gracious Sovereign'.[81] Secondly, they pulled at the heartstrings of the likely reader. Sailors on board the *Eleanor* tender, many of whom had volunteered for service, had been promised a bounty on arrival but had only received a third of it and made a point to mention 'our now doubly Distress[ed] families who are now deprived of us and in a most deplorable condition'. The crew of another ship asked for unpaid prize money and noted that it was 'the means of our providing, comfortably, for our wives & families that are at present in a most melancholy and abject distress at this juncture when every necessary article of life is so extravagantly dear'.[82]

Alongside these appeals to the heart, petitions were also an attempt by seamen to negotiate the terms of their service. One such document emphasised the sailors' 'good service' and 'laborious Industry' performed 'in defence of their King and Country', but it also noted that the British state had, so far, offered them little in return.[83] Most letters made clear that their continued loyalty was conditional. 'We have no Encouragement Either to serve King or Country with such Usage', wrote the sailors of the *Squirrel*, while another made clear that they 'never will fight Like British Subjects under the Command of these officers'.[84] According to the men of the *Nassau*, they could 'never be expected . . . to face our enemy with a cheerful Heart' when suffering 'under the hand of a Tyrant'.[85] Indeed, most petitions came with a threat. Some referred to the negative impact of continued poor treatment, pointing to incredibly high desertion rates. Others were quite arch in their meaning, such as the crew of the *Brunswick*, who referred to a 'Spirit of Discontent and disaffection' and pondered unmade 'fatal Consequences' were their demands not heeded.[86] In rare cases, the authors could be very explicit about their likely next steps. The men of the *Reunion* were resolute that 'we will Neither fight nor Sail any more' unless their hated officers were replaced, while the petitioners of the *Bellerophon* threatened 'the Great Necessity of Mutiny'. The crew of the *Shannon* raised the ruinous prospect of taking the ship into 'An Enemies Port'.[87]

Most alarming for the Admiralty was that sailors' petitions increasingly framed their service using political refrains about 'rights' and 'tyranny'. Traditionally, sailors' civil liberties were limited to those laid out in the Articles of War, and to demand anything further was deemed subversive. William Robinson commented that on joining the Navy, a seaman 'must take leave of the liberty to *speak*, or to act; he may *think*, but he must confine his thoughts to the *hold* of his mind'.[88] And yet, in the 1790s petitions were used to refer to fundamental privileges sailors could expect as Britons. The ship's company of the *Bellerophon* believed their treatment was shocking for men who considered themselves 'Free, willing & British Subjects', while those of the *Atlas* referred explicitly to their background as 'free born English subjects'.[89] This idea drew on a long intellectual tradition dating back to at least the seventeenth century, but sailors' petitions also appropriated more recent, radical language that aligned with the ideals set forth in Enlightenment thinking, and more recently in Paine's *Rights of Man*. 'We have neither Liberty not Dare we speke for our Rites', wrote the petitioner of the *Squirrel*.[90] The sailors of the *Shannon* quoted the Enlightenment philosopher Jean-Jacques Rousseau directly. 'We are Born free But Now we are Slaves', they stated, detailing their oppression and 'tyranny' at the hands of their captain, which was 'more than the Spirits and Harts of true English Man can Cleaverly Bear'.[91] In these documents, then, we see a range of different political strands of thought, from the traditional, to the intellectual, to the revolutionary, all applied directly in a naval context.

There is some evidence that sailors' petitioning could be successful. John Cook, a private marine who admitted writing a petition, said he did so because he had known of similar letters written from other ships 'and they had gotten relieved'.[92] In most cases, the Admiralty ordered officers to investigate the claims of the sailors, and they certainly took the threat of further protests seriously.[93] On the *Ceres*, sailors complained about harsh discipline and asked for 'speedy relief from our present sufferings' by transferring them to another ship. A few days later, three naval captains came on board and spent two and a half hours discussing the crew's grievances before promising to reply in a few days. Good news came shortly after, when their officers were moved to a different ship and a new captain, James Newman-Newman, was given command. Sailors' petitions could also be effective in limiting punishments. In 1795, James Anderson was found guilty of uttering mutinous expressions, a sentence that could carry the death penalty. The crew of his ship, the *Hebe*, wrote an impassioned petition on his behalf, pleading with the captain of the ship to pardon him and promising in return that he would 'never to be Guilty of any thing Inconsistent with his Duty' again. The clerk of the court noted their concern and saw to it that he received 'only' thirty-six lashes, a brutal punishment to be sure, but also an acknowledgement that petitioning could work.[94]

It remained a dangerous business, however, for in many cases a petition was seen as a direct assault on a captain's authority and character. While the *Venus* was at anchor at Torbay in 1796, a letter was sent to the Admiralty complaining of the sailors' treatment, prompting the Admiralty to write to the captain asking for an explanation. The furious officer called the crew on deck and demanded that the writer come forward, asking them if they had seen the letter or recognised the handwriting, threatening to have them 'tied up and flogged' so much that they 'would see [their] back bone' if the guilty party did not come forward.[95] More often, petitions were simply ignored, or accusations were swept under the carpet. On the *Reunion*, the sailors' complaints about their captain Henry William Bayntum were ignored, and his ship was wrecked on the Sunk Sand in the Thames Estuary the following month. On other ships, the failure to respond to their complaints forced sailors to take another, riskier path. In August 1793 the *Winchelsea's* sailors attempted to highlight their grievances to the Admiralty but received no response. They wrote again the following month asking to be put on another ship, making it clear that if they did not hear back they would be under 'the neccessity [sic] to free our selves from her as soon as Possible by some other mains'.[96] Three days later, certain that no response was coming, the ship's crew took the ultimate and most extreme step: mutiny.

No form of shipboard protest has excited as much historical and public attention as mutiny. Individual uprisings, such as that on the *Bounty* in 1789, have excited considerable popular and scholarly interest, and it represents the most extreme form of resistance possible on a warship: one sailor later recalled that to talk of mutiny on board was to 'rush on certain death', for even to 'breathe the idea' was to risk swinging at the yard arm.[97] In all likelihood this is in part due to a problem with the historical record: neither sailors nor officers had much to gain by reporting clashes that were resolved amicably, just as many official records failed to note instances when mutinies were narrowly avoided. The near mutiny on the *Blanche* in 1795, for instance, was not mentioned in the log, and we only know of it because a sailor happened to record it in his memoir later.[98] However, what is clear is that mutinies occurred more frequently in the 1790s than ever before. Whereas during the American War of 1775–83 there were 31 British mutinous acts recorded, an average of 3.75 per year, during the French Revolutionary Wars the number was 170, corresponding to an extraordinary average of 18.89 mutinies per year.[99] In the revolutionary 1790s, seamen were far more willing to take extreme measures.

The potential penalty of death for mutiny meant that there was a clear division between mutiny and other lesser acts of defiance such as disobedience and contempt; so long as it did not upset the hierarchy of the ship, a jury was usually content to apply the lower penalty. In 1796, for instance, John Clark openly refused to have his pay docked, but despite being charged with both mutiny and contempt, he was only found guilty of the latter.[100] There was also an important distinction between 'mutiny' and 'mutinous expressions'. The former constituted a deliberate collective attempt to take over the ship, while the latter represented words that discussed or incited upheaval. Either way, these were subjective terms that could be stretched to cover almost any resistance to authority. John Horsington, a marine of the *Europa*, was found guilty of mutinous expressions and given 100 lashes for calling the corporal a 'dirty rascal' and protesting that he had already 'done his Duty'.[101] For the most part, though, the Navy's need for skilled labour saw courts martial fall on the side of leniency.[102] Nonetheless, the charge of 'mutinous expressions' was a means by which commissioned officers could control the language used on board a ship by all members of the crew, including petty and warrant officers. In 1794, the purser of the *Regulus*, Cornelius Harrington, was found guilty of writing letters 'of mutinous tendency' and was dismissed from the ship.[103]

The act of mutiny, by contrast, was not something to be taken lightly and usually represented a final, extreme attempt to have a crew's grievances heard. The men of the *Winchelsea* had already written two petitions in 1793 demanding that disliked officers be removed, and it was only when it was clear their letters were being ignored that they took the more extreme step. The subsequent mutiny was the first ship-wide rebellion of the French Revolutionary Wars and conformed to a longer tradition of maritime protest, in which a mutiny resembled something akin to a strike, whereby sailors withdrew their labour until their grievances were met.[104] The mutiny was fundamentally peaceful, and as the sailors barricaded themselves below deck, they laid out their demands clearly and emphasised that 'they wished to hurt nobody'. It was the ship's captain who escalated the situation, firing a pistol into the hammocks, which was enough to scare the sailors into abandoning their rebellion. Two sailors, William Price and William Duggan, were accused of being the ringleaders, but in the court martial that followed it was acknowledged that they had offered no violence, and it proved impossible to identify their voices or to tie them to mutinous statements. They could only prove that the two men were present and 'did not use their utmost endeavour to suppress the same', which was enough to sentence them to 200 lashes each. The mutiny had achieved its aim, however. Nine days after the floggings, the captain, eight petty officers and eight of his followers were assigned to other ships.[105]

Equally successful was a second mutiny the following year on the *Windsor Castle*. On 9 November 1794, around 300 members of the crew rebelled against their officers, arming themselves with cutlasses, boarding pikes and handspikes, and prevented the officers from going below so as to maintain anonymity. The *Windsor Castle* was not a happy ship, and in a letter addressed to the commander-in-chief, Admiral William Hotham, the mutineers outlined repeated examples of oppression and cruelty by their new captain, John Shield, and Lieutenant George McKinley. Sailors had been punished for any slight lapse, to the extent that seamen were afraid to go aloft for fear of drawing punishment, while the most skilled sailors of all, the top men who operated in the rigging, had been made to scour the decks. This petty attack on expertise and fair play 'hurted us very much, as we never had the Like Usage Before', and in September and October the ship suffered a number of desertions. Hotham quickly arranged a court martial of the ship's officers, but unsurprisingly, no individual sailor was willing to come forward and testify for fear of being punished, and the charges were dismissed. However, the sailors steadfastly refused to return to their duties, and Hotham was left with no choice but to acquiesce to Shield and McKinley's request for a new ship.[106]

In the first year and a half of the war, the mutinies on the *Winchelsea* and the *Windsor Castle* represented the sole examples of ship-wide rebellion. Non-violent, moderate in their aims and with a successful settlement, these were textbook examples of how mutiny could be used by sailors to negotiate the terms of their service. The mutiny on the *Culloden* on 4 December 1794, however, transformed the way shipboard relations were conducted and perceived. With the ship at anchor in Portsmouth, between forty and fifty sailors took charge of the lower decks, disarming the marines – a shipboard police force tasked in part with subduing mutinous activity – and driving officers and loyalist sailors up on deck. Initially, it followed the patterns laid down on the

Winchelsea and the *Windsor Castle*. Ladders were removed and hammocks were brought together to create a barricade, while the crew peacefully laid out their demands. A letter was produced on the 'point of a stick' addressed to the commander of the Channel Fleet, Admiral Bridport, declaring that the ship was not fit for service and refusing to go to sea with the first lieutenant, who had referred to the crew as a 'set of Cowardly Rascalls', a slur that sat uneasily with crews who had recently fought at the Battle of the Glorious First of June. The petition followed traditional conventions, appealing to Bridport's good nature, and emphasised that the 'many Brave Sailors' on board had 'gladly embraced the favourable opportunity to distinguish our Courage and Valour, in so Glorious a Victory'. By the second day of the mutiny they had the support of around 250 men, paralysing the ship.[107]

Far more concerning was that the seamen were acting in a defiantly 'revolutionary' manner. The letter written by the seamen of the *Culloden* was signed 'A Delegate', a deliberate reference to the French Revolution and the representatives of the London Corresponding Society. The mutineers' petition declared that if they were forced to sea 'they would not fire a Shot' and instead would 'be taken by the French'. They also swore under oath not to desert the cause 'till it was all over' and promised not to divulge any secret[s]', while sailors encouraged their crewmates to swear, crying out 'Kiss the Book, kiss the Book'.[108] Political oaths of this nature were a long-standing form of dissent but became ever more symbolic in the tense climate of the 1790s; certainly, they were taken very seriously by the Navy, as they contradicted the sailors' oath to king and country.[109] In addition, the more radical mutineers were overheard discussing treasonous acts: both Cornelius Sullivan and Jeremiah Collins threatened to blow up the ship. The Navy grew increasingly desperate, and the Admiralty escalated matters further when they ordered two other warships to position themselves to fire on the *Culloden* if needed. It was only after five days, and the promise of a general pardon from Captain Pakenham, that the mutineers abandoned the mutiny.[110]

To the shock of the seamen, however, no sooner had they come up on deck than ten 'ringleaders' were apprehended and put on trial for mutiny. The court martial that followed was a fraught and dramatic affair. Some sailors, particularly those who had been heavily involved in the mutiny, displayed remarkable solidarity. A number of sailors offered testimony that helped those accused, arguing forcefully that there were no ringleaders. Maurice Dunn stated that 'I saw none they were all alike' and testified that there were no executive orders. His answers grew so vague that he was sent to Marshalsea prison for three months for gross prevarication. There was a limit to this solidarity, however; the trial also revealed a crew divided in aims and ideals. The mutineers had represented less than half the ship's company, and many loyal sailors were happy to testify against those deemed responsible. Some of the 'well-affected' men such as Solomon Bostock and John Banks had warned the officers that mutineers were threatening to blow up the ship, and they and others testified against the accused. Some claimed that Francis Watts had armed himself with a cutlass, placed sentries and administered the mutinous oath, while others reported that James Johnson had threatened sailors with a cutlass and written the petition. In this way, seamen contributed to the deaths of their crewmates: eight of those accused were found guilty of mutiny, five of whom – including Watts and Johnson – were hanged.[111]

The *Culloden* mutiny transformed the relationship between the men of the lower deck and their commissioned officers. If the mutinies of 1793–4 had demonstrated the willingness of seamen and officers to negotiate, the executions of the *Culloden* sailors who had been promised a pardon shattered the trust between them. The mood on the *Culloden* remained volatile: three men were flogged for riotous behaviour and insolence, and the captain had thirty-one seamen he suspected of involvement dispersed to other ships.[112] As news of the reprisals spread through the Navy, those planning similar revolts learned important lessons. In the second half of 1795, a series of separate mutinies on the *Terrible* (12 September 1795), the *Defiance* (18 October 1795) and the

Pompee (30 November 1795) took place. In each case, the crew's grievances were initially specific and moderate, and the sailors had worked
their way through less extreme options before resorting to mutiny. On
the *Terrible*, for instance, the crew had complained about the quality of
the bread, only to be told by the purser's mate, despite acknowledging
that some of the bread had been on board for eight months, that 'it was
of no use' complaining further. Their grievances ignored, the crew
started to take command of the ship, barricading themselves below
decks.[113] No longer were mutinies planned as fundamentally peaceful
affairs; from 1795 sailors ensured that they gathered arms and demonstrated a willingness to use them.

This represented a step change in sailors' tactics. Whereas before
mutinies had taken the form of a strike, largely without physical
confrontation, the rebellions of 1795 were aggressive and violent.[114] On
the *Terrible*, two of the lower-deck guns were pointed aft, while the
seamen collected muskets, cutlasses, tomahawks and half pikes, plus
boxes of powder. On the *Pompee* and the *Defiance* the crews rolled
cannon shot down the deck so as to 'endanger the life of every person
that went below'. On the latter, the crew broke into the magazine,
loaded two guns with grapeshot, primed them with matches burning
and pointed them, ready to be used against loyalist members of the
crew. When a group of marines from another ship attempted to come
on board, the seamen threw shot into the boats and pointed the lower-
deck guns at them until they beat a hasty retreat. One mutineer, John
Sullivan, threatened a lieutenant from the *Jupiter* with a boarding
pike.[115] The mutineers also learned other important lessons. In particular they found new ways to ensure that the anonymity of the organisers was maintained. On the *Terrible* the mutinying sailors spoke to the
ship's officers through a speaking trumpet 'in order to disguise their
voices'. On the *Pompee* and the *Defiance* the sailors knocked the candle
and lanterns out of the gunners' hands to avoid being identified. On the
latter, one sailor recalled how throughout the tumultuous events, 'all
[was] in darkness. There were no lights.'[116]

While sailors expanded the means at their disposal, they also ensured that their aims were more concrete and assertively communicated. The sailors of the *Terrible* framed their grievances not as 'humble requests' but as 'expectations':

> We do not wish to incur your displeasure nor to create any disturbance in the ship, but as Men we would wish to be treated and to have wholsom [sic] bread as proper application has been made several times and no redress given we are under the disagreeable necessity to take these measures which are as obnoxious to us as they are to your Honour.

> Our expectations are, an answer from under your hand that no Man shou'd be upbraided hereafter.

> No man to be punished, and serve us Bread and we will return to our Duty as usually.[117]

On the *Defiance*, an anonymous letter was written that made 'demands'. The authors reminded the officers in blunt terms about the conditional nature of their service: once their requests were met, they would 'with the greatest pleasure comply with any Terms confirmable to the Rules of His Majesty's Navy'.[118] Furthermore, throughout these mutinies there was remarkable camaraderie among the mutineers, and a carefully constructed appearance of unity. On the *Terrible*, the officers demanded that the crew give up the ringleaders, but they answered in no uncertain terms that 'There was no Ringleaders, but one and all'. Similarly, on the *Pompee*, Captain Vashon asked if there were any well-disposed men on board who would name the organisers, but the sailors replied 'No! No! damme we won't'.[119]

The mutinies of late 1795 revealed that a more extreme and politically motivated form of mutiny had emerged. The sailors framed their actions in clear political terms, particularly on the *Defiance*, where individual seamen cried out that they had been kept on board 'like convicts' and that 'they would have liberty'. This was a particular reference to shore leave, but the sailors felt comfortable using highly politicised language to make their point. Countless testimonies reported hearing them say they 'wanted liberty', that they 'repeatedly cried out for liberty', 'it was liberty he wanted & was determined to have it', 'liberty, liberty'. The seamen understood their rights and knew when these were not being met: one sailor was heard to say that 'they were too old or had been too long on board a Man of War to be kept on board as Prisoners'. The *Defiance* mutiny took on added significance when the mutineers referred to sections of the crew who had remained loyal to the ship's officers as 'Royalists' and enclosed a list of around 130 sailors whom they ordered to leave the ship. One sailor, William Handy, forcibly removed a number of them and proclaimed 'with an Oath that the World was nothing without liberty'.[120] A similar divide occurred on the *Terrible*. One seaman, Edward Masters, saw the mutiny in clear political terms, abusing one crewmate for 'fighting for our King and Country' when he 'would not for our rights'.[121]

If the naval revolts of 1795 represented an escalation of seamen's political efforts, they also augured a more uncompromising response from the naval establishment. Captain George Campbell of the *Terrible* was determined not to allow the concessions that had been granted earlier in the war, declaring that the uprising on the ship 'shall not be a Windsor Castle's business'. Campbell's aggressive response ensured that a peaceful solution was impossible and represented a heightening of the use of state violence in response to naval rebellion. He demanded that the crew give up 'the Planners of their villainous proceedings' and threatened 'unpleasant measures' if they did not do so. 'So far from promising them that no man should be punished ... I gave them my Word and Honour, every one concerned in it should be punished, and that very severely.' After waiting only a few minutes, he ordered his men to fire on the mutineers. Five sailors were wounded by musket balls in a series of gruesome injuries: William Miles was hit with a musket ball in the knee, George Wilkinson in the groin, and Mattio Ciantar, a Maltese sailor, was hit in the lungs.

Only the desperate cries of sailors not to fire brought the mutiny to an end.[122] Increasingly violent means were also used on the *Defiance* to bring the mutiny to an end. Marines were sent on board to retake control of the ship by force, and having done so, eight men who were deemed to have taken leading roles in the revolt were taken into custody.[123]

In the aftermath of the 1795 mutinies, the Navy too began to make a connection between political ideas and shipboard rebellion. The Admiralty started to use the state's language of repression in naval contexts; in 1795, for the first time words such as 'riotous' and 'seditious' were used to charge sailors with discordant behaviour.[124] By 1795 a seaman writing a 'publick letter' was deemed a mutinous act. As one court martial noted, 'the Writing, or being concerned in the Writing such Letters, is highly improper, and injurious to the publick service'. A year later, one sailor was punished with 300 lashes for having written such a petition.[125] The courts martial of the 1795 mutineers took place in this context of heightened tension and were especially brutal. Eight sailors of the *Defiance* were sentenced to hang, another four were given 300 lashes and three received 100 lashes. On the *Terrible* five sailors were hanged, and on the *Pompee* David Cumbers was found guilty of 'endeavouring to incite the people to mutiny' and sentenced to three hundred lashes.[126] These were not show trials – the trial of the *Defiance* mutineers alone lasted three weeks – and in each case sailors were acquitted of wrongdoing. However, the punishments handed out represented a deliberate attempt to use extreme violence to deter future rebellions. The sentence of the five hanged mutineers of the *Terrible* noted that it 'was a painful alternative' but declared that 'the occasion required a striking and forcible example'. They hoped that 'the general impression it may have made upon the minds of many will conduce to allay that turbulent Spirit and Dissatisfaction which of late has been but too prevalent'.[127]

Naval elites were soon disappointed. Throughout 1796 and into 1797, the objectives of seamen became ever more ambitious, and sailors' petitions ever more demanding. That of the *Eurydice* used the word 'Require' when listing the sailors' grievances, a long way from the humble, fawning petitions of the early 1790s.[128] The strategies of sailors also grew bolder. In April 1796, the sailors of the *Bermuda* concocted a plan to mutiny and take their ship to America. One naval captain lamented 'that there should exist an Englishman capable of forming so very wicked an intention'.[129] In November two seamen of the *Reunion*, John Lloyd and Peter Bavarot, were accused of organising a group of fifteen to twenty sailors on the quarterdeck, where Lloyd gave a speech laying out his criticism of the captain, demanded a new ship and told the rest of the crew, 'don't be afraid speak your mind'. The Navy's response was especially brutal: despite the charges only being 'proved in part', Lloyd was sentenced to 600 lashes and Baverot to 500 lashes.[130] These were death sentences in all but name; in each case, the victim was flogged until he was unconscious before being allowed to recover, only for the punishment to continue again. It is hard to believe that acts such as this did anything to salve relations between commissioned officers and other naval personnel.

By 1797, naval ships were established as political spaces in which sailors felt confident in offering criticism of both their officers and the British government. On the *Mermaid*, the seaman John Murray lost his temper with his captain, declaring that 'you are a pretty Fellow to be a Captain of a Man of War', and urged him to bring him to a court martial. The ship's commander, Robert Otway, duly obliged and Murray was punished with 300 lashes. A failed mutiny on the *Beaulieu* saw one sailor use the language of class struggle: he declared that 'he was neither a Lords Son or a Baronet, but he would be buggered if he did not make his officers repent putting him in Irons'.[131] Many members of the ships' crews read newspapers, wrote and exchanged letters, and engaged with politicised songs of both loyalist and radical bent. By 1797, ballads with clear radical political points were circulating on naval ships. In a tranche of papers found on board the *Repulse* in 1797, investigators discovered a series of what they termed 'insidious' songs that compared the working conditions of sailors with those on shore. They contrasted the 'rites of Freeman' with sailors who had been impressed:

Is this your proof of British rites
Is this rewarding bravery
Oh shame to boast your Tars Exploits
Then Doom those Tars to Slavery

It went on to critique the 'Minions of a Court' and those who supported the war, and it threatened a time when these 'Mean Baubles of Creation' would no longer be in power.[132] Another ballad found on the ship framed the sailors' predicament in terms of class and wealth, as well as in terms of rights lost:

... In Days of Yore when Rich and poor agreed
Poor served the Rich and Rich the poor Relived
No Despotic Tyrants then the womb produced
But mutual all, each loved, and none abus'd
But now How Dreadful is the scene revers'd
Were Blest with Birth but by oppression Curs'd.[133]

Most seditious literature would have been well hidden or destroyed, and these ballads offer a rare window into the everyday political lives of sailors. Even then, seditious papers continued to be found on naval ships throughout the 1790s.[134]

An astonishing series of exchanges on the *Atlas* reveals the ways in which political subjects could be discussed on board a ship. In February 1797, the sailor James McCoy felt comfortable enough to declare to the master's mate, George Box, that

twas highly necessary a Revolution should take place: and that it certainly would in a short time, as there was a great deal of Corruption and Bribery in the Higher Departments of Government; that the people were very much oppressed & assured me I should very soon see a Revolution in this Country

McCoy and Box had exchanged a newspaper in which they had both read about a recent strike in a Cornish mine and had come to very different conclusions about its significance. While McCoy imagined upheaval, Box offered a response that could have been taken directly from one of Hannah More's loyalist tracts. 'I argued with him upon the superior degree of Happiness the people of this Country enjoyed when compared with those of other nations,' he recalled. McCoy was adamant in his opinions and stated to other crewmates that 'as there was a great deal of Corruption and Bribery in the Higher Departments of Government . . . the people were very much oppressed' and that 'it was time that Government, has a reform, and that the heads of government ought not to be where they were'. He was just as forthcoming about his officers, for while 'he knew his Business . . . they did not know theirs'. For his seditious talk McCoy was punished with 300 lashes.[135]

Of course, not every sailor was a revolutionary. Many were loyal to their captains and did all they could to preserve order on board. One, Solomon Hines, threatened to knock down a sailor who protested having to go back to work.[136] It is notable that as part of James McCoy's defence for mutinous expression, he called on sailors to testify that he had often spoken 'in a very respectable manner of Wm. Pitt & the other principle officers in administration', and to his loyalty to the king and the present government.[137] Clearly this was the acceptable face of political discussion on board a ship. Indeed, it is often hard to establish exactly what proportion of a ship's crew was involved in the mutiny, and how many were opposed or indifferent. Mutinies usually began with a nucleus of sailors, perhaps only 20–30 per cent of the crew, enough to be successful if the remainder stayed neutral.[138] This certainly was the case in the 1790s – in the investigation into the near mutiny on the *Bermuda*, one sailor claimed that twenty men signed their names to a mutinous document, but that at least thirteen acknowledged being asked to sign but refused to and even suggested that it should be thrown overboard. On a brig sloop of eighty to a hundred men, these samples represented the minority of the crew, and it is likely that many seamen were keen to avoid declaring their loyalty either way. Certainly, whether through fear of punishment or genuine conviction, some went out of their way to prevent mutinies from occurring. Peter Stevenson reported to an officer that a plot was under way on his ship and identified two of his crewmates as agitators.[139]

Similarly, not every vessel was marked by discord in this period. To paraphrase Tolstoy, 'happy ships are all alike; every unhappy ship is different in its own way'. It seems likely that crews that secured significant prize money would have been more likely to submit to the conditions of naval life, and naval officers who treated their men favourably – who offered them 'good usage' – were less likely to face protests. For every captain like John Shield or George Campbell, there were others like Cuthbert Collingwood, whose distaste for corporal punishment meant beatings were rare and floggings were ordered sparingly. The memoirs of sailors writing after the war report any number of tyrants, but also officers who made genuine attempts to create bonds with their crew, and who were in turn respected by the sailors they commanded. William Richardson scorned the Admiralty's decision to try his commander William Cornwallis for disobeying orders and delighted when this 'great man' – fondly nicknamed 'Blue Billy' – escaped punishment.[140] After all, everyone on board a naval ship had a vested interest in maintaining some degree of harmony. Operating a machine as complex as a naval ship required collaboration across all ranks: in battle or on a stormy night, the lives of all rested on the men across warrant and commissioned rank making the right decisions, and on these orders being executed precisely by the men under their command.

What is notable, though, is how often across the 1790s this consensus broke down. In the face of severe punishment, sailors were prepared on numerous occasions to put obedience to one side and agitate to improve their lives. Indeed, the distinction between 'happy' and 'unhappy' ships simplifies a much more complex picture. Every ship housed a diverse political community, containing radicals, moderates, reformers and loyalists, alongside others more ambivalent about taking a stance. In this the full range of political persuasions was on display in the revolutionary 1790s. On vessels where grievances were felt, there was a range of different options open to sailors. There was rarely full agreement about the best course of action, as different individuals and cliques disagreed about means and ends. The decision to mutiny was the one most reluctantly taken, coming as it did with the threat of execution. It followed that conflict and debate among a ship's crew was normal. During the mutiny on the *Belliqueux* in 1796, Jonathan Harper urged the ship's company to 'rise and carry her into France', but his crewmates were not convinced: some pointed out to him that these words were 'wrong' and told him to 'refrain from using them again'.[141] The nomination of 'delegates' on board the *Culloden* was an attempt to work around these issues of political representation, creating a structure that allowed for the views of all men to be heard. Just as individuals across Britain called out for electoral reform and parliamentary representation, in the Navy, sailors took matters into their own hands.

We are left, then, with a complex picture of shipboard political culture in early 1797. The first four years of the Revolutionary Wars had revealed a community of sailors keen to register grievance, and who had an arsenal of customary forms of protest at their disposal. At the same time, we also know that those seamen demanding change did not always represent the entire workforce, and seamen were just as likely to take up more conservative, even reactionary stances. In this way, the various debates on ships mirrored those on shore, as the French Revolution prompted a new British political culture riven by disagreements between radicals and conservatives.[142] As on shore, those most likely to take part were not the labouring masses, but skilled men in positions of some authority, in particular experienced sailors and petty officers. The captain of the *Tartar*, Charles Elphinstone Fleming, told John

Clark, a boatswain's mate, that 'it was such men as him neither Seaman or Officer, that breeds disturbance in a Ship'.[143] The Admiralty, however, were slow to comprehend this changing landscape. In 1790 the naval officer Philip Patton had drawn up a document offering observations on naval affairs, in which he registered deep concern for the working conditions and pay of seamen and warrant officers. In the aftermath of the mutiny on the *Culloden* and while the rebellions of the *Terrible*, the *Defiance* and the *Pompee* were playing out, he revised his original ideas under the title 'Observations on Naval Mutiny', adding suggestions on how this might be prevented. It was presented to the First Lord of the Admiralty in April 1795, and while copies were sent to William Pitt, Henry Dundas and William Wilberforce, the government took no heed of his warnings. Despondent, Patton retired from public life to Fareham, Hampshire.[144]

It is not clear why the government failed to heed Patton's warnings, especially after reports of the mutinies of 1795 arrived at the Admiralty. Certainly, by 1797 it was clear to those in Whitehall that something far more concerning was afoot. Seamen were now acting collectively as they had never done before, on board individual ships but also exchanging ideas and tactics between vessels. As we heard at the start of this chapter, in March that year a petition landed on the Admiralty's desk signed 'We the seamen of His Majesty's Navy', signalling the new capacity of ships' crews to act together for a common good. Over the subsequent months, fleets stationed around the British Isles mutinied, paralysing the nation's naval defences. These were not isolated outbreaks of rebellion but the result of a wider transformation of sailors' political ideas and activity throughout the early years of the Revolutionary War. Ships were centres of political activity, with sailors sharing grievances with their peers on other vessels. Indeed, their political discussions were not confined on board. As the next chapter will show, the mobile nature of their work meant that sailors were an important part of a global network that helped spread news and revolutionary ideas around the world.

FOUR

TIDES, CURRENTS AND WINDS
Navy and Empire, 1793–7

The Age of Revolutions was truly global. In the last decades of the eighteenth century, ideas about liberty and individual rights travelled across and beyond national borders, and the 1790s offered countless examples of how easily news and information could spread and shape events around the world. The French Revolution of 1789 brought a language of rights and a model of action that were hugely influential, and global war in 1793 created opportunities for its ideals to proliferate further.[1] The best known occurred in the French colony of Saint-Domingue in the Caribbean, where a home-rule movement was transformed into a struggle for freedom, equality and independence by the island's free and enslaved people of colour.[2] The Haitian Revolution, as it came to be known, was a cradle of revolutionary activism in the Caribbean, and there were revolts across European colonial empires as exploited peoples defied imperial authority and agitated for rights and freedoms. Historians continue to discuss the precise relationship between events in Paris, Saint-Domingue and other sites of revolt, and in recent years they have moved the focus from Eurocentric explanations of the French Revolution's impact to studies of the enslaved and indigenous peoples who actively instigated and executed change.[3] These movements occurred in a global context, however, whereby uprisings in the Mediterranean, the Indian Ocean, the Caribbean and Latin America reinvented and re-applied the language and ideas of the Age of Revolutions for their own ends.[4]

For Britain's government, instability on this scale offered opportunities but also threats. In the opening months of the war, optimistic ministers looked forward to securing rich pickings in colonies where France, Spain and the Netherlands struggled to maintain authority. Initially at least, it appeared that Britain's own colonial position was secure: in 1793 colonists in Barbados, Grenada and Jamaica burnt effigies of Tom Paine in a deliberate attempt to dissuade would-be revolutionaries and identify themselves with loyalist ideals. However, as the war continued, Britain's imperial ventures were also unsettled by the wider currents of revolutionary change. In the Mediterranean and the Indian Ocean, the activities of Republican France sparked fears and anxieties that forced drastic responses from Britain.[5] In the Caribbean a series of revolts rocked the British-occupied islands of St Vincent, Grenada and Jamaica and took on the spectre of a widespread insurrection. These uprisings not only threatened the spread of revolutionary ideas but also targeted the economic system on which British colonialism in the West Indies depended: slavery. Enormous sums of capital were tied to the production of commodities produced by slave labour, such as sugar, coffee and tobacco, and despite a burgeoning movement for abolition, Britain's trade in human cargo continued unabated in the late eighteenth century: between 1781 and 1790, it is calculated that Britain transported 323,446 enslaved Africans to the Caribbean.[6] The rebellions of the 1790s threatened to overturn this economic system, prompting a determined and often brutal response.

The maintenance of Britain's colonial position was inconceivable without the Royal Navy. While it could also rely on its imperial infrastructure of governors, consuls and trading companies, and sparsely placed military regiments in key sites, only the Navy offered the organisational reach to protect commerce and project power on a global scale. In this, its actions were inherently traditional and spoke to a policy that had served Britain well throughout most of its eighteenth-century wars.[7] However, as the 1790s continued, this imperial activity became the British state's primary counter-revolutionary force as it attempted

to extend control into enemy colonies that had thrown off their imperial masters, while also subduing revolts in its own possessions. This
chapter explores the relationship between the Royal Navy and the
British Empire throughout the revolutionary 1790s, considering
Britain's attempts to extend – and increasingly protect – its imperial
footholds. In the late 1790s, the British commander-in-chief in the
Caribbean, Ralph Abercromby, described operations in the Caribbean
as a matter of 'tides, currents and winds'.[8] As we will see, this was an
accurate description of the logistical challenges of waging war in distant
theatres. At the same time, though, it stands as a powerful metaphor for
Britain's struggle against the global ebb and flow of revolutionary ideas
during the 1790s.

More than any other British institution, the Royal Navy was a 'global'
power. Even in peacetime, small detachments of naval ships were positioned around Britain's empire, ensuring the protection of its trade and,
more symbolically, offering a reminder to local dignitaries, merchants
and pirates of British imperial power.[9] With the coming of war in 1793,
the immediate threat from across the English Channel meant that the
attention of British ministers was firmly focused on operations in
Europe. It followed that in the first year of the conflict, these far-flung
imperial forces received little extra support as ships and regiments were
concentrated in home waters. A small Caribbean force was ordered to
capture the island of Tobago, and in the East Indies an equally slight
naval squadron took the French colony at Pondicherry in August 1793.
Only briefly in the opening weeks of the conflict, when it appeared that
a French naval force was sailing west across the Atlantic, did British
policymakers divert resources and dispatch a British fleet to Barbados.[10]
However, as the war continued – and as prospects of a breakthrough in
Europe diminished – attention turned to 'blue-water' targets. Imperial
forces were supplemented, and by October 1795 there were more than

forty ships stationed in the Caribbean, with small detachments also placed at Newfoundland and Nova Scotia. In the Indian Ocean there were 16 ships and over 5,000 naval sailors protecting British interests in the region.[11]

Britain's largest 'imperial' presence in this period was closer to home, in the Mediterranean. We have already seen how, in the first year of the war, naval operations here offered early success against the French revolutionary forces, not least the capture of Toulon in 1793. Actions to counter the seemingly inexorable spread of France's armies also created opportunities to extend Britain's imperial position. Just such an opportunity presented itself in the summer of 1793, following a nationalist revolt led by Pasquale Paoli that forced the French military garrison on Corsica behind the fortifications of San Fiorenzo, Calvi and Bastia on the north of the island. Britain seized the chance to secure an imperial outpost in the western Mediterranean, for while the island offered few commercial rewards, there was a tangible strategic boon, including rich resources of timber and a naval base from which Toulon could be blockaded. There were also hopes that Corsicans could be recruited into British military and naval forces.[12] Amphibious landings of British soldiers and naval marines took place in February 1794, supported by Corsican irregular fighters. San Fiorenzo was captured, and the French retreated to the capital, Bastia, with naval sailors playing a very active role in landing guns for the siege and manning batteries established onshore.[13] The French surrendered on 21 May 1794, and Paoli agreed a deal with the British envoy Gilbert Elliot that saw the island brought under British control in return for protection against French revolutionary forces.

The occupation of Corsica proved far more problematic than had first been imagined. Paoli was an unreliable partner and, as the costs of maintaining a strong position on Corsica rose exponentially, ministers and naval officers alike were critical of its usefulness. Horatio Nelson, who had played a role in the capture of the island, noted that its inhabitants were 'so greedy of wealth, and so jealous of each other, that it would require the patience of Job, and the riches of Croesus, to satisfy them', while his friend and colleague Cuthbert Collingwood criticised the 'immense expense' incurred in the occupation. Privately, he admitted that 'Miserable Corsica produced nothing but rebels . . . The favourable reports which have been made of this island are shameful falsehoods, and shew how blind people are to the truth.'[14] In terms that offer a surprisingly modern understanding of popular political support, the Home Secretary the Duke of Portland also noted that there was no public will to continue with further investment. Corsica's 'cost', he wrote,

> renders it unpopular. Our worthy citizens are not interested in foreign policy – they understand accounting and commercial speculation, but as regards power and security beyond the Channel, the mass of the population is incapable of seeing the necessity and understanding its worth.[15]

Its strategic function dubious, and with no popular support for a continued presence, in 1796 Corsica was abandoned. *The Times* noted that the troops on the island could be better employed somewhere more useful, but otherwise the evacuation passed with little comment.[16] It proved a revealing experiment in the use of empire to counteract the advance of revolution.

Corsica's loss was also a result of the revival of French naval power in the Mediterranean. The British capture of Toulon in 1793 had been a temporary setback for French naval forces, but by January 1795 there were reports of several new ships on the stocks almost ready for action.[17] Early French sorties saw the capture of the 74-gun *Berwick*, and in February a sizeable squadron was sent to sea. It was confronted by an equivalent force under the command of Vice Admiral William Hotham, and after an indecisive engagement the French retreated back to the safety of Toulon, having lost two ships to the British. Nelson, whose ship the *Agamemnon* had attacked the French for three hours, privately criticised his commander for not making more of the opportunity to destroy the French fleet.[18] Nonetheless, the French became ever more ambitious. In October 1795 a force under Rear Admiral Joseph de Richery captured thirty valuable merchant ships from a convoy bound from the Levant.[19] French military advances in northern Italy further weakened Britain's Mediterranean position, as General Bonaparte's Italian campaign captured Leghorn. The sailor Jacob Nagle witnessed the Royal Navy's fighting retreat, describing how his ship the *Blanche* escaped from under continual fire until it was out of reach of the French guns.[20] Britain's position worsened throughout 1796 as its Spanish and Neapolitan allies sued for peace, and in November the Navy withdrew from the Mediterranean altogether. With no warship inside the straits of Gibraltar, Britain's efforts to extend its empire into the Mediterranean had come to nought, and it was almost two years before the Navy returned.[21]

Britain's efforts in the Indian Ocean were far more successful. Imperial engagement with India and Southeast Asia had been growing in importance in the latter decades of the eighteenth century, and in 1793 John Bruce wrote extensively of the importance of this region to the British economy. Exports to India and China amounted to £1,500,000 per annum, and the duty on imported tea raised more than £1,000,000 each year out of a total government revenue of £18,732,000 in 1794.[22] From 1794, responsibility for protecting this trade was given to Commodore Peter Rainier, who had only a handful of small ships to cover the entire Indian Ocean – an area of 30 million miles – as well as the Dutch East Indies and China; in 1794, he had only five vessels of over 30 guns.[23] His chief task was protecting seasonal convoys to and from India and China, themselves governed by the monsoon, which created a narrow window during which ships could sail and a tempting target for Britain's enemies. During his eleven years in command, Rainier managed his resources and balanced his responsibilities well. Lacking the ships to guard every possible choke point, he used his few vessels to escort vast convoys across the Indian Ocean, and only seven East Indiamen were lost in his tenure, fewer than one a year.[24]

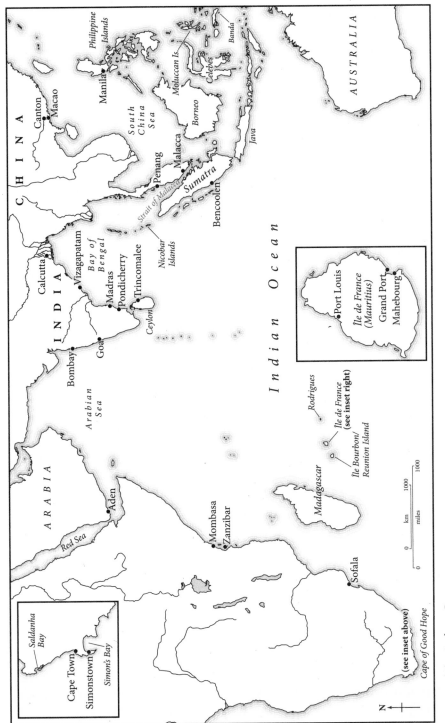

Map 3: The Indian Ocean.

The biggest thorn in Rainier's side was the French naval base at Mauritius in the southern Indian Ocean. Home to an excellent harbour at Port Louis, it served as a haven for French privateers who could leave port at will and prey on passing British trade. From 1794 it housed a prominent Jacobin club, allowing the island to also serve as a centre of revolt in the Indian Ocean.[25] Its distance from India (2,500 miles) meant that attempts to blockade the island were a logistical and organisational nightmare. Two of Rainier's ships, the *Diomede* and the *Centurion*, were sent to blockade Mauritius, and on 22 October 1794 they were engaged by a French squadron of four smaller ships. As at the Battle of the Glorious First of June, the British were taken aback at the ardour of the enemy. The French commander later explained that 'everyday the hymn of liberty sung on the deck produced a new elan' and described how the seamen cried 'Vive la République' and served their guns 'with incredible speed'.[26] The *Centurion* suffered heavy damage and Rainier was forced to abandon the blockade. By 1795, the British were resigned to navigating the southern Indian Ocean as best they could, with the Admiralty official Evan Nepean describing Mauritius as 'a nest of pirates, secure and unattackable'. Numerous plans were hatched in 1796 and 1797 to attack Mauritius but they were all dismissed as foolhardy, and it remained in French hands until the end of the conflict.[27]

The French occupation of the Netherlands and its transformation into the revolutionary Batavian Republic in 1795 created new opportunities for the naval forces operating in the northern Indian Ocean. Every Dutch colonial possession was suddenly up for grabs, and Sir Mark Wood was just one projector who offered suggestions for how Britain might secure Dutch possessions in the East Indies and prevent them falling into the hands of the French.[28] In the summer of 1795 the British embarked on such a plan. In August 1795 British naval forces seized Trincomalee: Rainier, now promoted to rear admiral, commented on 'the great advantage of obtaining possession of so important a fortification in an uninjured state' as well as 'the acquisition of the only safe Harbour this side of India'. A few days later a separate expedition landed forces at Malacca on the south-west coast of the Malayan peninsula, and the garrison surrendered without firing a shot. The Moluccan Islands were taken from the Dutch in February 1796, and Banda fell soon after. The commercial rewards on offer were notable, and the five captains present at the former were reported to have each received £15,000 in prize money, an astronomical sum for the time.[29]

Nonetheless, it was the strategic value of these ports that was uppermost in ministers' minds. Attention turned to the most important Indian Ocean base, the Dutch-occupied Cape of Good Hope, where Dutch colonists had in February 1795 proclaimed a republic. Henry Dundas, now Secretary of War and the architect of Britain's imperialist policies throughout the 1790s, had been agitating for an expedition to this 'key to the Indian and China Commerce' since the start of the war and with the Dutch now an enemy, an expedition went ahead under Vice Admiral Sir George Keith Elphinstone in 1795, comprising 6 warships and a regiment of 500 soldiers.[30] The fleet arrived in Simon's Bay in early July, and the troops were landed alongside 1,000 sailors, while defensive positions were attacked from the sea.

Simonstown quickly fell, and Cape Town followed soon after on 15 September after 5,000 troop reinforcements arrived. The British had secured a valuable base in a vital strategic position for defending and expanding the country's trade with Asia; in the words of Lord Macartney, the first governor of the Cape, it 'formed the master link of connection between the western and eastern world', and the 'great outwork of our Asian commerce and Indian Empire'.[31] Furthermore, as the only convenient port between Brazil and Southeast Asia, it was capable of housing a large naval force, supplying fleets and offering hospitals for seamen, and allowing for a more convenient blockade of Mauritius. A new naval station was created at the Cape that took over responsibility for blockading the French outpost, allowing Rainier to concentrate on the protection of the India and China trades: by April 1796 the East Indies force had 20 ships and over 6,000 seamen, the largest it had been in the war.[32]

In 1796, Britain's enlarged naval forces secured control of the Indian Ocean. A concerted Dutch attempt to retake the Cape failed ignominiously in August when, having slipped through the British blockade at the Texel and sailed north around Scotland, a Dutch fleet of eight warships under the command of Rear Admiral Engelbertus Lucas arrived at Saldanha Bay, fifty miles north of Simon's Bay. After a voyage of five months the fleet was in poor condition: in need of fresh supplies, with little water on board and many ill seamen, dissent had broken out on a number of Dutch vessels and many of their crews were close to mutiny. Keith moved quickly to intercept the Dutch with fourteen vessels (seven of them ships of the line), and on 16 August an officer was sent to Lucas demanding he surrender 'to spare an effusion of blood'. Otherwise, warned Keith, 'it will be my duty ... of making serious attack ... the issue of which is not difficult to guess'. Outnumbered and outgunned, the Dutch commander surrendered without a shot being fired.[33]

Only at Mauritius did the French remain a threat, where reinforcements of warships were sent throughout the year, and where the British continued to struggle to organise an effective blockade. The most successful of these reinforcements was Robert Surcouf, who early in 1796 took up a position on the Hooghli River and proved a recurring threat to passing commerce. That same year, a squadron of six heavy frigates under Rear Admiral Sercey arrived at Mauritius, though this squadron was gradually worn down through individual ship actions, weather and damage. By 1799, the last of the French squadrons had been lost.[34]

British imperial troubles in the Indian Ocean increasingly came not from the sea, but from the land. In 1793, John Bruce had noted that the Dutch at the Cape were 'almost all converts to the French Revolutionary principles', and having secured it, the British found that the revolutionary passions had not faded. One correspondent wrote to Dundas in 1795 that 'a spirit of revolt against all regular government seems to prevail and Jacobinism has taken root here', while British commander

General John Craig observed that the local population was 'infested with the rankest poison of Jacobinism'. In April 1796 there was a rebellion in the Graaf-Reinet district, formed 'upon the Idea which they have conceived of that which exists in France'.[35] Naval commanders had little doubt of the origins of these ideas: Roger Curtis noted that many of them were 'born and nurtured in Republican principles', while John Barrow opined that 'Jacobinism, or subversion of all order, has industriously been propagated by the ill-disciplined among the ignorant part of the colonists, both in the town and the country districts'.[36] Another attempt to found a free nation in Graaf-Reinet in 1799 adopted the slogan 'Liberty, Equality and Fraternity'. Forces were sent into rebellious districts to disarm rebels and enforce martial law, the revolt was brutally put down by British soldiers, and an oath of allegiance to the British monarch became a condition of migration.[37] Here, as in the Mediterranean, British imperialism was synonymous with opposition to the revolutionary ideas that circulated the globe.

The threat of revolutionary activity was even greater in the Caribbean. As early as 1791, the military governor of Dominica noted that 'Notions and opinions have certainly got root in the minds of slaves in general', which would prevent 'their ever being such faithful and contented servants they were formerly'.[38] An enslaved revolt on the island was brutally subdued, but the subsequent uprising in French Saint-Domingue was something entirely novel in the history of the Caribbean. Here people of colour, many of them formerly enslaved, risked cruel punishment and death to secure civil and political rights, and in August 1793 the General Emancipation Proclamation freed enslaved people across the territory. For colonial elites across the Caribbean, the spectre of politically inspired slave rebellion was a terrifying threat to their way of life.[39] In Britain, exaggerated reports of slave armies killing white captives did the rounds, followed by reports of revolutionary ideas spreading to nearby Jamaica, its richest colony in the western Caribbean. One Kingston correspondent noted in alarm that enslaved people were 'so different a people from what they were . . . I am convinced that the ideas of liberty have sunk so deep . . . that . . . they will rise'.[40] British colonists wrote despairing letters back to Cabinet ministers, while their French counterparts were prepared to take drastic steps to protect their incomes. Facing an apathetic – even hostile – reception in revolutionary France, planters from Saint-Domingue offered the sovereignty of their island to the British in return for the protection of the plantation system.[41]

The coming of war in 1793 saw Britain intervene on the side of royalism and counter-revolution, and in the Caribbean this meant it also intervened in defence of slavery. This was as much about hard economics as ideology. The importance of the Caribbean to the British economy was well established: by 1789, the West Indies collectively represented 21.9 per cent of Britain's imports and 9.6 per cent of its exports.[42] The loss of this trade augured ill both for merchants and for Britain's fiscal health, as government revenues were reliant on the taxation of this commerce.[43] It was for this reason that the West Indies were, in Dundas's view, 'the first point to make perfectly certain', and no sooner had war been declared than he started lobbying for Caribbean expeditions.[44] British aims in the region were not solely defensive, however; there was also opportunity. By 1789 France's possessions in the Caribbean were producing nearly half of the world's sugar and well over half of the world's coffee, tempting targets for avaricious policymakers and lobbyists alike.[45] *The Times* noted in February 1793 that were Britain to take control of France's 'rich commerce, which has so often excited her jealousy' . . . the degree of commercial prosperity to which the three kingdoms would then be elevated, would exceed all calculation'.[46] In this zero-sum colonial game, it calculated, Britain gained while France lost. Securing French colonies would deprive them of foreign trade and fatally undermine French sea power. Furthermore, even if Britain's occupation was temporary, these were assets that could

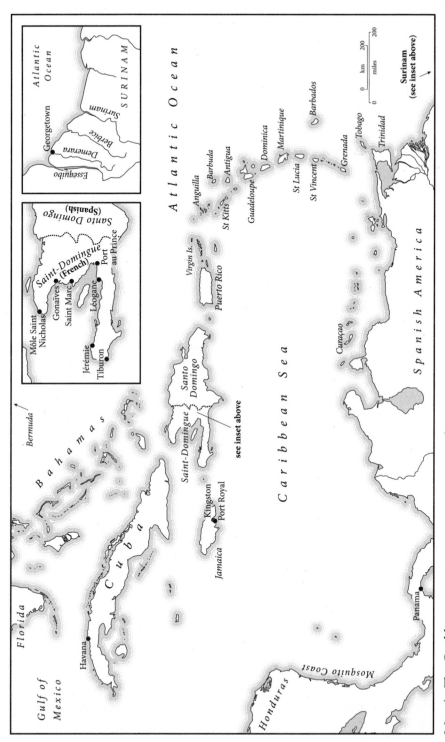

Map 4: The Caribbean.

be traded at the end of the war; in this way, expeditions were sent not to win the war, but to win the peace.[47]

In the Caribbean archipelago, Britain's operations relied on naval strength. Command of the waters allowed Britain to protect its own trade while harassing that of the enemy and preventing crucial supplies reaching its major maritime centres. Naval control also allowed troops to be landed quickly and speedily at decisive points, evidenced early in 1793 when Vice Admiral Laforey carried a force of soldiers from Barbados to Tobago, which was swiftly stormed and taken. Permanent control required significant resources, however, and initially the British found themselves outnumbered: at Jamaica they had only two frigates compared with four French ships of the line at Saint-Domingue, and it was only when the French squadron dispersed in July and August 1793 that an expedition to Saint-Domingue was possible.[48]

It was thanks to the Navy that the British secured a foothold there. On 20 September 1793, a force of 600 troops under the command of Colonel Whitelocke sailed from Jamaica and disembarked in Jérémie, where they were welcomed fulsomely by the local planters with banquets, twenty-one-gun salutes and shouts of 'Vivent les Anglais'. This was quickly followed by the surrender of the Môle Saint Nicolas on 22 September, one of the most important naval bases in the world. An initial attempt at capturing Tiburon was fought off on 4 October, but a more successful attempt was made a few months later under the covering fire of a naval frigate. In early January and again in March, Commodore Ford and his squadron appeared before Port au Prince and called on the French governor to surrender, threatening bombardment, but did not dare face the strong coastal batteries.[49]

The seizure of the key ports of Jérémie, Môle Saint Nicolas and Tiburon removed havens for French ships, while naval vessels blockading the island began to seize neutral vessels and their cargoes. French privateers operating out of other ports proved a persistent threat, however, helped by the maze of tiny islands and narrow passages where large warships could only penetrate at great risk to themselves; across the Caribbean, the Royal Navy remained chronically short of small, fast vessels to combat them. Just as threatening were the armed longboats sent out of Léogane and Gonaïves to board vessels becalmed off the coast. Naval resources were also stretched far and wide: the Jamaica station was responsible for patrolling, reconnoitring, moving supplies and providing logistical support off Saint-Domingue but also around Jamaica, Hondurus and the Bahamas.[50] Nonetheless, when directed strategically, naval forces could be incredibly effective. In December 1793 a British squadron under Captain Affleck arrived at Saint Marc, sailed into the harbour, seized a ship laden with £20,000 worth of produce and captured the town, forcing the republican mayor to escape into the hinterlands. Naval forces also proved essential for the survival of British-occupied outposts. On 16 April 1794, enemy forces attacked the recently captured Tiburon, but a naval frigate arrived the next day to replenish the defenders' supply of ammunition and provided seamen to stand guard while naval carpenters remounted guns that had been blown out of position. Carefully planned operations with the army also bore fruit: the following month, a land–sea expedition successfully attacked Port-au-Prince. Within only a few months, the British had occupied a third of Saint-Domingue.[51]

In London, the government was focused on the Windward Islands to the east. There, republican sympathisers had secured control of Guadeloupe on 9 February before any preparations could be made, and it was not until late March that a small squadron of seven battleships and two frigates under Rear Admiral Gardner set sail from Britain. The expedition brought with it a new military commander, Major General Thomas Bruce, and a group of royalist planters from Martinique, who like their peers in Saint-Domingue had successfully persuaded the British to occupy their island. However, they arrived to find a brutal war under way between competing royalist and republican factions. After an abortive landing, Bruce succeeded in getting 1,100 troops ashore, but the number of royalist troops that came forward to join him were too few, and a night ambush on 18–19 June demonstrated the difficulty of defeating the larger republican forces. Facing annihilation, Gardner was forced to evacuate his troops as well as a number of royalist insurgents who likely would have been put to death by the victorious republican forces. On 22 June 1793, a British fleet laden with troops and 5,000–6,000 refugees sailed away, leaving republican forces in control of the island.[52] Britain's 1793 campaign came to an end with its meagre military forces evacuating Martinique in the face of widespread republican opposition; for Britain to achieve its ends, a major expedition was required.

Dundas had been working on such an expedition, though it took time for it to move through the gears of Britain's war machinery. His plan was to augment the military garrison in the West Indies by transporting troops from Britain, Gibraltar and Ireland to the Caribbean, to be sent out in late September and arrive just as the 'rainy' or 'sickly' season (June–September) was ending. In late summer and early autumn heat, humidity and disease increased mortality rates among European soldiers and sailors exponentially, debilitating forces operating in the region, and it was hoped that arriving later would avoid the worst of this.[53] British plans were optimistic in the extreme, however. At one point Dundas envisaged sending 17,000 troops to capture all the French Caribbean islands, before returning to Europe to participate in an attack on one of the main French naval bases.[54] This was quickly deemed impractical, and there was considerable discord in Cabinet as ministers fought over military and naval resources. In July 1793 it finally approved a plan for an autumn expedition to the Caribbean to be commanded by Lieutenant General Sir Charles Grey and Admiral John Jervis. Initial plans focused on the French colonies in the Windward Islands, and particularly Martinique, but news of the capture of the Môle at Saint-Domingue brought hopes that he might achieve success in the Leeward Islands as well. As it happened, the expedition was significantly delayed and reduced in size as troops were diverted to Toulon and the Vendée (see p. 73), and it was not until 26 November that a force of 7,000 troops – rather than the 13,000 initially promised – set sail.[55]

The Grey/Jervis expedition focused first on Martinique, the scene of Britain's recent ignominious escape. A Royal Navy force of four ships of the line and eight frigates descended on the surrounding seas to ensure no French vessels could warn of their arrival, and on 5 February 1794, 7,223 troops were landed in multiple locations in a deliberate attempt to distract and confuse the French defenders. By 16 March most of the island had been captured, except for two forts, Bourbon and Royal, which held out. Naval gun crews were brought ashore to help in the siege and proved highly effective at getting guns into positions their military colleagues thought impossible.[56] Lieutenant Bartholomew James recorded the frantic attempts on both sides to concentrate their fire:

> The Effect of our fire on the works of Fort Bourbon was soon visible from the fall of houses and show of frequent explosions from our shells which hit them in all possible directions; but the enemy were not, however, deficient on their parts, for a most hot and incessant fire of shot and shells were kept up with the greatest vigilance the whole siege.[57]

The final assault came from the sea, when two squadrons of gunboats, flat-boats, barges and pinnaces were assembled to attack Fort Royal under supporting fire from two larger ships, the *Asia* and the *Zebra*. Captain Faulkner in the *Zebra* was able to sail right up under the defenders' guns and used scaling ladders as a bridge, allowing his crew to storm the parapet and take the fort. The fire of the besiegers then focused on Bourbon, which finally surrendered on 24 March 1794. It had taken seven weeks and considerable casualties, but the British had secured a rich colony and an important naval base. In London *The Times* described it as 'the keystone of that Archipelago, and the centre of command over all the Windward and Leeward Islands in the Caribbean Seas.'[58]

The expedition's late arrival and lengthy operations in Martinique meant that there was little time to secure Britain's other aims ahead of the sickly season. Grey and Jervis sailed south to St Lucia and again organised numerous landings to confuse the defenders: the island fell in five days without a casualty. On 11 April the squadron arrived at Guadeloupe, and the strong fortified position of Fleur d'Epée was successfully stormed by a mix of soldiers and sailors, with the rest of the island surrendering on 20 April. The expedition had run out of time to support further operations in Saint-Domingue as heat and disease began to take their toll: yellow fever meant that of the 518 troops sent from Martinique to Port-au-Prince only 290 arrived, with the rest having died at sea. Nonetheless, the British commanders could report considerable success: 'I have now the greatest satisfaction in informing you of the entire reduction of the French in these seas', wrote Jervis.[59] In Britain there were national celebrations, and the forty French colours captured at Martinique were paraded in front of the king and royal family, before being carried through the streets to be deposited at St Paul's Cathedral. More intriguing still were the economic calculations being made by British commentators. *The Times* declared that the acquisition of Tobago and Martinique far exceeded in value the cost of the war so far and opened to British manufacturers 'a source of riches, far beyond what was ever known to them'. By 21 July, they stated triumphantly that French commerce in the Caribbean 'is now no more'.[60]

No sooner had this been written than Britain's position in the West Indies began to unravel. Throughout the campaign of 1793–4, British forces operating in the Caribbean had taken every opportunity to plunder, capturing any shipping or personal property that either belonged to or was intended for the French Republic. A total of 307 merchant ships were seized, many of them sailing between neutral ports, and the inhabitants of St Lucia and Martinique paid vast sums of £150,000 and £250,000 in lieu of property confiscations.[61] This prompted public scorn in Britain, while the seizure of American shipping brought diplomatic protestations and briefly forced Grey to prepare for a US declaration of war.[62] At the same time, French defeats in the first half of 1794 brought revolutionary reprisals. In 1794 the French Convention abolished slavery throughout the empire in an attempt to encourage people of colour to come forward and fight the British invaders. As Danton put it, 'By casting loose liberty in the New World, it will yield abundant fruit . . . Pitt and his cronies shall be swept away into oblivion.'[63] If it had not been explicit before, the war in the Caribbean became one over the preservation or eradication of slavery. The emancipation decision rebalanced the manpower scales in the Caribbean, for while France was now able to recruit formerly enslaved people locally, Britain remained reliant on expensive and logistically cumbersome expeditions sent from the Channel. Reinforcements due to leave Europe in September 1794 were repeatedly driven back by storms and adverse winds, and a typhus outbreak meant only five of the ten regiments were healthy enough to embark. It was not until February 1795 that they arrived in the Caribbean.[64]

By the time they arrived, disaster had struck across the Caribbean. In Saint-Domingue, the talented Black leader Toussaint Louverture had embraced the revolutionary cause and joined forces with French republicans, placing the British firmly on the defensive.[65] Now facing a stronger and more united enemy, Britain also began to lose hundreds of troops to disease – over a thousand by the end of 1794 – and mortality among ships' crews was also incredibly high. Throughout the summer there were hundreds of sailors on the sick list, and by November the Jamaica station had lost over 440 men, leaving them at least 600 men short. The Navy's control of the surrounding waters loosened, allowing the republicans to transport in supplies and ammunition, while French privateers had considerable success raiding coastal ports in Saint-Domingue and Jamaica. Britain was left clinging on: Léogane was soon lost, and Tiburon fell to an assault on Christmas Day 1794. Only the timely arrival of a frigate at Saint Marc prevented further defeat. A similar disaster befell the British in the Windward Islands, where the arrival of a French squadron of nine ships in early June caught them entirely by surprise. The French landed an army commanded by the West Indian-born Jacobin Victor Hughes on Guadeloupe, which quickly recovered Point-a-Pitre, and over 500 soldiers and sailors were lost during Britain's attempt to retake the town. With British forces on the island decimated, the French retook control of Guadeloupe, and the defeated troops were evacuated by the Navy on 10 December 1794.[66]

Guadeloupe became the centre of resistance to the British empire in the Caribbean. Hughes emancipated enslaved people, executed royalists and launched a privateering war against the British that had a devastating impact on commerce. In early 1795 he began secretly sending small boats containing propaganda tracts and political operatives to the British-occupied islands with the aim of instigating rebellion among the enslaved populations. There followed a wave of rebellion across the British Windward empire: on St Lucia, republican insurgents forced British forces to evacuate, while at St Vincent a rebellion forced the British colonists to seek refuge in Kingstown; the rebels raised the tricolour on Dorsetshire Hill, which overlooked the town.[67] On Grenada, Julie Fédon led an anti-colonial, anti-slavery insurrection that took control of a number of towns, demanded a pro-French Republican government, and in the process secured the quasi-freedom of a large portion of the enslaved population.[68] Insurrection also spread to Jamaica in the west, where simmering tensions among the Maroon population exploded into outright resistance and guerrilla warfare.[69] The motivations that lay behind these revolts remain unclear, as no surviving accounts describe the subsequent rebellions in the insurgents' own words. What is evident is that each uprising sprang from decades of persecution of enslaved people and free people of colour, and that the revolutionary 1790s provided an opportunity to secure freedoms impossible a decade earlier.[70]

The loss of Guadeloupe and the wave of insurrection in 1795 placed the British firmly on the defensive in the Caribbean. Military garrisons in Grenada and St Vincent retreated behind fortifications, while the

Navy was stretched further than ever before, forced to abandon offensive manoeuvres and defend Britain's fragile position. In October 1795 the *Mermaid* intercepted two French ships taking troops to Grenada, but for the most part blockading French ports became increasingly difficult; in early 1795, a French convoy of fifteen ships sailed into Point-a-Pitre having been barely troubled by the Navy. In response, enemy naval forces grew more ambitious, and in 1795 French frigates captured eighteen ships from the Jamaica convoy. Just as problematic for the British was a chronic need for military manpower as soldiers succumbed to war and disease. Desperate times called for extraordinary measures, and in early 1795 Britain authorised the raising of 1,000 Black soldiers in a vain attempt to match French efforts to recruit local populations.[71] The absurdity of recruiting enslaved people to fight in a conflict for the preservation of slavery was not lost on contemporaries, and while some volunteers were lured by the promise of freedom after five years' service, most recruits were enslaved people purchased from West Indies merchants. Colonial assemblies in Grenada and Jamaica attempted similar schemes, and by the late 1790s other officials were lobbying for Black corps to be created around the Caribbean.[72] However, most colonists remained wary of arming enslaved people, and British hopes for additional manpower continued to rest on troops being sent out from home.

Reinforcements were sent from Britain in October 1795 in a desperate attempt to maintain Britain's position, though they were severely delayed by storms and adverse winds. Here too both army and Navy faced severe recruitment issues. What troops could be found were unwilling to be sent to the Caribbean, and there were army mutinies in Essex, Newcastle, Cork and Dublin. The uprising in the latter caused a 'continual scene of alarm and terror', according to *The Times*, and dragoons had to be sent in to break up rioting.[73] The Navy too struggled to find men: press gangs operated throughout the summer of 1795 and the first homeward convoys from the East and West Indies were scoured for men. A 'hot press' was declared, prompting protests and resistance.

In June, one press gang was attacked by London locals and fired upon by a merchant vessel; another gang boarded a ship on the Thames only to be attacked by the crew, who killed the lieutenant and threw the rest of the gang overboard. As in the early years of the war, the impress service took its powers too far: five members of a press gang operating at Sheerness were indicted and found guilty at the Kent Assizes the following year for a riot and assault on a publican, Joshua Rose.[74] Recruitment efforts were eased by widespread food shortages, which saw many desperate men come forward on the simple promise of a steady meal, and by late 1795 around 18,000 new troops were gathered at Nursling Common, just north of Southampton. This was far short of the original target of 30,000 but enough, the government hoped, to make a telling blow in the Caribbean.

For the first time in the war, Pitt's government made the West Indies its priority as it attempted to defend the institution of slavery and the economic wealth that went with it.[75] They had few other options for offensive action. By mid-1795, Britain had been all but defeated in Europe: its military forces had been forcibly removed, while Prussia, Spain and Sweden had made peace with Revolutionary France. Unable to do anything in Europe, it planned to concentrate its military resources first on crushing the rebellions in Grenada and St Vincent and retaking Guadeloupe and St Lucia, and to reinforce the position in Saint-Domingue. As in the Indian Ocean, France's new alliance with the Batavian Republic also presented opportunities to capture Dutch possessions in the West Indies, and there were hopes that Surinam, Berbice, Essequibo and Demerara could be captured.[76] From the outset, though, Britain's war machinery strained to breaking point, and there were delays as the Transport Board struggled to charter the requisite shipping to transport them across the Atlantic. Dundas was very critical of government bureaucracy, but in the subsequent inquiry it was found that any delays were the result of poor political communication and ministerial meddling rather than any administrative failings. In due course, the Board succeeded in chartering 100,000 tons of shipping in only a few months, and by 9 November the largest expedition ever to leave Britain was ready to sail.[77]

Hopes of a successful campaign were dashed almost immediately when the expedition was hit by a series of gales. On the night of 17–18 November, 5 ships were broken up on the shore at Chesil Beach and 249 troops were drowned, while the flagship *Prince George* was so damaged it could not continue. A second attempt at sailing was made on 9 December, but this too was hit by another storm. 'The night had been one of the most disastrous on record,' recorded William Dillon, as the expedition submitted to 'a succession of the most trying gales ever encountered in this part of the ocean'.[78] Ships found shelter at Cork and St Helens, but few made it to the Caribbean. A muster taken in February 1796 showed 11,000 men back in Portsmouth and 7,000 unaccounted for. British newspapers bewailed the turn of events. Ann Michaelson, writing to her friend Kitty Senhouse, said she had read of storms, tempests and high tides in the newspapers: 'Where the devastation of the West Indies expedition will end no one can say.'[79] Those vessels still seaworthy finally sailed on 28 February, now with only 8,000 men, and even then some ships failed to make it across the Atlantic. In one final drama, the flagship of William Cornwallis crashed into a transport, the *Bellisaris*, forcing it to return to port.[80] A lovesick sailor onboard wrote to his sweetheart following his short voyage, delighted to be home but scarred by what he had seen. His ship had come to the aid of the *Bellisaris*, saving around 118 men and women of the 400 on board, but the rest 'all went to the Bottom'. It was a 'scene of such distress . . . that you can have but a very faint Idea of How did my Heart my Angel bleed to see the poor miserable Creatures brought down to us bleeding and with their Limbs jamm'd to pieces'.[81]

With reinforcements arriving late and in reduced numbers, the 1796 campaign could not meet expectations. It began with an attack on Dutch Demerara by a force under Vice Admiral Laforey, which surrendered on 2 May 1796. It was at this point that the bulk of the expedition from Britain arrived, bringing 7,273 troops and extra ships, and

Abercromby's force proceeded to shore up Britain's position across the Windward Islands.[82] They faced hostile populations and often well-fortified positions and progress was slow. At St Lucia, disembarked troops began a lengthy siege, but it was only when the French stronghold at Castries was bombarded by five warships on 24 May that it finally submitted. The population continued to resist British occupation, however, and 4,000 troops had to be left to subdue those that continued to fight. In June forces moved to St Vincent, where British troops were able to leave their fortifications for the first time in months and take control of the island. Later that month, the expedition reached Grenada, where an attack on 19 June routed the insurgents, though Fédon himself escaped and reportedly perished at sea while attempting to escape by canoe to Trinidad. By this point, most of Abercromby's troops were tied down in garrison duty on the newly captured islands or fighting continued resistance in the hinterlands. He had neither the resources nor the will to make an attempt on Guadeloupe and, Demerara aside, the expedition had merely restored Britain to its 1794 position in the Windwards.[83]

The British quickly went about reasserting their authority in the recaptured islands. Slavery was reintroduced on St Lucia, and reprisals were severe. In an attempt to deter future rebellions, Dundas ordered that all British subjects who had taken up arms against the crown should be dealt with 'according to just severity of the law', which led to widespread deportations and executions. On St Vincent, barely half of the rebellious Carib population had survived the conflict following the systematic destruction of their houses, canoes and provisions, and in the aftermath of the rebellion, the remaining 2,248 were exiled to an island in Honduras by the naval ship *Experiment*.[84] On Grenada, the conflict had devolved into brutal fights between enslaved and enslaver, in which the usual rules of war were abandoned. Fédon had prisoners – including the governor Vivian Home – shot, while British colonists hanged captured rebels without trial or mercy. As many as 7,000 enslaved people, estimated at a quarter of the total population, were killed during rebellion, and those who survived found little quarter. Black soldiers were given summary executions, while there were brief show trials for prominent rebels who had refused to surrender. Fifty were condemned and fourteen were executed on 1 July 1796, while a further 500 were charged with bearing arms and sold off the island. Similar reprisals took place at Jamaica, where British troops' scorched-earth policy ensured that the Trelawny Town Maroons were unable to maintain their guerrilla campaign. Their land was put up for sale by the Jamaica Assembly, and those who had survived were deported to Sierra Leone on the west coast of Africa.[85]

In nearby Saint-Domingue, Britain fell back in the face of fanatical republican troops and the inspired leadership of Toussaint Louverture. An abortive attack on Léogane saw two ships of the line and two frigates damaged so extensively they had to retreat, after which Hyde Parker, short of seamen, refused to risk the lives of any more of his men. Desperate for more manpower, naval commanders were forced to apply to local imperial bodies for permission to send press gangs ashore: in August 1796, John Duckworth begged the Privy Council of Jamaica to be allowed to impress 1,500 sailors.[86] The chronic shortage of manpower had begun to affect operations, forcing the abandonment of the blockade of Saint-Domingue. In early 1796 the French sent two squadrons with reinforcements for their garrisons there, both of which delivered their cargoes and returned safely to France without being intercepted by British naval forces. At the same time, French privateers continued to wreak havoc off the coasts: in mid-July a vessel was actually cut out at the entrance to the harbour, while a flotilla of transports carrying 400 troops was seized at the Môle.[87]

By the end of 1796, Britain's Caribbean campaign had run its course. Losses to disease were extraordinary, with 14,000 deaths in the army destroying the bulk of the force sent out in 1795–6. Most were newly raised and unprepared for the Caribbean climate, and having arrived late at the start of the sickly season, they died in droves from malaria and yellow fever. What troops remained were tied down in garrison duty. The situation was no better at sea, and the surgeon of the *Alfred* recorded a 1796 shipboard epidemic in gruesome terms:

> The symptoms as they appeared on board the Alfred at the worst period were prostration of strength; heavy, sometimes acute pain of the fore-head; a severe pain of the loins, joints, and extremities; a glazy appear-ance of, with a bloody suffusion of the eye; nausea or vomiting of bilious, sometimes offensive black matter, not unlike coffee grounds.[88]

Back in Britain, reports of losses brought considerable public outcry and parliamentary critique, with Edmund Burke speaking for many when he denounced the sending of further troops out to 'the West Indian grave'. Dundas was forced to defend government policy in Parliament amid mounting condemnation.[89] The 'great' push organised in 1795–6 had clawed back some possessions that had been lost but had failed to offer the telling blow Dundas and other ministers had hoped for. War with Spain in 1796 offered the possibility of capturing a few more colonies, but there was no appetite in Britain to send more resources to support an attack on Guadeloupe, or to support Britain's faltering position in Saint-Domingue. From this point on there were no more expeditions from Britain – between August 1797 and March 1800 Britain sent only one regiment to the West Indies – and subsequent operations were conducted by naval and military forces already stationed in the Caribbean.[90]

Naval strength remained central to any activity. In February 1797 a squadron under Rear Admiral Henry Harvey carried troops to Spanish-occupied Trinidad, where they found four enemy ships of the line defended by a battery of twenty guns: in the face of overwhelming force, the Spanish burned their own ships, and after a successful landing the whole island capitulated. Naval action could also under-mine French offensive attempts. An attempted landing of French troops on the island of Anguilla was frustrated by the arrival of the 28-gun frigate *Lapwing*, prompting the immediate re-embarkation of French forces, and the British went on to capture one French vessel and destroy another.[91] Elsewhere, though, a British attack on Puerto Rico was repelled on 30 April by strong defences, and other ventures were deemed impractical. Abercromby guessed he would need 8,000–10,000 men to attack Guadeloupe, and 15,000–16,000 men to take Havana, numbers which by 1797 were fantastical. At sea, naval forces offered a more effective defence of Jamaica, and the Navy had increased success raiding French outposts along the coast of Saint-Domingue, cutting out merchant ships and gradually wearing down the naval force available to the republican forces. Toussaint's attack on Saint Marc was devastated by the guns of a sloop anchored offshore.[92]

The Navy could do little to affect operations further inland, though, where Britain faced overwhelming numbers and a hostile populace. By early 1798 the British government was desperate to extricate itself from Saint-Domingue and sent Brigadier General Thomas Maitland to make a deal with Toussaint that was 'not dishonourable'. In April, a secret convention saw the British withdraw in exchange for good treatment, the chance to remove guns from forts and a promise from Toussaint not to export his revolution to Jamaica. Troops were embarked throughout the autumn and the last British troops left the Môle in October 1798.[93] While Britain had been defeated militarily, its latent economic and maritime power in the region meant that Haiti remained dependent on British trade for supplies. Under the terms of the settlement it was agreed that British ships shared the monopoly on Saint-Domingue's foreign trade, while Saint-Domingue's coasting ships were restricted to sailing within a fifteen-mile radius of the coast. The Royal Navy strictly enforced this as part of a wider policy to isolate Saint-Domingue. In 1799 naval forces captured 'a small fleet of war' under Toussaint's orders heading to Port-au-Prince, now renamed Port Républican, alleging it had strayed beyond the fifteen-mile limit, while the following year it kidnapped 'between five and six hundred Sea-faring Men' for once again overstepping. Despite Toussaint's pleas that 'my ships be respected', cruisers of the Royal Navy frequently ignored these rules and further undermined Toussaint's authority.[94] In the aftermath of revolution, and thanks in no small part to the Navy's efforts, European imperialism remained alive and well in the Caribbean.

The imperial warfare of 1793–7 was in many ways the most brutal and politically charged of the entire conflict. In the Caribbean, terms such as 'liberty' and 'freedom' were not just abstract concepts but governed the reality of the daily lives of millions of enslaved people. As we have already seen, sailors could also see their service in terms of bondage, and sailors protesting impressment or negotiating for better usage were happy to deploy the rhetoric of 'slavery' to highlight their own plight. The political declaration with which this book started, authored by naval sailors in 1797, also used charged racial language to highlight their woes. The sailors, it argued, 'Labour under every Disagreement and affliction which African Slaves cannot endure'.[95] This conflation of sailors' experience with that of enslaved people indicates that sailors were well aware of the injustices of slavery, and also suggests engagement with the abolition movement of the 1780s led in Parliament by William Wilberforce. And yet, at the same time, it was naval sailors who served on the ships that restored the enslaved peoples of St Vincent, Grenada and Jamaica to bondage and removed – in some cases for a generation – the prospect of further freedom. How complicit were sailors in the Navy's repressive activities in imperial spheres – and particularly in the Caribbean – during the 1790s? More broadly, how did the imperial warfare of 1793–7 impact the sailors and officers of the Royal Navy who fought in it?

Royal Navy personnel were closely entangled with Britain's imperial and economic agendas. The Navy's role in defending trade meant they frequently worked alongside merchants and trading companies that were all too happy to reward those who helped their profit margin. In the Mediterranean, Samuel Hood was showered with thanks and gifts by the Levant Company and the British Factory of merchants in Smyrna following his actions protecting their trading vessels in 1795. In the Caribbean there was a long history of mercantile companies' assemblies voting large prizes of money and presentation swords for naval officers who performed well in the service of their interests.[96] For colonial elites, the Navy was often all that stood between an enemy invasion and the ruin of their economy, while it also provided opportunities for merchants to cash in by acting as naval agents, or through sizeable victualling contracts.

It followed that naval officers arriving at a station would be bombarded with fawning letters from local colonial officers in the hopes of winning favours in the future. White colonists provided hospitality for visiting naval officers in the form of meals, dances and prostitution, creating a strong social network that integrated the Navy into colonial society.[97] There were certainly moments of conflict between Navy and colony, and the Navy's impressment activities could irritate local imperial officials. However, this remained a relationship based on mutual reliance, and there is little doubt mercantile charm offensives worked. Nelson, who spent more time in the Caribbean than most and married into planter society, later wrote passionately about being a 'firm friend' to 'our present colonial system', and of 'the damnable and cursed doctrine of Wilberforce and his hypocritical allies'.[98]

Nelson's views on slavery are controversial, and it is hard to know how representative they are of the wider naval officer corps. Some naval officers returned from the Caribbean committed abolitionists, but countless others spoke out vehemently in defence of slavery during the 1790s, and their authority as naval officers certainly helped.[99] Many naval officers would have commanded people of colour, as naval ships were racial as well as national melting pots. It has been estimated that at least 3 per cent of seamen serving in the Navy during this period were people of colour, and the numbers on ships serving in the Caribbean were likely far greater: one prisoner exchange saw twenty-two 'White Men' and twenty-one 'Black Men' returned to Britain, suggesting that naval crews could have sizeable Black populations.[100] However, the widespread acceptance of Black labour does not mean the Navy was a colour-blind paradise. On the contrary, it was more a reflection of the Navy's desperate need for skilled workers. Olaudah Equiano, one of the most prominent abolition campaigners operating in Britain, was a former mariner, and the outbreak of war in 1793 saw him terrified of travelling to Bristol in case he was impressed.[101] Other Africans found that their freedom was taken away by naval officers. Joseph Emidy, originally enslaved in his native Guinea by Portuguese slave traders, was kidnapped in 1795 by Sir Edward Pellew to act as a musician on board his vessel. Pellew refused to let Emidy go on shore in case he escaped, and it was only after four years of captivity that he was finally released in Falmouth when Pellew moved to another ship.[102]

Sailors' ideas about slavery and race were similarly complex. Many had learned their trade on slaving voyages, which hardly suggests a community committed to abolition: one such sailor, William Richardson, later demonstrated some sympathy for the plight of those he helped enslave but was nonetheless happy to work on a ship that saw hundreds of Africans committed to bondage in North America.[103] Others, however, took a more moral stance. James McCoy, able seaman of the *Atlas*, castigated one of his officers for his prior involvement in the slave trade, 'that barbarous Traffick'.[104] If in some quarters there was sympathy, elsewhere we see sailors delivering violence to Black Caribbean populations. In early 1794, five seamen belonging to the *Vengeance* were put on trial for going on shore at Martinique and beating and ill-treating a Black man named Felix. In the court martial, he testified that the sailors had come into his home armed with cutlasses and a pike, stole four dollars and beat two women, Olive and April. Despite having a broken arm and bleeding wounds, Felix followed the sailors to their ship and reported them to their commanding officer. In the trial, the testimony of the three victims was heard and believed, and all the sailors were sentenced to hundreds of lashes in punishment.[105] Nor was this colonial violence limited to the Caribbean. The ship's log of the vessel the *Hope*, sailing off Madagascar, described how one sailor, Thomas

Johnson, was given fourteen lashes for striking an indigenous person 'without any provocation'.[106]

That said, there is evidence that naval service could bring understanding and acceptance between white sailors and people of colour. In the Caribbean, sailors and enslaved people came into constant contact, offering opportunities for small trading, bartering and exchanging news and experiences. The Irish merchant James Kelly noted that sailors and enslaved people 'are ever on the most amicable terms', describing a 'mutual confidence and familiarity' and 'a feeling of independence in their intercourse' which contrasted with the 'degradation' they both suffered in their everyday relationships with naval and colonial elites.[107] Naval sailors were one constituent part of the oceanic 'news pipeline' by which enslaved people received information carried on a tide of published and oral communication. Sailors brought books, newspapers and letters, and in French-speaking Grenada one colonist observed that 'the English news papers come in so great a number' that street conversation took on a British slant.[108] Kingston's *Royal Gazette* heavily censored its content to avoid mentioning the revolt on Saint-Domingue, but it could do nothing to stop the spread of information by word of mouth, with sailors again integral to its dissemination. Through such means, enslaved people on Grenada were 'immediately informed of every kind of news that arrives' and knew 'perfectly well every transaction' there, while songs sung by enslaved people at Jamaica referred to the rebellion.[109] While conversation and discussion might not denote allyship, in the revolutionary Caribbean both sailors and enslaved people came to rely on each other for information.

For some enslaved people, the Navy offered a potential escape from forced servitude, and an opportunity to improve their wealth and status.[110] Those who worked in naval dockyards became expert enough that they could secure wages for their efforts, and those who went to sea could use their maritime skills to enhance their own prospects of freedom.[111] In the Caribbean it was common for ships to employ local pilots to navigate tricky unknown waters, and as many of them were enslaved people of colour, this provided opportunities to invert the traditional racial and social hierarchy. James 'Jemmy' Darrell was one such pilot, whose knowledge of Bermuda's reef-encrusted seafloor prompted one of the Navy's hydrographers, Thomas Hurd, to employ him on a six-year survey of the archipelago that was conducted in the first half of the 1790s. On 17 May 1795, Darrell piloted Vice Admiral George Murray's flagship the *Resolution* through a channel called 'The Narrows', the first warship brought into Bermuda, allowing the establishment of a naval base there. On 1 March 1796, Darrell was freed from servitude in reward for his efforts and became Bermuda's first king's pilot, a respectable, royally appointed position that included a substantial salary and enabled him to purchase his own pilot boats and a small house.[112]

The 1790s also witnessed the extraordinary sight of a Black man taking command of a British naval vessel. John Perkins, the son of an enslaved woman, was used as a pilot due to his maritime knowledge of the waters of the Caribbean, and in 1781 he was entered into the Navy as a lieutenant. In what was a remarkable career, he served as a British spy during the early years of the Haitian Revolution and was briefly imprisoned before being given command of his own naval schooner in 1793. In 1797 he was promoted to the rank of captain and by 1802 he had secured the command of a frigate, the 32-gun *Tartar*, placing him in charge of 264 men, the majority of whom were white.[113] Perkins serves as an example of the remarkable meritocracy that could exist in the Royal Navy, and his skills allowed him to make a small fortune capturing enemy vessels in the Caribbean. However, it is worth remembering just how rare it was for a person of colour to command a naval ship: only two other Black men in this era rose even to the rank of midshipman.[114] Indeed, Perkins's ethnicity was clearly an issue for some of his men. One of his junior officers, Peter Chazotte, complained that it was 'a cursed disgrace for us British officers to be placed under the command of a blood-thirsty colored [sic] captain', and it seems as though Perkins resorted to harsh measures to maintain discipline. During one year in command of the *Drake* he ordered fourteen of the eighty-six sailors on board to receive floggings, which does not suggest a happy ship, or one in which he was accepted uncritically. While we might marvel that a man of colour was placed in charge of a naval ship amid a war for empire and slavery, Perkins's story is exceptional in almost every way, and reveals the limitations placed on Black aspiration in the Royal Navy.[115]

The Royal Navy was one of the major counter-revolutionary forces acting in the 1790s. Its actions helped both defend and extend Britain's colonial position: if empire itself was a 'counter-revolt', then the Navy was one of its major facilitators.[116] Saint Domingue proved an exception, and in all other European colonies around the world imperial rule remained secure.[117] Moreover, in the West Indies, the Navy acted as a defender not just of empire but also of slavery. The Caribbean campaigns of the 1790s seem to have held back the cause of abolition, as slave revolts linked abolition to radical ideologies, frightening many away from supporting changes to the Caribbean status quo. Despite the popularity of abolition in the House of Commons in the years before the outbreak of the war, it rejected the Abolition Bill in 1792 and continued to deny Wilberforce's motions during the war with Revolutionary France. While the Haitian Revolution was inspiring to some, the numerous atrocities that occurred were selectively reported, and ideas of 'barbarism' became more prominent in public discourse. Longer term, though, as fears of revolution abated into the 1800s and slave rebellions continued to break out, some scholars have suggested that resistance led by people of colour helped stimulate renewed debate about the abolition of slavery.[118] It was only in 1807, however, that the British Parliament abolished the slave trade, and slavery was not outlawed across the British Empire until 1833.

Britain's imperial campaigns from 1793–7 had little effect on the wider war. For all that Britain's colonial empire in the Indian Ocean grew, its attempts to gain a foothold in the Mediterranean failed, and its Caribbean campaigns had been incredibly costly. It has been calculated that 43,747 soldiers lost their lives through fighting or disease in the West Indies, roughly half of the force sent out, while the real figure may well have been higher as there is some suggestion the government falsified the casualty numbers in the last years of campaigning. The Navy suffered badly too: during 1794–8, 1,920 sailors died at Port Royal naval hospital. Nor was this confined to human lives. £16 million was spent on the West Indian expeditions, while trade with British colonies was devastated: at Grenada, sixty-five sugar and thirty-five coffee plantations were in ruins, and exports were severely impacted. Some revenues were recouped through taxation of colonial possessions, but this was a brief windfall, and at the Treaty of Amiens Britain surrendered its major conquests, Martinique and the Cape, in exchange for token gains in Europe.[119]

In 1795 and 1796 the West Indies had represented the focus of Britain's strategic attention, but from 1797, few in government were willing to risk further expeditions. Only once in the remaining years of the war did an imperial expedition leave Britain (to Egypt in 1800–1), and it is notable that in the Napoleonic Wars of 1803–15, Britain ordered no imperial expeditions to the Caribbean sent from Europe.[120] Colonial projectors continued to call for further campaigns to the Caribbean, and Dundas remained convinced of the importance of imperial warfare for the prosecution of the war.[121] By the end of 1796 these arguments were already falling on deaf ears, however, as the attention of policymakers turned to a renewed threat from across the English Channel.

FIVE

SPLINTERING THE WOODEN WALLS
The Threat of Invasion, 1796–8

In late December 1796, the French newspaper *Le Moniteur* signalled that a new front was opening in the war. Using defiant prose, it laid out 'the necessity of carrying the war into the British Empire' and described imminent plans for a French invasion of Ireland. A week later the London newspaper the *Star* translated and republished the article for its British audience, and it made for uncomfortable reading. Rumour and speculation about French troop build-ups were already dominating the British press, and the article served as confirmation that a full-fledged invasion was both imminent and achievable: 'The difficulty of landing in England, is not insurmountable as the English pretend,' it noted. The article also offered an astute critique of the British population's relationship with the Royal Navy. Britain's favourable geographical position, it argued, had inspired in its people 'an extreme confidence in their own security' and made them believe 'that they will always be sheltered from the calamities of war'. Moreover, their confidence in their Navy was foolhardy. 'It is absurd to pretend that the French can never pass the Channel,' it noted, and pointed to 1760 as the last instance when France had landed troops on British soil. While the British had been 'brought up on the idea, that the safety of Britain is in her wooden walls', a proper reading of their history should inform them 'that whoever has set foot in England, has achieved the conquest of it'.[1]

The threat of invasion was certainly not a new experience for the British people. With only the small stretch of the English Channel separating Britain from the European continent, attacks from across the 'narrow straits' had become a recurring reality for Britons across the eighteenth century, and major invasion efforts were gathered on at least eight occasions between 1688 and 1790.[2] However, just as *Le Moniteur* had predicted, war with Revolutionary France found Britons too confident in the strength of their 'wooden walls'. Maria Stanley spoke for many in 1794 when, in response to news of a French invasion attempt, she stated to her friend Ann Firth that she did not 'feel much alarmed', for 'I cannot think that our Navy is reduced so very low as to suffer the French to land in any number so as to do much damage'.[3] A range of popular culture agreed and repeatedly ridiculed the prospect of a French invasion. James Gillray's 1793 caricature *The French Invasion; – or – John Bull, bombarding the Bum-Boats* depicted John Bull defecating with wild abandon on France's attempts to invade, while the 1796 song 'The Patriot Briton; or, England's Invasion' declared proudly that 'Never shall the Storms of France / Rive, or blast, the British Oak!'[4] British faith in its Navy and natural geographic defences had become a powerful part of the national psyche.

More clear-sighted commentators, however, knew full well that the Navy could not make the Channel an impenetrable military frontier; on the contrary, it was a contested and fundamentally permeable space.[5] '[N]ever was a country assailed by so formidable a force,' wrote Collingwood in reference to the French invasion build-up, 'the thing is practicable'.[6] Those with military expertise attempted to raise awareness of the looming threat. John Ranby's 1794 *Short Hints on a French Invasion* cast doubt on the Navy's ability to defend Britain's shores, for 'whatever may be the number or strength of our fleets', they could not watch every port the whole year round, while strong winds and fogs could present the French with the thirty to forty hours they needed to effect a successful landing.[7] The following year, George Hanger published his *Military Reflections on the Attack and Defence of the City of London*, in which he argued persuasively that the British fleet was no guarantor of defence, citing the 1779 fiasco during the American Revolutionary War when combined French and Spanish fleets had threatened Plymouth.[8] An anonymous pamphlet that same year noted the accidents that could befall a naval ship and worried that 'the blow may be struck before the British fleet can arrive to give battle to the enemy'.[9] By October 1796 British confidence had been replaced by anxiety, and even Gillray had changed his mind about French military capabilities. That same month he produced his famous print *Promis'd Horrors of the French INVASION*, in which he depicted French troops – and friendly 'Jacobin' Whig politicians – running amok in London's streets.[10]

Between 1796 and 1798 France put *Le Moniteur's* proposition to the test, repeatedly challenging Britain's 'wooden walls' and finding them far more pliable than Britons expected. This was a campaign fought in the waters of the English Channel and Irish Sea, but it was also contested through the fears and anxieties of the British public, as repeated incursions forced the nation to question long-standing assumptions about its Navy. When it failed it revealed fundamental vulnerabilities, and in these years the government was able to use naval uncertainty to justify increasingly repressive legislative measures and an unprecedented build-up of military forces in Britain. When, on 17 December 1796, just weeks before the *Le Moniteur* article was first published, Home Secretary Henry Dundas called on the legislature to enact a new Militia Bill that would allow 60,000 men to be called up, he did so by emphasising that 'He knew for certain that the French ports were full of boats, and their troops in readiness' for an invasion attempt.[11] What initially appeared as a patriotic call to arms also revealed deeper insecurities about Britain's naval defences that were repeatedly exploited by the government over the next two years.

As *Le Moniteur* went to press in late 1796, an expedition was already under way destined for the south coast of Ireland, the first strike in a larger plan to invade Britain. Confronting it were overlapping layers of

British defences, the first and most important of which was the Royal Navy itself, tasked with blockading French ports that contained invasion flotillas and attacking any force that ventured out. The Channel Fleet was commanded by Lord Bridport, who in 1795 had taken over active command from the chronically ill Howe.[12] The chief responsibility of his fleet of twenty ships of the line was to guard Brest, France's major Atlantic base, protected by massive batteries and surrounded by a challenging coastline that made it hard for blockading squadrons to shelter. The vagaries of wind and weather meant that maintaining a permanent station was difficult, and its close blockade was entrusted to a smaller detached squadron, with the remainder of the main fleet stationed at Torbay or Spithead, ready to move if the French fleet made sail. Two other detached squadrons under Sir John Borlase Warren and Edward Pellew operated independently out of Falmouth and Plymouth, protecting incoming trade and making sorties towards Brest to inspect developments there. To the east a second, smaller fleet monitored the Dutch Navy off the Texel, and to the north a small collection of frigates constituted the Irish station, its primary concern the protection of convoys between England and Ireland.[13]

Behind these naval defences was a mixture of land-based military forces of varying quality and experience. Chief among these was the British Army, though it was worryingly small in comparison with its European equivalents. Supplementing this was a militia, encouraged by the government and designed to be used both for defence duties and for controlling domestic unrest. Militias were established through annual legislative acts, but up until 1796 recruitment was slow: would-be soldiers were deterred because they would be subject to military discipline and could be deployed outside the local community. What is more, far from helping to calm social tensions, the creation of militias sparked resistance, with riots occurring across the country in 1796–7 as parishes fought over scarce resources of manpower.[14] More successful was the embryonic 'Volunteer Movement', which began in 1793 when local associations requested arms and equipment from the government, and

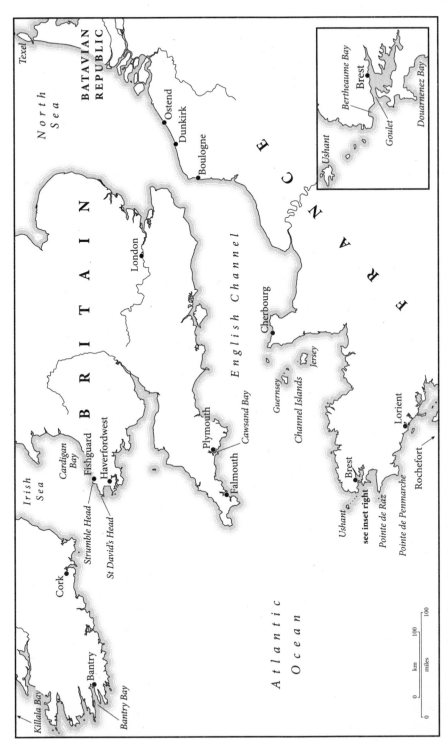

Map 5: The English Channel and Irish Sea.

took matters into their own hands when this was not forthcoming. The government belatedly rode this wave of localised patriotism and in 1794 pushed through the Volunteer Act to organise these volunteer forces for national defence. Even so, by 1796 there were still only 10,000 volunteers in the whole of England, and taken together the government could call on 25,000 men at most to repel an invasion in southern England. In Ireland the situation was not much better, with 2,000 troops and 17,000 militia and volunteers available for the defence of the entire country.[15]

The defensive system protecting Britain relied on coherent defence planning and high-quality intelligence to ensure the various components acted in tandem. Early in the war this was largely absent, and it was not until the mid-1790s that systematic defence planning began in earnest. Detailed assessments were made of the beaches most likely to be targeted by the French, and predictions made about likely landing spots. Ministers decided there was little likelihood of an invasion west of the Solent, since a south-west wind that assisted a flotilla sailing from Brest would throw up heavy surf on beaches on the west of England and make a landing almost impossible. In their eyes, the main areas of danger were the south coast of England between Suffolk and the Solent, and a French descent on Ireland. Establishing the nature of French plans was essential, and different ministries developed their own intelligence networks across Europe in an attempt to secure reliable information. Numerous agents were sent by the Home Office to France to spy on the French Revolutionary government, while the Admiralty ran secret agents abroad to assess the state of readiness of ships in French naval bases.[16] This was an imperfect system, however, and personal jealousies – as well as institutional rivalries – meant that timely communication of intelligence across departments was the exception rather than the norm.[17]

Most information about the readiness of French naval preparations came directly from warships blockading French ports. Captains were ordered to report their observations of enemy ships, as close attention to the height of an anchored vessel (for example whether it was weighed down by stores, or whether the topmasts were in place or sails bent on the yards), were concrete indicators of the imminent departure of a ship. Agents positioned around France picked up news of concentrations of seamen, or other indications that an enemy fleet was about to sail. In addition, specific individuals were entrusted with bespoke espionage missions. Captain Philippe d'Auvergne, for instance, acted under the dual control of the Admiralty and the War Office and commanded a small squadron operating in the Channel Islands where he kept a continuous watch on Le Havre, Brest, Lorient and Rochefort.[18] Another naval spy was William Sidney Smith, who commanded a small naval squadron off Normandy. From there he carried out intelligence operations, landing agents and money off the coast and liaising with local royalist resistance groups, all under the cover of his role as a naval officer. These were dangerous and risky operations, however. In April 1796 Sidney Smith was captured and imprisoned in the Temple prison as a spy, rather than as a prisoner of war.[19]

Britain's intelligence network had been scrutinising French invasion attempts throughout 1796, and by December they were sure an attempt was imminent. No ships had left Brest for a month, and the watching British commanders assumed that an embargo on seamen was under way. 'The account this morning from Brest looks as if the enemy meant to take the sea air', wrote Rear Admiral John Colpoys to the Admiralty on 7 December.[20] Four days later the French fleet at Brest was reinforced, and on 16 December, a force of 17 ships of the line, 13 frigates and 7 transports carrying 18,000 troops anchored for the night at the mouth of the Goulet and made sail on the following day. Edward Pellew, commanding the watching squadron, sent two frigates to warn Colpoys, who was stationed off Ushant, while another vessel was sent to inform the Admiralty. Already, though, the British defensive system had been splintered in heavy winter gales. Colpoys was blown off station, and on hearing the news of the French escape he mistakenly chased a smaller French squadron from Toulon that put into Lorient. The first Bridport heard of the escape was on 20 December, and despite increasingly agitated letters from the Admiralty urging him to go to sea and intercept the French fleet, an easterly wind and adverse tides prevented him leaving port. Several of his ships collided on leaving the anchorage, and it was not until 3 January that he was able to make sail.[21]

As these mishaps played out, on 29 December news arrived in London that the French expedition had set sail from Brest. '[T]he combined fleets have sailed from the ports of France,' explained the *Oracle and Evening Advertiser*, and it predicted that the fleet was intended for Ireland.[22] Over the next few days competing reports arrived, and the Whig-leaning *Telegraph* spread gloom about the possibilities of a French invasion, quoting letters from Dublin that the city was 'in a state of consternation'. It directed its ire squarely at the naval commanders who had allowed the French to escape: 'It is rather unfortunate,' it stated, 'that Admiral Colpoys should be obliged to put into port with a distressed fleet, short of water and provisions, at the very period of the attempted invasion.'[23] Ministerial papers such as the *True Briton* took a different line, describing the enthusiastic reports of Irish militias and volunteer forces to the news of an invasion attempt in what amounted to state-sponsored propaganda: 'The daring response of the French Fleet has produced a spirit of loyalty in the South, which will, we have no doubt, make the Invader repent his temerity,' it boasted. It described army, militia and volunteer regiments marching towards the enemy, while farmers burned their stocks of corn rather than let them fall into French hands. Two days later it reported admirals Bridport, Parker and Colpoys rushing to the scene to secure a victory.[24]

The reality, however, was quite different. Bridport's fleet had only just weighed anchor, and French force was able to make its way to Bantry Bay on the south coast of Ireland without harassment from Royal Navy vessels. The expedition was intended to be the first act in an invasion of the British Isles, taking advantage of widespread opposition to British rule in Ireland in response to a series of discriminatory penal laws. The Society of United Irishmen, a republican and non-sectarian coalition, was formed in the early 1790s seeking to secure 'an equal representation of all the people' and a national Irish government, through armed means if necessary.[25] French help was to be welcomed, and the invasion of 1796 was the brainchild of Lord Edward Fitzgerald and Arthur O'Connor, both United Irishmen, who convinced the French general Lazare Hoche of the value of an attempt. The Irish revolutionary leader Wolfe Tone travelled to Paris to appeal to the Directory in person and persuaded them that there were hundreds of thousands of Irishmen waiting to rise up. For the Directory, the Irish expedition would create an Irish Republic steeped in the ideals of the French Revolution, while Ireland would provide an ideal springboard for an invasion of England, Scotland and Wales.[26]

The French had evaded the Royal Navy, but they could not escape the weather. Once at sea the expedition was separated in a gale, and the largest group under Vice Admiral Joseph Bouvet set a course for Mizen Head in southern Ireland. It arrived in Bantry on 21 December, while the smaller groups – including the ship carrying Hoche – remained at sea, struggling in high winds and fog. That night the storm worsened further, as Atlantic gales brought blizzards that hid the shoreline and forced the French to anchor. By 25 December the situation had grown steadily worse, with violent waves breaking over the bows of the ships. The vessels at Bantry Bay were blown out into the Atlantic, dragging their anchors with them, and the largest vessel, the *Indomptable*, collided with the *Résolue*, both of which suffered severe damage. For another four days Bouvet's ships were battered further by high winds, unable to approach the shore without severe risk of being wrecked on the rocky coast.[27] Running low on supplies, on 29 December Bouvet decided to call off the operation, and the following day Hoche arrived in Bantry to find that the rest of the fleet had gone. Expecting Bridport's fleet to arrive at any moment, Hoche too decided to return to Brest, unaware that he was still stuck at anchor. Bridport would not arrive at Bantry Bay until 9 January, by which time the remnants of Hoche's invasion force were on their way back to the safety of Brest.[28]

The French expedition had been a calamity for almost everyone involved. The French had failed to land their army and lost a quarter of their vessels, while 2,230 sailors and soldiers had been killed or drowned.[29] Only one French ship had been lost to a British naval vessel, when two frigates under Pellew, the *Indefatigable* and the *Amazon*, intercepted the French battleship *Droits de l'Homme* on its return home to port on 13–14 January. In stormy conditions, in which the sea ran so high that the men fighting on the main decks of the frigates were up to their waists in water, the French ship was surrounded and bombarded with broadsides. The *Droits de l'Homme* and the *Amazon* were wrecked against the French coast, and it was only exceptional seamanship from Pellew that allowed the *Indefatigable* to escape without further loss of life.[30] This aside, the Royal Navy had played no part in the expedition's defeat. Neither Colpoys nor Bridport had been able to intercept the main French force, and only the winter weather had prevented a full-scale invasion of Ireland. At sea, the *Orion* and the *Caesar* lost their masts in the tempestuous conditions, and while they continued to pursue the French further south, they were unable to intercept.[31]

Pellew's victory was trumpeted in the national press, but this isolated success did little to comfort those in Britain. Panicked sightings of enemy transports were reported to the Admiralty for some time afterwards, and rather than calming fears, the Navy's indolence sparked substantive criticism. Lord Castlereagh, commanding in the Derry militia, questioned Colpoys's conduct and suggested that he 'might well have follow'd them to Ireland'.[32] In the Irish House of Commons Henry Grattan noted that the destination of the Brest expedition had been well publicised, and that despite having a superior force, 'our coasts had been left for sixteen days at the mercy of the Enemy'. He then asked the most important question of all: 'Where was the British Navy during this period? Absent. To what had our defence been committed? To the wind.'[33] The *Telegraph* published a letter from 'A British Seaman' which criticised both the Admiralty's deployments and the Navy's conduct in the hope of 'awakening in Government a proper attention for the safety and honour of these kingdoms; as their supineness has occasioned such universal murmuring and complaint'. Ministerial papers such as the *True Briton* avoided commenting on the delayed naval response and instead focused their attention on Pellew's victory and his 'gallantry and skill'.[34] Perhaps most revealing was the view of Wolfe Tone, who wrote in his journal that he was 'utterly astonished' not to see British ships of war during their passage.[35]

Public confidence in the Navy to protect the country was eroding fast. In the months after the operation, a range of literary works were produced that mocked the recent naval efforts and lampooned the Navy's commanders. A ballad called 'The Invasion' called to task the British admirals for not having annihilated the French Fleet:

Oh! where was Hood, and where was Howe,
And where Cornwallis then;
Where Colpoys, Bridport, or Pellew,
And all their gallant men?[36]

A poem by the Irish poet Patrick O'Kelly celebrated 'General Gale', the true deliverer of victory, who deserved all the plaudits, rather than the Royal Navy:

While Admiral Bridport lay at rest,
And Colpoys everywhere was peeping
Admirale de Galle stole from Brest,
And thought to catch the Irish sleeping.[37]

The weather had saved Britain this time, but as one pamphlet put it, 'Who can promise that upon future occasions the elements shall be so favourable to us?'[38] In the most visceral representation of the expedition, the caricaturist James Gillray's *End of the Irish Invasion* depicted French ships being destroyed in a tempest, blasted by winds blown from the mouths of leading Tory ministers.[39] The Royal Navy was conspicuous by its absence; for the first time in the war, it was an object of derision.

Worse was to follow, for by late February, anxiety over a second invasion had begun to take hold. The Admiralty received intelligence that the French were preparing another expedition at Brest – they learned that the enemy were 'using every exertion in the equipment of their ships' – and ordered Bridport to be watchful.[40] Once again the likely destination of this new invasion led to much speculation among the British reading public, though it was assumed by many that Ireland would once again be the target. 'If ever circumstances were alarming, it is at this moment', wrote one commentary; 'Ireland has lately narrowly escaped one invasion; but it may be its fate soon to oppose another much more formidable.'[41] Others pondered whether an attack on the English mainland would follow, and naval captains wrote in to newspapers with detailed plans to repel the expected expedition. In an attempt to calm public fears, newspapers with ministerial links endeavoured to play down the threat. The *True Briton* stated confidently on 25 February that 'we are sure there is no ground to apprehend any immediate Expedition' and that 'they will never make an attempt to invade this Kingdom'.[42] Their stance was soon made to look ridiculous, however, for that same day the Admiralty received further intelligence that French ships of the line had been spotted off Haverfordwest in south-west Wales.[43]

This second French sortie had originally been intended as a diversion from the Bantry attack. The plan was for a small, subsidiary force to be sent to Bristol under the command of the Irish-American William Tate to terrify the local populace and thus prevent reinforcements being sent to Ireland.[44] Following the failure of the Bantry expedition, it is unclear why this operation was sent, but a persuasive analysis in the *Critical Review* concluded that the French wanted to demonstrate the feasibility of an 'invasion of England'. In addition, the French ministry anticipated that the small number of troops would be joined by considerable numbers of the 'lower classes of the people' and spark an uprising among the local peasantry.[45] Whatever the aim, the second expedition went ahead, and on 16 February 1797 two large frigates, a corvette and a lugger escaped from Brest with a small army of 1,200 men, known as the Black Legion because of the colour of their uniforms. On the Admiralty's orders, a large part of Bridport's squadron had returned to port to fix defects and re-provision, leaving at sea only one ship of the line and five frigates, which were easily avoided by the escaping force.[46] Adverse winds forced the expedition to sail north of the Bristol Channel into Cardigan Bay, and they rounded St David's Head on 22 February, where they were spotted by retired Welsh seaman Thomas Williams, who raised the alarm. The French proceeded north, anchoring three miles from Fishguard, and disembarked the soldiers: for the first time in decades, the French had successfully landed troops on British soil.

The Royal Navy had again been found wanting, but this time the invasion attempt had immediate and damaging results. British finances had been steadily deteriorating under the pressure of war, and in December 1796 a desperate Pitt had launched a 'Loyalty Loan' in an attempt to raise more money. It was partially successful, and thanks to generous subscriptions from the East India Company, the Bank of England and many Cabinet members, £18 million was raised in the first four days.[47] However, this was not enough to solve the government's long-term problem, and it remained vulnerable to unexpected shocks; the French invasion of Wales in February 1797 could therefore not have come at a worse time. News of the French landing was as alarming as it was surprising. In Cardiganshire, the cobbler John Davies wrote of the 'great noise about the French landing in Pembrokeshire', while a local oral history recalled 'The terrible news extended throughout the country, like a wild fire burning up stubble'.[48] With confidence already low, crowds across the country rushed to withdraw money from banks, and the government was forced to intervene to prevent financial meltdown. On 26 February the Privy Council ordered the Bank of England to refuse cash payments, confirmed by an Act of Parliament (the Banks Restriction Act) on 3 May 1797. There was much criticism of the government for bringing Britain to the brink of bankruptcy, and petitions were sent calling on George III to dismiss his ministers for their prosecution of 'a long, disastrous, unjust and unnecessary war'.[49]

The government was spared further embarrassment by the speedy actions of the Welsh population and auxiliary forces. Local volunteer and yeomanry regiments were mobilised, along with 150 sailors provided by the Navy's regulating officer at Haverfordwest.[50] Still, the local commander Lord Cawdor could initially only muster 600 men and they could do little to halt early French depredations: the invading troops killed at least two people who refused to surrender their livestock and raped a local woman, Mary Williams. The reaction of the Welsh people was one of anger and violence, and locals joined the auxiliary forces in large numbers, arming themselves with scythes and pitchforks. The Duke of Rutland, who was travelling through Wales in 1797, later recalled that there were several instances of surrendered Frenchmen having to be saved from death by English officers, and guards had to be placed to protect prisoners 'in case the mob should attempt to rush in'.[51] Certainly, the French were shocked by the strength of the local resistance, and French morale plummeted further when their naval ships departed to harass trade off Dublin. According to Welsh legend, the final French loss of nerve was prompted by the appearance of large numbers of women wearing the traditional dress of red shawls and black hats, whom the French mistook for a British army regiment. Though likely a Victorian myth, the presence of a large, hostile crowd would certainly have confirmed local resistance to invasion, and either way, Tate surrendered to Cawdor's force on 24 February, just two days after the first landing.[52]

The news of the surrender came too late to avoid the run on the banks, and it was lost on no one that financial disaster was rooted in naval failure. 'If the maritime systems of Government are as impenetrable to the Enemy as they still continue to me,' wrote Howe, 'the happiest consequences may be looked for.'[53] The Royal Navy's response had been lethargic in the extreme, failing to prevent the escape of the expedition or to intercept it at sea, while the commanding officer of the Irish station, Vice Admiral Robert Kingsmill, had sent reinforcements from his squadron too late for them to have any effect. In the Commons, the radical MP Samuel Whitbread called for an inquiry into the 'palpable miscarriage in our naval administration' that had left the country defenceless, in which he placed the recent French escape as merely the latest in a series of naval failures, including the arrival of the Toulon squadron at Lorient, the escape to Bantry and Bridport's refusal to sail. 'Is not there a matter for alarm,' he asked, that 'despite possessing a Navy of above 100 sail of the line' and over 500 ships in commission, 'there was scarcely one expedition of the French Navy, that had not been successful?'[54] Secretary of War Dundas was forced to stand up in Parliament to defend the Navy's admirals and administration. He offered a stern defence of the Admiralty and a less effusive vindication of the leading admirals' conduct, blaming the wind and a 'concatenation of miracles' for the French escape. If anything, he argued, recent events had demonstrated the 'necessity of a superior Navy' and that 'Our confidence in our navy, so far from being diminished, should therefore be increased', and Whitbread's motion was dismissed along partisan lines, by a vote of 201 to 62.[55]

For all Dundas's bluster, Britons' faith in their Navy had been dented. Gone were triumphant declarations of naval prowess; instead, alarm about new invasions sprang up with the appearance of unidentified ships off the coasts, though in each case they turned out to be merchant or fishing vessels. Even the smallest sighting was magnified into a potential new French expedition: when a Royal Naval squadron was spotted off Strumble Head, it provoked fears of another invasion. Fears and rumours abounded, and a Somerset man noted that 'new news comes[s] in two or three times a day . . . I believe every person's imagination [sic] after spoken once to twice are put down for fact.'[56] Newspapers reported every scrap of news that suggested another invasion was nigh. In this environment, even naval successes were overlooked. On 9 March, Pellew's squadron intercepted and defeated two of the French warships that had recently dropped troops in Wales, the *Résistance* and *La Constance*.[57] It could do little to change the national debate, however, or overturn public concern about the competence of the Navy. Over the following months, the parliamentary opposition had a field day, using the recent failures to attack the sitting ministry. Fox noted that it was 'to fortune' that Britain owed its recent deliverance, and that 'our Fleet could not with prudence keep the Channel', while Lord Albemarle questioned why, despite Britain having 'such a superior navy', the French had been able to leave and get back to their ports in safety.[58]

When good news arrived, it came from further afield. In early March 1797, reports emerged of a naval victory off Cape St Vincent, at the south-west tip of Portugal. On 11 October 1796, Spain had declared war on Britain, significantly increasing the size of opposing naval forces to 123 ships of the line. Forced on the defensive, Britain's naval blockade of Cadiz was broken in February 1797 when a Spanish fleet under Vice Admiral José de Córdoba was sent to sea to convoy important supplies to its colonies in South America, before sailing north to join the French in an invasion of Britain. The British commander, Vice Admiral John Jervis, had a frigate watching the Spanish and signalled to his fleet to prepare for battle. Outnumbered, with only fifteen ships of the line to the Spanish twenty-three, he was conscious of the wider political situation: with Britain subsumed by fears of invasion, he knew that 'a victory is very essential to England at this moment'. He was also aware that the enemy was 'shockingly manned', ill-equipped and badly provisioned, something that became more evident as the two fleets approached.[59] Parsons described the British line as 'one of the most beautiful and close lines ever beheld', in contrast to the Spanish, who 'were making the most awkward attempt to form their line of battle, and they looked a complete forest huddled together'.[60] The strength of the Spanish fleet lay in its concentration of three-deckers, including six of 112 guns, each more powerful than the largest British ship, the

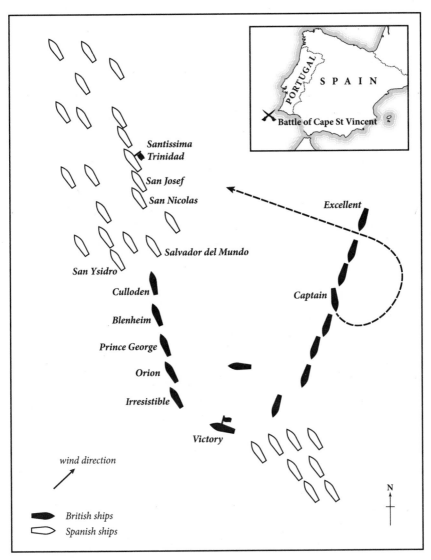

Map 6: The Battle of Cape St Vincent.

Victory. 'They loom like Beachy Head in a fog. By my soul, they are thumpers,' called down Lieutenant Henry Edgell of the *Barfleur*, who had gone aloft to get a better view.[61]

Jervis approached with the intention of following the traditional British tactic of rolling up the line and succeeded in cutting the Spanish force in two. 'We flew to them as a hawk to his prey,' wrote Collingwood, and 'separated them into two distinct parts.'[62] When the northern division attempted to unite with the southern, Jervis signalled all British ships to concentrate on the larger grouping to prevent them combining, but amid the chaos of battle, this was missed by Vice Admiral Charles Thompson. Commodore Horatio Nelson in the *Captain* was alive to the opportunity, and took his ship out of the line to intercept the Spanish. Accounts of the battle are confused and there is little consensus as to whether Nelson had seen Jervis's signal or was acting under his own initiative, but either way his decision turned the battle, preventing the Spanish from concentrating and mounting a strong defence.[63] The *Captain* was followed by two other ships, with Collingwood's *Excellent* forcing the surrender of the *San Isidro*. In the close action that followed, ship on ship, the British superiority in gunnery began to take hold, and Nelson's subsequent actions won even greater plaudits. The *Captain* was heavily damaged by the time it encountered two crippled Spanish ships that had become emmeshed with each other, which compelled him to use his initiative. Nelson led a boarding party that took control of the *San Nicolas* and from that vessel then proceeded to board and capture the second Spanish ship, the *San Josef.* The Spanish ultimately lost four ships of the line, and after five hours of fighting against superior gunnery in which they suffered severe casualties, they broke off the action.[64]

News of the victory offered a semblance of comfort for Britons at a crucial time in the war. James Oakes was one of those who heard of the victory on 4 March, and he delighted that 'At this Critical Juncture' it was 'perhaps the most providential & happiest Event that could have happened to this Kingdom'.[65] Jervis received the thanks of Parliament and was ennobled as Earl St Vincent, and a special thanksgiving was mandated for Sunday services. Elsewhere, though, there was a dawning realisation that the bulk of the Spanish fleet had lived to fight another day, and the victory had done nothing to affect French invasion plans in the north. Otherwise loyalist propagandists struggled to sell the battle's strategic legacy to the public.[66] Attention focused instead on the advent of a new naval hero who had captured two Spanish vessels, the first time since 1513 that a British flag officer had led a boarding party in person. To the annoyance of some of his fellow officers, Nelson ensured that his boldness and bravery were communicated to the public as fulsomely as possible. He sent home his own account of the battle ahead of Jervis's official dispatches and had it delivered to the War Office, which was only too happy to have a heroic version of the battle to present to the public. Nelson's 'Patent Bridge for boarding First Rates' later appeared in *The Times* and the *Sun* and his exciting narrative became the known version of the battle.[67] Nelson was promoted to rear admiral and catapulted to national stardom, a notable contrast to the bungling commanders directing the Channel Fleet.

Nelson aside, the actions of both the government and the wider population indicate that faith in the Navy was at a low ebb. By June, Dundas was telling Parliament that 'the best defence of any country against invasion was the voluntary inrolment [sic] of its inhabitants', as he advocated raising and embodying a militia force in Scotland.[68] Indeed, much to his delight, over the following months thousands of people from across the country flocked to join local volunteer forces. Volunteering was not new in 1797, but the events of 1797 prompted a truly national response on the part of the British people, in which the likelihood of a French landing was an important motivating factor. By late 1797, 51,000 men had joined, and thousands more came forward over the following months.[69] The Loyal Independent Sheffield Volunteers was formed 'to oppose the ferocious Enemy of this Country, in case of Invasion, or of very imminent danger thereof', while residents of Middlesex appointed a committee to consider forming and arming an association to aid national defence.[70] Volunteers were now willing to leave their local area if necessary. In Scotland, the Dunblane Volunteers 'unanimously offered their services in case of Invasion', wherever the government 'may have occasion to use them', while the Loyal Forfar Volunteers agreed to 'march to any part of the County of Angus; and in case of actual Invasion, to march to any part of Scotland'. To the south, the North East Devon Yeomanry Light Dragoons professed that 'in case of actual Invasion, or wherever the Enemy may attempt a Landing on any parts of our Coasts, we will most readily exert our best Services, and will chearfully [sic] act in any part of the Kingdom'.[71]

The best evidence for this new-found patriotic fervour came from the area that had most recently been threatened: Wales. Men along the Cambrian coastline flocked to join local volunteer forces, and the government was inundated with requests for additional protection by land and sea. Indeed, it seems that a higher proportion of Welshmen attached themselves to volunteer corps than Englishmen; of the thirteen militia regiments raised from England and Wales to be sent to Ireland, six were Welsh.[72] This response allowed some opportunistic writers to try to use the recent incursion to make a unifying point about the spirit of 'Ancient Britons'. An undated handbill, produced after the Fishguard invasion, appealed directly to the Welsh to take up arms alongside those from other parts of Britain: 'The blood of the ancient Briton pulsates through the veins of the whole of Britain; we are now one kingdom, and one people.'[73] In 1798 the loyalist Bishop of Llandaff Robert Watson produced a pamphlet that described how the Welsh 'of all denominations' had defeated the French intruders 'with the impetuosity of ancient Britons' before leading them to captivity. In his view, they had 'too ardent a love of their country to submit to a foreign yoke, under whatever specious promises of supporting the Rights of Men, of introducing Liberty and Equality, the Invaders may attempt to deceive them'. The Bishop of Landaff's pamphlet was widely admired among political elites, in part because it told the story of national loyalism they wanted to hear.[74]

Beneath the propaganda, though, the Fishguard invasion revealed concerns about the loyalty of the population. The gentry commanding volunteer regiments were as uneasy about the prospect of arming the Welsh peasantry as they were about the threat of French troops. On 1 March, shortly after the defeat of the French at Fishguard, General Rooke instructed Knox to search for the 3,000 stands of arms that had been landed by the French to ensure that they did not fall into the hands of the locals. The Duke of Rutland, who had earlier commented on the ferocity of the Welsh response to the invasion, was unsure of the loyalty of the armed 'country people' and noted the presence of 'disaffected' peasantry around the areas where the enemy had landed.[75] In the aftermath of the Fishguard invasion, two men of status within their communities – Thomas John, a farmer and Baptist preacher, and Samuel Griffith of Pointz Castle, a yeoman farmer – were charged with aiding and comforting the French and urging them not to surrender. The defendants were acquitted, but the trial itself was evidence of the ambivalence of Welsh identity during a time of war. More than this, it also reveals that the priorities of the British state were at once short term and often conflicting. While those in London could celebrate the enthusiastic response of the Welsh to the call for volunteers, this was at the same time undercut by doubts about the risks of arming a population whose allegiance could not be taken for granted.[76]

The invasion attempts at Bantry and Fishguard prompted considerable soul-searching for the Admiralty. The blockading fleets off Brest were unified under a single sea-going commander – Lord Bridport – in an attempt to avoid some of the communication and command issues that had bedevilled the fleet in recent months. Only Pellew was given a roving brief in charge of a small squadron charged with providing 'Quick and authentic information' on the French fleet at Brest, but in May even he was placed under Bridport's direct orders.[77] Criticisms and fresh ideas arose for making the Channel Fleet more effective, with both Warren and Pellew recommending the close blockade of Brest. Bridport was less keen, however, and continued to adhere to a more open system.[78] Over the course of 1797, Lord Spencer and the Admiralty gradually imposed government priorities on Bridport, taking advantage of the close proximity of his fleet to send communications that could be received the same day.[79] The Admiralty acted as a site of institutional memory, and as a centralised body capable of retaining and developing expertise. While early in their correspondence the civilian Lord Spencer deferred to Bridport's seamanship, from 1797 onwards he became increasingly assertive. By the end of the year, the Admiralty was giving Sir Roger Curtis, then commanding the squadron off Brest, the precise positions to station his ships and outlining the places on the coast of Ireland and England they were to resort to in the event of a breakout.[80]

Partly in response to this, relations between Bridport and the Admiralty grew more strained. In June Bridport noted that although 'the safety of England' depended on his fleet, he felt himself 'unsupported' by the Admiralty, noting peevishly that he would continue to 'do my best for the King and the Country'.[81] He spent much of the summer sending increasingly impolite letters to the Admiralty covering a range of objections, from the lack of flag officers, to his want of frigates, to critiques of his fellow commanders. Bridport was on stronger ground when complaining about the insufficient size of his fleet, especially as the French continued to concentrate their own naval forces in the Channel. Britain's abandonment of the Mediterranean in 1796 allowed part of the French Toulon fleet under Villeneuve to sail to Brest, and by July 1797 there were nineteen ships of the line stationed in the harbour.[82] The Admiralty did what it could, increasing Bridport's force to sixteen ships of the line, though with mutinies breaking out at the Nore and Yarmouth (see Chapter 6) they struggled to find extra resources. They were more successful in reinforcing Bridport's frigate fleets, and by the beginning of September their number had been increased to fifteen, enough for Bridport to maintain an effective watch on French invasion ports. The Admiralty expected little thanks, however. Evan Nepean noted wearily to Spencer that Lord Bridport 'ought to be pleased, though he is never likely to be so'.[83]

With its fleets close to breaking point, the British were fortunate that the French force at Brest was unable to make further invasion attempts that year. Political convulsions in Paris put a temporary halt to naval preparations, and the only serious invasion attempt came from the Netherlands. Following the failure at Bantry Bay, Wolfe Tone had gone to the Batavian Republic as part of a French plan to invade Ireland by sailing around the north coast of Scotland, and by July twelve ships of the line, thirty-nine smaller warships, twenty-eight transports and fifteen thousand French soldiers had collected. On 10 July the troops were embarked, but once again the French were foiled by the weather, with adverse winds preventing them from leaving port. Provisions were running low and so the troops were disembarked; another invasion plan had come to nought.[84] The Channel Fleet instead focused on its subordinate mission, protecting British trade while attacking that of the enemy. Here they had more success: in one notable triumph, Warren's strengthened frigate squadron captured the greater part of a convoy of naval stores, which greatly impeded important supplies getting to Brest. Equally pressing was the need to eliminate French privateers, for the Channel was a rich cruising ground for enemy commerce raiders. Many British merchant ships were taken, and it proved impossible to bottle up permanently every small French harbour. Privateers continued to pose a significant problem and a threat to British commerce through to the conclusion of the war.[85]

At end of 1797, the Directory again took up the idea of invading Britain. General Napoleon Bonaparte, recently returned from a series of military victories in Italy, was put in charge of surveying the embarkation ports, managing the construction of troop-carrying gunboats and drilling the 50,000 soldiers assembled. The British Cabinet received regular intelligence on French preparations, which fed exaggerated tales of invasion craft, fanned by uncertainty and rumour.[86] By late December 1797, the first reports of invasion rafts being built arrived in Britain. *Bell's Weekly Messenger* reported thirty under construction, made up of 'enormous quantities of timber', and included descriptions of cannon-proof parapets of timber and hides, artillery and furnaces to heat red-hot cannon balls, as well as ships that could carry over 10,000 men each.[87] Some of the reports verged on the ridiculous. The *Star* reported on 10 February 1798 that in St Malo

> a Raft, one quarter of a mile long, proportioned breadth, and seven balks deep, mounting a citadel in the centre, covered with hides, was nearly finished; and that a second upon a much larger scale, being near three quarters of a mile long, was constructing with unremitting activity ... desperate as an expedition of this nature appears, it is not impossible that they may attempt it.[88]

Not everyone was convinced, with more sceptical organs pouring scorn on the idea: 'We have seen Letters of a recent date from Jersey,' wrote one; 'There are no Boats ... nor have they the means of building any, much less a floating Machine of such magnitude as that represented.'[89] That said, even those who believed the French plans to be 'absurd' or 'chimerical' did not doubt that an attempt would soon be made.[90] Martha Saumarez, wife of a naval officer herself, wrote to her husband that 'Various are the accounts we hear of their Floating Machines', and while it was doubted 'if they are actually in existence ... it is beyond a doubt that they intend to attempt an invasion.'[91]

The great French 'Floating Machine' proved hard to dislodge from the public imagination. Printmakers competed to depict the most 'accurate' or 'correct' representation of the threat from across the Channel, invoking eyewitness accounts and offering geometrically precise designs and measurements to prove authenticity. Others offered more satirical and politically charged representations, creating absurdist configurations of windmills, paddlewheels, citadels and armaments; one interpreted the

French Floating Machine as a giant hot-air balloon – a citadel in the sky – complete with its own apartments, hospital and coffee house.[92] Artists such as Isaac Cruikshank and James Gillray used the revolutionary threat of these landing craft to make a political point, depicting the successful invasion as a contest between opposition politicians (shown pulling the craft towards Britain) and Prime Minister William Pitt, depicted blowing a patriotic wind to repel the invaders.[93] Playwrights also got in on the action, presenting theatregoers with numerous opportunities to view spectacular stage versions of these craft and inviting the audience to either ridicule French intentions or cheer their successful defeat. One production, *The Raft; Or, Both Sides of the Water*, gave its audience the opportunity to 'laugh at the projected invasion of this country by the French', while in Sadler's Wells, the audience was treated to a 'Musical Spectacle' called *The British Raft, or a Cheer for Old England*, which offered 'a striking contrast between British and French liberty'. One of its songs, 'The Island', proved particularly popular, and one reviewer hoped it 'might inspire a whole nation with the ardour of true patriotism'.[94]

While the idea of a full-scale invasion was sometimes greeted with ridicule, the Royal Navy's recent failures around the coast of Britain meant that even the most outlandish reports from across the Channel exploited a genuine fear of attack. In the first few months of 1798, newspapers provided up-to-date news on the state of French preparations and printed letters that described troops exercising landing their guns and practising manoeuvres '*day* and *night*' along the French coastline. By mid-April, fears reached a fever pitch: one newspaper noted that 'preparations for the Invasion of this Country are prosecuted with unremitting energy', while detailed reports from the invasion ports at Ostend and Dunkirk became numerous.[95] In May, a map of the intended French and Dutch invasion was published showing its projected track, while military experts such as the exiled French General Dumouriez described the likely landing spots to a nervous population, helpfully summarised in the national and local press. Havilland Le Mesurier, the

Commissary General for the Southern District of England, noted that 'The menace of a French Invasion, which formerly afforded a subject for ridicule, cannot now be treated in so light a manner'.[96] Gillray's print series *Consequences of a French Invasion* depicted various symbols of nationhood being overrun by Frenchmen: in one image the House of Commons is shown ransacked by marauding soldiers, while in another British farmers are forced to cultivate garlic.[97]

The government took the invasion threat very seriously, and its preparations assumed that the Navy would not be able to stop an attempt. The militia was extended to Scotland, while the full force was expanded to 116,000 individuals. The Defence of the Realm Act, passed in April 1798, significantly expanded the volunteer infantry as well as the yeomanry, adding both to the force available for national defence. Volunteers were given incentives to serve outside their localities, and the government authorised pay for training and a clothing allowance for those who came forward. For the first time, volunteers were to be properly armed and disciplined bodies, intended for military service rather than local policing. The response was impressive: in just four months, between April and July 1798, the volunteer establishment increased from 54,600 to 116,000, an extraordinary mobilisation.[98]

The government also created a new volunteer force designed to utilise the great mass of skilled maritime labour in Britain. Officially formed on 14 May 1798, the Sea Fencibles were formed to patrol beaches where a French invasion was expected and to maintain a fleet of armed commercial vessels that could capture enemy shipping and defend against invasion barges. Recruitment focused on seafaring men, such as fishermen and other mercantile sailors, though it seems many of these men volunteered in part because it allowed them to avoid impressment, and many refused to serve outside their local area.[99] Like much of the volunteer movement of the 1790s, service in the Fencibles was a way for Britons to demonstrate their patriotism, but this was also opportunistic and conditional.[100]

In the face of the French threat came calls for voluntary contributions from all quarters. One author appealed to 'The high and low, the rich and poor, the learned and unlearned, the supporters and opposers of Administration – nay the friends and foes of the Government and Constitution'. In this sense, it hoped that patriotism would trump politics, with the author declaring he would rather be condemned by a radical Corresponding Society than ordered to execution by a French general.[101] Collingwood was adamant that 'there never was a time that required so much the unanimity of a nation':

> The question is not merely, who shall be the conqueror ... but whether we shall any longer be a people, – whether Britain is still to be enrolled among the list of European nations, – whether the name of Englishmen is to continue an appellation of honour, conveying the idea of every quality which makes human nature respectable, or a term of reproach and infamy, the designation of beggars and of slaves. Men of property must come forward with purse and sword; for the contest must decide whether they shall have any thing, even a country, which they can call their own.[102]

Voluntary contributions did indeed flood in. Martha Saumarez was delighted that 'all descriptions of People have caught the generous flame ... it is truly delightful to see Patriotism surmounting avarice & all other selfish Passions'. It was proudly reported that the sailors and officers belonging to the Channel Fleet had subscribed a month's pay, while the queen donated £5,000, and the Bankers and Merchants of London came forward with contributions 'suitable to the spirit of Englishmen'.[103]

For all these efforts, the Royal Navy remained the first line of British defence, and for the first time began to offer a more effective barrier. By April it was evident that France would soon make another attempt to invade Ireland, likely with simultaneous expeditions. The Channel Fleet returned to sea to face the renewed invasion threat, with the main fleet taking up position off Ushant, while the Irish station was reinforced. Squadrons of ships under Seymour, Thompson and Gardner relieved one another off Ushant as a matter of routine.[104] The Admiralty gave clear priorities for commanders, establishing that careful observation of French invasion preparations was paramount. Such interference meant correspondence between Bridport and the Admiralty became ever more acrimonious. The admiral repeated earlier complaints about the number of ships at his disposal, to the frustration of the Admiralty, who felt he had more than adequate resources.[105] In truth, the concentration of warships off Brest made it much harder for the French to escape: the port was now kept under near-constant observation, with a strong frigate squadron stationed off Pointe de Penmarche and further frigates ranged along the whole of the French Atlantic coast, from off Cape Finisterre to the Channel. A more plausible complaint was the quality of these frigates, for after many years at sea and almost constant service, many were in urgent need of repairs and refitting.[106] With Admiralty resources stretched ever further in 1798, all naval commanders had to make do with the ships at their disposal.

One notable development in British strategic planning was the institution of pre-emptive strikes against French ports. This idea was put forward by Dundas in January 1798, and the first successful raid took place in May 1798, when the dashing – and at times delusional – Home Riggs Popham commanded a force that raided Ostend. Over the following months other naval vessels were involved in attacks on French invasion preparations, entering some of the most difficult French harbours to cut out French vessels. Captain Charles Hamilton commanded one such operation at Corigeou, where his ship attacked the port in the early morning hours of 3 August 1798. Amid bad light, heavy rain and 'vivid lightning', and under heavy fire from the town's batteries for over two hours, his crew boarded and took the brig anchored in the harbour, with the loss of one man.[107] Elsewhere, vessels continued to neutralise French privateers that emerged from enemy harbours. On 4 August Pellew intercepted and captured the French privateer *L'Heureux*, mounted with 16 guns and manned with 112 men, 'a very handsome ship ... in every respect fit for His Majesty's service'.[108] A few days later he captured another French vessel of 20 guns and 175 men, *La Vaillante*, which was also entered into British service.[109] Countless battered British ships cruised the waters outside French ports, gaining intelligence as best they could. Much of what they saw was encouraging. Stopford noted that enemy privateers were mostly laid up for want of sailors and suggested that the numerous desertions of French sailors did not augur well for French success.[110]

Britain's position was undermined by news of a major uprising in Ireland. Long-standing demands for political reform had been given new lustre by the efforts of the United Irishmen, and the failure of the 1796 Bantry expedition had done little to dissuade Wolfe Tone and his associates. Sailors serving off the coast of Ireland communicated ever more distressing scenes. Leonard Bullmer detailed the establishment of martial law and the invasive searches of the British army to his son: 'it is high Treason for a Girl to wear a green Ribbon or a man a green Handkerchief', he confided, and he predicted a 'bloody scene' to come.[111] Another sailor, John Flanigan, wrote that

... the times here are very troublesome, and every man is sworn to be true to one another over all Ireland, and that is what they call uniting or United Irishmen ... any man that will not be united is counted an Enemy to his Country, and he is in danger of being killed every minute, and his house is wrecked as they term it.[112]

In early 1798 the uprising spread into Wicklow in the north-east and Wexford in the south-east, and all told an estimated 50,000 United Irishmen took part in the revolt. In due course they faced around 40,000 militia, 25,000 yeomanry and 30,000 British Army regulars, as experienced soldiers were quickly sent to Ireland to subdue the rebellion.[113] Britain's great fear was that France would also send troops to the theatre to aid the Irish rebels, and in late May Bridport was urged to take up his station off Ushant to prevent French attempts to support the rebels and furnish them with supplies. He succeeded in driving back French ships that had taken station in Bertheaume Bay but made it clear to the Admiralty that his shortage of frigates and cutters made it unlikely he could prevent ships entering and leaving Brest.[114]

This formed the backdrop for four French expeditions launched in the second half of 1798. Captain D'Auvergne reported in late July that ships were preparing at Brest, with larger vessels being disarmed to equip the expedition force; a week later, Captain Richard Goodwin Keats counted a total of sixteen ships of the line, as well as twelve frigates and four corvettes, ready to sail.[115] However, it was from Rochefort that the first French attempt came: on 6 August three French frigates left port with 1,500 troops, sailing out into the Atlantic to avoid British cruisers operating off Cork and landing at Killala Bay in north-west Ireland.[116] Despite its small size, the invasion had momentous consequences, sparking a second rebellion that once again engulfed the country in chaos. Five thousand local rebels came forward to join the French troops, and the combined force achieved a notable early success over British forces at Castlebar. The victorious army declared a new 'Irish Republic' based on the revolutionary principles of 'Liberty, Equality and Fraternity'. There were further uprisings in Longford and Westmeath, and the combined army won another battle at Collooney before British troops finally defeated the rebellion at County Longford on 8 September 1798.[117] British defences had eventually worked, though once again this was no thanks to the Navy.

Many Britons hoped that the threat of a French invasion was now over. 'No farther attempt is likely to be made, for a long time at least, either at Insurrection, on the one hand, or Invasion, on the other,' wrote the *Oracle* in September, while the Admiralty complimented Bridport on his careful management of the blockade of Brest.[118] No sooner had they done so, though, when the force that had been collecting at Brest left port, carrying 3,000 troops and the Irish revolutionary leader Wolfe Tone. On this occasion the Royal Navy succeeded in intercepting the

French, though this owed more to the initiative of individual commanders than to any preconceived plan. The French shook off the pursuing squadron under Keats, but they were unfortunate to meet the British ship *Anson*, which tracked the French squadron for the following three weeks. On hearing the news of the French escape, Warren was sent with his squadron to reinforce the Irish station, and on 11 October he sighted the *Anson*, still pursuing the French force. After a general chase, Warren's squadron of three ships of the line and five frigates surrounded the French force off Tory Island, on the north coast of Ireland. He fought the flagship *Hoche* to a wreck and secured its surrender, along with three other frigates.[119] Tone was recognised as one of the prisoners, tried and convicted of treason, but he committed suicide before the death sentence could be carried out.

Just as the Battle of Tory Island was being fought, the French made a third attempt to invade. On 3 October four French frigates sailed from Rochefort, again slipping through the naval blockade, and made for Killala Bay. By the time they arrived the second Irish Rebellion had been quashed, and on learning of the fate of the previous expeditions, they returned home, successfully re-entering Rochefort following a skirmish with a British squadron off Broadhaven. A final unsuccessful effort was made on 24 October when the enemy frigates *Furie* and *Waakzaamheim* were dispatched to Ireland with military supplies. Within hours of leaving port, however, the ships were intercepted and captured by the British frigate *Sirius* under Captain Richard King.[120]

British newspapers increasingly began to offer assertive denunciations of recent French attempts: the *Chester Chronicle* noted of the second French attempt of 1798 that 'the troops landed can only expect a prison or a grave'. Others, however, continued to highlight alarm. '[T]he Daily Papers,' wrote one, continue to offer 'frequent alarms of invasion, accompanied, as usual, by assurances that every one is the last'. These arguments were founded on the 'crippled state' of the French navy and the frequent failure of the enterprises, but 'Neither of them seem to be good' justifications for the future.[121] Up to the end of

1798 and beyond, the fear of the French menace across the Channel remained.

The French expeditions of summer and autumn 1798 were the most sustained attempts to invade the British Isles during the Revolutionary War. The defeat of the Irish Rebellion in 1798 offered little prospect for further success, and for all their plans and schemes, the French had struggled to overcome the logistical and geographic challenges that confronted them. Halfway through 1798, the man entrusted with organising the French forces into an invading army had seen enough, and Napoleon Bonaparte persuaded the Directory that he should instead take his army to Egypt and there threaten Britain's interests in the East. This did not, however, put an end to the threat of invasion. 'The menace of invasion, I do not doubt will continue as long as the war,' wrote one insightful newspaper in 1798.[122] In early 1799, the Admiralty devoted significant naval resources to the blockade of French invasion ports, and the French continued to demonstrate that they had the wherewithal to escape port. The escape of Admiral Bruix's squadron from Brest on 26 April 1799 raised the spectre of an invasion attempt. The French fleet headed to the Mediterranean and remained at large for much of 1799, finally returning to Brest on 8 August.[123] Napoleon's seizure of power later that year once again raised the spectre of invasion as military forces were collected at Boulogne for 'Les Projets de Descente', the invasion of Britain. As we will see in Chapter 8, the government took it seriously, and only the arrival of peace preliminaries in September 1801 brought a degree of closure.

The threat of invasion continued precisely because the Royal Navy had shown itself to be incapable of reliably defending Britain's shores from a French attack. Time after time, French fleets had escaped from supposedly blockaded ports at will, and only a combination of the weather, unfortunate timing and poor communication between the

French and United Irishmen had prevented more serious consequences. The *Le Moniteur* article of late 1796 had been right to say that the British public were 'brought up on the idea, that the safety of Britain is in her wooden walls', but by 1798 the British public had been thoroughly disabused of that notion. Newspapers, poems, diaries and the fantastical satirical art of Gillray and Cruikshank reveal that the threat of invasion was very real throughout these years. One pamphleteer celebrated the fact that there had been no mass invasion, that there had been no 'interruption of our domestic quiet' while 'a great part of Europe has experienced all the horrors of War . . . its cities have been sacked, and its fields drenched with blood', which they put down to 'the immense superiority of our triumphant Navy'.[124] This bore little relation to the experiences of Britons, however, who had lived through the everyday emotional trauma of the threat of invasion, rooted in naval inadequacy.

What is more, the Navy's failure to defend Britain's shores had long-lasting consequences. Fears of a renewed French invasion helped bring about the Union of Britain and Ireland in 1801, confirming as one pamphlet put it, the 'impossibility of Ireland, particularly in her present state, maintaining a total independence amid such powerful neighbours'.[125] The ongoing threat of invasion served other political ends. Pitt and his government were able to use it to pass further repressive measures, not least a second suspension of habeas corpus in 1798.[126] Naval uncertainty also justified the creation of an 'Armed Nation' unprecedented in scale and scope, facing off against the terrifying threat of French Jacobinism. In 1797 and 1798 the embryonic volunteer movement of the early 1790s was transformed into a vast military build-up, and by 1800 there were hundreds of thousands of Britons in military uniform, whether as army regulars, militia or volunteers, all justified by the fear that the Navy might not be able to prevent a crossing.[127] The American Minister to Britain, Rufus King, noted the British government's practice of 'alarming the country in order that the means of prosecuting the war might more easily be obtained'.[128]

The invasion threats of 1796–8 also raised fundamental questions about the loyalty of the British population. Just as the arming of Welsh volunteers in the aftermath of the Fishguard invasion had precipitated concerns about their allegiance, these were magnified when implemented across the nation. Insurrection in Ireland in 1798 renewed fears of a wider revolutionary movement and that same year the British government commissioned surveys by its Lord Lieutenants to report on the disposition of its people; it was not reassured by what it found.[129] In government correspondence and loyalist literature it was assumed that there were people working to subvert Britain from within, and the great military mobilisation of the 1790s was designed in part with internal threats in mind. Public displays of militia, volunteer and fencible units were intended to comfort an anxious population, but also as an unsubtle demonstration of force. That said, what is most notable about this period is the remarkable resilience of popular loyalism. After all, there would be no revolution in Britain as there had been in France, and it seems likely that the invasion attempts of 1796–8 reset the calculations of many Britons who were shocked to see the French actually land troops on British soil.

Governmental paranoia makes more sense in the context of a series of rebellions that had recently taken place in the Navy itself, among the very people tasked with protecting the nation from enemies abroad. The invasion scare had only confirmed the centrality of naval sailors to the war effort, and in April 1797 they seized the opportunity to use this leverage, downing tools until their demands were met.

SIX

THE DELEGATES IN COUNCIL
The Naval Mutinies of 1797

In 1797 Britain was confronted with a series of naval rebellions unprecedented in their scale and scope. Mutinies, as we have seen, were not a rare occurrence in the revolutionary 1790s, and the uprisings on the *Culloden*, the *Terrible*, the *Defiance* and the *Pompee* earlier in the decade established practices of resistance that initially were closely adhered to during this momentous year. In terms of scale, though, the uprisings of 1797 dwarfed all that had come before as entire fleets came together to register grievances and seek redress. In total over 100 ships were immobilised along the south and east coasts of Britain, paralysing the forces stationed to protect Britain from invasion. The nature of these mutinies was also different. The conventions of shipboard society were inverted, as sailors commandeered spaces usually limited to officers, venturing onto the quarterdeck and even into the captain's cabin. Almost overnight, seamen became admirals. On the *Nassau*, the admiral's servant Theophilus King was appointed 'Admiral of the Ship', while one of the leading mutineers, George Gainier, was piped aboard by the rest of the crew, paying him 'as much respect as if I was the Admiral'.[1] This brave new world was quickly captured by Isaac Cruikshank, whose print *The Delegates in Council* depicted sailors sitting confidently around a captain's table while in the background, a portrait of Britannia hung upside down as a graphic reminder that the Navy's social order had been turned on its head.[2]

Cruikshank was one of many Britons who watched in horror as, for the first time in the war, the loyalty of Britain's sailors became a major public concern. Onlookers were shocked as the nation's 'sure shield' against invasion was transformed into its Achilles heel: Edmund Burke was not alone in thinking that the mutinies had rendered Britain so vulnerable that 'our only hope is in a submission to the enemy . . . [on] any terms', adding that 'as to our Navy, that has already perished with its discipline forever'.[3] The mutinies of 1797 took place on Britain's door-step and played out in the full gaze of a nervous public as reports arrived of sailors refusing orders, officers being sent ashore and, in due course, violence breaking out between the men of the lower and upper decks.[4] In particular, the lack of deference shown to officers and the mutineers' organisational sophistication terrified members of the ruling class. One writer thought the mutiny 'more . . . dangerous in its tendency than any thing of the kind that ever occurred in this, or perhaps any other country'.[5] Indeed, the 'revolutionary' nature of the mutinies was not lost on observers. The sailors elected delegates, wrote petitions, engaged with local newspapers and produced political addresses aimed at persuading the wider public that their cause was just, also threatening to spark further rebellious activity elsewhere. In due course newspapers announced the establishment of a 'Floating Republic', and for a few months in the summer of 1797, the nation waited with bated breath for news about the rebellious ships.[6]

The mutinies of 1797 were fundamentally political and only make sense when considered as part of Britain's Age of Revolutions. These were not isolated outbreaks of dissent, but one larger movement equivalent to the food riots of the 1790s, the campaigns of the Luddites in the 1810s or the Swing Riots of the early 1830s.[7] The mutinies at Spithead and the Nore are now infamous, but often neglected is a series of other contemporary naval rebellions further afield – and around the world – that shared similar aims and employed almost identical means.[8] Only by thinking about them together can we comprehend sailors' attempts to improve their working conditions, and the widespread public anxiety

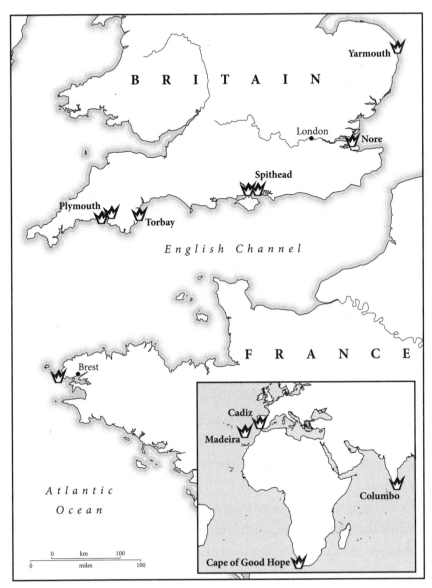

Map 7: The mutinies of 1797.

they prompted. Contemporaries struggled to come to terms with the fact that so many seamen had rebelled and instead blamed external culprits – French Jacobins, British radicals or United Irishmen, to name a few. In *The Delegates in Council*, Cruikshank depicted members of the Foxite opposition faction hiding under the captain's table, quietly orchestrating proceedings. As we shall see, however, sailors were closely enmeshed with shore-based political culture; it was their own capacity for political action that drove the mutinies.[9] Furthermore, just as the sailors' actions were shaped by wider currents, so too was the response of the state. The reprisals ordered by the government in the aftermath of the naval mutinies can only be understood in the context of a state growing in repressive power during Britain's Age of Revolutions.

The first rumblings of discontent arose in the Channel Fleet, stationed at Spithead, in February 1797. The men of the *Queen Charlotte* took the initiative and drew up a petition which was circulated to the rest of the fleet, allowing verbatim letters to be sent from different ships' companies to the shore-bound commander-in-chief, Lord Howe.[10] Their objection was over pay, for while the wages of the army and militia had been raised in 1795, sailors' salaries had not been increased since 1653.[11] This was grievance enough, but the food scarcities and rising prices of 1795–6 had only made matters worse, and the sailors calculated that those joining the Navy in 1793 had seen a 30 per cent drop in purchasing power. This was a genuine cost-of-living crisis, and it is notable that the petitions made much of the sailors' desire to 'support our wives and families in a more comfortable manner'.[12] Nor did the demand for improved wages come out of the blue. In 1793 Tyneside seamen had petitioned Parliament for a pay increase, and a scheme to regulate sailors' wages was proposed by the MP Rowland Burgon but was not taken up. As recently as December 1796, the naval officer Thomas Pakenham had urged the Admiralty to raise wages, conscious that administrators had 'lost sight' of the low wages of 'thoroughbred seamen'.[13]

What followed, however, was institutional inaction. Howe asked one of his flag captains to investigate the petitions and then sent them to the Admiralty, who in turn ignored them. The sailors' patience ran out, and on 16 April, coordinated cheering from the *Queen Charlotte* signalled the beginning of the protest.[14] Ship after ship refused to obey the order from Bridport, the Channel Fleet's active commander, to weigh anchor, resolving that they would not return to their duty until an Act of Parliament was passed increasing their pay, and a pardon issued from the king absolving them of any wrongdoing.[15] To achieve these ends, the crews followed the example laid down by the *Culloden* in 1794, electing 'delegates' to represent them. In total thirty-three representatives gathered in the cabin of the flagship to set out rules for the crews and draw up a new list of grievances. These were far more extensive than the initial call for increased pay and represented the most ambitious programme for naval reform ever proposed by sailors, including fairer allowances of food, more fresh vegetables and meat, improved care for the sick, a fairer system of prize money, better pensions and the possibility of shore leave. Ships were also given the opportunity to put forward any specific objections they might have, and at least fourteen crews came forward with complaints about 'bad Usage' or accusations against specific officers who had behaved 'tiranicaly'. Taken together, this was a coherent set of demands aimed at collectively improving the working conditions of all.[16]

That such a collaborative programme could be proposed by sailors was the result of careful planning over the preceding weeks and months. It remains unclear exactly how the sailors coordinated their actions, for messages between sailors were secretive and left little archival trail, but piecing together evidence reveals a network of communication taking place out of sight of officers. The boat crews of individual ships regularly moved between vessels when the fleet was at anchor, allowing sailors to meet but also to exchange hardships and grievances. At the same time, 'bum boat' women and slop sellers who plied their trades between ship and shore transmitted messages back and forth, while on individual ships, furtive conversations happened at night to avoid discovery.[17] It also seems likely that the prejudices of naval elites blinded them to what was going on. Howe's early inspections of sailors' petitions led him to believe that they were the complaints of a small few, rather than a majority of sailors, while Lord Spencer was astonished when he learned of the extent of sailors' plans, which he deemed 'more systematical than one would naturally expect from the common sailor'.[18] It was not until 15 April that Bridport learned that a correspondence was being 'secretly carried on between the different ships companies', by which time it was too late. Plans were already afoot, and his order to prevent intra-ship communication arrived just as the sailors were preparing a second round of petitions.[19]

If further evidence were needed of sailors' organisational ability, this was soon provided when another fleet to the west also mutinied. Sailors at Plymouth had received letters from their peers in Portsmouth, and when on 26 April news of the Spithead mutiny arrived, the crew of the *Atlas* presented its officers with a list of demands. Spokesmen from the vessel then went to the other ships stationed at Plymouth, and one by one the crews of the *Edgar*, the *Majestic* and the *Saturn* rebelled against their officers, sending them ashore while securing possession of the arms chests and the powder magazines. Their ultimatum followed 'the plan laid down at Spithead', as one petition put it, and in all other respects the sailors mirrored the activities of their 'brethren' further east. Delegates were elected on board each of the four ships, and on 27 April the *Atlas* was designated 'the Parliament Ship'. A delegation was sent to meet with the mutineers at Spithead, and the commander at Plymouth, Sir John Orde, hastily wrote to the Admiralty saying that eight men were travelling 'without leave'. However, there was little else he could do to prevent them departing, and he watched in alarm as the crews cheered from the gangways and forecastles as the delegates made sail to Portsmouth.[20]

RIGHTS OF MAN:

BEING AN

ANSWER TO MR. BURKE's ATTACK

ON THE

FRENCH REVOLUTION.

BY

THOMAS PAINE,

SECRETARY FOR FOREIGN AFFAIRS TO CONGRESS IN THE
AMERICAN WAR, AND
AUTHOR OF THE WORK INTITLED *COMMON SENSE.*

LONDON:
PRINTED FOR J. JOHNSON, ST PAUL's CHURCH-YARD.
MDCCXCI.

1. Born in Thetford, Norfolk, Thomas Paine played a leading role in the American and French Revolutions, and did his utmost to inspire one in Britain. His *Rights of Man*, published in two parts between 1791 and 1792, was banned by Pitt's government but its critique of the aristocracy and poverty was impossible to suppress.

2. The London Corresponding Society was a leading organisation calling for political change during the 1790s. It organised petitions, held open-air meetings and disseminated handbills like this one calling for parliamentary reform. The LCS eventually advocated a National Convention to replace the antiquated British Parliament.

REFORM IN PARLIAMENT.

LONDON CORRESPONDING Society,
APRIL 11, 1793.

A

PETITION

TO BE PRESENTED TO THE HONORABLE
The HOUSE of COMMONS,

PRAYING for a Radical Reform in the Reprefentation of the PEOPLE; now lies for the Reception of Signatures at the following Places. viz.

Mr. RIDGEWAY's Bookfeller, York-ftreet, St James's-fquare.

Mr. HARDY, No. 9, Piccadilly near the Hay-market.

Mr. LAMBATH's, No. 3, St. George's Mall, near the Dog-and-Duck.

Mr. EATON's, Bookfeller, No. 81, Bifhopfgate-Without.

Mr. SPENCE's, Bookfeller, No. 8, Little-Turnftile, Holborn.

The Office of the Morning Poft, Blake-Court, Catharine-Street, Strand;

And the Office of the Courier, No. 38, Charing-Crofs.

⁎⁎⁎ Near 3000 have already figned.

No Expence attends Signing.

3. John Nicol was one of many sailors who wrote a memoir of their maritime life. These publications were often sensationalistic but Nicol's account is marked not just by evocative story-telling but also brutal honesty, not least about his colourful romantic life and the emotional trauma brought about by his fear of the press gang.

4. Posters like this were pasted up across Britain in the hope of encouraging men to come forward and join the Navy. They offered clear incentives: a steady wage and the possibility of prize money. They also used patriotic language to encourage men to volunteer – this example called on those who 'love your country, and your liberty'.

5. While the Navy hoped for volunteers, it relied on impressment to ensure that its ships were adequately manned. Violence was often used to encourage compliance, and here we see one unfortunate victim being beaten as he resists. Wapping was a common hunting ground for press gangs – the nearby Tower of London is visible in the background.

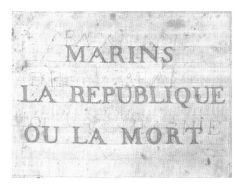

6. This massive command flag, flown from the British flagship during the Battle of the Glorious First of June, would have been visible to many combatants in the early stages of the action. The British succeeded in capturing six vessels and sinking another, but failed to prevent an important grain convoy reaching France.

7. This French Republic banner was captured during the Battle of the Glorious First of June when sailors from the vessel *L'Amerique* attempted to board the British ship *Leviathan*. It is embroidered with the words 'MARINS LA REPUBLIQUE OU LA MORT' (Sailors, the Republic or Death), a battle cry fit for a new age of ideological warfare.

8. After the battle the British commander Admiral Richard Howe returned to a hero's welcome. This image shows George III presenting him with a diamond sword in thanks for his efforts, while the great and good of British society – including Prime Minster William Pitt – look on.

9. Discipline was central to the maintenance of order on board a naval ship. The Articles of War laid out clear rules for all to follow, and punishments for any infraction. Floggings of hundreds of lashes, as depicted here, were extreme sentences but they became increasingly common in the 1790s.

10. This image painted by the naval officer Gabriel Bray during the American Revolution offers a rare window onto the lower decks of a naval ship. It was here that sailors would rest and recreate, but the darker recesses of the ships also offered opportunities to discuss grievances, write petitions and even plot mutinies.

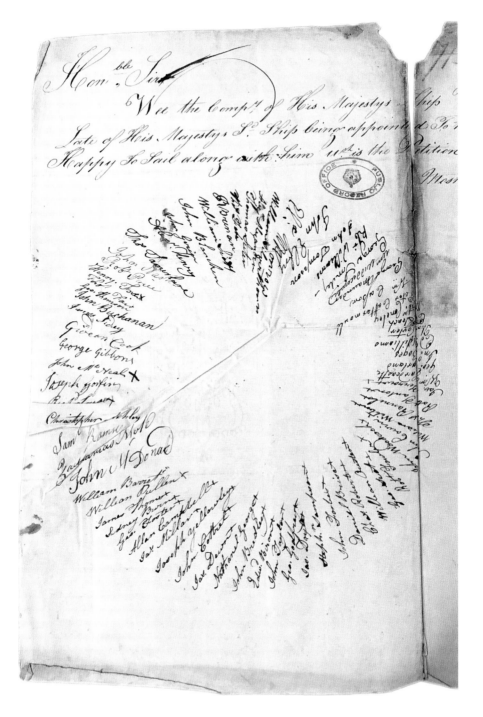

11. One common form of petition was the 'round robin', in which sailors signed their names in a circle to prevent ringleaders from being identified. Making any sort of demand was seen as dangerously subversive: in this example from the *Vestal*, the crew asked only that they be allowed to 'sail along with' a favourite officer who was moving to a different vessel. A few sailors marked their name with an 'x', but the majority were able to sign their own names, revealing the high rates of literacy on board a late-eighteenth-century naval ship.

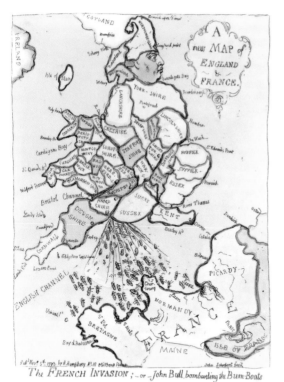

12. In 1793 Gillray offered this defiant print in response to rumours of a French invasion. The body of John Bull is reconfigured to match the geography of Britain and he enthusiastically unloads on French invasion preparations. Quite what the townspeople of Portsmouth made of their city's position in the image is unknown.

13. Gillray's images could be crude but his work was also political. In this caricature the attempted French invasion of Ireland in 1796 is re-imagined as a conflict between parliamentary leaders. Charles James Fox appears as the figurehead of an invading French vessel, about to be capsized by the patriotic waves created by William Pitt and his Cabinet colleagues.

14. By 1798, confidence in the Royal Navy was at a low ebb after a series of naval failures. Images of extravagant French invasion craft were circulated throughout Britain, complete with turrets, citadels, paddle wheels and windmills. These 'Floating Machines' were fantastical, but they revealed a genuine fear of invasion.

15. Gillray's series *Consequences of a Successful French Invasion* imagined the ruinous impact of a French conquest of Britain. In this print, the third of four, he depicted French Republicans forcing ordinary British people to cultivate garlic. Other prints in the series saw revolutionaries ransacking the Houses of Commons and Lords.

16. No image better demonstrates the latent political power of naval sailors. Initially drawn to show the ship's company of the *Queen Charlotte* saluting an admiral coming onboard, the sailors dominate the scene. The crew of this vessel were the first to defy orders during the Spithead mutiny of 1797.

17. Isaac Cruikshank was one of Britain's leading caricaturists and frequently made sailors the subject of his prints. *The Delegates in Council* depicts them turning the naval world upside down during the 1797 mutinies. The seated sailors are armed and threatening, while an image of Britannia hangs on its head in the background.

18. Richard Parker's education and maritime experience made him an obvious figure to act as spokesman for the rebellious sailors at the Nore. In this contemporary print he is shown taking on the role of 'President of the Committee of Delegates', confidently brandishing their list of demands.

19. In the aftermath of the 1797 mutinies there was a swathe of media that represented Richard Parker as a treasonous figure. Alongside these, though, came more sympathetic portraits. This likeness is shorn of subversive meaning and suggests that some Britons saw him in a much more positive light.

20. Jack Crawford was the first named sailor to be fêted by the British public. During the Battle of Camperdown he nailed his ship's fallen flag to the mast, an act of bravery that prompted celebratory prints like this one. He was subsequently used by Pitt's ministry to boost public confidence in the Navy.

21. The image of Crawford nailing a flag to the mast became a common sight in late 1797, depicted across a range of different material culture. Here the 'Hero of Camperdown' decorates a plate designed to be displayed in the home. Domestic ceramicware like this offers us an insight into the extent of his celebrity.

22. This painting depicts the surrender of the Dutch admiral after Camperdown. Unusually, Jack Crawford is placed centrally, carrying the marlin spike he used to nail the flag to the *Venerable*'s mast. The artist Daniel Orme reportedly took Crawford's likeness from a life sketch, a rare moment where an individual sailor was depicted in high art.

23. The 'Thanksgiving' of 1797 was an exercise in patriotic theatre. Jack Crawford played a central role in the procession to St Paul's Cathedral, and, as this image reveals, many thousands turned out to watch. For all the bombast, the event also saw violence and vocal criticism of the prime minister, William Pitt.

24. There was a determined effort to restore the image of the British sailor after the mutinies of 1797. In this image, Gillray depicts 'Jack Tar' punching the nation's latest military adversary, Napoleon Bonaparte, off the face of the world. This marked a return to the unproblematic stereotype of the loyal British seaman.

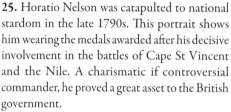

25. Horatio Nelson was catapulted to national stardom in the late 1790s. This portrait shows him wearing the medals awarded after his decisive involvement in the battles of Cape St Vincent and the Nile. A charismatic if controversial commander, he proved a great asset to the British government.

26. Nelson's victory at the Battle of the Nile prompted a fascination with 'Egyptian' culture. Here, the artist depicts two figures wearing ludicrous items of clothing, including a crocodile hat and muff, and webbed shoes. The print affectionately mocks the British public's celebration of Nelson while offering a pointed satire on sartorial excess.

27 and 28. The pendant and ribbon shown here are more restrained examples of 'Nelsonmania'. By the end of 1798 there was a fast-growing industry producing objects that catered to all classes and genders. These examples were aimed the higher end of the market, but every item allowed patriotic Britons to mark their affection for the latest naval hero.

29. Here Gillray captures the relationship between naval victories and the loyalist British public. His focus is firmly on naval officers: John Bull is shown almost fit to burst as he consumes French 'Frigasees' captured by Nelson, Duncan, Howe and others, while in the background opposition Whigs bewail the latest naval successes.

30. Nelson's fame made him a useful propaganda figure. This fictitious image depicts him recreating with his sailors, implying a return to shipboard harmony following the turbulent events of 1797. In reality, there remained clear social divisions between officers and their men, and 1798 saw more instances of shipboard discord than ever before.

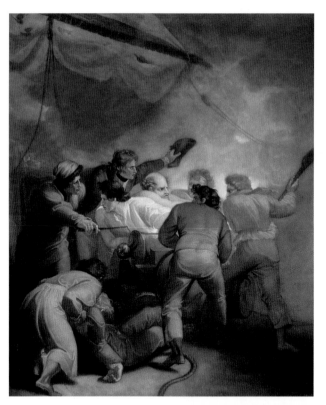

31. British naval success relied on the fighting spirit of the Navy's sailors. This dynamic print shows them frantically firing a gun, while one of their crewmates falls having paid the ultimate price. Trials in battle convinced sailors of their worth, and gave them ample justification to demand better wages and working conditions.

32. For many sailors, it was the conflict against the elements that proved the greatest danger. Here, seamen are shown cutting away rigging from a dismasted vessel, while a storm blows in the background. For those men employed on blockade or convoying duty, the vagaries of the weather were a daily concern.

33. Numerous plans were made to create a monument to commemorate the Navy, such as this spectacular 'naval pillar'. Subscriptions were established to fund these efforts, but organisers struggled to agree on form and location, and there were heated debates about whether sailors should be included.

34. Tens of thousands of British sailors were killed during the French Revolutionary War, leaving behind countless widows and orphans. Public subscriptions were set up to help alleviate the impact on families, and middle-class women could play a leading role in directing funds. The 'ladies subscriptions' referred to here were increasingly common.

35. This image offers a romanticised image of post-war lives. Four sailors regale each other with stories, while an intrigued onlooker listens intently. Many thousands of seamen did return home with the signing of peace preliminaries in 1801, but with the international situation uncertain, others were forced to remain at sea.

I. Mayfield.   J. Ward.   J. Chesterman.   J. Fitzgerald.

J. Rowland.   T. Jones.   T. Cross.   W. Cook.

C. White.   J. Collins.   J. Locker.   J. Cummins.

R. Page.   W. Hillier.   I. Dayley.   T. Piper.

PORTRAITS of the MUTINEERS

36. The *Temeraire* was one of several ships that mutinied following the end of the French Revolutionary War. This image portrays the sailors deemed to have organised the rebellion, circulated with a published version of their court martial in 1802. There was much sympathy within and without the Navy when six of the accused were hanged.

Word continued to travel, and on 7 May 1797 another fleet mutiny broke out at Torbay. Here a squadron under Sir Roger Curtis had received an excited message detailing events at Spithead, and they immediately began to remove unpopular officers. Once again, delegates were elected, oaths were sworn and demands were passed on to their officers. This time, though, fearful of Admiralty attempts to divide the different striking forces, the sailors chose not to send a delegation but instead decided to sail the entire fleet to Portsmouth as a show of support, with Curtis a virtual prisoner on board his own flagship.[21] Nor did the rebellions stop there. Another mutiny broke out in Sir John Borlase Warren's squadron sailing off Pointe de Raz on the coast of Brittany, where it was stationed blockading the French fleet at Brest. The crew of the *Galatea* received news of the Spithead mutiny, and keen to rid themselves of their own unpopular officers, they confined the captain, boatswain and master's mate to their quarters and put the ship under the command of First Lieutenant Charles Carter. The sailors swore on oath to bring the ship into port to secure their grievances and were joined by two other vessels, the *Artois* and the *Sylph*, also sailing off Brest. Upon their arrival at Plymouth the three crews presented petitions to the Admiralty declaring that they could 'no longer groan under such insupportable & cruel Tyranny'.[22] For the first time in the war, mutinying British ships had abandoned their station in the face of the enemy.

The naval establishment was rocked to its core. On hearing the first rumours of rebellion at Spithead the Admiralty had ordered Bridport to take 'the most vigorous and effectual measures for checking its progress and securing the Ringleaders', but the sailors presented a united front and refused to offer up any individual. An Admiralty deputation that included Spencer made hasty progress to Portsmouth and, finally understanding the magnitude of what was taking place, ordered Bridport on 20 April to give in to almost all of the sailors' demands.[23] The sailors were at this point negotiating directly with the British government, a remarkable expansion of the normal channels of protest,

and they well understood the leverage they had. They politely acknowledged the Admiralty's offer but continued to insist on individual ships'
grievances being met, as well as an Act of Parliament codifying an
increase in their wages and a King's pardon, 'published in the Daily
Papers'.[24] This last was an astute acknowledgement that the mutinies
were also being played out in the public presses, further forcing the
Admiralty's hand. Conservative newspapers emphasised the treasonous
nature of the sailors' conduct, especially as reports of further rebellions
to the west arrived. 'The Spirit of mutiny, which first broke out at
Portsmouth,' wrote the *Morning Post*, 'has spread throughout our whole
Navy, and threatens the most lamentable consequences.'[25] Many others
were more favourable, however, and conceded the justice of the seamen's
demands. Furthermore, the *London Chronicle* noted that the sailors had
conducted themselves 'with sobriety, steadiness, unanimity and determination', while *The Times* was gratified that 'nothing can exceed the
general good behavior and submission of the Seamen'.[26]

The government's difficulties controlling the media narrative were in
no small part due to the sailors' efforts to secure wide coverage of their
demands. Their initial petitions were sent to newspapers and the opposition leader Charles James Fox, and they also produced their own political documents that advanced their grievances and ensured that their
side of the debate was presented to the public. On 13 May, the sailors at
Spithead published an 'Address to the Nation' to ensure 'that our grateful
countrymen might not be deceived, or ourselves prejudiced by false
reports'. The address – later published by the *Oracle and Public Advertiser*
and the *Courier* – laid out their demands, labelling them 'moderate and
just', and placed the blame for the crisis firmly on the government.[27] The
sailors also developed close links with the local *Portsmouth Gazette*,
which joined them in bringing attention to the 'willfull and wicked'
perversions of recent events in some London newspapers. The sailors
even sent corrections when they felt their actions had been misrepre-
sented. They took particular issue with the pro-government *Sun*,
which printed the comments of an opposition MP who had accused

the sailors of being 'the basest and foulest traitors that ever disgraced a country'. In response, they calmly laid out their 'Wants and Wishes', all the while emphasising their love of country, making clear their willingness to meet the French in battle were they to leave port.[28] It was a canny, considered exercise in public relations.

It was in the national press that the sailors at Spithead learned of continued vacillation in Parliament over the pay legislation and the King's pardon.[29] Memories of former injustices loomed large in sailors' minds. 'Remember the *Culloden*', urged the lead mutineer at Spithead, Valentine Joyce, while letters were circulated through the fleet concerned that 'there [is] not the least reliance to be placed in their promises'.[30] Tensions were highest on the *London*, where Rear Admiral John Colpoys refused to allow delegates to come aboard. One of the ship's officers, Lieutenant Bower, fired his gun into a crowd and three sailors were killed in the subsequent affray; only the intervention of Joyce prevented Bower's lynching.[31] The mutinies had thus far been free of violence, but the outbreak on the *London* threatened to rupture the negotiations between the striking seamen and the government. Over a hundred officers were unceremoniously sent on shore, and those most culpable for the bloodshed were put on trial. Colpoys' case was heard by a fleet tribunal made up of sailors, who voted twelve to five for sending him ashore, rather than for a summary execution, while Lieutenant Bowers was handed over to the civil authorities on shore. The subsequent coroner's report of 'justifiable homicide' enraged the more militant ships, and for the first time divisions appeared among the Spithead mutineers. The crews of the *Mars* and the *Latona* accused the *London* delegates of treachery, while the crew of the *Duke* threatened to set sail and surrender the ship to the French.[32]

Further division was prevented by positive news from the west. It was at this point that the rebellious squadron from Torbay arrived with red flags of mutiny flying, joining the Spithead ships in demanding the expulsion of obnoxious officers. The mutineers also learned that another nineteen ships had mutinied at Plymouth, joining the naval uprising there and further strengthening the Spithead delegates' hand.[33] Facing an ever growing rebellion, the government caved. On 9 May Parliament passed legislation that increased sailors' pay and provisions, adding an extra £536,795 to the annual naval budget, while the Victualling Office agreed to the changes to provisions demanded by the mutineers. Coming at a time of deep financial concern and only a few months after the Fishguard invasion had come close to causing financial meltdown, this was no small gesture. What is more, the government made clear that these benefits – and the king's pardon – would be for all sailors currently serving.[34] The delegates accepted the Admiralty's caution that 'the present Revenues' would not allow for better pensions or a different system of prize money and quietly conceded these demands, but they insisted on the removal of unpopular officers. Lord Howe toured the ships at Spithead, acquiescing to their individual demands: in total, 113 unpopular officers were sent on shore. It took another couple of weeks for the news to be communicated along the south coast, where Sir John Orde was forced to make 'humiliating' and 'alarming' concessions to the sailors, including the removal of a further sixty-six officers, and it was not until 25 May that the sailors there returned to duty. The remaining rebellious fleet at Cawsand Bay consulted with their fellow sailors at Plymouth before agreeing to do the same.[35]

The south coast mutinies of 1797 represented one of the most successful labour disputes of the eighteenth century. Sailors had secured almost all their demands, including a substantial pay rise and improved working conditions, without anyone being subjected to naval discipline. The deaths of the sailors on the *London* tempered celebrations, and the funerals of those killed were held at Portsea in front of an 'immense' crowd, a further sign that public support for the sailors' actions was considerable. At Plymouth there was a real sense of achievement. One sailor wrote proudly of the rebellion, which had been accomplished 'with great success without any loss of men'.[36] For the naval authorities, it represented a shocking demonstration of sailors' latent strength. Colpoys, who had seen the stubbornness of sailors first-hand, reported with alarm that delegates had stated bluntly that 'we have the power'.[37] Nonetheless, it served everyone's interests to emphasise the renewed loyalty of the sailors, and following the resolution, there was a carefully coordinated display of devotion. Sailors sent a letter of thanks to Howe, signed by the two delegates of each ship, in which they referred to the mutiny as a 'recent disturbance', making clear that their conduct was 'not in the least owing to any disloyalty to His Majesty or disaffection to our Country'.[38] On 15 May, the sailors returned to duty amid cheering and the playing of 'Rule Britannia'. These ceremonies were designed to restore public faith in the Navy and were widely reported, but their staged nature was not lost on more astute observers.[39]

Hopes of a permanent resolution were dashed with the news of a fresh uprising at the Nore, an anchorage where the Thames Estuary meets the North Sea. In its form it followed the tactics laid down further west: planned in advance, sailors held secret meetings and signalled the start of the mutiny through a series of cheers. The red flag of mutiny was raised, ships' magazines were secured and each vessel elected two delegates to represent their views. As at Plymouth, the delegates arrived on the largest ship, this time the *Sandwich*, and renamed it the 'Parliament Ship'.[40] Perhaps conscious of the division that had crept in during the later stages of the mutinies further west, the delegates went one step further and elected a 'President' to act as spokesman for the fleet. The man selected, Richard Parker, was a former schoolmaster from Exeter who had served in the Navy as a master's mate before being dismissed in 1795 on a charge of disobedience (see p. 105). Forced through destitution to rejoin the Navy in 1797, his education and experience made him an ideal figurehead. It remains unclear how involved he was in the formation of mutineer policy, and he later claimed to have been a moderate of 'cool temper' who did much to oppose the demands of more radical sailors.[41] Certainly, though, he understood the symbolic nature of his role and was frequently seen walking about on shore with 'all the pomp of parade', waving the mutinous red flag and offering rallying speeches to different ships' companies, in one case haranguing the hands when 'they were not hearty in the cause'. Whether fair or not, he became the public face of the mutiny – the 'Robespierre of the Delegates', as some newspapers put it.[42]

The mutineers' demands at the Nore were both a reprise and an extension of those made earlier. They insisted on the same concessions as at Spithead, perhaps unaware that these had already been granted, or suspicious that the government would not follow through on its promises. They again asked for the grievance traded away at Spithead – a more equitable distribution of prize money – alongside further requests. These included more regular pay, advance wages for pressed men, a right to shore leave in port, a standing pardon for returning deserters, revisions to the Articles of War and what amounted to an effective veto over officers.[43] The Nore delegates were clearly emboldened by the success of the earlier mutinies and were confident that they too would be able to force the government to give in to their demands. Richard Parker came on shore and met with Admiral Charles Buckner, insisting that they would not 'give up the power they then had', while his fellow delegate John Davis told Buckner explicitly that 'the power was in their hands'.[44]

Compared with the Channel Fleet, however, the Nore squadron was small and of little strategic consequence, and having already granted the wishes of one set of sailors the Admiralty was unwilling to do the same again. Much of the intelligence received by the Admiralty suggested that the majority of seamen remained loyal, which was borne out on 29 May when two ships – the *Clyde* and the *St Fiorenzo* – escaped under fire from the mutineers.[45] The Lords of the Admiralty belatedly visited Sheerness to offer a pardon if the sailors returned to work, and they were shocked when the sailors made further demands, including the radical notion of courts martial being made up of sailors and marines, rather than officers. The Admiralty, deeming these to be 'of a nature so extravagant, & calculated so directly to overturn all Naval Discipline', rejected them without further discussion.[46]

These new demands were the result of new impetus breathed into the mutiny by the arrival of another rebellious fleet. At Yarmouth, the force commanded by Admiral Adam Duncan mutinied, and the rebellious ships made their way south to join the force at the Nore. Only two ships, Duncan's flagship the *Venerable* and the *Adamant*, remained loyal, and they sailed to the Texel where they performed a makeshift blockade of the enemy's invasion fleet. The remainder arrived at the Nore in late May and boosted the mutineers' prospects. Parker greeted the newly arrived vessels with thanks for 'so speedily' joining 'the good cause we are embarked in'.[47] Their arrival escalated the situation still further. The Admiralty made it illegal to communicate with the mutineers, and in response, the sailors cut off all correspondence with the shore. The government then ordered mortar batteries constructed at Sheerness, halted food supplies and brought in military reinforcements that patrolled the coastline with such efficiency that a lost Victualling Office official, Mr Beddingfield, was temporarily arrested as a mutineer.[48] Alarmed at the military build-up, the mutineers responded with equally extreme measures, blockading the River Thames until they received a 'satisfactory Answer from the Minister and Admiralty'. One of the leading mutineers, Thomas Jephson, predicted that 'before Saturday all London will be in uproar'.[49]

Both government and delegates understood that the conflict playing out at the Nore was also a battle for public hearts and minds. The government's military cordon proved very effective: unlike at Spithead, journalists were unable to get easy access to the mutineers, and the sailors themselves struggled to find avenues through which they could justify their demands in the press. Political declarations were composed, and papers found on board the rebellious ships in the aftermath of the mutinies reveal political treatises with which the mutineers hoped to justify their actions to 'our Country and the world at large' so that 'every thinking man' could see the validity of their demands.[50] Prior to the cordon going up, delegates were able to distribute handbills on shore: one of the mutineers, William Gregory, gave a merchant pilot money to print one and pin it up 'upon the Pillars of the Exchange in London as other publick places'.[51] For the most part, though, with the exception of more radical organs such as the *Courant*, *Manchester Gazette* and *Cambridge Intelligencer*, most newspapers followed the ministerial line, united in horror at the course of events; it was at this point that the mutiny was pejoratively dubbed the 'Floating Republic'.[52] Even those papers that had been initially sympathetic to the Nore mutineers' grievances struggled to maintain this position following the blockade of the Thames, and it certainly seems that among the middling and elite classes, government propaganda that emphasised the potentially calamitous nature of the mutinies was very effective. In a private letter to his masters in America, the US Minister Rufus King noted that 'The public anxiety cannot be described'.[53]

Less clear is how labouring and artisanal classes responded to the mutinies on the east coast. The government, perhaps aware that its version of events was finding favour, briefly allowed mail that offered 'good advice and exhortations to return to their duty' to reach the mutinying ships, and letters poured in cautioning the sailors to return to their duty.[54] These letters discussed the likelihood of severe punishment for those who had mutinied, and some offered political reflections that appealed for faith in Britain's constitution and way of life. John Cudlip preached to his brother serving on the *Belliqueux* of 'every privledge which is dear to us as Englishmen' including religion, liberty and 'our happy and glorious Constitution'.[55] Other sailors, though, received much more supportive messages. Thomas West received a letter stating that 'The lower Class of People in general wish the Sailors good Success', while Hardwick Richardson was told that 'People of all ranks' were applauding the mutineers' stance and 'think their demands very moderate'.[56] There is also evidence from across the country of a broader community of support. John Cantelo told customers at the George Inn, Christchurch, that 'the sailors were men of Spirit' and that the mutinies were 'the way to shake off the arbitrary Government', while John Leverit was tried for sedition for critiquing the government's attempts to 'starve the sailors at the Nore'. Ballads were circulated in Liverpool that praised the 'noble example' sailors were setting.[57] The best insight into the public divide came when a group of travellers on board a passenger boat sailing up the Thames cheered a mutinous ship as they passed it, which so enraged the others on board that a fight broke out.[58]

Isolated from the shore, and with public support unclear, the mutineers were forced into ever more extreme positions. Parker briefly lifted the blockade and attempted to reopen discussions with the government, offering a new petition to the king that contained a threat to take the ships to France. The government again refused to negotiate, and on 9 June Parker gave the order for the fleet to put to sea. No ship obeyed and conflicts broke out on individual vessels between the mutineers and more loyalist elements. On the *Iris* there was a shoot-out between the 'blue party' and the 'bloody party', while on the *Leopard* the boatswain's mate knocked down a leading mutineer and called for the ship to divide into its different factions; the subsequent fight saw several men wounded and twenty-five mutineers imprisoned. On the *Champion* the ship's company took a vote won by the loyalists, rejecting the delegates' calls to sail the ship to France and there join the 'Friends to the Liberty of mankind'. The crew of the *Sandwich* declared that the ship was to be given over to their officers, and in a moment pregnant with meaning, Parker was forced to hand over the keys to the magazine and was put in irons.[59] Other mutineers committed desperate acts: William Wallace fatally shot himself in the head rather than accept defeat, while the most extreme leaders discussed blowing up their vessels. Many ran away to escape retribution: mutineers on the *Inflexible* and the *Montagu* deserted, likely escaping to France. One by one, crews surrendered unconditionally, sending formal acknowledgement to Admiral Keith, and by 15 June every ship was once again under government control.[60]

The spell of naval rebellion was far from over, however. Across the summer months, ships that had taken part in the mutinies at Spithead and Plymouth were inspired by events at the Nore to mutiny again. For a few days in early June, a group of sailors on the *Pompee* tried to organise a rebellion that called for the removal of the Pitt ministry and an immediate peace with France, again threatening to hand the ship over to the French. On *La Revolutionaire* sailors refused to go to sea 'until they knew on what terms the poor fellows at the Nore, had given in, or what they had determined on'. The crew of the *Calypso* had been at sea and missed the opportunity to remove its officers, and so in June they refused to sail 'unless they find another Captain'.[61] New complaints manifested on other ships. The *Saturn* was taken over by a committee protesting their length of service, while on the *Beaulieu* the crew attempted to release two imprisoned seamen, seizing cutlasses and attacking officers before they were driven below by officers and apprehended.[62] There were also disturbances on the *Polyphemus*, the *Marlborough* and the *Mars*, and there were multiple attempts by sailors on the *Royal Sovereign* to take over the ship.[63] Perhaps most concerning for Pitt's ministry was a mutiny that broke out at the Stonehouse Barracks in Plymouth, where four marines were caught plotting to destroy the powder magazines and 'do everything in their power to overthrow the government'. The ringleader admitted being a member of the United Irishmen and claimed that the marines' coup was to be assisted by the nearby 58th Regiment and the crews of two men-of-war in the harbour.[64]

News of the mutinies was spread further around the world by sailors animated by recent events. A merchant fleet was convoyed to Madeira by the naval ship *Thames*, on board which an astonished onlooker noted how the men were 'doing exactly what they pleased', openly discussing taking command of the vessel while their officers were too terrified to impose discipline. On arrival at Madeira they also encouraged other naval ships to follow their lead, sending 'inflammatory papers' on board and explaining how ships at Spithead had removed unwanted officers. Crews reacted differently to these efforts: on the *Minerve* the sailors turned the papers over to their captain, but on the *Lively* there was a disturbance when sailors protested that they were not allowed on shore, which was put down through floggings and the arrest of a 'ringleader'.[65] In St Vincent's fleet, blockading Cadiz, the men of the *St George* mutinied, hoping to secure the freedom of three men whom they believed had been erroneously accused of buggery. The mutiny failed and the convicted men were hanged on the next available day, which happened to be a Sunday. Some officers, such as Vice Admiral Thompson, protested hanging men on the sabbath, but St Vincent cared little for such considerations and was determined to set an example. Horatio Nelson agreed: 'I would have executed them. We know not what might have been hatched by a Sunday's grog; *now* your discipline is safe.'[66]

Naval ships also brought news of the rebellions into the Indian Ocean, where sailors organised a mutiny that demanded, in the words of one officer, 'several outrageous propositions nearly similar to those made by Parker at the Nore'. It had taken months for reports of the mutinies to arrive in Columbo and, as at Madeira, different shipboard cultures interpreted the reports in contrasting ways. One vessel presented complaints of ill-usage from two officers and insisted they be put on shore, resulting in the arrest of the 'most culpable' eleven men, while a sailor on the *Carysfort* was also punished when he 'endeavoured to excite a similar disturbance'. By contrast, the ship's company of the *Suffolk* considered themselves 'upon an equilibrium with those at home' and demanded only the indulgences given to sailors in Britain, at the same time assuring their captain of 'their readiness to do their duty' and promising to inform on any shipmate that 'should hereafter attempt to excite any disturbance among them'. A paper with demands was delivered to a ship's officer asking for the same allowances for provisions, better care for the sick, as well as shore leave while in harbour, and insisting that 'there shall be no ill treatment suffered on board the ship'. A small minority were unpersuaded and, following further unrest, one ringleader, John Bray, was sentenced to hang, while another four sailors received hundreds of lashes each.[67]

The most extreme of the 'global' mutinies were those at the Cape of Good Hope. There sailors learned of the Nore mutiny before their superiors, a testament to the speed with which seditious information could travel outside the usual course of official communications.[68] On 5 October 1797, an unsigned letter was dropped on deck of the

Tremendous that detailed a series of abuses, and two days later eight ships rose in mutiny, demanding improved food and the removal of unwanted officers. Crews once again elected delegates and drew up lists of grievances, while each officer was brought forward and a vote was taken on whether to expel them or not.[69] Alarmed officers noted the similarity with the rebellions that had recently taken place in Britain, and the local commander was forced to enter into a dialogue with the sailors. He agreed to investigate cases of abuse, and two officers were put on trial; while Captain Stephens of the *Tremendous* was cleared of any wrongdoing, William Stewart of the *Rattlesnake* was convicted of tyranny, oppression and neglect of duty and was dismissed from the service.[70]

These actions, as well as a proclamation of 'pardon and amnesty', helped bring an end to the uprising, but imperial elites remained nervous about the impact of the 1797 mutinies. Lord Macartney compared them to the 'sweating sickness' of Tudor times. This was, he said, a 'national malady', one 'not content with its devastations in England' but instead to be visited 'at the most distant parts of the globe'.[71] In his view, the naval rebellion at the Cape was just the most recent symptom of a wider contagion. Not until the end of October did the symptoms disappear.

Those who have tried to explain the mutinies of 1797 have repeatedly looked for external instigators. Contemporaries assumed that because the rebellions were so well planned, and of such scale, they could not have been the work of 'simpleton' sailors. Pitt spoke for many of his class when he told the House of Commons on 2 June 1797 that the origins of the mutinies 'could not be in the hearts of British seamen' and instead blamed seditious revolutionaries who had poisoned the minds and 'perverted the principles of our sailors', a claim that helpfully absolved him and his allies in Cabinet of any blame for the outbreaks. The Duke of Portland blamed 'French agents', while Thomas Grenville suggested that the uprisings were 'deeply rooted in the influence of Jacobin emissaries and the Correspondence Society'.[72] Even those close to the Navy struggled to come to terms with the fact that sailors had political agency of their own. Cuthbert Collingwood blamed 'your Constitution and Corresponding Society men' for the rebellions of 1797.[73] The contemporary consensus was confirmed in a 1799 House of Commons Committee of Secrecy report into seditious activities that took for granted that the sailors were 'a brave and loyal body of men' who could only have been seduced from their duty by foreign dissidents.[74] Until recently, this has also formed a scholarly consensus, with historians ascribing the outbreak of mutiny to the influence – and intervention – of the United Irishmen or the London Corresponding Society.[75]

There is, however, very little evidence that directly connects these groups to the mutinies. Some mutineers certainly had links with the United Irishmen: Thomas Jephson had visited London prior to the mutinies and returned with quantities of literature printed at Belfast and addressed 'to the People of Ireland', and the mutineers at Plymouth marine barracks were explicitly identified as United Irishmen.[76] However, these associations do not explain the scale of the wider rebellions, and Irishmen were significantly underrepresented among the delegates and crews of the more radical ships.[77] We also know that some sailors – such as James Smart of the *Grampus* – were members of the LCS, and the organisation had strong support in naval ports such as Portsmouth.[78] However, there is again no evidence that any political organisation had a direct hand in instigating the mutinies. One peculiarly persistent myth is that the mutinies of 1797 were instigated by educated 'quota men', lured into the Navy from 1795 onwards by the promise of a bounty. Again, though, this is not borne out by the archive. The vast majority of the delegates were experienced sailors of long standing, and while Parker was a quota man, he was hardly a newcomer to the Navy and had at one point been on track to an officer's commission. The delegates were for the most part men who could combine maritime experience with either political nous or education. Smart was elected as a delegate owing to the fact that he was deemed to be a 'scholar and had been to sea before', while Matthew Hollister had previously been a delegate during the *Defiance* mutiny of 1795.[79]

The only convincing explanation for the mutinies is the sailors' own capacity for political action. Throughout the early years of the war they had demonstrated a persistent desire to call for redress, and what is striking about the mutinies of 1797 is how politically engaged many sailors were. They consumed media in large quantities, with Admiral Gardner noting that 'The Public Newspapers are read by almost everyone in the fleet'.[80] We know also that sailors sought a variety of idealogical literature. Later investigators found 'many cheap publications' on board the mutinous ships on 'subjects relating to Clubs and Societies of all descriptions', while a copy of Thomas Paine's *Rights of Man* was found on board the *Espion*.[81] Nor was this limited to what was written; there was a wider acknowledgement that sailors should be able to speak their mind on the issues of the day. In May 1797, as the mutinies played out, the bosun of the *Ceres* admonished his captain, stating 'If I can't speak, I can think'.[82] Sailors also understood their actions in the context of Britain's wider political culture. John Pickering directly referenced newspaper reports that the LCS was about to hold a meeting and induce 'a general rising' that would 'involve the nation in all the horrors of a Revolution'.[83] Furthermore, sailors' political education was evident in their demands, which demonstrated familiarity with legislative procedures, naval estimates, taxation and inflation, not to mention the progress of the war.[84] In an era of new ideas, reform and extra-parliamentary activity, it is not surprising that the nation's largest labour force was politically engaged.

A more interesting question is what kind of 'politics' was advocated by sailors throughout the mutinies of 1797. Here the answer is less clear cut, for among the tens of thousands of sailors who participated in the mutinies of 1797 there was a multiplicity of different views and agendas, and attempts to assign this heterogeneous community into categories are riven with difficulties. Nonetheless, it is helpful to think about three different factions on a given ship: those who were enthusiastic about mutiny, who took up positions as delegates or committeemen; loyalists who opposed it; and a larger mass of sailors whose support both sides sought. We are helped here by the fact that sailors also used the binary terminology of party and faction themselves to describe the divisions on board each ship. On the *Leopard*, John Habbigan accused John Slater of raising 'an opposition' in the ship, while others testified that the mutineers became concerned when 'an opposite party' made up of those who were for 'their King and Country' was formed.[85] Thomas Jephson of the *Sandwich* referred to those who opposed the mutiny specifically as 'Loyalists', while one such man, Peter Powell, made a clear distinction between the mutineers on board and those of 'our party'. Thomas Atkinson, another Nore mutineer, referred to 'an opposition party in . . . the *Inflexible* and the *Director*', while a petition from imprisoned mutineers later blamed the mutinies on the 'leaders of a dreadful Faction' who were responsible for 'extremist plans'.[86]

Establishing the number of sailors who subscribed to each stance is trickier still. Many sailors had good reason to claim to be 'loyalist' in the aftermath, and while some were imprisoned by the rebellious crews, many likely kept quiet. Nonetheless, it is clear that the 'mutineer' and 'loyalist' factions were both minorities on board. On the *Artois* the sailor John Lucy estimated there were about forty men involved in the mutiny, while on the smaller *Swan*, ten sailors were deemed to have 'entirely commanded' the ship's company during the mutiny.[87] The numbers of loyalists were equivalent. A post-mutiny report from the *Pylades* stated that sixteen men had remained 'steadfast in opposing the violent measures of the Delegates and Committee'.[88] Each faction could likely call on wider support as the mutiny progressed. On the *Pompee*, eighty-three sailors signed an oath committing them to agitate for peace and reform, while sixty-one sailors signed a counter-petition that acknowledged the cause but argued that this was not the time to press for it. Out of a complement of 640, this still left many men uncommitted, and persuading this larger mass of undecideds was crucial;

Thomas McCann of the *Sandwich* was but one delegate who 'went frequently into different berths to find out the sentiments of the people'.[89] This was a dynamic situation, and the number of men associating with a 'loyalist' mentality obviously grew towards the end of the Nore mutiny. As the mutineers lost control of the *Standard*, one of the ringleaders, Joseph Hudson, was heard to say that 'if he had his will he would hang one half of the ship's company'; while imprecise, it suggests that around half of the crew were of 'loyalist' bent by this point.[90]

Those most active in the mutinies used a variety of means to persuade others to the cause. Among the mutineers were skilled political operators capable of using their standing on the ship to persuade doubters, such as Abraham Nelson, who used his 'influence with the people' to encourage others to take part. Others used force of argument. William Gregory read out the Act of Parliament to suspicious sailors on the *Sandwich*, pointing out that none of their grievances had been redressed, but arguing that 'this can be altered in the course of a few hours'.[91] Delegates subtly altered their demands to help enlist the support of the marines. At Spithead the sailors ensured that marines were included in their stated grievances, after which the marine companies of the *Queen Charlotte*, the *Duke* and the *Royal George* promised their assistance and declared their 'Steadyness to their Cause'. At the Nore, the marines were promised a pay rise of 10 pence per day to ensure their support.[92]

Nor were mutineers afraid to use the 'dark arts'. The delegates of the *Leviathan* insisted that all private communications received were read first to either the ship's company or the delegates themselves, and on the *Pompee* the principal mutineers pretended they had more supportive signatures than they actually did.[93] Where persuasion failed, coercion also helped to 'encourage' recalcitrant crews. Here we must be careful, for in the aftermath all sailors had a vested interest in saying they had been compelled to take part, but it seems clear that the threat of force was frequently enlisted. During the mutiny on the *Artois*, for example, John Lucy was threatened with a 'trial by the ship's company' if he refused to sign his name, while Robert Dobson, a sailor on board the

Nassau, wrote that preparations were being made for hanging any man who refused to agree with the delegates' proposals.[94]

Sailors also drew on long-standing political traditions to help tie together mutinous crews. Oath-taking had long been a practice by which individuals could swear an allegiance, and during the French Revolution it became increasingly associated with political activity.[95] Across the rebellious fleets in 1797, sailors swore oaths to 'stand true to the fleet' until their grievances were won, 'To be true and faithful one to another' or until 'the Cause we have Undertaken we Persevere in till accomplished'.[96] Some ships framed their oaths in even more extreme language. On the *Pompee*, sailors promised to promote the 'cause of Freedom with Equity', a phrase that had been used in a range of radical literature including William Godwin's republican tome *Enquiry Concerning Political Justice* in 1793.[97] Some oaths used the rhetoric of martyrdom to advance their case. Sailors on the *Defiance* valued their oath as 'Equal to our lives', while at the Nore sailors swore to be true to the cause 'to the laying down of my life'.[98] It is not clear, however, whether the taking of an oath automatically denoted guilt. The Articles of War did not forbid oath-taking, and most sailors would have known that only a few ringleaders would be tried in any future court martial. It is far more likely that these oaths were means of asserting solidarity and allegiance among often divided crews, safe in the knowledge that punishing everyone who swore was a practical impossibility. We know sailors took the act very seriously, with sailors taking it in turns to come forward and theatrically 'kiss the book' – often a Bible – while swearing the oath.[99]

How radical, then, were the mutinies of 1797? At Spithead the sailors' stated aims were defined by their moderation, and Lord Spencer freely acknowledged that 'the wages were undoubtedly too low in proportion to the times'. Even at the Nore, many of the demands were incidental as much as structural and refined rather than overturned existing regulations.[100] It has often been noted that issues such as impressment were not mentioned, though it is clear that this is something sailors felt strongly about. A ballad found on the *Repulse* compared sailors' coercion to 'slavery' and pitied those who had been condemned to 'oppression' in the 'Tender's loathsome hole'. Addresses produced by sailors critiqued the policy of 'turning over' men as a 'disgrace to British Liberty', or declared themselves as 'Prisoners ever since the war Commenc'd'.[101] Nonetheless, the grievances put forward were marked for the most part by their pragmatic nature, and the sailors were conscious that a fundamental restructuring of maritime labour was ambitious. The other issues highlighted at the Nore – the right to shore leave while in port, revisions to the Articles of War, an effective veto over officers and courts martial being made up of sailors and marines – were chosen as they involved no extra funding from the government. They did, however, signify a fundamental challenge to the naval status quo, a line the Admiralty was not prepared to cross.[102]

If their aims represented a broad spectrum of achievable demands, the rhetoric used across the rebellion was often far more heated and avowedly political. Sailors at Spithead represented themselves as 'poor, but loyal' sailors who had been 'trampled under foot' by 'tyrannical and malicious men in office'. The petition of the *Nymphe* complained that its crew were 'kept more like convicts than free Born Britons'.[103] The public addresses of the Nore mutineers used similarly incendiary language. While their demands to the Admiralty stated plainly that 'every man on a Ship coming into Harbour shall have liberty ... to go and see their friends & families', their public declaration stated that 'Liberty' was the 'Invaluable Privilege ... of an Englishman, the pride & Boast of all Britain & the Natural Rights of all'. Similarly, their demand to remove unpopular officers became a critique of those who 'oppressingly & tyrannically' used sailors 'as a parcel of slaves', while their demand for courts martial made up of sailors criticised the 'Cruel Lordly Officers' who held sway over discipline on board.[104] Ballads written by the Nore mutineers swore that they would 'banish all Tyrants', remove 'a set of [base] Villians' or break the chains of 'Bondage'.[105]

It was in this heady climate that sailors' wrote the declaration with which this book opened. This document heralding the arrival of the 'Age of Reason' in the Navy perhaps best demonstrates sailors' interpretation of political philosophy, framing their actions as an attempt to secure 'common rights' that had been taken away. Indeed, the focus on 'rights' dominates the mutineers' writings throughout 1797. The earliest petitions of April called for assistance in 'Recovering their Lawful Rights', while the public declarations of Spithead mutineers demanded 'the Recovery of our rights'. At Torbay, the sailors declared they were 'freeing ourselves from the tiranny [sic] and arbitrary power' and determined to maintain their 'rights and privileges'.[106] At the Nore, an 'address to the nation' described liberty as 'That invaluable privilege more particularly inherent to an Englishman – the pride & Boast of a Briton, the natural Right of all', one that had been 'denied to us'. External observers were alive to this context: the *Annual Register* noted that mutinies came about 'by the contagion of a general spirit of inquiry into rights, natural and conventional'.[107] Sailors also explicitly mentioned this in their letters to their families. John Mileham wrote that 'seamen will have their Rights before they sail', while Joseph Thompson, serving on one of the ships that sailed to join the mutiny from Yarmouth, described their actions as 'sticking out for their Rights and Wages'. Some sailors quoted Tom Paine directly. On 7 July 1797, John Lloyd, quartermaster of the gun vessel *Friendship*, freely admitted that 'he would stick up for the Rights of Man, and that he was a true Republican'.[108]

This was seditious talk, and despite the often heated political rhetoric, the majority of mutineers were determined to refute accusations that they were 'Jacobin' or 'Republican'. Even the Nore mutineers claimed in their addresses to be 'affronted' at being represented as 'Jacobins & Traitors' and rejected the suggestion that their aim was to 'adopt the plan of a Neighbouring Nation'.[109] Instead, the mutineers attempted to frame their actions as a form of conditional patriotism, in which their brave conduct in the war so far deserved more reward. The first petition of the Spithead mutineers described their loyalty and courage as 'unquestionable . . . as their Enemys can testify', while on the *London* sailors saw their demand for an increase in pay as 'worthey of the Conqeurs of the Glorious First of June'. Throughout they determined they would return to their duty if the French left port, and they also insisted that they would happily sing 'God Save the King' and 'Rule Britannia' and fight again once their grievances had been met.[110] On the *Galatea*, the ship that had left its station off Brest, the sailors lamented that they had been forced into such measures but made clear 'there is not a Man in the Gallatea but would voluntarily shed his last blood for his Country'.[111] The Nore mutineers also harnessed the language of loyalism when it suited them, insisting initially that they would return to their duty if the Dutch fleet left port and claiming that 'we possess a Degree of Loyalty & Attachment to our King and Country that has and will on every proper Occasion Shew itself'.[112] This might also explain the mutineers' reluctance to include impressment as a grievance, something that could easily be construed by the wider public as a lack of patriotic fervour.

Beyond this, it is possible to identify different strands of ideological thought among the mutineers. There is evidence that some at Spithead saw themselves as moderate reformers, aligning with opposition policies. It was for this reason that they sent their initial petition to the Whig leader Charles James Fox, and it explains their identification of English sailors as the 'Legitimate Sons of Liberty'. They believed the English Constitution was 'admirable' and 'well Calculated' but felt that they no longer had protection from it. All they asked was for the people of Britain to 'suffer their Pockets' a little more to reaffirm this faith in king and country.[113] Added to this were common Whig critiques of the war and its cost. On the *Pompee* sailors spoke of reforming Parliament, dismissing the sitting ministry and ending the war, something that 'could only be brought about by the Sailors' and by which 'they would be doing an Act of Charity to the Nation'.[114] Critiques of the Tory government were also common throughout the Nore uprising, where mutineer declarations lambasted the conduct of the 'present Ministers' who were sending the country to ruin and laid the blame for 'a tedious disgraceful war' on William Pitt.[115] The prime minister came in for some pretty brutal treatment throughout. The sailor John Durack declared that the mutinies were 'that Bugger Billy Pitt's fault', and effigies of the prime minister were displayed and mocked on the *Sandwich* and fired at on the *Grampus*. Even loyalist sailors found the government at fault. Theophilus King despaired at the sight of mutiny but placed the blame firmly in Whitehall: 'see what a situation Mr Pitt brought England in', he wrote.[116]

Despite their declarations to the contrary, there is evidence that several of the mutineers harboured more radical ideologies. We know that some mutineers wore red cockades in their hats, a clear reference to the French Revolution and which for Morgan Jones was 'the same as hoisting the red flag which I knew did not belong to the English Government'. William Gregory referred to the sailors' 'tyrannical Country', while George Shave stated that 'the Country had been oppressed for these five years that the war had been too long and now was the time to get themselves righted'.[117] One of the marines at Plymouth offered a public confession in which he acknowledged that his mind had been 'poisoned by reading the works of Tom Payne [sic]'.[118] There are also countless examples of republicanism in the Navy's ranks. Charles Chant offered many treasonable sentences, such as 'Damn and Buggar the King' and 'We want no King', while Thomas Jephson refused to sing 'God Save the King' as it 'was an old tune and ought to have been done away long since'.[119] Thomas Ashley was a committed democrat, who had 'traced History & could not discover any Good quality belonging' to George III, while William Guthrie also dismissed the king as 'a Bad Man' whose reign 'meant the ruin of the Nation'. Colin Brown of the *Phoenix* placed the sailors' struggles in more idealistic, almost Romantic terms, stating that 'they would have no Government but their own will the sea being wide enough and any country better than their own'. Some saw the conflict in terms of class: Michael Collins talked of a time when 'there would be soon no Sirs amongst us'.[120] By the end of the Nore mutiny, it is clear that some were considering the treasonable step of sailing their ships to France and handing them over to the French Convention. As one mutineer put it, this was the 'only government that understands the rights of man'.[121]

For all this radical talk, though, many sailors remained loyal. In the early stages of the mutiny, sailors applied to the clerk on the *Sandwich* and asked to be sent ashore sick 'for the purpose of getting out of the way' and others escaped in small boats. It is also clear that among those who remained, many were unhappy. Joseph Devonish prayed to be freed 'from such an unhappy business', while Rous Mabson, a pilot on board the *Nassau*, found himself a prisoner: 'We are unhappy with our situation but can't help it now.'[122] Elsewhere we find there was a well of loyalism on board even the most radical ships. Martin Welsh refused to join the mutiny on the *Pompee* as he did not want to 'hurt my Parents at home and the nation by so doing', while John Mountain declared 'it was a very wrong piece of business'.[123] The radicalism of the last few days of the Nore was for many a step too far. On the *Sandwich*, Alias Broadbury declared that 'I would rather see his neck at the yard arm' than see the ship sail to France, while Thomas Wood on the *Leopard* said he would rather be 'under a black flag' (in other words a pirate) than a foreign one. By the end of the Nore mutiny it was these loyalists who came to the fore, and for the first time they were able to find enough support to take back the ship. Throughout the mutinies, sailors who had remained loyal risked severe punishments. John Frederick Waters of the *Monmouth* was assaulted, put in irons for five days and then put on trial for 'conspiracy against the ship's company' when he resisted the mutiny.[124] These were men of conviction, for whom the language of loyalism so abundant in the 1790s was not just propaganda, but genuine patriotic conviction.

It was through actions, as much as words, that sailors conveyed their politics. In some ways the mutinies of 1797 represented traditional forms of maritime protest, withdrawing their labour until their demands were secured. However, they were also conducted in ways that reveal the influence of the Age of Revolutions. The creation of delegates – a term borrowed from the LCS – was a democratic act in itself, providing two men from each ship who were 'Impowered to act for the ship Company', who discussed issues with their ships' companies before making decisions communally. Nor did it go unnoticed by the press, with the *Morning Chronicle* declaring 'Representative Government actually established on board the British fleet', astonished that the Admiralty had 'gone to treat with a Convention of Delegates'.[125] In true democratic style, delegates and committee men were subject to immediate recall if they failed to reflect the interests of their crew. James Robertson and Thomas Sterling, delegates of the *Leopard*, were recalled for returning from shore drunk, while James Smart, on the *Grampus*, was removed for neglecting orders while on shore. The *Monmouth* replaced half of its initial committee 'in consequence of some of the first Committee not being liked by the Ship's Company'.[126] There was a limit to this democracy, however, and the committees were themselves capable of purging those who had become 'obnoxious' to them. Thomas McCann and Charles McCarthy, for instance, were expelled from the committee of the *Sandwich* on 22 May, accused of 'enflaming the minds of the people against the Committee'.[127]

When it came to discipline, the mutineers both adopted but also subverted traditional norms. In the early stages of the mutinies, lists of rules to govern behaviour were circulated and pinned up, and for the most part the conventions of naval discipline were followed as if little had changed: mutinous ships continued to flog sailors for drunkenness.[128] However, in other ways, hierarchies and traditions were subverted, sometimes gratuitously. At Spithead, while officers were initially allowed to keep their watches and give orders, the mutineers established a 'Counter-Watch of Surveillance' to assess officer behaviour, shredding their authority.[129] Sailors also began to run their own courts, trying men for a range of offences from the mundane to the political, and men who had previously been in positions of authority were targeted. On the *Mars*, for instance, Samuel Nelson was found guilty of 'Betraying the Confidence' of his shipmates and was punished with twenty-four lashes, while the boatswain of the *Proserpine* was found guilty of abusing the crew and was rowed past the mutinying ships with a rope around his neck in a show of ritual humiliation.[130] Quartermaster Charles Bowen was given twelve lashes for attempting to take hold of the helm out of the hands of a mutineer. The most extreme cases of retributive violence came on the *Monmouth*, where the master's mate, two midshipmen and a sergeant of marines were flogged for refusing to assist the mutineers, while the ship's surgeon was tarred and feathered.[131]

This uprooting of the naval status quo compelled the government to make a committed response. Pitt's ministry was no stranger to suppressive measures and, alarmed at the extent and nature of the rebellions, passed legislation in the summer of 1797 designed to deter any future uprisings. The Mutiny Act that came into law in June made it a capital crime to communicate with a mutinous ship, and the subsequent Unlawful Oaths Act threatened transportation of up to seven years for anyone caught administering a mutinous or seditious oath.[132] These Acts were read to naval crews and on some ships were hung up on board for 'publick inspection', though they were not always welcomed by the crews. On the *Phoenix*, the seaman Colin Brown described the reading as a 'pretty speech' of such quality that the king was either asleep or 'fucking the Queen' at the time he made it, words for which he was subsequently hanged.[133] Aware that legislation alone could not hope to control sailors, the government also launched official investigations into the causes and motivations of the rebellions, with a particular focus on links with political organisations such as the London Corresponding Society. Two London magistrates, Aaron Graham and Daniel Williams, reported back in late June, and while they had plenty of evidence of political pamphlets being circulated, and anecdotal examples of men of 'mischievous dispositions' visiting the Nore, they concluded that no 'club or society in the kingdom . . . have in smallest degree been able to influence the proceedings of the mutineers'.[134]

Sailors would therefore have to pay the price. The mutineers of Spithead and Plymouth had received blanket pardons, but given the seriousness of the east coast mutinies, no such clemency was offered. The Admiralty planned to bring the mutineers to trial without delay, but they faced a quandary, for tens of thousands of men had been involved in the rebellions and it was logistically impossible to try more than a small minority.[135] Added to this, the perpetual shortage of maritime labour and continued concerns about the loyalty of the wider population meant that it was in the state's interest to portray the mutinies as the work of a dissident few rather than a vast rebellion. Here too the Admiralty had a problem, for establishing exactly who had been involved proved difficult. Those who had acted as delegates or committeemen were obvious candidates for trial, as were the authors of petitions and committee orders who could be identified by their handwriting. Additionally, lists of the sailors 'most conspicuous' in the mutinies were provided to authorities by naval officers returning to their ships. However, it was widely understood that many of the ringleaders had escaped or had been quietly operating behind the scenes. Captain John Knight of the *Montagu* noted pointedly that 'the greatest promoters' of the mutinies were 'generally the least conspicuous'. Keith's solution was to round up the 'ten most guilty men' on each ship, regardless of their degree of involvement in the mutiny, and in the end there was considerable randomness in deciding who was charged.[136]

The courts martial of the naval mutineers were dramatic events, closely monitored by the press and followed as assiduously as the famous 'Treason Trials' in the mid-1790s. On the face of it, they had the appearance of even-handedness: the defendants were given time to prepare their cases, and many of the trials lasted for days as evidence was heard. Elsewhere we find courts unwilling to be generous. Discursive defences, as might be allowed on land, were ruled out, with the president of one trial intervening to announce that 'We are not at the Old Bailey' and cautioning that 'The Court is not to be trifled with'.[137] In some of the more publicised cases there was little chance of an acquittal. The first man to be put on trial was the most famous mutineer of all, Richard Parker, whose guilt was assumed from the start. 'You may prove almost anything you like against him, for he has been guilty of everything that's bad,' wrote the Admiralty Secretary Evan Nepean, and he advised one court martial judge that the evidence was enough 'to dispose of a dozen scoundrels of Parker's Description'.[138] Queries about the legality of the charges were swept aside. Captain Riou, who took part in Parker's trial, received a note from a lawyer querying some of the evidence that had been admitted and hoping that 'Clamour & Prejudices' would not see a 'helpless undefended man' suffer.[139] These concerns were ignored, however, and no leniency was shown to the man who had become the face of the Nore mutiny. Parker was duly convicted and sentenced to hang. 'I am to Die a Martyr in the Cause of Humanity,' he stated proudly at his trail, and he was executed on 30 June 1797.[140]

This was the first act in what became a programme of unprecedented naval retribution. Four hundred and twelve sailors from the east coast fleets were held for trial: fifty-two were condemned to death, of whom twenty-nine were ultimately executed, with the remainder 'recommended for the king's mercy' and given a lesser punishment. A further twenty-nine men were imprisoned or transported.[141] Capital punishments were also awarded to sailors of individual ships at Plymouth and Spithead that had mutinied in May and June, including two men of the *Pompee*, eleven of the *Saturn*, two of the *Royal Sovereign* and four men who mutinied at the Cape. Of the four marines charged with mutiny at Plymouth, three were executed by firing squad, while the fourth was sentenced to 1,000 lashes. Deemed incapable of bearing more than 416, the punishment was halted and he was soon after transported to Botany Bay. In total an astonishing fifty-nine men were executed for mutiny in 1797, more than in any previous year, in what amounted to a shocking naval reckoning.[142]

The purpose of these executions was brutal deterrence, a warning to other seamen. Executions took place in front of assembled crews with sombre theatricality, while armed sailors from loyal ships were brought on board to ensure there were no disturbances. After the executions were carried out, the Articles of War were read to the crew, the whole event designed to impress on their minds 'the fatal Consequences that may arise from a Mutinous and disorderly Behaviour'.[143] Corpses became symbols. Two men of the *Saturn* were hung in chains where passing ships could see them, a violent reminder of what happened to those who erred in their duty.[144] The execution of the Plymouth marines was preceded by an hour-long march through the city's streets to the Hoe, in which the sentenced men were followed by their coffins and a band playing a funereal march. After the executions were carried out, their bloodied corpses were displayed to the marine regiments on duty, and in the aftermath a print was produced and circulated to locals offering a solemn commentary on their dying words.[145] Even displays of clemency were brutal in their theatre. Two mutineers of the *Pompee* were hooded and taken to the yard arm before the commutation of their sentences was announced; both men broke down on hearing the news.[146]

The response of naval officers was equally extreme. Some, such as Collingwood, were nervous about the precedent that had been set, concerned that some demands had been granted not as 'acts of favour' but 'as rights extorted from Government'.[147] Nelson, stationed in the Mediterranean, was also convinced that mutineers needed to be made an example of:

> If government gives in, what can we except of this fleet? ... Mankind are all alike and if these people find their brethren in England get their ignorant wishes complied with by being troublesome, it is human nature of others to take the same methods.[148]

In the subsequent months and years many became paranoid about the prospect of mutiny. On some ships severe steps had to be taken to break up unsettled crews, and the officers of the *Saturn* discharged twenty men perceived to be 'the most dangerous' and replaced the ship's entire party of marines. Captain Worsley turned the *Calypso* into an armed camp, posting marine sentries with drawn swords and loaded pistols everywhere, giving them orders 'to fire and kill' anyone moving about the ship without permission.[149] Even words out of place resulted in punishment: John Morrison on board the *Phoenix* was heard saying that 'the ship is as bad as a Convict Ship' and was given fifty lashes, while on the *Saturn*, James Diabell was given the same punishment for offering to speak for the crew.[150]

It is not clear how effective these policies of retribution were. Certainly the executions of 1797 put self-preservation at the forefront of many sailors' minds, and the incentive to inform on colleagues became ever greater. In August 1797, the 'great part' of the ship's company of the *Royal Sovereign* came forward to betray two sailors plotting a mutiny, and it was a seaman, John Hamnell, who told his captain that the ship's company of the *St George* were about to mutiny in July 1797.[151] On some ships attempts were made to repair relationships, and a number of crews sent petitions of apology to their officers. That these tended to come from the more 'radical' ships suggests that their purpose was tactical as much as a genuine call for forgiveness, and they used deliberately submissive language to make their point. The petition of the *Saturn* 'humbly [hoped] that whatever may have happened During these times may be forgoten', while others followed the government line and blamed the unrest on a few 'Ill Disposed' people.[152] The petition of the *Mars* saw 493 sailors sign their name underneath an apology for being 'in Open and Direct Violation to the laws of our Country'. Tensions and discontent remained, however. There were also countless trials for mutinous behaviour in the latter months of 1797, and incidents where sailors assaulted those who had testified against the mutineers.[153]

Perhaps most revealing is that naval officers were now more willing to order brutal punishments for anything that approached mutinous behaviour.[154] In early July 1797, sailors on board the *St George* presented a petition signed by 'a great number of men' asking that prisoners' lives be spared, signing an oath and asking that certain officers be sent from the ship and fresh ones appointed. These were demands no greater than those asked for at Spithead, but by this point leniency was long gone, and the four ringleaders were all hanged.[155] In the subsequent months, any act deemed preparatory to mutiny was punished with little mercy. William Docton was punished with 200 lashes for reading aloud a paper that protested an unfair punishment and calling on sailors to 'stand by one another', while Charles Duff, who had presented a round robin petition and complained of cruelty, 'bad bread' and prize money, was punished with 500 lashes.[156] By the same token, courts martial looked favourably on officers who had committed violent acts in defence. During a mutiny on the *Kingfisher*, Captain John Maitland killed one sailor and injured another five who had cheered and hissed at him. While the court martial judges accepted that he had reacted in a manner that was 'hasty', he was acquitted and praised for his 'spirited and successful' conduct.[157] If some sailors hoped that the mutinies' resolution would usher in a new era of understanding and consensus on board naval ships, these illusions were soon crushed.

The mutinies of 1797 represented the largest and most intense programme of naval protest in Britain's history. This was a movement in every sense, for while individual instances of rebellion occurred for specific reasons, each was intimately connected to the others.[158] The rebellions at Spithead directly influenced those that followed at Plymouth and Torbay, while the outbreaks at the Nore and Yarmouth took these initial ambitions further. Their global imitators at Madeira, the Cape and in the Indian Ocean were closely aligned in aims and deeds to the those that took place around the coast of Britain. The one constant throughout was the sailors' desire to improve their working conditions based on a firm understanding of their rights, and a reliance on their own capacity for action to force a result. In this, they were avowedly appropriating and redirecting the political culture of the time. Among the sailors who participated in the naval mutinies were radicals, reformers, republicans, loyalists and conservatives, alongside a mass of no fixed opinion. Here was Britain's Age of Revolutions, writ large in a maritime context. The retribution that followed must also be seen in the context of the British state's wider policy of political repression towards those who expressed dissent. Indeed, here the extremity of naval punishments allowed naval elites to punish miscreants in greater numbers – and in far more lethal fashion – than the British government's attempts to subdue political dissidents on shore.

The longer-term legacy of the mutinies also remained unclear. There would not be another fleetwide mutiny for a century, but the attempt to deter further naval rebellions failed. As we will see in the final chapter, mutiny and mutinous behaviour became *more* common in 1798. Perhaps the most damaging result, however, was the broken relationships between the Navy's sailors and the wider British public. The appearance of 'Delegates in Council' had prompted fears and anxieties that only grew stronger over the summer months, and Lord William Russell was not alone in wondering whether 'the people of England can rely on seamen ... for their future defence and protection?'[159] Government propaganda attempted to dismiss the mutinies as the machinations of a radical few who 'misguided the Seamen by false representations', but there was no escaping the momentous nature of what had happened.[160] One issue of Hannah More's *Cheap Repository Tracts*, a bastion of conservative thinking during the 1790s, compared the rebellions to a landlubber going to sea, with disastrous consequences for him and his family. It urged that every Briton should 'mind his place' and mocked the idea that Jack Tar had become 'a legislator'.[161] The sailor had become a potent political symbol, and the final months of 1797 saw a battle over its representation play out across British popular culture.

SEVEN

A TALE OF TWO SAILORS
Camperdown and Naval Propaganda

For Britain, 1797 was very much the worst of times. Financial paralysis, a manpower shortage, unrest in Ireland and the ever-present threat of invasion formed the backdrop to a year of crisis that appeared never-ending to those who lived through it. While newspapers reported calamity after calamity, those in government became almost inured to bad news. In May 1797, the young Pittite politician George Canning wrote a few ironic stanzas to Secretary at War William Windham, urging him to hold a celebration for a 'day of *no* disaster':

> Come, Windham! celebrate with me
> This day of joy and jubilee,
> This day of *no* disaster.
> Our government is *not* o'erturned—
> Huzza! Our fleet has *not* been burned,
> Our army's *not* the master.[1]

The naval mutinies mentioned in the penultimate line were therefore merely the latest in a series of blows to the government. Canning wrote this verse just as one set of uprisings were coming to a resolution at Spithead, and no sooner had he committed pen to paper than news of the mutiny at the Nore arrived in London, prompting further anguish on the part of Pitt's ministry. A few days later, the Yorkshire MP Sir William Milner stood up in Parliament to deplore the situation to which the country had been reduced: 'the ill success of the War, the

Mutiny of the Fleet, and the failure of the Bank', to the extent that 'he almost despaired of its ever retrieving its former prosperity'.[2] Adversity appeared to be never-ending. 'In this era of Revolutions, wrote the *Oracle*, 'events of the most important nature succeed each other with astonishing rapidity ... now the Mutiny at the Nore drives Ireland completely out of our heads.'[3]

If the naval mutinies were politically damaging, they also threatened a relationship that long pre-dated Pitt's government. As we saw in the previous chapter, the rebellions of 1797 offered the most concrete and significant example of sailors' political activity and shook the naval establishment to its core. More than that, though, the mutinies shattered the British public's confidence in the men protecting the country. Across the eighteenth century, the image of the sailor had been ubiquitous, channelled through the frequently caricatured figure of 'Jack Tar'. This was a complex and sometimes problematic representation, but for most Britons, the sailor was a comforting, patriotic figure.[4] The mutinies of 1797, however, showed him in an entirely different light. Arriving in the middle of Britain's *annus horribilis*, and in a political culture fraught with anxiety over the secretive meetings of Jacobin radicals, the sailors' actions were charged with revolutionary meaning. Far from the reassuring image of bluff manhood, the sailor became a subversive and potentially radical figure, capable of undermining Britain's constitution and way of life. At a stroke, a community that had hitherto been heralded as the natural defenders of British interests was transformed into something far more threatening.

The events of 1797 also prompted the British public to engage with sailors not as a generic mass, but as real individuals. Whereas previously artists and commentators had disseminated a fictional 'Jack Tar', in the summer and autumn of 1797 the actions of two individuals meant that the British sailor was given a real name and a face. The first of these was Richard Parker, the man elected 'President' of the sailors who mutinied at the Nore. He was one of the few mutineers to be publicly named, and in the months that followed his features became synonymous with subversive activity and treason. The second sailor to come to public prominence was Jack Crawford, who was publicly fêted after he performed a distinctive act of bravery during the Battle of Camperdown in October 1797, a few months after the mutinies had ended. These sailors offered two competing ideas of who the British sailor was, and what he symbolised. While Parker became a symbol of the Jacobin revolutionary, Crawford represented the honest and dutiful sailor, celebrated as a brave, noble and patriotic figure. In the highly charged atmosphere of Britain's 'year of disasters', these contrasting representations were taken up by journalists, pamphleteers, artists and engravers, each of whom had reasons to utilise the sailors' deeds for their own ends.[5] Most notably, politicians too intervened in this battle over representations, castigating Parker as an errant exception while celebrating Crawford as an exemplar of British naval manhood.

Sailors had long been the subject of public fascination. Robinson Crusoe was merely the most famous of early eighteenth-century depictions, while Tobias Smollett's novels of the mid-century used stereotypical representations of naval seamen to offer satirical commentary on emergent ideas of national identity.[6] The earliest visual representation of the sailor was produced in 1739 with the print *The British Hercules*, a hawkish satire on the unwillingness of Walpole's government to go to war with Spain which depicted a sturdy seaman impatiently waiting for orders.[7] In the decades that followed, the sailor became a staple of British culture, his centrality to British interests increasingly self-evident to a nation defined by its maritime prowess. This was by no means a consistent depiction, and he held many contradictory positions in the popular imagination. The sailor was frequently depicted as a romantic hero who suffered long separations from his loved ones but when on land could be transformed into a womanising reprobate. The unfortunate men who were press-ganged deserved the nation's pity, but the violent, trouble-making seamen on shore leave warranted only condemnation. By the late 1780s, the most common images were those that celebrated his aggressive masculinity, admirable when turned against Britain's enemies: Robert Sayer's print *An English Jack-Tar giving Monsieur a Drubbing* was representative of a wave of material culture that depicted burly sailors beating up their effeminate French equivalents.[8] If anything, these mixed images obscured any real effort to engage with the individuals who made up the Navy. For most people, they remained a faceless, anonymous mass, open to crude caricature.[9]

These cultural media all had one thing in common: the British sailor was fundamentally loyal. While he was sometimes overly aggressive – and while you might not want to be married to him – no one could doubt his fidelity and devotion to the nation. This image, however, was devastated by the impact of the French Revolutionary Wars, in which the British public was confronted with a much more threatening reality, one in which sailors were neither uncomplaining nor faithful. The appearance of resistance, and then widespread mutiny in the fleet, demonstrated that the British sailor's priorities were not aligned with those of the 'nation', and newspapers reacted with horror. When the *St James's Chronicle* reported the mutinies at the Nore, they revealed circumstances that 'reflect disgrace on the name of a British Seaman', while numerous other organs declared their disgust at the sailors' conduct.[10] Caricaturists replaced 'Jack Tar' with something far more menacing. Isaac Cruikshank, who in 1794 had produced a memorable image depicting sailors enthusiastically thrashing the French enemy at the Battle of the Glorious First of June, offered a new print, his *Delegates in Council*, in which sailors were portrayed as subversive dissidents.[11] Feelings ran high, and newspapers and citizens alike called for examples to be made of sailors. Writing to a friend, Elizabeth Carter spoke for many genteel Britons:

I was never so much alarmed by any circumstances of our political situation, as by the horrid mutiny of our sailors ... It may teach us humility . . . when, what we considered as our greatest human defence, was turned against ourselves . . . It must be hoped, that such as are the least guilty, and escape capital punishment, may be entirely banished from the country, which they have endeavoured to destroy.[12]

There is evidence that this chimed with the wider popular mood: the Admiralty received several letters from members of the public with suggestions for how they should punish the mutineers, including one recommending that they should be transported to Botany Bay along with their entire families.[13]

Not everyone saw these events in such black and white terms.[14] In the early weeks of the mutiny, a number of Whig and radical publications suggested that the sailor's grievances had some foundation: the *Evening Mail*, for instance, was happy to admit that many naval officers had been 'obnoxious' and deserved to be expelled from their ships.[15] The loyalist press initially attempted to represent Jack Tar as fundamentally faithful, if temporarily errant. Following the resolution of the Spithead mutiny, Martha Saumarez spoke for many when she explained how the sailors had been redeemed in her eyes:

Happily She [Britain] has <u>weather'd</u> one of the greatest perils that ever threaten'd her By the late alarming Mutiny in the Fleet, with heartfelt pleasure I acquaint Thee that Discipline & Order are once more restor'd . . . This Mutiny while it stands recorded as the most serious that ever has threatened this Country must at the same time excite the astonishment of the World at the Order & Regularity with which these men conducted themselves who at other times, when left to their own Conduct . . . are the most Disorderly Beings upon the Earth! It is a great satisfaction to perceive that there was no disaffection amongst them – for on the contrary they express as fully attach'd as ever to their Country & are gone to Sea with Hearty Wishes. They may have an opportunity of giving the French a sound Drubbing . . .[16]

The figure of the loyal sailor was certainly resilient, and throughout April and early May, numerous papers opted to take stances that maintained the image of the 'loyal tar'. Papers noted the ongoing maintenance of discipline on board and celebrated the sailors' return to their ships in May.[17]

The subsequent mutinies at the Nore and Yarmouth, however, saw public trust decimated, and condemnation of the sailor reached fever point. Some ministerial papers attempted to direct blame towards outside influence – the *True Briton*, for example, suggested that a radical attorney had infiltrated the fleet – but most condemned the Navy's sailors.[18] The *Morning Herald* critiqued those few papers that had offered 'fawning' treatments and pointed to 'The refractory spirit of the Seamen', which had been manifested

> in a manner that reflects very little credit on their boasted loyalty and attachment to their country's cause. What! the natural defenders of Old England refuse to put to sea, and sluggishly remain in port, under a frivolous pretext, when her coasts are menaced by a daring and enterprising foe! Such behaviour is surely unworthy the character of British Seamen.[19]

The *Oracle* critiqued those who attempted to 'soothe the mutineers' by extolling the virtues of the sailors, noting that the 'People of England' saw nothing but 'treachery, disloyalty, and at base a sordid selfishness' in those who were usually 'the most favoured portion of the community'. The following month, it noted more sagely that while sailors were once figures 'treated as the *favourite children of the public*', the mutinies had upturned the service's staging 'in the public estimation'.[20] Sailors were, in the eyes of one pamphleteer, 'but a shadow of the proudest bulwark of the country', characterised by 'confusion, disorder, irregularity, discontent, and oppression'. One organ described them as 'worse than the pirates – the monsters of the sea'.[21]

This new-found treasonous reputation was not lost on sailors themselves, who were only too aware that their character was being manipulated in the public press. They were active agents in the construction of their image, and during the mutinies they paid considerable attention to how they were being represented. The Spithead mutineers, for instance, responded to accusations that their actions were inconsistent with the 'characteristics as British Seamen'.[22] Individual sailors were also alive to the risk they were taking by rebelling. One worried that 'English sailors were once the ornament of their country', but now he was 'afraid they were about to do something which would clap a stamp on their character which would never be recovered'.[23] The Nore mutineers also attempted to control their image. One proclamation stated that those on shore 'ascribe Treason and Treachery to a British seaman. Good God what a Thought, a Thought that never enter'd the Brest of a British Tar'.[24] Parker was himself alive to the way his 'character' had been 'improperly represented in public prints', and this formed part of his court martial defence. Throughout, he adopted the mantle of the honest, bluff sailor: 'I hope nothing can be expected from me but plain facts', he stated, 'as I cannot be expected to dress up my defence in that pompous language which a Lawyer might have done.'[25]

Unique among the mutineers, Parker achieved the status of a celebrity criminal, and his actions spawned stories, rumours and a variety of material culture. It is not clear how far his deeds warranted this condemnation, for Parker seems to have had no role in planning or instigating the mutiny at the Nore, and, despite the grand title of 'President', his ability to shape policy was always doubtful and was certainly never absolute: the most recent study suggests that Parker's role was that of glorified spokesman.[26] Nonetheless, he became a subject of considerable fascination for the British public and in due course became a convenient scapegoat, much as Fletcher Christian had done following the mutiny on the *Bounty* in 1789.[27] This was in no small part due to the actions of the British government, who did all they could to maximise his notoriety. In the latter stages of the mutiny, 'wanted' notices for Parker were issued and widely circulated, and a £500 reward was offered for the capture of 'the Mutineer Chief at the Nore', who, it was said, 'stands charged with various acts of mutiny, treason, and rebellion'. These offered a detailed description, instructing the populace to look for a man of about thirty years of age, of a dark complexion, with a prominent nose and dark eyes, who dressed in a 'very slovenly manner' and wore his black hair untied and uncropped. To discredit him further Parker was mentioned 'not as a sailor, but as a *supernumerary seaman* on board the *Sandwich*'.[28] This was untrue, but it served to further isolate him as an exceptional, unique presence on board the nation's ships.

Parker's trial and execution on 30 June was an exercise in stage-managed scapegoating. As we have seen, he was given his own trial, and his execution took place a month before other sailors were sentenced to death for the same crime. Further steps were taken to ensure that he alone bore the brunt of the national anguish for the recent conduct of its sailors. An account of Parker's execution was widely circulated in the press – and subsequently in pamphlet form, bearing an image of the condemned man on the scaffold preparing to be hanged – portraying Parker as a penitent sinner. 'I acknowledge the justice of the sentence under which I suffer', he was reported to have said, 'and I hope that my death might be deemed a sufficient atonement, and save the lives of others.'[29] Images of Parker abounded, both in print form and as frontispieces for accounts of the trial and execution, which served a range of purposes. *The Execution of Richard Parker*, published on 8 July 1797, just days after his hanging, depicted a figure gesturing towards a gibbet in the far distance, a cautionary warning to other sailors who might follow a similar path. Other images offered a more positive view of the man: one had him tendering a list of grievances to Vice Admiral Buckner, while another popular print offered a sympathetic, even heroic, portrait. Their production and consumption spoke of a fascination with Parker and suggested a more complex figure than government propaganda suggested.[30]

Indeed, while Parker's vilification was effective in some circles, it was not fully successful. Parker's conduct during his trial and execution sparked considerable public sympathy, and it seems likely that many of those who consumed news of his final moments did so admiringly. Six days after Parker's death, the government-supporting *Oracle* questioned the intentions of those of their countrymen who had 'laboured so much to exalt the character of Parker' and despaired of those who were presenting his deeds as heroic.[31] There was intense public interest in the morbid story of his subsequent exhumation by his wife Ann to ensure he received the proper Christian burial denied him by the Navy – 'like a Gentleman, as he had been bred', noted the *Star*.[32] Initially buried in a nondescript naval graveyard at Sheerness, Ann secretly disinterred the body and took it to the Hoop and Horseshoe pub in Tower Hill, where crowds – many of them sailors – gathered to pay their respects. There was much governmental alarm about the sympathetic throngs that gathered to see his body as it was moved, which only dispersed when London's mayor personally obtained Ann's permission to have Richard's body buried in the vault of St Mary Matfelon (also known as St Mary, Whitechapel) in London's East End. Shaken by the response and ever conscious of the public mood, the government urged the Admiralty to ensure that subsequent executions of mutineers took place with much less fanfare and to 'prevent the bodies from being exposed to the public view'.[33]

The government's vilification of Parker was the first act in a wider effort to rehabilitate the image of 'Jack Tar'. One pamphlet noted how 'Every Lover of His Country has seen, with concern and regret, the spirit of MUTINY which has lately discovered itself in a part of the BRITISH NAVY' and how the manner and timing of the mutiny had been 'disgraceful to the promoters of it'. However, it hoped to 'cast a Veil over the past' by offering hints to 'BRITISH SEAMEN, who have a Character attached to them, which they should be ever proud to merit, – that of being respected at home, and feared abroad'.[34] Isaac Cruikshank, ever a useful weathervane for the cultural representation of the sailor, published a print in 1797 entitled *True Blue! Or Britain's jolly tars paid off at Portsmouth* that depicted the familiar, unthreatening image of the sailor being happy with his lot.

Newspapers also joined in these attempts, with one song published in the *Oracle* calling on Britons to forget the mutinous events and seek comfort in the prospect of future battles exhibiting British naval glory:

> Yet still respect the British Tar
> Remember his past merit
> And once again in hottest war
> He'll shew his daring spirit.[35]

A play by John Cartwright Cross entitled *The Raft; or, Both Sides of the Water* and performed in the aftermath of the mutinies was ostensibly about the ongoing threat of invasion from France. However, the attention of the audience was directed to the main protagonist, Patrick O'Bowling, a loyal Irish sailor who dutifully helped defend the British nation.[36] Taken together, these media represented a concerted push to restore the sailor to his previous prominence and reputation.

Once again, sailors played a role in controlling their public image. The 'apology' letters written by sailors after the Nore attempted to portray the mutinies as a temporary diversion. One such document referred to the recent 'unhappy event which has stained the character of the British tar' and hoped that their return to duties would provide an opportunity 'to be redeemed by future bravery and a steady perseverance in their country's cause. We sincerely wish the enemy may give us an opportunity of manifesting our loyalty to our King [and] our steady attachment to the Constitution.'[37] In October 1797, Britain's sailors were offered such a chance. Following years of blockade, the Dutch fleet stationed at the Texel finally left port and sailed towards Britain. The North Sea Fleet, which only months before had been in a state of mutiny, scrambled to repel the Dutch enemy, fighting a battle off the small village of Camperduin in north Holland. The subsequent victory, which became known by its anglicised name 'Camperdown', offered Britons a naval triumph after months of crisis and a narrative of formerly recalcitrant crews successfully fighting the enemy. It also delivered a story pregnant with symbolic meaning. During the action, a young sailor named Jack Crawford performed an act of bravery and provided a potential antidote to fears over the trustworthiness of sailors. With invasion fears escalating and public trust in the Navy and government at rock bottom, an alternative figure was needed to rehabilitate the image of the sailor. If Richard Parker was a bogeyman, in Crawford the state hoped to find a figure of redemption.

The Battle of Camperdown, fought on 12 October 1797, was conducted in the shadow of the naval mutinies. Britain's opponent was the new Batavian Republic, a key French ally established in 1795 by occupying revolutionary armies. Though it subscribed to similar democratic principles as France, it remained an independent nation with an autonomous foreign policy and, most troublingly for Britain, a powerful navy of twenty-eight ships with easy access to the North Sea. By 1797 Britain's North Sea Fleet had been blockading the Dutch fleet at the Texel River for two years, though it was a nondescript force made up of smaller ships of dubious seaworthiness.[38] What is more, the mutiny of the North Sea Fleet had decimated the forces under Vice Admiral Adam Duncan's control, and during the mutinies the blockade had been conducted by the two ships that had avoided all-out mutiny, his flagship the *Venerable* and the *Adamant*.[39] These two vessels sailed back and forth within sight of the Dutch coast, signalling to imaginary ships beyond the horizon in an (ultimately successful) attempt to persuade the Dutch that the blockade was continuing in full force.[40] It was not until October 1797 that the Dutch fleet successfully left port, and even then, it remains unclear why they did so. There was no prospect of a successful invasion attempt, nor was there any plan to connect with French naval forces further west. It seems most likely that the Batavian Committee for Foreign Affairs intended to fight the British North Sea

Fleet to make a gesture against Britain and re-establish Dutch honour following their defeat by the British at Saldanha Bay the previous year.[41]

The attempt was certainly opportunistic. In early October, Duncan returned with the fleet to Yarmouth to victual and refit, leaving only a small observation squadron, and the Dutch force took advantage of the opening: on 8 October 1797, fifteen Dutch ships of the line emerged into the North Sea. On hearing the news of the Dutch escape, Duncan got under way immediately, and by 12 October he had sighted the enemy fleet. Both fleets attempted to form a line of battle, but with the Dutch edging into shallow water, Duncan decided he did not have time for careful manoeuvring and hoisted the signal for a 'General chase' before directing his ships to 'pass through the Enemy's Line and Engage from Leeward'. The British ships approached the Dutch in two columns almost at a right angle, led by the flagship the *Venerable* and Richard Onslow's *Monarch*. In the subsequent battle there was little in the way of tactical sophistication, for the speed of the British approach – and the condition of Duncan's ships – meant maintaining order was all but impossible. A study of Duncan's log shows that he made no fewer than forty-four signals between 6.15 a.m. and 11.49 a.m., when the fleets finally clashed, but it seems they were largely ignored by his captains. The commander of the *Belliqueux* gave up attempting to follow Duncan's instructions, summarising the approach neatly as 'Dam . . . Up wi' the hel-lem and gang into the middle o'it'. In the chaos there were many instances of friendly fire, for example when the *Agincourt* fired into the *Monmouth*, and the *Lancaster* into the *Isis*.[42]

The battle broke down into a series of individual fights in which the heavier British guns began to have a telling effect.[43] It was one of the bloodiest actions fought during the Revolutionary Wars, as cannon balls smashed through timbers, creating vicious shards of wood that cut flesh to the bone. In total the British suffered 823 casualties and the Dutch 1,160, concentrated in the ships that were at the forefront of the action. The *Monarch*'s list of officers and men wounded lists 103 sailors from 599, a total of 17 per cent, significantly higher than other comparable

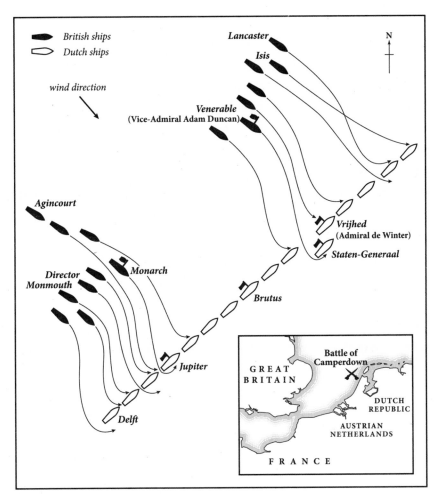

Map 8: Battle of Camperdown.

naval battles of the era.[44] The surgeon of the *Ardent*, Robert Young, has left a searing testimony that captures the damage inflicted on bodies:

> Melancholy cries for assistance were addressed to me from every side by the wounded and dying, and piteous moans and bewailing from pain and despair ... Many of the worst wounded were stoical beyond belief ... when news of the shattering victory was brought down to them, they raised a cheer and declared they regretted not the loss of their limbs.[45]

This last is hard to believe, but the fervour with which sailors fought was impressive. One by one, Dutch ships surrendered to the onslaught of gunnery, and by the end of the battle the British had captured seven ships of the line, one of which was wrecked, and two frigates. Duncan's dispatches acknowledge the 'truly British spirit' of his crews, though one notable omission was Captain John Williamson of the *Agincourt*, who had failed to engage the enemy at any stage. Later court-martialled for negligence, he was found guilty, demoted to bottom of the post captain list and denied the chance of further service.[46]

For most sailors involved, there was little pleasure in victory and there was considerable anger directed towards those ships that were seen to have shirked their duty. Joseph Samain reported to his parents that 'our admiral says it was the hardis [hardest] battle that was ever fought by two fleets' but noted pointedly that 'three of our ships did not come into the action not any thing to speak of w[h]ich did look cowardly'.[47] Richard Greenhalgh, who served on the *Powerful*, was pleased just to have come through alive. 'I am very happy to inform you that I got through this action with out any damage,' he wrote to his family, 'w[h]ich will bee of great satisfaction to you as well as my self.'[48] From the perspective of the officer corps, the valour of the sailors had gone some distance to overcoming doubts about their fidelity; in fact, it was a naval officer who came under fire for his conduct. Some officers made the chance for redemption explicit. As his ship closed on the enemy, Captain James Walker of the *Monmouth* exhorted his crew to take the opportunity of 'washing the stain off your characters in the blood of your foes', and he was not disappointed. In the aftermath of battle, he wrote to the Admiralty Secretary, Evan Nepean, to relay that 'All the officers and Men of His Majesty's Ship did their duty as became British Seamen', while 'the exertions of the Men strongly evinced how much they wished to expunge from the records of their Country the remembrance of their ever having forgot their duty'.[49]

Why did the sailors at Camperdown fight? How was it that a series of crews that only months earlier had been in open rebellion against the British state came to fight so fervently on its behalf? We have very few sources written by the sailors who took part, and the subsequent accounts by naval officers and administrators such as Nepean do not allow the most impartial window into the minds of their crews. Nonetheless, we can make some deductions. Firstly, we should highlight the genuine patriotic instincts of the majority of British sailors. Throughout the mutinies of 1797, most of those involved were adamant about their desire to fight for their country if their demands were met, and there is no reason to think these convictions disappeared following the defeat of the east coast mutinies: indeed, it is notable that it was the order to sail the fleet to France that brought them to an end. This is not to say all sailors were dedicated patriots, of course, but the prospect of further mass protests looked bleak in the autumn months of 1797. It seems likely that, as we saw when discussing the motivations of impressed sailors, many simply resigned themselves to their fate and focused their energies on finding ways to survive. This would explain the rash of 'apology' letters offered in the months after the mutinies, as well as the fervour with which the sailors at Camperdown fought.

It is useful also to make a distinction between the desire to protest and the will to fight. Even if sailors had doubts about their conditions of service, once at sea they had little control over the movement of their ship, and few alternatives when an enemy fleet appeared on the horizon. Their options were reduced to basic calculations of 'fight or flight', with the latter particularly difficult on a ship of the line. Sailors could hide in the lower reaches of a vessel, where they might avoid the worst ravages of enemy gunnery, but this was hardly a place of great safety, and likely a lethal one were the ship to sink. Added to these basic instincts was peer pressure and the genuine desire to help one's shipmates. In the heat of battle, the thoughts of combatants rarely turn to high politics; instead, the history of warfare tells us that protagonists fight not just because it offers the best chance of survival, but also for the men who stand beside them. Historians are still unpicking the layers of camaraderie that govern a unit's will to fight, and the frenzied emotions in the 'face of battle' are notoriously difficult to uncover.[50] However, it seems sensible to assume that, as with any number of military forces, sailors at Camperdown fought for their messmates and friends as much as they did for their king and country. We might even conjecture that while the recent mutinies had seen ships riven with internal conflict, specific cliques and messes on board ship might even have been hardened by the recent turmoil.

Whatever the reality, the government did everything it could in the aftermath of the battle to emphasise the sailors' new-found sense of duty. This was a deliberate attempt to rehabilitate the reputation of the sailor: in a telling act of political theatre, King George III travelled down to the Nore, the site of the recent mutiny, to welcome the sailors returning to their anchorage and publicly thanked 'those brave fellows . . . for defending me, protecting my people and preserving my country'.[51] His visit was subsequently immortalised in Andrew Franklin's musical entertainment *A Trip to the Nore*, first performed at Drury Lane on 9 November 1797, which avoided any mention of the mutinies.[52] Other steps were taken to correct the prevailing narrative of disloyalty. Duncan presented the king with a petition to pardon some 180 mutineers still in prison, which he granted, while the London Common Council announced that seamen were once again the 'guardians of the realm'.[53]

Newspapers also sought to use the battle to draw a line under the recent upheavals. The *Oracle* focused explicitly on the sailors' act of atonement. '[L]et us not forget the . . . gallant tars, who so bravely followed and executed the commands of their leaders,' it noted, and it made clear that the sailors had redeemed themselves:

> If they suffered in the opinion of the Public in a moment of delirium, when, seduced by designing men, they broke out in Mutiny and Rebellion; if the crews of Admiral Duncan's squadron were for a time more mutinous than others, who will say that they are not now entitled to forgiveness? Who will say that they have not by their zeal, their loyalty, and their bravery, atoned for their crime? And who will now, who indeed can, remember anything but the signal service which they have done their country?[54]

The *True Briton* agreed that the battle allowed the public 'to reflect additional lustre on that of our brave seamen', while the opposition *Morning Chronicle* saw sailors succeeding where the government had failed: 'However we may deplore the calamity, or condemn the impolicy of the war itself,' it wrote, 'it is with pride and pleasure . . . that we see our Country saved against the incapacity of Government by the courage of our Tars.'[55]

One sailor, above all, came to claim the limelight. This was Jack Crawford, serving on board Duncan's flagship the *Venerable*, who at the height of the battle performed a distinctive and famed act of bravery. The Union Flag flying from the mainmast of his vessel was shot away, and Crawford took it upon himself to take another flag up to the splintered masthead and nail it in place. Though the act went unreported in the admiral's dispatches, news of the incident reached the ears of London newspaper editors, and on 25 October the government-aligned organ *True Briton* related 'an anecdote worth remembering'. As they described it, a 'young lad' was ordered to replace the fallen flag, stating that he had nailed it to the mast with the words that 'it should not come down again'. This was, they declared, 'An instance of courage truly British'.[56] Subsequent reports were confused, suggesting that the incident may have taken place on a different ship, or that it was Duncan himself who had nailed the flag to the mast.[57] In a fuller report published in early November, the *True Briton* was able to offer more detail:

> In the heat of the action, the haulyards of Lord DUNCAN'S Flag were shot away, upon which one of his brave Crew went aloft, nailed the Flag to the Mast, and afterwards informed the Admiral what he had done, saying, 'that he was certain it must be agreeable to his Honour, as he knew that his Honour would never strike his Flag'.[58]

Again, though, no name was mentioned, and for weeks the sailor in question remained anonymous.

In the following months, however, there was a concerted effort by the British government to promote Jack Crawford as the sailor who had performed this act of bravery. This was propaganda designed to celebrate and promote the British sailor. Firstly, in December 1797, it arranged a 'National Thanksgiving Ceremony' to be held in London. Though intended to celebrate all Britain's naval victories of the previous years – including Cape St Vincent and the Glorious First of June – it was the recent victory at Camperdown that was fixed in the public's minds, and the action which the government played on the most. Jack Crawford was given a prominent place in the Thanksgiving ceremony, riding in the same carriage as the Dutch colours taken in the battle, to widespread popular acclaim.[59] Nor did Crawford's appropriation end here. After the victory procession he was formally presented to the king and given a government pension of £30 a year, an incredible sum for a sailor who only recently had been earning half of that figure annually. In the days before and after the ceremony, his name was circulated and his exploits widely publicised. This was a truly remarkable example of state munificence: sailors did not normally receive pensions from the government as rewards for meritorious service – they were usually reserved for officers and bureaucrats. There was no precedent of a sailor receiving such a large amount or playing such a prominent role in a victory parade.

The intervention of the government transformed Crawford from an unknown sailor into a naval celebrity. A wide range of newspapers, now mentioning him specifically by name, offered their congratulations when he was presented with a silver medal by his home town of Sunderland for his gallant services at Camperdown. The *London Packet or New England Post* described the 'elegant silver medal' gifted to Crawford 'who so heroically nailed Admiral Duncan's flag to the mast, in the glorious action off Camperdown'.[60] The *Sun* offered a detailed description of the design and inscriptions of the medal, showering further praise on the sailor in the process. On one side was engraved a view of two ships in action, with the motto *'Orbis est Dei'* and the following inscription underneath: 'The Town of Sunderland to John Crawford, for gallant services on the 11 October 1797.' The *True Briton*, the *Star and Evening Advertiser* and the *Observer* followed suit in the days that followed, and the next week local newspapers took up the story.[61] The following year a history of the war was published that retold the story in vibrant prose, relating how Crawford 'flew up' to replace the flag, 'for which act his name is celebrated'.[62] Just a few months after Richard Parker's execution, the British government had an alternative representation of the sailor ready for public consumption.

Crawford was also adopted by artists keen to get their own slice of this new naval hero. Daniel Orme published a print of Crawford intended to advertise his proposed painting of the Battle of Camperdown. This was again a deliberate attempt to return the sailor to the unthreatening, loyal image that he had enjoyed prior to the mutinies. The artist also took steps to ensure this was a recognisable image of a sailor: he is depicted not in the everyday clothes he would have worn during the battle, but in his smarter 'shore-going' rig that would have been familiar to the British public.[63] In the final painting depicting the surrender of the Dutch Admiral de Winter to Duncan, Crawford is given a prominent position, hanging over the naval officers in the shrouds with his marlin spike in hand. This was something entirely new, for a sailor had never before been placed at the centre of a work of marine art. Hitherto, sailors had been represented as anonymous scenery, a backdrop to the deeds of naval officers, but here a sailor was made a recognisable subject of a painting. Moreover, it seems this new take was popular: the *Sun*, reviewing the painting at the Royal Academy, noted approvingly that it portrayed 'the brave sailor, CRAWFORD, descending one of the main shrouds, with the Marlinspike in his hand'. In the subsequent months and years, there were countless other artworks depicting Crawford, each of them adopting the patriotic styling first depicted by Orme.[64]

Crawford's significance as a patriotic symbol gained further traction because of the nature of his act. Nailing the fallen colours to the mast was an act of bravery, made all the more so because its purpose was almost entirely symbolic. No lives had been saved, nor had his ship been restored to its full fighting function as a result of his actions. Instead, it was a statement of defiance, laden with meaning. British sailors fighting at the Glorious First of June had noted how French sailors had done the same even when their masts were reduced to 'stumps' (see p. 80), and Crawford's act of bravery was all the more significant because the ship's mast had been a site of contestation throughout the mutinies of 1797. At Plymouth, the rebellious crews of the *Atlas*, the *Saturn* and the *Majestic* nailed their rules and articles to the main mast in a direct repudiation of naval discipline. Similarly, at Portsmouth, the seamen of the *Sovereign* nailed the King's Proclamation to the mast with the phrase 'God Save the King' cut out as a form of protest, while on the *Mars* and the *Latona*, a blue flag of defiance was nailed to the mizzen-topmast head. Towards the end of the uprising, ships that refused to haul down their red flag instead 'had them nailed to the mast-head' in an act of further disobedience.[65] The mast, then, was a site of authority and resistance, and Crawford's act served to reclaim it for a more patriotic and loyalist purpose.

The act of nailing a fallen flag to the mast was not just meaningful, it was also impactful. In late 1800, the opposition politician Richard Brinsley Sheridan stood up to defend the rights of naval ships to search neutral vessels and referred to 'the Colours, which to allude to the common practice of our brave Sailors in action, should be nailed to the Mast of the Nation'.[66] From this point 'nailing your colours to the mast' became an English proverb. What is more, Crawford's actions seem to have had a telling effect on naval sailors too. In the three years following the battle, there were countless reports of sailors copying him by taking up a fallen flag and hammering it to a mast. In May 1798 the flag of the *Barbara* brig 'was three times shot away', and a sailor took it upon himself to nail the remnants to the maintop-gallant-masthead, 'the whole crew declaring at the same time, that they would rather perish than it should be struck'.[67] Later that year, a Scottish seaman on board the *Canada* 'ran aloft and nailed the colours to the mizzen-mast' in the midst of the engagement. In the action between the *Foudroyant* and the *Guillaume Tell* on 30 March 1800, Sir Edward Berry himself was reported to have nailed his ship's colours to the mast.[68] During the action of the *Dick* against a French privateer, the *Porcupine* newspaper noted that '. . . one of the brave Tars nailed the *Dick's* colours to the stump of the mizzen-mast, and they one and all were determined to fight the vessel as long as she would swim'.[69] Crawford's actions had set a new ideal of performative bravery.

Jack Crawford's appearance at the Naval Thanksgiving in December 1797 was an important part of a larger propagandist effort to boost popular support for the war. The Foreign Secretary, Lord Grenville, wrote of the need for the 'raising of people's spirits', noting that 'if we had done in this war half that our enemies have done to raise the courage and zeal of their people, we should not now be where we are'.[70] The government continued to hold sway over public opinion through press subsidies, and in November 1797 it went one better with the founding of the *Anti-Jacobin or Weekly Examiner*, a pro-government newspaper, created after a discussion with Pitt on 'Measures to be taken for keeping the public Mind right upon all Subjects by the Press'.[71] There was also a government-sponsored project for a national pillar, the first attempt to raise a heroic monument by public subscription. The government had proposed to erect statues in St Paul's Cathedral 'commemorating the nation's naval and military officer-heroes', but it was only after the events of 1797 that this project took hold. Prepared in parallel with the Naval Thanksgiving, the design competition ran into the new year alongside the passage of the Defence of the Realm Act, which made plans for civil defence, and the collection of Pitt's voluntary contribution scheme in spring 1798.[72] Through this, members of the public could donate sums of money to help pay for naval and military bounties and also to provide for the wives and families of sailors who had been injured or killed at Camperdown. On the day of the Thanksgiving these were advertised in numerous newspapers, with *The Times* printing a lengthy list of contributors to the fund, which had raised £34,390 for the 'Relief of the Widows and Children of the Brave Men who so nobly fought in the Service of their KING and COUNTRY'.[73] It eventually raised some £2.8 million.

It was the Naval Thanksgiving itself, though, that was the centrepiece of the government's efforts. The ceremony was ordered by the Home Secretary, the Duke of Portland, and organised by the Office of Works, which received notes from Lord Salisbury and Lord Spencer on how the ceremony might be organised.[74] The degree of micro-management was impressive: the prime minister, William Pitt, insisted on seeing a draft of the sermon and advised that sentences referring explicitly to the naval mutiny be omitted, a direction that was duly followed.[75] Another sermon read that day and later published offered up the idea of the 'ship' as a metaphor for the state. An effective ship relied on collaborative action and obedience to orders, as did the nation. In a call for deference, he stated that everyone was the servant of their king and country, and that the 'just performance of their duties, will consequently have a considerable and lasting effect, on the happiness of the community at large'. He reminded the nation that sailors were brave, selfless men undertaking great risk on behalf of the country:

Called up repeatedly in the night, when ... the howling blast, would agitate the most decided resolution; with a presence of mind, that baffles all description, the hardy Mariner points out the track, where preservation may be expected ... While every sense of danger is lost in a sense of Duty, and the real Horror of the scene is absorbed in the animating hope of National Glory.[76]

In this, the Tar was elevated to the level of national martyr. Rather than acknowledging the troubling events of the summer, the ceremony offered a significant expansion on earlier attempts to celebrate the battles of the Glorious First of June and Cape St Vincent and marked a concerted government campaign to mobilise the population behind the war effort.[77]

The organisation of the Thanksgiving revealed governmental insecurities not just about the connections between mutiny and radicalism, but also about the loyalty of the British people. The king's proclamation of 29 November 1797 declaring a day of national thanksgiving – subsequently announced in most newspapers and declared from church pulpits across the land – called for the public to recognise 'Almighty God' and Providence for the 'many signal and important Naval victories obtained in the present War'. It came with a warning that those who did not observe or participate ran the risk of punishment 'upon pain of suffering'.[78] The proclamation disseminated in Scotland revealed deeper anxieties. Copies were printed and displayed throughout the country and 'all other places needful', and it was ordered that the message should be read out in every church so that no one could pretend not to have heard it.[79] On the day of the Thanksgiving, extensive precautions were taken to keep popular enthusiasm – or worse, agitation – in check. The route of the procession to St Paul's, through Fleet Street and Ludgate Hill, was guarded by London-based regiments of volunteers and militia, and in total around 8,000 troops were on duty across the metropolis. The government were also not confident about the allegiance of those who were due to take part in the procession, and the sailors and marines due to participate were carefully selected and paid for their services.[80]

The government's unease was in part due to the mixed public reaction to recent civic events. At the Lord Mayor's Day a month earlier, the crowd had stoned the carriage of Pitt and the Secretary of State for War, Henry Dundas, and there was considerable nervousness about similar disturbances occurring.[81] The news of Camperdown had initially served as a comforting tonic, with Britons across the country arranging illuminations – decorative lanterns and lamps displayed prominently in domestic windows – as well as in opera houses, theatres and the Admiralty itself in celebration of the victory. In Plymouth, preparations were made for a general illumination as well as a grand display of fireworks on the Hoe, the site of the recent executions of naval marines.[82] Elsewhere, though, other Britons saw through the lustre of these public spectacles. In Surrey, for instance, a local magistrate not only refused to illuminate his house but also paraded through the streets of his town 'with a *posse of Constables*', with the aim of preventing his neighbours from 'shewing that sign of patriotic rejoicing'.[83] The most prominent recalcitrant was the radical Thomas Hardy, who, despite promptings from a crowd outside his house, refused to light an illumination. Rocks were thrown and nineteen panes of glass were destroyed before a group of Hardy's supporters from the London Corresponding Society arrived. The subsequent street battle was only extinguished by the arrival of troops.[84]

Preparations for the Thanksgiving also attracted much criticism. The opposition newspaper the *Morning Chronicle* termed it a '*Frenchified Farce*' – a direct comparison to the staged celebrations organised by the revolutionary government in Paris – and later compared the event to 'the amusements of *Bartholomew Fair*'. It denounced the government's threat to prosecute those who did not participate and predicted a 'terrible day for the metropolis', with London's citizens forced to observe the 'gilt procession' through London's streets.[85] It suggested that the recent naval victory paled into insignificance compared with the government's wider failings, for 'even the most brilliant successes afford to the people neither present relief nor hope of future benefit'.[86] Ten days later it published a mocking poem that made clear that the proposed celebrations meant little amid the futility and cost of the war:

COME ON, my brave Boys, and your voices all raise:–
We'll go to St Paul's, and there chaunt forth our praise;
We'll preach and we'll pray, and we'll glug as 'tis meet,
Huzza, and get drunk – *We have beat the Dutch fleet*! . . .

Never mind, my brave Boys, what our Victories cost,
Nor let your dull brains come on what we have lost;
For TWO HUNDRED MILLIONS (sum not very great)
Are very well spent – to have beat the Dutch fleet!

For TWO HUNDRED MILLIONS d'ye ask what we get?–
Why Taxes, and Peerships, and Contracts, and Debt;
Seven ships of the line: so, my lads, I entreat
You'll not count on ruin:–We've beat the Dutch fleet![87]

These criticisms prompted a backlash from loyalist papers, with *The Times* and the *Anti-Jacobin Weekly* defending the Thanksgiving's religious and patriotic purpose.[88] Elsewhere, though, plenty of others were less impressed. Thomas Rowlandson's *The Victorious Procession to St Pauls*, published the week before the Thanksgiving, satirised its crude attempts to cover up more fundamental failings, particularly the increasing burden of taxation. The playwright John O'Keefe followed up with a new musical farce entitled *Britain's Brave Tars; or, All for St Paul's*, in which wealthy citizens manoeuvred desperately for a sight of the procession to great comic effect.[89]

In the face of this mockery, every step was taken by the organisers to demonstrate military might and royal power. The procession began with a division of marines from Chatham barracks playing music, followed by sailors, lieutenants and petty officers who had fought at the Glorious First of June, Cape St Vincent and Camperdown battles, all walking with drawn swords. These were in turn followed by officers and admirals in their carriages, carrying colours taken from the enemy at the three battles, as well as the king and a collection of his ministers, including William Pitt and his Chancellor.[90] Extensive preparation went into the construction of the interior of St Paul's, with the leading architects James Wyatt and John Armstrong hired to erect seating and a throne for the king, while an immense furnace was created to warm the guests, consuming over one hundred sacks of charcoal every twenty-four hours.[91] Within St Paul's, efforts were taken to ensure distinctions of class and status were stringently observed. Specific galleries were created for naval officers (room for them was increased from fifty to ninety places at Lord Spencer's insistence), while explicit orders were given to arrange isolated spaces for more elite spectators 'so that Their Lordships may not be mixed with others'. The sailors' station under the dome was kept separate.[92] Newspapers commented approvingly on these arrangements, stating that the construction was 'deserving of high praise' and noting 'the accommodation which it afforded to every one present'.[93]

In the days after the Thanksgiving, loyalist newspapers attempted to outdo each other in their celebration of the event. *The Times* declared that 'Never perhaps was there so fine a spectacle exhibited as that of yesterday', while the *Oracle* printed three different eyewitness accounts that offered little extra in detail. 'The crowd in the street was perhaps the greatest that ever was known on any former occasion', noted the *Whitehall Evening Post*, while another noted that 'The crowd in the streets from St James's to the Cathedral was immense'.[94] Those papers with the closest connections to government trumpeted the impact the procession had had on those watching. 'UNDOUBTEDLY it must afford to every British Subject the most heartfelt satisfaction', wrote the *Anti-Jacobin Weekly*, 'that in the midst of the difficulties and dangers with which we have to contend, the Naval Superiority of the Country appears more conspicuous than at any former period of its History.'[95] The *London Chronicle* noted that 'all hearts seemed cheered and gladdened while they viewed the trophies achieved by the distinguished valour of their country'. Over the following few days, they also published accounts of Thanksgiving days across the country. That in Liverpool was 'observed here with every appearance of devotion'; shops were closed and volunteer forces paraded before large crowds.[96] At Shrewsbury, contributions to the subscription at Lloyd's for the relief of wounded seamen and their families on 11 October were raised to the tune of £76 7s 8d.[97]

A closer reading of the events of the day, however, suggests something far less harmonious. While naval heroes were celebrated, Pitt was hissed and booed as his carriage proceeded through the streets, and as it neared St Paul's his coachmen were attacked by people pelting them with mud.[98] The Chancellor of the Exchequer was similarly molested and had to be escorted home by the London Association after his coachman was pulled off the box and 'grossly abused' in the yard of St Paul's Cathedral.[99] More concerning still was the effigy of Pitt found hanging in Long Acre on the evening before the Thanksgiving, placed there by a group of mechanics suffering greatly under the ministry's war taxes. The *Morning Chronicle* commented on the quality of the likeness and described how a priest had begun to ring a tolling bell, calling on the stuffed figure to repent, while flammable materials were prepared around it. The effigy would have been burnt but for the intervention of police officers who confiscated it and took it to Bow Street, where instructions were given for the perpetrators of the 'wicked deed' to be arrested. While this attempt was prevented, tens of others went ahead, and one newspaper reported that Pitt's effigy had been burnt 'in 20 different parts of this Town and Suburbs'.[100]

Nor was public protest limited to effigy-burning. Some newspapers attempted to paint a picture of unprecedented harmony, but the reality was rather different.[101] The crowds were far from pliant: at one point the Islington Corps were obliged to form a line across the street with their bayonets fixed in the face of a discontented mob, while a man and a boy were taken into custody for spitting on the colours as they passed in the procession and throwing pieces of mortar.[102] At one point an ox was driven into the crowd to create confusion, prompting 'universal terror and dismay' and causing many injuries before it was killed by soldiers' bayonets in St Paul's churchyard.[103] Perhaps the most threatening moment came halfway through the procession, when troops spotted a red flag flying from the top of a house in Ludgate Hill. This symbol of mutiny was a worrying reminder of the summer's events, all the more so when men on the parapets began to throw bricks at the oncoming troops, one of which struck an East India Volunteer on the head.[104] The following week the newspaper published a correction, claiming that the flag was a handkerchief, and that the bricks had been 'accidently dislodged', an explanation that seems highly dubious.[105] Other newspapers focused on stories of human suffering. The *Morning Chronicle* told the story of a mother of three children who had been trampled so badly by one of the City Volunteers' horses that it was doubtful she would survive. Its rival the *Morning Post* noted pithily that the sum total of the Thanksgiving was that 'one man returned thanks to God Almighty and one woman was kicked to death'.[106]

The involvement of hundreds of naval sailors in the procession offered some crumbs of comfort for the organisers. In contrast to the other participants, sailors were seemingly heralded by both the populace and the newspapers who reported on the Thanksgiving procession. The sailors were 'every where received with a tumult of plaudits from the windows, lined with ladies, and from the populace in the street', noted one, while another commented that 'the Sailors and Marines were universally cheered by the populace'.[107] This appreciation straddled the political divide: the critical *Morning Chronicle* proudly noted that around 500 sailors would walk in the procession, while at the other end of the political spectrum, the *True Briton* commended the brave tars who had captured so many enemy colours and described them walking through the city 'amidst the loudest acclamations that perhaps ever were uttered by the greatest concourse of People ever assembled upon any former occasion'.[108] The inclusion of sailors added lustre to an event that otherwise came in for substantial mockery. Newspapers dutifully commented that 'these gallant sons of the ocean' standing with the 'trophies of their bravery . . . [was] . . . by far the most interesting part of the spectacle'. Chief among these was Jack Crawford himself, who received particular attention from the crowd.[109] In Crawford at least, Britons had an antidote to the recent mutinies, and an example for the future.

On the day of the Thanksgiving, a curious drawing was found on a wall next to the procession route. It displayed a ship, the *Britannia*, a visual representation of the British state, dis-masted and floundering. Underneath the image the following lines were written:

> A Vessel quite crazy, and almost a wreck,
> At her reins has a PILOT, unskill'd on the deck,
> Without Chart or Compass! – who ne'er heaves the lead;
> Who steers by his Stars, or false lights in his head.
> The Storm too increasing, 'midst Shoals and 'midst Shelves,
> Half the crew in despair making Rafts for themselves;
> Provisions all out – the last Water-cask stav'd-
> By a miracle only THAT Ship can be sav'd![110]

Maritime metaphors of this nature were common, and during Britain's 'worst year', Pitt's ministry was an easy target for those unhappy with the political direction of travel. However, displayed as it was amid a state-ordained Thanksgiving, this graffiti offered a politically potent message. As we have seen, alongside the celebrations and the heady propaganda was an undercurrent of subversion that surfaced in myriad ways. It remains unclear how far the Thanksgiving went to bolster loyalist spirits, and it is difficult for historians to gauge exactly what constituent sections of a crowd were thinking.[111] Even the seemingly universal celebration of sailors during the Thanksgiving becomes more complex when considered in the context of the 'year of disasters'. Richard Parker's contested popularity as a folk hero, and the appearance of a red flag of mutiny during the Thanksgiving, indicate that naval symbolism did not necessarily equate to loyalism. What is more, the British government's defensive public relations in late 1797 represented something of a belated victory for the mutineers. While many in the crowds were cheering the sailors for their exertions at Camperdown, for some they could also be a symbol of defiance.

The year 1797 therefore marked a conflict between two different versions of the British sailor – the disloyal mutineer and the dutiful fighter. That the sailor came to such public prominence speaks to Britain's ongoing interest in its maritime prowess, but also how in the Age of Revolutions the attention of the public turned away from elites to proletariat figures. This was also the age of the 'citizen', in which people of humble origins such as the actress Emma Hamilton and the Jewish boxer Daniel Mendoza became figures of public fascination. The comparison with Mendoza is particularly instructive: he was a man famed for his fighting abilities but who prompted public opprobrium in 1795 when an Old Bailey trial found him guilty of assault.[112] Like the sailors who came to prominence two years later, his pugilistic passion was acceptable when channelled in the right direction: at his height, he was so popular that one of his fights was organised by the Prince of Wales. However, the assault charge prompted a sharp decline in his popularity. He later landed in debtor's prison and, in a curious turn of events, ended up working in a London pub named after the admiral Horatio Nelson. Richard Parker had, in a similar way, come to represent everything that was wrong with the British sailor, directing his proletariat violence against the nation for which he fought. By contrast, Crawford represented the 'correct' version of working-class ambition.

Crawford's example helped restore the longer-standing idea of the loyal, dutiful 'tar'. As early as 1798, the *Sun* newspaper was once again calling on its readers to celebrate sailors as 'Our Nations true Defenders', and the sailor of the nineteenth century built firmly on the template laid down by Crawford.[113] Crawford later gained a new lease of life as a Victorian hero: in the 1870s and 1880s, he was reappropriated to meet the mores of a different age.[114] This redeemed version of the British sailor was a fictional construct, just as the depiction of 'Jack Tar' prior to the 1790s had been. Contemporaries found new ways to stereotype him as they attempted to reassure a worried public. From the late 1790s his blunt, dim-witted characteristics once again took hold as the sailor became a figure of fun. Just as the Nore mutiny was coming to an end, Laurie and Whittle's *The Sailor and Long-Back'd Horse* was published, in which the maritime protagonist was portrayed as an unthinking simpleton being fooled by a nefarious horse salesman.[115] Over the following years, hundreds of caricatures were produced that mocked the sailor for his simple ways, complex vernacular and foolish decision-making.[116] Popular interest in the real sailors fighting on British naval ships, briefly on view in the final years of the Revolutionary War, fell away. Crawford himself died almost forgotten in the cholera epidemic of 1831 and was buried in an unmarked pauper's grave.

Indeed, in the short term, fears over the loyalty of 'Jack Tar' remained evident, and it took time before the sailor was returned to his position as Britain's faithful defender, trusted unequivocally. The events of 1797, however, remain a crucial turning point because they witnessed for the first time an attempt by the state to control the image of the sailor for its own purposes. The vilification of Richard Parker, the celebration of Jack Crawford and the organisation of the Naval Thanksgiving were all part of the same programme of propaganda, designed to overcome deep public mistrust. In the subsequent years, the state went to great lengths to harness naval propaganda further. In 1798 the balladeer Charles Dibdin was given an annual pension to write songs celebrating the manly virtues of the heroic Tar, of which he wrote more than 100 in the subsequent years.[117] That same year, the caricaturist James Gillray (who also received a government pension) penned one of his most famous prints, *Fighting for the Dunghill*, which depicted a garrulous Jack Tar punching a French revolutionary off the face of the world.[118] Seamen became ever-present figures at the numerous naval celebrations and funerals organised during the 1800s, most notably at Nelson's funeral in early 1806.[119] However, as the next chapter will show, the government moved away from the celebration of individual sailors. Instead, as the French Revolutionary Wars reached their zenith, it turned to the familiar – and less problematic – image of the naval officer for succour.

EIGHT

BAD LUCK TO THE BRITISH NAVY!
Mutiny and Naval Warfare, 1798–1801

On 6 July 1798, John Stephens and John Mullins, sailors serving on board the naval ship *Adamant*, were sentenced to death. Only a few days earlier they had complained of ill-treatment on board their vessel, but their grievances were ignored, and they chose to take more drastic measures. Declaring 'one and all', they attempted to rouse the remainder of the ship's company, arguing that they should all refuse to go to sea until the ship's officers had been changed. Naval elites acted swiftly, however, putting them in irons and arranging a hasty court martial that found them guilty of mutiny.[1] Perhaps aware that his words would shortly be printed in the national press, the president of the court martial, Vice Admiral William Waldegrave, proclaimed in fiery prose the serious nature of their actions:

> You stand charged with the blackest and most heinous crimes, that of endeavoring to Stir up Mutiny and Sedition among your Shipmates, and this at a time when every heart and hand should be joined to oppose not only the Enemy of your Country, but the common Enemy of all Mankind.

With Britain still mired in an intense, ideological war with Revolutionary France, Waldegrave was alive to the political nature of this recent rebellion. 'Do not, my Lads, suffer yourselves any longer to be deluded by the deceitful sounds of Liberty and Equality,' he declared, which were 'only held forth to deceive and betray you.' In a final, cautionary note, he offered a warning to other sailors who might be tempted to rebel, directing their attention to 'the sad example now before our eyes' and hoping that this 'will be the last that we shall have occasion to make'.[2]

Waldegrave was disappointed, however, for British naval sailors continued to organise rebellions with great fervour. In the months that followed, there were numerous attempted uprisings across the fleet, and 1798 witnessed more courts martial for mutinous activity than in any previous year.[3] What is more, these mutinies were far more extreme than those that had come before, as crews abandoned negotiation and instead plotted to seize control of the ship in order to hand it over to Britain's enemies.[4] Such an idea had been mooted before – not least in the final, desperate stages of the Nore mutiny – but had been quashed through lack of support. In the aftermath of the 1797 rebellions, however, sailors – some of them claiming to be United Irishmen – abandoned any idea of securing their rights in the British Navy, and instead calculated that they would look to a foreign power for restitution. The sailors on the *Defiance*, for instance, swore an oath to 'defend their Rights to the last Drop of my Blood' and 'to carry the ship into Brest' while hiding handspikes – which they referred to as 'trees of liberty' – throughout the ship. This represented an abandonment of any notion of calculated patriotism or negotiation, and instead the adoption of aims that spoke ill of the Navy as an institution. On the *Defiance*, the sailor Thomas Derbyshire drank a toast to 'Bad Luck to the British Navy'; his crew-mate Nicholas Ryan called out 'Bad Luck to the British Fleet'.[5]

The latter years of the French Revolutionary War were in many respects a time of great success for the Navy. As we will see, the battles of the Nile and Copenhagen offered moments of triumph that were celebrated across the public sphere, contributing to a 'victory culture' that celebrated British arms in a way that often transcended partisan divisions.[6] However, the backdrop to these victories was a continuation of discord within the Navy's ranks and a brutal reaction from naval authorities. Derbyshire and Ryan of the *Defiance* joined Stephens and Mullins at the hangman's noose, among over fifty men executed for mutinous behaviour during the course of 1798.[7] The upswell in naval rebellion was also followed closely in the national press, which printed cautionary speeches such as Waldegrave's and reported British naval vessels being handed over to the enemy. In a headline of March 1800, *Lloyd's Evening Post* declared 'MUTINY ON BOARD THE DANAE' and bemoaned that reports of it being 'traitorously put into the hands of the Enemy' were all 'too true'.[8] This chapter seeks to explain this paradox, arguing that the Navy's achievements in 1798–1801 – and particularly those of Horatio Nelson – offered an antidote to the stories of continued rebellion in the Navy's ships. Up to the end of the war the loyalty of 'Jack Tar' remained uncertain, so the government refocused its propaganda efforts on Nelson as a new exemplar of naval heroism, harnessed by the government to restore the reputation of the Navy and calm public tensions as the conflict reached its conclusion.

The aftermath of the 1797 mutinies left naval crews divided. As Camperdown had shown, many sailors returned to their duty having accepted the settlement agreed after Spithead and fought bravely. Others had been cowed by the brutal reprisals seen after the Nore. In early 1798, sailors on the *Renommee* hatched a plot against the ship's officers and threw the captain out of the cabin window, but the reaction of most sailors was fear. William Allen told the ringleaders that 'it was foolish to think of that, and that surely every Man would be hung', while John Nicholas felt he had too much invested in the Navy to rebel. 'I am an Old man, and have a deal of Wages due to me,' he said, 'this is too hard, I cannot give you my Vote to it.'[9] Indeed, it is notable that many of the mutinous plots hatched in 1798 were reported by sailors, and later seamen testified against their rebellious crewmates.[10] The executions of 1797, however, had done nothing to quell the more radical sprits within the Navy. Robert Larkin, a sailor on the *Amelia*, was heard saying 'That if it was not for the Cowardly Buggers at Spithead, they should not now be in slavery', while French intelligence officers who interviewed captured British sailors found them disillusioned in the aftermath of the Nore executions and reported a large number of discontented Irish sailors.[11] Crews continued to organise, meeting in secret 'clubs' or arranging subscriptions for comrades imprisoned in the Marshalsea. For the remainder of the war, naval authorities continued to intercept letters exchanged between ships, suggesting that networks of communication endured.[12]

There remained, then, a community of sailors determined to organise and oppose naval authority. They did so using the revolutionary language of 'rights' and 'liberty' to advocate for better conditions, and in the early months of 1798 we see numerous examples that demonstrate that sailors were far from intimidated. Thomas Butler told an officer that 'he had as much right to talk' as him, and elsewhere sailors questioned the 'right' of the ship's officers to 'put any man in irons'. On the *Amelia*, twenty men shouted that they would 'have their Rights' and pledged to free themselves from 'bondage'. They called for a 'New Act', meaning a set of demands including the right to dispel unpopular officers.[13] The sailor Robert Jepsom, serving on the *Druid*, was punished with 150 lashes for singing a political song:

> We are the Boys
> That fear no noise
> Success to Liberty.[14]

Sailors continued to be explicitly political in their discourse, deploying the language of slavery and radicalism to critique their situation. James Anderson was heard 'damning the King and Country, damning all Englishmen, for they were no better than Slaves and soon would go into Slavery', declaring also that 'your Laws are very arbitrary'. Richard Forrester used similar language, comparing his officers to 'an arbitrary Government' and claiming that 'he was a Briton, that he had a spirit, and had read Magna Carta and the History of England'. William

Stevenson of the *St Albans* claimed he was serving with 'the Tyrants of the Seas' and called on all who disagreed to come to him, 'I will shew it them in print'.[15]

Just as worrying for naval authorities was evidence that sailors were now looking at Britain's enemies with sympathy, and even affection. The sailor John Daley, for instance, was overheard saying that 'it was a pity we were not like the French, to have no flogging at all', while Florence McCarthy felt that 'one country was as good to him as another'. Some refused outright to fight against the French. In early 1798, Bryan McMahon, a seaman of the *Albacore*, refused to fire on a Frenchman if the ship should come into action, a remark for which he was sentenced to 500 lashes. James Cluncy said he 'would sooner kill an Englishman than fire at a Frenchman'.[16] Other sailors spoke with their feet, deserting to the enemy when opportunity arose. This reflected the peripatetic nature of sailors' labour, but also revealed a community whose allegiance to Britain was by no means guaranteed. In late 1797, the trial of George Jay, found 'fighting against the subjects of this country' despite being 'a natural-born subject of this kingdom', was deemed of sufficient national importance to be reported in the national press.[17] The Admiralty had good reason to be worried about the loyalty of their sailors. The following year the *Mercury* was stationed off Ballywick in Ireland when one of its sailors, Jeremiah Dordau, jumped overboard and attempted to swim ashore. A man of strong republican convictions, he had hoped to join the Irish rebels and their French allies, whom he described as 'a fine liberal set of fellows', but was apprehended and interrogated. In his court martial more troubling objectives became clear, as other sailors reported his desire to 'be avenged on some of the English' and 'take a sword and kill' as many of the ship's company as possible.[18]

The best-known – and most extreme – example came in autumn 1797 with the mutiny of the frigate *Hermione* in the Caribbean. The crew of the ship had been subjected to a lengthy campaign of brutality from the ship's captain Hugh Pigot, who publicly demoted and flogged a popular midshipman, David O'Brien Casey, and threatened the ship's topmen – some of the most skilled sailors on board the ship – for not working quickly enough. Three fell to their deaths, after which the survivors were beaten at Pigot's orders.[19] Driven to extreme measures, on the night of the 21 September, around twenty sailors took over the ship, stabbing Pigot and throwing him overboard, and killing three other officers too. Political motivations were also evident. One of the leading mutineers, surgeon's mate Lawrence Cronin, read a paper stating that 'he had been a Republican ever since the War', that 'they were doing a good thing' and that 'all the Officers must be put to death'. Each officer was put on trial, his conduct assessed, and his fate decided by a general vote of the ship's company: the master Edward Southcott survived, but Lieutenant Macintosh did not – he was thrown overboard.[20] The mutineers then took the most radical step of all, sailing to La Guaira, on the coast of Venezuela, to request asylum and surrender the ship to the King of Spain.

Plots to take over a ship and take it to a foreign port were not new: in 1796, two sailors of the sloop *Bermuda* had conspired to take over the ship and carry it to an American port, only to be discovered. In the aftermath of the Nore mutiny, a group of diehard mutineers seized the merchant vessel *Good Intent* and sailed it to France. A few months later, John Harper, serving on the *Maidstone*, discussed the possibility of taking control of the ship to 'carry her into France'.[21] However, the mutiny on the *Hermione* represented the first time in the war that a British naval ship had successfully deserted to the enemy. The British public was outraged, and the Admiralty established a task force charged with tracking down the rebellious sailors. In February 1798, sailors captured at Samana Bay were mustered and inspected, and while no men from the *Hermione* were found, three other deserters who had served on the *Aquilon* between 1794 and 1797 were discovered, tried and sentenced to death.[22] In due course, participants in the *Hermione* mutiny were located as the searches became more widespread. Four sailors operating under false names were captured on board the *Valiant* after they were betrayed by their shipmates: following a trial, they were hanged and their bodies taken to specially built gibbets at Port Royal, Jamaica, for more prominent display. Overall, thirty-six sailors were apprehended, of whom twenty-four were hanged and two transported, with each sentence cheered in loyalist newspapers.[23]

It was in the interests of both the government and the conservative press to dismiss the *Hermione* mutiny as an isolated event. However, from late 1797 and into 1798, naval mutinies were planned that promised violence of a similar nature. A plot on board the *Amelia* aimed at the murder of superior officers, with the leading mutineers heard saying that they 'would kill every Bugger of an officer in the ship'.[24] In the summer of 1798, further conspiracies were discovered on ships stationed primarily in British waters, including on board the *Adamant*, *Haughty*, *Caesar*, *Defiance*, *Glory*, *Atlas*, *Queen Charlotte* and *Captain*. Each followed the *Hermione*'s model, seeking to take over the ship, kill the officers and sail the ship to an enemy port. None came to fruition, as loyal sailors alerted their officers to the conspiracies under way, and conspirators on board the *Caesar*, *Defiance* and *Glory* plateaued at around fifty men. Would-be mutineers came up against a majority of sailors stubbornly opposed to mutiny. On the *Glory*, for instance, Michael Keefe told William Regan 'it was a very bad thing to be done to take the ship into an Enemy's Country', and over a hundred crewmates wrote a petition stating they knew nothing about 'a horrid plot or conspiracy' by some 'designing men' in the ship. This did nothing to dissuade further plots later that year, however. In September, another conspiracy was discovered on the *Diomede* where two marines, John Wrights and George Tomms, concocted a plan to bribe the ship's company and carry the vessel into a French, Dutch or Irish port.[25]

It is not clear if the mutinies of 1798 were organised collectively, but they bore the hallmark of considerable planning. Many of the ships had been stationed together at Cawsand Bay in the preceding weeks, where communications had been passed between vessels, and sailors had met on shore. Furthermore, on some of the ships at least – certainly the *Caesar* and the *Defiance*, and likely the *Glory* too – men identifying as

United Irishmen were heavily involved.[26] Virtually every naval ship in the fleet had a sizeable proportion of Irish sailors, and as news of the 1798 Irish rebellion (see Chapter 5) arrived on board, their loyalties were torn. Irish sailors drank the health of rebels, damned the English and their king, and went as far as discussing supporting the rebels.[27] Sailors corresponded in Irish, allowing them to discuss matters without risk of being overheard, while Irish 'clubs' met regularly below deck to discuss political themes. One such debate contended that 'the Government of England had no right to the possession of Ireland'. Naval authorities attempted to control this discourse – the captain of the *Glory* banned clubs and directed that no conversation should be held in Irish – but it proved hard to police.[28] Dissenting activity was channelled into oaths, as sailors vowed 'to be true to the free and united Irishmen', to hoist green ensigns with harps depicted on them, to 'kill and destroy the protestants' and to 'carry the ship into Brest'.[29] The courts martial that followed the mutinies revealed a deep well of Irish resentment on board these ships. On the *Captain*, one sailor discussed the 'sweets of Liberty' and said that it was 'better for them to be hung at once' than to be 'used in the cruel manner the Irishmen often were'. Others sided openly with Irish nationalism. John Divine of the *Caesar* boasted that 'he was no Briton but a true Irishman' and a 'true catholic'.[30]

The mutinies of 1798 brought back fears of the previous year's crisis. Reports of the rebellion on the *Caesar* arrived in London in early August, with the *Sun* reporting that forty men had been confined on board.[31] The *Morning Herald* lamented that 'the Spirit of mutiny has manifested itself on board one of His Majesty's ships at Plymouth' and detailed the plot among Irish seamen on the *Caesar* to 'murder their Officers'. Matters were not helped by the news of separate mutinies in the Mediterranean, for which the United Irishmen also got the blame. 'The number of United Irishmen who have been forced to serve on board the fleet is astonishing,' continued the *Herald*. 'The mutinies on board Lord ST VINCENT'S squadron are therefore no matter of surprise.' 'Much discontent still continues on board the blockading fleet,' wrote *The Times* in late August. 'A great part of the crews, who are Irishmen, are at every moment ready to mutiny.'[32] Over the subsequent months, newspapers offered considerable detail on the progress of the courts martial, the crimes of the sailors and the severe punishments enacted, one noting solemnly that Lord St Vincent had been obliged 'to make some terrible examples'. More conservative organs delighted in the punishment handed out. 'The most able and active of the Boatswain's Mates were selected in each Ship,' wrote the *True Briton*, 'and they discharged their duty with such zeal, that one of the Culprits could receive only sixty lashes, in consequence of which . . . he expired.'[33]

The courts martial themselves revealed the continued divisions in the fleet, as a series of sailors and marines came forward to testify against the men who had plotted mutinies.[34] The motivations of these men are unclear. Some were no doubt sincere in their opposition to mutiny and chose to testify to preserve the shipboard status quo. Others likely had self-preservation in mind as they gave evidence. There are suggestions that some used their testimony to improve their own standing on board their ship. John Mahoney, a key witness in the *Caesar* trial, was accused by a defendant of inventing the plot to improve his relationship with the ship's captain: 'he expects to get to be a Nob [nobility] in the Navy by his Informations'.[35] These claims did not wash, however, and the executions were carried out in Plymouth in another deliberate act of deterrence. Officers across the fleet were ordered to lecture their crews on the 'Severity of the Crime of which these desperate Men were guilty', and patriotic literature was handed out to the fleet in a desperate attempt to sway hearts and minds. This was done in hope rather than expectation, and alongside this the Admiralty ordered a secret survey of all Irish sailors, with captains asked to report on the precise number who might be 'evil disposed'.[36] Officers filled in a template with spaces for American, French, Dutch, Spanish and 'other nations', in an unprecedented effort to collect information about the loyalty of sailors. The returns showed that of 1,517 seamen and 460 marines, 411 were deemed 'evil disposed', though they were concentrated on a few specific ships. The *Royal George's* captain deemed fifty-seven out of ninety-two Irish sailors untrustworthy, but on the *Saturn* and the *Royal Sovereign*, the officers reported no concerns.[37]

In the subsequent months, naval discipline hardened further, particularly as pro-Irish sentiments continued to be located. William Nugent of *Minerve* proudly declared that 'I am a United Irishman', while Philip Newsom, surgeon's mate of the *Nemesis*, described the Irish as 'oppressed' and commended the spirit of the United Irishmen, in contrast to 'Kiss Arse Englishmen'.[38] Officers watched on nervously. Collingwood noted that 'there are a great many ships where the reins of discipline are held very loosely', the effect of a long war, and an overgrown navy', a criticism of fellow officers but also an acknowledgement of the precariousness of naval discipline.[39] The crime of mutiny was stretched to incorporate almost any form of dissent, with even the most anodyne statement punished severely. In September 1798, George Smith complained to an officer that he 'was no Gentleman nor was there one amongst us' and opined that if others on the ship would take the same view, 'they would not be buggered in that manner'; he was punished with 300 lashes. Four marines of the *St George* were given the same when one of them drunkenly wished success to the United Irish and raised a toast to the tree of liberty.[40] Disciplinarians were placed in charge of crucial fleets. In 1800, Lord St Vincent replaced Bridport as commander-in-chief of the Channel Fleet, bringing with him a temperament wholly committed to eradicating dissent in the Navy's ranks, and punishments for resistance became harsher still.[41]

A common refrain from officers was that sailors should follow the 'proper channels' and ask for a court martial to make a complaint. As we saw in Chapter 3, on the face of it this offered a path to resolution, and some of the more humane officers encouraged their men to come forward with any grievances. However, for others, objections of this nature were considered to be attacks on their authority and prompted severe responses. On the *Boadicea*, Captain Keats invited his men forward to 'state their Grievances', but when a number of men did just that, saying they 'did not choose to go to sea again' with him, he had one of the men deemed 'particularly active' court-martialled and punished with 200 lashes.[42] It transpired that sailors who did make complaints could be punished as severely as if they had been involved in far more seditious behaviour. In 1798, John Haig brought charges against a lieutenant, and despite a number of sailors testifying to mistreatment, the officer was acquitted; Haig was then court-martialled for making false representations and was punished with 150 lashes. Sailors learned that there was little use in coming forward with grievances. Haig's crewmate John Parker noted archly that 'it was no use making any complaints to the Officers of this ship for he could not get redress'.[43] It was therefore no surprise that across the Navy, sailors avoided using the 'proper channels' and instead took more extreme actions.

For the remainder of the war, it seemed no ship was safe from the spectre of mutiny. The period 1797–8 represented the high point of mutinous activity, but even in 1799 and 1800 rebellions occurred that were deeply concerning for naval authorities.[44] On the *Impetueux*, sailors protested at excessive flogging and demanded a new captain and officers. Three men were hanged, but two lieutenants were put ashore, 'their continuance in the ship being judged highly dangerous to her safety'.[45] Another case in point was the mutiny that broke out on the sloop *Hope*, sailing off Madagascar in May 1799. The ship's captain, Augustus Brine, was informed of 'a Dangerous Plan' to confine the officers, take control of the ship and sail it to a French-controlled port. He confined some of the ringleaders but discovered that the conspiracy went much deeper and, unable to confine the entire ship's company, divided his officers into two armed watches to keep a constant look-out. Brine's officers were forced to maintain this watch for almost four weeks as they made sail for the Cape, a voyage of incredible tension during which Brine and his officers listened nervously to 'a good deal of Whispering among the People'. On 22 July, several officers and the few loyal sailors became very ill, and the ship's surgeon was convinced that an attempt had been made to poison them. It was not until 30 July that the ship finally reached Simon's Bay, at which point a mass of prisoners were sent on shore. In the trials that followed, ten sailors were accused of mutiny and a further twelve of concealing knowledge about the plot; five men were executed.[46]

By 1800, plots to take over naval vessels and sail them to enemy ports were once again successful. In March 1800, the *Danae* was taken into a French port, and a few months later the crew of the *Albanaise* took control of the vessel and deserted to the Spanish at Malaga. The following year, the *Gozo* was handed over to the Parthenopean Republic, formerly part of the Kingdom of Naples.[47] The rebellions followed a similar pattern, as crews took control of the ship with little warning. On the *Albanaise*, Captain Francis Newcome awoke to the sound of cutlasses clashing and a mutineer, Jacob Godfrey, whispering in his ear that 'if you spoke a word' he would be killed. On the *Gozo*, Lieutenant William Milne was woken by 'a number of people rushing on my Bed', who dragged him on deck and threatened to throw him overboard unless he acquiesced.[48] In each case there were around twenty participants in the mutiny, which on small ships was enough to take complete control, though on the latter vessel, Milne later testified that the whole crew were supportive of the mutiny.[49] There was no attempt to petition or negotiate, and on the *Gozo* at least there seem to have been strong political motivations. One mutineer, John King, was later spotted wearing a 'French Cockade', while Peter Jones admitted 'I am a true Republican'. On each ship, sailors had no compunctions about using violence, killing those who opposed them when necessary.[50]

The mutiny on the *Danae* received considerable public attention. In late March 1800 the *St James's Chronicle* announced that a successful mutiny had taken place and bewailed the ship being carried into Brest by the 'villains who obtained possession of her'. In a similar vein, the *Morning Post* reported the 'wanton barbarity' that had taken place on board the ship and blamed the rebellion on eleven French seamen who had supposedly entered as volunteers on board. It struggled to come to terms with the fact that later reports made clear that the mutiny was led by an Englishmen, and that the only Frenchmen on board were five prisoners of war.[51] Rumour and hearsay were reported as fact, which only raised further alarm at the prospect of further naval conspiracies. One newspaper reported that one of the seamen involved had earlier served on the *Hermione* and, having escaped punishment, had now 'overtaken his companions in villainy' through his actions on the *Danae*. Another stated that the leader of the mutiny had previously acted as a secretary to Richard Parker, the president of the Nore mutineers.[52] As with the *Hermione*, a search began for the guilty sailors, and Lieutenant Charles Niven was sent to tour the nation's ports and prisons to see if any of the *Danae* mutineers could be found. John Maret was discovered in Mill Prison the year after the mutiny took place, but most of the mutineers escaped into the murky maritime world; in total, only ten sailors involved in the mutinies of 1800–1 were caught.[53]

If the number of rebellious ships was smaller than in 1797–8, the Navy remained paranoid about the prospect of further upheaval. Two months after the news of the *Danae* mutiny arrived, and with rumours of 'Conversations' and 'Correspondence' being exchanged in the North Sea fleet, the Admiralty wrote to commanders instructing them to be constantly on their guard, especially when in port, against the 'machinations of wicked and designing men'. They directed commanders to take special measures to secure the hatchways on their ships and instructed that all communication between vessels was forbidden, 'as far as the duties of His Majesty's service will admit'.[54] Letter-writing within the fleet was cracked down upon. In February 1801, the ship's company of the *Active* wrote a letter complaining about the conduct of Captain Charles Sydney Davers and asking that Captain John Gifford be appointed instead. The Admiralty temporarily acceded but ordered Gifford to 'take every practicable means to endeavour to discover the writers thereof'. The investigation found a number of men who had been involved in writing the letter, three of whom were punished with between 300 and 500 lashes for 'endeavouring to make mutinous assemblies', and Davers was then reinstated as captain.[55] Three months later, three seamen of the *Glenmore* were hanged for writing a letter complaining of tyrannical conduct and asking either to be drafted or for their captain to be replaced.[56]

The last years of the war, then, found a Navy still contorted by internal strife. The mutinies that occurred between 1798 and 1801 are less famous than those at Spithead and the Nore that immediately preceded them, but in many respects they were more significant. Not only did these mutinies see British naval ships handed over to the enemy, but they also reflected the continuation of genuine grievances in the face of violent coercion. For all the punishments and executions, some sailors' desire to resist had not been broken, and many continued to believe that their rights could be secured. Gone was any attempt at claiming patriotic motivations, and anti-British sentiment was evident across the fleet. James Mahoney was heard in 1800 saying that he would be 'damned if I will be one of the British subjects to take up arms to fight in defence of the King, as he is the fellow, that was carrying on the war'.[57]

Not every seaman felt this way, of course, and countless thousands remained loyal to king and country whether through fear or personal conviction. The conservative press took every opportunity to highlight loyalism in the Navy's ranks: at the height of the 1798 mutinies, the *True Briton* published a letter, ostensibly from the sailors of the *Sans Pareil*, criticising the 'horrid designs and misguided conduct' of the sailors on board the vessel, stressing that there were Irishmen on board with 'unshaken Loyalty to our gracious King and Constitution'.[58] Nonetheless, the number and nature of the naval rebellions that occurred in the final years are significant, not least because it was in this climate of anxiety and uncertainty that the nation's gaze fixed upon a new naval hero: Horatio Nelson.

The continued upheaval across the Navy's ships occurred amid a string of naval victories unsurpassed in Britain's history. In the aftermath of

Camperdown, and following the failure of Britain's Caribbean campaigns, British attention focused on Europe, and in particular on the Mediterranean. Abandoned to the French two years earlier, a change in French strategy encouraged the Admiralty to send naval reinforcements to Lord St Vincent's fleet stationed off Cadiz. In the early months of 1798, France's leading general Napoleon Bonaparte had been stationed in the French Channel ports, helping to prepare troops for their mooted invasion of Britain, but in March it was decided that he would lead an expedition to Egypt. There, it was hoped, he could add new territories to the French empire and threaten Britain's imperial interests in India while putting considerable distance between Napoleon and the nerve centre of French politics in Paris. Reports of ships and soldiers collecting at Toulon reached Britain, but there was little clear intelligence on where the French fleet was heading. *The Times* of 24 April announced a 'FRENCH EXPEDITION TO EGYPT', quoting a long speech by a French deputy waxing lyrical about the potential new colony in the east, but most in government thought this was unlikely, instead anticipating a descent on Ireland. Only belatedly did the first Lord of the Admiralty, Lord Spencer, receive certain information that Egypt was the target, and naval commanders in the eastern Mediterranean were acting in the dark during the spring months of 1798 in what amounted to a serious failure of Britain's intelligence network.[59]

Regardless of its target, French preparations at Toulon needed to be watched, and a fleet under Rear Admiral Horatio Nelson was sent to observe the port. His exploits at the Battle of Cape St Vincent the year before had made him the emerging star of the Navy, and throughout the second half of 1797 he had been employed by John Jervis, now Lord St Vincent, on a series of assaults designed to restore naval morale after the damaging mutinies of that year. With confidence precarious, and following numerous acts of cowardice among officers and men, Nelson understood it was necessary that officers be seen to 'lead from the front'.[60] The blockade of Toulon served a more important strategic function, evidenced when, on 20 May, a fierce gale hit his fleet, damaging his flagship and allowing the French force to sail from port without opposition.[61] The French expedition sailed east, capturing Malta on 12 June after barely twenty-four hours of fighting, before arriving at Egypt and disembarking the troops. Nelson followed in pursuit, searching the Italian coast before guessing correctly that the French fleet was heading to Egypt. His squadron easily outpaced the slow-moving invasion expedition and indeed overtook it, arriving at Alexandria on 29 June to find an empty harbour. It was only after another month combing the eastern Mediterranean that he received concrete intelligence that the French were in Egypt, finally locating them at Aboukir Bay on the evening of 1 August 1798.[62]

Having tracked down the French fleet, Nelson decided to attack immediately. It was a bold decision that used the element of surprise and exploited a surprisingly poor French defensive position. The French naval commander, Vice Admiral François-Paul de Brueys d'Aigalliers, had failed to station frigates offshore to warn of an enemy arrival, and many of his ships were still encumbered with cargo destined for the new French colony. Even more problematic was his positioning of vessels at anchor some distance from the shore; only towards the rear of the line were cables placed between ships to prevent vessels sailing between them. As the leading British ship the *Goliath* approached, its captain Thomas Foley spotted the space inshore and ordered his ship to cross the head of the French line and attack from the landward side. Four others followed, while the remainder of the fleet, including Nelson in the *Vanguard*, attacked from the north. Foley's initiative allowed the British fleet to double up on the enemy, creating an overwhelming concentration of firepower as the two separate divisions attacked the French from both sides. The first two French ships were devastated before the last ships in the British fleet had entered the battle.[63]

Thus began the Battle of the Nile, and it quickly descended into fierce action. British ships worked down the French line, firing lethal broadsides into the enemy ships. Unable to flee, primal instincts guided both sailors and officers: 'theres no alternative we conquer or perish,'

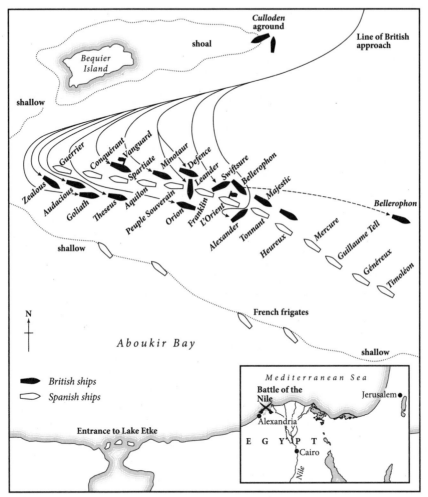

Map 9: Battle of the Nile.

remembered Thomas Wilkes on board the *Goliath*, describing 'The Roaring of the Guns, the Crashing of masts & the shrieks of Wounded'.[64] At the height of the battle, the French flagship *L'Orient* exploded, likely caused by Britain's use of combustible material, a highly controversial act outside the accepted rules of warfare.[65] The sailor John Jupp described to his parents how

> at 6 O Clock at Night began the bloody fray we continued a most thundering and tremendous Noise till near half past ten During which time we sett the L'Orient of 120 Guns on fire and Burnt her to the magazine and then she blue up ... the Explotion made the whole Element Shake and was a most Glorious Scean to us altho would have been teriable to people which had never seen the like or been acquained [acquainted] with the business of the firing.[66]

Despite the advantage secured in the early stages, some British ships suffered terribly, and Henry Harrop recalled how 'in 15 Minutes the Belerophon Was a mere Wreck Every Mast Gone and Cable Cut'.[67] French resistance was especially strong at the centre of the French line, where their most powerful ships were positioned. Nonetheless, the weight and accuracy of British gunnery took a brutal toll, and by midnight the *Tonnant* was the only French ship still able to fire.

The next morning, the sun rose to a scene of devastation. 'At Day light we find our Victory nearly Compleat,' wrote Wilkes, 'Immense wrecks in every quarter, & Dead Body's all around us.'[68] The scale of the British victory, however, was extraordinary. Of the thirteen French ships of the line that had started the battle, eleven had been captured or destroyed, while the British had lost none. Casualties on both sides reflected the fierceness of the action: the British fleet lost 202 seamen killed, but the French suffered more, with 2,012 dead and further thousands taken prisoner.[69] This was no ordinary battle, and the survivors understood that they had participated in something extraordinary. The French had experienced 'a Defeat as never was known in the world before', wrote Jupp. In a letter to his parents, he explained that this was a turning point in the war itself and, channelling the recent propaganda efforts on behalf of Crawford and the British sailor, called on them to direct the plaudits for victory to the seamen who had won the battle:

> My Brave Country men be not in Fear of an Invasion for the Lord will prosper your Island and Will in time Resolve peace ... let no false alarms frighten you think on the Wooden Walls and the Brave fellows that are in them Remember they are your Safety therefore when you see poor Jack Tar in Distress Relieve him as one good turn deserves another.[70]

Others hoped that the victory would bring about a speedy end to the war. 'Theire is Not the least Doubt but that theire Army will be Entirely Cutt off', wrote Harrop, concluding that he hoped 'this will bring about a speedy Peace'.[71]

In Britain, news of the battle brought relief. Over the preceding weeks and months the public had heard only depressing news of the course of the war, whether of the mutinies in home waters or the progress of the rebellion in Ireland. Nelson's first dispatches were captured on route to London, and without news of the French expedition's destination or fate, many in Britain had feared the worst. Cabinet ministers waited anxiously, and Dundas predicted the imminent loss of the British Empire.[72] In the absence of any reports, various organs were critical of the Admiralty's decision to send such a young admiral for such an important task, with the *Morning Chronicle* in particular pointing to Nelson's inexperience.[73] Others questioned his efforts to prevent the Toulon fleet from leaving port. Hester Piozzi noted pointedly that it was 'nearly miraculous' that a fleet of almost 400 ships had '*slipt unperceived*' past Admiral Nelson and his 'Fleet of *Observation*'.[74] The belated arrival of news of Nelson's victory, printed in the *London Gazette Extraordinary* on 2 October 1798, saw an explosion of joy among government and public alike. The First Lord, Spencer, fainted with relief on hearing the news, while newspapers competed with each other to offer the most triumphalist take. 'So complete a destruction has not occurred in the annals of our maritime glory since the overthrow of the Spanish Armada,' wrote one.[75]

After a summer of trials, the public celebrations that followed the Nile outdid anything that had come before. There were the usual bonfires and fireworks around the country: Humphrey Davy, travelling to Bristol, heard cheering throughout his journey, while every village he passed through glowed with candles. For the first time, festivities met with near-universal acclaim. Illuminations had typically been accompanied by window-breaking – as had occurred during the Camperdown celebrations the year before – but there were no reports of any such activities in October 1798, and the *Evening Mail* reported proudly that 'all ranks of people seemed to participate in the glorious news'. The celebration of a military hero was nothing new, of course, but the scale and extent of 'Nelsonmania' in late 1798 were unprece-dented.[76] An incredible range of manufactures were produced, with cultural production aimed directly at women in the form of fans, brooches, earrings, patch boxes, muslins and jewellery.[77] Ladies of fashion dressed 'A La Nelson', with ribbons and bonnets decorated with anchors, or with caps modelled on the Egyptian fez, adorned with Nelson's emblem.[78] In due course, concerts, songs, dances and panto-mimes were produced that celebrated Nelson and his victory. Thomas Dibdin's Francophobic play *The Mouth of the Nile* drew large crowds, while a theatre in Fleet Street was redesigned to allow its owners to stage mock sea battles.[79]

The public fascination with Nelson reflected a very real desire to celebrate the man who had won a singular victory that had transformed the war against Revolutionary France. The Battle of the Nile appeared to be that rare thing – a decisive naval victory – that restored Britain's prospects in the war. British naval supremacy in the Mediterranean was reinstated while Napoleon's army was trapped in Egypt. As promisingly, the Ottoman Empire, Austria and Russia were further encouraged to create a new alliance against Revolutionary France, helping to bring about the 'War of the Second Coalition'.[80] After years of defeat and frustration, finally Britain had a victory to rival those of the French Revolutionary armies. The battle, wrote the *Sun*, 'places Great Britain in a proud situation – the undoubted Mistress of the Ocean, and the Arbitress of Europe'. The *Morning Post* was equally giddy in its praise, suggesting that 'perhaps no victory was ever achieved at a more critical period', and that it would 'rouse the powers of Europe' to form a new coalition against Revolutionary France.[81] Nelson was ideally suited to reap the plaudits: he was aggressive, masculine and patriotic, in the long tradition of national naval heroes. However, where Vernon in the 1740s and Rodney in the 1780s were partisan figures, Nelson offered an embodiment of martial manliness that sat above factional politics.[82]

Certainly, different political groups attempted to claim Nelson as their own. Whigs such as Fox and Erskine toasted Nelson – while questioning Britain's wider strategy – and used the Nile to argue that the time was ripe for peace. Loyalists, by contrast, argued that the Nile brought opportunities for yet greater victory.[83] No one was more successful in harnessing Nelson's appeal than the British government, for whom he became a figurehead for mobilising patriotic fervour. The desire to focus attention on Nelson represented a marked change from 1797, when the government had made a strenuous effort to incorporate the figure of the British sailor – and particularly Jack Crawford – into celebrations. In the context of continued mutinies of 1798, sailors remained a troubling community, and so it instead whipped up patriotic pride in Britain's new naval hero, offering thanks in Parliament and encouraging public celebrations of the victory. The growth of the volunteers, which doubled in size in 1798, increased opportunities for public display, and for the second time in the war, the government set aside a weekday for a day of national thanksgiving, to be organised at a local level (St Paul's hosted the City of London's Thanksgiving ceremony).[84] Illuminations in 1797 had been relatively restrained, but in 1798 the government encouraged politically charged displays. A theatre displayed a transparency representing the figure of Britannia crushing 'Anarchy' and 'Rebellion' under her feet, which in the words of one newspaper 'had a very striking effect'.[85]

Seamen were not ignored, and newspapers lamented 'the number of brave men whose services the country has lost', or the 'gallant' or 'brave' Tars who had brought about victory.[86] Nelson's dispatches specifically thanked the 'high state of discipline' in the fleet and the efforts of the 'Officers and Men of every description', a deliberate attempt to paint a picture of a united and successful Navy. However, when newspapers discussed individuals, they focused on Nelson's captains at the battle – cleverly marketed by Nelson as his 'Band of Brothers' – or on specific officers such as Darby, whose *Bellerophon* had sustained heavy casualties in its attack on *L'Orient*.[87] Once again, subscriptions were raised for wounded seamen and their families, but enthusiasm for such schemes appeared to be on the wane. A subscription was opened at Lloyd's, but when surviving sailors began to club together to contribute to the subscription scheme, officers such as Collingwood became nervous at the prospect of 'accustoming great bodies of men ... to deliberate on any subject' or involve them in 'any political measure'.[88] Over 300 people happily attended a Nile ball and supper in Brighton, but hardly anyone turned up for a masquerade the following night, when the proceeds went to the subscription fund.[89]

The focus on Nelson presented an opportunity to restore Jack Tar to his former anonymous, unthreatening reputation. The mutinies of the summer and autumn of 1798 were fresh in people's minds, and prints of Nelson recreating with his 'Brave Tars' after the Nile were incredibly popular, offering as they did a sanitised representation of the British sailor.[90] The idea of Nelson enjoying drinks or music with his sailors stretched reality considerably, but it fitted with a need to have positive, unproblematic naval symbols. In the following years, instances where Nelson interacted with sailors were amplified for patriotic resonance. At a public celebration in Fonthill, Nelson happened upon two sailors who had served with him in 1797, one of whom had kept a fragment of Nelson's uniform following the amputation of his arm. This meeting was reported on extensively in the press, twinning Nelson's achievements and fate with those of the common seaman.[91] Other organs used Nelson's conduct more explicitly as an example to be followed. The *Gentleman's Magazine* opined that Nelson's actions must convince 'every British seaman … [that] courage alone will not lead him to conquest, without the aid of direction, exact discipline and order' and directed that 'submissive obedience' and 'willing subordination' were necessary.[92] Nelson, then, became a further tool in attempts to subdue discontent in the Navy's ranks.

In the aftermath of the Nile, the government's use of the Navy for propaganda purposes became ever more evident. In January 1799 this found literary form with the creation of the *Naval Chronicle*, a monthly miscellany 'comprehending all the Naval Circumstances of Great Britain'. Its creators, James Stanier Clarke and John McArthur, were both naval men with close links to government, determined to restore public confidence in its sailors. Clarke's *Naval Sermons*, published in 1798, had preached loyalist politics to the Navy's sailors, lecturing them on 'The Delusions which seduce Mariners from their Duty' and 'The Necessity of Advantages of Obedience'. The *Chronicle* was the next stage in Clarke's wider project of naval reform, containing biographical sketches, historical essays, obituaries and even naval poetry that helped extend ideas about British naval heroism beyond figures such as Nelson.[93]

Alongside this came the government's continued efforts to create a 'naval pillar', a monument intended to celebrate Britain's naval achievements in the war, which was given further impetus after the Battle of the Nile. Members of Cabinet initiated a public subscription, but the project fell apart amid disagreements over its location and discussions over what form of 'naval patriotism' to offer. The better-publicised proposals, such as that of John Flaxman, represented Nelson alongside other naval officers, but more radical proposals suggested it commemorate all those operating in the maritime sphere, including dockyard workers and carpenters. In the anxious climate of the late 1790s this was seen as too politically charged and, after many false starts and lacking wealthy donors, the project was finally abandoned in April 1801.[94]

Another form of state-sponsored navalism came through ship launches. This was a customary public ceremony through which the British public was awed by naval spectacle. Between 1790 and 1794 there had been twenty public ship launches, with that of the *Prince of Wales* attracting special attention during Britain's 'war of principle' (see p. 89).[95] By 1800, ship launches were tried and tested opportunities to demonstrate the skill and technical proficiency of British naval vessels, with one spectator that year describing the experience in terms of wonder. 'I went the other day to see a Ship-launch, which is a magnificent sight indeed', he wrote, as he watched the vessel 'dipping so grandly and so smoothly into its element . . . surely it must be considered, as the perfection of human art'.[96] Most importantly, though, launches were deeply patriotic events that drew large and enthusiastic crowds. One account from the 1790s told of people of all backgrounds coming together to see the launch:

> Every morning the new warship was surrounded by anxious hundreds, many of whom, allured by the trumpetings of fame, journeyed from the adjacent countryside . . . The eve of the launch was observed as a carnival, and parties were made up for the following day. Cousins from distant villages and towns were constantly arriving, and bustle and anticipation prevailed.[97]

Careful thought went into ship naming to exaggerate fundamental British characteristics. Royalty was a prominent theme, and the launch of the 74-gun *Plantagenet* in October 1801 'went off very finely, amidst the huzzas of a vast crowd of admiring spectators'. They also served to demonstrate British superiority over their French rivals. In June 1799, the French frigate *Courageux* was captured by the *Centaur*, but it was too damaged to continue in service. Instead, the British built a new, larger ship with the same French name. Launched in March 1800, this 'interesting, national spectacle' took place, reported newspapers, 'amidst the acclamations of an immense concourse of spectators'.[98]

By 1800, the Navy's role as a propaganda tool was rivalling its military function. British strategic attention continued to focus on Europe, but with the French armies dominant, limited troops and few allies following the failure of the second coalition, it struggled to find avenues where it could do real damage to the enemy. In 1799 an ambitious attempt was made to link up with a British-subsidised Russian army, and a number of Dutch vessels were captured at den Helder. However, the land campaign commanded by the Duke of York could not break out of the peninsula and was forced to evacuate, an embarrassing failure that gained the 'Grand Old Duke' immortality in the form of an unfavourable nursery rhyme.[99] The failures experienced by the British army meant that public attention fixated on the Navy, and individual ship actions, such as that by the *Centaur*, became moments for public celebration. This was especially true when it involved a storied vessel, and the recapture of the *Hermione* in October 1799 was trumpeted across the national press. Discovered at anchor in the harbour of Porto Cavallo, the British commander Captain Edward Hamilton reported that it was for 'The honour of my country, and the glory of the British navy' that he should attempt to cut out the ship. The subsequent action saw 119 enemy killed and 229 prisoners taken, while 35 of the *Hermione*'s sailors – likely including some of the original mutineers – escaped in a launch or swam ashore.[100]

Only in the Mediterranean, where Britain's new-found naval strength gave it relative impunity to act, were further advances possible. In October 1798 Britain laid siege to Malta, and it eventually succumbed in September 1800. The island of Minorca was also captured, presenting the Navy with a superb harbour in the western Mediterranean. Elsewhere, though, naval activity came with political challenges. Nelson's reputation in Whitehall was temporarily tarnished when he helped execute a Sicilian invasion of the Italian mainland, far exceeding his orders to give 'unlimited protection' to Britain's allies in the region and infuriating Britain's new Austrian partners.[101] A counter-offensive of French troops sparked a Jacobin uprising in Naples, and Nelson was forced to evacuate the Neapolitan court to Palermo, where they could be protected by naval ships. Italy descended into ideological warfare, and Nelson received further criticism when he executed an estimated 145 Neapolitan revolutionaries imprisoned on board British naval ships in a moment of political vengefulness. 'It is their infernal principles I dread,' wrote Nelson of the French, 'not their prowess.'[102] The most impressive feat of British arms was the invasion of Egypt, in which an expedition of 175 ships led by the experienced Lieutenant General Ralph Abercromby successfully landed 14,000 troops. The army defeated the remaining French troops that had remained stranded since Nelson's victory at Aboukir and removed any lingering threat to British imperial interests in India.[103]

The Navy's war was otherwise fought quietly in the background, protecting British trade and, where possible, attacking that of the enemy. French privateering efforts reached a peak of activity in 1797–8, partly as a consequence of the naval mutinies at Spithead and the Nore, which briefly encouraged the French to think that the Royal Navy's command of the seas had weakened. In total, French privateer attacks on British commerce cost the country £4 million in the first seven years of the war, a vast sum that contributed to the economic and financial uncertainty of 1797–8.[104] The British government took the threat seriously, however, and the increased aggression of French privateers led to the Convoy Act of 1798, which made sailing in a convoy compulsory while also imposing a tax upon merchantmen for naval protection. This commerce was escorted exclusively by the Navy on thankless but often highly dangerous convoying voyages that kept crucial trade – the lifeblood of the British economy – flowing. The insurers Lloyd's of London estimated that 3,639 ships were lost by capture between 1793 and 1800, compared with 2,967 lost from 'sea risk', but this was not enough to do decisive damage to the British economy. In 1799 alone there were 17,879 ships registered and the Secretary of Lloyd's estimated that the loss rate to the enemy was only around 2 per cent. It was this tireless and often tedious work that enabled Britain to stay in the conflict.[105]

The British public, however, had little interest in the mundane activity of convoy and trade protection. Nelson's return home to Britain in 1800, by contrast, generated considerable excitement. Throughout his visit he was followed by cheering crowds wherever he went and presented with freedoms of boroughs, decorative swords and silver plate. Nelson was bombarded with invitations, and the government ensured he remained as visible as possible, directing him to make numerous appearances to watch local volunteers parade.[106] They also used him to directly influence political campaigns. Nelson's martial prowess and loyalist credentials made him an ideal figure for the government to use against the Mayor of London, Harvey Christian Combe, who had been elected in 1799 on an anti-war platform. The government's initial attempts had focused on Captain Edward Hamilton, the man who had recaptured the *Hermione*, who had been given the freedom of the city on 6 March 1800. Hamilton's speech offered the expected anti-Jacobin sentiments, criticising the 'dissemination of those destructive principles which have deluged the world with blood', but he threw a spanner in the works when he went on to declare his support for Combe. Hamilton was quietly moved aside, and instead it was Nelson who was wheeled out at the Lord Mayor's Day on 10 November 1800. Nelson supposedly shook hands with over 2,000 people and pledged to use his sword 'to aid in reducing our implacable and inveterate enemy to proper and due limits' – playing his part as a more reliable agent of ministerial interests.[107]

In late 1800, Nelson was presented with one further opportunity to boost the government's prospects when a crisis emerged in the Baltic. Tsar Paul I of Russia, infuriated at the delay in restoring Malta to the Knights of St John and the continued British policy of inspecting neutral ships, persuaded Denmark-Norway, Prussia and Sweden to join him in a 'League of Armed Neutrality', reprising a tactic that had been successfully used during the American War. It struck directly at the heart of Britain's war effort, cutting off the supply of naval stores on which the navy relied, and which could not be secured from any other region.[108] The commercial and strategic consequences of the embargo were outlined succinctly by the London newspaper the *Albion and Evening Advertiser*:

> Its consequences must prove prejudicial not only to our trade but also to our national security . . . What we take from Russia . . . consists principally in naval merchandize and stores, such as timber for shipbuilding, masts, iron work, hemp, tar . . . the advantages accruing to England from our trade in all these important articles are incalculable; but the most prominent and essential advantages we derive from it is our possessing in Russia under our unobstructed management and controul [sic], an inexhaustible source of everything that contribute[s] to the creation to the reproduction, and the augmentation of a marine both military and commercial.[109]

Henry Dundas agreed, writing that 'in the Baltick we must act with vigor in the <u>Offensive</u>, for it is on such an exertion that the whole contest turns.'[110] The government response was swift, forming a committee charged with finding new sources of this material that was truly global in its scope. However, from its early stages it was clear that any success would take years to cultivate, and it was instead decided to send a fleet to the Baltic to open up the trade in naval stores by force.[111]

A British fleet of fifty-six vessels, including nine ships of the line, was sent under the command of the experienced Hyde Parker, whose knowledge of the Baltic waters was extensive. The Admiralty, wary of giving Nelson independent command after his actions at Naples but conscious of his operational abilities, sent him as Hyde Parker's second in command. Final instructions from the Admiralty were to target the destruction of the Danish fleet and, if necessary, proceed to Reval and Cronstadt to put pressure on Russia. The fleet approached Copenhagen via the Sound, a tricky passage that delayed their progress. Nelson's squadron sailed south, anchoring in the Middle Ground to the southeast of the Danish ships and fortifications, with the plan to concentrate at the southern end of the Danish line, with Hyde Parker's division attacking from the north. The delay had allowed the Danes to make the Copenhagen defences daunting, but as at the Nile, Nelson was confident a bold approach would bring success.[112] 'It looks formidable to those who are children at war,' he wrote to his lover Emma Hamilton, 'but to my judgement, with ten sail of the line, I think I can annihilate them.'[113] As Nelson's squadron approached on 2 April 1801, midshipman Millard of the *Monarch*, stationed towards the back of the British line, watched on: 'A more beautiful and solemn spectacle I never witnessed . . . A man of war under sail is at all times a beautiful object, but at such a time the scene is heightened beyond the powers of description . . . our minds were deeply impressed with awe, and not a word was spoken through the ship but by the pilot and the helmsman.'[114]

If the approach was serene, the battle itself was frantic. The British struggled to locate navigable channels and some ships grounded, while others fought at long range against stronger than expected Danish defences. So hard was the action that at around midday, Hyde Parker ordered Nelson to discontinue the action, an order that if followed would have forced Nelson to withdraw northwards, past Danish defences that were still fully operational. Nelson, astonished at the decision, proceeded to ignore it and continued signalling 'for Close Action'.[115] His determination paid off, and by 2 p.m. most Danish ships had suffered heavy casualties, and many were put out of action. It was at this point that Nelson sent a letter to the Crown Prince of Denmark, the effective head of government, threatening to burn every ship if they did not cease firing. 'I believe I told him such truths as seldom reaches the ears of princes,' he later confided.[116] Once again Nelson was overstepping his authority – and virtually ignoring Hyde Parker – but unlike in Naples his confidence paid off, and the Crown Prince submitted. Nelson had won another victory that saw

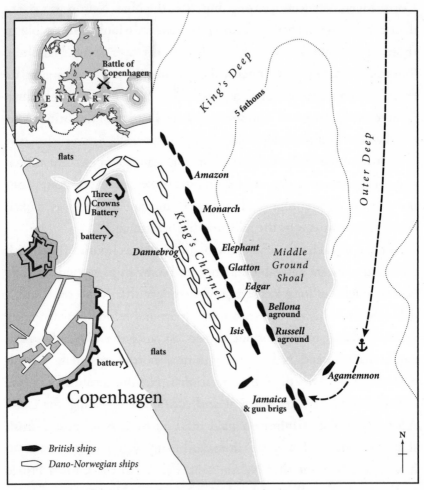

Map 10: Battle of Copenhagen.

three Danish ships of the line sunk or destroyed, and another six captured, alongside heavy casualties. Hyde Parker was quietly recalled, and Nelson proceeded to Reval, where he found that the Russian Tsar Paul had been killed in a coup. The League of Armed Neutrality fell apart, and British supplies of naval stores were restored.[117]

Following the victory at Copenhagen, Nelson was celebrated with greater fervour than ever before. The *Morning Post* proclaimed that Nelson had 'earned new laurels by his conduct', while its rival the *Morning Chronicle* proclaimed the battle as one that 'adds new glory to the naval annals of the country', ascribing some of the success to 'our gallant seamen' who had won 'fresh claims to the gratitude and admiration of their fellow citizens'.[118] One organ reported 'The glorious success of our navy, obtained by the unrivalled skill, intrepidity, and discipline of the officers and seamen', and stated confidently that 'the transcendent abilities and gallantry of the Naval Heroes' had outdone even the 'memorable battle of *Aboukir*'.[119] The *Caledonian Mercury* celebrated the 'DESTRUCTION OF THE DANISH FLEET' and an event 'glorious to the British Navy'. They took comfort from the fact that 'Our bombs are placed in such a way that we can destroy Copenhagen when we please'. Guns were fired at Green Park and the Tower of London, and 'a great sensation was felt throughout London, with the exultation the courage and skill of our tars were spoken of', while the capital's theatre audiences demanded 'Rule Britannia' be sung. As was now usual, a subscription for 'brave MEN and Wounded, and the FAMILIES of those who Fell in the Fleet under Command of Sir HYDE PARKER, in the Service of their King and Country, off Copenhagen, and in the Baltic in 1801'. 'Nelsonmania' returned, with newspapers hastily advertising busts of Nelson for sale across London.[120]

Ministers did their best to trumpet the success. Parliament once again voted its thanks, and Lord Grenville commended an achievement that he believed 'had terminated the war'. This, along with the victory at the Nile, were 'two of the most important and widest in their political consequences ever achieved'.[121] The campaign certainly heightened expectations that peace with France was nigh. In the midst of the Baltic crisis, Pitt had resigned over the king's opposition to Catholic Emancipation, bringing his almost two-decade-long term in office to an end. He was replaced by a ministry led by Henry Addington, whose first speech in Parliament on 25 March 1801 announced that he would try for peace. Recent successes in Egypt and Copenhagen had briefly tipped the scales in Britain's favour, and the new prime minister was well aware that Britain did not have the money to fund another year of warfare. Between 1798 and 1799 Pitt had brought in a series of new income taxes that temporarily restored national coffers, but by 1801 there was little prospect of continuing the war without raising expensive loans and increasing the already stretched national debt.[122] Addington sent out peace feelers to Napoleon Bonaparte, in the hope of sparing Britain further financial turmoil.

Negotiations took time, and the war meandered on for another few months. Naval squadrons continued to locate and fight enemy forces, and other naval heroes were also created; indeed, Rear Admiral Sir James Saumarez's victory at Algeciras in the summer of 1801 demonstrated the speed with which a naval officer could go from ruin to redemption. On 6 July, his force of six ships of the line met that of the French commander Charles Linois, who commanded three ships of the line and a frigate while also benefiting from fourteen Spanish gunboats and extensive shore batteries. After five hours of action the British fleet was forced to retire, having sustained severe damage and having lost the *Hannibal*, which ran aground. Saumarez wrote disconsolately to his wife Martha, knowing how the defeat would be reported in Britain and that this likely spelt the end of his career. A few days later he wrote again, apologising for the previous 'distressing letter', and detailed a remarkable turnaround. He had ordered his ships repaired, pursued the enemy and, despite finding them reinforced with vessels from Cadiz, took them by surprise in a night attack. Two enemy ships of the line were destroyed along with a frigate, and another was captured in what represented another example of British superiority of gunnery and seamanship.[123] In Britain, Saumarez was awarded the thanks of both Houses of Parliament and made a Knight of the Bath. His dispatches spread the praise among his officers, but like Nelson before him, he also took care to commend in generic terms the 'Discipline and Valour of British Seamen'.[124]

Alongside the victories at Copenhagen and Algeciras, the final months of the war were played out in the face of rumours of a new French invasion attempt. The new French leader, Napoleon Bonaparte, gathered vast armies at Boulogne, though it remains unclear how seriously he took this operation. Even if he did entertain the possibility of a fresh attempt to cross the English Channel, he also knew that a threatening force in northern France offered further leverage as his diplomats negotiated a more favourable deal in the post-war settlement; some French officers referred to it knowingly as *'un projet chimérique'*. Whatever his intention, this activity renewed invasion fears in Britain, and the anxieties of 1797–8 briefly returned. The government took steps to calm public concerns, parading 4,730 volunteers in Hyde Park on 21 July 1801 in front of 30,000 spectators. They also turned to their favourite naval placebo, when Nelson was sent to command the naval forces defending the coasts between Beachy Head and Orford Ness.[125] While he maintained publicly that France might attempt to invade, privately he ridiculed the idea. 'I can hardly believe they will be such fools as to make the attempt,' he wrote to Vice Admiral Lord Keith. Most of those in the Navy and government understood that Nelson's role was primarily to calm public fears. 'The public mind is so very much tranquillis'd by your being at your post,' wrote St Vincent, while Troubridge commented that 'Your being on the spot keeps the minds of all classes easy'.[126]

Characteristically, Nelson threw himself into making a show of the operation. A direct attack on French invasion preparations was planned, designed to give the appearance of strenuous activity. On 4 August 1801, 28 gunboats and 5 bomb boats fired between 750 and 850 shots at the invasion flotilla, watched by crowds on both sides of the Channel. The attack caused some French casualties but did little material damage. His plans for a second attack were undermined when they were reported in British newspapers, and a confused attempt to break into the anchorage on the night of 15 August was fought off.[127] An abortive attack was launched on Flushing towards the end of the month, after which further attacks were called off. Some opposition newspapers saw through the charade, doubting the prospect of an invasion attempt, but for the most part Nelson's flurry of activity achieved the government's aim of calming public fears. When Nelson came ashore, he was 'received by the Acclamations of the People who looked with mild but most affectionate amazement at him who was once more going to step forward in defence of this Country'.[128] Shortly afterwards, *The Times* described Nelson visiting the wounded sailors in Deal 'with that humanity which has characterized his naval career'.[129] Up to the end of the war, Nelson served as a political tool par excellence.

Thomas Derbyshire, the sailor who in 1798 had wished 'Bad Luck to the British Navy', had been brought up to believe that British victory in war rested on the Navy. He naturally hoped that rebellion in the fleet would corrupt Britain's war effort, and while his and many others' efforts to achieve this failed, it transpired that there was little the Navy could do to ensure British victory. The final four years of the French Revolutionary War were marked by a series of naval successes celebrated across the British nation, but positive results emanating from these seemingly 'decisive' actions proved fleeting. The peace preliminaries signed on 29 September 1801 represented a comprehensive defeat for Britain. None of Britain's war aims had been achieved: France remained dominant on the European continent, while Britain ceded most of its overseas conquests in return for assurances of goodwill from Bonaparte. It was exhausted in every possible way, and the last year of the war was fought against a backdrop of food riots and a manpower shortage that saw the Navy become ever more desperate in its search for trained sailors.[130] Addington's government had little prospect of funding the war for another season and there was no strategic plan for how Britain's limited military resources should be directed. Ministers had no intention of renewing the calamitous colonial campaigns of earlier in the decade and there was little scope for action in Europe. For all the celebratory trumpeting, then, the Navy's activities in the final years of the war – be it in battle, through trade protection or in its defence against invasion – bore little strategic dividend other than preventing an even more devastating defeat.

Derbyshire's words were nonetheless significant, demonstrating that disunity in the Navy's ranks continued long after the mutinies at the Nore. Indeed, the Navy's triumphs of the final years of the conflict were fought against a backdrop of continued naval dissent and rebellion. Of course, not every sailor was radically opposed to naval authority, and the majority did indeed conform to the post-Spithead settlement and fought with bravery and distinction. Richard Greenhalgh wrote proudly to his parents in early 1798 that 'we are a Dreadful scourge by sea and hope we will . . . continue it with the assistance of God'.[131] This was not mindless loyalism; it often reflected pragmatic decision-making. In the view of such sailors, the best way to secure release from the Navy was to win the war as quickly as possible; that was the motivation of John Nicol, who fought bravely at the Battle of the Nile.[132] Indeed, behind the patriotic rhetoric and carefully worded dispatches lay a more uneasy reality that suggests even the bravest sailor's loyalty was conditional and contingent. Among triumphalist accounts of battle came more discomforting reports of sailors refusing to fight. The poet Samuel Coleridge, who briefly acted as secretary to the naval officer Alexander Ball, recorded during the battle of Copenhagen that 'the men on board our most glorious Warships often run from their Quarters', though 'it was made a point to hush it up'.[133] Throughout this period, whether radical, Irish nationalist or loyalist, sailors continued to make precise calculations about their prospects and acted accordingly.

This was an unnerving situation for those in government, and the end of the war saw a much more comforting – and simplistic – view of the Navy projected. One print, published just as the preliminaries were signed, attempted to persuade the British public that a great victory had been achieved, and that the Navy had played a central role. 'PEACE!! THE RESULT OF OUR NAVAL VICTORIES', it boasted, celebrating the Navy's many 'Triumphs' since the commencement of the conflict by depicting them as fruit hanging from the branches of an allegorical 'Tree of Liberty'. Each victory was ascribed to the naval officer who had commanded it: Nelson was positioned on the highest branch, with Bridport, Howe, Duncan and Saumarez, among others, placed below.[134] This was the logical conclusion of the cultural politics of the late 1790s, when concerns over continued disorder in the fleet saw naval propaganda coalesce around the figure of the naval officer; Nelson's popularity and unquestionable loyalty made him the ideal ministerial hero for the Age of Revolutions. In the weeks that followed the print's publication, his fierce martial reputation proved useful once more as the government attempted to sell the peace to the public. In October 1801 Nelson was once again deployed at the London Guildhall during Lord Mayor's Day, this time with his sword sheathed, preaching the value of peace.[135]

The government's use of the Navy as a propaganda tool was hardly new, but the final years of the French Revolutionary War saw it deployed with more precision than ever before. How successful this policy was remains unclear, however. We know, for instance, that thousands turned out to see Nelson, but as with the Naval Thanksgiving of 1797, it is difficult to unpick the motivations and mentalities of all those who stood in the crowd and gazed at Britain's latest naval hero. Some no doubt saw Nelson as an opportunity to celebrate the victories achieved in the war, while others would have come to see one half of Britain's most prominent celebrity couple; by 1801 his affair with Emma Hamilton was widely known and the source of much conversation and mockery. It seems reasonable to suppose that many who attended the Lord Mayor's Day were simply relieved that the conflict with Revolutionary France was over. War-weary Britons had good reason to welcome peace, and since the announcement there had been numerous celebrations to mark the end of hostilities. Napoleon's emissary sent to deliver the French ratification of the Treaty of Amiens, as it would become known, was welcomed by a crowd that insisted on drawing his carriage through the streets of London.[136]

Not everyone was convinced by the carefully orchestrated and stage-managed public appearances. Elsewhere, we find moments of discord that suggest something quite different among the nation's population: a genuine concern for the health and wellbeing of sailors, and a more critical take on the attempt to heroise only the Navy's officers. During one excursion on shore in 1801 Nelson was accosted in the street of Deal by a 'vagabond' who critiqued his conduct 'in being careless of poor Seamen's lives'.[137] Some, it seems, were not swayed by the propaganda.

EPILOGUE

The end of the Revolutionary War in 1801 was welcomed in almost every quarter. For most sailors, the termination of their naval service beckoned, along with the prospect of reunions with loved ones ashore. In April 1801 the sailor Richard Buckley prayed that the 'furious Rages of this Distressing War Will not Last Longer' and hoped that he and other sailors could soon return 'and Chat to ther Espouses . . . by their fire side' [sic] alongside their children, who had all but forgotten their absent fathers.[1] The geopolitical situation, however, did not allow for a full demobilisation. The British government remained nervous about the reliability of the new French leader, Napoleon Bonaparte, and the Navy maintained a standing force of naval ships around the world, causing much anguish among sailors forced to remain at sea.

The pull of home was strong. Richard Greenhalgh, whom we last saw celebrating Britain's victory over the French at the Battle of the Nile, was much less enamoured of naval service by 1801, one of many thousands of sailors forced to continue serving in his warship. June found him nostalgic and homesick. 'I have not forget the names of the feilds [sic] yet,' he wrote disconsolately to his parents. Greenhalgh described naval life in crude terms, as 'hard usage', and complained that there was no prospect of setting 'his foot on shore'. By August 1802, many months after peace had been agreed, he finally lost patience and deserted to a merchant ship at Naples, calculating that this would eventually see him home. 'You need not answer this latter [sic],' he again wrote to his parents, 'as I Shall not bee there to recive [sic] it.'[2]

Greenhalgh was not alone in wanting to escape, and the arrival of peace in 1801–2 ushered in a series of mutinies organised by sailors who could not understand why they had not yet been released. The most famous was that of the *Temeraire*, stationed at Bantry Bay in south-west Ireland, the scene of the failed French invasion in late 1796. There, on 3 December 1801, homesick sailors heard the news of peace and demanded to be allowed to go home rather than sail to the West Indies as they had been ordered. They cheered, took command of the ship's ammunition, and then argued loudly and openly with the ship's captain, Thomas Eyles. There were divisions among the crew about whether to use violence to further their aims, and they failed to secure the support of the ship's marines; after a stand-off the ringleaders were apprehended and court-martialled. In response to the mutiny, Addington rushed to the country house of the new First Lord of the Admiralty, Lord St Vincent, where they agreed to give Vice Admiral Mitchell extraordinary powers regarding the death sentence for sailors. Six ringleaders were convicted and executed, punishments that sat uneasily with crews and officers alike. Collingwood, who sat at the trial, wrote that 'there are none more desirous than I am that they might return to their families'. In Edward Brenton's view, the leaders of the mutiny were 'the noblest fellows, with the most undaunted and prepossessing men, I ever beheld – the beau ideal of British sailors'.[3]

In the following months, further rebellions took place among naval crews desperate to return home. On the *Syren*, sailors swore an oath 'to be true to the Ship's Company to carry the ship home' – an extreme step following the clampdown on mutinous oaths that followed the 1797 rebellions – and admonished the captain for his treatment of them. The crew, they said, 'were used like men before . . . we are now thrashed like dogs'.[4] On the *Gibraltar*, the crew shouted out 'home! Home!', and sailors exchanged letters with other ships in the squadron.[5] A similar scenario occurred on the *Excellent*, where sailors also gathered together to call out 'Home, Home'. One sailor, Matthew Lovell, told Commodore Stopford that 'he himself had a mother that he wishes to sea [sic]' and that the ship's company had 'wives and Children they wished to sea [sic]'.[6] Mutinies at the conclusion of a war were not a new phenomenon, and both the Seven Years' War and American War had concluded with widespread uprisings among sailors determined to return home.[7] The rebellions that followed the arrival of peace in 1801 were therefore more traditional, and less politically charged, than the resistance and protest seen during the 1790s. However, if this hinted at the return of more customary modes of shipboard protest, the Navy responded with the same brutality that had marked their response throughout the preceding decade. In total thirteen men from the *Syren*, *Gibraltar* and *Excellent* were hanged, in addition to the six hanged from the *Temeraire*, with others receiving brutal floggings.[8]

CONCLUSION

In 1799 the sailor William Davis looked about his ship, the *Lowestoft*, and hoped he 'spied the Tree of Liberty' planted on board and 'extended thro' the British navy'.[1] Davis's hopes for the creation of a fairer and more egalitarian Navy came to naught, but his words offered a glimpse into how the Age of Revolutions had made its mark on the Royal Navy. First and foremost, it had shaped the lives of naval sailors, offering them a new language of resistance based on rights and fundamental liberties that could be deployed to demand improvements to their pay and working conditions. In an era of remarkable political engagement sailors proudly made their opinions known. Shortly after Davis's declaration a different sailor on the *Ganges*, Benjamin Thompson, spoke defiantly of his ability to write and communicate ideas to his shipmates: 'I have Open Ink and Paper and can make use of them as well as any of you, & will be heard.'[2] Nor was this limited to rhetoric. He and countless other sailors had their voices heard, whether through complaints to their superiors, courts martial, petitions and, in more extreme cases, through press-gang resistance, shipboard strikes and mutiny. These built on longer traditions of protest in the Navy, but they were turbo-charged in the context of the 1790s, becoming more extreme in nature and deploying the language of 'revolution' in a naval context. This represented a sea change in the way sailors engaged with politics.

It needs to be emphasised that not every sailor was a radical, but that ships had become a political space. Some sailors did subscribe to the ideas of Tom Paine and the London Corresponding Society, and

William Davis was one of those who understood his naval service in such terms. However, as this book has shown, sailors were not a homogeneous body of men but a conglomerate of different opinions and stances that reveal the wide-ranging political contours of the revolutionary era. Alongside radicals came more moderate reformers, Irish nationalists, and those who increasingly took an anti-war stance or who engaged with Whig critiques of Pitt's government. Some sailors deployed the more traditional language of 'usage' to advocate for improvements. Many – and in the final years of the war likely the majority – opposed petitioning, strikes and mutiny. It is notable that in the years after 1797 there were any number of mutinous conspiracies organised across the Navy's ships, but relatively few that were successfully executed. Indeed, by 1800 the Navy's crews were marked by vicious divisions between those who favoured resistance and those who did not. One sailor who had testified against the *Hermione* mutineers, known as 'Jack Catch', suffered abuse and threats from his crewmates. Thomas Nelson was given two years' imprisonment for abusing him, describing him as 'the bloody buggar belonging to the Hermione who hangs all the Men'.[3] As we have seen, though, in the latter years of the war sailors testifying against their crewmates was hardly a rare occurrence, and the majority of seamen actively avoided mutiny.

In this, the Navy reflected the wider currents of British political culture. Ultimately there was no revolution in the Navy, just as there was no revolution in Britain. How close either came to insurrection remains an exercise in counterfactual history, but understanding what happened in the Navy during the 1790s also helps us better understand Britain's wider Age of Revolutions. Both Navy and nation came close to radical upheaval, and sailors arguably got further than the LCS in securing a degree of democracy as they elected delegates and, for a brief few weeks in 1797, took charge of fleets stationed around Britain. This was short-lived, however, and much like the British reform movement, sailors struggled to maintain momentum in the face of a persistent culture of popular loyalism. On land, the activities of leading radicals had already been curtailed by the mid-1790s, and the invasion threat of 1796–8 seems to have been a decisive moment in which Britons chose to side with the constitutional devil they knew. It followed that sailors had the most success when they were able to place their actions in a patriotic light, most notably at Spithead and Plymouth, when the government was forced to cave to their demands. In contrast, the rebellion at the Nore, and particularly the more extreme mutinies that followed, could not be framed as patriotic events and met with public opprobrium.

The Navy's repression of sailors' protests across the 1790s can also be mapped onto Britain's Age of Revolutions. Just as radicals on land were imprisoned, deported or forced to withdraw from public life, sailors were violently impressed, flogged and hanged, as the British Admiralty become ever more extreme in its response to dissent in the Navy's ranks. In an era that saw suspensions of habeas corpus, the trial of political radicals, gagging acts and other forms of legislation that attempted to confine radical literary space, the Navy was another vital site for unprecedented state repression in the face of political dissent. The mere act of writing was laden with political significance and became a threat to be clamped down upon. Benjamin Thompson, who in 1799 had so proudly declared his ability to write and 'be heard', was punished with 500 lashes for his outburst.[4] Some aspects of this programme of naval retribution – not least the policies surrounding impressment – should be considered a form of state-sanctioned violence. By the end of the 1790s, the Navy's reputation for harsh discipline meant that political dissidents were being sent there as a deterrent. In 1801, a Lancashire magistrate suggested that men arrested at a seditious meeting should be impressed into the Navy as 'idle and disorderly persons'. While he acknowledged they would not be 'ideal recruits', he was confident that the threat of the Navy would discourage further meetings.[5]

Despite the brutal repression witnessed across the 1790s, the men of the lower deck had demonstrated that they could successfully force change. Throughout the 1790s, sailors acted collectively to secure better food, remove or constrain hated officers and, in rare cases, secure permanent improvements for the fleet, such as the increase in wages achieved in 1797. Sailors had shown themselves to be adept political actors, though the success of their efforts depended on timing, the nature of their demands and the public support they could call upon. Just as important was the dawning realisation of sailors' power, which forced institutional change: so common did the sight of the mutinous red flag become that the Navy dropped it entirely from its 1799 signal book.[6] It also prompted reforms to systems of reward and punishment. In 1808 the Navy belatedly recognised one of the Nore mutineers' demands, creating a more equitable system of prize money that saw the officers' share decreased and redistributed among the rest of the ship's company, particularly among skilled petty officers.[7] The Navy also banned some of the more ferocious forms of discipline, such as 'running the gauntlet' and 'starting'. Nor were sailors browbeaten by harsh discipline. Mutinies and shipboard protests continued after 1797–8, albeit in smaller numbers, and the end of the Napoleonic Wars in 1815 was met by a wave of sailors' strikes that once again panicked the government.[8] Naval elites were forced to come to terms with sailors' newfound power: seamen were now a 'thinking set of people', noted Captain Anselm Griffiths in 1824.[9]

While the Admiralty responded with violence and repression, it did not always work. In the latter years of the 1790s the Navy's severe response to dissent in the ranks initially seemed effective: in the aftermath of the 1797 executions, many sailors chose loyalty over protest, and it was this that made the naval victories in the final years of the war possible. How much the fear of harsh discipline motivated sailors' actions remains unclear, and we must recognise that some fought for patriotic reasons, or calculated that bringing the war to a speedy conclusion was their best chance of returning home. However, it is revealing that the punishments handed out in 1797 did not quell sailors' desire to rebel, and in 1798 more men were hanged for the crime of mutiny than in any previous year. Indeed, it seems likely that tighter discipline often had the opposite effect, forcing sailors to take more radical measures: it was after 1797 that more extreme mutinies took place, as British naval ships were handed over to the enemy. In this, the Navy's efforts and failure to quell protest again aligned with contemporary attempts by the British government to subdue dissent. The Combination Acts of 1799 responded to the creation of proto-trade unions, banning such 'combinations' in an attempt to prevent collective-bargaining efforts. This only encouraged further resistance and more sophisticated organisation by workers, and Parliament was forced to pass the Arbitration Act later that year, a compromise that allowed weavers to negotiate wages with their employers under the arbitration of a magistrate.[10]

A similar pattern can be found among the Navy's land-based workers. The naval dockyards employed thousands of skilled workers who had considerable bargaining power, especially during wartime, for without them the crucial processes of shipbuilding and refitting could not occur. Throughout the 1790s small-scale resistance had occurred in the Navy's yards, with workers engaged in quiet subversion as well as open revolt. This involved embezzling supplies and creative time accounting, but also the successful organisation of strikes by shipwrights to secure the release of colleagues who had been impressed or negotiating improved conditions.[11] Larger-scale strikes were avoided, though. At the height of fears about British Jacobinism, the government had discussed a bill to prevent 'combinations' in the naval dockyards, though it was not brought forward for fear of aggravating relations in the yards at a critical point of the war. It was only in 1799–1800, as the government responded to labour protests across the country, that more general prohibitions came into the yards. Unsurprisingly, the subsequent two years were marked by labour unrest on a scale hitherto unseen in the war. In spring 1801, dockyard workers at Plymouth and Sheerness became involved in food riots, and government figures were quick to blame 'the insinuations of evil disposing and designing men'. Three hundred and forty supposedly dangerous individuals were discharged from the yards, and a select few were prosecuted for assault and riot, but in the years that followed the Navy Board were fighting a losing battle. Between 1803 and 1805 shipwrights at Chatham, Portsmouth and Plymouth made seven complaints about their terms of employment, winning concessions on six occasions.[12]

Perhaps aware that repression could only achieve so much, the state devoted considerable attention to shaping public opinion through propaganda. Naval victories – particularly those at Camperdown and Aboukir Bay – allowed the Navy to be presented to the public as a victorious institution, commanded by skilled officers and brave, loyal Tars, helping the government construct a 'victory culture' that calmed public fears and boosted support for the war. Unlike the army, which suffered defeat after defeat throughout the 1790s, the Navy offered a series of striking successes. Thomas Erskine, MP for Portsmouth, agreed and noted its subsequent potential to shape identities:

> Would to God I were to look nowhere else than to the ocean for the military occurrences of Great Britain. We might then encrease [sic] every day the enthusiasm of Englishmen for their country & its Constitution.[13]

Central to this programme were naval officers, and in particular Horatio Nelson, who came to symbolise Britain's war against Revolutionary France. It is worth remembering, though, that this cultural outpouring sat alongside a much more complex and often negative depiction of naval events. Even the 'Glorious' victory of 1794 was satirised and, as this book has shown, sectors of the British population were resistant to the state's propaganda efforts. What is more, the government could do little to cover up naval failures, such as calamitous imperial campaigns that cost tens of thousands of lives, or the Navy's failure to reliably defend the British coastline from French invasion attempts. This serves to remind us of the limits of state power. We know that celebratory material reached countless Britons, but to what extent it shaped their world view remains unclear.

The renewed focus on naval officers was no coincidence. Alongside the 'victory culture' of the late 1790s came the continued spectre of mutinous, disloyal sailors, and the propaganda efforts in the aftermath of Camperdown were in many respects a last-ditch – and largely unsuccessful – attempt to resurrect the once-comforting figure of the sailor in British popular culture. For the remainder of the war, the sailor remained a contested figure associated with rebellion as much as valour. There were no celebrations of the individual sailors who had fought at the Nile or Copenhagen, and an image depicting the 1801 *Temeraire* mutineers was included in the trial proceedings that was published the following year, giving their names and likenesses. Throughout the Napoleonic Wars of 1803–15, the British populace were once again bombarded with a simplistic image of 'Jack Tar', a worthy ally in the war against the French emperor, but also a figure who was easily duped and required careful management.[14] It was not until the mid-nineteenth century that the common seaman was properly re-assimilated into the pantheon of British heroes and re-envisaged as a symbol of patriotic manhood. It is no surprise that Victorians once again returned to the story of Jack Crawford to help sell this image.[15]

The contested representation of the sailor was one legacy of this era. Another was a new understanding that naval power offered only so much in a war against a continental enemy in a conflict for national survival. Traditionally, Britain's 'blue-water' strategy had been very successful in the 'limited' wars of the eighteenth century, ensuring that imperial successes more than made up for any moderate European acquisitions made by a continental enemy. During the Revolutionary War, though, colonial gains could not make up for the European advances of France's revolutionary army. Winning naval battles maintained a command of the seas, though the strategic dividends of the Glorious First of June, the Nile and Camperdown were marginal. Naval blockade prevented calamitous French naval incursions, but the Egypt expedition from Toulon in May 1798 and the escape of French fleets in April 1799 and January 1801 demonstrated that French fleets could and did avoid the Navy's shackles.[16] There was no 'knock-out' blow against the French navy, and the Navy's successes across the period were largely ones of attrition. From 1793 to 1800 it captured 250,000 tons of prizes and the French a mere 48,000, which forced France to devote ever greater resources to shipbuilding, and secured a controlling influence over the ships of its allies. By the time of the peace in 1801, 371 French naval vessels had been lost including 55 ships of the line, representing 67 per cent of its battlefleet at the beginning of the war.[17]

British naval successes in this war were therefore fundamentally defensive. While the Navy's role in defending the territorial integrity of the British Isles is debatable, to say the least, its protection of British trade – the lifeblood of the British economy and financial system – proved more decisive. Here too there were cracks in the edifice of British naval might, and French privateers took some 5,600 British merchant ships between 1793 and 1801.[18] However, this represented a relatively small proportion of Britain's overall commerce, and by the late 1790s, with the privateer threat weakened and colonial conflict diminished, Britain's maritime trade was once again flowing at record levels. Between 1798 and 1802, imports increased 58.5 per cent over 1788–92 values, with West Indian sugar and coffee representing a significant proportion of this. Domestic exports rose 57.7 per cent in the same period, with re-exports growing a remarkable 187.2 per cent.[19] It was the revenues of these trades, alongside ever larger borrowing, that allowed Pitt and then Addington to finance the war as long as they did. Commerce alone could not win the war, however, and attempts to use the Navy in a more offensive way – through amphibious assaults and attacks on the French economy – were less successful and go some way to explaining Britain's willingness to agree terms in 1801. In the conflict that followed – another global war fought on an even larger scale – the protection of trade remained paramount, but the Navy proved far more adept at influencing the wider war through offensive operations.[20]

In other respects, too, the Napoleonic Wars of 1803–15 were entirely different. Unlike the conflict that was waged during the 1790s, they saw considerably fewer examples of maritime protest, and there was no outbreak of organised fleet mutinies like those of 1797. Shipboard society – and by extension resistance and rebellion – was always a product of contemporary political culture. The 1790s had been marked by deep ideological divisions between radicals and loyalists, reformers and moderates, war hawks and pacifists, as the Age of Revolutions shaped and reshaped the meaning and practice of politics. The 1800s, by contrast, witnessed remarkable political unanimity. Radicalism was consigned to the margins, and it was not until the late 1810s and 1820s that a revived movement for political reform once again re-emerged. For the most part the war against Napoleon was popular, and critiques of the war tended to focus on how – rather than whether – the conflict should be fought.[21] In an era of broad political consensus, it is perhaps not surprising that fewer sailors actively resisted naval authority or came to see their service in less political terms. Those sailors who did make 'political' statements were dismissed as abnormal rather than threatening. Only a few months into the Napoleonic Wars in 1803, a sailor who declared that he hated 'all kings' was let off a death sentence when a series of witnesses persuaded the court that he was insane.[22]

The 'tempest' experienced by the Navy in the 1790s, then, was a unique period of history. Afterwards, few protagonists – sailors, officers or government officials – had much to gain by raking over the upheavals of the period, barring the celebration of notable naval victories, and the Navy did all it could to confine the accompanying story of mutiny and rebellion to the recesses of history. The radical Thomas Spence was a rare individual who continued to hold up the naval mutinies of 1797 as a model of popular resistance, but his call for the abolition of private ownership of land was so naïve, and his following so small, that he was largely ignored.[23] Memories of the Navy's Age of Revolutions survived through folk memory, in songs that either celebrated the sailors' attempts to forge a better life for themselves ('The Floating Republic') or commemorated those who had suffered ('Here's the Tender Coming', 'Seventeen Bright Stars'). Otherwise, most Britons in the early nineteenth century engaged with the Navy through newspaper reports, or through staged patriotic events such as ship launches. Writing after the conflict, the sailor Samuel Leech noted that the average Briton 'has doubtless seen ships of war with their trim rigging . . . and his heart has swelled with pride as he has gazed upon these floating cities', but to its 'internal arrangements, however, he has been a stranger'.[24] It is hoped that this book has helped to recover the political lives of the men who worked these vessels, their attempts to strive for a better life and their relationship with the turbulent age in which they lived.

NOTE ON SOURCES

Tempest uses an array of untapped archival material. Perhaps most obviously, it employs official sources – in particular Admiralty records – to explore naval events. These include correspondence, registers and logs kept by captains, lieutenants and masters, as well as other administrative records assembled and preserved by the government and its bureaucracy. Care must be taken here, as these documents were often formulaic, one-sided and limited in their perspective. Even the most senior naval officers knew they could only offer a partial picture. Writing in 1794, Admiral Lord Howe noted that 'The Commander of a Fleet, their Lordships know, is unavoidably so confined in his view of the Occurrences in Battle, as to be little capable of rendering personal testimony'. Others were reticent about offering detail: John Jervis wrote that 'I would rather have an action with the enemy than detail one'.[1] We are also reliant on what the state chose to collect, and what subsequent governments have chosen to preserve. The Admiralty destroyed some of the documents seized at the Nore mutiny, leaving us only with sparsely catalogued digests and a large archival silence. Isaac Land rightly challenges us to think about government records much as we would any others, as partial records that reflect the aims and agendas of their creators.[2] Nonetheless, state collections remain the best way to access institutional priorities, as well as the views and ideas of seamen. The vast majority of sailors' political writings have only survived because they were deemed of sufficient (if alarming) importance.

Official correspondence is mixed with personal papers that tend to offer a more candid version of events. Here the balance of the archive leans heavily towards naval elites, whose letters have been preserved and conserved in great numbers. Writing was an important part of life for naval officers, who were frequently distant from friends and loved ones, providing a crucial means of maintaining connections and securing emotional comfort. They therefore offer a much more private window into thoughts and feelings and reveal networks of knowledge in which the domestic sphere acted as a 'nerve centre' of information capable of subsuming news and rumour.[3] Correspondents came to rely on regular letters, and when these failed to arrive, it was hard not to fear the worst. In early 1797, Martha Saumarez, wife of the naval officer Captain James Saumarez, wrote of her anxiety at not hearing from him and pleaded for news. She understood full well that this was emotional labour that often went unnoticed. 'Nobody pities me for the Distance of our separation!', she declared, and in language that upturned the usual gender roles, she wrote that '<u>considering all things</u> – I think I behave like a heroine'.[4] Letters were not always private and could be circulated among friends and family, so there remained a degree of self-censorship. Nonetheless, letter-writing was a daily activity for most naval officers, and we benefit from a profusion of officers' papers that offer rich insights into their objectives and experiences.

Letters from home offer one way of engaging with wider public views, but this book uses a variety of other materials to explore how Britons thought about the Navy, and how it shaped their lives, ranging from books to pamphlets, prints, plays, tracts and ballads. These were competing forms of cultural media that appealed to different audiences: while books were predominantly the preserve of the educated middle classes, ballads were more of a 'shared culture', reaching up and down the social spectrum. Taken together, they allow us to construct a sense of differing public mentalities, whether about the Navy, its officer corps or its sailors. These tended to follow more patriotic, loyalist tropes, for the 1790s was an age of censorship, and seditious material is less likely to have made its way into the historical record. Even plays were monitored closely for any problematic content.[5] Perhaps the most revealing material, then, are visual sources that were able to use images to make their points, making them virtually immune from prosecution for sedition, libel or obscenity. Caricatures of contemporary political and military affairs were routinely published within days of the events that inspired them, often appearing in tandem with, and even anticipating, the official dispatches and news reports that filled an ever growing number of daily and weekly papers. The journalistic concern for current affairs ensured that caricature served as both a barometer of, and a guiding force for, public opinion.[6]

More voluminous than any other form of cultural media were newspapers, ranging from the large nationals based in London to the hundreds of smaller, local organs that copied and adapted news reports before disseminating them to their immediate communities.[7] More than any other source, newspapers capture the diversity of opinion across Britain. Every newspaper claimed some degree of political objectivity, but most openly aligned themselves to a particular faction.[8] A number of ministerial newspapers, such as the *Sun* and *True Briton*, were founded just as war with France neared (in October 1792 and January 1793 respectively), offering loyalist takes that defended Pitt's government and denounced opposition newspapers such as the *Courier* and *Morning Chronicle* as Jacobin. Others were nakedly propagandist: from January 1798 to 1799 the editor of *The Times*, John Walter, received a subsidy of £300 a year from the Treasury to 'continue his general support of Government'.[9] These were designed to influence, and historians have debated how effective this propaganda was. Then as now, contemporaries learned not to trust everything they read in newspapers. One sailor writing to his son claimed they were little more than fake news: 'Assertions & Contradictions fill up every news paper that a man of veracity . . . must cease reading and guard against repeating what he hears'.[10]

For all the criticism of their journalistic integrity, however, newspapers offer an incredible window into the way Britons experienced war, and therefore how they engaged with the Navy. Newspapers provided fast and often detailed reportage of recent events and were the primary means through which individuals – both the public and sailors – consumed news. The speed with which information could be disseminated was incredible, and many sailors wrote home expecting that the events described in their letters would already be known to the recipient due to the speed with which newspapers could spread information. Following the Battle of the Nile in 1798, Henry Harrop wrote to his father anticipating that 'Before you receive this you will have heard of the action betwixt our Fleet and the French on our first coming up the Mediterranean'. Edward Nosworthy gave only an 'out line' of the battle, of 'which the particulars you must have long since been informed by the news papers'.[11] Certainly, we know that they reached a large swathe of the population. While the largest organs had circulations numbering in the low thousands, Hannah Barker has shown that news was often consumed communally or via establishments such as coffee houses and newspaper lenders, where a large group of people could read a paper's contents.[12]

If there are countless types of sources that reveal the lives and viewpoints of naval officers and popular elites, recovering the voices of sailors is a far trickier task. No 'personal papers' from men of the lower deck have survived, but it is nonetheless possible to locate the voice of the sailor through a range of other materials. By 1800, all ranks of society were participating in what one historian describes as a vibrant 'culture of letters', and as this book has shown, a high proportion of sailors were literate.[13] Others could ask more literate friends to help with their communications. In 1800, the sailor Richard Greenhalgh apologised to his parents for his 'bad writing' as the crewmate who usually helped him, Thomas Brown, had been drafted to another ship. For sailors such as Greenhalgh, naval service helped them develop their writing skills, and following Brown's departure he hoped that 'I shall write myself for the future'.[14] It follows that in recent years, hundreds of contemporary letters from sailors have been found and catalogued, offering a rare insight into the hearts and minds of the Navy's lower deck.[15]

As with the letters of naval officers, this correspondence gives an insight into the thoughts of individuals, rather than the collective. Tom Gill wrote that describing a battle was 'impossible'. 'An individual may know tolerably well what is going on in his own ship,' he wrote, 'but no more.'[16] Much like their officer counterparts, sailors could struggle to put their experiences into words. 'I Could Wich [wish] to Describ it Better to You,' wrote the sailor Samuel Willcock to his brother after a battle, 'But it Does Not Lye in My Power.'[17] Sailors tended to present a positive view of naval service, sparing loved ones the details of battles or gruesome conditions at sea. Richard Greenhalgh deliberately kept the 'many misfortunes that are daily happening' from his parents.[18] If there was a difference between sailors' and officers' correspondence, it was that sailors' letters were far more likely to be monitored by the state. In 1795 the British government passed an act that allowed sailors to send letters for only a penny, with the condition that they used their name, confirmed by the signature of the officer in command.[19] Censorship of this nature was not uncommon in the 1790s – the Post Office was given powers by the Secretary of State to intercept letters, which contributed to the 1794 prosecutions against Horn Tooke and Thomas Paine – and sailors were certainly aware that their post might be read.[20] Nonetheless, letters remain the best way to understand the thoughts and feelings of sailors at the time of their service.

Another source used for exploring sailors' lived experience is the memoir. From the 1820s onwards a number of sailors who had served throughout the Revolutionary and Napoleonic Wars set out their experiences for wider public consumption. There appears to have been a real market for these memoirs, with a number of published works emerging alongside shorter testimonials in weekly and monthly periodicals. The distance from the events being described has led some historians to question their accuracy, as well as the motivations of the sailors who wrote them.[21] Certainly some had a clear political agenda. *Nautical Economy*, published by William Robinson in 1836 amid a renewed movement for reform, critiqued the triumphalist books produced by '*epaulette* authors' and 'high-flown gentlemen-writers' and offered a very different picture of naval life based around the brutal realities of impressment and harsh discipline. His purpose was also clear: 'The order of the present day, *on land*, it seems is *reform*: – then why should the *sea-service* have its imperfections remain unattended to?'[22] Other motivations also propelled sailors into authorship. John Nicol published his memoir in 1822 in a desperate attempt to earn money, having been told by the Admiralty not to bother applying for a pension.[23] Some of these authors had axes to grind, and it may well be that there was a tendency towards exaggeration and sensationalism by authors hoping to sell copy. However, the experiences being described were not fictional: as we have seen, sailors were frequently impressed and exploited, and it seems churlish to discount their views and experiences because they wrote with literary flair.[24]

Another way to reconstruct the social fabric of the naval world is through courts martial. These naval trials allowed any member of a naval crew to be accused of wrongdoing under the guidelines set out by the Articles of War; for instance, any captain who lost his ship was given an automatic court martial.[25] More frequently, however, it was the men of the lower deck who were charged, generally for the most severe crimes. As a result, we have access to voluminous – and largely untapped – naval records that record the voice of the sailor: in most cases these acted as interviews, with the accused responding to the questioner's prompts, while other sailors could be called on to testify for or against a given individual. Every participant swore an oath to be truthful, but with severe punishments often at stake, participants had good reason to at least be flexible with the truth. We should also be aware that while we can hear the voice of the sailor in these records, it was a voice that was moderated by the naval elites. Nonetheless, David Featherstone's analysis of these records finds that the sailors were rarely diffident in their testimony and in fact used these court appearances as a way of challenging the strict hierarchical order of the ship.[26] Courts martial therefore remain a rich source for detailing the lives of sailors. They are particularly relevant because they frequently document the moment when sailors came into conflict with the naval authorities, and perhaps more than any other source they offer a compelling window into the political lives of sailors.

NOTES

PREFACE

1. TNA, ADM 1/5125, 'To the Delegates of the Different Ships Assembled in Council'.
2. Ibid.

INTRODUCTION

1. For some, the 'Age of Revolutions' begins with the American Revolution of 1775, but others have questioned its transformative impact and instead identify the French Revolution of 1789 or the Haitian Revolution of 1791 as marking its start. Eric Hobsbawm's *The Age of Revolutions* ignores the American Revolution altogether and sees the 1789–1848 period as the most transformative. The end date is similarly contested, and while the European revolutions of 1848 work as a sensible conclusion for many, others see dates in earlier decades. R.R. Palmer's *The Age of the Democratic Revolution* focused particularly on events in America and France and concluded in 1799, while Trevor Burnard's recent book on Jamaica during the Age of Revolutions concludes in 1788 (though he does acknowledge 'the defining crisis of the French Revolution' that followed, p. 9). See R.R. Palmer, *The Age of the Democratic Revolution* (Princeton, NJ: Princeton University Press, 1959); Eric Hobsbawm, *The Age of Revolution, 1789–1848* (London: Weidenfeld & Nicholson, 1962); Trevor Burnard, *Jamaica in the Age of Revolution* (Philadelphia: University of Pennsylvania Press, 2020).
2. Jonathan Israel, *Revolutionary Ideas: An Intellectual History of the French Revolution from The Rights of Man to Robespierre* (Princeton, NJ: Princeton University Press, 2014).
3. See for example David Armitage and Sanjay Subrahmanyam, eds, *The Age of Revolutions in Global Context, c. 1760–1840* (Basingstoke: Palgrave Macmillan, 2010); C.A. Bayly, *Imperial Meridian: The British Empire and the World, 1780–1830* (London: Routledge, 1989); C.A. Bayly, *The Birth of the Modern World, 1780–1914: Global Connections and Comparisons* (Oxford: Oxford University Press, 2004), esp. pp. 86–129; John Darwin, *After Tamerlaine: The Rise and Fall of Global Empires* (London, 2007).
4. *Morning Post*, 12 June 1795.
5. E.P. Thompson, *The Making of the English Working Class* (London: Penguin, 2013), p. 167.

6. See for instance Mark Philp, ed., *The French Revolution and British Popular Politics* (Cambridge: Cambridge University Press, 1991); Chris Evans, *Debating the Revolution: Britain in the 1790s* (London: I.B. Tauris, 2006).

7. John Barrell and Jon Mee, eds, 'Introduction', in *Trials for Treason and Sedition, 1792–1794*, Vol. 1 (London: Pickering and Chatto, 2006–7), pp. ix–x; Paul Langford, *A Polite and Commercial People: England 1727–1783* (Oxford: Oxford University Press, 1989), pp. 710–19.

8. Kathleen Wilson, 'The Crisis: Radicalism, Loyalism and the American War, 1774–85', in Kathleen Wilson, *Sense of the People: Politics, Culture and Imperialism in England, 1715–1785* (Cambridge: Cambridge University Press, 1995), pp. 237–84; Dror Wahrman, *The Making of the Modern Self: Identity and Culture in Eighteenth-Century England* (New Haven, CT and London: Yale University Press, 2007), pp. 218–64.

9. The classic work on the French Revolution remains William Doyle, *The Oxford History of the French Revolution* (Oxford: Oxford University Press, 1989). For a more modern take see Peter McPhee, *Liberty or Death: The French Revolution* (New Haven, CT and London: Yale University Press, 2016).

10. See Marilyn Butler, ed., *Burke, Paine, Godwin and the Revolution Controversy* (Cambridge: Cambridge University Press, 1984); Ian Hampsher-Monk, ed., *The Impact of the French Revolution: Texts from Britain in the 1790s* (Cambridge: Cambridge University Press, 2005); Norbert Schürer, 'The Storming of the Bastille in English Newspapers', *Eighteenth-Century Life*, Vol. 29, No. 1 (2005), pp. 50–81; Robert Hole, 'English Sermons and Tracts as Media of Debate on the French Revolution 1789–99', in Philp, ed., *The French Revolution and British Popular Politics*, pp. 1–17.

11. Nicholas Rogers, *Crowds, Culture and Politics in Georgian Britain* (Oxford: Clarendon Press, 1998), pp. 195–6.

12. Thomas Paine, *Rights of Man: Being an Answer to Mr Burke's Attack on the French Revolution*, edited by Mark Philp (London: Penguin, 2008), pp. vii, xvii–xxi, xxiii–xxiv, 162.

13. Mark Philp, 'Introduction', in Mark Philp, ed., *Resisting Napoleon: The British Response to the Threat of Invasion, 1797–1815* (Aldershot: Ashgate, 2006), p. 4; Thompson, *Making of the English Working Class*, pp. 93–118, 130–1; Rogers, *Crowds, Culture and Politics*, p. 196; Barrell and Mee, 'Introduction', p. xii.

14. Michael T. Davis, 'Introduction', in Michael T. Davis, ed., *London Corresponding Society, 1792–1799* (London: Pickering and Chatto, 2002), Vol. 1, pp. xxv–xlviii. On the radical movement more broadly see Pamela Clemit, ed., *The Cambridge Companion to British Literature of the French Revolution in the 1790s* (Cambridge: Cambridge University Press, 2011); Michael T. Davis and Paul Pickering, eds, *Unrespectable Radicals? Popular Politics in the Age of Reform* (London: Ashgate, 2008); Robert Maniquis, ed., *British Radical Culture of the 1790s* (San Marino, CA: Huntington Library Press, 2002); Rogers, *Crowds, Culture and Politics*, pp. 197–8.

15. For the most recent treatment see John Rees, *The Leveller Revolution: Radical Political Organization in England, 1640–1650* (London: Verso, 2016).

16. Barrell and Mee, 'Introduction', pp. xxii–xxiii; see J.R. Dinwiddy, 'Conceptions of Revolution in the English Radicalism of the 1790s', in J.R. Dinwiddy, *Radicalism and Reform in Britain, 1780–1850* (London: Hambledon Press, 1992), pp. 169–94, p. 177.

17. Mark Philp, 'The Fragmented Ideology of Reform', in Philp, ed., *The French Revolution and British Popular Politics*, pp. 50–77; Dinwiddy, 'Conceptions of Revolution', pp. 169–94; Katrina Navickas, *Loyalism and Radicalism in Lancashire, 1798–1815* (Oxford: Oxford University Press, 2009), pp. 4–6.

18. Steve Poole, *The Politics of Regicide in England, 1760–1850: Troublesome Subjects* (Manchester: Manchester University Press, 2000).

19. Hester Stanhope, *Memoirs of the Lady Hester Stanhope as Related by Herself in Conversations with her Physician; Comprising her Opinions and Anecdotes of Some of the Most Remarkable Persons of Her Time*, 3 vols (London: Henry Colburn, 1845), Vol. 2, p. 22.

20. *The Times*, 19 July 1791; Mark Philp, 'Disconcerting Ideas: Explaining Popular Radicalism and Popular Loyalism in the 1790s', in Glenn Burgess and Matthew Festenstein, eds, *English Radicalism, 1550–1850* (Cambridge: Cambridge University Press, 2007), p. 159.

21. Nicholas Rogers, 'Burning Tom Paine: Loyalism and Counter-Revolution in Britain, 1792–93', *Social History*, Vol. 32, No. 64 (November 1999), pp. 139–71, p. 141.

22. Rogers, *Crowds, Culture and Politics*, pp. 204–5; John Dinwiddy, 'Interpretations of Anti-Jacobinism', in Philp, ed., *The French Revolution and British Popular Politics*, pp. 18–37, p. 205.

23. J.E. Cookson, *The British Armed Nation 1793–1815* (Oxford: Clarendon Press, 1997), p. 26; Robert R. Dozier, *For King, Constitution and Country* (Lexington, KY: University Press of Kentucky, 1983), pp. 55–64; Elizabeth Sparrow, *The Secret Service: British Agents in France 1792–1815* (Woodbridge: Boydell Press, 1999), pp. 10–12.

24. Frank O'Gorman, 'English Loyalism Revisited', in Allan Blackstock and Eoin Magennis, eds, *Politics and Political Culture in Britain and Ireland 1750–1850* (Belfast: Ulster Historical Foundation, 2007), pp. 223–41; Mona Scheuerman, *In Praise of Poverty: Hannah More Counters Thomas Paine and the Radical Threat* (Lexington, KY: University Press of Kentucky, 2002); Kevin Gilmartin, *Writing Against Revolution: Literary Conservatism in Britain, 1790–1832* (Cambridge: Cambridge University Press, 2007); Dinwiddy, 'Interpretations of Anti-Jacobinism'; Gary Kelly, 'Revolution, Reaction and the Expropriation of Popular Culture: Hannah More's Cheap Repository', *Man and Nature*, Vol. 6 (1987), pp. 147–59; Kevin Gilmartin, ' "Study to Be Quiet": Hannah More and Counterrevolutionary Moral Reform', in Gilmartin, ed., *Writing Against Revolution*, pp. 55–95.

25. Hampson, *Perfidy of Albion*, pp. 96–7, quoted in Roger Knight, *Britain Against Napoleon: The Organization of Victory* (London: Allen Lane, 2013), p. 62.

26. National Maritime Museum (NMM), NEP/3. Secret Service accounts, 'Government Account with the Rt Hon. Henry Dundas', 2 March 1795; Elizabeth Sparrow, 'The Alien Office, 1792–1806', *Historical Journal*, Vol. 33, No. 2 (1990), pp. 361–84; Sparrow, *Secret Service*, pp. 19–20, 286; Knight, *Britain Against Napoleon*, p. 127; Clive Emsley, 'The Home Office and Its Sources of Information and Investigation, 1791–1801', *English Historical Review*, Vol. 94 (1979), pp. 532–61, see p. 539 and its note.

27. Sparrow, *Secret Service*, pp. 7–9, 27–8; Rogers, *Crowds, Culture and Politics*, p. 200.

28. Hampsher-Monk, *The Impact of the French Revolution*, p. 19; Barrell and Mee, 'Introduction', pp. xiii–xx.

29. Rogers, *Crowds, Culture and Politics*, p. 210.

30. Barrell and Mee, 'Introduction', pp. xxvi–xxviii. See also John Barrell, *Imagining the King's Death: Figurative Treason, Fantasies of Regicide 1793–1796* (Oxford: Oxford University Press, 2000).

31. David Worrall, *Radical Culture: Discourse, Resistance and Surveillance, 1790–1820* (Detroit, MI: Wayne State University Press, 1992), pp. 9–14; Clive Emsley, 'An Aspect of Pitt's "Terror": Prosecutions for Sedition during the 1790s', *Social History*, Vol. 6, No. 2 (May 1981), pp. 155–84.

32. Barrell and Mee, 'Introduction', pp. xxi–xxii, xxxii–xxxiv.

33. Edward Hughes, ed., *The Private Correspondence of Admiral Lord Collingwood* (London: Navy Records Society, 1957), p. 43.
34. Emma Vincent Macleod, *A War of Ideas: British Attitudes to the Wars Against Revolutionary France, 1792–1802* (Aldershot: Ashgate, 1998), pp. 1–2, 202–3; Philp, 'Introduction', p. 4.
35. Philip Harling, 'A Tale of Two Conflicts: Critiques of the British War Effort, 1793–1815', in Philp, ed., *Resisting Napoleon*, pp. 19–40. See also Macleod, *A War of Ideas*.
36. Mark Philp, 'Disconcerting Ideas: Explaining Popular Radicalism and Popular Loyalism in the 1790s', in Glenn Burgess and Matthew Festenstein, eds, *English Radicalism, 1550–1850* (Cambridge: Cambridge University Press, 2007), pp. 160–1; Philp, 'Introduction', p. 11.
37. For this point see Dinwiddy, 'Interpretations of Anti-Jacobinism', p. 48; Rogers, *Crowds, Culture and Politics*, p. 211.
38. Nick Mansfield, *Soldiers as Citizens: Popular Politics and the Nineteenth-Century British Military* (Liverpool: Liverpool University Press, 2020); Joseph Cozens, 'The Experience of Soldiering: Civil–Military Relations and Popular Protest in England', Unpublished PhD thesis, University of Essex (2020); Cookson, *British Armed Nation*; Matthew McCormack, *Embodying the Militia in Georgian England* (Oxford: Oxford University Press, 2015); Philp, ed., *Resisting Napoleon*; J.E. Cookson, 'The English Volunteer Movement of the French Wars, 1793–1815: Some Contexts', *Historical Journal*, Vol. 32, No. 4 (December 1989), pp. 867–91; Austin Gee, *The British Volunteer Movement 1794–1814* (Oxford: Clarendon Press, 2003); Kevin B. Lynch, ' "A Citizen and Not a Soldier": The British Volunteer Movement and the War Against Napoleon', in Alan Forrest, Karen Hagerman and Jane Rendell, eds, *Soldiers, Citizens and Civilians: Experiences and Perceptions of the Revolutionary and Napoleonic Wars, 1790–1820* (Basingstoke: Palgrave Macmillan, 2009), pp. 205–21.
39. Cookson, *British Armed Nation*, p. v.
40. Isaac Land, *War, Nationalism and the British Sailor, 1750–1805* (London: Palgrave Macmillan, 2009), p. 1.
41. NMM, ACG/B/26, John Jupp to his father and mother, 26 November 1798.
42. See Sara Caputo, 'Alien Seamen in the British Navy, British Law, and the British State, c. 1793–c. 1815', *Historical Journal*, Vol. 62, No. 4 (2019), pp. 685–707; Sara Caputo, 'Scotland, Scottishness, British Integration and the Royal Navy, 1793–1815', *Scottish Historical Review*, Vol. 97, No. 1 (2018), pp. 85–118; and Sara Caputo, *Foreign Jack Tars: The British Navy and Transnational Seafarers during the Revolutionary and Napoleonic Wars* (Cambridge: Cambridge University Press, forthcoming). For the specific data see J. Ross Dancy, *The Myth of the Press Gang: Volunteers, Impressment and the Naval Manpower Problem in the Late Eighteenth Century* (Woodbridge: Boydell Press, 2015), pp. 49–53.
43. Brian Vale, 'The Post Office, the Admiralty and Letters to Sailors in the Napoleonic Wars', *Mariner's Mirror*, Vol. 105, No. 2 (2019), pp. 148–61; Helen Watt and Anne Hawkins, eds, *Letters of Seamen in the Wars with France, 1793–1815* (Woodbridge: Boydell Press, 2016), pp. 20–5.
44. TNA, ADM 1/5340, court martial of John Goody et al. of the *Saturn*, 19–27 July 1797.
45. Evan Wilson, *A Social History of British Naval Officers, 1775–1815* (Woodbridge: Boydell Press, 2016); Sam Cavell, *Midshipmen and Quarterdeck Boys in the British Navy, 1771–1831* (Woodbridge: Boydell Press, 2012); Richard Blake, *Evangelicals in the Royal Navy 1775–1815* (Woodbridge: Boydell Press, 2008); Ellen Gill, *Naval Families, War and Duty in Britain, 1740–1820* (Woodbridge: Boydell

Press, 2016); Cheryl A. Fury, *The Social History of Seamen 1650–1815* (Woodbridge: Boydell Press, 2017).

46. Wilson, *Social History*, pp. 87, 83–104.

47. Henry Lloyd, *A Political and Military Rhapsody on the Invasion and Defence of Great Britain and Ireland. Illustrated with three copper-plates. By the Late General Lloyd. To which is annexed, an introduction, and a short account of the author's life* (London, 1790), pp. 14–15.

48. Knight, *Britain Against Napoleon*, pp. 21–39; B.R. Mitchell, *British Historical Statistics* (Cambridge: Cambridge University Press, 1988), pp. 579–81.

49. Kathleen Wilson, 'Empire, Trade and Popular Politics in Mid-Hanoverian Britain: The Case of Admiral Vernon', *Past and Present*, Vol. 21 (November 1988), pp. 74–109; Gerald Jordan and Nicholas Rogers, 'Admirals as Heroes: Patriotism and Liberty in Hanoverian England', *Journal of British Studies*, Vol. 27, No. 3 (July 1989), pp. 201–24, pp. 208–10.

50. Anon., *An Address to the Seamen in the British Navy* (London: W. Richardson, 1797), pp. 5–6.

51. Michael Lewis, *A Social History of the Navy, 1793–1815* (London: Allen & Unwin, 1960), p. 124; Stephen Taylor, *Sons of the Waves: The Common Seaman in the Heroic Age of Sail* (New Haven, CT and London: Yale University Press, 2020), p. xvii.

52. TNA, ADM 1/5339, court martial of William Guthrie et al. of the *Pompee*, 20–23 June 1797.

53. N.A.M. Rodger, *The Wooden World: An Anatomy of the Georgian Navy* (London: Collins, 1986).

54. Marcus Rediker, *Between the Devil and the Deep Blue Sea: Merchant Seamen, Pirates and the Anglo-American Naval World, 1700–1750* (Cambridge: Cambridge University Press, 1987), pp. 154–5; Peter Linebaugh and Marcus Rediker, *The Many-Headed Hydra: The Hidden History of the Revolutionary Atlantic* (London: Verso, 2000), pp. 143–4, 154–6.

55. Niklas Frykman, *The Bloody Flag: Mutiny in the Age of Atlantic Revolution* (Oakland: University of California Press, 2020).

56. For critiques of Rediker's work see Ronald Schultz, 'Pirates and Proletarians: Authority, Labour and Capital Accumulation in the First British Empire', *Radical History Review*, Vol. 44 (1989); Daniel Vickers et al., 'Roundtable: Reviews of Marcus Rediker, Between the Devil and the Deep Blue Sea', *International Journal of Maritime History*, Vol. 1 (1989), pp. 311–57; Seth Rockman, 'Work in the Cities of Colonial British North America', *Journal of Urban History*, Vol. 33 (2007); Land, *War, Nationalism and the British Sailor*, pp. 3–4, 14–28.

57. TNA, ADM 1/5339, court martial of Daniel Campbell of the *Tartar*, 30 May 1797.

58. N.A.M. Rodger, *Safeguard of the Sea: A Naval History of Britain, Vol. 1: 660–1649* (London: Allen Lane, 1997), p. 322; N.A.M. Rodger, 'Mutiny or Subversion? Spithead and the Nore', in T. Bartlett, D. Dickson, D. Keogh and K. Whelan, eds, *1798: A Bicentenary Perspective* (Dublin: Four Courts Press, 2003), pp. 549–64, p. 563. See also Karel Davids, 'Seamen's Organizations and Social Protest in Europe, c. 1300–1825', *International Review of Social History*, Vol. 39, Supplement 2: Before the Unions: Wage Earners and Collective Action in Europe, 1300–1850 (1994), pp. 145–69.

59. Michel Foucault, 'Of Other Spaces', *Diacritics*, Vol. 16 (1986), p. 27.

60. Richard Sheldon, 'The London Sailors' Strike of 1768', in Andrew Charlesworth et al., eds, *An Atlas of Industrial Protest in Britain, 1750–1990* (London: Macmillan, 1996).

61. Notable exceptions are Robert Gardiner's two volumes that cover this period: Robert Gardiner, ed., *Fleet Battle and Blockade: The French Revolutionary War 1793–1797* (London: Chatham, 1996); Robert Gardiner, ed., *Nelson Against Napoleon: From the Nile to Copenhagen, 1798–1801* (London: Chatham, 1997).

62. NMM WYN/109/7, Philip Patton, Observations on Naval Mutiny, presented in April 1795.

63. On finance see John Brewer, *The Sinews of Power: War Money and the English State 1688–1783* (New York, 1989); Aaron Graham and Patrick Walsh, eds, *The British Fiscal-Military States, 1660–c.1783* (London: Routledge, 2016); N.A.M. Rodger, 'From the "Military Revolution" to the "Fiscal-Naval State"', *Journal for Maritime Research*, Vol. 13, No. 2 (November 2011), pp. 119–28. On logistics and naval administration see Knight, *Britain Against Napoleon*; Roger Morriss, *The Foundations of British Maritime Ascendancy: Resources, Logistics and the State, 1755–1815* (Cambridge: Cambridge University Press, 2011); Clive Wilkinson, *The British Navy and the State in the 18th Century* (Woodbridge: Boydell Press, 2004); Roger Morriss, *The Royal Dockyards during the Revolutionary and Napoleonic Wars* (Leicester: University of Leicester Press, 1983); Roger Knight and Martin Wilcox, *Sustaining the Fleet: War, the British Navy and the Contractor State 1793–1815* (Woodbridge: Boydell Press, 2010); James Davey, *The Transformation of British Naval Strategy: Seapower and Supply in Northern Europe, 1808–1812* (Woodbridge: Boydell Press, 2012); Gareth Cole, *Arming the Royal Navy, 1793–1815: The Office of Ordnance and the State* (London: Pickering and Chatto, 2012); Jonathan Coad, *Support for the Fleet: Architecture and Engineering of the Royal Navy's Bases 1700–1914* (London: English Heritage, 2013).

64. Roger Wells, *Wretched Faces: Famine in Wartime England, 1793–1801* (Gloucester: Allan Sutton, 1988); Carl J. Griffin, *The Politics of Hunger: Protest, Poverty and Policy in England, c. 1750–c. 1840* (Manchester: Manchester University Press, 2020); Chris Evans, 'Hunger and Political Economy', in Evans, *Debating the Revolution*; Michael T. Davis, 'Food Riots and the Politics of Provision in Early-Modern England and France, the Irish Famine and World War I', in Michael T. Davis, ed., *Crowd Actions in Britain and France from the Middle Ages to the Modern World* (London: Palgrave Macmillan, 2015), pp. 101–23; John Bohstedt, *The Politics of Provisions: Food Riots, Moral Economy, and Market Transition in England, c. 1550–1850* (Aldershot: Routledge, 2010).

65. One recent exception is Thomas Malcomson, *Order and Disorder in the British Navy 1793–1815: Control, Resistance, Flogging and Hanging* (Woodbridge: Boydell Press, 2016), which focuses on the 1812–15 period.

66. Stuart Andrews, *The British Periodical Press and the French Revolution, 1789–99* (Basingstoke: Palgrave, 2000), pp. 72, 108; Mark Philp, Roz Southey, Caroline Jackson-Houlston and Susan Wollenberg, 'Music and Politics, 1793–1815' in Philp, ed., *Resisting Napoleon*, pp. 173–204, p. 174.

67. For the idea of the Navy as a cultural tool see Timothy Jenks, *Naval Engagements: Patriotism, Cultural Politics, and the Royal Navy 1793–1815* (Oxford: Oxford University Press, 2006).

68. Catriona Kennedy, *Narratives of the Revolutionary and Napoleonic Wars: Military and Civilian Experience in Britain and Ireland* (London: Palgrave Macmillan, 2013); Alan Forrest, Karen Hagerman and Jane Rendall, eds, *Soldiers, Citizens and Civilians: Experiences and Perceptions of the Revolutionary and Napoleonic Wars, 1790–1820* (London: Palgrave Macmillan, 2009); Jenny Uglow, *In These Times: Living in Britain Through Napoleon's Wars, 1793–1815* (London: Faber and Faber, 2014).

69. Jenks, *Naval Engagements*; Margarette Lincoln, *Representing the Royal Navy: British Seapower 1750–1815* (Aldershot: Routledge, 2002); Geoff Quilley, *Empire to Nation: Art, History and the Visualisation of Maritime Britain* (New Haven, CT and London: Yale University Press, 2011).
70. Quintin Colville and James Davey, eds, *A New Naval History* (Manchester: Manchester University Press, 2019).

1 LAWLESS MOBS AND A GORE OF BLOOD: NAVAL MOBILISATION AND IMPRESSMENT

1. John Nicol, *The Life and Adventures of John Nicol, Mariner* (London: William Blackwood, 1822), pp. 157–60.
2. For an example of the more relaxed recruitment policies followed during peacetime see Huntington Library (HL), Hamond Collection, Box 16 (12), 'Regulations for Carrying on the Impress Service, also at Dover, Folkestone, Ramsgate, Deal and Margate, with Remarks', 11 May 1790. The document sought to find 'the most Economical' solution to competition between the naval and merchant service, and to 'prevent *by any means*' irregularity or improper conduct'. As this chapter suggests, in wartime these concerns were notable by their absence.
3. Nicol, *Life and Adventures*, p. 205. See also Lincoln, *Representing the Royal Navy*.
4. For wider scholarship on impressment and sailors' labour see Dancy, *Myth of the Press Gang*; Rediker, *Devil and the Deep Blue Sea*; Denver Brunsman, *The Evil Necessity: British Naval Impressment in the Eighteenth-Century Atlantic World* (Charlottesville and London: University of Virginia Press, 2013). For critiques of Dancy see Isaac Land, 'New Scholarship on the Press Gang', parts 1 and 2, http://porttowns.port.ac.uk/press-gang-1/ and http://porttowns.port.ac.uk/press-gang2/; Christopher P. Magra, *Poseidon's Curse: Naval Impressment and Atlantic Origins of the American Revolution* (Cambridge: Cambridge University Press, 2016); Nicholas Rogers, 'British Impressment and Its Discontents', *International Journal of Maritime History*, Vol. 30, No. 1 (2018), pp. 52–73. This follows his earlier work: Nicholas Rogers, *The Press Gang: Naval Impressment and Its Opponents in Georgian Britain* (London: Continuum, 2007).
5. Nicol, *Life and Adventures*, pp. 171–2.
6. NMM, PBB7084, Naval Recruitment poster, c. 1797.
7. Christopher Lloyd, *The British Seaman 1200–1860: A Social Survey* (Cranbury, NJ: Associated University Presses, 1968), p. 121.
8. Cambridge University Library, Madden collection, 8,833, *British Tars* (J. Pitts, London).
9. Anon., *Songs, Naval and National, of the Late Charles Dibdin; With a memoir and Addenda. Collected and arranged by Thomas Dibdin, with Characteristic sketches by George Cruickshank* (London: John Murray, 1841). See also James Davey, 'Singing for the Nation: Balladry, Naval Recruitment, and the Language of Patriotism in Eighteenth-Century Britain', *Mariner's Mirror*, Vol. 103, No. 1 (2017), pp. 43–66; Land, *War, Nationalism and the British Sailor*, p. 5.
10. Nicol, *Life and Adventures*, p. 4.
11. When his prior employer complained, the Admiralty discharged him and forced him to pay costs. TNA, ADM 1/3683, Oath of John Gibbs, 5 July 1793.
12. *Trewman's Exeter Flying Post*, 13 and 27 December 1792; Rogers, 'British Impressment and Its Discontents', p. 70, referencing the *Sun*, 5 January 1793; *True Briton*, 23 February 1793; *Whitehall Evening Post*, 7–9 March 1793.

13. TNA, ADM 1/5336, court martial of John Johnston, Edward McGuire and John McGuire of the *Castor*, 2 May 1796; NMM, AML/K/7, Letter of Attorney from Thomas Ottery, 20 October 1797.

14. That said, food and shelter mattered little if a sailor had a family on land that needed support, and agricultural workers – for example farm servants – could also receive food and lodgings as perquisites. On average sailors stood to benefit from prize money, but in reality this was concentrated among a lucky few. On ships of the line, the captain's share of prize money was about 550 times that received by a seaman, and preliminary research by Dan Benjamin suggests that while on average captains could expect to earn more from prize money than they could from monthly wages (even more so if they commanded a frigate), for the rest of the officers and men prize money was a supplement, not a living. Daniel K. Benjamin, 'Golden Harvest: The British Naval Prize System, 1793–1815', Clemson University and PERC (unpublished), 2009. I am grateful to Professor Benjamin for sharing his work.

15. Calculations of cash and real wages are complex and disputed. These comparisons are taken from averages in Gregory Clark, 'What Were the British Earnings and Prices Then' (New Series), MeasuringWorth, 2021, which are in turn based on the following works: Gregory Clark, 'Farm Wages and Living Standards in the Industrial Revolution: England, 1670–1869', *Economic History Review*, Vol. 54, No. 3 (August 2001), pp. 477–505; Charles H. Feinstein, 'Pessimism Perpetuated: Real Wages and the Standard of Living in Britain During and After the Industrial Revolution', *Journal of Economic History*, Vol. 58, No. 3 (September 1998), pp. 625–58; Charles H. Feinstein, 'Wage-Earnings in Great Britain during the Industrial Revolution', in Iain Begg and S.G.B. Henry, eds, *Applied Economics and Public Policy* (Cambridge: Cambridge University Press, 1998), pp. 181–208; A.L. Bowley, 'The Statistics of Wages in the United Kingdom during the last Hundred Years. Part I. Agricultural Wages', *Journal of the Royal Statistical Society*, Vol. 61 (1898), pp. 702–22. It is worth adding that these series and averages are indicative, and in recent years economic historians have suggested that wages paid to London workers may have been different to those previously estimated: see Judy Z. Stephenson, '"Real" Wages? Contractors, Workers, and Pay in London Building Trades, 1650–1800', *Economic History Review*, Vol. 71, No. 1 (2018), pp. 106–32; J. Hatcher, 'Seven Centuries of Unreal Wages', in J. Hatcher and J.Z. Stephenson, eds, *Seven Centuries of Unreal Wages* (London: Palgrave, 2018), pp. 15–69. The data on number of days worked in a year comes from Jane Humphries and Jacob Wiesdorf, 'Unreal Wages? Real Income and Economic Growth in England, 1260–1850', *Economic Journal*, Vol. 129 (2019), pp. 2867–87, which suggests that by the end of the eighteenth century the number of days worked per year was over 300 (data at p. 2880). I have used 300 days as an infinitive figure, though again it is worth mentioning that employment was irregular and much more seasonal than current estimates of income infer. See Judy Z. Stephenson, 'Working Days in a London Construction Team in the Eighteenth Century: Evidence from St Paul's Cathedral', *Economic History Review*, Vol. 32, No. 2 (2020), pp. 409–30.

16. Ralph Davis, *The Rise of the English Shipping Industry in the Seventeenth and Eighteenth Centuries* (Liverpool: Liverpool University Press, 2012), pp. 145, 151–2. William Atkinson boasted to his mother that he was earning £2 per month (40 shillings) working on a slave ship, as well as a share of the profits. NMM, AGC/A/6, William Atkinson to his mother, 4 July 1798; The Trans Atlantic Slave Trade Database (http://slavevoyages.org/tast/database/search/faces), quoted in Watt and Hawkins, eds, *Letters of Seamen*, p. 146.

17. Knight, *Britain Against Napoleon*, p. 77; Christopher Oprey, 'Schemes for the Reform of Naval Recruitment 1793–1815', Unpublished MA thesis, University of Liverpool (1961), quoted in Rodger, 'Mutiny or Subversion?', p. 560.
18. For Carnarvon see the *Chester Chronicle*, 14 June 1793, where 3 guineas were collected for every able seaman, 2 guineas for every ordinary seaman and 1 guinea for all others. For Great Yarmouth see the *Norfolk Chronicle*, 2 March 1793, which allowed 2, 1.5 and 1 guineas for the same, as did Ashburton, the full appeal of which can be found in TNA, HO 42/24, f. 526. For Wrexham, which raised 40 shillings for every sailor that volunteered, and Newcastle, which raised a total sum of £235, see *True Briton*, 16 February 1793. At the Isle of Wight, Governor Thomas Orde was recorded as donating £50 alone; see *True Briton*, 20 February 1793.
19. *True Briton*, 23 February 1793; *True Briton*, 28 February 1793.
20. Brian Lavery, *Nelson's Navy; The Ships, Men and Organization*, revised edition (London: Conway, 2013), p. 125.
21. Roy Adkins and Lesley Adkins, *Jack Tar: The Men Who Made Nelson's Navy* (London: Little, Brown, 2008), p. 59.
22. Dorset History Centre, 10H/109, 'Men Raised for the Navy', 1795–8.
23. Dorset History Centre, 10H/109, 'Men Raised for the Navy', 1795–8. On categories of race in the eighteenth century see Roxann Wheeler, *The Complexion of Race: Categories of Difference in Eighteenth-Century British Culture* (Philadelphia: University of Pennsylvania Press, 2000).
24. NMM PLT/1/2, Impressment orders for John Platt of HMS *Alligator*, Thomas Affleck Esq. Commander; Lavery, *Nelson's Navy*, p. 120.
25. Brunsman, *Evil Necessity*, p. 10.
26. Michael Duffy, *Parameters of British Naval Power* (Liverpool: Liverpool University Press, 1992), p. 7; Brunsman, *Evil Necessity*, pp. 89–90.
27. HL, HO 154, Howe to Curtis, 11 June 1793.
28. Crosbie Garstin, ed., *Samuel Kelly: An Eighteenth Century Seaman whose days have been few and evil, to which is added remarks etc. on places he visited during his pilgrimage in this wilderness* (New York: Frederick A. Stokes Company, 1925), pp. 194–5. See also the account of William Henry Dillon, who records working both with captains who followed the rules and with those who interpreted them less precisely: Michael Lewis, ed., *A Narrative of My Professional Adventures (1790–1839) By William Henry Dillon* (London: Navy Records Society, 1953), Vol. 1, pp. 368, 375.
29. NMM, PLT/1/2, Impressment orders for John Platt of HMS *Alligator*, Thomas Affleck Esq. Commander. See also Lavery, *Nelson's Navy*, pp. 118–19; Brunsman, *Evil Necessity*, pp. 6–7, 65–6. The exemption certificate for Richard Dunn stated 'we have received testimony, that the Bearer Richard Dunn has bound himself Apprentice to Serve at Sea, by indenture dated the 28th June 1796 and that he never used the Sea before that time; and he being entitled to a Protection, in pursuance of the Said Act of Parliament, to free and exempt him being impressed for the space of Three Years from the aforementioned date of his indenture; We do hereby require and direct all Commanders of His Majesty's Ships, Pressmasters, and others whom it doth or may concern, not to impress him into His Majesty's service during the said space of Three Years.' NMM, ADL/J/20, Impressment exemption certificate for Richard Dunn.
30. In the UK National Archives there are extensive volumes listing protections given to thousands of men – the majority of whom were apprentices of one form or another – who were given exemption from naval service. See ADM 7/398, Register of protections from being pressed. Apprentices, Foreigners and others, 1795–1801. An estimate based on 232 pages and an average of twenty entries per

page suggests that around 4,640 sailors were given exemption from impressment in this period.

31. See TNA, ADM 1/1509, Jaheel Brenton to John Ibetson, Esq., 19 June 1794; TNA, ADM 1/2743, William Yeo to Philip Stephens, 16 March 1794.

32. Officers were instructed that if they had reason to suspect fraud, they had the right 'immediately to cause the parties to be impressed'. NMM, PLT/1/2, 'Impressment orders for John Platt'.

33. Garstin, *Samuel Kelly*, p. 251; TNA, ADM 1/5335, court martial of Prince Edward (alias Jackson) and Abraham Ramsden (alias Lennox) of the *Ann* tender, 2 April 1796.

34. Dancy, *Myth of the Press Gang*, pp. 38–9.

35. NMM, PLT/1/2, 'Impressment orders for John Platt'. For a detailed critique of Dancy's arguments and methodology see Rogers, 'British Impressment and Its Discontents', pp. 67–8.

36. Dillon, *My Professional Adventures*, Vol. 1, pp. 391–2.

37. TNA, ADM 7/302, Case 22, 24 September 1795. The solicitor made it clear that 'the practice of pressing apprentices with the hope of getting them afterwards to enlist, ought to be discontinued. There is no doubt, that the pressing of them in the first instance is directly in opposition to the Statute and there, when this illegal hold has been obtained of them, to tempt them by the offer of a bounty to desert their masters, can hardly be considered as creditable to the service.'

38. TNA, ADM 1/1618, report of William Carthew, 30 September 1793; Rogers, 'British Impressment and Its Discontents', p. 70.

39. TNA, ADM 1/5335, court martial of Jacob Berry of the *Edgar*, 29 March 1796.

40. John Rattenbury, *Memoirs of a Smuggler, compiled from his diary and journal* (Sidmouth: J. Harvey, 1837), p. 15.

41. Dancy, *Myth of the Press Gang*, pp. 38–9.

42. Spencer Childers, ed., *A Mariner of England: An Account of the Career of William Richardson From Cabin Boy in the Merchant Service to Warrant Officer in the Royal Navy [1780 to 1819] As Told By Himself* (London: John Murray, 1908), pp. 65–6, 96–7; William Robinson, *Nautical Economy; Or, Forecastle Recollections of Events during the Last War. Dedicated to the Brave Tars of Old England, By a Sailor, Politely Called by the Officers of the Navy, Jack Nasty-Face* (London: William Robinson, 1836, repr. London 1973), pp. 2–3.

43. Thomas Trotter, *A Practicable Plan for Manning the Royal Navy and Preserving our Maritime Ascendancy, without Impressment* (Newcastle: Longman, 1819), p. 40; Thomas Trotter, *Medicina Nautica: An Essay on the Diseases of Seamen* (London, 1797), p. 44.

44. Nicol, *Life and Adventures*, pp. 200–1.

45. Brunsman, *Evil Necessity*, p. 153.

46. A. Beckford Bevan and H. B. Wolryche-Whitmore, eds, *A Sailor of King George: The Journals of Captain Frederick Hoffman, RN, 1793–1814* (London: John Murray, 1901), p. 11.

47. TNA, ADM 1/5331, Court martial of John Marlow of the *Bellerophon*, 19 February 1794.

48. TNA, ADM 1/5119/16, Petition of Mary Quick, 23 April 1791.

49. Childers, ed., *A Mariner of England*, p. 121.

50. Rogers, *Press Gang*, 118. See also Douglas Hay and Nicholas Rogers, *Eighteenth-Century English Society* (Oxford: Oxford University Press, 1997), p. 158.

51. Robinson, *Nautical Economy*, p. 1.

52. For the data on number of turned over men see Dancy, *Myth of the Press Gang*, p. 78. For the Richardson quote see Childers, ed., *A Mariner of England*, p. 111.

53. Brunsman, *Evil Necessity*, pp. 143-4.
54. See N.A.M. Rodger, *Command of the Ocean* (London: Allen Lane, 2014), pp. 397, 492; Dancy, *Myth of the Press Gang*, pp. 152-3; Brunsman, *Evil Necessity*, pp. 12-13.
55. Childers, ed., *A Mariner of England*, p. 67.
56. Childers, ed., *A Mariner of England*, pp. 96-7.
57. William Spavens, *The Narrative of William Spavens*, introduction by N.A.M. Rodger (London: Chatham, 1998), p. 36.
58. Nicol, *Life and Adventures*, pp. 171-2.
59. TNA 1/5125, Petition from HMS *Shannon*, 16 June 1796.
60. TNA 1/5125, declaration of sailors at the Nore, June 1797.
61. Brunsman, *Evil Necessity*, pp. 35, 43-4; Rogers, *Crowds, Culture, and Politics*, pp. 85-121. See Land, *War, Nationalism and the British Sailor*, p. 106.
62. James Oglethorpe, *Sailors Advocate* (London, 1728), pp. 4-5 and 10-11; Rogers, 'British Impressment and Its Discontents', p. 56.
63. Samuel Collings, *Manning the Navy* (London: Bentley and Company, 1790).
64. Sir Frederic Madden Collection, University of Cambridge (hereafter 'Madden'), Vol. 5, No. 1561, *The Press'd Sailor's Lamentation: A New Song*; No. 1841, *True Blue, Or, the Press Gang*; Oscar Cox Jensen, *Napoleon and British Song, 1797-1822* (London: Palgrave Macmillan, 2015), p. 94.
65. See for example the 1791 pamphlet by Rev. James Cochrane, *Thoughts Concerning the Proper Constitutional Principles of Manning & Recruiting the British Navy and Army* (York: Wilson, Spence, and Mawman, 1791). Cochrane suggested an embargo on all trade until the naval ships were filled to 'encourage' merchant ships to volunteer men, but he ignored the disastrous economic impact this would have, let alone the agency of the sailors themselves. See also the 1786 pamphlet by John Mackenzie, *Impress of Seamen: Considerations on its legality, policy and operation. Applicable to the motion intended to be made in the House of Commons on Friday, 12 May, 1786 by William Pulteney, Esq.* (London: J. Debrett and J. French, 1786), quoted in full in J.S. Bromley, ed., *The Manning of the Royal Navy: Selected Public Pamphlets 1693-1873* (London: Navy Records Society, 1974), pp. 124-40.
66. *Sun*, 16 November 1793; *World*, 2 October 1793.
67. For a more detailed discussion of the plays and their representation of impressment see Jenks, *Naval Engagements*, pp. 39-40, 48-9. See also *World*, 10 May 1794.
68. Thomas Paine, *Rights of Man, Common Sense and Other Political Writings* (Oxford: Oxford University Press, 1995, re-issued 2008), p. 321.
69. John Stevenson, *Popular Disturbances in England, 1700-1832*, 2nd edition (London: Longman, 1992), pp. 208-12.
70. Charles Pigott, *A Political Dictionary: explaining the true meaning of words illustrated & exemplified in the lives, morals, character & conduct of ... illustrious personages* (London: D.I. Eaten, 1795).
71. William Shephard, ed., *Poems and Other Writings by the Late Edward Rushton* (London: Effingham Wilson, 1824), Vol. 6, pp. 115-16. For analysis see Franca Dellarosa, *Talking Revolution: Edward Rushton's Rebellious Poetics, 1782-1814* (Liverpool: Liverpool University Press, 2014), pp. 51-61.
72. Mary Wollstonecraft, *Maria: Or, the Wrongs of Women* (London, 1797); Brunsman, *Evil Necessity*, p. 156.
73. On the audience for these texts see Mark Philp, 'Introduction' to *Rights of Man and Common Sense*, pp. vii-xxvii; Bernard Vincent, *The Transatlantic Republican: Thomas Paine and the Age of Revolutions* (Amsterdam: Rodopi, 2005); Edward

Larkin, *Thomas Paine and the Literature of Revolution* (Cambridge: Cambridge University Press, 2005); Christopher Hitchens, *Thomas Paine's Rights of Man: A Biography* (London: Atlantic Books, 2006); Butler, *Burke, Paine, Godwin and the Revolution Controversy*; Dellarosa, *Talking Revolution*, pp. 51–61; Stuart Curran, 'Women Readers, Women Writers', in Stuart Curran, ed., *The Cambridge Companion to British Romanticism*, 2nd edition (Cambridge: Cambridge University Press, 2010), pp. 169–86; Cora Kaplan, 'Mary Wollstonecraft's Reception and Legacies', in Claudia L. Johnson, ed., *The Cambridge Companion to Mary Wollstonecraft* (Cambridge: Cambridge University Press, 2002); Gary Kelly, 'Revolutionary and Romantic Feminism: Women, Writing and Cultural Revolution', in Keith Hanley and Raman Selden, eds, *Revolution and English Romanticism: Politic and Rhetoric* (Hemel Hempstead: St Martin's Press, 1990), pp. 107–30; Barbara Taylor, *Mary Wollstonecraft and the Feminist Imagination* (Cambridge: Cambridge University Press, 2003); Ralph M. Wardle, *Wollstonecraft: A Critical Biography* (Lincoln: University of Nebraska Press, 1951), p. 316.

74. John Ford to Philip Stephens, 14 April 1794, ADM 1/245; quoted in Julius S. Scott, *The Common Wind: Afro-American Currents in the Age of the Haitian Revolution* (London and New York: Verso, 2018), p. 41.

75. J.D.M. Robertson, *The Press Gang in Orkney and Shetland* (Orkney: The Orcadian, 2011), pp. 94–103; Dillon, *My Professional Adventures*, Vol. I, pp. 375–6; John C. Dann, ed., *The Nagle Journal: A Diary of the Life of Jacob Nagle, Sailor, From the Year 1775 to 1841* (New York: Weidenfeld & Nicolson, 1988), p. 183.

76. TNA, ADM 1/3683, James Dyson to Stephens, 8 January 1795.

77. TNA, ADM 1/3683, James Dyson to Stephens, 6 January 1795.

78. TNA, ADM 1/3683, James Dyson to Stephens, 13 January 1795.

79. United States National Archives (USNA), M30, Despatches from U.S. Ministers to Great Britain, 1791–1906, Roll No. 4, Despatches from U.S. Minsters to Great Britain, 10 August 1796–28 December 1797, A2 Cab. 21/10, Rufus King to Timothy Pickering, 8 September 1796; Rufus King to Timothy Pickering, 13 April 1797; Brunsman, *Evil Necessity*, pp. 176–7.

80. Lloyd, *British Seaman*, p. 163.

81. TNA, ADM 1/5330, Court martial of Lieutenant Ralph Ridley, 21 September 1793.

82. TNA, ADM 7/302, Case 8, 17 June 1793.

83. Brunsman, *Evil Necessity*, p. 194. Paul Halliday argues that there were more than a thousand habeas corpus cases in the last four decades of the century; 80 per cent of them were successful, much higher than the 50 per cent dismissal rate for prisoners overall. Costello suggests that release rates decreased during the 1790s in response to the wider political situation, but almost all the Admiralty cases I consulted were successful appeals. See Paul D. Halliday, *Habeas Corpus: From England to Empire* (Cambridge, MA: Belknap Press of Harvard University Press, 2010), pp. 23–37, 115–16, 133–4. See also Kevin Costello, 'Habeas Corpus and Military and Naval Impressment, 1756–1816', *Journal of Legal History*, 29 (2008), pp. 239–40.

84. TNA, ADM 1/3683, letters from James Dyson to Alexander Stephens. Edward Willis, Richard Forster, George Thompson and James Tyzens, released as apprentices, 12 January 1795. George Fletcher, employee of the coal trade, released, 3 March 1795; unnamed sailor, over the age of eighteen, could be legally detained, 16 January 1795; unnamed sailor, apprenticed to his father, released, 22 January 1795; Hennick Loughnaugh, foreigner and impressed out of an East India Company ship, released, 1 February 1795; William Davison, apprentice, released, 17 March 1795; unnamed sailor, underage, released, 18 March 1795;

Josephus Grubalva, a subject of the King of Spain, released, 26 March 1795; John Spaven and John Usher, apprentices, released, 16 April 1795; Henry Alliston, apprentice, released, 23 April 1795; Thomas Emslie, apprentice, released, 21 May 1795; Gilbert Story and Samuel Falkons, apprentices, released, 13 June 1795; John Ridley, apprentice, released, 27 June 1795. For Dyson's irritated letter see TNA, ADM 1/3683, James Dyson to Evan Nepean, March 1795.

85. TNA, ADM 1/3683, James Dyson to Alexander Stephens, 7 January 1795. See also Rogers, *Press Gang*, p. 30.

86. HL, Hamond Collection, Box 74, 'List of Men Imprest at Mahon'; *London Packet of Evening Post*, 12 September 1800.

87. *The Times*, 19 November 1793.

88. TNA, ADM 1/1508, 'An Account of the number of men procured for His Majesty's Fleet by Captain Jaheel Brenton . . .', 26 July and 1 August 1793.

89. TNA, ADM 2/1063/426-7, 19 June 1793; Garstin, *Samuel Kelly*, pp. 270-1.

90. *Newcastle Courant*, 23 November 1793; *London Chronicle*, 18-20 March 1794; *Newcastle Chronicle*, 15 March 1794.

91. TNA, ADM 1/5335, court martial of Prince Edward (alias Jackson) and Abraham Ramsden (alias Abraham Lennox) of the *Ann* tender, 2 April 1796.

92. There is a tendency among historians to diminish the role violence played in coercing men into the Navy. See for example Rodger, *Wooden World*, p. 182; Dancy, *Myth of the Press Gang*, pp. 136, 140. For a critique of this see Land, 'New Scholarship', part 2.

93. I am indebted to Professor Rogers for sending me his working list of anti-impressment affrays and riots for the long eighteenth century. For more context see Rogers, *The Press Gang*, pp. 13, 39. See also Land, 'New Scholarship', part 2.

94. TNA, HO 42/24, ff. 315-16, James Rudman to Henry Dundas, 31 January 1793.

95. Rogers, 'Burning Tom Paine'. For Liverpool as a site of radicalism see Navickas, *Loyalism and Radicalism*, p. 38.

96. TNA, HO 28/9, 68, John Shortland Philip Stephens, Whitby, 26 January 1793.

97. TNA, HO 28/9, 70-1, John Oaks to Admiralty, Guisborough, 28 January 1793; TNA, HO 42/24, ff. 351-6, James Rudman to Dundas, 4 February 1793; Rogers, *Press Gang*, p. 56.

98. TNA, HO 28/9, Magistrates' declaration, 26 January 1793; Rogers, *Press Gang*, p. 56.

99. Collingwood to Nelson, 14 November 1792, in G.L. Newnham Collingwood, ed., *A Selection From the Public and Private Correspondence of Vice-Admiral Lord Collingwood: Interspersed with Memoirs of his Life*, 2 vols (5th edition, containing some new letters, 1837), Vol. 1, pp. 24-5; TNA, HO 42/23, 1, Christopher Blackett to Home Office, 22 November 1792.

100. TNA, HO 28/9, Sailor's declaration, Newcastle Upon Tyne, January 1793, 63-5; TNA, HO 42/24, f. 365, Charles Branding and Rowland Burdon [MPs for Newcastle Upon Tyne and County Durham respectively], to Dundas, 5 February 1793.

101. *Newcastle Courant*, 23 February 1793; Rogers, *Press Gang*, pp. 53-4.

102. *Newcastle Courant*, 30 March 1793; Rogers, *Press Gang*, p. 107.

103. See TNA, HO 42/23/351, 1793, ff. 770-1, James Rudman, Mayor of Newcastle Upon Tyne to Henry Dundas, 11 February 1793; TNA, HO 42/24, f. 365, Charles Branding and Rowland Burdon [MPs for Newcastle Upon Tyne and County Durham respectively] to Dundas, 5 February 1793.

104. TNA, HO 42/24, 1793. f. 356, 'Friends and Fellow Seamen!'.

105. TNA, HO 42/24, ff. 351-6, James Rudman to Dundas, 4 February 1793.

106. TNA, HO 42/24, 1793, f. 354, Letter from 'Sunderland Sailors'.

107. TNA, HO 42/24, 1793. f. 356, 'Friends and Fellow Seamen!'.

108. TNA, HO 42/24/218, ff. 538–9, 'T.S.' [Thomas Sanderson] to Rowland Burdon [MP for County Durham], Sunderland, 19 February 1793; Rogers, *Press Gang*, p. 53.

109. TNA, ADM 1/1508, Jaheel Brenton to Philip Stephens, 3 February 1793; TNA, ADM 1/1508, Jaheel Brenton to Philip Stephens, 28 February 1793; TNA, ADM 1/1508, Jaheel Brenton to Philip Stephens, 6 June 1793.

110. TNA, ADM 1/1508, Jaheel Brenton to Philip Stephens, 14 March 1793; TNA HO 28/23, Brenton to Evan Nepean, 4 October 1797.

111. TNA, ADM 1/1508, Jaheel Brenton to Philip Stephens, 14 November 1793.

112. TNA, HO 28/13, 13 November 1793; Land, 'New Scholarship', part 2.

113. I am grateful to Nicholas Rogers for providing this example. See TNA, HO 42/27/499–502; *Morning Chronicle*, 2 November 1793; *E. Johnson's British Gazette and Sunday Monitor*, 3 November 1793; *London Packet, or New Lloyd's Evening Post*, 1–4 November 1793; *York Courant*, 28 October 1793; Clive Emsley, *British Society and the French Wars 1793–1815* (London: Macmillan, 1979), pp. 32, 35; *Williamson's Liverpool Advertiser*, 21 October 1793; *Newcastle Courant*, 2 November 1793; *Bath Journal*, 28 October 1793.

114. Keith Mercer, 'The Murder of Lieutenant Lawry: A Case Study of British Naval Impressment in Newfoundland, 1794', *Newfoundland and Labrador Studies*, Vol. 21 (2006), pp. 255–98; Keith Mercer, 'Northern Exposure: Resistance to Naval Impressment in British North America, 1775–1815', *Canadian Historical Review*, Vol. 91 (2010), p. 214.

115. For the newspaper quote see *Sun*, 21 August 1794. For the 'crimping riots' see Stevenson, *Popular Disturbances in England*, pp. 208–12.

116. On the wider policy of state surveillance see H.T. Dickinson, 'Conservative Reaction and Government Repression', in H.T. Dickinson, *British Radicalism and the French Revolution* (London: Wiley-Blackwell, 1985), pp. 25–42; Barrell and Mee, 'Introduction', pp. ix–xli; Boyd Hilton, 'Pitt's Terror', in Boyd Hilton, *A Mad, Bad, and Dangerous People: England 1783–1846* (Oxford: Clarendon Press, 2006), pp. 65–74; Worrall, *Radical Culture*.

117. Some examples of reports sent in late 1792 and early 1793 include the following: in Norwich it was reported that 'things wear a very threatening aspect', while at Bainham 'the minds of the lower people are attempted to be perverted, by persons who came about selling Paines & other libels'. In Leicester a printer named Phillips distributed Thomas Paine's book (*Rights of Man*) among the soldiery, and 'the society are emply'd in printing 10,000 copies of the abstract, to be distributed gratis on Market day'. At Ipswich, 8 November, 'above a dozen Clubs in that town, where Paine's books are read and explained'. See TNA, HO 42/23 for all.

118. TNA, HO 42/23, John Stockdale to the Home Office, 1 December 1792.

119. TNA, HO 42/23, Nepean to the Rev. W. Sproule, 1 December 1792.

120. See TNA, HO 42/23 for these examples.

121. Troops were concentrated in eight districts: Plymouth, Portsmouth, Kent, London, Harwich and Yarmouth, Newcastle 'Interior' and West coast. TNA HO 42/24, ff. 307–8, 'Proposed Distribution of the Troops in South Britain', 1793.

122. Adam Zamoyski, *Phantom Terror: Political Paranoia and the Creation of the Modern State, 1789–1848* (New York: Basic Books, 2015), p. 55.

123. Jane Austen, *Northanger Abbey* (Oxford: Oxford University Press, 2003), p. 145.

124. Old Bailey Proceedings Online (www.oldbaileyonline.org, version 8.0, 20 January 2021), October 1793, trial of Richard Tuart (t17931030-66). For more information on Old Bailey proceedings and their reportage of trials see S. Devereaux,

'The City and the Sessions Paper: "Public Justice" in London, 1770–1800', *Journal of British Studies*, Vol. 35, No. 4 (October 1996), pp. 466–503; Robert Shoemaker, 'The Old Bailey Proceedings and the Representation of Crime and Criminal Justice in Eighteenth-Century London', *Journal of British Studies*, Vol. 47, No. 3 (2008), pp. 559–80.

125. Old Bailey Proceedings Online (www.oldbaileyonline.org, version 8.0, 20 January 2021), October 1793, trial of Richard Tuart (t17931030-66); *World*, 2 November 1793.

126. London Metropolitan Archives, Middlesex Sessions Papers – Justices Working Documents, LMSMPS508910124, December 1793, accessed via londonlives.org (https://www.londonlives.org/browse.jsp?id=LMSMPS50891_ n924-10&div=LMSMPS50891PS508910124#highlight), 20 January 2021.

127. Old Bailey Proceedings Online (www.oldbaileyonline.org, version 8.0, 20 January 2021), October 1793, trial of Richard Tuart (t17931030-66).

128. TNA, HO 47/16/23, Reports on Criminals, Correspondence, 9 April 1793.

129. See *Sun*, 2 November 1793; *World*, 2 November 1793.

130. TNA, ADM 1/2743, William Yeo to Philip Stephens, Poole, 2 January 1794; TNA, ADM 1/2743, William Yeo to Philip Stephens, 6 April 1794. See also TNA, ADM 1/2743, William Yeo to John Lester, 23 May 1794.

131. *Courier*, 16 December 1794.

132. *Courier*, 16 December 1794.

133. TNA, ADM 1/3683, James Dyson to Alexander Stephens, 28 February 1795; TNA, ADM 1/3683, James Dyson to Evan Nepean, 7 March 1795.

134. *Courier and Evening Gazette*, 16 December 1794; *Sun*, 2 December 1794; *Oracle and Public Advertiser*, 5 December 1794; *Morning Chronicle*, 11 June 1795; *Morning Post*, 2 July 1795. I am grateful to Nick Rogers for these references.

135. TNA, ADM 1/3683, James Dyson to Nepean, 28 July 1795.

136. TNA, ADM 1/3683, James Dyson to Evan Nepean, 15 July 1795; TNA, ADM 1/3683, James Dyson to Evan Nepean, 28 July 1795; *Whitehall Evening Post*, 6 August 1795.

137. TNA, ADM 1/2743, William Yeo to Evan Nepean, 8 August 1795.

138. *Bristol Gazette*, 20 February 1794.

139. J.J. Sheehan, *History of Kingston-upon-Hull*, 1864, p. 148; referenced in Lavery, *Nelson's Navy*, p. 118; *Bell's Weekly Messenger*, 6 August 1797; *Courier*, 5 August 1797.

140. Old Bailey Proceedings Online (www.oldbaileyonline.org, version 8.0, 20 January 2021), January 1799; trial of Charles Eyres (t17990109-5); TNA HO 47/23/7 ff. 27–30; HO 43/27/9. See also Margarette Lincoln, *Trading in War: London's Maritime World in the Age of Cook and Nelson* (New Haven, CT and London: Yale University Press, 2018), pp. 202–5.

141. Francisco Herreros, '"The Full Weight of the State": The Logic of Random State-Sanctioned Violence', *Journal of Peace Research* (2006); Jeffrey Ian Ross, *An Introduction to Political Crime* (Bristol: Policy Press, 2012); Jeffrey Ian Ross, *The Dynamics of Political Crime* (Thousand Oaks, CA: SAGE, 2003); Melvin Delgada, *State-Sanctioned Violence: Advancing a Social Work Social Justice Agenda* (Oxford: Oxford University Press, 2020); Eric W. Shoon, 'The Asymmetry of Legitimacy: Analyzing the Legitimation of Violence in 30 Cases of Insurgent Revolution', *Social Forces*, Vol. 93, No. 2 (December 2014), pp. 779–801. Much historical literature on state-sanctioned violence has concentrated on issues of race and gender: see for example Treva B. Lindsey, 'Post-Ferguson: A "Herstorical" Approach to Black Violability', *Feminist Studies*, Vol. 41, No. 1 (2015),

pp. 232–7; Tyson E.J. Marsh, 'Critical Pedagogy for Black Youth Resistance', *Black History Bulletin*, Vol. 79, No. 1 (Spring 2016), pp. 14–23.

142. Troy Bickham and Ian Abbey, '"The Greatest Encouragement to Seamen": Pay, Families, and the State in Britain during the French Wars, 1793–1815', *Journal of Social History*, Vol. 56, No. 1 (2022), pp. 1–31.

143. TNA, ADM 8/68–70, 78.

144. Nicol, *Life and Adventures*, pp. 172, 179, 185–99.

2 WAR OF PRINCIPLE: NAVAL CONFLICT IN EUROPE, 1793–5

1. On British war aims and policy see Michael Duffy, 'British Policy in the War Against Revolutionary France', in Colin Jones, ed., *Britain and Revolutionary France: Conflict, Subversion and Propaganda* (Exeter: Exeter Studies in History, 1983), pp. 11–26; Michael Duffy, 'British Diplomacy and the French Wars, 1789–1815', in Dickinson, ed., *British Radicalism*, pp. 127–45; Rodger, *Command of the Ocean*, p. 426.

2. For an overview of this operation see Michael Duffy, '"A Particular Service": the British Government and the Dunkirk Expedition of 1793', *English Historical Review*, Vol. 91 (1976), pp. 529–54. See also Knight, *Britain Against Napoleon*, pp. 67–9.

3. P. Kelly, 'Strategy and Counter-Revolution: The Journal of Sir Gilbert Elliot on 8–9 September 1793', *English Historical Review*, Vol. 98 (1983), p. 340; Michael Duffy, *Soldiers, Sugar and Seapower: The British Expeditions to the West Indies and the War Against Revolutionary France* (Oxford: Clarendon Press, 1987), p. 5.

4. TNA, ADM 8/69. The sizes of the respective fleets in October 1793 were East Indies (1), Jamaica (8), Leeward Islands (18), Newfoundland (9), Nova Scotia (3), Overseas (10), Mediterranean (44), Channel Fleet (40), Home Waters (121). Thirty ships were on convoy duty, while a further ten had no known location. On the European concentration being traditional see Rodger, *Command of the Ocean*, p. 429; Stephen Conway, 'Empire, Europe and British Naval Power', in David Cannadine, ed., *Empire, the Sea and Global History: Britain's Maritime World, c. 1760–c. 1840* (Basingstoke: Palgrave Macmillan, 2007), pp. 22–40.

5. William Pitt budget speech, 17 February 1792, *The Speeches of the Right Honourable William Pitt in the House Commons* (London: Longman, Hurst, Rees and Orne, 1806), Vol. 2, p. 36. See also Philip Scofield, 'British Politicians and French Arms: The Ideological War of 1793–1795', *History*, Vol. 77, No. 250 (1992), pp. 183–201.

6. Anon, *Objections to the War Examined and Refuted by a Friend of Peace* (London, 1793), p. 3.

7. For British observance of events in France see Schürer, 'Storming of the Bastille'; Emma Macleod, 'British Spectators of the French Revolution: The View from across the Channel', *Gonriek*, Vol. 197 (2013), pp. 377–92. For more general takes on Britain's response to the revolution see Butler, *Burke, Paine, Godwin and the Revolution Controversy*; Philp, ed., *The French Revolution and British Popular Politics*; Evans, *Debating the Revolution*.

8. Historians have debated the extent to which this conflict can be termed a 'total war'. For my purposes, I take the line that the war was more 'total' than those that preceded it, for all that it built on – and in some ways mirrored – traditions and practices established earlier in the century. For the leading proponent of the 'total war' idea see David A. Bell, *The First Total War: Napoleon's Europe and the Birth of Modern Warfare* (London: Bloomsbury, 2007), esp. pp. 7–10. For a corrective, see in particular Roger Chickering and Stig Förster, eds, *War in an Age of Revolution, 1775–1815* (Cambridge: Cambridge University Press, 2010), which suggests

that the transition in European warfare from the eighteenth to the nineteenth century was 'marked less by rupture than by continuity, the playing out of dynamics that were already evident in the ancient régime, the testing of ideas long articulated and institutions long anticipated' (p. 7).

9. Bell, *First Total War*, p. 143; Sibylle Scheipers, 'The Status and Protections of Prisoners of War and Detainees', in Hew Strachan and Sibylle Scheipers, eds, *The Changing Character of War* (Oxford: Oxford University Press, 2011), pp. 394–409, p. 398.

10. Bell, *First Total War*, pp. 143–4.

11. On British attempts to starve the French see Silvia Marzagalli, 'Sea Power and Neutrality', in David Morgan-Owen and Louis Halewood, eds, *Economic Warfare and the Sea: Grand Stratégies for Maritime Power* (Liverpool: Liverpool University Press), pp. 101–20, p. 101, quoting Pierrick Pourchasse, 'La Guerre de la faim: l'approvisionement de la Republique, le blocus britannique, et bonnes affaires des neutres au course des guerres revolutionnaires (1793–1795)', HdR thesis, Universite de Bretagne Sud, 2010.

12. Bell, *First Total War*, p. 145; Burke to Portland, 1 August 1793, in Thomas W. Copeland, eds, *The Correspondence of Edmund Burke, 1729-1797*, 10 vols (Cambridge: Cambridge University Press, 1958–78), Vol. 7, pp. 380–1.

13. Robert Nares, *Man's Best Right: A Solemn Appeal in the name of Religion* (1793), pp. 45–7.

14. Collingwood to Nelson, 14 November 1792, in Collingwood, *Public and Private Correspondence*, Vol. 1, pp. 24–5.

15. Duffy, *Soldiers, Sugar, Seapower*, pp. 3–4.

16. William S. Cormack, *Revolution & Political Conflict in the French Navy, 1789-1794* (Cambridge: Cambridge University Press, 1995), pp. 108–9, 86–7, 215–41.

17. Sam Willis, *The Glorious First of June: Fleet Battle in the Reign of Terror* (London: Quercus, 2011), pp. 12, 14, 18.

18. Rear Admiral George Bowyer noted that a number of ships were 'short in their Complements of Men than they ought to be'. TNA, ADM 1/100, ff. 56–56v, Bowyer to Howe, 27 January 1794. For the estimate of crews see Willis, *First of June*, pp. 117–18.

19. TNA, ADM 1/5330, Court martial of Lieutenant Horace Pine, 2 August 1793; TNA, ADM 1/100, f. 263, Howe to Stephens, 22 April 1794 (see also ff. 266–266v, Colonel Innes to Howe; f. 264, Pasley to Howe); Willis, *First of June*, p. 131.

20. Hughes, *Collingwood Correspondence*, p. 36.

21. Sam Willis, *In the Hour of Victory: The Royal Navy at War in the Age of Nelson* (London: Atlantic Books, 2014), pp. 35–6.

22. See for example Huntington Library (HL), HO 166, Howe to Curtis, 30 December 1793.

23. Other onlookers were more sympathetic. In January 1794 one correspondent, Edward Stokes, wrote to Howe and commiserated with his 'late unsuccessful endeavors to capture the Scattered Fleet of Our Savage Enemy's [sic]' and reminded him that 'Disappointment . . . happens to every One'. He enclosed a large Stilton cheese to improve Howe's spirits and went so far as to advise him on its consumption: 'If you can spare your knife from the Cheese a couple of Months, it will be more ripe & pleasant to your palate than at the present . . .'. Whether Howe heeded this advice is unknown. See NMM, AGC/VI, Edward Stokes to Howe, 8 January 1794.

24. Jenks, *Naval Engagements*, p. 30. For the Gillray caricature see James Gillray, *A French Hail Storm, - or - Neptune losing sight of the French fleet* (London: Hannah Humphrey, 10 December 1793).

25. HL, HO 140, Howe to Curtis, 9 April 1793.
26. Gardiner, *Fleet Battle and Blockade*, pp. 17–20; Stephen Taylor, *Commander: The Life and Exploits of Britain's Greatest Frigate Captain* (London: Faber and Faber, 2012), pp. 68–71; Willis, *First of June*, p. 133.
27. Christopher Ware, 'The Glorious First of June: The British Strategic Perspective', in Michael Duffy and Roger Morriss, eds, *The Glorious First of June 1794: A Naval Battle and Its Aftermath* (Exeter: University of Exeter Press, 2001), pp. 25–42, p. 30.
28. Horatio Nelson to Fanny Nelson, 27 September 1793, in G.P.B. Naish, ed., *Nelson's Letters to His Wife and Other Documents 1785–1831* (London, 1958), p. 92. Another young captain, Sidney Smith, witnessed a similar incident in Leghorn a few months later; see NMM, CRK/11/7, Smith to William Hamilton, 2 December 1793.
29. Roger Knight, *The Pursuit of Victory: The Life and Achievement of Horatio Nelson* (London: Allen Lane, 2006), pp. 161–2.
30. 'Secret Instructions', 18 May 1793, quoted in J. Holland Rose, *Lord Hood and the Defence of Toulon* (Cambridge: Cambridge University Press, 1922), pp. 96–7.
31. Cormack, *Revolution & Political Conflict*, pp. 176, 179–83.
32. Malcolm Crook, *Toulon in War and Revolution: From the Ancien Regime to the Restoration, 1750–1820* (Manchester: Manchester University Press, 1991), esp. pp. 126–59; Cormack, *Revolution & Political Conflict*, pp. 191–2, 195–6, 212.
33. *London Chronicle*, 14–17 September 1793; *Sun*, 18 September 1793; *St James's Chronicle*, 14–17 September 1793.
34. *Sun*, 18 September 1793; *London Chronicle*, 14–17 September 1793; also printed verbatim in *St James's Chronicle*, 14–17 September 1793.
35. Though undoubtedly opportunistic, Toulon was a target for British policymakers. In a document produced before news of the capture of Toulon arrived in Britain, Prime Minister Pitt drew up a military strategy for 1794 in which an 'attack on Toulon' with 50,000 troops was listed. See PRO, 30/8/I95, 28 August 1793, f. 49; Jennifer Mori, 'The British Government and the Bourbon Restoration: The Occupation of Toulon, 1793', *Historical Journal*, Vol. 40, No. 3 (1997), pp. 699–719.
36. *St James's Chronicle*, 19 September 1793.
37. Mori, 'British Government and the Bourbon Restoration', pp. 700–1, 715–16.
38. TNA, HO 50/455, O'Hara to D. Dundas, 22 November 1793; Rose, *Defence of Toulon*, pp. 34, 40–5, 50–2, 55–68, 69–75, 88, 124.
39. Of the thirty-one ships initially captured, eight were destroyed by the British on 18 December, four were commissioned into the Royal Navy, four were sent with prisoners to French ports, and fifteen escaped and continued to serve as French naval ships. See William James, *The Naval History of Great Britain from the Declaration of War by France in 1793 to the Accession of George IV*, 6 vols (London: Richard Bentley, 1837). Vol. 1, pp. 66–84.
40. Rose, *Defence of Toulon*, pp. 75–9, 80–1.
41. Nelson to William Suckling, 31 October 1794, in Nicholas Harris Nicolas, ed., *The Dispatches and Letters of Vice Admiral Lord Viscount Nelson*, 7 vols (Cambridge: Cambridge University Press, 2011; first published 1844–6), Vol. 1, p. 500.
42. Cormack, *Revolution & Political Conflict*, p. 173.
43. For orders of ships to Cherbourg and Guernsey see BL, Add. MS. 35194, ff. 251–2, Howe's instructions for the conduct of the ships stationed at St Helen's, 5 February 1794.
44. TNA, ADM 1/100, ff. 133–133v, Captain Sir Andrew Douglas to Howe, 4 March 1794.

45. Somerset Heritage Centre (SHC), DD\AH\61/2/1–4, Copy of *London Gazette*, 18–22 February 1794; SHC, DD\AH\61/2/1–4, Captain Samuel Hood to Lord Hood, 13 January 1794; SHC, DD\AH\61/2/1–4, Letter from Samuel Hood to the Admiralty, 16 January 1794.

46. Cormack, *Revolution & Political Conflict*, pp. 253, 277; Willis, *First of June*, pp. 25, 34–5, 37.

47. Cormack, *Revolution & Political Conflict*, pp. 242–90.

48. Willis, *First of June*, pp. 39–40.

49. See Ware, 'British Strategic Perspective', p. 25; N. Hampson, *La Marine de l'an II: mobilisation de la flotte de l'Océan 1793–1794* (Paris: Librairie Marcel Rivière & Cie, 1959), pp. 21–3, 72, 81–6.

50. Laurence Evans, 'The Convoy, the Grain and their Influence on the French Revolution', in Duffy and Morriss, eds, *Glorious First of June*, pp. 120–31, p. 122. Evans goes on to suggest that the convoy was less important than historians have suggested – the French transportation system was bad, and one shipment was not a long-term solution to the problem. There can be no doubt, however, about the importance that Robespierre and the Committee of Public Safety placed on the safe arrival of the convoy. See Evans, 'The Convoy', pp. 128–9. There is also debate about the value of the convoy. *The Times* of 30 April stated the value of the convoy to be £1.5 million, while the precise number of merchantmen is unclear: different sources state that there were 110, 116, 124, 127, 130 and even 170 vessels in the convoy. See Michael Duffy, 'The Man Who Missed the Grain Convoy: Rear Admiral George Montagu and the Arrival of Vanstabel's Convoy from America in 1794', pp. 101–19, p. 105, and André Delaporte, 'The Prairial Battles: The French Viewpoint', pp. 12–24, pp. 12–13, both in in Duffy and Morriss, eds, *Glorious First of June*.

51. Ware, 'British Strategic Perspective', p. 28.

52. TNA ADM 2/125, pp. 504–6, Board of Admiralty to Howe, 7 March 1794; TNA ADM, 1/100, ff. 177–177v, Douglas to Howe, 14 March 1794.

53. For the intelligence see TNA ADM 1/100, ff. 216–216v, Captain Candler of the brig *Unity* of Boston, intelligence report, 2 April 1794; Duffy, 'Montagu and the Arrival of Vanstabel's Convoy', p. 102. For the Admiralty order see TNA ADM 2/1347, Secret, Lords of the Admiralty to Howe, 17 April 1794.

54. TNA ADM 1/100, ff. 320–1, Howe to Stephens, 14 May 1794; Michael Duffy, 'Montagu and the Arrival of Vanstabel's Convoy', p. 104.

55. TNA ADM 1/100, ff. 346–7, Rear Admiral George Montagu, signed report of intelligence obtained by his squadron 15–29 May 1794; Ware, 'British Strategic Perspective', pp. 32–3. For Admiralty intelligence see TNA ADM 2/1347, Stephens to Howe, 21 May 1794. For intelligence sent to Montagu see BL, Add. MSS 23207, ff. 15–16, 'Intelligence obtained by the ships of the squadron under the command of Rear Admiral Montagu at Sea', May 1794. See also TNA ADM 1/100, ff. 331–2.

56. Willis, *First of June*, pp. 113–16, 121, 123.

57. Lewis, *Narrative*, Vol. 1, p. 120.

58. Midshipman Dillon saw the *Demourisque* destroyed, which 'made my heart ache when I saw flames spreading over her, in fact hurling her to destruction'. Lewis, *Narrative*, Vol. 1, p. 120.

59. Willis, *First of June*, pp. 141–2; Willis, *Hour of Victory*, p. 36.

60. HL, HO 185, Howe to Curtis, 8 March 1794.

61. Oliver Warner, *Glorious First of June* (London: Batsford, 1961), p. 92.

62. Delaporte, 'Prairial Battles', pp. 12–13.

63. HL, HO 75, Howe to Curtis, 14 October 1789. For other thoughts on tactical concerns see HL, HO 66, Howe to Curtis, 27 July 1788; HL, HO 67, Howe to Curtis, 23 October 1788; HL, HO 104, Howe to Curtis, 21 February 1791; HL, HO 124, Howe to Curtis, 5 January 1793.

64. Rodger, *Command of the Ocean*, p. 430; Willis, *Hour of Victory*, pp. 57–8; Willis, *First of June*, pp. 64–6.

65. Howe to Stephens, 6 June 1794, quoted in Willis, *Hour of Victory*, p. 52.

66. Willis, *First of June*, pp. 149, 153–6, 158–9.

67. N.A.M. Rodger, 'Image and Reality in Eighteenth-Century Naval Tactics', in *Mariner's Mirror*, Vol. 89 (2003), pp. 280–96; Willis, *First of June*, pp. 159–63, 163–7; Lewis, *Narrative*, Vol. 1, p. 124.

68. Willis, *First of June*, pp. 168–9.

69. Willis, *First of June*, pp. 187–8, 191–2; Lewis, *Narrative*, Vol. 1, pp. 128–9.

70. Serving on board the *Brunswick* was Mary Anne Talbot, disguised as John Taylor. She was hit by grapeshot in the ankle that exposed bone, then shot by musket ball. She survived the battle but was never able to remove a piece of grapeshot close to the tendons, and it remained in her ankle for the rest of her life. Mary Anne Talbot, *The Life and Surprising Adventures of Mary Anne Talbot, in the name of John Taylor* (London, 1809), p. 155.

71. Willis, *First of June*, pp. 193–4, 195–6, 198–9.

72. Unknown seamen, likely of *Alfred*, shortly after 1 June 1794, quoted in Watt and Hawkins, eds, *Letters of Seamen*, p. 81.

73. C.H.H. Owen, 'Letters from Vice Admiral Lord Collingwood, 1794–1809', in Susan Rose, ed., *The Naval Miscellany*, Vol. 6 (London: Navy Records Society, 2003), pp. 156–60; NMM, PAR/193, William Parker to his father, 17 June 1794.

74. Jonathan Wilkinson to John Clark, 2 July 1794. See Roger Morriss, 'The British View of the Actions of 28, 29, and 1 June 1794', in Duffy and Morriss, eds, *Glorious First of June*, pp. 80–1; see also *Mariner's Mirror*, Vol. 43 (1957), p. 324.

75. TNA, ADM 1/100, f. 290; BL, Add. Ms. 23207, ff. 10, 98; Willis, *First of June*, pp. 241–2.

76. Lewis, *Narrative*, Vol. 1, p. 131.

77. The battle smoke was described by one French onlooker in poetic terms: 'the cloud which enveloped us was produced by the burning of a hundred thousand barrels of gunpowder; it did not in any way resemble the sea fog of previous days; instead of a uniform grey, colour it carried not only in tint but in intensity according to the circumstances. Sometimes it was a thick sooty black, gleaming with sparks and suddenly stabbed with flame; then again it was transparent, giving to the light of day the appearance of moonlight and blotting out objects by a fantastic sort of mirage. It was frequently sown with brownish circles, floating upwards horizontally, which recalled those traced by medieval painters above the heads of saints.' See Willis, *The Glorious First of June*, p. 205.

78. Willis, *First of June*, pp. 207–12.

79. Morriss, 'British View', pp. 66–7; Willis, *First of June*, pp. 197, 200–1, 203.

80. Unknown seamen, likely of *Alfred*, shortly after 1 June 1794, quoted in Watt and Hawkins, eds, *Letters of Seamen*, p. 81.

81. John Morris to his parents, 14 June 1794, quoted in Watt and Hawkins, eds, *Letters of Seamen*, p. 90; Willis, *First of June*, p. 202.

82. Willis, *First of June*, pp. 202–3; Morriss, 'British View', pp. 66–7.

83. John Davies to his parents, 15 June 1794 [Caesar], quoted in Watt and Hawkins, eds, *Letters of Seamen*, p. 93.

84. Jonathan Wilkinson to John Clark, 2 July 1794. See Morriss, 'British View', pp. 80–1.
85. See TNA, ADM 36/11363, referenced by Morriss, 'British View', p. 82.
86. Ware, 'British Strategic Perspective', pp. 38–40.
87. Willis, *First of June*, p. 306.
88. Evan Wilson, 'The Naval Defence of Ireland during the French Revolutionary and Napoleonic Wars', *Historical Research*, Vol. 92, No. 257 (August 2019), pp. 570–1; Willis, *Hour of Victory*, p. 72.
89. Roger Morriss suggests that Howe's victory would have been more impressive had he not allowed the French to tow away four of their dis-masted ships; Sam Willis, by contrast, argues persuasively that a more active pursuit was beyond the capabilities of Howe's disordered ships. See Morriss, 'British View', pp. 67–8; Willis, *First of June*, pp. 221–2. For contemporary criticism of Howe see Lewis, *Narrative*, Vol. 1, p. 136. For the Nelson quote see Thomas Sturges Jackson, *Logs of the Great Sea Fights, 1794–1805*, Vol. 1 (Navy Records Society, 1899), p. 6.
90. Willis, *First of June*, pp. 203–4; Willis, *Hour of Victory*, pp. 58–9.
91. For Howe's long dislike of Molloy see HL, HO 193, Howe to Curtis, 11 April 1794, in which he mocks 'Our friend Molloy' who 'seems rather unfortunate in the multiplicity of important Family & other Concerns, in which he is so frequently engaged'. For Howe's work behind the scenes see HL, HO 209, 20 December 1794; HO 210, 24 December 1794; 17 April, 17/18 April, 20 April, 21 April (HO 220–3). The jurors are listed at TNA, ADM, 1/5332, f. 382.
92. Lord Vincent noted in 1800 that 'there is an insuperable bar to your being employed in any way', likely the criticism of George III. See Duffy, 'Montagu and the Arrival of Vanstabel's Convoy', pp. 112–14.
93. TNA, ADM 1/100, ff. 361–3, Howe to Stephens, 2 June 1794.
94. For Caldwell's anger see HL, HO 202, Howe to Curtis, 28 July 1794. For Collingwood's quote see Hughes, *Collingwood Correspondence*, pp. 49–52; Willis, *First of June*, p. 265.
95. See HL, HO 196, Howe to Curtis, 18 July 1794; John Ehrman, *The Younger Pitt*, 3 vols (London, 1969–96), Vol. 2, p. 409; Willis, *First of June*, p. 272; Rodger, *Command of the Ocean*, p. 430.
96. P. Jupp, ed., *The Letter Journal of George Canning, 1793–1795* (London: Camden Fourth Series, Vol. 41, 1991), p. 121.
97. *St James's Chronicle*, 12–14 June 1794; Jenks, *Naval Engagements*, p. 27; Willis, *First of June*, pp. 232–3.
98. *The Times*, 12 June 1794.
99. *The Times*, 12 June 1794; Jenks, *Naval Engagements*, pp. 44–5; Duffy and Morriss, 'Introduction', in Duffy and Morriss, eds, *Glorious First of June*, p. 2.
100. Willis, *First of June*, p. 233.
101. *Oracle*, 12 June 1794.
102. *Official Documents and Interesting Particulars of the Glorious Victory Obtained over the French Fleet, on Sunday June 1, 1794, by the British Fleet, Under the Command of Admiral Lord Howe: Illustrated with an accurate engraving of the manoeuvering [sic] and line of battle of the two fleets on that memorable day* (London: J. Debrett, 1794); Pieter van der Merwe, 'The Glorious First of June: A Battle of Art and Theatre', in Duffy and Morriss, eds, *Glorious First of June*, pp. 132–58, pp. 133–4.
103. Its explanatory banners contained 'a neat compendium of English Naval History, very happily introduced, and easily read and remembered'. See *Oracle*, 1 July 1794.

104. *Lord Howe they run or the British Tars giving the Carmignols a Dressing on Memorable 1st of June 1794* (Cruikshank, 1794).

105. Van der Merwe, 'Battle of Art and Theatre', pp. 152–4; Jenks, *Naval Engagements*, pp. 37–42, 46–50.

106. *Songs, Duetts, Choruses, &c. in A New and Appropriate Entertainment, called the Glorious First of June. Performed for the first time, by His Majesty's Servants, at the Theatre Royal, Drury-Lane, on Wednesday, July 2ns 1794 for the Benefit of the Widows and Orphans of the brave Men who fell in the late Engagements under Earl Howe* (London: C. Lowndes, 1794, first edition), p. 7.

107. It was repeated for another six nights, which took in smaller sums of £220–£320. See van der Merwe, 'Battle of Art and Theatre', pp. 152–4. For the Farington quote see Kenneth Farlick and Angus Macintyre, eds, *The Diary of Joseph Farington*, 16 vols (New Haven, CT and London: Yale University Press, 1978–84), Vol. 1, p. 211.

108. *Sun*, 28 February 1793; see also *Morning Herald*, 1 March 1793; *Reading Mercury*, 4 March 1793. For amounts raised see *Sun*, 15 April 1793; *World*, 15 January 1794. For the Foundling Hospital see *Sun*, 21 February 1794. See also *World*, 14 June 1794.

109. There were also personal donations. Midshipman William Parker asked his father to set up a subscription for the wife and children of one seaman, George Graham, who had helped Parker in the early stages of his naval career. Graham had been killed at the Glorious First of June, 'in a manner too shocking to mention to a tender hearted parent'. See Willis, *First of June*, p. 236; and Morriss, 'British View', p. 90.

110. For Lloyd's see TNA ADM 2/605, pp. 396–8, Stephens to Howe, 16 June 1794; for Trinity House see *Oracle*, 21 June 1794; *Oracle*, 15 September 1794. For St Martin in the Fields see *Oracle*, 15 September 1794. For the ladies' subscriptions see *St James's Chronicle*, 12 March 1793.

111. *The Times*, 18 July 1794; *Oracle*, 28 June 1794; *Oracle*, 15 August 1794; *The Times*, 10 September 1794. On philanthropy in the eighteenth century see Helen Berry, *Orphans of Empire* (Oxford: Oxford University Press, 2019), pp. 79, 84. See also Donna Andrews, *Philanthropy and Police: London Charity in the Eighteenth Century* (Princeton, NJ: Princeton University Press, 1989); David L. Wykes, ed., *Protestant Dissent and Philanthropy in Britain, 1660–1914* (Woodbridge: Boydell Press, 2020).

112. Lewis, *Narrative*, Vol. 1, pp. 149–50.

113. Jenks, *Naval Engagements*, pp. 30–1.

114. *Morning Chronicle*, 13 June 1794; *Morning Chronicle*, 17 June 1794; Jenks, *Naval Engagements*, pp. 28, 46–50.

115. Willis, *First of June*, pp. 237–8. For more on the complexity of loyalist rhetoric in the aftermath of the battle see Jenks, *Naval Engagements*, pp. 46–50. See also Dozier, *For King, Constitution, and Country*, p. 156; Ehrman, *The Younger Pitt*, Vol. 2, pp. 349–50, 401; Mark Philp, 'Vulgar Conservatism, 1792–3', *English Historical Review*, Vol. 110 (1995), pp. 42–69; Kevin Gilmartin, 'In the Theatre of Counterrevolution: Loyalist Association and Conservative Opinion in the 1790s', *Journal of British Studies*, Vol. 41 (2002), pp. 291–328.

116. Delaporte, 'Prairial Battles', pp. 19–20; Willis, *First of June*, pp. 242–4.

117. Richard Vesey Hamilton and John Knox Laughton, eds, *Recollections of James Anthony Gardner, R.N. 1755–1814* (London: Navy Records Society, 1906), pp. 158–9; Willis, *First of June*, p. 301.

118. Scofield, 'The Ideological War of 1793–1795', p. 198.

119. Roger Morriss, ed., *The Channel Fleet and the Blockade of Brest, 1793–1801* (London: Ashgate for Navy Records Society, 2001), pp. 73–4, 78; Gardiner, *Fleet Battle and Blockade*, pp. 44–9.

120. Morriss, *Blockade of Brest*, pp. 73–4; Spencer to Bridport, 29 June 1795, in Morriss, *Blockade of Brest*, p. 87.

121. I am grateful to Nick Rogers for these examples. References for each affray are in turn: Kenneth J. Logue, *Popular Disturbances in Scotland, 1780–1815* (London: John Donald, 1979), pp. 121–3; *Philadelphia Gazette,* 24 April 1795; Nicholas Rogers, ed. *Manning the Royal Navy in Bristol: Liberty, Impressment and the State, 1739–1815* (Bristol: Bristol Record Society, 2014), no. 280; TNA, ADM 1/3283, 18 June 1795.

122. John Barrell, *Spirit of Despotism: Invasion of Privacy in the 1790s* (Oxford: Oxford University Press, 2006), pp. 44–5; Knight, *Britain Against Napoleon,* p. 63.

123. Emsley, 'An Aspect of Pitt's "Terror"'; Hilton, 'Pitt's Terror'. For a detailed study of the trials for sedition in this period see John Barrell and Jon Mee, eds, *Trials for Treason and Sedition,* 2 vols (London: Pickering and Chatto, 2006–7).

124. The Duke of Portland to Edmund Burke, 11 June 1794, Marshal and Woods, eds, *Correspondence of Edmund Burke* (Cambridge: Cambridge University Press, 1958), Vol. 7, p. 549.

125. TNA, ADM 2/604, pp. 437–8, Stephens to Howe, 18 April 1794.

126. TNA, ADM 1/100, ff. 268–268v, Howe to Stephens, 23 April 1794.

127. Barrell and Mee, 'Introduction', pp. xxiv–xxv. Ann Coats makes the point that the term 'delegate' had early antecedents, and that it can be traced to merchant seamen's disputes of the earlier eighteenth century. However, as Howe's response demonstrates, its usage in 1794 was novel enough, and naval authorities clearly interpreted the word as having 'revolutionary' undertones. See Ann Coats, 'The 1797 Mutinies in the Channel Fleet: A Foreign-Inspired Revolutionary Movement?' in Ann Coats and Philip MacDougall, eds, *The Naval Mutinies of 1797: Unity and Perseverance* (Woodbridge: Boydell and Brewer, 2011), pp. 126–42, p. 126.

128. HL, HO 207, Howe to Curtis, 8 December 1794.

3 'WE THE SEAMEN': PROTEST AND RESISTANCE AT SEA

1. Samuel Leech, *Thirty Years From Home* (Boston: Tappan & Dennet, 1843), pp. 39–40.

2. TNA, ADM 1/5125, Petition to the Admiralty, 1 March 1797.

3. James C. Scott, *Domination and the Arts of Resistance: Hidden Transcripts* (New Haven, CT and London: Yale University Press, 1990). On 'everyday violence' see for example Jonathan Saha, 'Histories of Everyday Violence in British India', *History Compass,* Vol. 9, No. 1 (2011), pp. 844–53.

4. Leech, *Thirty Years From Home*, pp. 39–40.

5. Vale, 'Post Office'; Mary Favret, 'War Correspondence: Reading Romantic War', *Prose Studies: History, Theory, Criticism,* Vol. 19, No. 2 (1996), pp. 173–85; Watt and Hawkins, eds, *Letters of Seamen*, pp. 10–11.

6. TNA, ADM 1/5336, court martial of Bryan McDonnough of the *Eurydice*, 8 July 1796.

7. Markus Eder, *Crime and Punishment in the Royal Navy of the Seven Years' War, 1755–1763* (Aldershot: Ashgate, 2004), pp. 161–4. This was also mentioned in courts martial, for example TNA, ADM 1/5333, court martial of Dennis Kelly et al. of the *Bellerophon*, 29 September 1795.

8. TNA, ADM 1/5330, court martial of Lieutenant Horace Pine of the *Colossus*, 2 August 1793.

9. As they noted, 'We should have Represented the Case to Admiral Linzee Before we had proceeded thus, But we very seldom have the opportunity of Seeing him, and no petition is admitted to him'. TNA, ADM 1/5331, court martial of Captain John Shield and Lieutenant George McKinley, of the *Windsor Castle*, 11 November 1794.

10. TNA, ADM 1/5333, court martial of Dennis Kelly et al. of the *Bellerophon*, 29 September 1795; TNA, ADM 1/5125, Petition of crew of the *Squirrel*, 24 February 1795; TNA, ADM 1/5330, court martial of William Batty of the *Illustrious*, 9 October 1793.

11. TNA, ADM 1/5335, court martial of Thomas Brown of the *Excellence*, 26 March 1796.

12. TNA, ADM 1/5342, court martial of John Cooper of the *Pelter* gun vessel, 16 October 1797; TNA, ADM 1/5347, court martial of David Coleman of the *Babek*, 12 November 1798.

13. TNA, ADM 1/5336, court martial of Lieutenant Humphrey Faulkner of the *Petterell*, 2 July 1796; TNA, ADM 1/5337, court martial of John Grant, master at arms of the *Janus*, 4 October 1796; TNA, ADM 1/5330, court martial of Lieutenant Horace Pine of the *Colossus*, 2 August 1793.

14. Childers, *A Mariner of England*, p. 106.

15. Patrick Underwood, Steven Pfaff and Michael Hechter, 'Threat, Deterrence, and Penal Severity: An Analysis of Flogging in the Royal Navy, 1740–1820', *Social Science History*, Vol. 42, No. 3 (2018), pp. 414, 423; Steven Pfaff and Michael Hechter, *The Genesis of Rebellion: Governance, Grievance and Mutiny in the Age of Sail* (Cambridge: Cambridge University Press, 2020), p. 183. See also Alan Jamieson, 'Tyranny of the Lash: Punishment in the Royal Navy during the American War, 1776–1783', *Northern Mariner*, Vol. 9, No. 1 (1999). This appears to be part of a longer trend: Thomas Malcomson finds much more severe punishment in the 1810s than John Byrn found in the 1780s. See Malcomson, *Order and Disorder*; John D. Bryn, *Crime and Punishment in the Royal Navy: Discipline on the Leeward Islands Station 1784–1812* (Aldershot: Scholars Press, 1989).

16. TNA, ADM 1/5332, court martial of John Connor of the *Fortitude*, 12 January 1795.

17. Bridges was subsequently dismissed for verbally abusing his officers and questioning their expertise. TNA, ADM 1/5332, court martial of Captain Richard Bridges and Lieutenant William Cooke of the *Fairy*, 4–12 March 1795.

18. TNA, ADM 1/5330, court martial of William Batty of the *Illustrious*, 9 October 1793; TNA, ADM 1/5330, court martial of James Allen of the *Medusa*, 30 July 1792.

19. TNA, ADM 1/5335, court martial of Thomas Brown of the *Excellence*, 26 March 1796.

20. TNA, ADM 1/5331, court martial of Jeremiah Squirrel of the *Thetis*, 24 November 1794; David Featherstone, 'Counter-Insurgency, Subalternity and Spatial Relations: Interrogating Court-Martial Narratives of the Nore Mutiny of 1797', *South African Historical Journal*, Vol. 61, No. 4 (2009), pp. 766–87.

21. TNA, ADM 1/530, court martial of Edward Patten of the *Porcupine*, 15 April 1793.

22. TNA, ADM 1/5333, court martial of Hugh Irwin et al. of the *Terrible*, 25 September–3 October 1795.

23. TNA, ADM 1/5347, court martial of George Anderson et al. of the *Sheerness*, 26–27 October 1798.

24. See for example Childers, *A Mariner of England*, p. 106.
25. TNA, ADM 1/5337, court martial of William Scruton of the *Crachefeu,* 19 December 1796.
26. Elin Jones, 'Space, Sound and Sedition on the Royal Naval Ship, 1756–1815', *Journal of Historical Geography*, Vol. 70 (2020), p. 72.
27. TNA, ADM 1/5330, court martial of William Price, William Duggan and Robert Field of the *Winchelsea*, 1 October 1793.
28. Jones, 'Space, Sound and Sedition', p. 69; J. Heinsen ' "Nothing but Noyse": The Political Complexities of English Maritime Soundscapes', *Radical History Review*, Vol. 121 (2015), p. 115.
29. Bruce Buchan, 'Civility at Sea: From Murmuring to Mutiny', *Republic of Letters*, Vol. 5, No. 2 (2017), pp. 6–7; Jones, 'Space, Sound and Sedition', pp. 68–9; Taylor, *Sons of the Waves*, p. 228; referencing TNA, ADM 51/1130, Log of *Culloden*.
30. *St. James's Chronicle or the British Evening Post*, 22–25 April 1797.
31. Jones, 'Space, Sound and Sedition', p. 65.
32. TNA, ADM 1/5330, court martial of William Price, William Duggan and Robert Field of the *Winchelsea*, 1 October 1793; TNA, ADM 1/5333, court martial of Hugh Irwin et al. of HMS *Terrible*, 25 September–3 October 1795; TNA, ADM 1/5333, court martial of David Cumbers and Murdock Hughes of the *Pompeé*, 28 December 1795.
33. Jones, 'Space, Sound and Sedition', p. 65.
34. G. Russell, 'Hissing the King: The Politics of Vocal Expression in 1790s' Britain', in P. Denny, B. Buchan, D. Ellison and K. Crawley, eds, *Sound, Space and Civility in the British World, 1700–1850* (London and New York: Routledge, 2019), p. 147.
35. TNA, ADM 1/5336, court martial of Richard Parke of the *Gibraltar*, 17–18 June 1796.
36. TNA, ADM 12/22, digest of court martial convictions, 1755–1806, D-Dis.
37. TNA, ADM 1/5330, court martial of Richard Parker of the *Assurance*, 12 December 1793.
38. TNA, ADM 1/5332, court martial of Henry Jackson of the *Fairy*, 24 June 1795; TNA, ADM 1/5330, court martial of Michael Passmore of the *Deadalus*, 30 August 1793.
39. TNA, ADM 1/5332, court martial of Edward Chambers and Thomas Diggins of the *Marlborough*, 4 April 1795.
40. TNA, ADM 1/5331, court martial of John Dick, carpenter of *La Concorde*, 9 September 1794; TNA, ADM 1/5331, court martial of George Passmore, Master of the *Woolwich*, 10 March 1794; TNA, ADM 1/5331, court martial of John Barry of the *Europa*, 4 March 1794.
41. TNA, ADM 1/5330, court martial of Richard Parker of the *Assurance*, 12 December 1793.
42. TNA, ADM 1/5125, petition of ship's company of the *Ceres*, 3 July 1795.
43. TNA, ADM 1/5335, court martial of John Packwood et al. of the *Sampson*, 6 February 1796; TNA, ADM 1/5336, court martial of David Read and William Read of the *Pandour*, 12 September 1796.
44. For examples of sailors fooling officers see TNA, ADM 1/5331, court martial of John Marlow of the *Bellerophon*, 19 February 1794; TNA, ADM 1/5335, court martial of John Bartlet and Thomas Williams of the *Abergavenny*, 13 April 1796; TNA, ADM 1/5335, court martial of John McBean of the *Abergavenny*, 13 April 1796. For the latter two examples of sailors taking command of the ship's boats see TNA, ADM 1/5338, court martial of James Coleman of the *Nassau*, 13 February 1797; TNA, ADM 1/5337, court martial of William Saunders of the *Theseus*, 2 October 1796.

45. TNA, ADM 1/5336, court martial of John Phlips and Daniel McHorsal of the *Malabar*, 13 June 1796. For examples of sailors taking command of the ship's boats see TNA, ADM 1/5331, court martial of John Green of the *Pilote*, 22 August 1794; TNA, ADM 1/5335, court martial of Thomas Moore, seaman of *La Bait*, 13 April 1796.

46. TNA, ADM 1/5338, court martial of William Taylor of the *George*, 14 March 1797.

47. TNA, ADM 1/5125, petition of ship's company of the *Ceres*, 3 July 1795; TNA, ADM 1/5337, court martial of John Skene of the *Hermes*, 21 November 1796; TNA, ADM 1/5337, court martial of Charles Colquhan, alias James Donald and William Dixon, alias William Spaughton of the *Maidstone*, 10 December 1796.

48. TNA, ADM 1/5338, court martial of James McCoy of the *Atlas*, 28 February 1797.

49. TNA, ADM 1/5331, court martial of Samuel Moules and George White of the *Marlborough*, 19 February 1794.

50. TNA, ADM 1/5335, court martial of Stephen William of the *Etrusco*, 10 March 1796; TNA, ADM 1/5335, court martial of Dominick Mullany and James Burgess of the *Lion*, 19 March 1796. For reference to the Act of Parliament see TNA, ADM 1/5338, court martial of William Kidman and Thomas Lewis of the *Weazle*, 11 February 1797.

51. TNA, ADM 1/5336, court martial of David Read and William Read of the *Pandour*, 12 September 1796.

52. TNA, ADM 1/5335, court martial of John Packwood et al. of the *Sampson*, 6 February 1796; TNA, ADM 1/5338, court martial of John Hayes and John Matthews of the *St George*, 16 January 1797.

53. Rodger, *Wooden World*, pp. 229–324.

54. TNA, ADM 1/5125, petition of the crew of the *Syren*, 20 March 1797.

55. Thomas Sokoll, *Essex Pauper Letters, 1731–1837 – Records of Social and Economic History (New Series)*, Vol. 30 (Oxford: Oxford University Press, 2006). See also the research project 'The Power of Petitioning', https://petitioning.history.ac.uk/. See also Jason Peacey, *Print and Public Politics in the English Revolution* (Cambridge: Cambridge University Press, 2013); A. J. Whiting, *Women and Petitioning in the Seventeenth-Century English Revolution: Deference, Difference and Dissent* (Turnhout: Brepolis, 2015); Tania Robles Ballesteros, 'Englishwomen's Petitioning Strategies during the 17th Century', *Culture and History*, Vol. 7, No. 2 (2018); Edward Vallance, 'Harrington, Petitioning and the Construction of Public Opinion', in D. Wiemann and G. Mahlberg, eds, *Perspectives on English Revolutionary Republicanism* (Aldershot: Ashgate, 2014), pp. 119–32.

56. Henry Miller, 'Introduction: The Transformation of Petitioning in the Long Nineteenth Century (1780–1914)', *Social Science History*, Vol. 43, No. 3: The Transformation of Petitioning (2019), pp. 409–29. See also Mark Knights, ' "The Lowest Degree of Freedom": The Right to Petition, 1640–1800', in Richard Huzzey, ed., *Pressure and Parliament: From Civil War to Civil Society* (London: John Wiley, 2018), pp. 18–34; Philip Loft, 'Petitioning and Petitioners to the Westminster Parliament, 1660–1788', *Parliamentary History*, Vol. 38, No. 3 (2019), pp. 342–61; Richard Huzzey, 'Petitions, Parliament and Political Culture: Petitioning the House of Commons, 1780–1918', *Past and Present*, Vol. 248, No. 1 (2020), pp. 123–64.

57. James E. Bradley, *Popular Politics and the American Revolution in England: Petitions, the Crown and Public Opinion* (Mercer, GA: Mercer University Press, 1986), pp. 121–2.

58. John R. Oldfield, *Popular Politics and British Anti-Slavery: The Mobilisation of Public Opinion against the Slave Trade 1787–1807* (Manchester: Manchester University Press, 1995); Seymour Drescher, 'Public Opinion and Parliament in the Abolition of the British Slave Trade', in Stephen Farrell, Melanie Unwin and James Walvin, eds, *The British Slave Trade: Abolition, Parliament and People* (Edinburgh: Edinburgh University Press, 2007), pp. 42–65. On the abolition movement more broadly see Christopher Leslie Brown, *Moral Capital: Foundations of British Abolitionism* (Chapel Hill, NC: University of North Carolina Press, 2006); Farrell, Unwin and Walvin, *British Slave Trade*.

59. *An Address to the Prime Minister of Corsica . . . demonstrating that the Constitution which was so graciously ratified in June last, to His Majesty's Corsican Subjects, contains, in Principle, that very System of Representation, which has so long and unsuccessfully sought to be obtained by the People of Great Britain and Ireland, from a Parliamentary Reform* (1795), in *Critical Review* (June 1795), pp. 217–18.

60. TNA, ADM 1/5125, petition of the ship's company of the *Nassau*, 19 August 1795; TNA, ADM 1/5125, petition of crew of the *Fly*, 28 January 1795; TNA, ADM 1/5125, petition of ship's company of the *Ceres*, 3 July 1795; TNA, ADM 1/5334, petition of sailors of the *Defiance*, admitted as part of the court martial of William Parker et al. of the *Defiance* for mutiny, 20 January to 11 February 1796.

61. TNA, ADM 1/5125, petition of the *Reunion*, 15 November 1796; TNA, ADM 1/5336, court martial of Bryan McDonnough of the *Eurydice*, 8 July 1796.

62. TNA, ADM 1/5337, court martial of Thomas Ryan of the *Caesar*, 26 November 1796.

63. TNA, ADM 1/5334, court martial of William Parker et al. of the *Defiance*, 20 January to 11 February 1796.

64. Rediker, *Devil and the Deep Blue Sea*, pp. 234–5; Davids, 'Seamen's Organizations', pp. 160–1.

65. TNA, ADM 1/5125, petition of crew of the *Lady Taylor* armed sloop, 30 March 1794; TNA, ADM 1/5125, petition of ship's company of the *Vestal*.

66. Duffy, *Soldiers, Sugar and Seapower*, p. 187.

67. TNA, ADM 1/5338, court martial of James McCoy of the *Atlas*, 28 February 1797; TNA, ADM 1/5336, court martial of Bryan McDonnough of the *Eurydice*, 8 July 1796.

68. TNA, ADM 1/5337, court martial of Thomas Ryan of the *Caesar*, 26 November 1796.

69. TNA, ADM 1/5333, court martial of Hugh Irwin et al. of the *Terrible*, 25 September–3 October 1795.

70. TNA, ADM 1/5338, court martial of James McCoy of the *Atlas*, 28 February 1797.

71. TNA, ADM 1/5125, petition of the crew of the *Lady Taylor* armed sloop, 30 March 1794.

72. TNA, ADM 1/5125, petition of the ship's company of the *Nassau*, 19 August 1795; TNA, ADM 1/5125, petition of the company of *Weasle* sloop, 16 August 1795; TNA, ADM 1/5125, petition of the *Emerald*, December 1796; TNA, ADM 1/5125, petition of the company of the *Crescent*, 23 December 1795.

73. TNA, ADM 1/5338, court martial of James McCoy of the *Atlas*, 28 February 1797.

74. TNA, ADM 1/5125, petition of the crew of the *Fly*, 28 January 1795; TNA, ADM 1/5125, petition of the crew of the *Syren*, 20 March 1797; TNA, ADM 1/5125, petition of the crew of the *Squirrel*, 24 February 1795.

75. The sailors noted that 'we have too great a Reason to believe that he labors under a degree of inability with respect to Friendly Interest'. TNA, ADM 1/5125, petition of the crew of the *Alfred* to Admiralty, 2 May 1794.

76. TNA, ADM 1/5125, petition of the crew of the *Fly*, 28 January 1795.
77. See Naomi Tadmor, *Family and Friends in Eighteenth-Century England: Household, Kinship, and Patronage* (Cambridge: Cambridge University Press, 2001).
78. TNA, ADM 1/5125, petition of the *Reunion*, 15 November 1796.
79. TNA, ADM 1/5338, court martial of James McCoy of the *Atlas*, 28 February 1797; TNA, ADM 1/5125, petition of the crew of the *Fly*, 28 January 1795; TNA, ADM 1/5125, petition of the ship's company of the *Nassau*, 19 August 1795.
80. TNA, ADM 1/5125, petition of the ship's company of the *Ceres*, 3 July 1795; TNA, ADM 1/5125, petition of the *Winchelsea*, 18 August 1795.
81. TNA, ADM 1/5338, court martial of James McCoy of the *Atlas*, 28 February 1797.
82. TNA, ADM 1/5125, petition of the *Eleanor* tender, 15 March 1797; TNA, ADM 1/5125, petition of the ship's company of the *Royal William*, 25 September 1796.
83. TNA, ADM 1/5125, petition to the Admiralty, 1 March 1797.
84. TNA, ADM 1/5125, petition of the crew of the *Squirrel*, 24 February 1795; TNA, ADM 1/5125, petition of the *Winchelsea*, 14 September 1795.
85. TNA, ADM 1/5125, petition of the *Nassau*, 19 August 1795.
86. TNA, ADM 1/5125, petition of the crew of the *Squirrel*, 24 February 1795; TNA, ADM 1/5125, petition from the *Shannon*, 16 June 1796; TNA, ADM 1/5125, petition of ship's company of the *Brunswick*, 1 July 1796.
87. TNA, ADM 1/5125, petition of the *Reunion*, 15 November 1796; TNA, ADM 1/5125, petition of the ship's company of the *Bellerophon*, 6 May 1795; TNA, ADM 1/5125, petition from the *Shannon*, 16 June 1796.
88. Robinson, *Nautical Economy*, p. 1.
89. TNA, ADM 1/5125, petition of the ship's company of the *Bellerophon*, 6 May 1795; TNA, ADM 1/5338, court martial of James McCoy of the *Atlas*, 28 February 1797.
90. TNA, ADM 1/5125, petition of the crew of the *Squirrel*, 24 February 1795.
91. TNA, ADM 1/5125, petition from the *Shannon*, 16 June 1796.
92. TNA, ADM 1/5333, court martial of Dennis Kelly et al. of the *Bellerophon*, 29 September 1795.
93. See for example TNA ADM 1/5125, petition of the ship's company of the *Nassau*, 19 August 1795; petition of the company of the *Crescent*, 23 December 1795; petition from the *Shannon*, 16 June 1796; petition of the ship's company of the *Brunswick*, 1 July 1796; petition of the *Emerald*, December 1796; petition of ship's company of the *Royal William*, 25 September 1796.
94. TNA, ADM 1/5125, petition of the ship's company of the *Ceres*, 3 July 1795; TNA, ADM 1/5125, petition of the ship's crew of the *Ceres*, 15 July 1795; TNA, ADM 1/5333, court martial of James Anderson of the *Hebe*, 15 September 1795.
95. TNA, ADM 1/5336, court martial of Michael Glynn et al. of the *Venus*, 24 September 1796.
96. TNA, ADM 1/5125, petition of the *Reunion*, 15 November 1796; TNA, ADM 1/5125, petition of the *Winchelsea*, 18 August 1795; TNA, ADM 1/5125, petition of the *Winchelsea*, 14 September 1795.
97. Robinson, *Nautical Economy*, p. 89–90.
98. Dann, *Nagle Journal*, p. 211.
99. This data represents every case of 'mutiny' or 'mutinous expression' recorded during the period. See TNA, ADM 12/24.
100. Though he was given the unusually harsh sentence of 150 lashes. TNA, ADM 1/5336, court martial of John Clark of the *Tartar*, 10 June 1796. By the same token, in 1796 John Hoile was found innocent of mutiny but guilty of contempt towards one of his lieutenants. TNA, ADM 1/5337, court martial of John Hoile of the *Speedy*, 30 December 1796.

101. TNA, ADM 1/5331, court martial of John Horsington of the *Europa*, 18 October 1794.

102. In 1794, the boatswain George Dunning told his officer to 'kiss his backside' and was demoted to the rank of seaman. TNA, ADM 1/5331, court martial of George Dunning, boatswain of the *Swan*, 12 August 1794.

103. He accused his captain of behaving in a 'Tyranny, Cruel, Oppressive and Fraudulent Manner'. See TNA, ADM 1/5331, court martial of Charles Watson of the *Rattlesnake*, 23 December 1794; TNA, ADM 1/5331, court martial of Edward Bowater of the *Regulus*, 26–29 December 1794.

104. Rodger, 'Mutiny or Subversion?'.

105. TNA, ADM 1/5330, court martial of William Price, William Duggan and Robert Field of the *Winchelsea*, 1 October 1793; Frykman, *Bloody Flag*, p. 111.

106. TNA, ADM 1/5331, court martial of John Shield and George McKinley of the *Windsor Castle*, 11 November 1794. See also Frykman, *Bloody Flag*, pp. 112–13. For the desertions see TNA, ADM 1/5331, court martial of Joseph Gray and Andrew Greenan of the *Windsor Castle*, 4 October 1794.

107. Frykman, *Bloody Flag*, pp. 114–16; TNA, ADM 1/5331, court martial of Francis Watts et al. of the *Culloden*, 14–20 December 1794.

108. TNA, ADM 1/5331, court martial of Francis Watts et al. of the *Culloden*, 14–20 December 1794.

109. Francesco Buscemi, 'The Importance of Being Revolutionary: Oath-Taking and the "Feeling Rules" of Violence (1789–1794)', *French History*, Vol. 33, No. 2 (2019), pp. 218–35.

110. Frykman, *Bloody Flag*, pp. 117–18; TNA, ADM 1/5331, court martial of Francis Watts et al. of the *Culloden*, 14–20 December 1794.

111. TNA, ADM 1/5331, court martial of Francis Watts et al. of the *Culloden*, 14–20 December 1794.

112. Taylor, *Sons of the Waves*, p. 232.

113. TNA, ADM 1/5333, court martial of Hugh Irwin et al. of the *Terrible*, 25 September–3 October 1795.

114. N.A.M. Rodger, 'The Inner Life of the Navy, 1750–1800: Change or Decay?', in *Guerres et paix 1660–1815* (Vincennes: Service Historique de la Marine, 1987), pp. 172–3. This is contested: Rediker argues that mutinies more frequently used violence; Rediker, *Devil and the Deep Blue Sea*, p. 228.

115. TNA, ADM 1/5333, court martial of Hugh Irwin et al. of the *Terrible*, 25 September–3 October 1795; TNA, ADM 1/5333, court martial of David Cumbers and Murdock Hughes of the *Pompee*, 28 December 1795; TNA, ADM 1/5334, court martial of William Parker et al. of the *Defiance*, 20 January–11 February 1796. For an overview of the *Defiance* mutiny see Gavin Kennedy, 'Bligh and the Defiance Mutiny', *Mariner's Mirror*, Vol. 65, No. 1 (1979), pp. 65–8.

116. TNA, ADM 1/5333, court martial of Hugh Irwin et al. of the *Terrible*, 25 September–3 October 1795; TNA, ADM 1/5333, court martial of David Cumbers and Murdock Hughes of the *Pompee*, 28 December 1795; TNA, ADM 1/5334, court martial of William Parker et al. of the *Defiance*, 20 January–11 February 1796.

117. TNA, ADM 1/5333, court martial of Hugh Irwin et al. of the *Terrible*, 25 September–3 October 1795.

118. TNA, ADM 1/5334, petition of sailors of the *Defiance*, admitted as part of the court martial of William Parker et al. of the *Defiance*, 20 January–11 February 1796.

119. TNA, ADM 1/5333, court martial of Hugh Irwin et al. of the *Terrible*, 25 September–3 October 1795; TNA, ADM 1/5333, court martial of David Cumbers and Murdock Hughes of the *Pompee*, 28 December 1795.

120. TNA, ADM 1/5334, court martial of William Parker et al. of the *Defiance*, 20 January–11 February 1796; Frykman, *Bloody Flag*, p. 123.
121. TNA, ADM 1/5333, court martial of Hugh Irwin et al. of the *Terrible*, 25 September–3 October 1795.
122. TNA, ADM 1/5333, court martial of Hugh Irwin et al. of the *Terrible*, 25 September–3 October 1795. See also 'A List of mutineers who were wounded on board His Majesty's Ship Terrible on the 12th of September 1795', entered as part of proceedings. TNA, ADM 1/5333, court martial of Hugh Irwin et al. of the *Terrible*, 25 September–3 October 1795.
123. TNA, ADM 1/5334, petition of sailors of the *Defiance*, admitted as part of the court martial of William Parker et al. of the *Defiance*, 20 January–11 February 1796.
124. For 'riotous' see TNA, ADM 1/5333, court martial of Thomas Caviner of the *Fortune*, for 'riotous behaviour' and TNA, ADM 1/5333, court martial of David Walker of the *Beaulieu* for behaving 'in a most riotous manner', 5 September 1795; TNA, ADM 1/5333, court martial of John Fullarton and John Harrison of the *Weasle* for 'riotous and mutinous behaviour', 19 September 1795. For 'seditious' see TNA, ADM 1/5333, court martial of David Cumbers of *Pompee* for 'riotous and seditious speeches', and Murdock Hughes of the *Pompee*, 28 December 1795; TNA, ADM 1/5336, court martial of Richard Parke of the *Gibraltar* for 'making use of seditious speeches', 17–18 June 1796.
125. TNA, ADM 1/5333, court martial of Dennis Kelly et al. of the *Bellerophon*, 29 September 1795; TNA, ADM 1/5338, court martial of James McCoy of the *Atlas*, 28 February 1797.
126. TNA, ADM 1/5334, court martial of William Parker et al. of the *Defiance*, 20 January–11 February 1796; TNA, ADM 1/5333, court martial of Hugh Irwin et al. of the *Terrible*, 25 September–3 October 1795; TNA, ADM 1/5333, court martial of David Cumbers and Murdock Hughes of the *Pompee*, 28 December 1795.
127. TNA, ADM 1/5334, court martial of William Parker et al. of the *Defiance*, 20 January–11 February 1796; TNA, ADM 1/5333, court martial of Hugh Irwin et al. of the *Terrible*, 25 September–3 October 1795.
128. TNA, ADM 1/5336, court martial of Bryan McDonnough of the *Eurydice*, 8 July 1796.
129. TNA, ADM 1/5336, court martial of George Harvey and William Gleeson of the *Bermuda*, 27–28 May 1796.
130. TNA, ADM 1/5337, court martial of John Lloyd and Peter Bavarot of the *Reunion*, 5 December 1796.
131. TNA, ADM 1/5337, court martial of John Murray of the *Mermaid*, 3 November 1796; TNA, ADM 1/5333, court martial of David Walker of the *Beaulieu*, 5 September 1795.
132. TNA, 1/727, Letters from the *Repulse*, No. 2 'An Insidious Song'.
133. TNA, ADM 1/727, Letters from the *Repulse*, No. 35, 'A Copy of Verses on the Seamen Displaying their Noble Spirit in the Year 1797'.
134. See for example TNA, ADM 1/5347, court martial of Charles O'Neal and Patrick Molloy of the *Queen Charlotte*, 9 November 1798.
135. TNA, ADM 1/5338, court martial of James McCoy of the *Atlas*, 28 February 1797.
136. TNA, ADM 1/5335, court martial of George Johnson of the *Trident*, 28 March 1796.
137. TNA, ADM 1/5338, court martial of James McCoy of the *Atlas*, 28 February 1797.
138. Rediker, *Devil and the Deep Blue Sea*, pp. 228–9.

139. TNA, ADM 1/5336, court martial of George Harvey and William Gleeson of the *Bermuda*, 27–28 May 1796.
140. See Childers, *A Mariner of England*, p. 128.
141. TNA, ADM 1/5336, court martial of Jonathan Harper of the *Belliqueux*, 27 July 1796.
142. Philp, 'Fragmented Ideology of Reform', pp. 38–49; Chris Evans, 'Political Mobilization and the People in the 1790s', in Evans, *Debating the Revolution*, pp. 45–66; Dinwiddy, 'Conceptions of Revolution'; Roger Wells, *Insurrection: The British Experience, 1795–1803* (Gloucester: Allan Sutton, 1986); O'Gorman, 'English Loyalism Revisited'; Ian R. Christie, 'Conservatism and Stability in British Society', in Philp, *The French Revolution and British Popular Politics*, pp. 169–87
143. TNA, ADM 1/5336, court martial of John Clark of the *Tartar*, 10 June 1796.
144. NMM, TUN/212, Philip Patton, 'Observations on Naval Mutiny, presented in 1795'; WYN/109/7, Philip Patton, 'Observations on Naval Mutiny. Presented in April 1795' (mss version).

4 TIDES, CURRENTS AND WINDS: NAVY AND EMPIRE, 1793–7

1. Janet Polasky, *Revolutions Without Borders: The Call to Liberty in the Atlantic World* (New Haven, CT and London: Yale University Press, 2015); Douglas Hamilton, '"Sailing on the same uncertain sea": The Windward Islands of the Caribbean', in Douglas Hamilton and John McAleer, eds, *Islands and the British Empire in the Age of Sail* (Oxford: Oxford University Press, 2021), pp. 77–96, p. 93.
2. Laurent Dubois, *A Colony of Citizens: Revolution & Slave Emancipation in the French Caribbean, 1787–1804* (Chapel Hill, NC: University of North Carolina Press, 2004); Johnhenry Gonzalez, *Maroon Nation: A History of Revolutionary Haiti* (New Haven, CT and London: Yale University Press, 2019), esp. pp. 49–83; David Geggus, 'The Caribbean in the Age of Revolution', in Armitage and Subrahmanyam, eds, *The Age of Revolutions in Global Context*, pp. 83–100, p. 87.
3. Sujit Sivasundaram, *Waves Across the South: A New History of Revolution and Empire* (London: William Collins, 2020), p. 37; Suzanne Desan, Lynn Hunt and William Max Nelson, 'Introduction', in Suzanne Desan, Lynn Hunt and William Max Nelson (eds), *The French Revolution in Global Perspective* (Ithaca, NY: Cornell University Press, 2013), p. 2; Armitage and Subrahmanyam, *The Age of Revolutions in Global Context*. See also Robert Travers, 'Imperial Revolutions and Global Repercussions: South Asia and the World, c. 1750–1850', in Armitage and Subrahmanyam, *The Age of Revolutions in Global Context*, pp. 144–66. On the Caribbean see Michael Craton, *Testing the Chains: Resistance to Slavery in the British West Indies* (Ithaca, NY and London: Cornell University Press, 1982), pp. 180–223; Dubois, *A Colony of Citizens*. There is also a vast debate as to the origins of the Haitian Revolution, and the extent to which it was in turn influenced by events in France. See John D. Garrigus, *Before Haiti: Race and Citizenship in French Saint-Domingue* (New York: Macmillan, 2006); Carolyn E. Fick, *The Making of Haiti: The Saint Domingue Revolution from Below* (Knoxville: University of Tennessee Press, 1990).
4. Sivasundaram, *Waves Across the South*, p. 38.
5. For the burning of Tom Paine effigies in the Caribbean see Scott, *Common Wind*, pp. 49, 155–6. For ideas about the overlooked 'revolutionary Mediterranean' see Ian Coller, 'The Revolutionary Mediterranean', in Peter McPhee, ed., *A Companion to the French Revolution* (Chichester: Blackwell, 2013), pp. 419–34, p. 420. See also Joshua Meeks, *France, Britain, and the Struggle for the Revolutionary Western Mediterranean* (London: Palgrave Macmillan, 2017).

6. Burnard, *Jamaica in the Age of Revolution*, p. 6; Philip D. Curtin, *The Atlantic Slave Trade: A Census* (Madison, WI: University of Wisconsin Press, 1969), pp. 136, 170; as revised by Roger Anstey in 'The Volume and Profitability of the British Slave Trade, 1761–1807', in S.L. Engerman and E.D. Genovese, eds, *Race and Slavery in the Western Hemisphere: Quantitative Studies* (Princeton, NJ: Princeton University Press, 1975), pp. 3–32, p. 12; quoted in Duffy, *Soldiers, Sugar, and Seapower*, p. 14; David Geggus, 'The Anglo-French Conflict in the Caribbean in the 1790s', in Colin Jones, ed., *Britain and Revolutionary France: Conflict, Subversion and Propaganda* (Exeter: Exeter Studies in History, 1983), pp. 27–39, p. 27.

7. Daniel A. Baugh, 'Great Britain's "Blue-Water" Policy, 1689–1815', *International History Review*, Vol. 10, No. 1 (1998), pp. 33–58.

8. Duffy, *Soldiers, Sugar and Seapower*, p. 219.

9. Sarah Kinkel, *Disciplining the Empire: Politics, Governance and the Rise of the British Royal Navy* (Cambridge, MA: Harvard University Press, 2018).

10. F.J. Cardew, 'The Taking of Tobago 1793', *Journal for the Royal United Services Institution*, Vol. 70 (1925), pp. 411–14; Duffy, *Soldiers, Sugar and Seapower*, pp. 5–6, 30, 34–5; C. Northcote Parkinson, *War in the Eastern Seas, 1793–1815* (London: George Allen & Unwin, 1954), p. 62.

11. TNA, ADM 8/71, 'Admiralty List Books'. The precise numbers for October 1795 were: East Indies (16 ships, 5,768 men), Jamaica (21 ships, 5,760 men), Leeward Islands (24 ships, 6,927 men), Newfoundland (5 ships, 918 men) and Nova Scotia (14 ships, 3,579 men).

12. TNA, FO 20/20, Sir Gilbert Elliot to Henry Dundas, 4 February 1794 (No. 13).

13. Gardiner, *Fleet Battle and Blockade*, pp. 109–10.

14. Horatio Nelson to William Lockyer, 5 November 1796; Nicolas, ed., *Dispatches and Letters of Nelson*, Vol. 2, p. 298; Collingwood, *Public and Private Correspondence*, Vol. 1, p. 3; Collingwood to Blackett, 11 May 1796, in Collingwood, *Public and Private Correspondence*, Vol. 1, p. 43.

15. Duke of Portland quoted in Desmond Gregory, *The Ungovernable Rock: A History of the Anglo-Corsican Kingdom and Its Role in Britain's Mediterranean Strategy during the Revolutionary War (1793–97)* (London: Associated University Presses, 1985), p. 175.

16. *The Times*, 30 August 1796, quoted in Gregory, *Ungovernable Rock*, p. 175.

17. Huntington Library (HL), DUN 16, Lord Minto (Gilbert Elliot, Earl of) to Henry Dundas, 19 January 1795.

18. Nelson criticised Hotham for being happy with only the two prizes. While Hotham said that 'We must be contented, we have done very well', Nelson wrote to his wife that 'had we taken ten sail, and allowed an eleventh to escape when it had been possible to have got at her, I would never have called it well done: we should have had such a day, as I believe the annals of England never produced'. See Nicolas, ed., *Dispatches and Letters of Nelson*, Vol. 2, pp. 25–6.

19. The following year, Richery followed this up with an even more audacious raid on Newfoundland, where he destroyed fishing vessels and buildings and equipment ashore and threatened St John's. The British press fulminated over the French admiral's 'predatory incursions on the coast of Newfoundland . . . heroically committing acts for which a common plunderer would long since have been gibbetted'. See Roger Knight, *Convoys: The British Struggle Against Napoleonic Europe and America* (New Haven, CT and London: Yale University Press, 2022), pp. 21–2.

20. Dann, *Nagle Journal*, p. 200.

21. James Davey, 'Britain's European Island Empire, 1793–1815', in Hamilton and McAleer, *Islands and the British Empire*, pp. 35–54.
22. John Bruce, *Historical Views of plans, for the Government of British India and the regulation of trade to the East Indies* (London, 1793), pp. 272–3; John McAleer, *Britain's Maritime Empire: South Africa, the South Atlantic and the Indian Ocean, 1763–1820* (Cambridge: Cambridge University Press, 2017), p. 42; B.R. Mitchell and P. Deane, *Abstract of British Historical Statistics* (Cambridge, 1971), p. 388; quoted in Peter Ward, *British Naval Power in the East, 1794–1805: The Command of Admiral Peter Rainier* (Woodbridge: Boydell Press, 2013), p. 9.
23. Parkinson, *War in the Eastern Seas*, pp. 68–70.
24. Ward, *British Naval Power in the East, 1794–1805*, pp. 122, 137, 142
25. Sivasundaram, *Waves Across the South*, pp. 101–3.
26. Original: 'tous les jours l'hymne de la liberté chantée sur le pont produisait de nouveau Elan'. Parkinson, *War in the Eastern Seas*, p. 75.
27. McAleer, *Britain's Maritime Empire*, pp. 64, 97; Gardiner, *Fleet Battle and Blockade*, p. 73.
28. HL, DUN 17, Sir Mark Wood. Cursory suggestions, which are most respectfully submitted to Mr Dundas, for the purpose of getting Possession of the Dutch Eastern Possessions, and for preventing them from falling under the Dominion of the Enemies of his Country, 25 January 1795.
29. Parkinson, *War in the Eastern Seas*, p. 80; Gardiner, *Fleet Battle and Blockade*, p. 73; Rodger, *Command of the Ocean*, pp. 435–6.
30. Dundas to Spencer, 5 November 1797, quoted in McAleer, *Britain's Maritime Empire*, p. 64.
31. Thean Potieger and Albert Grundlingh, 'Admiral Elphinstone and the Conquest and Defence of the Cape of Good Hope, 1795–6', *Scientia Militaria: South African Journal of Military Studies*, Vol. 35, No. 2 (2007), 39–67; TNA, WO 1/329, p. 17, Lord Macartney to Dundas, 10 July 1797, in McAleer, *Britain's Maritime Empire*, p. 2.
32. For number of ships and seamen see TNA, ADM 8/72, 'Admiralty List Books, 1796'; John McAleer, 'Atlantic Periphery, Asian Gateway: The Royal Navy at the Cape of Good Hope, 1785–1815', in John McAleer and Christer Petley, eds, *The Royal Navy and the British Atlantic World, c. 1750–1820* (London: Palgrave Macmillan, 2016), pp. 173–96, p. 175; McAleer, *Britain's Maritime Empire*, pp. 64–7; Parkinson, *War in the Eastern Seas*, pp. 85–8, 112–13.
33. Potieger and Grundlingh, 'Conquest and Defence of the Cape of Good Hope', pp. 55–8.
34. Gardiner, *Fleet Battle and Blockade*, pp. 60, 71; Ward, *British Naval Power in the East, 1794–1805*, pp. 142–3; Parkinson, *War in the Eastern Seas*, pp. 120–31.
35. Richard Gott, *Britain's Empire: Resistance, Repression and Revolt* (London: Verso, 2011), p. 121; McAleer, *Britain's Maritime Empire*, pp. 134–5, 137–8.
36. Curtis to Spencer, 10 October 1800, in Julian Corbett and H.W. Richmond, eds, *The Private Papers of George, 2nd Earl Spencer*, 4 vols (London, 1913–24), Vol. 4, p. 235; John Barrow, *An Account of Travels into the Interior of Southern Africa, in the Years 1797 and 1798*, 2 vols (London: T. Cadell and W. Davies, 1801–4), Vol. 1, p. 52; quoted in McAleer, *Britain's Maritime Empire*, p. 139.
37. Sivasundaram, *Waves Across the South*, pp. 90–2.
38. Gott, *Britain's Empire*, pp. 104–6, quote at p. 106.
39. Geggus, 'The Caribbean in the Age of Revolution', pp. 91–7; David Geggus, *Slavery, War and Revolution: The British Occupation of Saint Domingue, 1793–1798* (Oxford: Oxford University Press), pp. 77–80, 86–7.
40. Quoted in Geggus, 'The Anglo-French Conflict', p. 31.

41. Duffy, *Soldiers, Sugar and Seapower*, pp. 28–9, 32–3.
42. Phyllis Deane and W.A. Cole, *British Economic Growth, 1688–1959* (Cambridge: Cambridge University Press, 1962), p. 87; Duffy, *Soldiers, Sugar and Seapower*, pp. 7, 10.
43. For Dundas, a loss in the Caribbean – and particularly Jamaica – was more significant than an invasion of Britain. In 1796 he commented that he would 'much rather hear that 15,000 men were landed in Ireland or even in Great Britain, than hear that the same number were landed in Jamaica with a fleet there superior to ours'. Corbett and Richmond, eds, *Spencer Papers*, Vol. 1, p. 318.
44. Dundas to Grenville, May 1793, *Historical Manuscripts Commission 14th Report, Appendix Part V: The Manuscripts of J.B. Fortescue Esq. Preserved at Dropmore* (London, 1894), Vol. 2, p. 408.
45. Geggus, 'The Anglo-French Conflict', pp. 27, 29.
46. *The Times*, 8 February 1793.
47. Duffy, *Soldiers, Sugar and Seapower*, p. 369.
48. Gardiner, *Fleet Battle and Blockade*, pp. 59, 62; Geggus, *Slavery, War and Revolution*, p. 98.
49. Geggus, *Slavery, War and Revolution*, pp. 98, 105–11.
50. Geggus, *Slavery, War and Revolution*, pp. 97, 107, 153; Gardiner, *Fleet Battle and Blockade*, p. 68.
51. Geggus, *Slavery, War and Revolution*, p. 66–7, 112–14.
52. Duffy, *Soldiers, Sugar and Seapower*, pp. 34–7; Gardiner, *Fleet Battle and Blockade*, pp. 59, 63.
53. On the impact of the 'rainy' or 'sickly' season see Coriann Convertito, 'The Health of British Seamen in the West Indies, 1770–1806', Unpublished PhD thesis, University of Exeter (2011), pp. 62–3, 144–5. See also J.R. McNeill, *Mosquito Empires: Ecology and the War in the Greater Caribbean 1620–1914* (Cambridge: Cambridge University Press, 2010), p. 246.
54. Kelly, 'Strategy and Counter-Revolution', p. 340.
55. Rodger, *Command of the Ocean*, p. 428; Duffy, *Soldiers, Sugar and Seapower*, pp. 44–58, 60, 86–7; Geggus, *Slavery, War and Revolution*, pp. 86–7, 111.
56. Duffy, *Soldiers, Sugar and Seapower*, pp. 68, 70–3, 78; Gardiner, *Fleet Battle and Blockade*, p. 64.
57. Duffy, *Soldiers, Sugar and Seapower*, p. 82.
58. *The Times*, 2 May 1794.
59. Gardiner, *Fleet Battle and Blockade*, pp. 64–5; Duffy, *Soldiers, Sugar and Seapower*, pp. 89, 90, 91, 95, 104, quote at p. 95.
60. Duffy, *Soldiers, Sugar and Seapower*, p. 104.
61. Individual profits were vast: Grey and Jervis secured at least £11,000 each, an incredible sum, while Lieutenant James made 3,000 guineas in two months as a prize commissioner on Martinique. Naval officers at sea could also do very well: one young frigate captain, Josias Rogers, made no less than £10,000 in early 1794. Willis, *First of June*, p. 108; Duffy, *Soldiers, Sugar and Seapower*, p. 113.
62. Willis, *First of June*, p. 108; Duffy, *Soldiers, Sugar and Seapower*, pp. 106–11.
63. Geggus, 'The Anglo-French Conflict', p. 33.
64. Duffy, *Soldiers, Sugar and Seapower*, pp. 118–20, 128–9, 137–9.
65. For the most recent biography of Toussaint Louverture see Sudhir Hazareesingh, *Black Spartacus: The Epic Life of Toussaint Louverture* (London: Allen Lane, 2020). For details of his alliance with France in 1794 see pp. 60–6.
66. See Farrar, 'Health of British Seamen', p. 320; ADM 102/426 and 730; Geggus, *Slavery, War and Revolution*, pp. 121, 128–31, 153–4; Gardiner, *Fleet Battle and Blockade*, pp. 59, 64–5.

67. Geggus, 'The Anglo-French Conflict', pp. 142–3.
68. John Angus Martin, 'Citizens and Comrades in Arms: The Congruence of Fédon's Rebellion and the Grenada Revolution', in Nicole Philip-Dowe and John Angus Martin, eds, *Perspectives on the Grenada Revolution, 1979–1983* (Cambridge: Cambridge Scholars Publishing, 2017), pp. 1–17, pp. 3–4.
69. Helen McKee, 'From Violence to Alliance: Maroons and White Settlers in Jamaica, 1739–1795', *Slavery and Abolition*, Vol. 39, No. 1 (2018), pp. 27–52; Michael Sivapragasam, 'After the Treaties: A Social, Economic and Demographic History of Maroon Society in Jamaica, 1739–1842', Unpublished PhD thesis, University of Southampton (2018), pp. 123–35.
70. Tessa Murphy, 'A Reassertion of Rights: Fedon's Rebellion, Grenada, 1795–6', *Économie politique et Révolution française*, No. 14 (2018), pp. 1–26, at p. 14. The debate is particularly marked in regard to Grenada, where many historians, such as Edward L. Cox, John Angus Martin and Kit Candlin, see the Grenada rebellion as a direct result of the Age of Revolution. More recently, Tessa Murphy has argued against this, emphasising the local nature of the conflict and the long-standing grievances on Grenada, and seeing it instead as part of a broader contest over democratic participation in both the French and British empires. Certainly, the rebellion was happy to take advantage of French help and present itself in a revolutionary light: the initial supply of arms, ammunition and finances came Guadeloupe, and Fédon was given a French commission while adopting the slogan of 'Liberté, equalité ou la mort', and they used the French tricolour as their own flag. See Edward L. Cox, "Fédon's Rebellion, 1795–96: Causes and Consequences', *Journal of Negro History*, Vol. 67, No. 1 (1982); Martin, 'Citizens and Comrades'; Kit Candlin, 'The Role of the Enslaved in the "Fedon Rebellion" of 1795', *Slavery and Abolition*, Vol. 39, No. 4 (2018), esp. p. 691; Murphy, 'Reassertion of Rights'. David Geggus has warned against seeing a direct link between the movements, which he argues is more easily 'imagined rather than demonstrated'. See David Geggus, 'Slavery and the Haitian Revolution', in D. Eltis, S.L. Engerman, S. Drescher and D. Richardson, eds, *The Cambridge World History of Slavery, 1804–AD 2016* (Cambridge: Cambridge University Press, 2017), Vol. 4, pp. 321–43, quote at p. 341. For the longer history of resistance to slavery in the British empire see Craton, *Testing the Chains*. On Grenada, for example, the rebellion originated from more than a century of slave resistance and discontent over British rule since 1763. See M. Jacobs, 'Fédon Rebellion', in R.N.M. Juang and N. Morrissette, eds, *Africa and the Americas: Culture, Politics and History: A Multidisciplinary Encyclopaedia* (Oxford: ABC Clio, 2008), pp. 448–9. On Jamaica, there was a long history of slave rebellion: see Vincent Brown, *Tacky's Revolt: The Story of an Atlantic Slave War* (Cambridge, MA: Belknap Press, 2020).
71. Gardiner, *Fleet Battle and Blockade*, pp. 60, 79; Duffy, *Soldiers, Sugar and Seapower*, pp. 141, 155; Geggus, *Slavery, War and Revolution*, pp. 176–7.
72. HL, DUN 22: Andrew James Cochrane Johnstone to Henry Dundas, 20 January 1796. For attempts in Grenada and Jamaica see Candlin, 'Role of the Enslaved', pp. 699–700; Duffy, *Soldiers, Sugar and Seapower*, pp. 242–3, 245; Roger N. Buckley, *Slaves in Red Coats: The British West India Regiments, 1795–1815* (New Haven, CT: Yale University Press, 1979).
73. Duffy, *Soldiers, Sugar and Seapower*, pp. 136–7, 170–6.
74. For the first example see TNA, ADM 1/3283, 18 June 1795; ADM 2/1064/328, 10 June 1795; ADM 2/1064, 339, 19 June 1795; for the second example see *Hampshire Chronicle*, 15 June 1795; *Morning Chronicle*, 9 June 1795. For the third see TNA, ADM 2/1064/346–7, 26 June 1795; ADM 2/1065/56–7, 24 March 1796. I am grateful to Nick Rogers for these examples. See also Duffy, *Soldiers, Sugar and*

Seapower, pp. 183–4; TNA, ADM 2/1064/346–7, 26 June 1795; ADM 2/1065/56–7, 24 March 1796.

75. Candlin, 'Role of the Enslaved', p. 687.
76. Duffy, *Soldiers, Sugar and Seapower*, pp. 199–200.
77. See Robert Sutcliffe, *British Expeditionary Warfare and the Defeat of Napoleon, 1793–1815* (Woodbridge: Boydell Press, 2016), pp. 102–6. See also Rodger, *Command of the Ocean*, p. 434; Duffy, *Soldiers, Sugar and Seapower*, pp. 194–6, 199.
78. Lewis, *Narrative*, Vol. 1, pp. 214, 216.
79. Knight, *Britain Against Napoleon*, pp. 73–4; Duffy, *Soldiers, Sugar and Seapower*, pp. 203–5, 207, 208; Uglow, *In These Times*, p. 156.
80. The ship was forced to return to Britain, where Cornwallis refused to follow the convoy in a frigate and wait for his ships to be repaired. The First Lord of the Admiralty, Lord Spencer, stripped him of his command, ordering a court martial, though he was eventually acquitted. See TNA, ADM 1/5335, Court Martial of William Cornwallis, 7–8 April 1796.
81. NMM, XAGC/H/32, J. Harrison to Miss Butler, 16 March 1796.
82. The main body of the expedition arrived at Barbados on 14–15 April. See Duffy, *Soldiers, Sugar and Seapower*, p. 221.
83. Cox, 'Fedon's Rebellion', p. 9; Duffy, *Soldiers, Sugar and Seapower*, p. 240.
84. Gott, *Britain's Empire*, p. 115; Duffy, *Soldiers, Sugar and Seapower*, pp. 258, 259, 260–3, 259–60; Uglow, *In These Times*, p. 156.
85. Martin, 'Citizens and Comrades in Arms', p. 4; Duffy, *Soldiers, Sugar and Seapower*, pp. 146, 258; Sivapragasam, 'After the Treaties', pp. 143–4, 147–9.
86. Hazareesingh, *Black Spartacus*, p. 99; Geggus, *Slavery, War and Revolution*, p. 194; Gardiner, *Fleet Battle and Blockade*, p. 79; HL, Hamond Collection, Box 73, No. 2, John Thomas Duckworth to the Governor and Privy Council of Jamaica, 19 August 1796.
87. Gardiner, *Fleet Battle and Blockade*, p. 79; Geggus, *Slavery, War and Revolution*, pp. 195–6.
88. TNA, ADM 101/87/3, quoted in McNeill, *Mosquito Empires*, p. 248.
89. Duffy, *Soldiers, Sugar and Seapower*, pp. 295, 296; Geggus, 'The Anglo-French Conflict', p. 36; Geggus, *Slavery, War and Revolution*, pp. 212–13.
90. Duffy, *Soldiers, Sugar and Seapower*, pp. 311, 313.
91. Gardiner, *Fleet Battle and Blockade*, pp. 79–81.
92. Duffy, *Soldiers, Sugar and Seapower*, pp. 270, 291; Geggus, *Slavery, War and Revolution*, pp. 224–6.
93. Hazareesingh, *Black Spartacus*, pp. 127–8, 135–8.
94. Scott, *Common Wind*, pp. 206–8. For a discussion of Haiti's place in the aftermath of the revolution, see in particular chapters 3 and 5 of Julia Gaffield, *Haitian Connections in the Atlantic World: Recognition after Revolution* (Chapel Hill, NC: University of North Carolina Press, 2015), pp. 93–123, 153–82.
95. TNA, ADM 1/5125, declaration of sailors at the Nore, June 1797.
96. In particular, they thanked him for 'his gallant conduct, and unremitting attention to the Protection of the Company's Factories and Trade in the Levant Seas'. Somerset Heritage Centre, DD\AH\61/7/1, Extract of the Minutes of a General Court of the Governor and Company of Merchants of England trading into the Levant held at Salters Hall on Tuesday the 29th September 1795; Somerset Heritage Centre, DD\AH\61/7/2, Letter to Samuel Hood, 2 December 1795, written in Smyrna from the British Factory of Merchants there. For the Caribbean see John McAleer, 'Eminent Service: War, Slavery and the Politics of Public Recognition in the British Caribbean and the Cape of Good Hope c. 1782–1807', *Mariner's Mirror*, Vol. 95, No. 1 (2009), pp. 33–51.

97. For naval agents and contracting see Frank A.J.L. James, 'Making Money from the Royal Navy in the Late Eighteenth Century: Charles Kerr on Antigua "Breathing the True Spirit of a West India Agent"', *Mariner's Mirror*, Vol. 107, No. 4 (November 2021), p. 402–19; Knight and Wilcox, *Sustaining the Fleet*, pp. 155–76. For commanders being bombarded by locals see for example the vast number of letters addressed to John Duckworth on arriving to take command in the Caribbean in 1800. Within the space of a week he received letters from the Presidents of Antigua and Barbados that lauded his abilities while also unsubtly asking for naval protection. See HL, Hamond Collection, Box 77, No. 2, Edward Bryan, President of Antigua, to John Duckworth, 5 August 1800; HL, Hamond Collection, Box 77, No. 6, W. Bishop to Duckworth, 1 August 1800. On the links between the navy and planter society see Sian Williams, 'The Royal Navy and Caribbean Colonial Society during the Eighteenth Century' in McAleer and Petley, *The Royal Navy and the British Atlantic World*, pp. 27–50, pp. 14–15, 31–4.

98. Christer Petley, 'The Royal Navy, the British Atlantic Empire and the Abolition of the Slave Trade', in McAleer and Petley, eds, *The Royal Navy and the British Atlantic World, c. 1750–1820*, pp. 97–122, p. 107; Horatio Nelson to Simon Taylor, 11 June 1805; John Knox Laughton, *The Naval Miscellany* (London: Navy Records Society, 1902), Vol. 1, pp. 438–9. A version with Wilberforce reference redacted is available in Nicolas, ed., *Dispatches and Letters of Nelson*, Vol. 6, pp. 450–1. See Petley, 'Royal Navy', pp. 97, 114.

99. Petley, 'Royal Navy'; Duffy, *Soldiers, Sugar and Seapower*, p. 391, n. 36.

100. For the idea of ships as ethnic melting pots see Linebaugh and Rediker, *Many-Headed Hydra*, p. 151. For estimates of the number of Black sailors serving in the Navy (the data covers a survey from 1784–1812) see Philip D. Morgan, 'Black Experiences in Britain's Maritime World', in Cannadine, ed., *Empire, the Sea and Global History*, pp. 105–33, reference at p. 118. See also Stephen D. Behrendt, 'Human Capital in the British Slave Trade', in David Richardson, Suzanne Schwarz and Anthony Tibbles, eds, *Liverpool and Transatlantic Slavery* (Liverpool: Liverpool University Press), pp. 66–97, pp. 78–9; Costello, *Black Salt*, pp. 35, 68. For the cartel agreement see HL, Hamond Collection, Box 80, No. 12, 'A List of the men received on board His Majesty's Ship *Daphne* from the French Cartel on the 24 January 1801, in exchange for the Crews of the L'Eclair National Schooner, and L'Hereux French Sloop'.

101. Costello, *Black Salt*, pp. 26–8.

102. Emidy became the leader of the Falmouth Harmonic Society, writing chamber works and symphonies and spending the rest of his life in Cornwall. Costello, *Black Salt*, pp. 46–7; Adkins and Adkins, *Jack Tar*, pp. 334–5.

103. Richardson's views on African people were complex. He noted numerous instances of deceiving African leaders with poor quality goods but also spoke of them as 'civil, harmless, and obliging . . . they were sober and industrious, and a credit to many Europeans in their morals'. He recorded feeling sorry for 'poor slaves with their eyes full of tears, looking to the land as long as a bit of it was to be seen; the females wept bitterly' but at no point did he question the institution of slavery. The closest he came was noting that he 'hated tyranny' but he also wrote that he and none of his 'had reason to complain'. Childers, ed., *A Mariner of England*, pp. 46, 50, 54, 56, 60–3.

104. TNA, ADM 1/5338, court martial of James McCoy of the *Atlas*, 28 February 1797.

105. TNA, ADM 1/5331, court martial of John Bell et al. of the *Vengeance*, 11 and 14 March 1794.

106. NMM, ADM/L/H121, Lieutenant's Log Book of the *Hope*, 1796–1800.
107. James Kelly, *Voyage to Jamaica, and Seventeen Years' Residence in that Island: Chiefly Written with a View to Exhibit Negro Life and Habits*, 2nd edition (Belfast, 1838), pp. 17, 29–30; quoted in Scott, *Common Wind*, p. 42.
108. Here I paraphrase Scott's 'transatlantic news pipeline'; see Scott, *Common Wind*, p. 118. For wider points about the spread of news see Scott, *Common Wind*, pp. xvi, 39, 76–7, 129. For the links between sailors and enslaved people see also Geggus, *Slavery, War and Revolution*, pp. 38–9.
109. Williamson to Dundas, 18 September 1791, 6 November 1791; Scott, *Common Wind*, pp. 143–4.
110. Costello, *Black Salt*, p. 73. See also W. Jeffrey Bolster, *Black Jacks: African American Seamen in the Age of Sail* (Cambridge, MA: Harvard University Press, 1998), p. 28.
111. Henry Snow, 'Fugitive Harbour: Labour, Community, and Marronage at Antigua Naval Yard', *Slavery and Abolition*, Vol. 42, No. 4 (2021), p. 819; Douglas Hamilton, '"A Most Active, Enterprising Officer": Captain John Perkins, the Royal Navy and the Boundaries of Slavery and Liberty in the Caribbean', *Slavery and Abolition*, Vol. 39, No. 1 (2018), p. 81. See also Bolster, *Black Jacks*; Charles S. Foy, 'The Royal Navy's Employment of Black Mariners and Maritime Workers, 1754–1783', *International Journal of Maritime History*, Vol. 28, No. 1 (2016), pp. 6–35.
112. Kevin Dawson, 'Enslaved Ship Pilots in the Age of Revolutions: Challenging Notions of Race and Slavery between the Boundaries of Land and Sea', *Journal of Social History*, Vol. 47, No. 1 (2013), pp. 72–83.
113. Douglas Hamilton, 'Captain John Perkins', pp. 84–5, 87–8; Costello, *Black Salt*, pp. 97–9.
114. Foy, 'Black Mariners and Maritime Workers', pp. 15–16.
115. Hamilton, 'Captain John Perkins', pp. 85, 89.
116. Sivasundaram, *Waves Across the South*, p. 39.
117. Geggus, 'The Caribbean in the Age of Revolution', p. 84
118. Roger Anstey, *The Atlantic Slave Trade and British Abolition 1760–1810* (Atlantic Highlands, NJ: Humanities Press, 1975), pp. 276–8; Petley, 'Royal Navy', p. 109; Duffy, *Soldiers, Sugar and Seapower*, p. 391; David Geggus, 'British Opinion and the Emergence of Haiti, 1791–1805', in James Walvin, ed., *Slavery and British Society, 1776–1848* (London: Macmillan, 1982), pp. 123–49, pp. 130. On the impact of Grenada see Candlin, 'Role of the Enslaved', p. 687. On the wider impact of slave rebellions on British politics and abolition see Robin Blackburn, *The Overthrow of Colonial Slavery, 1776–1848* (London: Verso, 1988), pp. 526–9; Robin Blackburn, 'The Force of Example', in David Geggus, ed., *The Impact of the Haitian Revolution in the Atlantic World* (Columbia, SC: University of South Carolina Press, 2001), pp. 15–20; Seymour Drescher, *Econocide: British Slavery in the Era of Abolition* (Chapel Hill, NC: University of North Carolina Press, 1977; 2nd edition, 2010), pp. 168–9; Drescher, *Capitalism and Antislavery: British Mobilization in Comparative Perspective* (Oxford: Oxford University Press, 1997), pp. 96–9, 105–6.
119. For figures see Charles Consolvo, 'The Prospects and Promotion of British Naval Officers 1793–1815', *Mariner's Mirror*, Vol. 91, No. 2 (2005), pp. 147, 155; TNA, ADM 102/426 and 427, passim; Geggus, *Slavery, War and Revolution*, p. 363; Duffy, *Soldiers, Sugar and Seapower*, p. 156; Geggus, 'The Anglo-French Conflict', p. 38. For the suggestion that the government falsified casualty returns see McNeill, *Mosquito Empires*, p. 247. For the peace terms see John Grainger, *The Amiens Truce: Britain and Bonaparte, 1801–1803* (Woodbridge: Boydell Press, 2003); Duffy, *Soldiers, Sugar and Seapower*, p. 389.

120. James Davey, *In Nelson's Wake: The Navy and the Napoleonic Wars* (London and New Haven, CT: Yale University Press, 2015), pp. 114–15; Michael Duffy, 'World-Wide War and British Expansion', in P.J. Marshall, ed., *The Oxford History of the British Empire*, Vol. 2: *The Eighteenth Century* (Oxford: Oxford University Press, 1998), pp. 184–207, p. 204.

121. For colonial projectors see for example Andrew James Cochrane Johnstone, who repeatedly demanded an expedition to attack Guadeloupe. HL, DUN39: Andrew James Cochrane Johnstone to Henry Dundas, 19 January 1799; HL, DUN 72: Andrew James Cochrane Johnstone to Henry Dundas, 26 November 1800 (at Martinique). Around the same time, Dundas continued to plead the colonial case. In 1799 he noted that 'Great Britain can at no time propose to maintain an extensive and complicated war but by destroying the colonial resources of our enemies and adding proportionally to our own commercial resources, which are, and ever must be, the sole basis of our maritime strength'. Dundas to Wellesley, 31 October 1799, in McAleer, *Britain's Maritime Empire*, p. 9.

5 SPLINTERING THE WOODEN WALLS: THE THREAT OF INVASION, 1796–8

1. *Le Moniteur*, 29 December 1796, quoted in the *Star*, 5 January 1797.

2. Serious invasion attempts were planned or executed in 1689, 1692, 1708, 1715, 1719, 1745, 1759–60 and 1779.

3. Maria Josepha Holroyd Stanley to Ann Firth, 18 February 1794, in Jane Henrietta Adeane (ed.), *The Girlhood of Maria Josepha Holroyd, Lady Stanley of Alderley: Recorded in Letters of a Hundred Years Ago, from 1776 to 1796* (London, 1896), p. 399.

4. James Gillray, *The French Invasion; – or – John Bull, bombarding the Bum-Boats* (London, 1793); James Davey and Richard Johns, *Broadsides: Caricature and the Navy, 1756–1815* (Barnsley: Seaforth, 2012), p. 41; Anon., *The Patriot Briton; or, England's Invasion* (London: Printed for Richard White, Printed by James Bateson, 1796), p. 5.

5. Renaud Morieux, *The Channel: England, France and the Construction of a Maritime Border in the Eighteenth Century* (Cambridge: Cambridge University Press, 2016). For analysis of the Channel as a military frontier see in particular pp. 109–49.

6. Collingwood to Blackett, 26 January 1798, in Collingwood, *Public and Private Correspondence*, Vol. 1, pp. 85–6.

7. John Ranby, *Short Hints on a French Invasion* (London: John Stockdale, 1794), pp. 3–4. See also George Hanger, *Military Reflections on the Attack and Defence of the City of London* (1795).

8. Hanger, *Military Reflections*, pp. 7–17, 128; quoted in Knight, *Britain Against Napoleon*, pp. 87–8.

9. Anon., *On the defence of Ireland: Including Observations on some other subjects connected therewith* (Dublin: P. Byrne, 1795), pp. 7–9.

10. James Gillray, *Promis'd Horrors of the French INVASION or Forcible Reasons for negotiating a Regicide PEACE. Vide, the Authority of Edmund Burke* (London, 20 October 1796).

11. *Bell's Weekly Messenger*, 18 December 1796. For details on the Militia Bill of 1796 see Cookson, *British Armed Nation*, p. 28.

12. By April 1795 Howe was using crutches to get around, and by June he was describing 'the weakness in my affected limbs'. See HL, HO 218, Howe to Curtis, 13 April 1795, 17 June 1795.

13. Morriss, *Blockade of Brest*, pp. 131–2; Gardiner, *Fleet Battle and Blockade*, pp. 140, 142–4, 152; Wilson, 'Naval Defence of Ireland', pp. 570–1.
14. Knight, *Britain Against Napoleon*, pp. 78–80; Navickas, *Loyalism and Radicalism*, pp. 62–3.
15. Linda Colley uses the term 'popular patriotism'; see Linda Colley, *Britons: Forging the Nation 1707–1837* (London and New Haven, CT: Yale University Press, 1992), pp. 285–319; Cookson, 'English Volunteer Movement'; Cookson, *British Armed Nation*, pp. 26–8, 32, 209–45; Gee, *British Volunteer Movement*. Other scholars – most noticeably Nicholas Rogers – suggest that volunteering was a less patriotic act: there were frictions between local and national, and volunteering allowed citizens to escape military or naval service (especially impressment). Nicholas Rogers, 'The Sea Fencibles, Loyalism, and the Reach of the State', in Philp, ed., *Resisting Napoleon*, pp. 41–60; Davey, *In Nelson's Wake*, chap. 7. For the situation in Ireland see Wilson, 'Naval Defence of Ireland', pp. 577–8.
16. Knight, *Britain Against Napoleon*, pp. 88, 150; Sparrow, *Secret Service*.
17. Knight, *Britain Against Napoleon*, p. 126. Roger Knight goes so far as to say of the 1790s that 'the verdict on the overall defence intelligence performance must be one of continual failure'. Knight, *Britain Against Napoleon*, p. 150.
18. Sparrow, *Secret Service*, pp. 84, 271–2, 335–7; Morriss, *Blockade of Brest*, pp. 165–6; Knight, *Britain Against Napoleon*, p. 123.
19. Tom Pocock, *A Thirst for Glory: The Life of Sir Sidney Smith*, 2nd edition (London: Pimlico, 1998), pp. 36–42; Sparrow, *Secret Service*, pp. 84, 87.
20. Colpoys to Spencer, 11 December 1796, Morriss, *Blockade of Brest*, p. 160; Colpoys to Spencer, 7 December 1796; Morriss, *Blockade of Brest*, pp. 159–60.
21. Morriss, *Blockade of Brest*, pp. 163–4. On Bridport hearing the news see Admiralty to Bridport, 21 December 1796, in Morriss, *Blockade of Brest*, pp. 168–9. For Bridport's final departure see Bridport to Admiralty, 3 January 1797, in Morriss, *Blockade of Brest*, pp. 175–6.
22. *Oracle and Public Advertiser*, 30 December 1796.
23. *Telegraph*, 3 January 1797.
24. *True Briton*, 3 January 1797; *True Briton*, 5 January 1797.
25. For literature on Ireland in the 1790s see Jim Smyth, ed., *Revolution, Counter-Revolution and Union: Ireland in the 1790s* (Cambridge: Cambridge University Press, 2000); Kevin Whelan, *Fellowship of Freedom: The United Irishmen and the 1798 Rebellion* (Cork: Cork University Press, 1998); Patrick Geoghegan, 'Rising and Union, 1791–1801', in Alvin Jackson, ed., *The Oxford Handbook of Modern Irish History* (Oxford: Oxford University Press, 2014), pp. 497–513; Ultán Gillen, 'Constructing Democratic Thought in Ireland in the Age of Revolution, 1775–1800', in Joanna Innes and Mark Philp, eds, *Re-imagining Democracy in the Age of Revolutions* (Oxford: Oxford University Press, 2013), pp. 149–61.
26. H.F.B. Wheeler and A.M. Broadley, *Napoleon and the Invasion of England: The Story of the Great Terror* (London, 1908; new edn. Stroud: Nonsuch, 2007), pp. 32–3; Gardiner, *Fleet Battle and Blockade*, p. 138.
27. James, *Naval History*, Vol. 3, pp. 7–9.
28. Morriss, *Blockade of Brest*, pp. 163–5; Wheeler and Broadley, *Invasion of England*, pp. 34–6; Gardiner, *Fleet Battle and Blockade*, p. 138.
29. Morriss, *Blockade of Brest*, p. 164.
30. James, *Naval History*, Vol. 2, p. 20; Gardiner, *Fleet Battle and Blockade*, pp. 158–9; Wheeler and Broadley, *Invasion of England*, pp. 35–6.
31. Suffolk Record Office (SRO), SA/3/1/2/1, James Saumarez to Martha Saumarez, 14 and 17 January 1797.

32. Morriss, *Blockade of Brest*, p. 164; Knight, *Britain Against Napoleon*, pp. 85–6.
33. *Oracle and Public Advertiser*, 24 January 1797.
34. *Telegraph*, 27 January 1797; *True Briton*, 21 January 1797.
35. P.M. Kerrigan, 'The French Expedition to Bantry Bay, 1796, and the Boat from the *Résolue*', *Irish Sword*, Vol. 21 (1999), pp. 65–84, quoted in Wilson, 'Naval Defence of Ireland', p. 572.
36. This ballad, probably first printed in a newspaper, appears in *A Collection of Constitutional Songs* (Cork: A. Edwards, 1799), Vol. I, p. 80. See T. Crofton Croker, *Popular Songs, Illustrative of the French Invasions of Ireland* (London: Percy Society, 1847), part 3, p. 13.
37. Wheeler and Broadley, *Invasion of England*, p. 36.
38. Anon, *General Observations on the State of Affairs in Ireland and its Defence against an Invasion. By a Country Gentleman* (Dublin: George Johnson, 1797), p. 9.
39. James Gillray, *End of the Irish invasion; – or – the destruction of the French Armada* (London: Hannah Humphrey, 20 January 1797).
40. Admiralty to Bridport, 26 February 1797; Morriss, *Blockade of Brest*, pp. 181–2.
41. Anon, *General Observations on the State of Affairs in Ireland*, pp. 2–4.
42. *True Briton*, 24 February 1797; *True Briton*, 25 February 1797.
43. *Oracle and Public Advertiser*, 25 February 1797.
44. For instructions see Instructions for Colonel Tate, in *Report of the Committee of the House of Commons, in consequence of the several motions relative to the treatment of prisoners of war. Including the whole of the examinations taken before the Committee, the correspondence relative to the exchange of prisoners; the instructions of Colonel Tate* (London, 1798), p. 127; Marianne Elliott, *Partners in Revolution: The United Irishmen and France* (New Haven, CT and London: Yale University Press, 1982), pp. 113–18, 134.
45. *Critical Review* 24 (1798), pp. 252–3.
46. Admiralty to Bridport, 28 January 1797; Morriss, *Blockade of Brest*, p. 177.
47. Knight, *Britain Against Napoleon*, pp. 83–4.
48. Both quoted in Davies, 'Terror, Treason and Tourism: The French in Pembrokeshire 1797' in Mary-Ann Constantine and Dafydd Johnston, *Footsteps of 'Liberty and Revolt': Essays on Wales and the French Revolution* (Cardiff: University of Wales Press, 2013), pp. 247–70, p. 250.
49. *Annual Register* 1797, p. 89. For parliamentary discussion see *Oracle and Public Advertiser*, 1 March 1797. The suspension of the gold standard was supposed to be a temporary measure, but it was renewed by successive governments until 1821. Emsley, *British Society*, p. 57.
50. For specifics of the campaign see E. Quinalt, 'The French Invasion of Pembrokeshire in 1797', *Welsh History Review*, Vol. 19 (1999), pp. 618–42; Richard Rose, 'The French at Fishguard: Fact, Fiction and Folklore', *Transactions of the Honourable Society of Cymmrodorion* (2002), pp. 74–105; J.E. Thomas, *Britain's Last Invasion: Fishguard, 1797* (Stroud, 2007); J.D. Davies, *Britannia's Dragon: A Naval History of Wales* (Cheltenham: History Press, 2013), pp. 75–6.
51. John Henry Manners (Duke of Rutland), *Journal of a tour through north and south Wales, the Isle of Man* (London: J. Triphook, 1805), pp. 128–9, 184.
52. Rose, 'The French at Fishguard', pp. 74–105; Davies, 'Terror, Treason and Tourism', pp. 251–5; Davies, *Britannia's Dragon*, p. 76.
53. HL, HO 334, Howe to Curtis, 1 March 1797.
54. Davies, *Britannia's Dragon*, pp. 76–7; *Oracle and Public Advertiser*, 4 March 1797; *True Briton*, 4 March 1797.
55. *Oracle and Public Advertiser*, 4 March 1797.

56. A.K. Hamilton Jenkin, ed., *News from Cornwall* (1951), p. 45; quoted in Emsley, *British Society*, p. 56.

57. For anxious newspaper reports see *True Briton*, 7 March 1797; *Oracle and Evening Advertiser*, 13 March 1797, 14 March 1797. For Pellew's victory see Gardiner, *Fleet Battle and Blockade*, p. 160; Davies, *Britannia's Dragon*, p. 77. The *Résistance* was taken into the Royal Navy and named *Fishguard* in recognition of Britain's latest deliverance from invasion.

58. *True Briton*, 5 April 1797; *Lloyd's Evening Post*, 15 March 1797.

59. Rodger, *Command of the Ocean*, pp. 438–9; Knight, *Pursuit of Victory*, pp. 219–21; Jedediah Stephens Tucker, ed., *Memoirs of Admiral the Right Hon. The Earl of St Vincent*, 2 vols (London: Richard Bentley, 1844), Vol. 1, p. 255.

60. George Parsons, ed., *Nelson Reminiscences* (London, 1843), p. 323.

61. Rodger, *Command of the Ocean*, p. 439.

62. Collingwood to Lady Collingwood, 17 February 1797, in Collingwood, *Public and Private Correspondence*, Vol. 1, pp. 46–7.

63. Willis, *Hour of Victory*, pp. 91–3; Knight, *Pursuit of Victory*, pp. 222–3, 226–7; N.A.M. Rodger, 'Nelson and the British Navy', in David Cannadine, ed., *Nelson: Context and Legacy* (Basingstoke: Palgrave Macmillan, 2005), pp. 7–29, pp. 12–13.

64. Knight, *Pursuit of Victory*, pp. 224–5. For the *Excellent's* progress see Collingwood to Lady Collingwood, 17 February 1797, in Collingwood, *Public and Private Correspondence*, Vol. 1, p. 49. For Nelson's conduct see Knight, *Pursuit of Victory*, pp. 222–5; Willis, *Hour of Victory*, p. 93.

65. Quoted in Uglow, *In These Times*, p. 174.

66. Jenks, *Naval Engagements*, p. 128. For a similar naval opinion see HL, HO335, Howe to Curtis, 4 May 1797.

67. See *The Times*, 21 March 1797; *Sun*, 22 March 1797; Willis, *Hour of Victory*, pp. 93, 96–7, 99; Knight, *Pursuit of Victory*, pp. 227–8.

68. *Oracle*, 3 June 1797.

69. Gee, *British Volunteer Movement*, p. 11. John Cookson argues that what he calls 'national defence patriotism' emerged only episodically, with the threat of invasion in 1798, 1801 and 1803–5. Cookson, *British Armed Nation*, pp. 210–11.

70. *Sun*, 24 April 1798; *True Briton*, 2 May 1798.

71. *Sun*, 11 April 1798; *Sun*, 12 April 1798.

72. Emsley, *British Society*, p. 57; Colley, *Britons*, p. 293; Davies, 'Terror, Treason and Tourism', p. 261.

73. Quoted in Davies, 'Terror, Treason and Tourism', pp. 259–60.

74. *The Bishop of Llandaff's Thoughts on the French Invasion, Originally Addressed to the Clergy of his Diocese* (London: James Asperne, June 1798). For its reception see SRO, SA/3/1/2/1, Martha Saumarez to James Saumarez, 2 February 1798.

75. Thomas Knox, *Some account of the proceedings that took place on the landing of the French near Fishguard, in Pembroke shire, on the 22nd February 1797 . . .* (London: A. Wilson, 1800), p. 28; Manners, *Journal*, p. 129.

76. Davies, 'Terror, Treason and Tourism', pp. 257–8; Colley, *Britons*, pp. 289–301; Philp, 'Introduction', p. 5.

77. Morriss, *Blockade of Brest*, p. 165. For Admiralty's orders regarding Pellew see Spencer to Pellew, 28 March 1797, in Morriss, *Blockade of Brest*, p. 188; Admiralty to Bridport, in Morriss, *Blockade of Brest*, 15 May 1797, pp. 244–5.

78. See for example Warren to Spencer, 30 December 1796, NRS, pp. 172–3. Warren had this idea sown by officers who had blockaded Brest during the Seven Years' War. See Morriss, *Blockade of Brest*, p. 165. Bridport noted that it was hard to keep station off the Goulet in easterly winds, and that observations made down the Channel could be deceptive, while information gleaned from French seamen was

liable to be propaganda put out by the French authorities. The blockade would still have to be abandoned in the worst winter weather. See Bridport to Spencer, 30 March 1797, in Morriss, *Blockade of Brest*, p. 188.

79. Morriss, *Blockade of Brest*, p. 238. For examples of letters arriving by packet within twenty-four hours see Acknowledged in Bridport to Admiralty, 14 July 1797, 15 July 1797, NRS, pp. 255–6.

80. For letter doing this see Admiralty to Bridport, 11 November 1797, in Morriss, *Blockade of Brest*, pp. 271–2. For the wider point about developing Admiralty expertise see Morriss, *Blockade of Brest*, p. 241.

81. Bridport to Admiralty, 18 June 1797, NRS, p. 250.

82. For complaints see Bridport to Spencer, 30 June 1797, NRS, p. 253; Bridport to Spencer, 27 July 1797, NRS, pp. 259–60; Bridport to Admiralty, 8 August 1797, NRS, pp. 262–3. Intelligence from Captain John Gore in July put the number of French vessels ready for sea at nineteen, with 40,000 soldiers 'who are expected daily at Brest to embark on an expedition against Ireland'. The following month, Pellew's cruise towards Brest put the number at 'upwards of twenty', while Duckworth counted eighteen to twenty. See Captain John Gore to Warren, 24 July 1797, NRS, pp. 258–9; Bridport to Spencer, 6 August 1797, NRS, p. 262. See also John Duckworth to Bridport, 3 September 1797, NRS, pp. 267–8 for similar numbers.

83. The Admiralty noted pointedly that 'you will not be likely to be exposed to any difficulty in making the detachments mentioned in their Lordships' order to you'. See Admiralty to Bridport, 8 September 1797, in Morriss, *Blockade of Brest*, pp. 268–9. For Nepean's tart response see Nepean to Spencer, 11 September, NRS, p. 269.

84. C.J.M. Kramers, 'The Batavian Republic and Ireland, 1797', *Irish Sword*, Vol. 20 (1996), pp. 145–7; Wilson, 'Naval Defence of Ireland', p. 572; Gardiner, *Fleet Battle and Blockade*, pp. 138–9.

85. Morriss, *Blockade of Brest*, pp. 239, 241; Gardiner, *Fleet Battle and Blockade*, pp. 141, 155.

86. For intelligence received relating to French intentions, and for the proposal for the defence of Britain and Ireland, February–April 1798, see Corbett and Richmond, *Private Papers of George, 2nd Earl Spencer*, Vol. 2, pp. 221–36.

87. *Bell's Weekly Messenger*, 24 December 1797.

88. *Star*, 10 February 1798.

89. *True Briton*, 12 February 1798.

90. See for example *Sun*, 23 April 1798; Anon., *Invasion of Britain: An Address to the People of Great Britain, On the Subject of a French Invasion. Dulce et decorum est pro patria mori. By a patriot.* (London: J. Fairburn, 1798), p. 5.

91. Suffolk Record Office, SA/3/1/2/1, Martha Saumarez to James Saumarez, 2 February 1798.

92. Robert Dighton, *An Accurate Representation of the Floating Machine Invented by the French for Invading England* (London, 1798); Samuel Fores, *A Correct Plan and Elevation of the Famous French Raft. Constructed on purpose of the Invasion of England* (1 February 1798); Davey and Johns, *Broadsides*, p. 44.

93. Cruikshank and Gillray produced two very similar prints within days of each other, with Gillray offering his own idiosyncratic take on Cruikshank's original. See Isaac Cruikshank, *The Raft in Danger or the Republican Crew Disappointed* (London, 28 January 1798); James Gillray, *The Storm Rising; – or – The Republican Flotilla in Danger* (1 February 1798).

94. *Morning Post*, 20 March 1798 and 31 March 1798. The description comes from *Oracle*, 2 April 1797. See also *Star and Evening Examiner*, 13 April 1798. For the

Sadler's Wells production see *Sun*, 11 April 1798. For 'The Island' see *Observer*, 15 April 1798.

95. *Observer*, 8 April 1798; *Observer*, 15 April 1798; *Oracle*, 16 April 1798; *Hereford Journal*, 18 April 1798.

96. See *Star and Evening Advertiser*, 12 April 1798; General Dumouriez, *Thoughts on the French Invasion of England* (1798); extracts were printed in the *Oracle*, 2 May 1798; *Hereford Journal*, 9 May 1798; *Chester Chronicle*, 11 May 1798. Havilland Le Mesurier, Esq., *Thoughts on a French Invasion with reference to the probability of its success, and the proper means of resisting it* (Edinburgh: Mundell and Sons, 1798), pp. 3, 5, 9.

97. James Gillray, *Consequences of a Successful French Invasion*, Nos 1–4 (London: 1 March 1798). Anthony Aufrére published a list of cruelties Britons could expect to be inflicted by French soldiers and officers, describing numerous pillages, thefts and murders committed by French troops. See Anthony Aufrére, *A Warning to Britons Against French Perfidy and Cruelty: Or a short account of the treacherous and inhuman Conduct of the French Officers and Soldiers towards the Peasants to Suabia, during the Invasion of Germany in 1796. Selected and translated from a well-authenticated German publication, By Anthony Aufrére, Esq. With an Address to the People of Great Britain, by the translator* (London: T. Cadell, Jun. and W. Davies in the Strand; and J. Wright and J. Hatchard, in Piccadilly, 1798).

98. Cookson, *British Armed Nation*, pp. 71, 107.

99. In 1801, Horatio Nelson ordered the Sea Fencibles to man their vessels but was told that they would only venture out if genuine 'assurances' were given that 'they should be returned to their homes, when the danger of Invasion is passed'. It is also not clear how reliable the 'immunity' from impressment was in practice. Thomas Troubridge, Lord of the Admiralty, wrote to Nelson in July 1801: 'I most sincerely hope that the Fencibles will embark if not we will impress them but keep this to yourself'. See Nicolas, ed., *Dispatches and Letters of Nelson*, Vol. 4, p. 432; quoted in Rogers, 'The Sea Fencibles', p. 49; NMM, CRK/13/49, Troubridge to Nelson, 28 July 1801; Knight, *Pursuit of Victory*, p. 404.

100. Rogers, 'The Sea Fencibles', pp. 51, 53.

101. Anon., *An Appeal to the Head and Heart of Every Man and Woman in Great Britain, Respecting The Threatened French Invasion, and the Importance of Immediately Coming Forward with Voluntary Contributions* (London: J. Wright, 1798), pp. 3, 14.

102. Collingwood to Blackett, 26 January 1798, in Collingwood, *Public and Private Correspondence*, Vol. 1, pp. 85–6.

103. SRO, SA/3/1/2/1, Martha Saumarez to James Saumarez, 14 February 1798.

104. For intelligence see 'Intelligence respecting the enemy collected by Commodore Sir John Borlase Warren', 14 March 1798, in Morriss, *Blockade of Brest*, p. 285; Admiralty to Bridport, 15 April 1798, in Morriss, *Blockade of Brest*, pp. 290–1. For views on British strategy see Spencer to Bridport, 5 March 1798, in Morriss, *Blockade of Brest*, pp. 283–4: 'Whenever the enemy shall be prepared to make the threatened attack on this country they will probably make it several parts at once', and likely towards Ireland. As such, the Admiralty aimed to keep the main naval force 'in a body to move as occasion may require'.

105. As the Admiralty noted: 'It does not appear from the information we have at present of the force of the enemy at Brest that a larger number of ships than are at present with your Lordship are immediately requisite', Spencer to Bridport, 1 May 1798, in Morriss, *Blockade of Brest*, p. 293. Bridport's response was typically graceless: 'With respect to the number of ships necessary for watching the port of Brest that object must be left to those who know the state of the enemy at that port . . . if

this plan is finally fixed what relief can I expect during the whole campaign? But I will stand it as long as I can with zeal and fidelity let the difficulties be what they may.' Bridport to Spencer, 17 May 1798, in Morriss, *Blockade of Brest*, p. 296.

106. Bridport to Admiralty, 28 June 1798, in Morriss, *Blockade of Brest*, p. 310; Bridport to Admiralty, 31 July 1797, in Morriss, *Blockade of Brest*, p. 322; Morriss, *Blockade of Brest*, p. 301.

107. Ward, 'French Revolutionary and Napoleonic Wars', quoting Dundas to Spencer, 20 Jan 1798, TNA, WO 30/64; Knight, *Britain Against Napoleon*, p. 88; Sir Charles Hamilton to Bridport, 4 August 1798, in Morriss, *Blockade of Brest*, pp. 322–3.

108. Pellew to Gardner, 5 August 1798, in Morriss, *Blockade of Brest*, p. 324.

109. The prisoners so dwarfed his own crew that Pellew was forced to land them on the French shore rather than attempt to transport them to Britain. Pellew to Gardner, 8 August 1798, in Morriss, *Blockade of Brest,* p. 326.

110. Stopford to Gardner, 5 June 1798, in Morriss, *Blockade of Brest*, pp. 307–8.

111. Leonard Bullmer to his son Reginald Bullmer, serving on the *Sandwich*, 30 May 1797, in Watt and Hawkins, eds, *Letters of Seamen*, pp. 410–11.

112. John Flanigan to his son James Flanigan, serving on the *Nassau*, 3 June 1797, in Watt and Hawkins, eds, *Letters of Seamen*, pp. 445–6.

113. For scholarship on the Irish Rebellion of 1798 see Bartlett et al., *Bicentenary Perspective*; Whelan, *Fellowship of Freedom*; Geoghegan, 'Rising and Union, 1791–1801'.

114. Admiralty to Bridport, 31 May 1798, in Morriss, *Blockade of Brest*, pp. 305–6; Bridport to Admiralty, 11 June 1798, in Morriss, *Blockade of Brest*, p. 308.

115. 'Substance of information respecting force at Brest and its neighbourhood transmitted by Captain D'Auvergne, 30 July 1798', in Morriss, *Blockade of Brest*, p. 321; 'Report of enemy's force in Brest water, reconnoitred by His Majesty's ships Boadicea and Mermaid, 6 August 1798', in Morriss, *Blockade of Brest*, pp. 324–5.

116. Wilson, 'Naval Defence of Ireland', pp. 572–3. For the first news of this arriving in London see *Whitehall Evening Post*, 25–28 August 1798: 'Yesterday arrived a mail from Ireland, which brought important intelligence, that a squadron of French frigates had entered the Bay of Killala . . . on the evening of the 2nd inst. and landed a body of troops, nearly 1,000 in number.'

117. For a more detailed examination of the episodes of cultural memory see Guy Beiner, *Remembering the Year of the French: Irish Folk History and Social Memory* (Madison, WI: University of Wisconsin Press, 2007).

118. *Oracle*, 13 September 1798; Admiralty to Bridport, 3 September 1798, NRS, p. 333.

119. Morriss, *Blockade of Brest*, p. 303.

120. Morriss, *Blockade of Brest*, p. 303; Gardiner, *Nelson Against Napoleon*, p. 115.

121. *Chester Chronicle*, 31 August 1798; *Bell's Weekly Messenger*, 4 November 1798.

122. *Oracle*, 21 July 1798.

123. A.N. Ryan, 'In Search of Bruix, 1799', in *Français et Anglais en Méditeraneé de la Révolution français a l'indépendence de la Grèce (1789–1830)* (Paris: Service Historique de la Marine, 1992), pp. 81–90; Knight, *Britain Against Napoleon*, pp. 148–9; Wilson, 'Naval Defence of Ireland', p. 573.

124. Anon., *An Appeal to the Head and Heart of Every Man and Woman*, p. 18.

125. Anon., *Observations by a Country Gentleman*, p. 18.

126. Philp, 'Introduction', p. 3; Knight, *Britain Against Napoleon*, p. 94.

127. The literature on this subject is vast, but see in particular Cookson, 'English Volunteer Movement'; Cookson, *British Armed Nation*; Colley, *Britons*.

128. United States National Archives (USNA), M30, Despatches from U.S. Ministers to Great Britain, 1791–1906, Roll No. 4, Despatches from U.S. Minsters to Great Britain, 10 August 1796–28 December 1797, A2 Cab. 21/10, Rufus King to Timothy Pickering, 5 March 1797. The sentence 'alarming the country in order that the means of prosecuting the war might more easily be obtained' was written in code but decoded by the receiver.
129. Colley, *Britons*, pp. 289–301.

6 THE DELEGATES IN COUNCIL: THE NAVAL MUTINIES OF 1797

1. Theophilus G. King to his wife, 1 June 1797, and George Gainier to Jenny Gent, 2 June 1797, in Watt and Hawkins, eds, *Letters of Seamen*, pp. 426, 436. See also Callum Easton, 'Counter-Theatre during the 1797 Fleet Mutinies', *International Review of Social History*, Vol. 64 (2019), pp. 389–411.
2. Isaac Cruikshank, *The Delegates in Council or Beggars on Horseback* (London: Samuel Fores, 9 June 1797). For further discussion of this print see Davey and Johns, *Broadsides*, p. 60.
3. J.P. Gilson, ed., *Correspondence of Edmund Burke and William Windham* (Cambridge: Cambridge University Press, 1910), p. 241. I am grateful to Quintin Colville for first suggesting the 'sure shield' and 'Achilles heel' comparison.
4. For a detailed study of the reportage of mutinies see David W. London, 'Mutiny in the Public Eye: The Role of Newspapers in the Mutiny at Spithead', Unpublished PhD thesis, University of London (2000).
5. *Sussex Weekly Advertiser*, 19 June 1797.
6. This term was first reported in the *Courier* but was quickly picked up by other organs: see for example *Chester Chronicle*, 9 June 1797; *Reading Mercury*, 12 June 1797. See also G.E. Manwaring and Bonamy Dobrée, *The Floating Republic: An Account of the Mutinies at Spithead and the Nore in 1797* (London: Frank Cass & Co., 1966), p. 183.
7. For recent studies of these social movements see Griffin, *Politics of Hunger*; Jeff Horn, 'Machine Breaking and the "Threat from Below" in Great Britain and France during the Early Industrial Revolution', in Davis, ed., *Crowd Actions*, pp. 165–78; Adrian Randall, '"Engines of Mischief": The Luddite Disturbances of 1811–12' in his *Riotous Assemblies: Popular Protests in Hanoverian Britain* (Oxford: Oxford University Press, 2006), pp. 271–302; Peter Jones, 'Finding Captain Swing: Protest, Parish Relations, and the State of the Public Mind in 1830', *International Review of Social History*, Vol. 54 (2009), pp. 429–58; Carl J. Griffin, 'The Violent Captain Swing?', *Past & Present*, Vol. 209, No. 1 (November 2010), pp. 149–80; Carl J. Griffin, *The Rural War: Captain Swing and the Politics of Protest* (Manchester: Manchester University Press, 2012).
8. For detailed studies of the mutinies at Spithead and the Nore see Conrad Gill, *The Naval Mutinies of 1797* (Manchester: Manchester University Press, 1913); Manwaring and Dobrée, *Floating Republic*; James Dugan, *The Great Mutiny* (New York: Putnam, 1965); Coats and MacDougall, eds, *Naval Mutinies*. Recent studies are Frykman, *Bloody Flag*, esp. pp. 127–64; and Callum Easton, 'A Social and Economic History of the 1797 Fleet Mutinies at Spithead and the Nore', Unpublished PhD thesis, University of Cambridge (2020). See also Niklas Frykman, 'Connections between Mutinies in European Navies', *International Review of Social History*, Vol. 58 (2013), pp. 87–107. A rare exception to the focus on Spithead and the Nore is Nick Rogers's recent article on the mutiny on the *Pompee*. See Nicholas Rogers, 'The Politics of Mutiny: The *Pompee* at Spithead and Beyond', *International Journal of Maritime History*, Vol. 33, No. 3 (2021), pp. 464–88.

9. Discussions of the mutinies tend to devolve into debates about whether the sailors were fundamentally 'radical' or 'loyalist'. For discussions of the sailors' radicalism see Thompson, *Making of the English Working Class*; esp. pp. 183–5; Wells, *Insurrection*, pp. 85–103; Frank Mabee, 'The Spithead Mutiny and Urban Radicalism in the 1790s', *Romanticism*, Vol. 13 (2007), pp. 133–44. For historians who emphasise the loyalty of sailors see Rodger, 'Mutiny or Subversion?', pp. 549–64; Ian R. Christie, *Stress and Stability in Late Eighteenth-Century Britain: Reflections on the British Avoidance of Revolution* (Oxford: Clarendon Press, 1984). Ann Coats and Philip MacDougall take slightly different views in Coats and MacDougall, eds, *Naval Mutinies*, with Coats emphasising the sailors' loyalty, and MacDougall acknowledging the influence of political ideologies.

10. TNA, ADM 1/5125, 'A detail of the Proceedings on Board H.M. Ship Queen Charlotte'. See also 'Petition to Howe from seamen and marines of *Queen Charlotte* (28 February), *Ramillies*, 28 February 1797, *Formidable* (28 February), *Royal George* (28 February), *Audacious* (4 March), *Triumph* (7 March), *Sans Pariel* (7 March), *Theseus* (8 March) and *Bellerophon* (10 March)'.

11. Not mentioned, but surely observed, was the fact that naval lieutenants and captains had also had their wages increased in 1796. See Philip MacDougall, ' "We went out with Admiral Duncan, we came back without him": Mutiny and the North Sea Squadron', in Coats and MacDougall, eds, *Naval Mutinies*, pp. 24–63, p. 254.

12. TNA, ADM 1/5125, Petition to Howe from seamen and marines of the *Queen Charlotte*; TNA, ADM 1/5125, 'The Right Honble and Honble the Lords Commissioners of the Admiralty'. For analysis of the wage disparity and recent food shortages see Wells, *Insurrection*, p. 85; Wells, *Wretched Faces*, pp. 128–31, 135, 140. Callum Easton's detailed study of naval wages finds that the sailors' claims were broadly very accurate. See Easton, 'Fleet Mutinies', p. 81.

13. Coats, 'The Delegates: a Radical Tradition', in Coats and MacDougall, eds, *Naval Mutinies*, pp. 39–60, pp. 46, 51; Pakenham to Spencer, 11 December 1796, in Corbett and Richmond, *Private Papers of George, 2nd Earl Spencer*, Vol. 4, pp. 105–9.

14. Not every ship followed suit. One hundred thirty-one sailors and sixteen marines on the *Garland* signed a declaration on 1 April – after most ships had sent a petition of demands – stating that they would not take part in 'any Assembly', and that they would 'act with the Captain in endeavouring to suppress such meeting or Assembly'. Such conduct, they suggested, befitted 'good and loyal subjects' exerting themselves 'in the service of our King and Country'. TNA, ADM 1/5125, Declaration from sailors of the *Garland*, 1 April 1797.

15. TNA, ADM 1/5125, petition from 'Delegates of the Fleet', 19 April 1797.

16. TNA, ADM 1/5125, 'The Right Honble and Honble the Lords Commissioners of the Admiralty' [no date but likely mid-April 1797]; these quotes come from TNA, ADM 1/5125, petition of sailors on the *Glory*, 17 April 1797; TNA, ADM 1/5125, letter from petitioners on the *Cumberland*, 21 April 1797. For the list of complaints from different ships see TNA, ADM 1/5125, 'Ships Objections against their officers'.

17. NMM, COO/2/A, 'Reflections on the Spithead Mutiny', pp. 39–40; TNA, ADM 1/5125, petition of the *Nymphe*, 22 April 1797; Alexander Hood, see NMM, MKH/15, Hood to unknown, 10 July 1797.

18. Lord Spencer to John Jervis, 4 May 1797, in Corbett and Richmond, eds, *Spencer Papers*, Vol. 3, pp. 298–300.

19. NMM, BRP/18, Admiralty to Bridport, 15 April 1797.

20. Gill, *Naval Mutinies*, pp. 91–2, 103–4; Manwaring and Dobrée, *Floating Republic*, pp. 71–3.

21. Manwaring and Dobrée, *Floating Republic*, p. 87.

22. See NMM, WAR/7, petition of ship's company of the *Galatea*, 18 May 1797; David Crawford to John Crawford, 1 June 1797, in Watt and Hawkins, eds, *Letters of Seamen*, p. 425; NMM, WAR/7, petition of ship's company of the *Galatea*, *Artois* and *Sylph*, no date.

23. NMM, BRP/18, Admiralty to Bridport, 15 April 1797; NMM, WYN/109/7, Admiralty to Bridport, 20 April 1797.

24. NMM, WYN/109/7, 'First reply made by the Spithead fleet to the very liberal offer made by the Admiralty', no date but April 1797; TNA, ADM 1/107, 224, 'The Seamen's Second Reply', 22 April 1797; NMM, MKH/15, unnamed letters, c. May 1797; Ann Coats, ' "Launched into Eternity": Admiralty Retribution or the Restoration of Discipline', in Coats and MacDougall, eds, *Naval Mutinies*, pp. 209–25, p. 218.

25. *Morning Post*, 18 May 1797.

26. *London Chronicle*, 19 April 1797; *The Times*, 18 April 1797.

27. *Address to the Nation, By the Seamen At St Helen's* (Edinburgh: G. Mudie and Son, South Bridge, 1797). For more on Mudie see Ezra Greenspan and Jonathan Rose, eds, *Book History*, Vol. 1 (University Park: Penn State University Press, 1988), pp. 68–73. For the letter to Fox see TNA, ADM 1/107, 15 April 1797, quoted in Coats, 'Retribution or Restoration', pp. 215–16.

28. For links with *Portsmouth Gazette* see David W. London, 'What Really Happened on Board HMS London', in Coats and MacDougall, eds, *Naval Mutinies*, pp. 61–78, pp. 75–6; Philip MacDougall, 'Reporting the Mutinies in the Provincial Press', in Coats and MacDougall, eds, *Naval Mutinies*, pp. 161–78, p. 165; Rogers, 'Politics of Mutiny', p. 481. For corrections sent to newspapers see *Sun*, 19 April 1797, referred to in *Address to the Nation*, p. 13; NMM, MID/1/207, Charles Middleton Papers, folder containing loose letters from unsigned persons regarding mutinies, 1797.

29. London, 'HMS London', p. 68. For reportage in the press see *Star*, 8 May 1797.

30. Gill, *Naval Mutinies*, pp. 37, 56. See also *Morning Post*, 9 May 1797; Coats, 'Radical Tradition', pp. 53–4.

31. London, 'HMS London', pp. 61–78; NMM, COO/2/A, 'Reflections on the Spithead Mutiny', pp. 12–14

32. *Address to the Nation*, p. 11; Rogers, 'Politics of Mutiny', p. 479; Frykman, *Bloody Flag*, p. 137.

33. TNA, ADM 1/811, petition of 'Ships of the Hamoaze', 16 May 1797.

34. NMM, WYN/109/7, 'By the King. A Proclamation . . ', 11 May 1797; WYN/109/7, Admiralty proclamation, 14 May 1797; NMM, RUSI NMM 235/ER/5/1, Victualling Office Declaration, 18 May 1797. See also Rif Winfield, *British Warships in the Age of Sail, 1793–1817* (Barnsley: Seaforth Publishing, 2010), p. 6; Easton, 'Fleet Mutinies', p. 111.

35. NMM, BRP/18, Admiralty to Bridport, 24 April 1797. For Orde's concessions see TNA, ADM 1/811, John Orde to Admiralty, 18 May 1797; for the removal of officers see TNA, ADM 1/812, John Orde to Admiralty, 24 May 1797; for the return to duty see TNA, ADM 1/812, John Orde to Admiralty, 25 May 1797. For the fleet at Cawsand Bay see NMM, WAR/7, Charles Carter to Admiralty, 22 May 1797; NMM, WAR/7, Charles Carter to Admiralty, 23 May 1797.

36. For the funeral see *Hampshire Chronicle*, 13 May 1797, quoted by Rogers, 'Politics of Mutiny', p. 480. For the sailors' letter see Richard Greenhalgh to his parents, 5 July 1797, quoted in Watt and Hawkins, eds, *Letters of Seamen*, p. 128.

37. TNA, ADM 1/107, 8 May 1797.

38. TNA, ADM 1/5125, sailors' letter of thanks to Howe, 13 May 1793.

39. Martha Saumarez was one individual who understood that it was for show: 'They were carried on with great pomp & solemnity no doubt to make them the more impressive', she wrote to her husband. Suffolk Record Office, SA/3/1/2/1, Martha Saumarez to James Saumarez, 18 May 1797.
40. For details of the origins of the mutinies at the Nore see TNA, ADM 1/5340, court martial of Thomas McCann of the *Sandwich*, 20–21 July 1797; Philip Mac-Dougall, 'The East Coast Mutinies: May–June 1797', in Coats and MacDougall, eds, *Naval Mutinies*, pp. 150–1.
41. BL, MS G197, Declaration of Richard Parker, executed 30 June 1797. On Parker's background and character see Taylor, *Sons of the Waves*, pp. 256–7, 259. For Parker's dismissal see p. 105.
42. TNA, ADM 1/5486, evidence of Charles Buckner; NMM, AGC/24/5, 'Memorandum Sir Charles Grey to Mr Dundas on the Mutiny at the Nore, dated from Barham Court', 25 June 1797; TNA, ADM 1/339, court martial of Richard Parker, *Sandwich*, 22–26 June 1797; TNA, ADM 1/5340, court martial of John Durrack et al. of the *Montagu*, 20–25 July 1797; *Kentish Gazette*, 8 June 1797; *Kentish Chronicle*, 9 June 1797, quoted in MacDougall, 'Reporting the Mutinies', p. 174.
43. Rodger, *Command of the Ocean*, p. 447; MacDougall, 'The East Coast Mutinies: May–June 1797', in Coats and MacDougall, eds, *Naval Mutinies*, pp. 147–60, p. 153.
44. TNA, ADM 1/339, court martial of Richard Parker, *Sandwich*, 22–26 June 1797.
45. For intelligence suggesting sailors' loyalty see for example NMM, RUSI NMM 235/ER/5/1, 'Resolution of the Officers of His Majesty's Navy', which suggested strongly that the mutiny was the result of 'the instigation of the Enemy and some hired Mercenary Incendiaries under the denomination of Englishmen', and that 'the greater part of those Ships' Companies now in a state of Rebellion and Committing Acts of Robbery, Cruelty and Piracy, are composed of Honest, Brave and Sensible Men'. These reports continued: sailors escaping from the *Grampus* wrote to the Admiralty of the many hundreds who would 'willingly accept the same and return to their duty, had they the Opportunity of doing it'; see TNA, ADM 1/5125, letter from sailors of the *Grampus*, 9 June 1797.
46. NMM, HSR/Z/33/3, Richard Parker to Lord Northesk, 6 June 1797; NMM, BRP/18, Admiralty to Bridport, 10 June 1797.
47. MacDougall, 'Mutiny and the North Sea Squadron', p. 243; NMM, HSR/B/12, William John Gore, 'Journal of the Mutiny at the Nore', 1797; TNA, ADM 1/727, Letters from the *Repulse*, No. 37, By Order of the Delegates of the Whole Fleet, 31 May 1797.
48. NMM, RUSI/NM/203, Committee of the *Swan*, 1 June 1797; NMM, HSR/B/12, William John Gore, 'Journal of the Mutiny at the Nore', 1797.
49. TNA, 1/727, letters from the *Repulse*, No. 26, order of Committee of the *Sandwich*, 1 June 1797; TNA, ADM 1/727, letters from the *Repulse*, No. 31, order sent to vessels from the *Sandwich* 'To the Committee', 2 June 1797; Joseph B. Devonish to his wife Jane Devonish, 31 May 1797, in Watt and Hawkins, eds, *Letters of Seamen*, pp. 421–2; TNA, ADM 1/5340, court martial of Thomas Jephson of the *Sandwich*, 27 July 1797.
50. For the journalistic cordon see *London Evening Post*, 3–6 June 1797. For political documents written by Nore mutineers see for example TNA, ADM 1/5125, letter from Nore mutineers, 1797; TNA, ADM 1/727, letters found on the *Repulse*, No. 1; TNA, 1/727, letters from the *Repulse*, No. 20: Address from the British Seamen & Marines at the Nore to their Brethren and Fellow Subjects on Shore. A declaration entitled 'To a discerning and loyal nation' was circulated on the *Sandwich*; see TNA, ADM 1/5340, court martial of William Gregory et al. of the *Sandwich*, 6–19 July 1797. See also MacDougall, 'Reporting the Mutinies', p. 172.

51. TNA, ADM 1/727, 12 June 1797, no. 20. For Gregory's order see TNA, ADM 1/5340, court martial of William Gregory et al. of the *Sandwich*, 6–19 July 1797.

52. Wells, *Insurrection*, p. 117.

53. United States National Archives (USNA), Despatches from U.S. Ministers to Great Britain, 1791–1906, Roll No. 4, Despatches from U.S. Minsters to Great Britain, 10 August 1796–28 December 1797, A2 Cab. 21/10, Rufus King to Timothy Pickering, 5 June 1797.

54. Not always correctly. Charlotte Osbaldeston wrote a furious letter to James Gregory, believing him to be one of the prominent mutineers on board the *Sandwich*. She admonished him for his disloyalty. 'Where was your Loyalty to your King and Country? And what could be your Reflections for your Wife and Child?' It was actually William Gregory who was a leading mutineer on the *Sandwich*, and we don't know what James made of this furious missive. See Charlotte Osbaldeston to James Gregory serving on board the *Montagu*, 24 June 1797, in Watt and Hawkins, eds, *Letters of Seamen*, pp. 566–7.

55. John Cudlip to his brother Peter Cudlip serving on the *Belliqueux*, 5 June 1797, in Watt and Hawkins, eds, *Letters of Seamen*, pp. 454–5.

56. J. & M. West to their brother Thomas West, 5 June 1797, and Agnes Maitland to Hardwick Richardson, 6 June 1797, in Watt and Hawkins, eds, *Letters of Seamen*, pp. 454, 457–8.

57. Leverit was sentenced to one year in prison for sedition, while the author of the ballad, Thomas Lloyd, and the printer, John Thacker Saxton, were arrested, tried and sentenced to two years and one year in prison respectively. See Emsley, *British Society*, pp. 60–1; and Wells, *Insurrection*, p. 117.

58. *Sussex Weekly Advertiser*, 12 June 1797; Wells, *Insurrection*, p. 118.

59. Frykman, *Bloody Flag*, p. 151; *Kentish Chronicle*, 16 June 1797, quoted by MacDougall, 'East Coast Mutinies', p. 157; *Memoirs of Richard Parker*, p. 20; Wells, *Insurrection*, p. 136; TNA, ADM 1/339, court martial of Richard Parker, *Sandwich*, 22–26 June 1797.

60. Frykman, *Bloody Flag*, p. 152; TNA, ADM 1/5341, court martial of John Burrows et al. of the *Standard*, 22–25 August 1797; TNA, ADM 1/727, descriptions of deserters from the *Inflexible*; TNA, ADM 1/5340, court martial of John Durrack et al. of the *Montagu*, 20–25 July 1797; Frykman, *Bloody Flag*, p. 156; TNA, ADM 1/727, see numerous letters (crews of the *Champion*, *Proserpine*, *Pylades*); Lord Keith to Admiralty, 14 June 1797.

61. TNA, ADM 1/5341, court martial of Michael Collins of *La Revolutionaire*, 24–26 August 1797; TNA, ADM 1/5340, court martial of Joseph Wells et al. of the *Calypso*, 14 July 1797; TNA, ADM 1/5339, court martial of William Guthrie et al. of the *Pompee*, 20–23 June 1797. For a detailed study of this mutiny see Rogers, 'Politics of Mutiny'.

62. TNA, ADM 1/5340, court martial of John Goody et al. of the *Saturn*, 19–27 July 1797; Frykman, *Bloody Flag*, pp. 159–60; Pfaff and Hechter, *Genesis of Rebellion*, p. 8.

63. TNA, ADM 1/5341, court martial of William Lee and Thomas Preston of the *Royal Sovereign*, 28–29 August 1797; Henry Hardy to his brother Andrew Hardy, 3 June 1797, in Watt and Hawkins, eds, *Letters of Seamen*, pp. 447–9; TNA, ADM 1/5340, court martial of John McCoy of the *Mars*, 19 July 1797; Roger Wells, *Insurrection*, p. 132.

64. See Lee-Jane Giles, ' "All That You Refuse to Do Is Mutiny": Contextualising the Marine Mutiny at Plymouth, 1797', Unpublished BA thesis, University of Plymouth, 2017. I am grateful to Lee for sending me a copy of her dissertation.

65. TNA, ADM 1/5341, court martial of John Crystal et al. of the *Thames*, 14–15 August 1797; Roger Morriss, 'Crew Management and Mutiny: The Case of *Minerve*, 1796–1803', in Coats and MacDougall, eds, *Naval Mutinies*, pp. 108–10.

66. Nelson to Calder, 9 July 1797, in Nicolas, ed., *Dispatches and Letters of Nelson*, Vol. 2, pp. 409–10. For details on the mutiny see Rodger, *Command of the Ocean*, p. 451.

67. TNA, ADM 1/5345, court martial of John Bray et al. of the *Suffolk*, 5–6 June 1798. See also Parkinson, *War in the Eastern Seas*, pp. 134–5.

68. Niklas Frykman, Clare Anderson, Lex Heerma van Voss and Marcus Rediker, 'Mutiny and Maritime Radicalism', *International Review of Social History*, Vol. 58 (2013), pp. 1–14, p. 10.

69. TNA, ADM 1/56, Pringle to Nepean, 13 October 1797, in McAleer, *Britain's Maritime Empire*, p. 180. For more on the mutiny at the Cape see Nicole Ulrich, 'International Radicalism, Local Solidarities: The 1797 Naval Mutinies in Southern African Waters', *International Review of Social History*, Vol. 58 (2013), pp. 61–85.

70. Ulrich, 'Naval Mutinies in Southern African Waters', pp. 61–85; Frykman, *Bloody Flag*, pp. 162–3; McAleer, *Britain's Maritime Empire*, pp. 178–9.

71. McAleer, *Britain's Maritime Empire*, p. 181.

72. Pitt quoted in Easton, 'Fleet Mutinies', p. 55. For the Portland quote see Coats and MacDougall, 'Spithead Mutiny: Introduction', p. 33; Manwaring and Dobrée, *Floating Republic*, pp. 100–1.

73. Hughes, *Collingwood Correspondence*, p. 85.

74. *Report of the Committee of Secrecy of the House of Commons* (Dublin: John Ex Shaw, 1799).

75. For this point see Rodger, 'Mutiny or Subversion?', p. 557. For examples of historians who see the mutinies as evidence of external influence see Thompson, *Making of the English Working Class*, p. 147; Wells, *Insurrection*, pp. 111, 125, 128–30; Elliot, *Partners in Revolution*; Linebaugh and Rediker, *Many-Headed Hydra*, pp. 275–8.

76. Wells, *Insurrection*, p. 128.

77. Only four of the thirty-three delegates at Spithead were Irish, and arguably the most radical ship at Portsmouth, the *Mars*, had the lowest proportion of Irish-born seamen among the Spithead fleets (14.9 per cent). See Coats, 'Spithead Mutiny: An Introduction'; and Coats, 'The 1797 Mutinies in the Channel Fleet', in Coats and MacDougall, eds, *Naval Mutinies*, pp. 21–2, 59, 133, 137; Christopher Doorne, 'A Floating Republic?', in Coats and MacDougall, eds, *Naval Mutinies*, pp. 185–6, p. 193.

78. TNA, ADM 1/5340, court martial of James Smart, John Taylor, John Preston, Joseph Croskele, Robert Hardy and Thomas Franklin, of *Grampus*, 10–12 July 1797; Wells, *Insurrection*, pp. 125–7; Featherstone, 'Interrogating Court-Martial Narratives', pp. 778–9.

79. NMM, COO/2/A, 'Reflections on the Spithead Mutiny', p. 40; Featherstone, 'Interrogating Court-Martial Narratives', p. 776; Frykman, *Bloody Flag*, p. 153.

80. Gardner to Nepean, 8 May 1797, quoted in Wells, *Insurrection*, p. 127.

81. TNA, ADM 1/4172, Graham and Williams to Portland, 26 June 1797; Gill, *Naval Mutinies*, p. 300.

82. TNA, ADM 1/5343, court martial of Roger Kirby, *Ceres*, 1 January 1798.

83. John Pickering to his brother, 29 May 1797, in Watt and Hawkins, eds, *Letters of Seamen*, pp. 409–10. See also *Whitehall Evening Post*, 27–30 May 1797. See also John Wells to his wife, 31 May 1797, in Watt and Hawkins, eds, *Letters of Seamen*, p. 418.

84. TNA, ADM 1/5125, petition from 'Delegates of the Fleet', 19 April 1797; TNA, ADM 1/5125, petition with Spithead demands, 1 May 1797.

85. TNA, ADM, 1/5339, court martial of Dennis Sullivan et al. of the *Leopard*, 28 June–4 July 1797.

86. TNA, ADM 1/5340, court martial of Thomas Jephson of the *Sandwich*, 27 July 1797; Wells, *Insurrection*, pp. 134–5.

87. John Cox to his wife, 31 May 1797, in Watt and Hawkins, eds, *Letters of Seamen*, p. 420; TNA, ADM 1/5339, court martial of Joseph Lydiard of the *Artois*, 27 June 1797; TNA, ADM 1/727, 'A Statement of the behavior of the crew of His Majesty's Ship Swan during the Mutiny at the Nore'.

88. TNA, ADM 1/727, 'A List of Men under description of Delegates from HM Sloop Pylades'.

89. For the *Pompee* see BL, Add. MS 35,197, Vashon to Bridport, 5 June 1797; Rogers, 'Politics of Mutiny', p. 483. A separate letter suggests the number of signatures was eighty-six rather than eighty-three. For the *Sandwich* see TNA, ADM 1/5340, court martial of Thomas McCann of the *Sandwich*, 20–21 July 1797.

90. TNA, ADM 1/5341, court martial of John Burrows et al. of the *Standard*, 22–25 August 1797.

91. TNA, ADM 1/5340, court martial of Abraham Nelson et al. of the *Beaulieu*, 6–17 July 1797; TNA, ADM 1/5340, court martial of William Gregory et al. of the *Sandwich*, 6–19 July 1797.

92. Coats, 'Radical Tradition', pp. 53–4; NMM, HSR/Z/33/3.

93. James Calloway told the sailor Michael Bowen that 560 men has already sworn an oath, most of whom were now resting 'and he didn't want to disturb them'. Bowen signed, saying 'I would not go against the ship's company'. John Livingstone was told 'almost all of the Ships Company had taken the oath'. This seems to have worked. James Kirkwood said he was told 'every one of the ship's company' had agreed; he said 'if the whole Ship's Company was so I mist be likewise'. TNA, ADM 1/5339, court martial of William Guthrie et al. of the *Pompee*, 20–23 June 1797; Rogers, 'Politics of Mutiny', p. 483. For the *Leviathan* tactic see TNA, ADM 1/811, 'Orders to be observed and strictly complied with by the Leviathan Ship's Company'.

94. TNA, ADM 1/5339, court martial of Joseph Lydiard of the *Artois*, 27 June 1797; Robert Dobson to his wife, 30 May 1797, in Watt and Hawkins, eds, *Letters of Seamen*, p. 410. This is supported by court martial evidence, in which one sailor recalled a rope being rove to the yard arm on the *Leopard* to hang any person who disobeyed the mutineers. See TNA, ADM, 1/5339, court martial of Dennis Sullivan et al. of the *Leopard*, 28 June–4 July 1797.

95. Buscemi, 'Oath-Taking and the "Feeling Rules" of Violence'.

96. See TNA, ADM 1/5125, petition of the *Nymphe*; TNA, ADM 1/5340, court martial of John Goody et al. of the *Saturn*, 19–27 July 1797; Coats, 'Radical Tradition', p. 49.

97. TNA, ADM 1/5339, court martial of William Guthrie et al. of the *Pompee*, 20–23 June 1797; Rogers, 'Politics of Mutiny', p. 482.

98. Coats, 'Radical Tradition', p. 53; TNA 1/727, letters from the *Repulse*, No. 7, example of an oath taken by the sailors at the Nore.

99. I am grateful to Callum Easton for the point about sailors' awareness that only a few would be prosecuted. For the 'kiss the book' quote see TNA, 1/5339, court martial of William Guthrie et al. of the *Pompee*, 20–23 June 1797.

100. Spencer to Jervis, 4 May 1797, in Corbett and Richmond, eds, *Spencer Papers*, Vol. 3, pp. 298–300.

101. TNA, 1/727, letters from the *Repulse*, No. 2, 'An Insidious Song'; TNA, ADM 1/727 C370, 'Address from the British Seamen and Marines at the Nore to their Brethren and Fellow Subjects on shore', papers found on the *Repulse*, 12 June 1797; TNA, ADM 1/5125, 'To the Delegates of the Different Ships Assembled in Council'.
102. Frykman, *Bloody Flag*, p. 143.
103. *Address to the Nation*, pp. 7–8; TNA, ADM 1/5125, 22 April 1797.
104. TNA, 1/727, papers found on board the *Repulse*, No. 20, Address from the British Seamen & Marines at the Nore to their Brethren and Fellow Subjects on Shore.
105. TNA, ADM 1/727, letters from the *Repulse*, No. 29, 'An Insidious Song'; TNA, ADM 1/727, letters from the *Repulse*, No. 35, 'A Copy of Verses on the Seamen Displaying their Noble Spirit in the Year 1797'.
106. TNA, ADM 1/5125, 'To the Delegates of the Different Ships Assembled in Council', c. June 1797; TNA, ADM 1/5125, 'The Seamen of the Fleet at Spithead to the Spirit of Kempenfelt'; Manwaring and Dobrée, *Floating Republic*, p. 87.
107. TNA, ADM 1/727, papers found on board the *Repulse*, No. 2; *Annual Register*, 1797, pp. 208, 209, quoted in Gill, *Naval Mutinies*, p. 307.
108. John Mileham to his parents, 31 May 1797, in Watt and Hawkins, eds, *Letters of Seamen*, pp. 417–18; Joseph Thompson to his mother, 2 June 1797, in Watt and Hawkins, eds, *Letters of Seamen*, pp. 442–3; TNA, ADM 1/5341, court martial of John Lloyd, 4 August 1797.
109. For Spithead see TNA, ADM, 1/5125, petition to Howe from men of *Jason*'s ships company, 13 May 1797; *Address to the Nation*, pp. 13, 15; NMM, MID/1/207, Charles Middleton Papers, folder containing loose letters from unsigned persons regarding mutinies, 1797. For the Nore see TNA, ADM 1/5125, 'To the Delegates of the Different Ships Assembled in Council'; TNA, ADM 1/727, letters from *Repulse*, No. 36, Final Determination of the Delegates of the Whole Fleet.
110. TNA, ADM 1/5125, petition to Howe from seamen and marines of *Ramillies*, 28 February 1797; Coats, 'Radical Tradition', pp. 50–1; TNA, ADM 1/5125, Letter to the Editor of the *Sun*, from 'Seamen of the Fleet' on *Queen Charlotte*, 21 April 1797.
111. NMM, WAR/7, petition of ships' companies of the *Galatea*, *Artois* and *Sylph*, no date.
112. TNA, ADM 1/5125, Proclamation of Nore Mutineers, 1797; see also TNA, 1/727, letters from the *Repulse*, No. 20, Address from the British Seamen & Marines at the Nore to their Brethren and Fellow Subjects on Shore; TNA, ADM 1/5341, court martial of William Holdsworth, Henry Freeman, John alias Jonathan Davis, Bartholomew Connery, William Jones, Sampson Harris and Thomas Paul of the *Standard*, 17–21 August 1797.
113. TNA, ADM 1/5125, Letter to the Editor of the *Sun*, from 'Seamen of the Fleet' on the *Queen Charlotte*, 21 April 1797.
114. For the *Saturn* see TNA, ADM 1/5340, court martial of John Goody et al. of the *Saturn*, 19–27 July 1797. For the *Pompee* see TNA, ADM 1/5339, court martial of William Guthrie et al. of the *Pompee*, 20–23 June 1797; Rogers, 'Politics of Mutiny', p. 465.
115. TNA, ADM 1/5125, letter from Nore mutineers, 1797; see also TNA, 1/727, letters found on the *Repulse*, No. 1; Seamen of Nore to George III, 6 June 1797.
116. TNA, ADM 1/5340, court martial of John Durrack et al. of the *Montagu*, 20–25 July 1797; Gill, *Naval Mutinies*, pp. 189, 305; Featherstone, 'Interrogating Court-Martial Narratives', p. 774; Theophilus G. King to his wife, 1 June 1797, in Watt and Hawkins, eds, *Letters of Seamen*, p. 426.

117. Thomas Leonard was one of those who wore a red cockade. TNA, ADM 1/5340, court martial of John Durrack et al. of the *Montagu*, 20–25 July 1797. For Morgan Jones see TNA, ADM, 1/5339, court martial of Dennis Sullivan et al. of the *Leopard*, 28 June–4 July 1797. For the Gregory and Shave quotes see TNA, ADM 1/5340, court martial of William Gregory et al. of the *Sandwich*, 6–19 July 1797; TNA, ADM, 1/5339, court martial of Dennis Sullivan et al. of the *Leopard*, 28 June–4 July 1797.

118. Anon, *The victims of Tom Payne who were shot on the Hoe, or Love's Hill, Thursday, July 6, 1797* (Plymouth, 1797).

119. See TNA, ADM 1/5340, court martial of William Gregory et al. of the *Sandwich*, 6–19 July 1797; TNA, ADM 1/5340, court martial of Thomas Jephson of the *Sandwich*, 27 July 1797.

120. For Ashley see TNA, ADM 1/5339, court martial of William Guthrie et al. of the *Pompee*, 20–23 June 1797. For Brown see TNA, ADM 1/5340, court martial of Colin Brown of the *Phoenix*, 2–7 July 1797. For Collins see TNA, ADM 1/5341, court martial of Michael Collins of *La Revolutionaire*, 24–26 August 1797.

121. Papers of the *Inflexible*, quoted in Gill, *Naval Mutinies*, p. 306. For other evidence that the sailors were considering deserting to the French see MacDougall, 'Mutiny and the North Sea Squadron', p. 259; Gill, *Naval Mutinies*, pp. 222–3.

122. TNA, ADM 1/5340, court martial of William Gregory et al. of the *Sandwich*, 6–19 July 1797; Joseph B. Devonish to his wife, 31 May 1797, and Rous Mabson to his wife, 2 June 1797, in Watt and Hawkins, eds, *Letters of Seamen*, pp. 421, 440.

123. TNA, ADM 1/5339, court martial of William Guthrie et al. of the *Pompee*, 20–23 June 1797.

124. TNA, ADM 1/5486, court martial papers, Nore mutiny; TNA, ADM, 1/5339, court martial of Dennis Sullivan et al. of the *Leopard*, 28 June–4 July 1797; John Frederick Waters to his father, 18 June 1797, in Watt and Hawkins, eds, *Letters of Seamen*, pp. 461–2.

125. Coats, 'Radical Tradition', p. 49; Coats, 'Admiralty Retribution', p. 215; *Morning Chronicle*, 22 April 1797.

126. For the *Leopard* see TNA, ADM 1/5339, court martial of Dennis Sullivan et al. of the *Leopard*, 28 June–4 July; for the *Grampus* see TNA, ADM 1/5340, court martial of James Smart et al. of the *Grampus*, 10–12 July 1797; TNA, ADM 1/5340, court martial of Richard Brown et al. of the *Monmouth*; Frykman, *Bloody Flag*, pp. 144–5.

127. TNA, ADM 1/5340, court martial of Thomas McCann of the *Sandwich*, 20–21 July 1797.

128. TNA, ADM 1/339, court martial of Richard Parker of the *Sandwich*, 22–26 June 1797; Mutineer's log book of the *Comet*, for 4 June 1797, quoted in Dugan, *Great Mutiny*, p. 477 and Watt and Hawkins, eds, *Letters of Seamen*, p. 383; Coats, 'Spithead Mutiny: An Introduction', pp. 24–5.

129. NMM, COO/2/A, 'Reflections on the Spithead Mutiny', pp. 3–4.

130. NMM, MKH/15, trial of Samuel Nelson on board the *Mars*, 12 May 1797; TNA, ADM 1/5339, court martial of Dennis Sullivan et al. of the *Leopard*, 28 June–4 July 1797; for the provision of councilors see TNA, ADM 1/727, papers found on the *Repulse*, No. 9 and No. 11, 12 June 1797.

131. TNA, ADM, 1/5339, court martial of Dennis Sullivan et al. of the *Leopard*, 28 June–4 July 1797; TNA, ADM 1/5340, court martial of Richard Brown et al. of the *Monmouth*, 29 July–5 August 1797. See also James Anderson to Ann Brof, 2 June 1797, and John Linton to John Drinkald, 2 June 1797, in Watt and Hawkins, eds, *Letters of Seamen*, pp. 443–5; NMM, HSR/B/12, William John Gore, 'Journal of the Mutiny at the Nore, 1797'.

132. NMM, WYN/109/7, *An Act for more effectually restraining Intercourse with the Crews of certain of His Majesty's Ships now in a State of Mutiny and Rebellion, and for the more effectual Suppression of such Mutiny and Rebellion*, 6 June 1797; *London Gazette*, 7 June 1797; Easton, 'Fleet Mutinies', pp. 183–4.

133. TNA, ADM 1/5340, court martial of Joseph Wells et al. of the *Calypso*, 14 July 1797; TNA, ADM 1/5340, court martial of Colin Brown of the *Phoenix*, 2–7 July 1797.

134. TNA, HO 42/41, ff. 213–14, 'Report on the Nore Mutiny' by Aaron Graham and Daniel William to the Duke of Portland, 24 June 1797; Doorne, 'A Floating Republic?', pp. 181–2, 192–3.

135. NMM, BRP/18, Admiralty to Bridport, 14 June 1797; Easton, 'Fleet Mutinies', p. 177.

136. For studies of handwriting and petitions see NMM, MKH/15, Alexander Hood to unknown, 10 July 1797 and TNA, ADM 1/5341, court martial of John Burrows et al. of the *Standard*, 22–25 August 1797. For quote from Captain Knight see TNA, ADM 1/5340, court martial of John Durrack et al., 20–25 July 1797. For Keith's decisions see Coats, 'Admiralty Retribution', p. 211; MacDougall, 'East Coast Mutinies', p. 158; Taylor, *Sons of the Waves*, pp. 272–3.

137. TNA, ADM 1/5341, court martial of John Burrows, Joseph Hudson, William Redfern, Thomas Lunnifs, alias Linnes, Bryan Finn alias Fenn, and Joseph Glaves, of the *Standard*, 22–15 August 1797; Featherstone, 'Interrogating Court-Martial Narratives', pp. 775–6.

138. Evan Nepean to Pasley, President of Parker's court martial, in Gill, *Naval Mutinies*, p. 247, quoting TNA ADM 1/727; TNA, ADM 1/727, Evan Nepean to Admiral Sir Thomas Pasley, 19 June 1797.

139. NMM, RUSI NMM 235/ER/5/1, letter to Captain Riou from W. Firth, of Temple, London (no date).

140. TNA, ADM 1/339, court martial of Richard Parker, *Sandwich*, 22–26 June 1797.

141. There is a considerable academic debate about the nature of the naval punishments of 1797. Easton argues that the courts martial conformed closely to the rationale of civilian justice at the time, whereby only a few would be severely punished to act as a deterrent example, while the vast majority of those guilty were treated more leniently; see Easton, 'Fleet Mutinies', pp. 167–208. Others take a more cynical view. Taylor emphasises the legal flaws, describing them as 'show trials', while Frykman refers to them as an 'unprecedented campaign of shipboard terror'. See Taylor, *Sons of the Waves*, pp. 256, 259; Frykman, *Bloody Flag*, pp. 155, 163. For numbers of sailors executed see Admiralty Rough Minutes, 1797, TNA, ADM 3/137, ff. 306–22; Easton, 'Fleet Mutinies', p. 15; MacDougall, 'East Coast Mutinies', p. 158; Coats, 'Admiralty Retribution', p. 211.

142. TNA, ADM 1/812, Richard King to Admiralty, 22 August 1797; Rogers, 'Politics of Mutiny', p. 465; TNA, ADM 1/5342, court martial of Colin McKelly and Abraham Mason of the *Grampus*, 20 October 1797; Frykman, *Bloody Flag*, p. 163; Giles, 'Contextualising the Marine Mutiny'.

143. For the theatre of executions see NMM, AGC/30/4/2, George Thompson to Mrs Thompson (his wife), 9 September 1797, written at Torbay; NMM, BRP/18, Gardner to Bridport, 4 September 1797; WYN/109/6, Bridport to his officers, 3 September 1797.

144. TNA, ADM 1/5340, court martial of John Goody et al. of the *Saturn*, 19–27 July 1797.

145. Anon., *The victims of Tom Payne who were shot on the Hoe, or Love's Hill, Thursday, July 6, 1797* (Plymouth, 1797).

146. Rogers, 'Politics of Mutiny', p. 486.

147. Collingwood to Blackett, 22 May 1797, in Collingwood, *Public and Private Correspondence*, Vol. 1, p. 60.

148. Nelson to Fanny, 30 June 1797, in Naish, *Nelson's Letters*, p. 328.

149. TNA, ADM 1/812, Richard King to Admiralty, 1 August 1797; Richard King to Admiralty, 5 August 1797; TNA, ADM 1/812, Richard King to Admiralty, 27 August 1797; Frykman, *Bloody Flag*, p. 160.

150. TNA, ADM 1/5340, court martial of John Morrison of the *Phoenix*, 8 July 1797; TNA, ADM 1/5341, court martial of James Diabell of the *Saturn*, 1 August 1797.

151. TNA, ADM 1/5341, court martial of William Lee and Thomas Preston of the *Royal Sovereign*, 28–29 August 1797; TNA, ADM 1/5340, court martial of John Anderson et al. of the *St George*, 7–8 July 1797.

152. TNA, ADM 1/812, petition of the *Saturn* [early July 1797]; NMM, WAR/7, petition of ship's company of the *Galatea*, 8 June 1797.

153. NMM, MKH/15, 'An Address to Alexander Hood Esq. and his Officers Commanding On Board HMS *Mars*', 25 June 1797; TNA, ADM 1/5341, court martial of William Moore of the *Royal William*, 6 September 1797.

154. Pfaff and Hechter, *The Genesis of Rebellion*, pp. 218–21, 225.

155. TNA, ADM 1/5340, court martial of John Anderson et al. of the *St George*, 7–8 July 1797.

156. TNA, ADM 1/5341, court martial of Philip James, William Docton and Samuel Shore of the *Powerful*, 29 August 1797; TNA, ADM 1/5342, court martial of Charles Duff of the *Swallow*, 7 October 1797.

157. See TNA, 1/5340, court martial of Thomas Leach and John Sayle of the *Kingfisher*, 10–11 July 1797; court martial of John Maitland of the *Kingfisher*, 12 July 1797.

158. See Jones, 'Finding Captain Swing'.

159. *Morning Herald*, 8 May 1797.

160. Anon., *An Address to the Seamen in the British Navy*, p. 4.

161. Z [Hannah More], *CHEAP REPOSITORY. THE SHOPKEEPER turned SAILOR; OR, THE Folly of going out of our Element. SHEWING What a clever Man John the SHOPKEEPER was in his own Business, and what a rash Step he took in resolving to upon the Water* (Cheapside, London: J. Marshall, 1796/ Bath: S. Hazard, 1796 [published date inaccurate as refers to events in 1797], pp. 4–5, 8.

7 A TALE OF TWO SAILORS: CAMPERDOWN AND NAVAL PROPAGANDA

1. Canning to Windham, 12 May 1797, in Herbert Jenkins, ed., *The Windham Papers: The Life and Correspondence of the Rt. Honourable William Windham* (London: Maynard Small, 1913), Vol. 2, p. 53. See also Emsley, *British Society*, p. 59.

2. *Oracle*, 20 May 1797.

3. *Oracle*, 8 June 1797.

4. See Quilley, *Empire to Nation*, esp. pp. 167–88; Lincoln, *Representing the Royal Navy*; Land, *War, Nationalism and the British Sailor*; Davey and Johns, *Broadsides*, pp. 30–9.

5. For literature on the state's propagandist efforts during the 1790s see Holger Hoock, *Empires of the Imagination: Politics, War, and the Arts in the British World, 1750–1850* (London: Profile, 2010); Holger Hoock, '"The Cheap Defence of Nations": Monuments and Propaganda', in Philp, ed., *Resisting Napoleon*; Jenks, *Naval Engagements*; Jordan and Rogers, 'Admirals as Heroes'.

6. See Juliann Elizabeth Reineke, 'Three Sheets to the Wind: The Jolly Jack Tar and Eighteenth-Century British Masculinity', Unpublished PhD thesis, Carnegie Mellon University (2018).

7. Anon., *The British Hercules*, 1739.

8. Land, *War, Nationalism and the British Sailor*, pp. 91–2.

9. See for example one officer's comments: 'When left himself at sea, [the sailor] becomes careless of his person, dirty and indolent. When on shore, however, few like to appear smarter. – A blue jacket, a silk handkerchief round the neck, white trousers, and silver buckles, shew him off to the best advantage. Happy then in his mistress, fiddle, and grog, Jack Tar cares not a fig for the rest of the world.' Anon., *A Letter to a Naval Officers from a Friend* (London: Murray and Highley, 1797), p. 11.

10. *St. James's Chronicle or the British Evening Post*, 6–9 May 1797. See also *True Briton*, 25 May 1797.

11. Isaac Cruikshank, *Lord Howe they run or the British Tars giving the Carmigols a Dressing on Memorable 1st of June 1794* (London, 1794).

12. Elizabeth Carter to Elizabeth Robinson Montagu, 23 June 1797, in *Letters from Mrs Elizabeth Carter to Mrs Montagu Between the Years 1755 and 1800 Chiefly on Literary and Moral Subjects* (London, 1817), Vol. 3, p. 358.

13. TNA, ADM12/75, 'Admiralty Correspondence Digests'. I am grateful to Callum Easton for making me aware of these records.

14. Jenks, *Naval Engagements*, p. 89.

15. *Evening Mail*, 26–29 May 1797.

16. SRO, SA 3/1/2/1, Martha Saumarez to James Saumarez, 18 May 1797.

17. Jenks, *Naval Engagements*, pp. 90–2. For papers celebrating the return to duty see for example *True Briton*, 19 April 1797 and 22 April 1797; *St James's Chronicle*, 20–22 April 1797.

18. *St James's Chronicle*, 11–13 May 1797, 29 June–1 July 1797, 1–3 July 1797; *True Briton*, 12 May, 13 May 1797.

19. *Morning Herald*, 9 May 1797.

20. *Oracle*, 3 June 1797; *Oracle*, 28 July 1797.

21. *A Fair Statement of the Real Grievances Experienced by Officers and Sailors in the Navy of Great Britain with a Plan of Reform . . . in a letter to the Rt. Hon. Henry Dundas, Treasurer of the Navy, by a Naval Officer* (London, 1797), p. 1, quoted in Jenks, *Naval Engagements*, p. 107; *Analytical Review*, 26 (1797), p. 303, quoted in Jenks, *Naval Engagements*, p. 108.

22. *Address to the Nation, By the Seamen At St Helen's* (Edinburgh: G. Mudie and Son, South Bridge, 1797), p. 13

23. Taylor, *Sons of the Waves*, p. 261.

24. TNA, ADM 1/5125, Declaration of Nore Mutineers, June 1797.

25. TNA, ADM 1/339, court martial of Richard Parker of the *Sandwich*, 22–26 June 1797.

26. Easton, 'Fleet Mutinies', p. 214.

27. See Ruth Scobie, 'Consuming the Bounty Mutiny', in Ruth Scobie, *Celebrity Culture and the Myth of Oceania in Britain 1770–1823* (Woodbridge: Boydell Press, 2019), pp. 97–129.

28. For a deeper analysis of Portland's response see Easton, 'Social and Economic History', pp. 215; see also *Lloyd's Evening Post* (London), 12 June 1797.

29. *True and Particular Account of the Execution of Richard Parker* (London, 1797).

30. See for example *The Whole Trial and Defence of Richard Parker* (London: G. Thompson, 1797); NMM CUN/3, Sir Charles Cunningham, 'A Narrative of Occurrences that took place during the Mutiny at the Nore in the Months of May and June, 1797'; NMM, PAH5441, *The Execution of Richard Parker* (London, 1797). It seems likely that the figure is Parker, for while he is wearing something approximating a naval uniform, suggesting he might be a generic naval officer,

this could also be an acknowledgement of Parker's status as 'President'. Easton has highlighted the figure's 'odd pose' and effeminate, delicate appearance, suggesting also that the small pistol positioned at his belt was a further attempt to emasculate him. I am not convinced that the representation is feminised in the way outlined here, but this seems a very plausible explanation of the print's meaning. See Easton, 'Fleet Mutinies', p. 220.

31. *Oracle and Public Advertiser*, 6 June 1797.
32. *Star*, 4 July 1797, 6 July 1797.
33. See Callum Easton, 'The Unusual Afterlife of Richard Parker', *History Today* (October 2017); Frykman, *Bloody Flag*, pp. 156–7; Jenks, *Naval Engagements*, p. 106.
34. Anon., *An Address to the Seamen in the British Navy*, p. 3.
35. *Oracle*, 22 June 1797.
36. I am indebted to Lizzie Lawrence for this point. Her assessed presentation in March 2022 offered a detailed analysis of this source.
37. Lloyd and Anderson, *St Vincent and Camperdown*, p. 129.
38. For a more detailed discussion of the Batavian Republic's relationship with Revolutionary France see Simon Schama, *Patriots and Liberators: Revolution in the Netherlands 1780–1813* (New York: Alfred A. Knopf, 1977), pp. 271–88. For the threat of the Dutch fleet see Willis, *Hour of Victory*, pp. 119–21, 124.
39. Both ships came close to mutinying, however. Eighteen days before the outbreak of mutiny, sailors on the *Venerable* challenged Duncan's authority with three orchestrated cheers, which were repeated by the sailors of the *Adamant*. Order was only restored on the latter when Duncan himself came aboard the ship, seized on the would-be mutineers and held a ringleader over the side of the ship, declaring 'My Lads – look at this fellow – he who dares to deprive me of command of the fleet'. The uprising was swiftly quelled. See MacDougall, 'Mutiny and the North Sea Squadron', p. 250.
40. Willis, *Hour of Victory*, p. 122.
41. For the pressures and agendas weighing on the Committee for Foreign Affairs see Schama, *Patriots and Liberators*, pp. 281–3. See also Gardiner, *Fleet Battle and Blockade*, pp. 173–5; Willis, *Hour of Victory*, pp. 119–20, 125–6.
42. Willis, *Hour of Victory*, pp. 132–3, 135; Gardiner, *Fleet Battle and Blockade*, p. 175–6; Lloyd and Anderson, *St Vincent and Camperdown*, p. 141.
43. Gardiner, *Fleet Battle and Blockade*, pp. 175–6, 178.
44. HMS *Victory* at Trafalgar, for instance, suffered 12 per cent casualties. See Willis, *Hour of Victory*, pp. 116, 140–6.
45. L. Brockliss, J. Cardwell and M. Moss, *Nelson's Surgeon: William Beatty, Naval Medicine and the Battle of Trafalgar* (Oxford, 2005), p. 113; Lloyd and Anderson, *St Vincent and Camperdown*, p. 147.
46. TNA, ADM 1/5341, court martial of John Williamson, 11 December–1 January 1797.
47. NMM, AGC/24/6, Joseph Samain to his parents, 18 October 1797.
48. Richard Greenhalgh to his parents, 17 October 1797; NMRN, 546/84 (17), quoted in Watt and Hawkins, eds, *Letters of Seamen*, p. 132.
49. J. Ralfe, *The Naval Biography of Great Britain* (London, 1828), Vol. 4, p. 160; Willis, *Hour of Victory*, pp. 151–2.
50. The classic work here is John Keegan, *The Face of Battle: A Study of Agincourt, Waterloo and the Somme* (London: Jonathan Cape, 1976).
51. Dugan, *Great Mutiny*, p. 419.
52. Quilley, *Empire to Nation*, p. 183.
53. *Northampton Mercury*, 28 October 1797.

54. *Oracle*, 14 October 1797.
55. *True Briton*, 6 November 1797; *Morning Chronicle*, 17 October 1797.
56. *True Briton*, 25 October 1797.
57. *True Briton*, 30 October 1797; *True Briton*, 7 November 1797.
58. *True Briton*, 6 November 1797.
59. *Bell's Weekly Messenger*, 24 December 1797.
60. *London Packet or New Evening Post*, 21–23 March 1798.
61. *Sun*, 24 March 1798; *True Briton*, 26 March 1789; *Star and Evening Advertiser*, 28 March 1798; *Observer*, 1 April 1798. For local organs see for example *Chester Chronicle*, 6 April 1798.
62. Anon., *An impartial history of the war, from the commencement of the Revolution in France. Containing an Accurate Description of the Sea Engagements, Sieges, Battles, Expeditions and Conquests, of the Various Contending powers. Including an Account of the General Mutiny among the Seamen, at Spithead and the Nore. Together with a particular narrative of the rise, progress, and various events accompanying the Rebellion in Ireland* (Manchester: Sowler and Russell, 1799), p. 378.
63. NMM PAD3447, Daniel Orme, *John Crawford of Sunderland Durham. The Sailor who Nailed the Flag to the Main Top Gallant mast head, on board the Venerable, Lord Duncan's Ship, after being once Shot away by the Dutch Admil de Winter. Drawn by Mr Orme on board for the Express purpose of Introducing into his Picture of Ld Duncan's Victory now Engraving by Subscription & which includes Portraits of the Admirals & Officers who so Gloriously Distinguished themselves on the ever Memorable 11th of October 1797*, 21 November 1797.
64. *Sun*, 1 December 1798; NMM, PAD3446, 'John Crawford, Nailing the Flag to the Main top gallant mast head, on board the Venerable, October 11th 1797', 20 November 1804; NMM, BHC3100, 'Duncan Receiving the Surrender of de Winter at the Battle of Camperdown', 11 October 1797; NMM, AAA4498, Mug depicting 'Jack' Crawford, early nineteenth century; NMM, ZBA4377, Plate depicting 'Jack' Crawford, early nineteenth century.
65. *True Briton*, 1 May 1797; *True Briton*, 13 May 1797; *London Chronicle*, 13 May 1797.
66. *Porcupine*, 3 December 1800.
67. *Sun*, 4 May 1798; also reported in *Oracle and Public Advertiser* and *True Briton* on 5 May, verbatim.
68. *True Briton*, 26 October 1798; *London Packet or New Evening Post*, 9–11 June 1800; *Bell's Weekly Messenger*, 15 June 1800.
69. *Porcupine*, 5 December 1800; also reported in *Oracle*, 5 December 1800.
70. Grenville to Lord Spencer, 13 October 1797, in Corbett and Richmond, eds, *Spencer Papers*, Vol. 2, p. 196.
71. Canning's diary, 18–21 October, quoted in Ehrman, *The Younger Pitt*, Vol. 3, p. 111. For the elaborate steps taken to disguise the publishing operation and conceal the identity of contributors see Emily Lorraine de Montluzin, *The Anti-Jacobins 1798-1800* (London: Macmillan, 1988), p. 22. See also Andrews, *British Periodical Press*, p. 72.
72. Hoock, '"Cheap Defence of Nations"', pp. 161–3; Hoock, *Empires of the Imagination*, p. 138; Alison Yarrington, *Commemoration of the Hero, 1800-1864: Monuments to the British Victors of the Napoleonic Wars* (New York and London: Garland, 1988), pp. 61–78, 338–46, quoted in Quilley, *Empire to Nation*, p. 184.
73. *The Times*, 19 December 1797.
74. TNA, WORK 4/18, Minutes of the Office of Works, 24 November 1797; TNA, WORK 4/18, Minutes of the Office of Works, 1 December 1797.

75. Hoock, *Empires of the Imagination*, p. 139. The sermon itself quoted from the 22nd chapter of the 2nd Book of Samuel, and parts of the 1st, 2nd and 3rd verses. It included the lines 'And God of my rock, in him I will trust, he is my shield and the horn of my salvation', so while it did not explicitly refer to the mutinies, it did offer some recognition of regrets and redemption. For details of the sermon see *The Times*, 20 December 1797.

76. James Stanier Clarke, *Naval Sermons, preached on board His Majesty's Ship the Impetueux, in the Western Squadron, during its Services off Brest: to which is added a Thanksgiving Sermon for Naval Victories; preached at Park-Street Chapel, Grosvenor Square, Dec. 19 M,DCC,XCVII* (London: T. Payne, B White, 1798), pp. 145–7, 214–15; see also Quillley, *Empire to Nation*, p. 185.

77. Quilley, *Empire to Nation*, p. 185; Jenks, *Naval Engagements*, p. 110.

78. TNA, PC/1/40/130, 'Proclamation for a General Thanksgiving for the many signal and important victories obtained in the present war', 29 November 1797. For newspaper reportage see for example *Oracle* and *True Briton* on 4 December 1797.

79. TNA, PC/1/40/130, 'Proclamation for a General Thanksgiving to be observed in Scotland', 29 November 1797.

80. TNA, PC/1/40/130, 'Proclamation for a General Thanksgiving to be observed in Scotland', 29 November 1797; *The Times*, 18 December 1797; *Hampshire Chronicle*, 23 December 1797.

81. Jenks, *Naval Engagements*, p. 121, referencing *Morning Chronicle*, 10 November 1797. The *Morning Chronicle* delighted in the fact that while Duncan and the naval Captain Trollope's carriages were cheered, Pitt's, sandwiched in between, received hisses; see *Morning Chronicle*, 15 November 1797.

82. *Oracle*, 17 October 1797; *True Briton*, 19 October 1797.

83. 'The people were so disgusted that they followed him with *hissings* and *hootings* . . .'; *True Briton*, 18 October 1797.

84. See *Oracle*, 19 October 1797; *Morning Chronicle*, 18 October 1797; *True Briton*, 18 October 1797. The latter joked that 'Upon such an occasion of public rejoicing as that of the Victory lately achieved by the British Fleet, it would certainly be worth the while of a Jacobin to weigh the difference of expence between two or three pounds weight of candles, and that of having all his windows to repair'.

85. *Morning Chronicle*, 9 December 1797; *Morning Chronicle*, 20 December 1797.

86. *Morning Chronicle*, 12 December 1797.

87. *Morning Chronicle*, 18 December 1797.

88. *The Times*, 19 December 1797; *Anti-Jacobin or Weekly Examiner*, 18 December 1797.

89. Thomas Rowlandson, *The Victorious Procession to St Pauls. Or Billy's Grand Triumphal Entry a Prelude* (11 December 1797). For *Britain's Brave Tars*, the *True Briton* found that the production was 'tediously protracted, but was not wholly destitute of humour', while the *Morning Chronicle* delighted in its mockery, which chimed so readily with its own views. See *True Briton*, 20 December 1797; *Morning Chronicle*, 21 December 1797.

90. For a description of the procession see *The Times*, 18 December 1797 and 20 December 1797; *Leeds Intelligencer*, 25 December 1797. A surprisingly detailed account of the ceremony was also published in the *Hampshire Chronicle*, 23 December 1797.

91. TNA, WORK 4/18, Minutes of the Office of Works, 23 December 1797; *London Chronicle*, 19–21 December 1797; *Morning Post*, 11 December 1797; Quilley, *Empire to Nation*, p. 183.

92. TNA, WORK 4/18, Minutes of the Office of Works, 1 December 1797; TNA, WORK 4/18, Minutes of the Office of Works, 8 December 1797; *Hampshire Chronicle*, 23 December 1797.
93. *True Briton*, 20 December 1797.
94. *The Times*, 20 December 1797; *Oracle*, 20 December 1797; *Whitehall Evening Post*, 19–21 December 1797.
95. *Anti-Jacobin or Weekly Examiner*, 25 December 1797.
96. *London Chronicle*, 19–21 December 1797; *True Briton*, 23 December 1797.
97. *Observer*, 24 December 1797.
98. While a number of newspapers noted Pitt's unpleasant reception, the extent of the hissing and booing is not clear and offers an insight into the way organs with competing agendas could report the same news. Some newspapers were open about the fact, for example the *Hampshire Chronicle* (23 December 1797), which noted 'Mr Pitt was hissed by populace on his way to the cathedral', in consequence of which he did not return in his carriage. Some newspapers hedged their bets: the *Leeds Intelligencer* (25 December 1797) noted that the plaudits bestowed on Pitt 'silenced and overpowered the hisses of a few scattered malcontents, planted in different places, apparently for the purpose of insulting him', while the *Morning Chronicle* (20 December 1797) noted that Pitt was met 'with a mixture of applause and hissing'.

    The *True Briton* stated evasively that his reception was 'such as a Minister of this Country might, in the peculiar moment . . . be proud to receive' (20 December 1797). *The Times* was in full denial, observing 'with pleasure' that Pitt was met with 'very general applause', *The Times*, 20 December 1797.
99. *Oracle*, 20 December 1797.
100. *London Chronicle*, 19–21 December 1797; *St James's Chronicle*, 19–21 December; *Morning Chronicle*, 19 December 1797; *Morning Chronicle*, 21 December 1797.
101. The *Oracle* noted that 'There was not expression of any unbecoming sentiment, nor any breach of decorum' while *Bell's Weekly Messenger* stated that 'there was very little mobbing or riotous behaviour'. See *Oracle*, 20 December 1797; *Bell's Weekly Messenger*, 24 December 1797.
102. The man was released after 'confessing his errors', but the boy was ordered to remain in custody. *The Times*, 20 December 1797; *Whitehall Evening Post*, 19–21 December 1797.
103. *The Times*, 20 December 1797.
104. *Bell's Weekly Messenger*, 24 December 1797. The event is also mentioned by Jordan and Rogers, 'Admirals as Heroes', p. 213; and Jenks, *Naval Engagements*, p. 122, though the latter takes the explanation at its word.
105. *Bell's Weekly Messenger*, 31 December 1797.
106. *Morning Chronicle*, 20 December 1797; *Morning Post*, 25 December 1797.
107. *Leeds Intelligencer*, 25 December 1797; *Whitehall Evening Post*, 19–21 December 1797. The precise number of sailors in attendance is unclear: the *Morning Chronicle* noted 500, while the *True Briton* thought it to be 200, with fifty marines. See *Morning Chronicle*, 9 December 1797; *True Briton*, 20 December 1797.
108. *Morning Chronicle*, 9 December 1797; *True Briton*, 20 December 1797.
109. *Hampshire Chronicle*, 23 December 1797.
110. *Morning Chronicle*, 21 December 1797.
111. Jordan and Rogers, 'Admirals as Heroes', p. 213.
112. For the account of the assault see *London Packet or New Lloyd's Evening Post*, 28 October 1795.

113. *Sun*, 8 November 1798.
114. See Joanne Begiato, *Manliness in Britain, 1760–1900: Bodies, Emotion and Material Culture* (Manchester: Manchester University Press, 2020), esp. chap. 3. I am very grateful to Joanne for sharing her chapter on Crawford prior to its publication.
115. Robert Laurie and James Whittle, *The Sailor and Long-Back'd Horse* (London, 10 June 1797).
116. Davey and Johns, *Broadsides*, pp. 30–9.
117. Land, *War, Nationalism and the British Sailor*, p. 5.
118. James Gillray, *Fighting for the DUNGHILL: or Jack Tar settling Citoyen Francois* (London, 20 November 1798).
119. See Timothy Jenks, 'Contesting the Hero: The Funeral of Admiral Lord Nelson', *Journal of British Studies*, Vol. 39 (2000); Davey, *In Nelson's Wake*, pp. 106–10.

8 BAD LUCK TO THE BRITISH NAVY! MUTINY AND NAVAL WARFARE, 1798–1801

1. TNA, ADM 1/5345, court martial of John Stephens, John Mullins and Cornelius Kelly of the *Adamant*, 6 July 1798.
2. *Oracle*, 9 July 1798; see also *St James's Chronicle*, 7–10 July 1798; *Evening Mail*, 9–11 July 1798.
3. TNA, ADM 12/24. In 1798 there were forty-three courts martial for mutiny or mutinous behaviour, compared with forty-two in 1797, eight in 1796 and 1795, four in 1794 and two in 1793.
4. Frykman, *Bloody Flag*, p. 167.
5. TNA, ADM 1/5346, court martial of the mutineers of the *Defiance*, 8–14 September 1798.
6. Colley, *Britons*, pp. 204–28; Cookson, *British Armed Nation*, pp. 209–45. Timothy Jenks and Jordan and Rogers offer a more complex picture which emphasises how military success could be contorted to fit more partisan agendas. See Jenks, *Naval Engagements*, p. 125; Jordan and Rogers, 'Admirals as Heroes'.
7. Leonard F. Gutteridge, *Mutiny: A History of Naval Insurrection* (Annapolis, MD: Naval Institute Press, 1992), p. 75.
8. *Lloyd's Evening Post*, 26–28 March 1800.
9. Four ringleaders were sentenced to hang. TNA, ADM 1/5343, court martial of John McDonald, Patrick Hymes, Thomas Hennigan and Gabriel Johnson of the *Renommee*, 20 March 1798.
10. See for example the court martial following an attempted mutiny on the *Pluto*, in which it was predominantly sailors rather than officers who testified against other sailors. TNA, ADM 1/5345, court martial of John Brian and William Whiley of the *Pluto*, 14 July 1798.
11. TNA, ADM 1/5343, court martial of Dennis Broughall, Robert Larkin and William Haye of the *Amelia*, 8–9 March 1798; Frykman, *Bloody Flag*, pp. 177–8.
12. Frykman, *Bloody Flag*, p. 159. For clubs see also TNA, ADM 1/5343, court martial of Dennis Broughall, Robert Larkin and William Haye of the *Amelia*, 8–9 March 1798.
13. For Thomas Butler quote see TNA, ADM 1/5343, court martial of Thomas Butler of the *Romulus*, 1 February 1798; TNA, ADM 1/5343, court martial of Joseph Robinson and Charles Crawley, 3 January 1798; for *Amelia* see TNA, ADM 1/5343, court martial of Dennis Broughall, Robert Larkin and William Haye of the *Amelia*, 8–9 March 1798.
14. TNA, ADM 1/5347, court martial of Robert Jepsom of the *Druid*, 22–23 October 1798.

15. TNA, ADM 1/5345, court martial of James Anderson of the *Perdrix*, 1 June 1798; TNA, ADM 1/5344, court martial of Richard Forrester of the *Monarch*, 9 April 1798; TNA, ADM 1/5345, court martial of William Stevenson of the *St Albans*, 18–19 June 1798.

16. TNA, ADM 1/5341, court martial of John Crystall et al. of the *Thames*, 14–15 August 1797; TNA, ADM 1/5352, court martial of Florence McCarthy and William Grace of the *Phoebe*, 7 April 1800; TNA, ADM 1/5343, court martial of Bryan McMahon of the *Albacore*, 3 January 1798; TNA, ADM 1/5346, court martial of mutineers of the *Caesar*, 16–23 August 1798.

17. *Whitehall Evening Post*, 19–21 December 1797. Jay was sentenced to hang.

18. TNA, ADM 1/5346, court martial of Jeremiah Dordau of the *Mercury*, 28 September 1798.

19. Niklas Frykman, 'The Mutiny on Hermione: Warfare, Revolution, and Treason in the Royal Navy', *Journal of Social History*, Vol. 44, No. 1 (2010), pp. 159–87; Frykman, *Bloody Flag*, pp. 167–8. See also Angus Konstam, *Mutiny on the Spanish Main: HMS Hermione and the Royal Navy's revenge* (London: Osprey, 2020).

20. Frykman, *Bloody Flag*, pp. 165–6.

21. TNA, ADM 12/24, court martial of George Harvey and William Gleeson, 27 May 1796; TNA, ADM, 12/24, court martial of John Harper, 27 July 1796; Anthony Brown, 'The Nore Mutiny: Sedition or Ship's Biscuit?', *Mariner's Mirror*, Vol. 92 (2006), pp. 60–74.

22. TNA, ADM 1/5344, court martial of John Perry, Timothy Cardigan and James Kelly of the *Aquilon*, 17 May 1798.

23. Reports of the *Hermione* mutiny were first reported in January 1798; see *London Packet or New Evening Post*, 1–3 January 1798. For an example of the close attention paid to the attempts to recapture mutinous sailors see *Oracle*, 16 March 1798. For figures on number of executions see Frykman, *Bloody Flag*, p. 171; Gutteridge, *Mutiny*, pp. 75, 81–2.

24. TNA, ADM 1/5343, court martial of Dennis Broughall, Robert Larkin and William Haye of the *Amelia*, 8–9 March 1798.

25. TNA, ADM 1/5347, court martial of the mutineers of the *Glory*, 1–9 October 1798; TNA, ADM 1/5347, court martial of John Wrights and George Tomms of the *Diomede*, 29–30 October 1798; Frykman, *Bloody Flag*, p. 181.

26. During the court martial of the *Caesar* mutineers it was heard that men 'were engaged with Correspondence with other Ships of the Fleet then at anchor, in order to induce the crews of those ships to join with them in the said oath'. During the trial of Captain John McKenna, one sailor discussed the 'United Irishmen who had been selected on board and on shore and wished me to become one of them'. See TNA, ADM 1/5346, court martial of mutineers of the *Caesar*, 16–23 August 1798; TNA, ADM 1/5347, court martial of the mutineers of the *Captain*, 5–8 December 1798. On identification of United Irishmen see Rodger, 'Mutiny or Subversion?', p. 558. On the 1798 mutinies more generally see Philip MacDougall, 'Lord Love the Irish and Damnation to the English: The Naval Mutinies of 1798', *Mariner's Mirror*, Vol. 108, No. 4 (November 2022), pp. 423–38, which was published just as this book went to press.

27. TNA, ADM 1/5346, court martial of the mutineers of the *Defiance*, 8–14 September 1798.

28. For sailors speaking in Irish see TNA, ADM 1/5346, court martial of mutineers of the *Caesar*, 16–23 August 1798; TNA, ADM 1/5346, court martial of the mutineers of the *Defiance*, 8–14 September 1798. For discussion of clubs see TNA, ADM 1/5347, court martial of the mutineers of the *Glory*, 1–9 October 1798. See also Frykman, *Bloody Flag*, pp. 179–80.

29. TNA, ADM 1/5346, court martial of mutineers of the *Caesar*, 16-23 August 1798; TNA, ADM 1/5346, court martial of the mutineers of the *Defiance*, 8-14 September 1798. On Irish oath-taking see Michael Durey, 'Loyalty in an Age of Conspiracy: The Oath-Filled Civil War in Ireland 1795-1799', in Davis and Pickering, *Unrespectable Radicals?*, pp. 71-89.

30. TNA, ADM 1/5347, court martial of mutineers of the *Captain*, 5-8 December 1798; TNA, ADM 1/5346, court martial of mutineers of the *Caesar*, 16-23 August 1798.

31. *Sun*, 4 August 1798; *Lloyd's Evening Post*, 3-6 August 1798.

32. *Morning Herald*, 3 August 1798; *The Times*, 24 August 1798.

33. *Reading Mercury*, 24 September 1798; *True Briton*, 29 September 1798.

34. See TNA, ADM 1/5346, court martial of mutineers of the *Caesar*, 16-23 August 1798; TNA, ADM 1/5347, court martial of the mutineers of the *Captain*, 5-8 December 1798.

35. TNA, ADM 1/5350, court martial of John Maloney, 23 July 1799.

36. Admiralty to Bridport, 14 August 1798, in Morriss, *Blockade of Brest*, pp. 328-9.

37. NMM, BEL/1, port orderbook, Plymouth, 1798-1799, General Order by Sir Rich. King, Commander in Chief of HM vessels at Plymouth, 29 August 1798, 14 September 1798; Morriss, *Blockade of Brest*, p. 329, n. 1. For the *Royal Sovereign*, Captain Bedford stated, 'From my own observations and the best information I can collect I have not the least reason to suspect any of them to be evil disposed'; see Bedford to Gardner, 21 August 1798, in Morriss, *Blockade of Brest*, pp. 329-30.

38. TNA, ADM 1/5347, court martial of William Nugent, *La Minerve*, 1 October 1798; TNA, ADM 1/5347, court martial of Philip Newsom of the *Nemesis*, 1-2 October 1798.

39. Collingwood to A. Carlyle, 5 December 1799, quoted in Hughes, *Collingwood Correspondence*, p. 108.

40. TNA, ADM 1/5346, court martial of George Smith of the *Seahorse*, 18 September 1798; TNA, ADM 1/5348, court martial of Patrick Townsend et al. of the *St George*, 15 January 1799.

41. Some naval officers were delighted at this arrival. Edward Pellew reported that 'we are to have a new commander in chief, heaven be praised. The old one is scarcely worth drowning, a more contemptible or more miserable animal does not exist. I believe there never was a man so universally despised by the whole Service. A mixture of ignorance, avarice and spleen.' See Pellew to A. Broughton, 1 December 1799, in C. Northcote Parkinson, *Edward Pellew, Viscount Exmouth, Admiral of the Red* (London: Methuen, 1934), p. 228.

42. For calls to follow the 'proper channels' see TNA, ADM 1/5340, court martial of Joseph Wells et al. of the *Calypso*, 14 July 1797. For the example on the *Boadicea* see TNA, ADM 1/5342, court martial of John Burn of the *Boadicea*, 14 December 1797.

43. TNA, ADM 1/5347, court martial of John Haig of the *Diomede*, 16-17 October 1798; TNA, ADM 1/5347, court martial of John Parker of the *Diomede*, 25 October 1798.

44. There were twenty-nine recorded instances of mutiny or mutinous behaviour in 1799, and twenty in 1800. TNA, ADM 12/24.

45. E.H. Stuart Jones, 'Mutiny in Bantry Bay', *Irish Sword*, No. 3 (1951-2), pp. 202-9; Rodger, *Command of the Ocean*, p. 451.

46. NMM, ADM/L/H121, Lieutenant's Log Book of the *Hope*, 1796-1800, May-July 1799; TNA, ADM 1/5351, court martial of James Gilbert et al. of the *Hope*, 3 January 1800.

47. For mutiny on the *Danae* see TNA, ADM 1/5353, court martial of Lord Proby of the *Danae*, 17 June 1800; TNA, ADM 1/5354, court martial of John Maret of the

Danae, 2 September 1800; TNA ADM 1/5358, court martial of John Williams of the *Danae*, 12 September 1801. For the mutiny on the *Albanaise* see TNA, ADM 1/5356, court martial of Francis Newcombe of the *Albanaise*, 17 June 1801; TNA, ADM 1/5360, court martial of Jacob Godfrey of the *Albanaise*, 11 January 1801. See also J.D. Spinney, 'The *Albanaise* Affair', *Mariner's Mirror* (1957), pp. 194–202. For the mutiny on the *Gozo* see TNA, ADM 1/5359, court martial of William Milne et al. of the *Gozo*, 26 November 1801; TNA ADM 1/5359, court martial of Peter Jones, Stephen White and John King of the *Gozo*, 14–15 December; TNA, ADM 1/5360, court martial of Duncan Drummond alias William Gibson et al. of the *Gozo*, 23 February 1802.

48. For the *Albanaise* see TNA, ADM 1/5356, court martial of Francis Newcombe of the *Albanaise*, 17 June 1801; TNA, ADM 1/5360, court martial of Jacob Godfrey of the *Albanaise*, 11 January 1801; Spinney, 'The *Albanaise* Affair', pp. 194–202. For the *Gozo* see TNA, ADM 1/5359, court martial of William Milne et al. of the *Gozo*, 26 November 1801; TNA ADM 1/5359, court martial of Peter Jones, Stephen White and John King of the *Gozo*, 14–15 December; TNA, ADM 1/5360, court martial of Duncan Drummond alias William Gibson et al. of the *Gozo*, 23 February 1802.

49. TNA, ADM 1/5359, court martial of William Milne et al. of the *Gozo*, 26 November 1801.

50. TNA ADM 1/5359, court martial of Peter Jones, Stephen White and John King of the *Gozo*, 14–15 December; TNA, ADM 1/5356, court martial of Francis Newcombe of the *Albanaise*, 17 June 1801.

51. *St James's Chronicle or the British Evening Post*, 27–29 March 1800; *Morning Post*, 29 March 1800. See also *True Briton*, 29 March 1800; *Star and Evening Advertiser*, 28 March 1800; *Star and Evening Advertiser*, 2 April 1800. See also *Whitehall Evening Post*, 1–3 April 1800; *The Times*, 2 April 1800.

52. For the *Hermione* link see *Reading Mercury*, 31 March 1800. For the connection to Parker see *St James's Chronicle or the British Evening Post*, 8–10 April 1800; *Lloyd's Evening Post*, 7–9 April 1800.

53. For Maret's punishment see TNA, ADM 1/5354, court martial of John Maret, *Danae* for Mutiny, 2 September 1800. For the search for the *Danae* mutineers see TNA, ADM 1/5354, court martial of John Maret of the *Danae* for Mutiny, 2 September 1800. For the punishments see TNA, ADM 1/5354, court martial of John Maret and John Williams of the *Danae*; court martial of Jacob Godfrey and Henry Kennedy of the *Albanaise* and the court martial of Peter Jones et al. of the *Gozo*; TNA, ADM 1/5360, court martial of Jacob Godfrey of the *Albanaise*, 11 January 1801; TNA, ADM 1/5362, court martial of Henry Kennedy of the *Albemaise* [sic], 5 October 1802; TNA ADM 1/5359, court martial of Peter Jones et al. of the *Gozo*, 14–15 December 1801; TNA, ADM 1/5360, court martial of Duncan Drummond alias William Gibson et al. of the *Gozo*, 23 February 1802.

54. NMM, MRK/101/1, Markham Papers, Lord St Vincent to Captain Markham, 13 June 1800.

55. TNA, ADM 1/5356, court martial of John Betham et al. of the *Active*, 9 April 1801.

56. TNA, ADM ADM 1/5358, court martial of Joseph Williamson et al. of the *Glenmore*, 1 October 1801.

57. TNA, ADM 1/5353, court martial of James Mahoney of the *Veteran*, 23 June 1800.

58. *True Briton*, 29 September 1798.

59. *The Times*, 24 April 1798; Rodger, *Command of the Ocean*, pp. 457–8; Knight, *Pursuit of Victory*, pp. 144–7, 275–7; Michael Duffy, 'British Naval Intelligence

and Bonaparte's Egyptian Expedition of 1798', *Mariner's Mirror*, Vol. 89 (1998), pp. 278–90.

60. Rodger, 'Nelson and the British Navy', pp. 9–10; Rodger, *Command of the Ocean*, p. 454.

61. The sailor John Jupp recorded how for two days 'the Gale lasted tossing us up and down like a pig in a string', with the damaged flagship 'a most dismal Sight'. NMM, AGC/J/9, John Jupp to his father and mother, 26 November 1798.

62. Willis, *Hour of Victory*, p. 166; Gardiner, *Nelson Against Napoleon*, pp. 21, 30; Rodger, *Command of the Ocean*, p. 459; Knight, *Pursuit of Victory*, pp. 282–9.

63. Knight, *Pursuit of Victory*, pp. 290–1; Rodger, *Command of the Ocean*, pp. 459–60; Willis, *Hour of Victory*, p. 168.

64. NMM, AGC/W/2, Thomas Wilkes to his cousin, 15 August 1798.

65. Knight, *Pursuit of Victory*, pp. 292–3, 296.

66. NMM, AGC/J/9, John Jupp to his father and mother, 26 November 1798.

67. NMM, AGC/H/28, Henry Harrop to his father, 24 August 1798.

68. NMM, AGC/W/2, Thomas Wilkes to his cousin, 15 August 1798.

69. Knight, *Pursuit of Victory*, p. 297.

70. NMM, AGC/J/9, John Jupp to his father and mother, 26 November 1798.

71. NMM, AGC/H/28, Henry Harrop to his father, 24 August 1798.

72. Rodger, *Command of the Ocean*, p. 461.

73. Terry Coleman, *Nelson: The Man and the Legend* (London: Bloomsbury, 2002), p. 155.

74. Hester Piozzi to Penelope Sophia Pennington, 14 September 1798, quoted in Uglow, *In These Times*, p. 234.

75. *Star and Evening Advertiser*, 3 October 1798; Knight, *Pursuit of Victory*, p. 301.

76. Uglow, *In These Times*, pp. 237–9; Jenks, *Naval Engagements*, p. 139. For the quote see *Evening Mail*, 3 October 1798.

77. As Nelson's likeness was not well known, many bore an uncanny resemblance to Admiral Rodney, a naval hero from the 1780s. See Marianne Czisnik, 'Nelson, Navy, and National Identity', in Quintin Colville and James Davey, eds, *Nelson, Navy and Nation: The Royal Navy and the British People, 1688–1815* (London: Conway, 2013), pp. 188–207, p. 189.

78. For female consumption see Kate Williams, 'Nelson and Women: Marketing, Representations and the Female Consumer', in Cannadine, ed., *Nelson: Context and Legacy*, pp. 67–89, p. 69. For an example of dress 'a la Nelson' see *Morning Post*, 5 October 1798.

79. Thomas Dibdin, *The mouth of the Nile; or, the glorious first of August, a musical entertainment; as performed at the Theatre-Royal, Covent Garden* (London: J. Barker, 1798). See also Uglow, *In These Times*, p. 237; Czisnik, 'Nelson, Navy, and National Identity', p. 189; Knight, *Pursuit of Victory*, p. 301.

80. Knight, *Pursuit of Victory*, pp. 295, 302–3.

81. *Sun*, 4 October 1798; *True Briton*, 4 October 1798; *Morning Post*, 3 October 1798.

82. Kathleen Wilson, 'Nelson and the People', in Cannadine, ed., *Nelson: Context and Legacy*, pp. 49–66, pp. 50–1; Wilson, 'Empire, Trade and Popular Politics'; Jordan and Rogers, 'Admirals as Heroes'.

83. Jenks, *Naval Engagements*, pp. 148–52.

84. One volunteer who participated in the victory celebrations in October 1798 was delighted to see 'a pretty decent crowd' collect to watch the parade but was somewhat put out the next day when a similarly sized crowd turned out to inspect a dead pig. *St James's Chronicle*, 2–4 October 1798.

85. Jenks, *Naval Engagements*, pp. 129, 141; *True Briton*, 29 November 1798; *Oracle*, 6 October 1798.

86. *The Times*, 3 October 1798; *London Chronicle*, 2–4 October 1798; *Star and Evening Advertiser*, 4 October 1798; *Lloyd's Evening Post*, 1–3 October 1798.

87. For dispatches see Horatio Nelson to Earl St Vincent, 3 August 1798, in Nicolas, ed., *Dispatches and Letters of Nelson*, Vol. 3, pp. 56–60; Willis, *Hour of Victory*, p. 174. For newspaper reportage see for example *Star and Evening Advertiser*, 3 October 1798.

88. For newspaper discussion see *Lloyd's Evening Post*, 1–3 October 1798; *True Briton*, 3 October 1798; *Morning Herald*, 4 October 1798; *Morning Post*, 4 October 1798; *Oracle*, 4 October 1798; Colley, *Britons*, p. 274. For Collingwood's concerns see Collingwood to Blackett, 1 May 1798, in Collingwood, *Public and Private Correspondence*, Vol. 1, pp. 88–9.

89. *Oracle*, 17 October 1798, referenced in Jenks, *Naval Engagements*, p. 136.

90. Thomas Rowlandson, *Admiral Nelson recreating with his Brave Tars after the Glorious Battle of the Nile* (London, 20 October 1798).

91. Wilson, 'Nelson and the People', pp. 58–9.

92. *Gentleman's Magazine*, Vol. 69 (1799), pp. 67–70.

93. Jenks, *Naval Engagements*, pp. 159–66.

94. See NMM, PAD3896, *Naval Pillar*, after John Flaxman (London: Richard Elsam and Thomas Tagg, 1804; Jenks, *Naval Engagements*, pp. 168–82.

95. Margarette Lincoln, 'Naval Ship Launches as Public Spectacle, 1773–1854', *Mariner's Mirror*, Vol. 83 (1997), pp. 466–72. See also NMM, PAD6038, *An exact Representation of Launching the Prince of Wales Man of War, before their Majesties, at Portsmouth, 1794* (London, 1794).

96. Anon, *The hospital pupil's guide through London, in a seres [sic] of letters; from a pupil at St. Thomas's Hospital to his friend in the country; recommending the best manner of a pupils employing his time, and interspersed with amusing anecdotes relative to the history and oconomy of hospital's* (London, 1800). See also James Davey, 'The Ship as Object: The Launch of the Queen Charlotte', in Adriana Craciun and Simon Schaffer, eds, *The Material Cultures of Enlightenment Arts and Sciences* (London: Palgrave, 2016), pp. 99–101.

97. Henry Francis Whitfield, *Plymouth and Devonport: in Times of War and Peace* (1900), p. 198.

98. For the *Plantagenet* see *Morning Chronicle*, 24 October 1801. For the *Courageux* see *Lloyd's Evening Post*, 26–28 March 1800; *Hampshire Chronicle*, 31 March 1800. See also *Oracle*, 28 March 1800.

99. Gardiner, *Nelson Against Napoleon*, pp. 122–3.

100. See for instance *Morning Post*, 22 January 1800; *Whitehall Evening Post*, 20–23 January 1800; *Sun*, 22 January 1800; *Oracle*, 22 January 1800; *Caledonian Mercury*, 25 January 1800.

101. Davey, 'Britain's European Island Empire'; Knight, *Pursuit of Victory*, p. 311.

102. Nelson to William Hamilton, 16 May 1799, in Alfred Morrison, ed., *The Collection of Autograph Letters . . . The Hamilton and Nelson Papers*, 2 vols (London, 1893–4), Vol. 2, p. 48; Knight, *Pursuit of Victory*, pp. 319–22, 324–7.

103. Sutcliffe, *Expeditionary Warfare*, pp. 124–5; Gardiner, *Nelson Against Napoleon*, pp. 79–81.

104. Knight, *Convoys*, pp. 21–2; Patrick Crowhurst, *The French War on Trade: Privateering, 1793–1815* (London: Scholar Press, 1989), pp. 46–78, 199, 203–4; Christopher D. Hall, *British Strategy in the Napoleonic War, 1803–1815* (Manchester: Manchester University Press, 1992), p. 187.

105. Knight, *Convoys*, pp. 23–4; Alfred Thayer Mahan, *The Influence of Seapower Upon the French Revolution and Empire, 1793–1812*, 2 vols (London: Sampson,

Low, Marston, 1893), pp. 205, 226; Rodger, *Command of the Ocean,* p. 561; Sutcliffe, *Expeditionary Warfare*, pp. 75–6.

106. Wilson, 'Nelson and the People', p. 68.
107. Jenks, *Naval Engagements*, pp. 219–22.
108. James Davey, 'Securing the Sinews of Sea Power: British Intervention in the Baltic 1780–1815', *International History Review*, Vol. 33, No. 2 (2011), pp. 161–84.
109. *Albion and Evening Advertiser*, 9 August 1800.
110. TNA, ADM 1/4186, Dundas to Nepean, 9 January 1801.
111. James Davey, 'Serving the State: Empire, Expertise and the British Hemp Crisis, 1800–1801', *Journal of Imperial and Commonwealth History*, Vol. 46, No. 4 (2018), pp. 651–75.
112. Rodger, *Command of the Ocean*, pp. 468–9; Knight, *Pursuit of Victory*, pp. 374–6.
113. Morrison, *Hamilton and Nelson Papers*, Vol. 2, p. 132.
114. Knight, *Pursuit of Victory*, p. 376.
115. The most famous Nelson story of all – that Nelson put his telescope to his blind eye and said 'I really do not see the signal' – is a myth. See Knight, *Pursuit of Victory*, pp. 378–9.
116. HL, HM34216, Nelson to Troubridge 4 April 1801.
117. Knight, *Pursuit of Victory*, pp. 379–82, 385–410; Rodger, *Command of the Ocean*, p. 470.
118. *Morning Post*, 16 April 1801; *Morning Chronicle*, 16 April 1801.
119. *Bell's Weekly Messenger*, 19 April 1801.
120. *Caledonian Mercury*, 18 April 1801; *Morning Post*, 16 April 1801, 17 April 1801, 18 April 1801.
121. *Morning Post*, 17 April 1801.
122. Knight, *Britain Against Napoleon*, pp. 83–4; Charles John Fedorak, 'Catholic Emancipation and the Resignation of William Pitt in 1801', *Albion: A Quarterly Journal Concerned with British Studies*, Vol. 24, No. 1 (1992), pp. 49–64.
123. SRO, SA/3/1/2/1, S to M, 10 July 1801; SRO, SA/3/1/2/1, S to M, 13 July 1801.
124. SHC, DD\AH/61/11/6, James Saumarez to Samuel Hood, 15 July 1801.
125. Knight, *Pursuit of Victory*, pp. 403–4; Uglow, *In These Times*, p. 282.
126. NMM, KEI/18/4, Nelson to Keith, 14 September 1901; NMM, AGC/J/1, St V to Nelson, 8 August 1801; NMM, CRK/1/54, Troubridge to Nelson, 7 August 1801.
127. Knight, *Pursuit of Victory*, pp. 407–8, 411–12; Uglow, *In These Times*, p. 283.
128. Knight, *Pursuit of Victory*, pp. 405, 413, 414–15.
129. Knight, *Pursuit of Victory*, pp. 405, 413, 414–15; Uglow, *In These Times*, p. 283.
130. Rodger, *Command of the Ocean*, p. 472; Gardiner, *Fleet Battle and Blockade*, pp. 58–9.
131. Richard Greenhalgh to his parents, 1 January 1798, quoted in Watt and Hawkins, eds, *Letters of Seamen*, p. 140.
132. Nicol, *Life and Adventures*, pp. 184–9.
133. Coleman, *Nelson*, p. 162, quoting Kathleen Coburn, ed., *The Notebooks of Samuel Taylor Coleridge* (New York and London: Routledge & Kegan Paul, 1962), Vol. 2, p. 188.
134. NMM, PAH7487, *Peace!! The Result of our Naval Victories . . . From the commencement of the war to the signing Preliminaries, Oct 1, 1801, The British Tree of Liberty* (London: John Wallis, 28 September 1801).
135. Jenks, *Naval Engagements*, pp. 223–4.
136. Harling, 'A Tale of Two Conflicts', in Philp, ed., *Resisting Napoleon*, pp. 20–1.
137. Knight, *Pursuit of Victory*, p. 416.

EPILOGUE

1. Richard Buckley to his parents, 16 August 1801, in Watt and Hawkins, eds, *Letters of Seamen*, p. 183.

2. Richard Greenhalgh to his parents, 20 June 1801, in Watt and Hawkins, eds, *Letters of Seamen*, p. 181; Richard Greenhalgh to his parents, 29 August 1802, in Watt and Hawkins, eds, *Letters of Seamen*, pp. 186–7. His desertion is registered in TNA, ADM 36/16192; see Watt and Hawkins, eds, *Letters of Seamen*, p. 187.

3. Sam Willis, *The Fighting Temeraire: Legend of Trafalgar* (London: Quercus, 2009), pp. 145–69; Leonard F. Gutteridge, *Mutiny: A History of Naval Insurrection* (Annapolis, MD: Naval Institute Press, 1992), p. 83; Edward Pelham Brenton, *Life and Correspondence of John Jervis, Earl St Vincent*, 2 vols (London: Henry Colburn, 1838), Vol. 2, p. 102.

4. TNA, ADM 1/5360, court martial of Henry Ross et al. of the *Syren*, 23–25 February 1802; court martial of Selon Ross of the *Syren*, 27 February–1 March; court martial of Richard Croft of the *Syren*, 4–5 March 1802.

5. TNA, ADM 1/5362 court martial of Thomas Bean and James Silk of the *Gibraltar*, 1–3 November 1802.

6. TNA, ADM 1/5362, court martial of 23 men of the *Excellent*, 27–29 December 1802.

7. Ann Coats, 'Spithead Mutiny: Introduction', in Coats and MacDougall, eds, *Naval Mutinies*, pp. 47–8; Rodger, *Command of the Ocean*, p. 404; Rodger, *Wooden World*, pp. 240–1.

8. On the *Syren* seven were hanged, on the *Gibraltar* two men were hanged, and on the *Excellent* four were hanged.

CONCLUSION

1. TNA, ADM 1/5348, court martial of William Davis of the *Lowestoft*, 24 January 1799.

2. TNA, ADM 1/5348, court martial of Benjamin Thompson of the *Ganges*, 22 February 1799.

3. TNA, ADM 1/5353, court martial of Thomas Nelson of the *Royal William*, 30 July 1800.

4. TNA, ADM 1/5348, court martial of Benjamin Thompson of the *Ganges*, 22 February 1799.

5. TNA, HO 42/62/34, 1801, letter from Ralph Fletcher, Lancashire magistrate, ff. 87–8.

6. Frykman, *Bloody Flag*, p. 148.

7. Grahame Aldous, 'The Law Relating to the Distribution of Prize Money in the Royal Navy', Unpublished PhD thesis, King's College London (2020).

8. See Evan Wilson, *The Horrible Peace: British Veterans and the End of the Napoleonic Wars* (Amherst, MA: University of Massachusetts Press, 2023), chap. 11, 'Sailors on Strike'. I am grateful to Evan for letting me see an advance draft of this book.

9. Rodger, *Command of the Ocean*, p. 491; Brian Lavery, ed., *Shipboard Life and Organization 1731–1815* (London: Navy Records Society, 1998), p. 355.

10. Navickas, *Loyalism and Radicalism*, pp. 176, 179, 182–6. See also Malcolm Chase, *Early Trade Unionism: Fraternity, Skill and the Politics of Labour* (Aldershot: Routledge, 2000); J. Orth, *Combination and Conspiracy: A Legal History of Trade Unionism, 1721–1906* (Oxford: Clarendon Press, 1991); James A. Jaffe, 'Industrial Arbitration, Equity, and Authority in England, 1800–1850', *Law and History Review*, Vol. 18, No. 3 (2000), pp. 525–58.

11. Snow, 'Fugitive Harbour', p. 809; Morriss, *Royal Dockyards*, pp. 120–1. See also Roger Morriss, 'Labour Relations in the Royal Dockyards, 1801–1805', *Mariner's Mirror*, Vol. 62. No. 4 (1976), pp. 337–46.
12. Morriss, *Royal Dockyards*, pp. 121–5. For an example of the state's response to the 1801 incidents see HO 42/61/190, 1801, f. 558, 'Copy of a notice addressed to the dockyard workers at Sheerness by [Aaron Graham], magistrate, clarifying his and their obligations under the Riot Act and setting out how they could and should have behaved in seeking to have their colleague released from impressment'.
13. Willis, *First of June*, p. 233.
14. Davey and Johns, *Broadsides*, pp. 30–9.
15. Land, *War, Nationalism and the British Sailor*, p. 9; Mary A. Conley, *From Jack Tar to Union Jack: Representing Naval Manhood in the British Empire, 1870–1918* (Manchester: Manchester University Press, 2009); Begiato, *Manliness in Britain*, chap. 3.
16. Gardiner, *Nelson Against Napoleon*, p. 11.
17. Jan Glete, *Navies and Nations: Warships, Navies and State Building in Europe and America, 1500–1860*, 2 vols (Stockholm: Almqvist and Wiksell, 1994), Vol. 2, pp. 382–4.
18. Crowhurst, *French War on Trade*, p. 31.
19. Gardiner, *Nelson Against Napoleon*, p. 12.
20. Davey, *In Nelson's Wake*.
21. Peter Spence, *The Birth of Romantic Radicalism: War, Popular Politics and English Radical Reformism, 1800–1815* (Aldershot: Scholars' Press, 1996), pp. viii, 21, 23; Hilton, *A Mad, Bad, Dangerous People*, pp. 104–5; Philp, ed., *Resisting Napoleon*, p. 7.
22. TNA, ADM 1/5354, court martial of Patrick Murphy, October 1803.
23. See Dinwiddy, 'Conceptions of Revolution', pp. 190–1.
24. Leech, *Thirty Years From Home*, p. 47.

NOTE ON SOURCES

1. Willis, *Hour of Victory*, pp. 54, 81.
2. Land, *War, Nationalism and the British Sailor*, p. 27. For the destruction of Nore documents see Wells, *Insurrection*, p. 120.
3. Favret, 'War Correspondence'.
4. Suffolk Record Office (SRO), SA/3/1/2/1, Martha Saumarez to James Saumarez, 31 January 1797.
5. David Worral, *Theatric Revolutions: Drama, Censorship, and Romantic Period Subcultures 1773–1832* (Oxford: Oxford University Press, 2006).
6. Diana Donald, *The Age of Caricature: Satirical Prints in the Reign of George III* (New Haven, CT and London: Yale University Press, 1997); Tamara L. Hunt, *Defining John Bull: Political Caricature and National Identity in Late Georgian England* (Aldershot: Ashgate, 2003); Vic Gattrell, *City of Laughter: Sex and Satire in Eighteenth-Century London* (London: Atlantic Books, 2006); Davey and Johns, *Broadsides*.
7. Andrews, *British Periodical Press*; Victoria E.M. Gardner, *The Business of News in England, 1760–1820* (Basingstoke: Palgrave Macmillan, 2016).
8. See for example the *Manchester Herald*. Its first issue on 31 March 1792 declared that 'The POLITICAL complexion of our Paper shall neither be MINISTERIAL nor ANTI-MINISTERIAL . . . we shall have little inducement to favour any cause but the *cause of the public*'. More realistically, it also acknowledged the 'dangerous

and unconstitutional extent of LIBEL' and warned that the paper was not keen to 'incur the lash of the law'. *Manchester Herald*, 31 March 1792.

9. Arthur Aspinall, *Politics and the Press, c. 1780–1850* (London: Home and Van Thal, 1949), pp. 74–5.

10. Patrick Robertson to his son William Robertson serving on the *Brilliant*, 25 June 1797, in Watt and Hawkins, eds, *Letters of Seamen*, p. 469.

11. NMM, AGC/H/28, Henry Harrop to his father, 14 August 1798; NMM, BGY/N/10, Edward Nosworthy to his wife, 2 October 1798.

12. Hannah Barker, *Newspapers, Politics and Public Opinion in Late Eighteenth-Century England* (Oxford: Oxford University Press, 1998), p. 31.

13. Susan E. Whyman, *The Pen and the People: English Letter Writers 1600–1800* (Oxford: Oxford University Press, 2009), p. 5. See also Lindsey O'Neil, *The Opened Letter: Networking in the Early Modern British World* (Philadelphia: University of Pennsylvania Press, 2015).

14. Richard Greenhalgh to his parents, 20 May 1800, NMRN, 546/84 (28), quoted in Watt and Hawkins, eds, *Letters of Seamen*, p. 174.

15. Helen Watt and Anne Hawkins have compiled a total of 255 letters of seamen and marines from the 1793–1815 period. See Watt and Hawkins, eds, *Letters of Seamen*.

16. Uglow, *In These Times*, p. 174.

17. Samuel Willcock to his brother, shortly after 21 April 1798, quoted in Watt and Hawkins, eds, *Letters of Seamen*, pp. 142–3.

18. Richard Greenhalgh to his parents, 24 July 1794, quoted in Watt and Hawkins, eds, *Letters of Seamen*, p. 95.

19. Vale, 'Post Office'; Watt and Hawkins, eds, *Letters of Seamen*, p. 10.

20. Kenneth Ellis, *The Post Office in the Eighteenth Century: A Study in Administrative History* (London, 1958), pp 60–72, 139. For sailors' awareness of their post being read see John Condren to Jonathan Greenwood, 28 April 1797, in Watt and Hawkins, eds, *Letters of Seamen*, p. 403; William Shoveller to his brother, 31 May 1797, in Watt and Hawkins, eds, *Letters of Seamen*, pp. 423–4.

21. Spavens, *Narrative*, p. vii.

22. *Nautical Economy; Or, Forecastle Recollections of Events during the Last War. Dedicated to the Brave Tars of Old England, By a Sailor, Politely Called by the Officers of the Navy, Jack Nasty-Face* (London: William Robinson, 1836), pp. iii–v.

23. John Nicol, *Adventures of John Nicol* (Edinburgh: William Blackwood, 1822), pp. 208–10.

24. See also Matilda Greig and Stephen Taylor, whose recent books offer robust defences of the use of memoirs: Matilda Greig, *Dead Men Telling Tales: Napoleonic War Veterans and the Military Memoirs Industry, 1808–1914* (Oxford: Oxford University Press 2021); Taylor, *Sons of the Waves*.

25. See John D. Byrn, ed., *Naval Courts Martial* (London: Navy Records Society, 2009).

26. Featherstone, 'Interrogating Court-Martial Narratives, p. 777.

BIBLIOGRAPHY

PRIMARY SOURCES

The National Archives (TNA)

ADM 1/100, Letters from Flag Officers, Channel Fleet: 1794, nos. 1–240.

ADM 1/107, Letters from Flag Officers, Channel Fleet: 1797, nos. 1–408.

ADM 1/727, Letters from Commanders-in-Chief, Nore: 1797, nos. 16–400.

ADM 1/811–12, Letters from Commanders-in-Chief, Plymouth: 1797, nos. 1–397, 403–925.

ADM 1/1508–9, Letters from Captains, Surnames B, 1793–4.

ADM 1/3683, Letters from the Solicitor of the Admiralty and other Crown legal officers, 1790–5.

ADM 1/4172, Letters from Secretary of State, 1797.

ADM 1/4186, Letters from Secretaries of State, 1801.

ADM 1/5119, Law Officers' Opinions, 1791.

ADM 1/5125, Petitions of Sailors, 1793–1801.

ADM 1/5330–62, 5486, 5488, Courts Martial Papers, 1792–1802.

ADM 2/125, Admiralty: Out-Letters. Lords Letters: Orders and Instructions, 1793–4.

ADM 2/604, Admiralty: Out-Letters. Secretary's Letters: Public Officers and Flag Officers, 1794.

ADM 2/1063–5, Admiralty: Out-Letters, Legal Correspondence, 1790–7.

ADM 2/1347, Admiralty: Out-Letters. Secret Letters, 1794.

ADM 7/302, Law Officers Opinions, 1793–5.

ADM 7/398, Register of protections from being pressed. Apprentices, Foreigners and others, 1795–1801.

ADM 8, Admiralty List Books, containing monthly returns compiled in the Admiralty Office for the information of the Board.

ADM 12/22, Analysis and digest of court martial convictions, arranged by offence: D-Dis.

ADM 12/24, Analysis and digest of court martial convictions, arranged by offence: J-N.

ADM 12/75, Admiralty Correspondence Digests, 1797.

HO 20/20, Home Office: General Correspondence before 1906, Corsica 1795–6.

HO 28/9–11, 13 Home Office: Admiralty Correspondence, 1793.

HO 28/23–4, Home Office: Admiralty Correspondence, 1797–8.

HO 42/16, 23–4, 27, 32, 41, 61–2, Home Office: Domestic Correspondence, 1790–1801.

HO 50/455, Home Office: Military Correspondence, Mediterranean Military Expedition, 1793.

PC 1/38/122, Papers relating to mutiny at the Nore, near Sheerness, Kent, 1797.

PC/1/40, Privy Council and Privy Council Office: Miscellaneous Unbound Papers.
WORK 4/18, Office of Works: Minutes, 1793–9.

The Caird Library, National Maritime Museum (NMM)

ADL/J/20, Impressment exemption certificate for Richard Dunn.
ADM/L/H121, Lieutenant's Log Book of Hope, 1796–1800, May–July 1799.
AGC/24/6, Joseph Samain to his parents, 18 October 1797. An Account of the Battle of Camperdown.
AGC/30/4/2, George Thompson to Mrs Thompson (his wife), 9 September 1797, written at Torbay.
AGC/A/6, William Atkinson to his mother, 4 July 1798.
AGC/B/26, John Jupp to his father and mother, 26 November 1798.
AGC/H/28, Henry Harrop to his father, 24 August 1798.
AGC/J/1, John Jervis, Lord St Vincent, to Horatio Nelson, 8 August 1801.
AGC/J/9, John Jupp to his father and mother, 26 November 1798.
AGC/W/2, Thomas Wilkes to his cousin, 15 August 1798.
AML/K/7, Letter of Attorney from Thomas Ottery, 20 October 1797.
BEL/1, port orderbook, Plymouth, 1798–9.
BGY/N/10, Edward Nosworthy to his wife, 2 October 1798.
BRP/18, Items about the mutiny at the Nore, April–September 1797.
COO/2/A, Admiral Sir Edward Campbell Rich Recollections concerning the Mutiny in the Channel Fleet in April, and at St Helens in May 1797, especially as relates to the transactions on board the London, 1825.
CRK, Croker Papers.
CUN/3, Sir Charles Cunningham, 'A Narrative of Occurrences that took place during the Mutiny at the Nore in the Months of May and June, 1797'.
HSR/B/12, William John Gore, 'Journal of the Mutiny at the Nore, 1797'.
HSR/Z/33/3, Richard Parker to Lord Northesk, 6 June 1797.
KEI: Papers of George Keith Elphinstone, 1st Viscount Keith, 1772–1815.
MID, Charles Middleton Papers.
MKH, Hood Family Papers.
MRK: Papers of Admiral John Markham.
NEP/3, Secret Service account book of the Admiralty, kept by Charles Wright, 1785–1804 signed by Evan Nepean.
PAR, William Parker Papers.
PLT/1/2, Impressment orders for John Platt of HMS *Alligator*, Thomas Affleck Esq. Commander.
RUSI/NM/235, Riou Family Papers.
RUSI/NM/203, Document by the mutineer's Committee of HMS *Swan* forbidding the officers to go ashore, 1 June 1797.
TUN/212, Philip Patton, 'Observations on Naval Mutiny, presented in 1795'.
WAR/7, Letters relating to the *Galatea*'s Mutiny 1797.
WYN/109/7, Philip Patton, Observations on Naval Mutiny, presented in April 1795.
XAGC/H/32, J. Harrison to Miss Butler, 16 March 1796.

The National Maritime Museum (NMM) Object Collections

AAA4498, Mug depicting 'Jack' Crawford, early nineteenth century.
BHC3100, 'Duncan Receiving the Surrender of de Winter at the Battle of Camperdown', 11 October 1797.

PAD3446, *John Crawford, Nailing the Flag to the Main top gallant mast head, on board the Venerable, October 11th 1797*, 20 November 1804.

PAD3447, Daniel Orme, *John Crawford of Sunderland Durham. The Sailor who Nailed the Flag to the Main Top Gallant mast head, on board the Venerable, Lord Duncan's Ship, after being once Shot away by the Dutch Admil de Winter. Drawn by Mr Orme on board for the Express purpose of Introducing into his Picture of Ld Duncan's Victory now Engraving by Subscription & which includes Portraits of the Admirals & Officers who so Gloriously Distinguished themselves on the ever Memorable 11th of October 1797*, 21 November 1797.

PAD3896, *Naval Pillar*, after John Flaxman (London: Richard Elsam and Thomas Tagg, 1804).

PAD6038, *An exact Representation of Launching the Prince of Wales Man of War, before their Majesties, at Portsmouth, 1794* (London, 1794).

PAH5441, *The Execution of Richard Parker* (London, 1797).

PBB7084, Naval Recruitment poster, c. 1797.

ZBA4377, Plate depicting 'Jack' Crawford, early nineteenth century.

The Huntington Library (HL)

DUN 1–104, Henry Dundas Papers.

HC, Hamond Collection.

HM 34180–207, 34208–83, Letters from Horatio Nelson.

HO 1–408, Letters from Admiral Richard Howe to Roger Curtis.

STW, Stowe Collection.

United States National Archives (USNA)

USNA, M30, Despatches from U.S. Ministers to Great Britain, 1791–1906, Roll No. 4, Despatches from U.S. Minsters to Great Britain, 10 August 1796–28 December 1797.

British Library

BL, Add. MS 23207, The Original Despatches communicating the principal victories obtained by the British Navy over the fleet of France and her allies in the course of the Revolutionary Wars, 1794–1806.

BL, Add. MS 35194, Correspondence between Admiral Alexander Hood, Viscount Bridport and Richard Howe, Lord Howe.

BL, Add. MS 35197, Sir Evan Nepean correspondence with Lord Bridport, 1796–7.

BL, MS G197, Declaration of Richard Parker, executed 30 June 1797.

Suffolk Record Office

SA/3/1/2/1, Correspondence between James and Martha Saumarez, 1797–1801.

Dorset History Centre

10H/109, 'Men Raised for the Navy', 1795–8.

Somerset Heritage Centre

DD\AH\61\1-2, Papers of Samuel Hood, 1794–5.

University of Cambridge Library

Sir Frederic Madden Ballad Collection.

Digital Sources

London Metropolitan Archives, Middlesex Sessions Papers – Justices Working Documents.
Old Bailey Proceedings Online (www.oldbaileyonline.org, version 8.0, 20 January 2021).
UK Parliamentary Papers, *Parliamentary Debates* and *Journals of the House of Commons*.

Newspapers and Periodicals

Albion and Evening Advertiser
Annual Register
Anti-Jacobin or Weekly Examiner
Bath Journal
Bell's Weekly Messenger
Bristol Gazette
Caledonian Mercury
Chester Chronicle
Cobbett's Parliamentary History
Courier and Evening Gazette
Critical Review
E. Johnson's British Gazette and Sunday Monitor
Evening Mail
Gentleman's Magazine
Hampshire Chronicle
Hereford Journal
Leeds Intelligencer
Lloyd's Evening Post
London Chronicle
London Evening Post
London Gazette
London Packet or New Lloyd's Evening Post
Morning Chronicle
Morning Herald
Morning Post
Newcastle Chronicle
Newcastle Courant
Norfolk Chronicle
Northampton Mercury
Observer
Oracle and Public Advertiser
Porcupine
Reading Mercury
St James's Chronicle or the British Evening Post
Star and Evening Examiner
Sun
Sussex Weekly Advertiser
Telegraph
The Times
Trewman's Exeter Flying Post

True Briton
Whitehall Evening Post
World
York Courant

Contemporary printed material

Anon, *Address to the Nation, By the Seamen At St Helen's* (Edinburgh: G. Mudie and Son, South Bridge, 1797).

Anon, *An Address to the Seamen in the British Navy* (London: W. Richardson, 1797).

Anon, *An Appeal to the Head and Heart of Every Man and Woman in Great Britain, Respecting The Threatened French Invasion, and the Importance of Immediately Coming Forward with Voluntary Contributions* (London: J. Wright, 1798).

Anon, *An impartial history of the war, from the commencement of the Revolution in France. Containing an Accurate Description of the Sea Engagements, Sieges, Battles, Expeditions and Conquests, of the Various Contending powers. Including an Account of the General Mutiny among the Seamen, at Spithead and the Nore. Together with a particular narrative of the rise, progress, and various events accompanying the Rebellion in Ireland* (Manchester: Sowler and Russell, 1799).

Anon, *A Letter to a Naval Officer from a Friend* (London: Murray and Highley, 1797).

Anon, *General Observations on the State of Affairs in Ireland and its Defence against an Invasion. By a Country Gentleman* (Dublin: George Johnson, 1797).

Anon, Instructions for Colonel Tate, in *Report of the Committee of the House of Commons, in consequence of the several motions relative to the treatment of prisoners of war. Including the whole of the examinations taken before the Committee, the correspondence relative to the exchange of prisoners; the instructions of Colonel Tate* (London, 1798).

Anon, *Invasion of Britain: An Address to the People of Great Britain, On the Subject of a French Invasion. Dulce et decorum est pro patria mori. By a patriot* (London: J. Fairburn, 1798).

Anon, *Memoirs of Richard Parker, the Mutineer: Together with an account at large of his trail by court martial, defence, sentence, and execution, and a narrative of the mutiny at the Nore and Sheerness from its commencement to its final termination* (London: George Cawthorn, 1797).

Anon, *Objections to the War Examined and Refuted by a Friend of Peace* (London, 1793).

Anon, *Official Documents and Interesting Particulars of the Glorious Victory Obtained over the French Fleet, on Sunday June 1, 1794, by the British Fleet, Under the Command of Admiral Lord Howe: Illustrated with an accurate engraving of the manoeuvering [sic] and line of battle of the two fleets on that memorable day* (London: J. Debrett, 1794).

Anon, *On the defence of Ireland: Including Observations on some other subjects connected therewith* (Dublin: P. Byrne, 1795).

Anon, *Peace!! The Result of our Naval Victories . . . From the commencement of the war to the signing Preliminaries, Oct 1, 1801, The British Tree of Liberty* (London: John Wallis, 28 September 1801)

Anon, *Report of the Committee of Secrecy of the House of Commons* (Dublin: John Ex Shaw, 1799).

Anon, *Songs, Duetts, Choruses, &c. in A New and Appropriate Entertainment, called the Glorious First of June. Performed for the first time, by His Majesty's Servants, at the Theatre Royal, Drury-Lane, on Wednesday, July 2ns 1794 for the Benefit of the Widows and Orphans of the brave Men who fell in the late Engagements under Earl Howe* (London: C. Lowndes, 1794, first edition).

Anon, *The British Hercules* (London, 1739).

Anon., *The hospital pupil's guide through London, in a seres [sic] of letters; from a pupil at St. Thomas's Hospital to his friend in the country; recommending the best manner of a pupils employing his time, and interspersed with amusing anecdotes relative to the history and oconomy of hospital's* (London, 1800).

Anon., *The Patriot Briton; or, England's Invasion* (London: Printed for Richard White, Printed by James Bateson, 1796).

Anon., *The victims of Tom Payne who were shot on the Hoe, or Love's Hill, Thursday, July 6, 1797* (Plymouth, 1797)

Anon., *The Whole Trial and Defence of Richard Parker* (London: G. Thompson, 1797).

Anon., *True and Particular Account of the Execution of Richard Parker* (London, 1797).

Aufrére, Anthony, *A Warning to Britons Against French Perfidy and Cruelty: Or a short account of the treacherous and inhuman Conduct of the French Officers and Soldiers towards the Peasants to Suabia, during the Invasion of Germany in 1796. Selected and translated from a well-authenticated German publication, By Anthony Aufrére, Esq. With an Address to the People of Great Britain, by the translator* (London: T. Cadell, Jun. and W. Davies in the Strand; and J. Wright and J. Hatcheard, in Piccadilly, 1798).

Bruce, John, *Historical Views of plans, for the Government of British India and the regulation of trade to the East Indies* (London, 1793).

Clarke, James Stanier, *Naval Sermons, preached on board His Majesty's Ship the Impetueux, in the Western Squadron, during its Services off Brest: to which is added a Thanksgiving Sermon for Naval Victories; preached at Park-Street Chapel, Grosvenor Square, Dec. 19 M,DCC,XCVII* (London: T. Payne, B. White, 1798).

Cochrane, James, *Thoughts Concerning the Proper Constitutional Principles of Manning & Recruiting the British Navy and Army* (York: Wilson, Spence, and Mawman, 1791).

Collings, Samuel, *Manning the Navy* (London: Bentley and Company, 1790).

Cruikshank, Isaac, *The Delegates in Council or Beggars on Horseback* (London: Samuel Fores, 9 June 1797).

— *Lord Howe they run or the British Tars giving the Carmignols a Dressing on Memorable 1ˢᵗ of June 1794* (London: Samuel Fores, 25 June 1794).

— *The Raft in Danger or the Republican Crew Disappointed* (London, 28 January 1798).

Dibdin, Thomas, *The mouth of the Nile; or, the glorious first of August, a musical entertainment; as performed at the Theatre-Royal, Covent Garden* (London: J. Barker, 1798).

Dighton, Robert, *An Accurate Representation of the Floating Machine Invented by the French for Invading England* (London, 1798).

Fores, Samuel, *A Correct Plan and Elevation of the Famous French Raft. Constructed on purpose of the Invasion of England* (1 February 1798).

Gillray, James, *Consequences of a Successful French Invasion*, Nos 1–4 (London: 1 March 1798).

— *End of the Irish invasion; – or – the destruction of the French armada* (London: Hannah Humphrey, 20 January 1797).

— *Fighting for the DUNGHILL: or Jack Tar settling Citoyen Francois* (London: Hannah Humphrey, 20 November 1798).

— *A French Hail Storm, – or – Neptune losing sight of the French fleet* (London: Hannah Humphrey, 10 December 1793).

— *The French Invasion; – or – John Bull, bombarding the Bum-Boats* (London: Hannah Humphrey, 1793).

— *Promis'd Horrors of the French INVASION or Forcible Reasons for negotiating a Regicide PEACE. Vide, the Authority of Edmund Burke* (London: Hannah Humphrey, 20 October 1796).

— *The Storm Rising; – or – The Republican Flotilla in Danger* (London: Hannah Humphrey, 1 February 1798).

Hanger, George, *Military Reflections on the Attack and Defence of the City of London* (1795).

Knox, Thomas, *Some account of the proceedings that took place on the landing of the French near Fishguard, in Pembroke shire, on the 22nd February 1797* . . . (London: A. Wilson, 1800).

Laurie, Robert and Whittle, James, *The Sailor and Long-Back'd Horse* (London, 10 June 1797).

Le Mesurier, Esq., Havilland, *Thoughts on a French Invasion with reference to the probability of its success, and the proper means of resisting it* (Edinburgh: Mundell and Sons, 1798).

Lloyd, Henry, *A Political and Military Rhapsody on the Invasion and Defence of Great Britain and Ireland. Illustrated with three copper-plates. By the Late General Lloyd. To which is annexed, an introduction, and a short account of the author's life* (London, 1790).

Mackenzie, John, *Impress of Seamen: Considerations on its legality, policy and operation. Applicable to the motion intended to be made in the House of Commons on Friday, 12 May, 1786 by William Pulteney, Esq.* (London: J. Debrett and J. French, 1786).

Nares, Robert, *Man's Best Right: A Solemn Appeal in the name of Religion* (London, 1793).

Oglethorpe, James, *Sailors Advocate* (London, 1728).

Paine, Thomas, *Rights of Man, Common Sense and Other Political Writings* (London: J.S. Jordan, 1791–2; Oxford: Oxford University Press, 1995, re-issued 2008).

Pigott, Charles, *A Political Dictionary: explaining the true meaning of words illustrated & exemplified in the lives, morals, character & conduct of* . . . *illustrious personages* (London: D.I. Eaten, 1795).

Ranby, John, *Short Hints on a French Invasion* (London: John Stockdale, 1794).

Rowlandson, Thomas, *Admiral Nelson Recreating with his Brave Tars after the Glorious Battle of the Nile* (London, 20 October 1798).

— *The Victorious Procession to St Pauls. Or Billy's Grand Triumphal Entry a Prelude* (London, 11 December 1797).

[Watson, Richard], *The Bishop of Llandaff's Thoughts on the French Invasion, Originally Addressed to the Clergy of his Diocese* (London: James Asperne, June 1798).

Wollstonecraft, Mary, *Maria: Or, the Wrongs of Women* (London, 1797).

Z [Hannah More], *CHEAP REPOSITORY. THE SHOPKEEPER turned SAILOR; OR, THE Folly of going out of our Element. SHEWING What a clever Man John the SHOPKEEPER was in his own Business, and what a rash Step he took in resolving to upon the Water* (Cheapside, London: J. Marshall, 1796/ Bath: S. Hazard, 1796 [published date inaccurate as refers to events in 1797]).

Published Primary Sources

Adeane, Jane Henrietta, ed., *The Girlhood of Maria Josepha Holroyd, Lady Stanley of Alderley: Recorded in Letters of a Hundred Years Ago, from 1776 to 1796* (London, 1896).

Anon., *Songs, Naval and National, of the Late Charles Dibdin; With a memoir and Addenda. Collected and arranged by Thomas Dibdin, with Characteristic sketches by George Cruickshank* (London: John Murray, 1841).

Austen, Jane, *Northanger Abbey* (London: John Murray, 1818; Oxford: Oxford University Press, 2003).

Bevan, A. Beckford and Wolryche-Whitmore, H. B., eds, *A Sailor of King George: The Journals of Captain Frederick Hoffman, RN, 1793–1814* (London: John Murray, 1901).

Brenton, Edward Pelham, *Life and Correspondence of John Jervis, Earl St Vincent*, 2 vols (London: Henry Colburn, 1838).

Bromley, J.S., ed., *The Manning of the Royal Navy: Selected Public Pamphlets 1693–1873* (London: Navy Records Society, 1974).

Byrn, John D., ed., *Naval Courts Martial* (London: Navy Records Society, 2009).

Childers, Spencer, ed., *A Mariner of England: An Account of the Career of William Richardson From Cabin Boy in the Merchant Service to Warrant Officer in the Royal Navy [1780 to 1819] As Told By Himself* (London: John Murray, 1908).

Collingwood, G.L. Newnham, ed., *A Selection From the Public and Private Correspondence of Vice-Admiral Lord Collingwood: Interspersed with Memoirs of his Life*, 2 vols (5th edition, containing some new letters, 1837).

Copeland, Thomas W., ed., *The Correspondence of Edmund Burke, 1729–1797*, 10 vols (Cambridge: Cambridge University Press, 1958–78).

Corbett, Julian and Richmond, H.W., eds, *The Private Papers of George, 2nd Earl Spencer*, 4 vols (London, 1913–24).

Croker, T. Crofton, *Popular Songs, Illustrative of the French Invasions of Ireland* (London: Percy Society, 1847).

Dann, John C., ed., *The Nagle Journal: A Diary of the Life of Jacob Nagle, Sailor, From the Year 1775 to 1841* (New York: Weidenfeld & Nicolson, 1988).

Farlick, Kenneth and Macintyre, Angus, eds, *The Diary of Joseph Farington*, 16 vols (New Haven, CT and London: Yale University Press, 1978–84).

Garstin, Crosbie, ed., *Samuel Kelly: An Eighteenth Century Seaman whose days have been few and evil, to which is added remarks etc. on places he visited during his pilgrimage in this wilderness* (New York: Frederick A. Stokes Company, 1925).

Gilson, J.P., ed., *Correspondence of Edmund Burke and William Windham* (Cambridge: Cambridge University Press, 1910).

Hamilton, R. Vesey and Laughton, John Knox, eds, *Recollections of James Anthony Gardner, Commander, R.N. 1775–1814* (London: Navy Records Society, 1906).

Hathaway, W.S., ed., *The Speeches of the Right Honourable William Pitt in the House of Commons*, 4 vols (London: Longman, Hurst, Rees and Orne, 1806).

Historical Manuscripts Commission, *The Manuscripts of J.B. Fortescue Esq. Preserved at Dropmore*, 2 vols (London, 1894).

Hughes, Edward, ed., *Private Correspondence of Admiral Lord Collingwood* (London: Navy Records Society, 1957).

Jackson, Thomas Sturges, ed., *Logs of the Great Sea Fights, 1794–1805*, 2 vols (London: Navy Records Society, 1899).

Jenkins, Herbert, ed., *The Windham Papers: The Life and Correspondence of the Rt. Honourable William Windham* (London: Maynard Small, 1913).

Jupp, Peter, ed., *The Letter Journal of George Canning, 1793–1795* (London: Camden Fourth Series, Vol. 41, 1991).

Laughton, John Knox, *The Naval Miscellany*, Volume 1 (London: Navy Records Society, 1902).

Lavery, Brian, ed., *Shipboard Life and Organization 1731–1815* (London: Navy Records Society, 1998).

Leech, Samuel, *Thirty Years From Home* (Boston: Tappan & Dennet, 1843).

Lewis, Michael A., *A Narrative of My Professional Adventures (1790–1839) By William Henry Dillon*, 2 vols (London: Navy Records Society, 1953).

Lloyd, Christopher, ed., *The Keith Papers: Selected from the Papers of Admiral Viscount Keith*, 3 vols (London: Navy Records Society, 1926–55).

Manners, John Henry (Duke of Rutland), *Journal of a tour through north and south Wales, the Isle of Man* (London: J. Triphook, 1805).

Morrison, Alfred, ed., *The Collection of Autograph Letters . . . The Hamilton and Nelson Papers*, 2 vols (London, 1893–4).

Morriss, Roger, ed., *The Channel Fleet and the Blockade of Brest, 1793–1801* (London: Ashgate for Navy Records Society, 2001).

Naish, G.P.B., ed., *Nelson's Letters to His Wife and Other Documents 1785–1831* (London, 1958).

Nicol, John, *The Life and Adventures of John Nicol, Mariner* (London: William Blackwood, 1822).

Nicolas, Nicholas Harris, ed., *The Dispatches and Letters of Vice Admiral Lord Viscount Nelson*, 7 vols (Cambridge: Cambridge University Press, 2011; first published 1844–6).

Parsons, George S., ed., *Nelson Reminiscences* (London, 1843).

Pennington, Montagu, ed., *Letters from Mrs Elizabeth Carter to Mrs Montagu, between the years 1755 and 1800, chiefly upon Literary and Moral Subjects*, 3 vols (London: F.C. & J. Rivington, 1817).

Rattenbury, John, *Memoirs of a Smuggler, compiled from his diary and journal* (Sidmouth: J. Harvey, 1837).

Robinson, William, *Nautical Economy; Or, Forecastle Recollections of Events during the Last War. Dedicated to the Brave Tars of Old England, By a Sailor, Politely Called by the Officers of the Navy, Jack Nasty-Face* (London: William Robinson, 1836).

Rose, Susan, ed., *The Naval Miscellany*, Volume 6 (London: Navy Records Society, 2003).

Shephard, William, ed., *Poems and Other Writings by the Late Edward Rushton* (London: Effingham Wilson, 1824).

Spavens, William, *The Narrative of William Spavens*, introduction by N.A.M. Rodger (London: Chatham, 1998).

Stanhope, Hester, *Memoirs of the Lady Hester Stanhope as Related by Herself in Conversations with her Physician; Comprising her Opinions and Anecdotes of Some of the Most Remarkable Persons of Her Time*, 3 vols (London: Henry Colburn, 1845).

Trotter, Thomas, *Medicina Nautica: An Essay on the Diseases of Seamen* (London, 1797).

— *A Practicable Plan for Manning the Royal Navy and Preserving our Maritime Ascendancy, without Impressment* (Newcastle: Longman, 1819).

Tucker, Jedediah Stephens, ed., *Memoirs of Admiral the Right Hon. The Earl of St Vincent*, 2 vols (London: Richard Bentley, 1844).

Ward, A.W., ed., *The Works of Mrs Gaskell*, Vol. 6: *Sylvia's Lovers* (London: John Murray, 1920).

Watt, Helen and Hawkins, Anne, eds, *Letters of Seamen in the Wars with France, 1793–1815* (Woodbridge: Boydell Press, 2016).

SECONDARY SOURCES

Adkins, Roy and Adkins, Lesley, *Jack Tar: The Men Who Made Nelson's Navy* (London: Little, Brown, 2008).

Aldous, Grahame, 'The Law Relating to the Distribution of Prize Money in the Royal Navy', Unpublished PhD thesis, King's College London (2020).

Andrews, Donna, *Philanthropy and Police: London Charity in the Eighteenth Century*. (Princeton, NJ: Princeton University Press, 1989).

Andrews, Stuart, *The British Periodical Press and the French Revolution, 1789–99* (Basingstoke: Palgrave, 2000).

Anstey, Roger, *The Atlantic Slave Trade and British Abolition 1760–1810* (Atlantic Highlands, NJ: Humanities Press, 1975).

Armitage, David and Subrahmanyam, Sanjay, eds, *The Age of Revolutions in Global Context, c. 1760–1840* (Basingstoke: Palgrave Macmillan, 2010).

Aspinall, Arthur, *Politics and the Press, c. 1780–1850* (London: Home and Van Thal, 1949).

Barker, Hannah, *Newspapers, Politics and Public Opinion in Late Eighteenth-Century England* (Oxford: Oxford University Press, 1998).

Barrell, John, *Imagining the King's Death: Figurative Treason, Fantasies of Regicide 1793–1796* (Oxford: Oxford University Press, 2000).

— *Spirit of Despotism: Invasion of Privacy in the 1790s* (Oxford: Oxford University Press, 2006).

Barrell, John and Mee, Jon, eds, *Trials for Treason and Sedition, 1792–1794*, 5 vols (London: Pickering and Chatto, 2006–7).

Bartlett, Thomas, Dickson, David, Keogh, Dáire Keogh and Whelan, Kevin, eds, *1798: A Bicentenary Perspective* (Dublin: Four Courts Press, 2003).

Baugh, Daniel A., 'Great Britain's "Blue-Water" Policy, 1689–1815', *International History Review*, Vol. 10, No. 1 (1998), pp. 33–58.

Bayly, C.A., *The Birth of the Modern World, 1780–1914: Global Connections and Comparisons* (Oxford: Oxford University Press, 2004).

— *Imperial Meridian: The British Empire and the World, 1780–1830* (London: Routledge, 1989).

Begiato, Joanne, *Manliness in Britain, 1760–1900: Bodies, Emotion and Material Culture* (Manchester: Manchester University Press, 2020).

Beiner, Guy, *Remembering the Year of the French: Irish Folk History and Social Memory* (Madison, WI: University of Wisconsin Press, 2007).

Bell, David A., *The First Total War: Napoleon's Europe and the Birth of Modern Warfare* (London: Bloomsbury, 2007).

Benjamin, Daniel K., 'Golden Harvest: The British Naval Prize System, 1793–1815', Clemson University and PERC (unpub.), 2009.

Berry, Helen, *Orphans of Empire* (Oxford: Oxford University Press, 2019).

Bickham, Troy and Abbey, Ian, '"The Greatest Encouragement to Seamen": Pay, Families, and the State in Britain during the French Wars, 1793–1815', *Journal of Social History*, Vol. 56, No. 1 (2022), pp. 1–31.

Blackburn, Robin, *The Overthrow of Colonial Slavery, 1776–1848* (London: Verso, 1988).

Blackstock, Allan and Magennis, Eoin, eds, *Politics and Political Culture in Britain and Ireland 1750–1850* (Belfast: Ulster Historical Foundation, 2007).

Blake, Richard, *Evangelicals in the Royal Navy 1775–1815* (Woodbridge: Boydell Press, 2008).

Bohstedt, John, *The Politics of Provisions: Food Riots, Moral Economy, and Market Transition in England, c. 1550–1850* (Aldershot: Routledge, 2010).

Bolster, W. Jeffrey, *Black Jacks: African American Seamen in the Age of Sail* (Cambridge, MA: Harvard University Press, 1998).

Bowley, A.L., 'The Statistics of Wages in the United Kingdom during the Last Hundred Years. Part I. Agricultural Wages', *Journal of the Royal Statistical Society*, Vol. 61 (1898), pp. 702–22.

Bradley, James E., *Popular Politics and the American Revolution in England: Petitions, the Crown and Public Opinion* (Mercer, GA: Mercer University Press, 1986).

Brewer, John, *The Sinews of Power: War, Money and the English State, 1688–1783* (New York and London: Routledge, 1989).

Brockliss, Laurence, Cardwell, John and Moss, Michael, *Nelson's Surgeon: William Beatty, Naval Medicine and the Battle of Trafalgar* (Oxford: Oxford University Press, 2005).

Brown, Anthony, 'The Nore Mutiny: Sedition or Ship's Biscuit?', *Mariner's Mirror*, Vol. 92 (2006), pp. 60–74.

Brown, Christopher Leslie, *Moral Capital: Foundations of Abolitionism* (Chapel Hill, NC: University of North Carolina Press, 2006).

Brown, Randy, *Surviving Slavery in the British Caribbean* (Philadelphia: University of Pennsylvania Press, 2017).

Brown, Vincent, *Tacky's Revolt: The Story of an Atlantic Slave War* (Cambridge, MA: Belknap Press, 2020).

Brunsman, Denver, *The Evil Necessity: British Naval Impressment in the Eighteenth-Century Atlantic World* (Charlottesville and London: University of Virginia Press, 2013).

Buchan, Bruce, 'Civility at Sea: From Murmuring to Mutiny', *Republic of Letters*, Vol. 5, No. 2 (2017), pp. 1–14.

Buckley, Roger N., *Slaves in Red Coats: The British West India Regiments, 1795–1815* (New Haven, CT: Yale University Press, 1979).

Burgess, Glenn and Festenstein, Matthew, *English Radicalism, 1550–1850* (Cambridge: Cambridge University Press, 2007).

Burnard, Trevor, *Jamaica in the Age of Revolution* (Philadelphia: University of Pennsylvania Press, 2020).

Buscemi, Francesco, 'The Importance of Being Revolutionary: Oath-Taking and the "Feeling Rules" of Violence (1789–1794)', *French History*, Vol. 33, No. 2 (2019), pp. 218–35.

Butler, Marilyn, ed., *Burke, Paine, Godwin and the Revolution Controversy* (Cambridge: Cambridge University Press, 1984).

Byrn, John D., *Crime and Punishment in the Royal Navy: Discipline on the Leeward Islands Station 1784–1812* (Aldershot: Scholar Press, 1989).

Candlin, Kit, 'The Role of the Enslaved in the "Fedon Rebellion" of 1795', *Slavery and Abolition*, Vol. 39, No. 4 (2018), pp. 685–707.

Cannadine, David, ed., *Admiral Lord Nelson: Context and Legacy* (London: Palgrave Macmillan, 2005).

— ed., *Empire, the Sea and Global History: Britain's Maritime World, c. 1760–c. 1840* (Basingstoke: Palgrave Macmillan, 2007).

Caputo, Sara, 'Alien Seamen in the British Navy, British Law, and the British State, c. 1793–c. 1815', *Historical Journal*, Vol. 62, No. 4 (2019), pp. 685–707.

— 'Scotland, Scottishness, British Integration and the Royal Navy, 1793–1815', *Scottish Historical Review*, Vol. 97, No. 1 (2018), pp. 85–118.

Cardew, F.J., 'The Taking of Tobago 1793', *Journal for the Royal United Services Institution*, Vol. 70 (1925), pp. 411–14.

Cavell, Sam, *Midshipmen and Quarterdeck Boys in the British Navy, 1771–1831* (Woodbridge: Boydell Press, 2012).

Charlesworth, Andrew, Gilbert, David and Randall, Adrian, eds, *An Atlas of Industrial Protest in Britain, 1750–1990* (London: Macmillan, 1996).

Chase, Malcolm, *Early Trade Unionism: Fraternity, Skill and the Politics of Labour* (Aldershot: Routledge, 2000).

Chickering, Roger and Förster, Stig, eds, *War in an Age of Revolution, 1775–1815* (Cambridge: Cambridge University Press, 2010).

Christie, Ian R., 'Conservatism and Stability in British Society', in Mark Philp, ed., *The French Revolution and British Popular Politics* (Cambridge: Cambridge University Press, 1991), pp. 169–87.

— *Stress and Stability in Late Eighteenth-Century Britain, Reflections on the British Avoidance of Revolution* (Oxford: Clarendon Press, 1984).

Clark, Gregory, 'Farm Wages and Living Standards in the Industrial Revolution: England, 1670–1869', *Economic History Review*, Vol. 54, No. 3 (August 2001), pp. 477–505.

Clemit, Pamela, ed., *The Cambridge Companion to British Literature of the French Revolution in the 1790s* (Cambridge: Cambridge University Press, 2011).

Coad, Jonathan, *Support for the Fleet: Architecture and Engineering of the Royal Navy's Bases 1700–1914* (London: English Heritage, 2013).

Coats, Ann and MacDougall, Philip, eds, *The Naval Mutinies of 1797: Unity and Perseverance* (Woodbridge: Boydell Press, 2011).

Cole, Gareth, *Arming the Royal Navy, 1793–1815: The Office of Ordnance and the State* (London: Pickering and Chatto, 2012).

Coleman, Terry, *Nelson: The Man and the Legend* (London: Bloomsbury, 2002).

Colley, Linda, *Britons: Forging the Nation 1707–1837* (New Haven, CT and London: University of Yale Press, 1992).

Colville, Quintin and Davey, James, eds, *Nelson, Navy and Nation* (London: Conway, 2013).

— eds, *A New Naval History* (Manchester: Manchester University Press, 2019).

Conley, Mary A., *From Jack Tar to Union Jack: Representing Naval Manhood in the British Empire, 1870–1918* (Manchester: Manchester University Press, 2009).

Consolvo, Charles, 'The Prospects and Promotion of British Naval Officers 1793–1815', *Mariner's Mirror*, Vol. 91, No. 2 (2005), pp. 137–59.

Convertito, Coriann, 'The Health of British Seamen in the West Indies, 1770–1806', Unpublished PhD thesis, University of Exeter (2011).

Cookson, J.E., *The British Armed Nation 1793–1815* (Oxford: Clarendon Press, 1997).

— 'The English Volunteer Movement of the French Wars 1793–1815: Some Contexts', *Historical Journal*, Vol. 32, No. 4 (1989), pp. 867–91.

Cormack, William S., *Revolution & Political Conflict in the French Navy, 1789–1794* (Cambridge: Cambridge University Press, 1995).

Costello, Kevin, 'Habeas Corpus and Military and Naval Impressment, 1756–1816', *Journal of Legal History*, Vol. 29 (2008), pp. 215–51.

Costello, Ray, *Black Salt: Seafarers of African Descent on British Ships* (Liverpool: Liverpool University Press, 2012).

Cox, Edward L., 'Fedon's Rebellion 1795–96: Causes and Consequences', *Journal of Negro History*, Vol. 67, No. 1 (1982), pp. 7–19.

Cox Jensen, Oscar, *Napoleon and British Song, 1797–1822* (London: Palgrave Macmillan, 2015).

Cozens, Joseph, 'The Experience of Soldiering: Civil–Military Relations and Popular Protest in England', Unpublished PhD thesis, University of Essex (2020).

Craciun, Adriana and Schaffer, Simon, eds, *The Material Cultures of Enlightenment Arts and Sciences* (London: Palgrave, 2016).

Craton, Michael, *Testing the Chains: Resistance to Slavery in the British West Indies* (Ithaca, NY and London: Cornell University Press, 1982).

Crook, Malcolm, *Toulon in War and Revolution: From the Ancien Regime to the Restoration, 1750–1820* (Manchester: Manchester University Press, 1991).

Crowhurst, Patrick, *The French War on Trade: Privateering, 1793–1815* (London: Scholar Press, 1989).

Curran, Stuart, 'Women Readers, Women Writers', in Stuart Curran, ed., *The Cambridge Companion to British Romanticism*, 2nd edition (Cambridge: Cambridge University Press, 2010), pp. 177–95.

Curtin, Philip D., *The Atlantic Slave Trade: A Census* (Madison, WI: University of Wisconsin Press, 1969).

Dancy, J. Ross, *The Myth of the Press Gang: Volunteers, Impressment and the Naval Manpower Problem in the Late Eighteenth Century* (Woodbridge: Boydell Press, 2015).

Darwin, John, *After Tamerlaine: The Rise and Fall of Global Empires* (London: Penguin, 2007).

Davey, James, *In Nelson's Wake: The Navy and the Napoleonic Wars* (London and New Haven, CT: Yale University Press, 2015).

— 'Securing the Sinews of Sea Power: British Intervention in the Baltic 1780–1815', *International History Review*, Vol. 33, No. 2 (2011), pp. 161–84.

— 'Singing for the Nation: Balladry, Naval Recruitment, and the Language of Patriotism in Eighteenth-Century Britain', *Mariner's Mirror*, Vol. 103, No. 1 (2017), pp. 43–66.

— *The Transformation of British Naval Strategy: Seapower and Supply in Northern Europe, 1808–1812* (Woodbridge: Boydell Press, 2012).

Davey, James and Johns, Richard, *Broadsides: Caricature and the Navy, 1756–1815* (Barnsley: Seaforth, 2012).

Davids, Karel, 'Seamen's Organizations and Social Protest in Europe, c. 1300–1825', *International Review of Social History*, Vol. 39, Supplement 2: Before the Unions: Wage Earners and Collective Action in Europe, 1300–1850 (1994), pp. 145–69.

Davies, J. D., *Britannia's Dragon: A Naval History of Wales* (Cheltenham: History Press, 2013).

Davis, Michael T., ed., *Crowd Actions in Britain and France from the Middle Ages to the Modern World* (Basingstoke: Palgrave Macmillan, 2015).

— ed., *London Corresponding Society, 1792–1799*, 6 vols (London: Pickering and Chatto, 2002).

Davis, Michael T. and Pickering, Paul A., eds, *Unrespectable Radicals? Popular Politics in the Age of Reform* (Abingdon: Ashgate, 2008).

Davis, Ralph, *The Rise of the English Shipping Industry in the Seventeenth and Eighteenth Centuries* (Liverpool: Liverpool University Press, 2012).

Dawson, Kevin, 'Enslaved Ship Pilots in the Age of Revolutions: Challenging Notions of Race and Slavery between the Boundaries of Land and Sea', *Journal of Social History*, Vol. 47, No. 1 (2013), pp. 71–100.

Deane, Phyllis and Cole, W.A., *British Economic Growth, 1688–1959* (Cambridge: Cambridge University Press, 1962).

Delgada, Melvin, *State-Sanctioned Violence: Advancing a Social Work Social Justice Agenda* (Oxford: Oxford University Press, 2020).

Dellarosa, Franca, *Talking Revolution: Edward Rushton's Rebellious Poetics, 1782–1814* (Liverpool: Liverpool University Press, 2014).

Denny, P., Buchan, B., Ellison, D. and Crawley, K., eds, *Sound, Space and Civility in the British World, 1700–1850* (London and New York: Routledge, 2019).

Desan, Suzanne, Hunt, Lynn and Nelson, William Max, eds, *The French Revolution in Global Perspective* (Ithaca, NY: Cornell University Press, 2013).

Devereaux, S., 'The City and the Sessions Paper: "Public Justice" in London, 1770–1800', *Journal of British Studies*, Vol. 35, No. 4 (October 1996), pp. 466–503.

Dickinson, H.T., *British Radicalism and the French Revolution* (London: Wiley-Blackwell, 1985).

Dinwiddy, J.R., *Radicalism and Reform in Britain, 1780–1850* (London: Hambledon Press, 1992).

Donald, Diana, *The Age of Caricature: Satirical Prints in the Reign of George III* (New Haven, CT and London: Yale University Press, 1997).

Doyle, William, *The Oxford History of the French Revolution* (Oxford: Oxford University Press, 1989).

Dozier, Robert R., *For King, Constitution and Country* (Lexington, KY: University Press of Kentucky, 1983).

Drescher, Seymour, *Capitalism and Antislavery: British Mobilization in Comparative Perspective* (Oxford: Oxford University Press, 1997).

— *Econocide: British Slavery in the Era of Abolition* (Chapel Hill, NC: University of North Carolina Press, 1977; 2nd edition, 2010).

Dubois, Laurent, *A Colony of Citizens: Revolution & Slave Emancipation in the French Caribbean, 1787–1804* (Chapel Hill, NC: University of North Carolina Press, 2004).

Duffy, Michael, 'British Naval Intelligence and Bonaparte's Egyptian Expedition of 1798', *Mariner's Mirror*, Vol. 89 (1998), pp. 278–90.

— *Parameters of British Naval Power* (Liverpool: Liverpool University Press, 1992).

— *Soldiers, Sugar and Seapower: The British Expeditions to the West Indies and the War Against Revolutionary France* (Oxford: Clarendon Press, 1987).

— ' "A Particular Service": The British Government and the Dunkirk Expedition of 1793', *English Historical Review*, Vol. 91 (1976), pp. 529–54.

Duffy, Michael and Morriss, Roger, eds, *The Glorious First of June 1794: A Naval Battle and Its Aftermath* (Exeter: University of Exeter Press, 2001).

Dugan, James, *The Great Mutiny* (New York: Putnam, 1965).

Easton, Callum, 'Counter-Theatre during the 1797 Fleet Mutinies', *International Review of Social History*, Vol. 64 (2019), pp. 389–411.

— 'A Social and Economic History of the 1797 Fleet Mutinies at Spithead and the Nore', Unpublished PhD thesis, University of Cambridge (2020).

— 'The Unusual Afterlife of Richard Parker', *History Today* (October 2017), online.

Eder, Markus, *Crime and Punishment in the Royal Navy of the Seven Year's War, 1755–1763* (Aldershot: Ashgate, 2004).

Ehrman, John, *The Younger Pitt*, 3 vols (London: Little, Brown, 1969–96).

Elliott, Marianne, *Partners in Revolution: The United Irishmen and France* (New Haven, CT and London: Yale University Press, 1982).

Ellis, Kenneth, *The Post Office in the Eighteenth Century: A Study in Administrative History* (Oxford: Oxford University Press, 1958).

Eltis, D., Engerman, S. L., Drescher, S. and Richardson, D., eds, *The Cambridge World History of Slavery, 1804–AD 2016*, Vol. 4 (Cambridge: Cambridge University Press, 2017).

Emsley, Clive, 'An Aspect of Pitt's "Terror": Prosecutions for Sedition during the 1790s', *Social History*, Vol. 6, No. 2 (May 1981), pp. 155–84.

— *British Society and the French Wars 1793–1815* (London: Macmillan, 1979).

— 'The Home Office and Its Sources of Information and Investigation, 1791–1801', *English Historical Review*, Vol. 94 (1979), pp. 532–61.

Ennis, Daniel James, *Enter the Press Gang: Naval Impressment in Eighteenth Century British Literature* (Newark: University of Delaware Press, 2002).

Evans, Chris, *Debating the Revolution: Britain in the 1790s* (London: I.B. Tauris, 2006).

Farrell, Stephen, Unwin, Melanie and Walvin, James, eds, *The British Slave Trade: Abolition, Parliament and People* (Edinburgh: Edinburgh University Press, 2007).

Favret, Mary, 'War Correspondence: Reading Romantic War', *Prose Studies: History, Theory, Criticism*, Vol. 19, No. 2 (1996), pp. 173–85.

Featherstone, David, 'Counter-Insurgency, Subalternity and Spatial Relations: Interrogating Court-Martial Narratives of the Nore Mutiny of 1797', *South African Historical Journal*, Vol. 61, No. 4 (2009), pp. 766–87.

Fedorak, Charles John, 'Catholic Emancipation and the Resignation of William Pitt in 1801', *Albion: A Quarterly Journal Concerned with British Studies*, Vol. 24, No. 1 (1992), pp. 49–64.

Feinstein, Charles H., 'Pessimism Perpetuated: Real Wages and the Standard of Living in Britain During and After the Industrial Revolution', *Journal of Economic History*, Vol. 58, No. 3 (September 1998), pp. 625–58.

— 'Wage-Earnings in Great Britain during the Industrial Revolution', in Iain Begg and S.G.B. Henry, eds, *Applied Economics and Public Policy* (Cambridge: Cambridge University Press, 1998), pp. 181–208.

Fick, Carolyn E., *The Making of Haiti: The Saint Domingue Revolution from Below* (Knoxville: University of Tennessee Press, 1990).

Forrest, Alan, Hagerman, Karen and Rendell, Jane, eds, *Soldiers, Citizens and Civilians: Experiences and Perceptions of the Revolutionary and Napoleonic Wars, 1790–1820* (Basingstoke: Palgrave Macmillan, 2009).

Foucault, Michel, 'Of Other Spaces', *Diacritics*, Vol. 16 (1986), p. 27.

Foy, Charles S., 'The Royal Navy's Employment of Black Mariners and Maritime Workers, 1754–1783', *International Journal of Maritime History*, Vol. 28, No. 1 (2016), pp. 6–35.

Frykman, Niklas, *The Bloody Flag: Mutiny in the Age of Atlantic Revolution* (Oakland: University of California Press, 2020).

— 'Connections between Mutinies in European Navies', *International Review of Social History*, Vol. 58 (2013), pp. 87–107.

— 'The Mutiny on Hermione: Warfare, Revolution, and Treason in the Royal Navy', *Journal of Social History*, Vol. 44, No. 1 (2010), pp. 159–87.

Frykman, Niklas, Anderson, Clare, van Voss, Lex Heerma and Rediker, Marcus, 'Mutiny and Maritime Radicalism', *International Review of Social History*, Vol. 58 (2013), pp. 1–14.

Fury, Cheryl A., *The Social History of Seamen 1650–1815* (Woodbridge: Boydell Press, 2017).

Gaffield, Julia, *Haitian Connections in the Atlantic World: Recognition after Revolution* (Chapel Hill, NC: University of North Carolina Press, 2015).

Gardiner, Robert, ed., *Fleet Battle and Blockade: The French Revolutionary War 1793–1797* (London: Chatham, 1996).

— ed., *Nelson Against Napoleon: From the Nile to Copenhagen, 1798–1801* (London: Chatham, 1997).

Gardner, Victoria E.M., *The Business of News in England, 1760–1820* (Basingstoke: Palgrave Macmillan, 2016).

Garrigus, John D., *Before Haiti: Race and Citizenship in French Saint-Domingue* (New York: Macmillan, 2006).

Gattrell, Vic, *City of Laughter: Sex and Satire in Eighteenth-Century London* (London: Atlantic Books, 2006).

Gee, Austin, *The British Volunteer Movement 1794–1814* (Oxford: Clarendon Press, 2003).

Geggus, David, ed., *The Impact of the Haitian Revolution in the Atlantic World* (Columbia, SC: University of South Carolina Press, 2001).

— *Slavery, War and Revolution: The British Occupation of Saint Domingue, 1793–1798* (Oxford: Oxford University Press).

Giles, Lee-Jane, '"All That You Refuse to Do Is Mutiny": Contextualising the Marine Mutiny at Plymouth, 1797', Unpublished BA thesis, University of Plymouth (2017).

Gill, Conrad, *The Naval Mutinies of 1797* (Manchester: Manchester University Press, 1913).

Gill, Ellen, *Naval Families, War and Duty in Britain, 1740–1820* (Woodbridge: Boydell Press, 2016).

Gilmartin, Kevin, 'In the Theatre of Counterrevolution: Loyalist Association and Conservative Opinion in the 1790s', *Journal of British Studies*, Vol. 41 (2002), pp. 291–328.

— *Writing Against Revolution: Literary Conservatism in Britain, 1790–1832* (Cambridge: Cambridge University Press, 2007).

Glete, Jan, *Navies and Nations: Warships, Navies and State Building in Europe and America, 1500–1860*, 2 vols (Stockholm: Almqvist and Wiksell, 1994).

Gonzalez, Johnhenry, *Maroon Nation: A History of Revolutionary Haiti* (New Haven, CT and London: Yale University Press, 2019).

Gott, Richard, *Britain's Empire: Resistance, Repression and Revolt* (London: Verso, 2011).

Graham, Aaron and Walsh, Patrick, eds, *The British Fiscal-Military States, 1660–c. 1783* (London: Routledge, 2016).

Grainger, John, *The Amiens Truce: Britain and Bonaparte, 1801–1803* (Woodbridge: Boydell Press, 2003).

Gregory, Desmond, *The Ungovernable Rock: A History of the Anglo-Corsican Kingdom and Its Role in Britain's Mediterranean Strategy during the Revolutionary War (1793–97)* (London: Associated University Presses, 1985).

Greig, Matilda, *Dead Men Telling Tales: Napoleonic War Veterans and the Military Memoirs Industry, 1808–1914* (Oxford: Oxford University Press 2021).

Griffin, Carl, *The Politics of Hunger: Protest, Poverty and Policy in England, c.1750–c.1840* (Manchester: Manchester University Press, 2020).

— *The Rural War: Captain Swing and the Politics of Protest* (Manchester: Manchester University Press, 2012).

— 'The Violent Captain Swing?', *Past & Present*, Vol. 209, No. 1 (November 2010), pp. 149–80.

Gutteridge, Leonard F., *Mutiny: A History of Naval Insurrection* (Annapolis, MD: Naval Institute Press, 1992).

Hall, Christopher D., *British Strategy in the Napoleonic War, 1803–1815* (Manchester: Manchester University Press, 1992).

Halliday, Paul D., *Habeas Corpus: From England to Empire* (Cambridge, MA: Belknap Press of Harvard University Press, 2010).

Hamilton, Douglas, ' "A Most Active, Enterprising Officer": Captain John Perkins, the Royal Navy and the Boundaries of Slavery and Liberty in the Caribbean', *Slavery and Abolition*, Vol. 39, No. 1 (2018), pp. 80–100.

Hamilton, Douglas and McAleer, John, eds, *Islands and the British Empire in the Age of Sail* (Oxford: Oxford University Press, 2021).

Hampsher-Monk, Ian, ed., *The Impact of the French Revolution: Texts from Britain in the 1790s* (Cambridge: Cambridge University Press, 2005).

Hanley, Keith and Selden, Raman, eds, *Revolution and English Romanticism: Politic and Rhetoric* (Hemel Hempstead: St Martin's Press, 1990).

Harding, Richard, ed., *Naval History 1650–1850* (London: Routledge, 2006).

Hatcher, J. and Stephenson, J.Z., eds, *Seven Centuries of Unreal Wages* (London: Palgrave, 2018).

Hay, Douglas and Rogers, Nicholas, *Eighteenth Century English Society* (Oxford: Oxford University Press, 1997).

Hazareesingh, Sudhir, *Black Spartacus: The Epic Life of Toussaint Louverture* (London: Allen Lane, 2020).

Heinsen, J., ' "Nothing but Noyse": The Political Complexities of English Maritime Soundscapes', *Radical History Review*, Vol. 121 (2015), pp. 106–22.

Herreros, Francisco, ' "The Full Weight of the State": The Logic of Random State-Sanctioned Violence', *Journal of Peace Research*, Vol. 43, No. 6 (2006), pp. 671–89.

Hewitt, Rachel, *A Revolution of Feeling: The Decade That Forged the Modern Mind* (London: Granta, 2017).

Hilton, Boyd, *A Mad, Bad, and Dangerous People: England 1783–1846* (Oxford: Clarendon Press, 2006).

Hitchens, Christopher, *Thomas Paine's Rights of Man: A Biography* (London: Atlantic Books, 2006).

Hobsbawm, Eric, *The Age of Revolution, 1789–1848* (London: Weidenfeld & Nicolson, 1962).

Holland Rose, J., *Lord Hood and the Defence of Toulon* (Cambridge: Cambridge University Press, 1922).

Hoock, Holger, *Empires of the Imagination: Politics, War, and the Arts in the British World, 1750–1850* (London: Profile, 2010).

Humphries, Jane and Wiesdorf, Jacob, 'Unreal Wages? Real Income and Economic Growth in England, 1260–1850', *The Economic Journal*, Vol. 129 (2019), pp. 2867–87.

Hunt, Tamara L., *Defining John Bull: Political Caricature and National Identity in Late Georgian England* (Aldershot: Ashgate, 2003).

Huzzey, Richard, 'Petitions, Parliament and Political Culture: Petitioning the House of Commons, 1780–1918', *Past and Present*, Vol. 248, No. 1 (2020), pp. 123–64.

— ed., *Pressure and Parliament: From Civil War to Civil Society* (London: John Wiley, 2018).

Innes, Joanna and Philp, Mark, eds, *Re-imagining Democracy in the Age of Revolutions* (Oxford: Oxford University Press, 2013).

Israel, Jonathan, *Revolutionary Ideas: An Intellectual History of the French Revolution from The Rights of Man to Robespierre* (Princeton, NJ: Princeton University Press, 2014).

Jackson, Alvin, ed., *The Oxford Handbook of Modern Irish History* (Oxford: Oxford University Press, 2014).

Jaffe, James A., 'Industrial Arbitration, Equity, and Authority in England, 1800–1850', *Law and History Review*, Vol. 18, No. 3 (2000), pp. 525–58.

Jaffer, Aaron, *Lascars and Indian Ocean Seafaring, 1780–1860: Shipboard Life, Unrest and Mutiny* (Woodbridge: Boydell Press, 2015).

James, Frank A.J.L., 'Making Money from the Royal Navy in the Late Eighteenth Century: Charles Kerr on Antigua "Breathing the True Spirit of a West India Agent"', *Mariner's Mirror*, Vol. 107, No. 4 (November 2021), pp. 402–19.

James, William, *The Naval History of Great Britain from the Declaration of War by France in 1793 to the Accession of George IV*, 6 vols (London: Richard Bentley, 1837).

Jamieson, Alan, 'Tyranny of the Lash: Punishment in the Royal Navy during the American War, 1776–1783', *Northern Mariner*, Vol. 9, No. 1 (1999), pp. 53–66.

Jenks, Timothy, *Naval Engagements: Patriotism, Cultural Politics, and the Royal Navy 1793–1815* (Oxford: Oxford University Press, 2006).

— 'Contesting the Hero: The Funeral of Admiral Lord Nelson', *Journal of British Studies*, Vol. 39 (2000), pp. 422–53.

Johnson, Claudia L., ed., *The Cambridge Companion to Mary Wollstonecraft* (Cambridge: Cambridge University Press, 2002).

Jones, Colin, ed., *Britain and Revolutionary France: Conflict, Subversion and Propaganda* (Exeter: Exeter Studies in History, 1983).

Jones, E.H. Stuart, 'Mutiny in Bantry Bay', *Irish Sword*, Vol. 3 (1951–2), pp. 202–9.

Jones, Elin, 'Masculinity, Materiality and Space on board the Royal Naval Ship, 1756–1815', Unpublished PhD thesis, Queen Mary University of London (2016).

— 'Space, Sound and Sedition on the Royal Naval Ship, 1756–1815', *Journal of Historical Geography*, Vol. 70 (2020), pp. 65–73.

Jones, Peter, 'Finding Captain Swing: Protest, Parish Relations, and the State of the Public Mind in 1830', *International Review of Social History*, Vol. 54 (2009), pp. 429–58.

Jordan, Gerald and Rogers, Nicholas, 'Admirals as Heroes: Patriotism and Liberty in Hanoverian England', *Journal of British Studies*, Vol. 28, No. 3 (July 1989), pp. 201–24.

Juang, R.N.M. and Morrissette, N., eds, *Africa and the Americas: Culture, Politics and History: A Multidisciplinary Encyclopaedia* (Oxford: ABC Clio, 2008).

Keegan, John, *The Face of Battle: A Study of Agincourt, Waterloo and the Somme* (London: Jonathan Cape, 1976).

Kelly, Gary, 'Revolution, Reaction and the Expropriation of Popular Culture: Hannah More's Cheap Repository', *Man and Nature*, Vol. 6 (1987), pp. 147–59.

Kelly, P., 'Strategy and Counter-Revolution: The Journal of Sir Gilbert Elliot on 8–9 September 1793', *English Historical Review*, Vol. 98 (1983), p. 340.

Kennedy, Catriona, *Narratives of the Revolutionary and Napoleonic Wars: Military and Civilian Experience in Britain and Ireland* (London: Palgrave Macmillan, 2013).

Kennedy, Gavin, 'Bligh and the Defiance Mutiny', *Mariner's Mirror*, Vol. 65, No. 1 (1979), pp. 65–8.

Kinkel, Sarah, *Disciplining the Empire: Politics, Governance and the Rise of the British Royal Navy* (Cambridge, MA: Harvard University Press, 2018).

Knight, Roger, *Britain Against Napoleon: The Organization of Victory* (London: Allen Lane, 2013).

— *Convoys: The British Struggle Against Napoleonic Europe and America* (New Haven, CT and London: Yale University Press, 2022).

— *The Pursuit of Victory: The Life and Achievement of Horatio Nelson* (London: Allen Lane, 2006).

Knight, Roger and Wilcox, Martin, *Sustaining the Fleet: War, the British Navy and the Contractor State 1793–1815* (Woodbridge: Boydell Press, 2010).

Konstam, Angus, *Mutiny on the Spanish Main: HMS Hermione and the Royal Navy's revenge* (London: Osprey, 2020).

Land, Isaac, *War, Nationalism and the British Sailor, 1750–1805* (London: Palgrave Macmillan, 2009).

— 'New Scholarship on the Press Gang', parts 1 and 2, http://porttowns.port.ac.uk/press-gang-1/ and http://porttowns.port.ac.uk/press-gang2/.

Langford, Paul, *A Polite and Commercial People: England 1727–1783* (Oxford: Oxford University Press, 1989).

Larkin, Edward, *Thomas Paine and the Literature of Revolution* (Cambridge: Cambridge University Press, 2005).

Lavery, Brian, *Nelson's Navy: The Ships, Men and Organization*, revised edition (London: Conway, 2013).

LeJacq, Seth Stein, 'Run Aflou: Sodomy, Masculinity, and the Body in the Georgian Royal Navy', Unpublished PhD thesis, Johns Hopkins University (2016).

Lewis, Michael, *A Social History of the Navy, 1793–1815* (London: Allen & Unwin, 1960).

Lincoln, Margarette, 'Naval Ship Launches as Public Spectacle, 1773–1854', *Mariner's Mirror*, Vol. 83 (1997), pp. 466–72.

— *Representing the Royal Navy: British Seapower 1750–1815* (Aldershot: Ashgate, 2002).

— *Trading in War: London's Maritime World in the Age of Cook and Nelson* (New Haven, CT and London: Yale University Press, 2018).

Lindsey, Treva B., 'Post-Ferguson: A "Herstorical" Approach to Black Violability', in *Feminist Studies*, Vol. 41, No. 1 (2015), pp. 232–7.

Linebaugh, Peter and Rediker, Marcus, *The Many-Headed Hydra: Sailors, Slaves, Commoners, and the Hidden History of the Revolutionary Atlantic* (Boston: Beacon Press, 2000).

Lloyd, Christopher, *The British Seaman 1200–1860: A Social Survey* (Cranbury, NJ: Associated University Presses, 1968).

— *St Vincent and Camperdown* (London: Batsford, 1963).

Loft, Philip, 'Petitioning and Petitioners to the Westminster Parliament, 1660–1788', *Parliamentary History*, Vol. 38, No. 3 (2019), pp. 342–61.

Logue, Kenneth, J., *Popular Disturbances in Scotland, 1780–1815* (London: John Donald, 1979).

London, David W., 'Mutiny in the Public Eye: The Role of Newspapers in the Mutiny at Spithead', Unpublished PhD thesis, University of London (2000).

Mabee, Frank, 'The Spithead Mutiny and Urban Radicalism in the 1790s', *Romanticism*, Vol. 13 (2007), pp. 133–44.

McAleer, John, *Britain's Maritime Empire: South Africa, the South Atlantic and the Indian Ocean, 1763–1820* (Cambridge: Cambridge University Press, 2017).

— 'Eminent Service: War, Slavery and the Politics of Public Recognition in the British Caribbean and the Cape of Good Hope c. 1782–1807', *Mariner's Mirror*, Vol. 95, No. 1 (2009), pp. 33–51.

McAleer, John and Petley, Christer, eds, *The Royal Navy and the British Atlantic World, c. 1750–1820* (London: Palgrave Macmillan, 2016).

McCormack, Matthew, *Embodying the Militia in Georgian England* (Oxford: Oxford University Press, 2015).

MacDougall, Philip, 'Lord Love the Irish and Damnation to the English: The Naval Mutinies of 1798', *Mariner's Mirror*, Vol. 108, No. 4 (November 2022), pp. 423–38.

McKee, Helen, 'From Violence to Alliance: Maroons and White Settlers in Jamaica, 1739–1795', *Slavery and Abolition*, Vol. 39, No. 1 (2018), pp. 27–52.

Macleod, Emma, 'British Spectators of the French Revolution: The View from across the Channel', *Gonriek*, Vol. 197 (2013), pp. 377–92.

Macleod, Emma Vincent, *A War of Ideas: British Attitudes to the Wars Against Revolutionary France, 1792–1802* (Aldershot: Ashgate, 1998).

McNeill, J.R., *Mosquito Empires: Ecology and the War in the Greater Caribbean 1620–1914* (Cambridge: Cambridge University Press, 2010).

McPhee, Peter, ed., *A Companion to the French Revolution* (Chichester: Blackwell, 2013).

— *Liberty or Death: The French Revolution* (New Haven, CT and London: Yale University Press, 2016).

Magra, Christopher P., *Poseidon's Curse: Naval Impressment and Atlantic Origins of the American Revolution* (Cambridge: Cambridge University Press, 2016).

Mahan, Alfred Thayer, *The Influence of Seapower Upon the French Revolution and Empire, 1793–1812*, 2 vols (London: Sampson, Low, Marston, 1893).

Malcomson, Thomas, *Order and Disorder in the British Navy 1793–1815: Control, Resistance, Flogging and Hanging* (Woodbridge: Boydell Press, 2016).

Maniquis, Robert, ed., *British Radical Culture of the 1790s* (San Marino, CA: Huntington Library Press, 2002).

Mansfield, Nick, *Soldiers as Citizens: Popular Politics and the Nineteenth-Century British Military* (Liverpool: Liverpool University Press, 2020).

Manwaring, G.E. and Dobrée, Bonamy, *The Floating Republic: An Account of the Mutinies at Spithead and the Nore in 1797* (London: Frank Cass & Co., 1966).

Marsh, Tyson E.J., 'Critical Pedagogy for Black Youth Resistance', *Black History Bulletin*, Vol. 79, No. 1 (Spring 2016), pp. 14–23.

Marshall, P.J., ed., *The Oxford History of the British Empire*, Volume 2: *The Eighteenth Century* (Oxford: Oxford University Press, 1998).

Meeks, Joshua, *France, Britain, and the Struggle for the Revolutionary Western Mediterranean* (London: Palgrave Macmillan, 2017).

Mercer, Keith, 'The Murder of Lieutenant Lawry: A Case Study of British Naval Impressment in Newfoundland, 1794', *Newfoundland and Labrador Studies*, Vol. 21 (2006), pp. 255–98.

— 'Northern Exposure: Resistance to Naval Impressment in British North America, 1775–1815', *Canadian Historical Review*, Vol. 91 (2010), pp. 199–232.

Miller, Henry, 'Introduction: The Transformation of Petitioning in the Long Nineteenth Century (1780–1914)', *Social Science History*, Vol. 43, No. 3: The Transformation of Petitioning (2019), pp. 409–29.

Mitchell, B.R., *British Historical Statistics* (Cambridge: Cambridge University Press, 1988).

Montluzin, Emily Lorraine de, *The Anti-Jacobins 1798–1800* (London: Macmillan, 1988).

Morgan, Philip D., 'Black Experiences in Britain's Maritime World', in David Cannadine, ed., *Empire, the Sea and Global History* (Basingstoke: Palgrave Macmillan, 2007), pp. 86–110.

Morgan-Owen, David and Halewood, Louis, eds, *Economic Warfare and the Sea: Grand Strategies for Maritime Power* (Liverpool: Liverpool University Press, 2020).

Mori, Jennifer, 'The British Government and the Bourbon Restoration: The Occupation of Toulon, 1793', *Historical Journal*, Vol. 40, No. 3 (1997), pp. 699–719.

Morieux, Renaud, *The Channel: England, France and the Construction of a Maritime Border in the Eighteenth Century* (Cambridge: Cambridge University Press, 2016).

Morriss, Roger, *The Foundations of British Maritime Ascendancy: Resources, Logistics and the State, 1755–1815* (Cambridge: Cambridge University Press, 2011).

— 'Labour Relations in the Royal Dockyards, 1801–1805', *Mariner's Mirror*, Vol. 62, No. 4 (1976), pp. 337–46.

— *The Royal Dockyards during the Revolutionary and Napoleonic Wars* (Leicester: Leicester University Press, 1983).

Murphy, Tessa, 'A Reassertion of Rights: Fedon's Rebellion, Grenada, 1795–6', *Économie politique et Révolution française*, Vol. 14 (2018), online.

Navickas, Katrina, *Loyalism and Radicalism in Lancashire, 1798–1815* (Oxford: Oxford University Press, 2009).

Oldfield, John R., *Popular Politics and British Anti-Slavery: The Mobilisation of Public Opinion against the Slave Trade 1787–1807* (Manchester: Manchester University Press, 1995).

O'Neil, Lindsey, *The Opened Letter: Networking in the Early Modern British World* (Philadelphia: University of Pennsylvania Press, 2015).

Orth, J., *Combination and Conspiracy: A Legal History of Trade Unionism, 1721–1906* (Oxford: Clarendon Press, 1991).

Palmer, R.R., *The Age of the Democratic Revolution* (Princeton, NJ: Princeton University Press, 1959).

Parkinson, C. Northcote, *Edward Pellew, Viscount Exmouth, Admiral of the Red* (London: Methuen, 1934).

— *War in the Eastern Seas, 1793–1815* (London: George Allen & Unwin, 1954).

Peacey, Jason, *Print and Public Politics in the English Revolution* (Cambridge: Cambridge University Press, 2013).

Petley, Christer, *White Fury: A Jamaican Slaveholder and the Age of Revolution* (Oxford: Oxford University Press, 2018).

Pfaff, Steven and Hechter, Michael, *The Genesis of Rebellion: Governance, Grievance and Mutiny in the Age of Sail* (Cambridge: Cambridge University Press, 2020).

Philip-Dowe, Nicole and Martin, John Angus, eds, *Perspectives on the Grenada Revolution, 1979–1983* (Cambridge: Cambridge Scholars Publishing, 2017).

Philp, Mark, ed., *The French Revolution and British Popular Politics* (Cambridge: Cambridge University Press, 1991).

— 'Vulgar Conservatism, 1792–3', *English Historical Review*, Vol. 110 (1995), pp. 42–69.

— ed., *Resisting Napoleon: The British Response to the Threat of Invasion, 1797–1815* (Aldershot: Ashgate, 2006).

Pocock, Tom, *A Thirst for Glory: The Life of Sir Sidney Smith*, 2nd edition (London: Pimlico, 1998).

Polasky, Janet, *Revolutions Without Borders: The Call to Liberty in the Atlantic World* (New Haven, CT and London: Yale University Press, 2015).

Poole, Steve, *The Politics of Regicide in England, 1760–1850: Troublesome Subjects* (Manchester: Manchester University Press, 2000).

Potieger, Thean and Grundlingh, Albert, 'Admiral Elphinstone and the Conquest and Defence of the Cape of Good Hope, 1795–6', *Scientia Militaria: South African Journal of Military Studies*, Vol. 35, No. 2 (2007), pp. 39–67.

Quilley, Geoff, *Empire to Nation: Art History and the Visualisation of Maritime Britain 1768–1829* (New Haven, CT and London: Yale University Press, 2011).

Quinalt, E., 'The French Invasion of Pembrokeshire in 1797', *Welsh History Review*, Vol. 19 (1999), pp. 618–42.

Randall, Adrian, *Riotous Assemblies: Popular Protests in Hanoverian Britain* (Oxford: Oxford University Press, 2006).

Rediker, Marcus, *Between the Devil and the Deep Blue Sea: Merchant Seamen, Pirates and the Anglo-American Naval World, 1700–1750* (Cambridge: Cambridge University Press, 1987).

Rees, John, *The Leveller Revolution: Radical Political Organization in England, 1640–1650* (London: Verso, 2016).

Reineke, Juliann Elizabeth, 'Three Sheets to the Wind: The Jolly Jack Tar and Eighteenth-Century British Masculinity', Unpublished PhD thesis, Carnegie Mellon University (2018).

Richardson, David, Schwarz, Suzanne and Tibbles, Anthony, eds, *Liverpool and Transatlantic Slavery* (Liverpool: Liverpool University Press, 2007).

Robertson, J.D.M., *The Press Gang in Orkney and Shetland* (Orkney: The Orcadian, 2011).

Rockman, Seth, 'Work in the Cities of Colonial British North America', *Journal of Urban History*, Vol. 33 (2007), pp. 1021–32.

Rodger, N.A.M., *The Command of the Ocean: A Naval History of Britain* (London: Allen Lane, 2004).

— 'From the "Military Revolution" to the "Fiscal-Military State"', *Journal for Maritime Research*, Vol. 13, No. 2 (November 2011), pp. 119–28.

— 'Image and Reality in Eighteenth-Century Naval Tactics', *Mariner's Mirror*, Vol. 89 (2003), pp. 280–96.

— 'The Inner Life of the Navy, 1750–1800: Change or Decay?', in *Guerres et paix 1660–1815* (Vincennes: Service Historique de la Marine, 1987).

— *The Safeguard of the Sea: A Naval History of Britain*, Volume 1: *660–1649* (London: Allen Lane, 1997).

— *The Wooden World: An Anatomy of the Georgian Navy* (London: Collins, 1986).

Rogers, Nicholas, 'British Impressment and Its Discontents', *International Journal of Maritime History*, Vol. 30, No. 1 (2018), pp. 52–73.

— 'Burning Tom Paine: Loyalism and Counter-Revolution in Britain, 1792–93', *Social History*, Vol. 32, No. 64 (November 1999), pp. 139–71.

— *Crowds, Culture and Politics in Georgian Britain* (Oxford: Clarendon Press, 1998).

— 'The Politics of Mutiny: The *Pompée* at Spithead and Beyond', *International Journal of Maritime History*, Vol. 33, No. 3 (2021), pp. 464–88.

— *The Press Gang: Naval Impressment and Its Opponents in Georgian Britain* (London: Continuum, 2007).

— ed., *Manning the Royal Navy in Bristol: Liberty Impressment and the State, 1739–1815* (Bristol: Bristol Record Society, 2014).

Rose, Richard, 'The French at Fishguard: Fact, Fiction and Folklore', *Transactions of the Honourable Society of Cymmrodorion* (2002), new series, Vol. 9 (2003), pp. 74–105.

Ross, Jeffrey Ian, *The Dynamics of Political Crime* (Thousand Oaks, CA: SAGE, 2003).

— *An Introduction to Political Crime* (Bristol: Policy Press, 2012).

Ryan, A.N., 'In Search of Bruix, 1799', in *Français et Anglais en Méditerranée de la Révolution français a l'indépendence de la Grèce (1789–1830)* (Paris: Service Historique de la Marine, 1992), pp. 81–90.

Saha, Jonathan, 'Histories of Everyday Violence in British India', *History Compass*, Vol. 9, No. 1 (2011), pp. 844–53.

Schama, Simon, *Patriots and Liberators: Revolution in the Netherlands 1780–1813* (New York: Alfred A. Knopf, 1977).

Scheuerman, Mona, *In Praise of Poverty: Hannah More Counters Thomas Paine and the Radical Threat* (Lexington, KY: University Press of Kentucky, 2002).

Schultz, Ronald, 'Pirates and Proletarians: Authority, Labour and Capital Accumulation in the First British Empire', *Radical History Review*, Vol. 44 (1989), pp. 167–74.

Schürer, Norbert, 'The Storming of the Bastille in English Newspapers', *Eighteenth-Century Life*, Vol. 29, No. 1 (2005), pp. 50–81.

Scobie, Ruth, *Celebrity Culture and the Myth of Oceania in Britain 1770–1823* (Woodbridge: Boydell Press, 2019).

Scofield, Philip, 'British Politicians and French Arms: The Ideological War of 1793–1795', *History*, Vol. 77, No. 250 (1992), pp. 183–201.

Scott, James C., *Domination and the Arts of Resistance: Hidden Transcripts* (New Haven, CT and London: Yale University Press, 1990).

Scott, Julius S., *The Common Wind: Afro-American Currents in the Age of the Haitian Revolution* (London and New York: Verso, 2018).

Shoemaker, Robert, 'The Old Bailey Proceedings and the Representation of Crime and Criminal Justice in Eighteenth-Century London', *Journal of British Studies*, Vol. 47, No. 3 (2008), pp. 559–80.

Shoon, Eric W., 'The Asymmetry of Legitimacy: Analyzing the Legitimation of Violence in 30 Cases of Insurgent Revolution', *Social Forces*, Vol. 93, No. 2 (December 2014), pp. 779–801.

Sivapragasam, Michael, 'After the Treaties: A Social, Economic and Demographic History of Maroon Society in Jamaica, 1739–1842', Unpublished PhD thesis, University of Southampton (2018).

Sivasundaram, Sujit, *Waves Across the South: A New History of Revolution and Empire* (London: William Collins, 2020).

Smyth, Jim, ed., *Revolution, Counter-Revolution and Union: Ireland in the 1790s* (Cambridge: Cambridge University Press, 2000).

Snow, Henry, 'Fugitive Harbour: Labour, Community, and Marronage at Antigua Naval Yard', *Slavery and Abolition*, Vol. 42, No. 4 (2021), pp. 802–26.

Sokoll, Thomas, *Essex Pauper Letters, 1731–1837*, Records of Social and Economic History (New Series) 30 (Oxford: Oxford University Press, 2006).

Sparrow, Elizabeth, 'The Alien Office, 1792–1806', *Historical Journal*, Vol. 33, No. 2 (1990), pp. 361–84.

— *The Secret Service: British Agents in France 1792–1815* (Woodbridge: Boydell Press, 1999).

Spence, Peter, *The Birth of Romantic Radicalism: War, Popular Politics and English Radical Reformism, 1800–1815* (Aldershot: Scholars' Press, 1996).

Spinney, J.D. 'The *Albanaise* Affair', *Mariner's Mirror*, Vol. 43 (1957), pp. 194–202.

Stephenson, Judy Z., ' "Real" Wages? Contractors, Workers, and Pay in London Building Trades, 1650–1800', *Economic History Review*, Vol. 71, No. 1 (2018), pp. 106–32.

— 'Working Days in a London Construction Team in the Eighteenth Century: Evidence from St Paul's Cathedral', *Economic History Review*, Vol. 32, No. 2 (2020), pp. 409–30.

Stevenson, John, *Popular Disturbances in England, 1700–1832*, 2nd edition (London: Longman, 1992).

Strachan, Hew and Scheipers, Sibylle, eds, *The Changing Character of War* (Oxford: Oxford University Press, 2011).

Sutcliffe, Robert, *British Expeditionary Warfare and the Defeat of Napoleon, 1793–1815* (Woodbridge: Boydell Press, 2016).

Tadmor, Naomi, *Family and Friends in Eighteenth-Century England: Household, Kinship, and Patronage* (Cambridge: Cambridge University Press, 2001).

Taylor, Barbara, *Mary Wollstonecraft and the Feminist Imagination* (Cambridge: Cambridge University Press, 2003).

Taylor, Stephen, *Commander: The Life and Exploits of Britain's Greatest Frigate Captain* (London: Faber and Faber, 2012).

— *Sons of the Waves: The Common Seaman in the Heroic Age of Sail* (New Haven, CT and London: Yale University Press, 2020).

Thomas, J.E., *Britain's Last Invasion: Fishguard, 1797* (Stroud: The History Press, 2007).

Thompson, E.P., *The Making of the English Working Class* (London: Penguin, 2013).

Uglow, Jenny, *In These Times: Living in Britain through Napoleon's Wars, 1793–1815* (London: Faber and Faber, 2014).

Underwood, Patrick, Pfaff, Steven and Hechter, Hechter, 'Threat, Deterrence, and Penal Severity: An Analysis of Flogging in the Royal Navy, 1740–1820', *Social Science History*, Vol. 42, No. 3 (2018), pp. 411–39.

Vale, Brian, 'The Post Office, the Admiralty and Letters to Sailors in the Napoleonic Wars', *Mariner's Mirror*, Vol. 105, No. 2 (2019), pp. 148–61.

Vickers, Daniel et al., 'Roundtable: Reviews of Marcus Rediker, Between the Devil and the Deep Blue Sea', *International Journal of Maritime History*, Vol. 1 (1989), pp. 311–57.

Vincent, Bernard, *The Transatlantic Republican: Thomas Paine and the Age of Revolutions* (Amsterdam: Rodopi, 2005).

Wahrman, Dror, *The Making of the Modern Self: Identity and Culture in Eighteenth-Century England* (New Haven, CT and London: Yale University Press, 2007).

Walvin, James, ed., *Slavery and British Society, 1776–1848* (London: Macmillan, 1982).

Ward, Peter, *British Naval Power in the East, 1794–1805: The Command of Admiral Peter Rainier* (Woodbridge: Boydell Press, 2013).

Wardle, Ralph M., *Wollstonecraft: A Critical Biography* (Lincoln: University of Nebraska Press, 1951).

Warner, Oliver, *The Glorious First of June* (London: Batsford, 1961).

Wells, Roger, *Insurrection: The British Experience, 1795–1803* (Gloucester: Alan Sutton, 1986).

— *Wretched Faces: Famine in Wartime England, 1793–1801* (Gloucester: Alan Sutton, 1988).

Wheeler, H.F.B. and Broadley, A.M., *Napoleon and the Invasion of England: The Story of the Great Terror* (Stroud: Nonsuch, 2007; originally published London, 1908).

Wheeler, Roxann, *The Complexion of Race: Categories of Difference in Eighteenth-Century British Culture* (Philadelphia: University of Pennsylvania Press, 2000).

Whelan, Kevin, *Fellowship of Freedom: the United Irishmen and the 1798 Rebellion* (Cork: Cork University Press, 1998).

Whitfield, Henry Francis, *Plymouth and Devonport: In Times of War and Peace* (Plymouth: E. Chapple, 1900).

Whiting, A. J., *Women and Petitioning in the Seventeenth-Century English Revolution: Deference, Difference and Dissent* (Turnhout: Brepols, 2015).

Whyman, Susan E., *The Pen and the People: English Letter Writers 1600–1800* (Oxford: Oxford University Press, 2009).

Wiemann, Dirk and Mahlberg, Gary, eds, *Perspectives on English Revolutionary Republicanism* (Aldershot: Ashgate, 2014).

Wilkinson, Clive, *The British Navy and the State in the 18th Century* (Woodbridge: Boydell Press, 2004).

Willis, Sam, *The Fighting Temeraire: Legend of Trafalgar* (London: Quercus, 2009).

— *The Glorious First of June: Fleet Battle in the Reign of Terror* (London: Quercus, 2012).

— *In the Hour of Victory: The Royal Navy at War in the Age of Nelson* (London: Atlantic Books, 2013).

Wilson, Evan, *The Horrible Peace: British Veterans and the End of the Napoleonic Wars* (Amherst, MA: University of Massachusetts Press, 2023).

— 'The Naval Defence of Ireland during the French Revolutionary and Napoleonic Wars', *Historical Research*, Vol. 92, No. 257 (August 2019), pp. 568–84.

— *A Social History of British Naval Officers, 1775–1815* (Woodbridge: Boydell Press, 2016).

Wilson, Kathleen, 'Empire, Trade and Popular Politics in Mid-Hanoverian Britain: The Case of Admiral Vernon', *Past and Present*, Vol. 21 (November 1988), pp. 74–109.

— *The Sense of the People: Politics, Culture and Imperialism in England, 1715–1785* (Cambridge: Cambridge University Press, 1995).

Winfield, Rif, *British Warships in the Age of Sail, 1793–1817* (Barnsley: Seaforth Publishing, 2010).

Worrall, David, *Radical Culture: Discourse, Resistance and Surveillance, 1790–1820* (Detroit, MI: Wayne State University Press, 1992).

— *Theatric Revolutions: Drama, Censorship, and Romantic Period Subcultures 1773–1832* (Oxford: Oxford University Press, 2006).

Wykes, David L., ed., *Protestant Dissent and Philanthropy in Britain, 1660–1914* (Woodbridge: Boydell Press, 2020).

Yarrington, Alison, *Commemoration of the Hero, 1800–1864: Monuments to the British Victors of the Napoleonic Wars* (New York and London: Garland, 1988).

Zamoyski, Adam, *Phantom Terror: Political Paranoia and the Creation of the Modern State, 1789–1848* (New York: Basic Books, 2015).

INDEX